The Paramount Story

JOHN DOUGLAS EAMES

CROWN PUBLISHERS, INC.
NEW YORK

The Paramount Story

Contents

Paramount Consultant
William S. Kenly

First published 1985 by Octopus Books Limited
59 Grosvenor Street, London W1

Illustrations of movies 1916-1928, 1949-1984
copyrighted by Paramount Pictures Corporation,
and of movies 1929-1948 copyrighted by
MCA Publishing, a division of MCA, Inc.
Reproduction by permission only.

First published 1985 in the United States of America
by Crown Publishers, Inc.
One Park Avenue, New York, New York 10016

Inquiries should be addressed to Crown Publishers, Inc.

Library of Congress Catalog Card Number 85-3745

ISBN 0-517-55348-1

10 9 8 7 6 5 4 3 2 1

First Edition

Printed in Hong Kong

Paramount Pictures Corporation is
a Gulf & Western Industries, Inc. company

This book is for BARRY WALKER

PREFACE

I must make two long-delayed personal apologies to Paramount. The first is for disrupting, in 1923, a New York premiere performance of *The Ten Commandments* to which my father took his seven-year-old offspring, under the impression that it would be a suitable Biblical lesson. He regretted it when, in one of the awe-inspiring moments of silence held by the symphony orchestra in the pit as Moses produced each of his holy tablets on the screen, I piped up, loud and clear, 'What is adultery, Daddy?' and brought the house down. ('Tell you later' he muttered, red-faced.) Any Paramount personnel then present must have shuddered, but DeMille's epic managed to survive this disgraceful incident.

So did I, and ten years later I began my career in the film industry with Paramount, taking a job in London which consisted entirely of dipping stills into a fixing solution in a dank cellar. After one day of this monotony I walked out without notice and defected to MGM (where I remained for four decades), leaving the Paramount stills dungeon unmanned. I hope that this book makes amends for such shameful conduct, because from childhood onwards I was enthralled by Paramount's glamour, fascinated by that studio's stars, and hardly ever missed one of its pictures. Something of this youthful fan-worship lingers on, so that working on the book has been, like the writing of my previous book in this series, 'The MGM Story', mostly a labour of love.

Although Paramount's history is one of the longest of any in the motion picture industry – its sources date back more than seven decades – you will find it comprehensively surveyed in this volume. Those sources (chiefly Adolph Zukor's Famous Players and Jesse Lasky's Feature Play companies) came together in 1916 to form the organization that remains one of the 'majors' of the film world to this day. Since then it has entertained the public with almost three thousand feature-length films – all of them covered in the following pages.

The extent to which each film is covered varies: the ideal of describing, commenting upon and illustrating every single one would have made the book (even if it were possible to produce it, many of the early movies and their stills having disappeared forever) too expensive to buy – and too heavy to hold! However, a large proportion of the total is surveyed fully in this way while the rest is listed with titles, leading players, directors, producers and story references. These shorter entries are nearly always of the comparatively minor 'B' pictures, but occasionally a more important one has had to be relegated by the exigencies of page and chapter layouts. The dates given are, as closely as could be ascertained,

the years of American release or first public showing, often one and the same.

As usual in this series, the author's first problem was to decide on a criterion for inclusion as a Paramount picture. Especially in recent years, all the major companies distribute, along with their own product, outside films made by foreign producers or domestic independents, sometimes co-sponsored or financed from the start, sometimes picked up after production. The distribution may apply to some countries and not to others. There are instances of two major studios producing a picture in partnership and splitting the international territorial rights. Once a common practice was making movies overseas purely for local consumption (these were known in Britain as 'quota quickies'). Since the advent of television, ownership of old product has passed from one major to another, further confusing the issue. Where does one draw the line? It was finally decided to include all the features that have been released by Paramount in the United States, its home country and the world's most important film market. (A very few films produced at Paramount but released by others are also included and are noted in the text.)

Having set down that yardstick, I picked up the pen – and would have written precious little with it if I had not had the help of the innumerable individuals, organizations and publications consulted during my research and composition. Most of all, I am grateful to supervising editor David Burn, a master of the art of shaping a multiplicity of details into a smooth whole; and to general editor Robyn Karney, who couples remarkable expertise with a sense of humour, plus a talent for encouragement. She is also blessed with a tireless assistant in Tammy Collins, who decoded my scribblings. Material and guidance were provided without stint by Paramount Pictures in Hollywood, Paramount in New York (especially by eagle-eyed William S. Kenly, who combed every line for factual accuracy), and United International Pictures in London. Elusive details were unearthed and my memory gaps filled by the endlessly helpful British Film Institute's library staff. Among many other periodicals, the files of *Variety* and the *New York Times* were particularly rich sources of information. Hundreds of books contributed to research and verification; Leslie Halliwell's 'Film Guide', DeWitt Bodeen's 'From Hollywood' and 'More from Hollywood', Ephraim Katz's 'International Film Encyclopedia' and the catalogues of the American Film Institute proved indispensable in this respect. To all these, and too many more than space will allow me to name separately, a deep bow of gratitude.

John Douglas Eames

PUBLISHER'S ACKNOWLEDGEMENTS

Producing a book such as this is simply not possible without the help of a large number of people. Our deepest gratitude must go to William S. Kenly, senior publicist and archivist in Paramount's Motion Picture Division, who has acted as our consultant expert throughout the project. His knowledge and experience have been invaluable to us in our attempt to ensure the accuracy of text and illustrations alike. For the countless hours he has spent poring over the mountain of paper we burdened him with, we are more than grateful.

Our thanks, too, to many other members of Paramount's New York staff who have contributed in one form or another: these include Peter Bankers, Mike Berman, Bruce Hosmer, Lloyd Ibert, Marty Kutner, Peter Mattair, Tamara Rawitt and LaVerne Williams. From Paramount's studios in Hollywood we have received much cooperation and advice from Helene Johnson, executive head of the Merchandising and Licensing Division; and for help in supplying stills we have appreciated the part played by Michael Noval, 'king of the back room' in Cliff Hauser's Advertising and Promotion

Division. Robert Isenberg took the photographs which appear on pages 3–5. For many of the pre-1949 talkies stills we must record our thanks to Universal Studios – in particular to ever-helpful Paul Lindenschmid, and to David Darley who allowed us access to his TV Syndication promotion files under the guidance of Dan Silverman. Archivist and film historian Vernon Harbin, who is no stranger to this series (he was consultant editor on 'The RKO Story'), provided valuable information on releases of the silent period. Other illustrations were kindly supplied by United International Pictures, the National Stills Archive of the British Film Institute, The Museum of Modern Art in New York, the Kobal Collection, the Topham Picture Library, William S. Kenly and Fortune Magazine (photographer Robert Mack).

Finally, we should like to record our warmest thanks to the author himself, not only for the industry, dedication and cooperation which he has displayed throughout, but also for originating the concept for this series of Hollywood studio histories.

Introduction
THE MEN WHO MADE PARAMOUNT

ADOLPH ZUKOR The Mastermind

The first 15 of Adolph Zukor's 103 years were lived in Hungary. The last 64 were spent in establishing and – latterly in title only – heading one of the biggest organizations in the history of the entertainment industry.

He was born in 1873 in Risce where, while his family was not poverty-stricken, there was plenty of room for improvement. He sought a better future – like millions of his fellow Europeans in the late 19th century – by venturing westward to America, the land of opportunity. He arrived in New York in 1888 with $40 sewn inside his waistcoat. What followed was pure Horatio Alger: 'Rags to Riches' or 'Broom Boy to Boss'.

Adolph got a job in an East Side fur store where his chief assignment was to keep the floors swept. A glutton for work and quick to learn, he was soon promoted to salesman and within a few years he had mastered all the intricacies and chicaneries of the fur trade. When the new century began Zukor found himself the owner of a thriving fur business in Chicago – a self-made man. And a restless one.

Friendship with Marcus Loew, a New York furrier who made frequent visits to Chicago, inspired Zukor to return to the bigger city. While looking for new investment opportunities, he met Mitchell Mark, an operator of penny arcades. These novelties – open-front 'parlors' lined with machines which responded to a penny in the slot with a brief moving picture – were drawing in the passing crowds so fast that the pennies became dollars, turning profits by the minute. Zukor and Mark formed the Automatic Vaudeville Company, opening its first arcade on 14th Street in 1903, and soon spreading its operations to Boston, Philadelphia and Newark, with Loew as an additional investor.

Two years later the ex-furrier friends were full-time showmen, running their own separate companies as proprietors of nickelodeons. These were an advance on penny arcades, giving their goggle-eyed customers short shows consisting of the one-reel movies being churned out by pioneer studios like Biograph, Vitagraph and Edison. The price of admission was five cents, a bargain considering that such films were usually exhibited in the comparatively expensive vaudeville theatres then dominating the mass entertainment scene. A nickelodeon made a cheap investment, too, requiring only a rented shop installed with a screen, projector, and as many chairs or benches as could be crammed in.

Among such other budding entrepeneurs in this prosperous field as Carl Laemmle, William Fox and the Warner brothers – all destined to become Hollywood moguls – Zukor and Loew were outstandingly successful. To the basic 'store show' concept they added innovations like Hale's Scenic Tours (travel films shown in a simulated railroad carriage with conductor and swaying seats), Humanova (actors speaking or shouting dialogue from behind the movie screen, a crude forerunner of talkies) and, between the films, live performances of singers accompanied by pianists and slides.

These last developed into full-scale variety shows for Loew and Zukor, combining movies and vaudeville acts. Aimed at the family trade, they were presented in real theatres with tip-up seats, and ticket prices soared to 25 cents. To further this progress the two friends and their associates pooled their holdings and, in 1910, established Loew's Consolidated Enterprises with Loew as president, Zukor as treasurer and Nicholas Schenck (later Loew's successor as the czar of MGM for three decades) as secretary. By 1912, just a few years past their penny arcade period, they controlled a circuit of theatres, including the prestigious American Music Hall on 42nd Street.

But Zukor grew restless once more. Now he was fascinated by the challenge of film production, and the idea that its future lay in longer pictures. Until that year, the length of a movie had been arbitrarily limited to one reel, around ten minutes, by the Motion Picture Patents Company, a consortium of the largest producing and renting companies which virtually controlled the industry by licensing the use of patented cameras and projectors. In 1912, regardless of this, more and more two-reelers were being made (three years later the MPPC, better known as the Trust and a frank attempt at monopoly, was crushed by vigorous independents, especially Laemmle and Fox, via government decree).

Zukor departed from the Loew concern with good wishes and a hefty profit from the sale of his shares. $35,000 of it went to Paris. He had been told by Edwin S. Porter, whose *Great Train Robbery* had been the nickelodeons' biggest attraction (and still stands as a milestone today), that French director Louis Mercanton had filmed Sarah Bernhardt in *Queen Elizabeth* – in four reels, no less! Bernhardt was then the most famous actress in the world; she had recently broken box-office records in a tour across the USA, and the American distribution rights of her film were for sale. Recognising a good thing when he saw one, Zukor didn't hesitate.

He went to the eminent Broadway producer and theatre owner,

Daniel Frohman, and, waving Bernhardt's name like a banner, got him to agree to give the film a gala premiere at his Lyceum Theatre. Its success handed the movies a tremendous up-market boost. Hitherto regarded as a pastime for the ignorant masses, the motion picture became socially respectable. Even more important, it became acceptable to the top talents of the American stage, who had previously considered it undignified to appear in a movie. Now, if the divine Sarah could do it with impunity, so could they.

Nothing could have been more helpful in furthering Adolph Zukor's keenest ambition: to make films starring the foremost names of the theatre in their greatest vehicles. It was not a new idea. Indeed, it was the very formula under which the French company responsible for *Queen Elizabeth* had been operating since 1908, and the cameras of Film d'Art had recorded all the actors of the Comedie Francaise in most of their repertoire. America deserved a similar display of its theatrical gems, Zukor grandly told reporters, as he became the centre of a contract-signing, bank-borrowing whirlwind. He equipped a New York studio on West 26th Street and announced that Famous Players In Famous Plays was ready to begin production.

His chief lieutenants were the inventive Edwin Porter, appointed as head of direction and photography; high-pressure salesman Al Lichtman, who was selling the Bernhardt picture as a roadshow around the country; B.P. Schulberg, publicity director, who left Zukor after a few years but returned in the 20s to become Paramount's studio boss; and Albert Kaufman, general manager. Playing safe, Zukor put them to work first on two old stage reliables, *The Count Of Monte Cristo*, perennial vehicle of James O'Neill (who was later immortalized in his son Eugene's masterpiece, *Long Day's Journey Into Night*), and *The Prisoner Of Zenda*, with matinee idol James K. Hackett and a budget of $50,000, almost four times the amount spent on any American film to date.

These were followed by Lily Langtry in *His Neighbor's Wife*, Minnie Maddern Fiske in *Tess Of The d'Urbervilles*, and a succession of other ageing stars in stiffly photographed plays which, predictably, became a drug on the market. In 1913 Zukor, always adaptable, shifted the focus of Famous Players to younger faces that the camera – and the public – preferred. Still drawing on Broadway talent, though, he signed 31-year-old John Barrymore to make his movie debut in *An American Citizen*; also Mary Pickford, at 20 already well known in films and plays. It was one of the latter, *A Good Little Devil*, that brought her to Zukor, whose screen version of it was so weak that he held back its release until she had made three more, *In The Bishop's Carriage*, *Caprice* and *Hearts Adrift*. All four, however, were box-office disappointments.

But Mary's $500 weekly salary, big in those days, seemed cheap at the price when her fifth for Famous Players appeared: *Tess Of The Storm Country*, directed by Porter, registered a huge hit, establishing her as a major star and Zukor's most valuable asset. Ranking after her on his contract list were Marguerite Clark, Pauline Frederick, Henry Ainley, Gaby Deslys, Marie Doro, Harold Lockwood, Jack Pickford (Mary's brother) and Owen Moore (her first husband). The company dropped 'In Famous Plays' from its ponderous title and increased its output to 30 pictures a year.

A big adventure begins: executives of Famous Players and Lasky Feature Plays on the day of their merger in 1916. From left – Jesse Lasky, Adolph Zukor, Samuel Goldfish (Goldwyn) and Albert Kaufman.

Thanks largely to Zukor's enterprise, feature length – four, five or even six reels – was now the norm for films, but the customary method of selling them to exhibitors, via middlemen on a regional basis, was still clumsy and inadequately rewarding to the producers. Zukor, along with several other film-makers, including Jesse Lasky, Oliver Morosco and Hobart Bosworth, accepted the offer of central distribution by W.W. Hodkinson's Paramount Company late in 1914. This improvement on the old 'states-rights' system looked so good to Zukor that he, alone among its new suppliers, insisted on part ownership. He was allowed to buy 10% of the releasing firm's shares, and began to figure out how to get a great deal more.

His grand design was only temporarily sidetracked by a disastrous fire which gutted the 26th Street studio in 1915, destroying all the equipment and film stores of Famous Players. Digging deep into the company's funds, Zukor promptly bought a former riding academy on 56th Street and converted it into a studio larger than his old one. Meanwhile he was cultivating a friendship with Jesse Lasky, the most important of Hodkinson's other product sources. Eventually, the two studio chiefs agreed on a merger.

The creation of the industry's biggest production combine, Famous Players-Lasky, was the first of two great consolidations masterminded by Zukor in 1916. Although a quiet man, small in stature and reserved in manner, he was driven by a Napoleonic need for total power. While he dominated the new studio amalgamation as its president, he still possessed only 10% of the non-producing concern which controlled the sale of his output. Hodkinson could still play the ace on Zukor's king. Hodkinson would have to go. And, after his partners had been induced to sell a majority of Paramount's shares to Famous Players-Lasky (Zukor having obtained the backing of Wall Street giant and patron of the arts Otto Kahn), Hodkinson went.

Thus the integration of production and distribution was brought about in September 1916, two months after the Famous Players-Lasky merger. The Paramount that still flourishes seven decades later, was born.

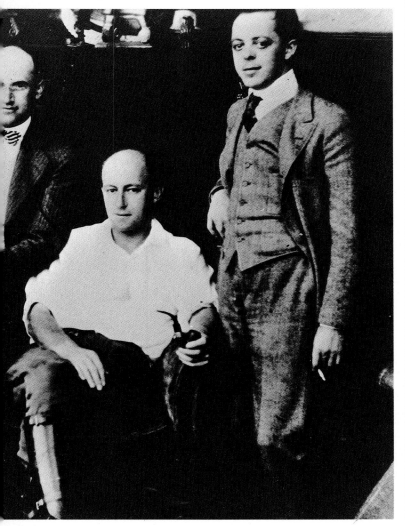

JESSE L. LASKY Winner of the West

While Adolph Zukor was making his first fortune in a Chicago fur emporium, Jesse Lasky was seeking his with a pickaxe in Alaska. Seven years younger than his future partner, he saw the 20th century dawn over a frozen wasteland which he had reached with thousands of other adventurers in the great gold rush. It yielded him nothing. He had to earn his fare back home by playing a cornet in a Nome honkytonk, and this musical talent kept him precariously employed in third-rate gigs around his native San Francisco, supporting his sister and widowed mother.

It was sister Blanche who showed him the way out of the poverty trap. She too learned to play the cornet, and they set out on a career as a double act. They played only the cheapest of vaudeville houses, but Jesse was delighted to be in real show business – an enthusiasm he retained for over 40 years, and which he passed on to his son, writer Jesse Lasky Jr.

Gradually the Laskys' bookings got better. They tooted their trumpets into the big time on a 40-week tour with magician Hermann the Great, who then made Jesse his manager. The ex-prospector began to find genuine gold at last as a vaudeville agent and producer, talent-spotting dancer Ruth St Denis, singer Al Jolson and a host of other stars-to-be. While Blanche, who had never relished performing, ran his New York office, he zipped around the country, fixing contracts, staging novelty acts and throwing out ideas like sparks from a catherine wheel.

His most extravagant notion was to put on a revue that would out-Ziegfeld the Follies in a lavish, specially built New York theatre-restaurant, to be called 'The Folies Bergère'. A showman friend, Henry Harris, agreed to put up half the money, and to supervise the construction on a 46th Street site just off Broadway while Lasky sailed to Europe to gather talent. He brought back specialty performers and entire troupes from London's Alhambra music hall, the Berlin Wintergarten and the Casino de Paris. The show's opening was a razzle-dazzling furore, a highlight of the 1911 season, but the overheads were so enormous that it couldn't last. In a few months Lasky had lost his $100,000 savings, Harris even more, and there was only the theatre left to show for their efforts. (They renamed it the Fulton; much later it was re-renamed the Helen Hayes, and after decades of renown it was demolished in 1982 to make way for a hotel.)

Scaling down his ambition a trifle, Lasky decided to produce an operetta. Armed with a title – *California* – and the rough outline of a story, he went to a well-known play broker, Beatrice de Mille, and asked if he could engage her son William, who had several successes to his credit, to write the libretto. William was busy, she replied, but how about her younger son, Cecil? He had done a little playwriting too. Before he could say thanks a lot but no thanks, Jesse was introduced to Cecil, who immediately evidenced such enthusiasm and inventiveness that a Lasky-DeMille collaboration began. It was destined to take them to unimagined heights.

Their ultimate rise was triggered off not by *California* (although that was a hit, as were their subsequent vaudeville creations) but by Zukor's trail-blazing for full-length films with *Queen Elizabeth*. Contemptuous of the one- and two-reel movies to which the Trust had limited the industry (vaudeville people called them 'chasers' because they cleared out the audience at the end of each variety show), Lasky felt his imagination stirred by the possibilities of photoplays as long as plays.

In a chance meeting with actor Dustin Farnum who had just scored a Broadway triumph in *The Virginian*, Lasky and DeMille talked about starring him in a film that would take an hour to screen. He suggested a recent stage hit, *The Squaw Man*, and Lasky threw himself into a characteristic frenzy of activity. He took an option on the play's movie rights from its author, Edwin Milton Royle, got a licence from the Trust, and organized the Jesse L. Lasky Feature Play Company. Its ownership was split four ways: to himself as president, to DeMille as director general, to Farnum as star – and to one Samuel Goldfish, who was not only a formidable salesman, but had the added advantage of being Blanche Lasky's husband. An important contributor to the company's scraped-together capitalization of $20,000, he was given the title of general manager.

Farnum, accustomed to a weekly salary in the theatre, promptly

A 1923 portrait of Jesse L. Lasky (1880–1958).

handed back his 25% of the Lasky stock and demanded its cash value of $5,000 before he would face a camera. The new company, which already owed Royle $15,000 for his *Squaw Man*, seemed ready for collapse before it started, until other Lasky relatives bought Farnum's share. In years to come it would have brought him millions. This first film alone netted over ten times its cost after its New York premiere in February 1914, which drew many congratulatory messages to Lasky, including one from Adolph Zukor. He invited Jesse to lunch, and the two men began a long friendship.

It was also a rivalry, because the new producer had to bid against Famous Players for stories and stars to send to the ramshackle property on the outskirts of Los Angeles which became his studio. DeMille transformed the place into a bustling film factory, turning out 21 features in its first year. The most successful were *Brewster's Millions*, Lasky's second picture (later remade twice by Paramount); *Rose Of The Rancho*, a romantic vehicle for rising star Bessie Barriscale; and *The Ghost Breaker*, starring H.B. Warner. It was a healthy company that joined with Famous Players and the smaller producers in the Hodkinson releasing system.

In its second year Lasky Feature Plays stepped up the pace to 36 pictures. Jesse signed up new stars like Blanche Sweet and Wallace Reid, and an established celebrity of the first rank: Geraldine Farrar, the world-famous Metropolitan Opera diva. A beauteous brunette, still youthful, she was ready to do some silent acting between opera seasons. Lasky gave her the industry's first supercolossal publicity campaign, starting with New York-to-Hollywood transportation in the 1915 version of Cleopatra's barge – a private railroad car containing Geraldine, her relatives, managers, beauticians, servants and fiancé (Lou Tellegen, Bernhardt's leading man in *Queen Elizabeth*) – and culminating in a series of box-office hits for the company.

Lasky chalked up two other firsts that year. He made an unprecedented deal with the great Broadway producer-playwright David Belasco for ten plays that had filled his theatre. The price was $100,000 against 50% of the films' profits. And when he wanted the Famous Players star Marguerite Clark for *The Goose Girl*, he arranged to borrow her from Zukor – the first instance of a practice that became commonplace among the Hollywood studios.

Such co-operation was, of course, part of Zukor's strategy in his plan to bring the fast-growing Lasky outfit into his orbit. His offer of a 50-50 partnership in a combined Famous Players-Lasky fell on receptive ears in 1916. Flattered, and correctly foreseeing a prosperous future for the mighty amalgamation, Lasky didn't mind being demoted from top boss to second man, with Zukor as president, himself as vice-president in charge of production, DeMille as director general and Goldfish as chairman of the board. He was equally willing to back Zukor's elimination of Hodkinson and the creation of an integrated Paramount.

CECIL B. DeMILLE Pioneer with Megaphone

Would Hollywood ever have been Hollywood without Cecil Blount DeMille? Probably, because there were already some makers of short movies scattered around that area when he arrived. But it's unlikely to have been quite such an exciting place. His zeal and boldness sparked a creative glow that spread to all those around him, from the moment he set out to film the first Lasky Feature Play until he died 46 years and 70 pictures later.

The Squaw Man was originally intended for production in New Jersey, a ferry trip away from Lasky's New York office. That seemed dull to the adventurous DeMille, especially since the story called for hordes of red Indians, who were decidedly thin on the ground in New Jersey. He thought Flagstaff, Arizona, sounded more suitable, and he headed west forthwith, accompanied by star Dustin Farnum, leading lady Winifred Kingston (soon to be Mrs Farnum), co-director Oscar Apfel and cameraman Alfred Gondolfi. When their train reached Flagstaff there was not an Indian in sight – and it was snowing!

Next day Lasky received a telegram: FLAGSTAFF NO GOOD FOR OUR PURPOSE. HAVE PROCEEDED TO CALIFORNIA. WANT AUTHORITY TO RENT BARN IN PLACE CALLED HOLLYWOOD FOR SEVENTY-FIVE DOLLARS A MONTH. CECIL. His request approved, DeMille and company started shooting Hollywood's first full-length picture in that barn on Vine Street on December 29, 1913. They completed it in 18 days. Most of it was directed by Apfel, who knew much more about film-making than DeMille (incidentally, the only one in his family to spell their name that way), but Cecil learned fast. He was particularly adept at writing scenes as and when needed, the de Milles having writer's ink in their blood: not only was brother William a noted playwright, but their mother and clergyman father had written plays too.

During production of *The Squaw Man* Lasky arrived to see what they were up to, liked what he saw, and sent such enthusiastic

DeMille working on a 1914 script, in front of a poster for his trail-blazing hit The Squaw Man, *the first feature film to be made in Hollywood.*

reports back to New York that Sam Goldfish was able to garner $60,000 worth of advance contracts from states' rights bookers. The film was costing only one third of that sum, so the Lasky company was already in clover. But a nasty shock lay ahead. When the finished film was previewed, its horrified creators saw the pictures constantly jiggling around and crawling up the screen. It was unwatchable. DeMille was close to apoplexy until, having rushed the movie to a Philadelphia laboratory for investigation, he was told he had perforated the sprocket holes inaccurately, through using a hand-held punch for economy's sake. Making a correct print was a simple matter, and the spectre of ruin vanished.

The instant success of this picture, and the go-ahead from Lasky to make more movies, fired DeMille and everybody else at the Vine Street barn with renewed energy. The studio was enlarged to accommodate several stages for simultaneous shooting, while additional acreage was leased for outdoor scenes. The overworked Apfel directed eight of the next ten pictures, one every three or four weeks; DeMille, more painstaking, made the other two, giving them new artistic touches. He and Gondolfi experimented with photographic light and shade, creating dramatic shadows instead of relying on the flat glare considered essential in 1914. When the first result reached New York, Goldfish exploded with protests that he couldn't sell such a dark film to exhibitors. 'Tell 'em it's Rembrandt lighting,' said DeMille, and Sam thereupon upped the rental terms for 'an art special'.

Three more directors, George Melford, Fred Thompson and James Neill, were brought in to relieve the pressure. And Hollywood precedents were set by the appointment of an art director and a story editor. The first was Wilfred Buckland, celebrated on Broadway for his spectacular designs for David Belasco. Per-

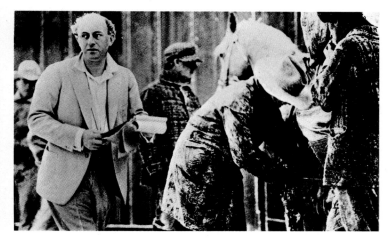

Here DeMille directs an outdoor scene for The Call Of The North. *He had a very busy year in 1914.*

suaded to join the Lasky company by Beatrice de Mille, he headed a staff of designers and, by introducing interior stage lighting to an industry that had always depended on the sun, greatly improved the rather crude artistic effects DeMille had attempted. The story editor was also sent out by Mrs de Mille: he was her elder son William. Although doubtful about following Cecil's desertion of the theatre, he agreed to try Hollywood for three months in order to organise its first story department. He stayed for 41 years, most prominently as a director, until his death in 1955.

Hits streamed from DeMille's cameras to the enrichment of the Jesse Lasky Feature Play Company with gratifying regularity. They included Dustin Farnum in *The Virginian*, Robert Edeson in *The Call Of The North*, Mabel Van Buren *The Girl Of The Golden West*, Ina Claire in *The Wild Goose Chase*, Blanche Sweet in *The Warrens Of Virginia* (William de Mille's play, whose New York cast had featured Mary Pickford and Cecil himself), Edgar Selwyn in *The Arab*, and Geraldine Farrar in *Carmen* and *Maria Rosa*. Biggest winner of all was *The Cheat*, a sensational drama which drew raves for Cecil's direction, Buckland's scenic effects and the performances of Fannie Ward and Hollywood's only Japanese star, Sessue Hayakawa. By the time of their merger, Lasky's product was considered to be at least the equal of Zukor's, in both quality and money-making strength.

THE SUPPORTING CAST in order of appearance

The man most instrumental in helping Zukor to transform Famous Players from dream to reality in 1912 was **Daniel Frohman**. He lent his theatre, the Lyceum, to launch *Queen Elizabeth*, and then used his influence to bring Broadway plays and players to Zukor's studio, which at first could not function because Adolph was refused a licence by the all-powerful Trust. Frohman went to Thomas Edison, whose patents were what the Trust lived on, and persuaded him to support the tyro producer's application. He also gave Zukor's early productions the prestige of his name, allowing the titles to be preceded by 'Daniel Frohman presents . . .', and he induced his even more famous brother, Charles, to follow suit. Daniel came to the rescue when at one point Zukor was scraping the bottom of the financial barrel and needed a $50,000 loan, yet he declined to become an investor in or a director of the company. Without him, motion pictures might have missed the driving force of Zukor and of Paramount as we know it, but Daniel Frohman remained a man of the theatre.

One can almost hear, as one relegates him to the supporting cast, **Samuel Goldwyn** crying from the great beyond, 'Include me out!' However, the name of Goldwyn is not to be found in the annals of Paramount, and his association with its founders was comparatively brief. He entered as Samuel Goldfish, successful glove salesman and Lasky's brother-in-law – and a dedicated movie fan whose encouragement nudged Jesse towards his first steps into the film jungle. As a partner in Lasky's firm he displayed even more gusto and shrewdness in selling movies than he had in filling glove counters. But his low boiling point led to frequent clashes with Lasky and DeMille and, later, when that hot temper came into contact with the icy dignity of Zukor, the effect was calamitous. 'Famous Players-Lasky is not large enough to hold both Mr Goldfish and myself,' Adolph announced, and paid him off with $900,000. Sam joined the Selwyn brothers to form Goldwyn Pictures shortly afterwards, adopting the company's name as his own; but it was only the name – not Sam which, in 1924, became part of Metro-Goldwyn-Mayer. He had already made another exit, to start a long career, unfettered by partners, as the industry's most brilliant independent film-maker.

At first glance it seems equally capricious to omit **W.W. Hodkinson** from star billing. After all, he did name Paramount (after an apartment house he happened to pass) and he gave it its trade-mark (while doodling mountains and stars on a blotter). He also provided, as we have seen, a distribution outlet for the early works of Famous Players and Lasky. But his was not the still-surviving Paramount that they created, and his connection with them lasted only two years. An astute, straight-dealing businessman, Hodkinson was a thriving member of the states' rights fraternity when he left San Francisco for New York with the idea of banding together other territorial franchise holders into a central sales organization. To keep it supplied with product, he signed contracts with various producers. It was his hard luck that one of these was Zukor, who couldn't rest until he dominated any business he touched. After he was ousted from Paramount, Hodkinson started another distribution network, then became an aircraft manufacturer.

Hiram Abrams, one of Hodkinson's partners, was used to overthrow him, having received a promise that he would then be rewarded with the presidency. Zukor kept that promise, but soon discovered that Abrams wasn't content to be a figurehead. His services were dispensed with. The independent production companies of **Oliver Morosco** and **Hobart Bosworth**, also participants in the Famous Players-Lasky-Paramount merger, proved similarly redundant to Zukor's plans and therefore also dropped out of the picture.

And how can one demote the stars themselves to the 'supporting cast'? Beyond doubt, it was they whose names and personalities generated the vast mass appeal of the company and, indeed, of Hollywood itself. To the filmgoing millions, any one of them was more important than the most influential of executives (except perhaps DeMille, always a ticket-selling name). But the stars' careers, along with those of hundreds of other men and women who helped to make Paramount paramount, will be covered in the pages that follow.

The Best Show in Town
1916-1925

Hectic activity marked the early years of the newly combined company – not least in production, which accelerated to such a tempo that, from 1916 to 1921, every week saw the emergence of two or three new pictures from Famous Players-Lasky. That name didn't slip from the public's tongue with the greatest of ease, so Adolph Zukor decided to use Paramount, the subsidiary distribution firm's name and trade-mark in advertising and publicity – and 'If It's a Paramount Picture It's the Best Show in Town' became the most familiar slogan in the movie world. The ego of each partner was cushioned by prefixing the main titles with 'Jesse L. Lasky presents' on the West Coast productions and 'Adolph Zukor presents' on those made in the East. Actually they were all produced under Lasky's aegis, with Hugh Ford supervising the East Coast studios and Hector Turnbull those in Hollywood which, increasingly, became the more productive and stretched the 'Barn' to the limits of its resources.

Lasky got off to a bad start in the new set-up by giving Mary Pickford what she (and many others) considered the worst picture of her career, *Less Than The Dust*, but her subsequent vehicles were all hits, confirming her position at the very apex of stardom. 'America's Sweetheart', as they now called the little charmer, had a keen brain under her blonde curls. She also had an even shrewder mother. Ambushed between the two of them, even Zukor was outbargained, and before long Mary's $500 weekly had soared to $10,000, plus a percentage of her films' profits. He had to keep her on to maintain Paramount's policy of block-booking, whereby exhibitors had to take a large group of pictures, sight unseen, to be sure of getting the big ones like Pickford's.

He also needed her to withstand the rivalry of Harry Aitken. This upstart, who had made a fortune by backing D.W. Griffith's *Birth Of A Nation*, put together a giant company, Triangle Pictures, consisting of top producers Griffith, Thomas Ince and Mack Sennett. In 1917 Zukor started luring all three into the Paramount fold, along with some of their best stars: Griffith's Douglas Fairbanks and the Gish sisters, Lillian and Dorothy, Ince's William S. Hart, Charles Ray and Dorothy Dalton, and Sennett's Roscoe 'Fatty' Arbuckle. He put most of them into Artcraft Pictures, a company (formed in 1916 to handle Pickford's films) which might more accurately have been called Paramount-Plus Pictures, calling for higher rental terms than the studio's regular product. Aitken's Triangle Pictures went into a rapid decline, and exhibitors went into hysterics. The enlargement of Artcraft, on top of block-booking, was just too much for them.

'Stop Zukor!' (or ruder words to that effect) became the exhibitors' rallying cry. A formidable number of them, led by circuit owners J.D. Williams and Thomas Tally, joined forces and plunged into the production maelstrom, creating First National Pictures, a more dangerous threat to Paramount's supremacy than Triangle had been. Its initial triumph was to sign up the only box-office attraction comparable to Pickford, Charlie Chaplin, for the unheard-of sum of $1,075,000 a year. Already stung by First National's ability to bar Paramount from its theatres, Zukor then suffered the unkindest cut from this rival which offered Mary $1,100,000 (including a $50,000 bonus for Ma, so that Pickford could top Chaplin) and got her.

Adolph retaliated by adopting the exhibitors' ploy in reverse. To Paramount's vast production-distribution organization he started to add a theatre chain. With the aid of a $10 million issue of preference shares to Wall Street banks, he built or bought showplaces for Paramount all over the map: first the Rialto and the Rivoli on Broadway (where his old penny arcade partner Mitchell Mark had begun the super-cinema vogue with the Strand), then theatres around the country – and even in Europe, with the Paris Paramount and the London Plaza opening in 1924. Meanwhile, distribution branches grew into a worldwide network. Studios also proliferated: in 1920 all New York production was shifted to a big new plant at Astoria, Long Island, and a London studio at Islington turned out several movies, although its chief claim to fame is having given Alfred Hitchcock his first film job, designing subtitles. Paris, Berlin and Bombay were other Paramount studio outposts.

In 1917 the queen of the screen was Mary Pickford, and a power behind the throne was her mother. They are seen on the set of Poor Little Rich Girl.

Never the mind the clothes; look at the model. In 1925 he had been a superstar for four years; after one more he died, aged 31. But the Valentino legend lives on.

DeMille (seated at table) directing the 1921 hit The Affairs of Anatol *with, from left, Wallace Reid, Agnes Ayres, Monte Blue, Charles Ogle, Theodore Kosloff.*

In 1919 Zukor invented a third brand name for his company. While the bulk of releases carried the Paramount label and the more expensive were dubbed Artcraft, Realart was a lower-budget category with a cheaper price tag for exhibitors – and this time not one was heard to utter a word of protest. Also in 1919, Zukor talked William Randolph Hearst into bringing to Paramount his Cosmo-politan Productions, his star Marion Davies, and invaluable pub-licity in his great newspaper chain. Within five years, all those subsidary names had disappeared from the release lists. Para-mount was enough.

While his partner was thus exercising as much acquisitive zeal as an itchy-tentacled octopus, Lasky kept production roaring ahead. Always seeking more stories and plays, he became the unpublicized head of the Broadway stage empire of Charles Frohman (who died in the 1915 *Lusitania* sinking), and signed New York and London producer Gilbert Miller to run it as a major source of hits for many years, with Paramount as silent partner. On a transatlantic trip Lasky bought the film rights to ten plays by Sir James Barrie, paying the famous Scot $100,000 plus 50% of profits, the same deal as he had made with Belasco. Another wholesale story buy was for the entire output of Western novelist Zane Grey.

The first Barrie play filmed, *The Admirable Crichton*, became *Male And Female* ('Why didn't I think of that title?' said Sir James, tongue well in cheek), one of a succession of lavish Cecil DeMille winners, which reached their peak with *The Ten Commandments* in 1923. That same year brought another blockbuster in *The Covered Wagon*, the first Western epic. By this time the biggest stars shining over the Paramount mountain were Gloria Swanson, Rudolph Valentino and a newcomer imported from Germany, Pola Negri.

But it was the studio's celebrities who cast a dark shadow over Hollywood's image. The first scandal broke in September 1921 when Fatty Arbuckle, the Sennett shorts comedian who had moved up to feature stardom at Paramount, was accused of the rape and manslaughter of a party girl. He was acquitted after two trials which got months of headline attention, but his career was short-cir-cuited. So was that of Mary Miles Minter, a star in innocently girlish roles, who was involved in the murder case, with sinister sex and dope revelations, of director William Desmond Taylor in Feb-ruary 1922. Both were Paramount contractees. The enormously popular Wallace Reid was a Paramount star too, and the other shocks had not subsided when this ideal specimen of clean-cut American manhood confessed to being a drug addict. He soon died, aged 32.

These events caused a public outcry, intensified by church groups and newspapers, against movie immorality, both on and off the screen. An industry self-censorship board was established, with august politician Will Hays at its head. Cecil DeMille's spec-tacular depictions of sin came under a cloud, and after a 1924 row with Zukor and sales chief Sidney Kent over his budget-bursting production costs, he left the company he had helped to create.

Another headache began to throb as the first half of the Twen-ties drew to a close. Paramount's steady annual profit of over $5 million – twice that of Fox, three times Universal's, five times more than Warners' – was now being equalled by the new Metro-Goldwyn-Mayer, put together in 1924 by none other than Zukor's old friend Marcus Loew. MGM was far too big to be subdued like Triangle and First National. Paramount had to move over and make room at the top.

Fatty Arbuckle (right) and lawyers conferring during the trials that both ended his starring career and helped bring Hollywood's morality into disrepute.

1916

▽ By far the most ambitious production of Famous Players-Lasky's early years, **Joan The Woman** was the first of the super-spectacles which made Cecil B. DeMille a legendary name in movie history. The title role was played by Geraldine Farrar (centre) with every ounce of the physical bravura and spiritual intensity required, surprising many who had thought Joan of Arc too demanding an assignment for the world-famous opera singer who had made her silent screen debut only the year before. She was surrounded by a huge cast which included Wallace Reid, Theodore Roberts, Raymond Hatton, Hobart Bosworth, Tully Marshall, James Neill, Lillian Leighton, Cleo Ridgely, Marjorie Daw, Walter Long and (by the publicity department's count) 1,000 extras. Jeanie Macpherson's script gave full scope to DeMille's flair for mass appeal, but – as usual with this story – public response was disappointing.

△ Audiences were more willing to suspend disbelief in 1916 than they were in later years, so Marie Doro was as readily accepted in the title role of **Oliver Twist** (left) as she was in the character of Rose Fairlie (right). Sheer acting skill, as well as a petite figure dressed in boy's clothes, assisted the illusion. Miss Doro had been enchanting theatre audiences for years before becoming one of the first actresses to be starred by Zukor and Lasky. In fact, she had scored one of her biggest Broadway hits as Oliver Twist in the 1912 dramatisation of Dickens's novel. As in the subsequent screen versions (by First National in 1922, Monogram in 1933; and the two best, Rank-United Artists in 1948 and, as the musical *Oliver!*, Romulus-Columbia in 1968, both British) much of the book's voluminous plot had to be elided, but enough was left to make a gripping drama. James Young directed the star's contrasting performances, with colourful support from Tully Marshall as Fagin, the fence whose thieves' den shelters Oliver; Raymond Hatton as his slickest pickpocket, the Artful Dodger; Hobart Bosworth as Bill Sikes, the brute who menaces Oliver, and Elsie Jane Wilson as Nancy, Bill's frightened doxy who is sympathetic to Oliver.

△ Although never achieving the stratospheric heights of popularity reached by Mary Pickford, Marguerite Clark (illustrated), another purveyor of perennial youth, came a good second at Famous Players after Zukor signed her in 1914 for three years at $1,000 a week. Five years later, when she left, he was paying her nearly six times as much. One of her best loved movies, **Snow White**, displayed her captivating charm, delicate technique, and ability to convince as a young girl when she was actually in her thirties. Winthrop Ames, who wrote the script from the Grimms' fairy tale, had produced it on Broadway in 1912 with Marguerite, then at the peak of her stage career. Creighton Hale, Dorothy Cumming and Lionel Braham supported her under J. Searle Dawley's direction in the film, the company's big-city release for Christmas 1916. In his book *From Hollywood* DeWitt Bodeen wrote: 'When Walt Disney, more than a score of years later, compiled his production of *Snow White*, he confessed that he deliberately modelled much of its treatment on the Marguerite Clark film.'

FOR THE OTHER PRODUCTIONS OF 1916 SEE PAGE 323.

1917

▽ **Rebecca Of Sunnybrook Farm** started a succession of five major Mary Pickford hits screenwritten by Frances Marion and directed by Marshall Neilan. With a strong supporting cast, including Eugene O'Brien, Helen Jerome Eddy, Charles Ogle, Marjorie Daw, Mayme Kelso, Josephine Crowell, Jane Wolff and Jack MacDonald, Mary (illustrated) had an ideal role as one of a large family of New England youngsters who is sent by her poverty-harassed mother (Wolfe) to live with a pair of strait-laced aunts (Kelso and Crowell). She shocks them with her pranks but makes friends with a neighbour (O'Brien) who, after she has been sent to boarding school and returns as a poised young lady, falls in love with her. Further joy comes to her family when the railroad decides to build through Sunnybrook Farm, bringing them prosperity. The story originated in a 1903 best-selling novel by Kate Douglas Wiggin, which was turned into a play in 1910 by the author and Charlotte Thompson. It was filmed twice more by Fox, in 1932 with Marian Nixon and in 1938 with Shirley Temple.

▽ Fifteen years before Paramount filmed George M. Cohan's talkie debut in *The Phantom President* (and wished they hadn't), the idolised Broadway actor-playwright-songsmith starred in three silents under the company's Artcraft banner. The one that really clicked at the box-office was **Seven Keys To Baldpate**, which had been a 1913 money-spinner for him on the stage. In 1917 Hugh Ford directed the Cohan adaptation of Earl Derr Biggers's book about a writer of best-sellers (Cohan, left) who boasts that he can complete a 10,000-word novel in 24 hours. A friend, making a bet that he can't, gives him the key to his Baldpate Inn, closed for the winter, where he can enjoy complete seclusion. The author settles down to write, only to be interrupted by a succession of key bearers who turn the inn into a frantic centre of criminal and romantic activities, which he records as a novel, thus winning his bet. Cohan's leading ladies were Anna Q. Nilsson (right), Hollywood's first Swedish import to become a star, and Elda Furry, who changed her name to Hedda Hopper and acted for many years before terrorising Tinseltown as a gossip-columnist. The Biggers story achieved the remarkable total of five film versions, the remakes coming from Paramount in 1925, and RKO in 1929 (Richard Dix's first real starrer), 1935 and 1947.

▽ An unabashed flag-wagger, **The Little American**'s wartime propaganda was irresistibly sweetened by the presence of Mary Pickford in the title role. The combination of America and America's Sweetheart was a double-strength magnet for moviegoers' cash, and the customers were well satisfied by Jeanie Macpherson's complicated screenplay, which ranged from disaster spectacle – the sinking of the 'Lusitania' – to romantic drama, in which the heroine (Mary, left) was emotionally torn between a German/American (Jack Holt, right) and a French/American (Raymond Hatton). No prize for guessing which man won her. Also featured under Cecil B. DeMille's direction were Hobart Bosworth, Walter Long, James Neill, Guy Oliver, Edythe Chapman and Ben Alexander. Adolph Zukor had persuaded Mary to leave the East Coast studio and move to DeMille's Hollywood headquarters, where the two most important Paramount talents could work together. She did so in February 1917, and made this and another DeMille picture (*Romance Of The Redwoods*) in an unhappy atmosphere in which the well-developed egos of star and director were often at loggerheads. Although she was then being paid $10,000 weekly, four times the salary of DeMille's other superstar, Geraldine Farrar, Mary began negotiating with First National for an even fatter contract.

△ Although his star contract was sniffed at by some as nepotism, Jack Pickford made almost as many movies as his sister Mary, and a number of them were very popular. One of the best was **Tom Sawyer**, in which Jack, aged 21, had no trouble in looking and acting like the much younger lad immortalised by Mark Twain. Julia Crawford Ivers, in her screen adaptation, smoothly integrated the book's episodic adventures, and William Desmond Taylor's direction caught their rural, youthful spirit. Among the highlights were the celebrated fence-painting incident, the transformation of Tom for Sunday school (seen here, centre, with, left to right, Alice Marvin, George Hackathorne and Edythe Chapman), and his disappearance with Huckleberry Finn (Robert Gordon) to a pirate island, and thought dead by the community, only to show up at their own funeral. Louise Huff, Clara Horton, Antrom Short and Helen Gillmore rounded out the cast. A year later Paramount reissued Pickford and Gordon in *Tom And Huck*, and revived the characters again in 1930 (*Tom Sawyer*), 1931 (*Huckleberry Finn*) and 1938 (*Tom Sawyer, Detective*). Pickford's life, marked by scandals and divorces, ended in 1933; Mary outlived him by 46 years.

△ In 1917 Geraldine Farrar returned to Hollywood for two more Artcraft productions under Cecil B. DeMille's direction to follow the four she had made in 1915–16. **The Woman God Forgot** was the first and more successful of the pair, after which the Metropolitan Opera diva left Paramount for a Goldwyn contract. In this gloriously melodramatic spectacle, the Spanish conquest of Mexico, circa 1520, succeeded mainly because Mme Farrar (right) as Aztec ruler Montezuma's daughter, loved Wallace Reid (centre) as invader Cortez's emissary, who was captured by warrior Theodore Kosloff (left), her betrothed; whereupon Farrar fled in the dead of night to the Spanish camp and led Cortez's army back inside the city before Reid could be offered as a sacrifice to the gods. Thus was the 300-year Aztec nation destroyed – or so the rich imagination of scenarist Jeanie Macpherson would have you believe. Two other regular DeMille collaborators, cameraman Alvin Wyckoff and set designer Wilfred Buckland, contributed some of their most eye-filling work to this extraordinary movie, whose cast (including Raymond Hatton as Montezuma, Hobart Bosworth as Cortez, Walter Long as a high priest and Julia Faye as a handmaiden) held nothing back in their grand-style silent emoting.

FOR THE OTHER PRODUCTIONS OF 1917 SEE PAGE 323.

1918

▽ Nobody in Hollywood was busier than William S. Hart during 1918. **Riddle Gawne** was generally considered the best of no fewer than eight features he completed in that year, as both star and director. An interest-holding drama by Charles Alden Seltzer from his story *The Vengeance Of Jefferson Gawne*, it traced a feud to the death between tough westerner 'Riddle' Gawne (Hart, seen here) and badman Bozzam (Lon Chaney) who, having killed Gawne's brother, runs off with his faithless wife. Two of Bozzam's gang abduct another girl (Katherine MacDonald) whom Gawne rescues; they fall in love, and she nurses him back to health after a violent fight in which Bozzam, assuming Gawne to be mortally wounded, has admitted his crimes and been strangled by the hero. Hart loped through all this with his usual impressive rigidity and a face that might have been carved on Mount Rushmore; his direction, however, emphasised action and, as always, eschewed horse-opera glamour to depict the West as it really was. Gertrude Short, Gretchen Lederer, E.P. Tilton, Milton Ross, George Field and Leon Kent completed his cast.

▽ 'One of Mr Griffith's best films,' said Lillian Gish about **The Greatest Thing In Life** in her autobiography. But it arrived rather late in a period overloaded with war pictures, and it was received with less rapture than the great D.W.'s pictures of the following year starring Miss Gish, *True Heart Susie* and *Broken Blossoms*. In this one she played a New York newspaper-seller's daughter whose beauty and vivacity catch the eye of a rich dilettante (Robert Harron). Fascinated, but too class-conscious to consider a proposal, he pays for her father's return to his native France with the girl. There they meet again during the war, in which the playboy is serving as a soldier and father and daughter are underground agents; battle-weary, his snobbery eradicated, Harron finds humility and love with Lillian. The latter is seen here with David Butler (an actor until he became a prolific director, 1927–67). Adolphe Lestina (the father), Elmo Lincoln, Kate Bruce, Edward Piel and Peaches Jackson also had parts in the screenplay by Captain Victor Marier (a Griffith pseudonym) and S.E.V. Taylor. Two years after making this, one of his many Griffith films, Harron died at the age of 26 from a gunshot wound. Coroner's verdict: accidental death.

▽ A major star whose fame now glimmers only faintly through the six decades since her last silent picture (she returned for one 1930 talkie), Elsie Ferguson had an excellent acting technique to augment the movie requisites of beauty and charm. She made 22 films for Paramount between 1917 and 1922, most of them successful, and distinguished by the company's 'Artcraft' label, as befitted an already established stage star. One of her best performances was as Nora (illustrated) in **A Doll's House**, directed by Maurice Tourneur, with Holmes Herbert, Ethel Grey Terry and Alex Shannon also cast in Charles Maigne's adaptation of the Ibsen classic about a Norwegian housewife who realised that 'house' and 'wife' need not be the limits of a woman's life. But its total lack of action (until the heroine slammed the final door on her claustrophobic marriage) repelled the fans and it was a box-office failure – like its other film versions in 1917 (Dorothy Phillips), 1922 (Nazimova) and 1973 (Jane Fonda and Claire Bloom).

△ **La Tosca** fitted Pauline Frederick's grand manner and dramatic intensity to perfection. Victorien Sardou wrote it for Sarah Bernhardt, whose 1887 triumph in it preceded the addition of Puccini's music by thirteen years. The florid passions of its characters – beautiful prima donna in love with a fugitive captured by a wicken police chief – swept it to its climax of torture, seduction and murder, with enough of its stage excitement intact on the silent screen to enthrall 1918 moviegoers. Frederick (right) was supported by Jules Raucourt (left), Frank Losee and Henry Herbert in this Charles Whittaker adaptation, directed by Edward Jose. The most glamorous star that Zukor had lured from Broadway, the leading lady was in the last of her four years with Famous Players, during which she made 28 pictures (they didn't fool around in those days), and she remained a prominent film name until 1937.

△ Exhibitors lucky enough to book it found Marguerite Clark and **Uncle Tom's Cabin** a money-in-the-bank combination. The petite star was natural casting as Little Eva (left) but this role hardly gave fans their money's worth of Marguerite, so she slapped on dark greasepaint and played Topsy, Eva's naughty black playmate as well – courtesy of double-exposure photography. J. Searle Dawley wrote and directed this efficient adaptation of Harriet Beecher Stowe's 1852 novel, wringing every teardrop from the long, sad story of Uncle Tom (Frank Losee, right) whose master (Thomas Carnahan Jr) has to sell him and another slave, Eliza (Florence Carpenter), who escapes with her child across the icy Ohio river. Tom is taken South with his new master (J.W. Johnston) and saves the life of Eva en route. Her parents (Augusta Anderson and Henry Stamford) buy Tom and he is happy until both Eva and her father die. Sold to brutal Simon Legree (Walter Lewis), Tom is literally tortured to death, and a mistreated slave girl (Ruby Hoffman) kills Legree. This bundle of fun has been unwrapped by film-makers seven times since 1903, not counting the condensed Siamese version in *The King And I*.

△ Cecil B. DeMille, who had a weakness for remaking his old hits, waited only a little over four years to give his first one another whirl. **The Squaw Man**, having already penetrated every town and hamlet either as Edwin Milton Royle's 1905 play or C.B.'s 1914 movie, had no surprises left, but there was enough dramatic muscle in the story to give this version, scripted by Beulah Marie Dix, renewed box-office stamina. Elliott Dexter (centre) played Jim who, having taken the blame for his cousin's theft because he loves the latter's wife (Katherine MacDonald), leaves England for Wyoming, where he saves an Indian girl (Ann Little, right) from the clutches of an outlaw (Jack Holt). She marries him, saves him from death, bears him a son, and kills his arch-enemy the outlaw. When accused of the latter's murder, she commits suicide. Jim's first love arrives from England with news that her husband has died, thereby making Jim an earl by inheritance, and they return home with Jim's son. In the large cast were Thurston Hall (the cousin), Theodore Roberts, Noah Beery, Tully Marshall (left), Herbert Standing, Monte Blue and Julia Faye. Still not as tired of the story as the public had become, DeMille filmed it for a third time in 1931, burdening MGM with a talkie flop.

▷ An extraordinary movie for its time, **The Whispering Chorus** had a melodramatic plot that would have stretched credulity to breaking point if the viewer had not been mesmerised by the imaginative treatment accorded to it by Cecil B. DeMille and his cinematographer, Alvin Wyckoff. Jeanie Macpherson's script, from a novel by Perley Poore Sheehan, concerned an embezzler (Raymond Hatton) who fakes his death to avoid imprisonment: finding a body floating in the river, he dresses it in his clothes and effects, and mutilates its face. After years of wandering and degradation, he is arrested and charged with his own murder; the truth is realised only by his mother (Edythe Chapman) who begs him to remain silent, and by his wife (Kathlyn Williams, right) who fears what the scandal may do to her new husband (Elliott Dexter, left) who is the State Governor, and their unborn baby. He keeps silent and is executed. What made all this so distinctive were the remarkable scenes of the man's conscience haunting him in the form of ghostly faces, swirling about him (via multi-exposure camera work) as inescapable accusers. Also impressive throughout was the performance of Hatton, who played hundreds of roles in his 55-year screen career, but none so powerful as this.

◁ Here, in the title role of **Stella Maris**, is the Mary Pickford adored by millions all over the world: the lovely, sunny-natured, dimple-smiled, sausage-curled girl whose box-office magnetism has rarely been equalled, never surpassed. Imagine the consternation of studio executives when she insisted on playing not only Stella, the pampered invalid heroine of William J. Locke's novel, but also the ugly drab whom Stella rescues from destitution and who sacrifices herself in a tragic climax of murder and suicide. Helped by superb scriptwriting and direction by Frances Marion and Marshall Neilan, respectively, Mary carried off both characterisations with great *éclat*. Her supporting cast included Conway Tearle, Ida Waterman, Herbert Standing, Camille Ankewich and Josephine Crowell. Particular praise went to the double-exposure effects, remarkably flawless in sustaining the illusion of two Pickfords on screen at the same time.

FOR THE OTHER PRODUCTIONS OF 1918 SEE PAGE 324.

1919

▽ **The Girl Who Stayed At Home** was Clarine Seymour (left) as the high-spirited fiancée of dough-boy Robert Harron (right) who played one of two American brothers fighting in France during World War I. He might have guessed she'd be as anxiety-making as the enemy's shellfire: her character's name was Cutie Beautiful. His brother (Richard Barthelmess) was similarly distracted meanwhile by a French girl (Carol Dempster) in imminent danger of rape and/or death by the Huns. However, the scenario by S.E.V. Taylor and D.W. Griffith had the two pairs of lovers safely reunited before its muddled narrative ran out of steam. The muddle was caused by the Armistice. Griffith had just finished directing the picture when its original purpose – dramatic propaganda to stimulate recruitment – suddenly became outdated, as did its hate-the-Hun element. He had to rearrange several sequences, and inserted some sympathy for the Germans (one of them a soldier who kills Carol's would-be rapist) which didn't please the public too well, and the movie's belated release in 1919 drew less than the usual Griffith crowds. With Kate Bruce, Tully Marshall and George Fawcett in the cast were several dignitaries appearing as themselves: Secretary of War Newton Baker, Chief of Staff General Peyton March and Provost-Marshal General E.H. Chowder.

△ One of the last pictures D.W. Griffith made for Paramount release under the Artcraft label during his 1917–19 association with the company turned out to be the best of the lot. **True Heart Susie** inspired superlative praise from the critics and brought in not only the habitual movie fans but also (in spite of a title that was pretty icky even for that era) the more discriminating customers. Scenes of young love played with delicacy and charm by Lillian Gish and Robert Harron (both illustrated) were chiefly responsible for its success. These were interrupted by a dramatic interlude in which Susie Trueheart's devotion to the boy is severely tested. Having furthered his ambition to be a clergyman by financing (without his knowledge) his college education, Susie welcomes him back, only to see him captivated by a worthless flirt (Clarine Seymour). He marries this girl, but her dissolute ways soon cause illness and death and he realises that Susie is his true love. Griffith and his renowned cameraman Billy Bitzer imbued Marian Fremont's screenplay with a simple, rustic beauty. The stars were supported by George Fawcett, Carol Dempster, Kate Bruce, Wilbur Higby, Loyola O'Connor and Raymond Cannon.

▷ Hosannas and hallelujahs echoed through Paramount's accounts department as religious faith overcame the force of evil in **The Miracle Man**, the story of a gang of crooks conspiring to cash in on the work of a blind healer, whose spiritual influence eventually regenerates them. Corn of the ripest sort, of course, but so beautifully served by director George Loane Tucker that it was relished by enormous audiences. It brought stardom to Betty Compson, as a girl of the underworld (here with Joseph Dowling as the Miracle Man) and to Lon Chaney as a derelict pretending to be a paralysed cripple. It boosted the career of Thomas Meighan, already well known, and began that of Elinor Fair, making her debut as a 17-year-old ingenue. Meighan, a friend of George M. Cohan, brought the latter's play, based on a novel by Frank Packard, to the attention of Tucker, who wrote the screenplay and filmed it in twelve weeks. A talking remake in 1932 failed to measure up.

▷ At the age of 17 Mary Miles Minter, already a popular star and veteran of stage and screen, was given a $1 million contract by Paramount. It began with **Anne Of Green Gables**, a shrewd choice to establish a Mary Pickford substitute for the studio. The adventures of Anne (left), her puppy-love sweetheart (Paul Kelly), her foster-parents, and other folksy characters, had already generated four best-selling books by L.M. Montgomery from which ace scenarist Frances Marion extracted an irresistible dollop of molasses for the masses. It was still a crowd-pleaser when RKO remade it as a talkie in 1934. Mary continued for three years as the strongest attraction under the Realart banner; then her career was cut short by her involvement in the scandals surrounding William Desmond

Taylor's murder. He directed this movie, with George Stewart, Frederick Burton (right), Marcia Harris, Lincoln Stedman and Albert Hackett (later a top screenwriter) in the cast.

△ Sir James Barrie must have been shaken to his Scottish core when he saw what DeMille had wrought from his play, *The Admirable Crichton*. Not only had its title been hotted up to **Male And Female** (although it kept the original one for British release), but Cecil B. had managed to insert one of his customary 'visions' – this time a sequence of king and slave girl in ancient Babylon, climaxed by her being cast into an arena full of lions. The excuse for this fantasy was the reading of Henley's verse, 'I was a king in Babylon and you were a Christian slave', by Thomas Meighan (right) to Gloria Swanson (left). No reason beyond DeMille's box-office flair was required for the elaborate depiction of Gloria taking a bath, which kept the fans agog with its unfulfilled promise of nudity. Otherwise Barrie's comedy of shipwrecked aristocrats having to take orders from their butler managed to survive Jeanie Macpherson's screenplay more or less intact. Bebe Daniels, Theodore Roberts and Lila Lee supported the two stars in the biggest hit of the year.

◁ The second of four movie versions of **Little Women**, made in 1918 by World, an independent company established by the prominent Broadway producer William A. Brady (father of Alice), was a very popular 1919 release for Paramount/Artcraft. Director Harley Knoles took his cast – Henry Hull (left) as the professor and Conrad Nagel (right) as Laurie (both destined for Hollywood fame for decades), Lillian Hall, Isabel Lamon (left), Kate Lester, Dorothy Bernard (right), Florence Flimm and George Kelson – to Concord, Massachusetts, and filmed the phenomenal Louisa May Alcott best-seller in and around the author's home where it was written fifty years before. The sentimental tale centred on a mother and her four daughters – their joys, sorrows and romances, with the Civil War rumbling in the distance. Remade by RKO in 1933 and MGM in 1948.

FOR THE OTHER PRODUCTIONS OF 1919 SEE PAGE 326.

1920

△ Gloria Swanson, Thomas Meighan (right) and Bebe Daniels (left) shone in a typical 1920 Cecil B. DeMille comedy, **Why Change Your Wife?** Stemming from a story by brother William, it gave Cecil scope for extravagantly dressing – and undressing – the leading ladies in boudoirs, bedrooms and bathrooms while flirtations and jealousies were volleyed by husband (Meighan), wife (Swanson), other woman (Daniels) and other man (Theodore Kosloff). This was the first starring role for Bebe, who had come to Paramount to play opposite Meighan in the Babylonian flashback sequence of *Male And Female*. She had begun her half-century in films as a child actress, was in hundreds of shorts (many as Harold Lloyd's heroine), then 51 Paramount features, and was a long-established star of London show business with her husband, Ben Lyon, when she died in 1971. She, and others, in this racy screenplay by Olga Printzlau and Sada Cowan made it a prime example of DeMille for the millions.

▽ Millions of ladies sobbed happily through **Humoresque** as a young concert violinist (Gaston Glass, right) emerged from the New York slums to the glittering world of Park Avenue, went to fight in the war and returned wounded. He tells his sweetheart (Alma Rubens) he can no longer follow his career and so will not marry her. Heartbroken, she faints, and while helping her he finds he can use his injured arm after all. Happy ending. More impressive were earlier sequences in the ghetto, where the boy's mother sustains her poverty-stricken family while dreaming of his becoming a successful musician. In this role, the warm performance of Vera Gordon (left) was the best thing in the picture. Adapted by ace screenwriter Frances Marion from the title tale in the book of short stories that began Fannie Hurst's best-sellership in 1919, it was directed by that maestro of the tear-ducts, Frank Borzage. (All three combined their talents in 1922 for another cosmopolitan production, *Back Pay*, with less success.) The cast included Dore Davidson, Sidney Carlyle and Miriam Battista. In the much-revised Warner Bros. remake, 27 years later, Joan Crawford and John Garfield were teamed in the Rubens and Glass roles.

▷ All the time he was making **Dr Jekyll And Mr Hyde** at the New York studio, John Barrymore (right) was rehearsing *Richard III* on Broadway, where he had recently triumphed in *The Jest*. There were reminders of both plays in the film. One of the elaborate *Jest* sets he particularly liked was transported uptown to the cameras; and his spidery Mr Hyde showed distinct traces of Shakespeare's twisted king. His transformations from Dr Jekyll owed little to make-up, much to cinematography and most of all to Barrymore's artistry, which illuminated his whole performance. John S. Robertson's direction of the Clara Beranger screenplay managed to combine a moody atmosphere with a brisk tempo, and drew effective work from Martha Mansfield as Jekyll's girl and Nita Naldi, then unknown, as Hyde's; also Louis Wolheim (left), Brandon Hurst, Charles Lane, Cecil Clovelly and J. Malcolm Dunn. (Barrymore offered a role to another unknown, Tallulah Bankhead, with a gesture to the casting couch, which she declined. Tallulah was very young in 1920...) Many versions of Robert Louis Stevenson's spellbinder have been filmed, from the primitive (by Universal in 1913) to the *outré* (Hammer's 1971 *Dr Jekyll And Sister Hyde*), and the farcical (Paramount's *Jekyll And Hyde Together Again*, 1983).

△ Lionel Barrymore's career, the longest of his fabulous family's, reached two peaks with **The Copperhead**. The first came in 1918, when he was given 15 curtain calls by the enraptured audience at the play's Broadway opening; the second followed two years later when his performance on film (illustrated) was acclaimed internationally. The title role in the drama by Augustus Thomas was actually named Milt Shanks, a rock-hard character who enrages his patriotic fellow small-towners in Illinois by voicing pro-Southern sympathies and becoming a conscientious objector during the Civil War. Forty years later, realising his beloved granddaughter (Anne Cornwall) is tainted by the town's hatred of him, he reveals that he had been appointed by Abraham Lincoln to infiltrate the Copperheads (Southern conspirators in the North) during the War, and sworn to lifelong secrecy. Doris Rankin, Barrymore's first wife, played Ma Shanks; Richard Carlyle, Arthur Rankin, Leslie Stowe, William Carlton and Frank Joyner were also cast, and Charles Maigne directed. In 1926, Barrymore, who had been alternating theatre and movie work in New York since 1909, revived *The Copperhead* in Los Angeles. It was his last stage appearance: MGM saw it and gave him a contract that lasted 28 years until his death.

▽ This was how they advertised one of the many enjoyable little comedies Dorothy Gish (left) starred in for D.W. Griffith's production company and Paramount release. It was a sprightly trifle whipped up by scenarist Dorothy Elizabeth Carter, about a vivacious girl who, in a series of comic episodes, teaches her smug husband to appreciate her. It was less interesting for its content than for the circumstances of its making. To begin with, **Remodeling Her Husband** is the only known instance of a picture whose star and director were sisters. Lillian Gish, who had handled occasional scenes for Griffith in the past, got his per-mission to direct an entire film, but was dismayed to find that she had to make it in his partly-built new studio at Mamaroneck, near New York, while he went West on another project. To add insult to injury, she was asked simultaneously to supervise the completion of the studio's construction. The deceptively frail-looking Lillian, having polished off both tasks with aplomb, stuck to acting for the next sixty odd years. Dorothy liked the way James Rennie (right) played her remodelled husband (in a cast including Marie Burke, Downing Clark and Frank Kingdon) so much that she married him.

△ Of all the 56 American movies Maurice Tourneur made in America between 1914 and 1926, none was more popular than **Treasure Island**. A never-failing story anyway, it was given powerful additional appeal by Tourneur's pictorial talent, as this shot exem-plifies. Throughout his long career, which began and finished in the studios of his native France, he ranked in the top echelon of directors by virtue of this exquis-ite visual style. And he was no slouch as a tale-spinner: smooth pacing enhanced the Jules Furthman-Stephen Fox screenplay treatment of the classic Robert Louis Stevenson swashbuckler charting a search for pirates' buried loot. One department in which this production compared unfavourably with the later versions made by MGM in 1934 and Walt Disney (for RKO) in 1950 was casting. For un-fathomable reasons Tourneur, who also produced it, indulged in the eccentricities of assigning a female star, Shirley Mason (second right), to play Jim Haw-kins, and Lon Chaney (centre) to play two roles, Pew and Merry. Others present included Charles Ogle, Josie Melville, Bull Montana, Charles Hill Mailes and Wilton Taylor.

FOR THE OTHER PRODUCTIONS OF 1920 SEE PAGE 327.

1921

▽ One of the less renowned but still profitable products of the art of Cecil B. DeMille was **Forbidden Fruit**, the title of which, according to Jeanie Macpherson's heavy-breathing screenplay, referred to the temptations of luxury assailing a working girl when she mixed with the rich. Agnes Ayres (right) starred as a gambler's wife elevated from seamstress to dinner guest by her employer to replace a non-arrival. She scores a social success, especially with oil magnate Forrest Stanley (left), but before she reaches the fade-out clinch in his arms she has to endure scandalous gossip, not to mention the embarrassment of her hostess (Kathlyn Williams) being robbed by the wastrel husband (Clarence Burton) who is killed in a struggle with his confederate, the butler (Boris Karloff). Agnes' chic headgear was by actor Theodore Kosloff, who both appeared in the movie (a remake of DeMille's 1915 *The Golden Chance*) as the butler's accomplice, and designed the costumes.

▷ Now listen carefully, and don't interrupt. In **Fool's Paradise** Conrad Nagel (right), a World War I soldier recuperating from an eye wound, fell in love with a French dancer (Mildred Harris, left; off-screen, Charlie Chaplin's first wife) who rejected him. Later, he is attracted to another French dancer in a US-Mexico border town (Dorothy Dalton), but her jealousy is kindled by his memories of the first girl, so she gives him an explosive cigar which blinds him completely. Contrite, she begs him to marry her, and takes him to a surgeon who restores his sight. Spurning Dorothy, however, he goes in search of Mildred and finds her living with a prince in Siam (John Davidson). Unable to choose between the two men, Mildred throws her gloves into a crocodile pit, promising herself to the one who retrieves them. The prince is first in, and is about to be devoured when Conrad leaps to his rescue, then gives him the gloves – and Mildred. Conrad returns to Dorothy, who is now passionately involved with a Mexican dancer (Theodore Kosloff); in a three-cornered fight she is badly hurt, but recovers to find Conrad awaiting her. Basing their script on a Leonard Merrick story, this Cecil B. DeMille production was co-written by Beulah Marie Dix and Sada Cowan. Give the girls a great big hand.

▽ Wallace Reid (centre) ranked as one of the most popular stars in the business when he made **The Charm School**, the first of 15 movies he carried to success during the last two years of his life. Overwork must have contributed to his fatal dependence on drugs, but neither was apparent in this light-hearted tale of a car salesman inheriting a girls' school. He switches its purpose from academic study to the acquisition of charm, grace and poise, thus shocking the faculty and delighting the students, until he is dispossessed by the discovery of a later will. James Cruze directed it in breezy style, with Lila Lee (horizontal), Adele Farrington, Beulah Bains, Edwin Stevens, Grace Morse and Lincoln Stedman also cast. Alice Duer Miller's story, which she and Robert Milton had turned into a stage hit in 1920, inspired more movies than any other Paramount property. After this 1921 Reid vehicle, the inherited college plot served Charles 'Buddy' Rogers in *Someone To Love* (1928), Nancy Carroll in *Sweetie* (1929), Jack Oakie in *Collegiate* (1936), Burns and Allen in *College Swing* (1938), and doubtless a few more heavily disguised reworkings.

▷ While no rivals at the box-office to brother Cecil's lavish romps, William C. de Mille's quieter productions were invariably made with care and integrity. Sometimes they appealed more strongly to the critics than to the mass of moviegoers, but they rarely failed to add quality to the Paramount programme. **Miss Lulu Bett**, starring (left to right) Theodore Roberts, Lois Wilson and Milton Sills, was one of his best. Its drab heroine, a drudge in her sister's home until carried away by a marriage that turns out to be bigamous, was perfectly played by Miss Wilson, a luminous performance. The two male stars, as well as Clarence Burton, Helen Ferguson, Mabel Van Buren and Ethel Wales, also gave full value to Clara Beranger's script, which came from the warm study of small-town life Zona Gale wrote as a novel, then turned into a Broadway play that won the 1920–21 Pulitzer Prize.

△ Company executives present at the projection room screenings of **The Sheik** were far from enthusiastic; in fact, there were dire predictions of a flop. They needn't have worried. Public response was instantaneous; warm from the start, it rapidly worked up a head of steam that shot the movie to the top of the hit list, made the title a synonym for the romantic male, and catapulted Rudolph Valentino to the highest rank of stardom. Paramount, having taken him from Metro after his hit in *The Four Horsemen Of The Apocalypse*, was none too sure of his box-office appeal and gave him second billing to Agnes Ayres. Workhorse director George Melford filmed the stagey Monte Katterjohn adaptation of Edith Hull's purple 1919 novel, with Adolphe Menjou, Walter Long and Lucien Littlefield featured. Here we see Rudy and Agnes, surrounded by a set-dresser's smorgasbord, enjoying a quiet moment after she, an English lady, had been abducted by the Sheik, escaped into the desert from a fate worse than death, was attacked by Arab bandits, rescued by her original captor, and has at last succumbed (along with several million female fans) to the spell of those flashing eyes, those flaring nostrils.

◁ Another of the four pictures William C. de Mille directed in 1921 also came from a stage hit, the more famous **What Every Woman Knows** by Sir James Barrie, and again starred Lois Wilson. With a rare gift for investing unglamorous roles with beauty and strength of character, Lois was kept busy year after year at Paramount, and her Maggie, the woman behind the success of her politician husband, was among her top portrayals. Conrad Nagel (right), too, scored as the railway station porter who agrees to marry a wealthy man's spinster daughter in exchange for an education; temporarily infatuated by a society beauty (Lillian Tucker, left), he later realises he loves the wife to whom he owes his career. Olga Printzlau's screenplay had good scenes for Charles Ogle, Guy Oliver, Winter Hall and Claire McDowell. Although a perennial winner as a play, this Barrie charmer generated only mild cinema grosses, both in this version and in MGM's 1934 talking remake.

△ Contemplating the end of one of **The Affairs Of Anatol**: Wallace Reid as the incorrigibly amorous Anatol and Wanda Hawley as one of his conquests. Still considered pretty shocking 28 years after Arthur Schnitzler wrote it (and nine years after John Barrymore played it on Broadway), this comedy of sexual entanglements among the smart set was given a little moral uplift by Cecil B. DeMille and his scenarist, Jeanie Macpherson, who devoted much footage to Anatol's wife (Gloria Swanson) to whom the wayward hero always returned. So much footage, indeed, that the following Swanson-Reid vehicle, *Don't Tell Everything*, consisted almost entirely of left-overs from *Anatol*. DeMille's lavish sets and costumes looked great in photography by two top cameramen, Alvin Wyckoff and Karl Struss, as did a cast including Elliott Dexter, Bebe Daniels (as Satan Synne, the wickedest woman in New York), Agnes Ayres, Theodore Roberts and Monte Blue.

◁ Exemplifying the company's output trademarked Realart Productions, **The March Hare** bounded along in its unpretentious way. These low-budget pictures fitted nicely into programmes, invariably turned a profit, and served as a grooming ground for talent. Bebe Daniels (left) made several in the early twenties, meanwhile being cast as a featured player in bigger Paramount movies; within a few years she was a major star. In this little comedy, running less than an hour, she was a rich girl from Los Angeles visiting New York, where she poses as a flower seller in a restaurant in order to win a bet that she can manage to live on 75 cents a week. In the eaterie she attracts a young millionaire, whom she marries after she has disposed of a butler who is trying to steal her aunt's jewels. Percy Heath scripted this from an Elmer Harris brainwave, and it was directed by Maurice Campbell, with Herbert Sherwood, Mayme Kelso, Helen Jerome Eddy (right), Sidney Bracey and Harry Myers also in it.

◁ Emil Jannings (right) as Henry VIII and Henny Porten (left) as Anne Boleyn were directed by Ernst Lubitsch in **Deception** at UFA's Berlin studio. Adolph Zukor bought the American release rights following the extraordinary success in the USA of Lubitsch's *Passion*, which also starred Jannings, together with Pola Negri. Zukor wanted both those stars and the director for Paramount, and eventually got them. His first direct association with Lubitsch began in 1921 when he invested in EFA, a German combine formed by Lubitsch and others, and took two of the director's EFA pictures, *The Loves Of Pharaoh* (with Jannings) and *Montmartre* (with Negri) for USA release, together with his earlier UFA film, *The Eyes Of The Mummy*. Meanwhile, *Deception* had grossed respectable 1921 figures and made a strong impression with its depiction, both intimate and spectacular, of the Tudor drama. The Hans Kraly-Fred Orbing scenario followed Anne Boleyn from her wooing by Henry while he was still married to Katherine of Aragon (Hedwig Pauly) to her execution when she had produced only (!) Elizabeth instead of a male heir. Good supporting work by Aud Egede Nissen (as Jane Seymour), Ludwig Hartau and Paul Hartmann; handsome photography by Theodor Sparkuhl.

△ Your suspension of disbelief had to be in good working order for full enjoyment of **The Witching Hour**, which had wowed Broadway audiences in 1907 with its heady brew of murder, hypnotism and mental telepathy. The Augustus Thomas play was filmed by an independent company in 1916 with C. Aubrey Smith in the lead, successfully enough for Famous Players-Lasky to remake it only five years later. (By 1934, when Paramount gave it another whirl, its theatricality creaked.) Now Elliott Dexter (centre right) starred as the gambling house operator at whose party a neurotic young man (Edward Sutherland, centre left, later a top comedy director at the studio, 1925–1938) is taunted into hysteria by another guest (Charles West) and kills him. After the youth's trial and sentence to death, the gambler, a whiz at mental telepathy, proves that the deed had been done under the influence of a sinister lawyer (Robert Cain, right), who tries to shoot him during a second trial. His trigger finger was stopped by the gambler's psychic power, the youth was acquitted, and large audiences went home happy with their money's worth of melodrama. Ruth Renick (left), Winter Hall and Mary Alden figured in the Julia Crawford Ivers screenplay, directed by William Desmond Taylor, whose own real-life murder drama hit the headlines a year later.

FOR THE OTHER PRODUCTIONS OF 1921 SEE PAGE 329.

▷ At the opposite end of the romantic spectrum from *The Sheik*, another 1921 winner celebrated the spiritual rather than the carnal aspect of love. It was **Forever**, George Fitzmaurice's beautifully made adaptation of George du Maurier's 1891 novel *Peter Ibbetson* and Nathaniel Raphael's stage version which starred Constance Collier and John and Lionel Barrymore in 1917. Their roles were played by Elsie Ferguson (left), Wallace Reid (right) and Montagu Love, respectively, with George Fawcett, Dolores Cassinelli, Elliott Dexter, Paul McAllister and Barbara Dean in support. Ibbetson is a French orphan who, after his adoption by an English rake, grows up in an atmosphere of easy morals – except for a true love for his childhood sweetheart. When he is convicted of murder after a violent quarrel with his uncle, she uses her influence as the Duchess of Towers to have Ibbetson's sentence commuted to life imprisonment. Physically separated, the lovers – not unlike Heloise and Abelard – remain linked in thoughts and dreams, until death unites their souls. So much spirituality was hard for mass audiences to take, and they gave the movie less than its box-office due.

1922

▽ One of the most frequently filmed properties in the Paramount library is **The Ghost Breaker**. Starting as a Broadway success by Paul Dickey and Charles Goddard, it went to the company's cameras first in 1914, was remade in 1922, again in 1940 as *The Ghost Breakers*, then twice more in 1945 and 1953 as *Scared Stiff*. The 1922 edition had the benefit of the charm of Wallace Reid (right) in the title role and Lila Lee (left) as the Spanish heiress who persuades him to help rid her father's castle of a ghost invasion. After a few reels of haunted house shenannigans, the spectres were revealed as hirelings of a neighbour seeking the treasure supposed to be hidden there. White comedian Walter Hiers played a black servant, not an odd procedure in those days; Arthur Edmund Carewe, J. Farrell MacDonald and Snitz Edwards also featured in the Jack Cunningham–Walter De Leon screenplay, directed by Alfred E. Green.

▷ Of all the Marion Davies movies into which publishing czar William Randolph Hearst poured his millions, **When Knighthood Was In Flower** was the most lavish. He loved to see her in the elaborate trappings of historical romance, while she (and nearly everyone else) preferred her in modern comedy. This costume piece, however, was highly enjoyable because, like its star, it had the saving grace of a sense of humour. As the heroine of Charles Major's old novel, Miss Davies (centre foreground) was Mary Tudor, who eloped with a commoner rather than obey the command of her brother, Henry VIII, to marry Louis XII of France. When the lovers were captured she agreed to the match, providing she could choose her second husband if Louis predeceased her. He did and she did. Forrest Stanley, Lyn Harding, Theresa Maxwell Conover, Pedro De Cordoba, William Powell and Gustav von Seyffertitz supported the star, and Robert Vignola directed the Luther Reed screenplay in sets created by the renowned Joseph Urban at the Cosmopolitan studio in New York.

△ Thomas Meighan, one of the earliest Famous Players-Lasky star discoveries, continued to be a dependable drawing-card until the end of the twenties. A good actor, too, as demonstrated in **Back Home And Broke**. This story, by the celebrated Middle-West humourist George Ade, concerned a man shunned by his townsfolk when his supposedly wealthy father dies leaving nothing. He goes West, strikes it rich in oil, returns pretending to be broke, and secretly buys up most of the town. Lila Lee played the only one who never lost faith in him; Frederick Burton, Laurence Wheat, Cyril Ring and Maude Turner Gordon supported. It was the most popular of seven pictures Alfred E. Green directed Meighan in during 1922–3.

▽ One of the early releases of the year, **The Little Minister** had to compete with another version of the same story issued in the last week of 1921 by Vitagraph, who had originally filmed it in 1913, starring Clara Kimball Young. The extraordinary personality of Katharine Hepburn was to make the 1934 RKO remake the most celebrated version, but Betty Compson (left) did a fine job for Paramount as J.M. Barrie's gypsy heroine, who is saved from arrest by the young minister of Thrums when they side with the local weavers in their violent struggle with the manufacturers. Romance ensues, to the outrage of the kirk elders who threaten to unfrock the minister, but back down when the gypsy reveals that she is really Lady Barbara, daughter of the district's baron-magistrate. George Hackathorne (right) in the title role, Edwin Stevens, Nigel Barrie and Guy Oliver supported the star in Elfrid Bingham's screenplay, directed by Penrhyn Stanlaws. *The Little Minister* was twice a landmark in Barrie's career: in 1891 it made his name as a novelist, and its dramatisation established him as a playwright at the turn of the century.

▷ Flappers' pulses raced; matinée ladies' blood-pressure soared; paybox cashiers' fingers worked overtime . . . Gloria Swanson (left) and Rudolph Valentino (right) were making love in **Beyond The Rocks**! This one and only appearance together of the king and queen of Hollywood glamour even had an added attraction in the author of their drama: Elinor Glyn, than whom nobody wrote more fervid romances. Scenarist Jack Cunningham re-heated her 1906 dish of *chile con carne* to suit modern tastes, and director Sam Wood served it up with showmanlike flourish. Only a fastidious few (the critics, for instance) failed to relish the tale of a millionaire's wife desired by a lord after he rescues her from a slip on an Alp. His jealous mistress switches a letter the lady wrote to her husband with one (hot) to the lord. The husband, stung, heads for Arabia, where he is killed by bandits, leaving wife and lord to pursue their amour. Gertrude Astor, Robert Bolder, Edythe Chapman, Alec B. Francis, Mabel Van Buren and Helen Dunbar acted in it, too.

△ Now approaching the end of his 32 years, Wallace Reid (illustrated) looked exhausted, but delivered another delightful performance in **Clarence** as an ex-soldier hired to do odd jobs in a household populated by charming eccentrics. He survived their assorted flirtations, jealousies, moods and mischiefs to win the love of the family's governess and to clear himself of the suspicion of being a deserter. Booth Tarkington's comedy had been a Broadway hit in 1921 and was still touring successfully when William C. de Mille's film version, adapted by Clara Beranger, opened in 1922. A few months later the public was shocked by the headlined news of Reid's death, a result of long addiction to morphine. He was sorely missed: during eight years at Paramount this popular, handsome man had made more movies than any other star. In this one he was supported by Agnes Ayres, May McAvoy, Adolphe Menjou, Kathlyn Williams, Edward Martindel, Robert Agnew and Mayme Kelso.

△ Looked at today, Rudolph Valentino's performance in **Blood And Sand** is decidedly hammy, but the star quality remains. You can see why his sleek handsomeness and potent screen presence, with its suggestion of violent passion barely held in check, inspired such public idolatry that, in spite of his relatively short career, he remains a legend. The 1908 Vicente Blasco Ibanez story, turned into a play by Tom Cushing in 1921, about a young matador led into dissipation and disgrace by a voluptuous temptress, ranked alongside *The Sheik* among Valentino's Paramount vehicles as a box-office smash. The June Mathis script originally ended with his death in the bullring; director Fred Niblo directed a more popular finish in which he recovered, aided by his faithful wife. Nita Naldi, stupendously concupiscent as the vamp, Lila Lee as the wife, Walter Long, George Field, Rosa Rosanova and Leo White supported Rudy.

▽ A potent money-maker for 1922 exhibitors, **Manslaughter** starred Leatrice Joy (left) as a rich and reckless woman, and Thomas Meighan (with her here) as a District Attorney who falls in love with her while investigating a case of theft which lands her maid (Lois Wilson) in jail. Before long Leatrice, having killed a policeman with her speeding car, is also in the slammer, sent there reluctantly by DA Meighan, whereupon both undergo personality changes. She becomes a charity worker and he takes to the bottle. Alice Duer Miller's book, adapted by Jeanie Macpherson, provided a happy ending, and director Cecil B. DeMille enjoyed himself by inserting a Roman orgy sequence, cued in by one of Leatrice's pre-reformation parties. Julia Faye, George Fawcett, Dorothy Cumming, Raymond Hatton and Edythe Chapman were featured; so were splendid sets by Paul Iribe, now DeMille's chief designer.

△ Anything less like the sophisticated frolics of Ernst Lubitsch than **The Loves Of Pharaoh** it would be hard to imagine. Such passion-swept amours, such damn-the-budget mob scenes would seem to belong to the master of depravity and spectacle, Cecil B. DeMille, but several Lubitsch pictures of his German period were of this type, and very successful they were too. Produced in Berlin with assistance from his frequent collaborators, writers Hans Kraly and Norbert Falk and cinematographer Theodor Sparkuhl (with Alfred Hansen on this occasion), this Egyptian epic gave Emil Jannings one of the sadistic roles which he relished as much as the masochistic (or Blue Angelic) ones he more often essayed. He was the ruthless Pharaoh about to contract a marriage with the daugher (Lyda Salmonova) of the King of Ethiopia (Paul Wegener) when his lustful eye falls upon her beautiful Greek serving girl (Dagny Servaes, right). He forces her to wed him, or forfeit the life of her lover (Harry Liedtke, left) who is sent to the slave quarries, but emerges to become a hero in Egypt's victory after the enraged Ethiopian ruler declares war. The new queen appoints her lover as Pharaoh when the old tyrant has apparently been killed in battle, but he reappears for a prolonged Jannings death scene before the audience could go home. Besides the director and star, Kraly, Sparkuhl and supporting players Albert Bassermann and Mady Christians all emigrated to Hollywood subsequently.

FOR THE OTHER PRODUCTIONS OF 1922 SEE PAGE 330.

1923

▽ The all-star casts that became fashionable in the early talkie era when every studio threw all its contractees into one revue, were long preceded by a silent comedy called **Hollywood**. It had Agnes Ayres, Mary Astor, Noah Beery, William Boyd, Betty Compson, Ricardo Cortez, Viola Dana, Cecil and William de Mille, William S. Hart, Jack Holt, Leatrice Joy, Lila Lee, May McAvoy, Thomas Meighan, Owen Moore, Nita Naldi (centre), Pola Negri, Anna Q. Nilsson, Jack Pickford, Will Rogers, Anita Stewart, Gloria Swanson, Lois Wilson and, in fictional roles, Luke Cosgrave (left), George K. Arthur and Hope Brown. The last played a movie-struck girl who couldn't get a studio job after arriving in Hollywood, chaperoned by her grandfather who was promptly signed up as a character actor. Frank Condon's slight story, adapted by Tom Geraghty, was spiced with satire on the film city's people and customs. James Cruze's direction had great panache and the movie was a big hit.

▽ **Zaza** already had decades of success behind it when Gloria Swanson (right) took it on in 1923. Adapted by David Belasco from a Paris hit by Pierre Berton and Charles Simon, it became a perennial American winner for Mrs Leslie Carter, and in 1915 was filmed by Famous Players with Pauline Frederick. Gloria moved from Hollywood to the Astoria studio (some said she wanted a continent between her and Pola Negri) to make it as her first of several pictures there under Allan Dwan's direction. She spark-

led brilliantly as the Paris music hall soubrette who falls in love with a highly ranked diplomat (H.B. Warner), believing him to be unmarried, then learns otherwise from a jealous showgirl. He offers to get a divorce but she refuses to mar his career, and they part until his wife dies. Mary Thurman, Ferdinand Gottschalk (left), Lucille La Verne (centre), Yvonne Hughes and Riley Hatch populated Albert LeVino's screenplay – a winner all the way. Claudette Colbert starred as the third screen *Zaza* in 1939.

▽ Gloria Swanson, who swung back and forth between drama and comedy with the greatest of ease, followed *Prodigal Daughter* by soaring into the high comedy of Alfred Savoir's **Bluebeard's Eighth Wife**, which had been a Broadway hit starring Ina Claire in 1921. Considered quite risqué in those days, it was about an aristocratic French girl, nudged into marrying a rich American by her impoverished family, and discovering that he has been divorced seven times. Outraged, she keeps him on the tenterhooks of unsatisfied husbandhood until he convinces her that this time it's for keeps. Huntley Gordon (right) played opposite Gloria (left) with Paul Weigel, Robert Agnew, Frank Butler, Irene Dalton and Charles Green supporting in the Sada Cowan screenplay. It was the star's tenth picture directed by Sam Wood, and her last for several years in Hollywood; she moved to New York and Paramount's Astoria studio.

△ Originally scheduled as a run-of-the-studio item to be directed by George Melford with Mary Miles Minter starring, **The Covered Wagon** was upped to higher status when Lasky turned it over to James Cruze with a bigger budget, ex-Griffith stalwart Karl Brown as cinematographer, Dorothy Arzner as editor, and as much time as they needed to make the first epic Western. Which they did. It thrilled worldwide audiences with its outdoor spectacle and impressed critics with its documentary-like depiction of a mid-19th century trek by America's pioneers. Author Emerson Hough, whose book was adapted to the screen by Jack Cunningham, wrote from personal experience of crossing the western plains by covered wagon. It was the documentary element, so magnificently shot by Brown on locations in Utah and Nevada, that made the film so memorable, rather than the often Hollywooden fiction enacted by J. Warren Kerrigan (left), Lois Wilson (right), Ernest Torrence, Alan Hale, Tully Marshall and Charles Ogle. Outstanding sequences: the river crossing by 400 wagons, the buffalo hunt, the runaway horse, and the Indian attack on the wagon-train camp.

△ **The Enemies Of Women** came from the prolific pen of Vicente Blasco Ibanez, whose passion-drenched dramas enjoyed a great vogue among producers and moviegoers of the twenties after his Four Horsemen Of The Apocalypse. William Randolph Hearst published many of his stories in *Cosmopolitan* magazine and produced this one, via the film-making unit of the same name, for Paramount. It was Cosmo-politan's last for that firm; by the time it was released Hearst had switched his unit to Goldwyn Pictures. The lavish production, directed by Alan Crosland in New York and designed by Joseph Urban, creator of Broadway spectaculars, had a script by John Lynch and a cast headed by Lionel Barrymore (right), Alma Rubens (left), Pedro De Cordoba (centre), Gareth Hughes, Gladys Hulette and William Collier Jr. Loaded with romantic conflict in glamorous settings, the story followed a libertine prince and his mistress (Barrymore and Rubens) from Russia to Paris, where he accuses her of consorting with a younger man. They part, but meet again in Monte Carlo where she fatally wounds the young man, whom she reveals to be her secret son. During the World War their paths cross once more: he begs her forgiveness and, true to the convention of such tales, receives it.

▽ Emotions ran high in the studio of war-wounded artist Percy Marmont (right), struggling to complete his masterpiece before his failing eyesight gives way completely. His street-girl model, enraged by his having warned his best friend to resist her charms, is about to slash the painting. This was the big scene in **The Light That Failed**, well acted by Marmont and ex-Ziegfeld Follies beauty Jacqueline Logan (left), both very popular in the silent twenties. Ronald

Colman and Ida Lupino would do it even better in the 1939 talking remake; in 1916 the Pathe company's version was the first filmed from Rudyard Kipling's story. David Torrence, Sigrid Holmquist, Mabel Van Buren and Luke Cosgrave were cast in this 1923 adaptation by F. McGrew Willis and Jack Cunning-ham, which was directed by George Melford (known as 'Whispering George' because his voice was so loud it often disrupted scenes on adjacent sets).

▽ Enter Pola Negri. The German cinema's famous Polish actress was the first of the many big names Hollywood lured from Europe. Already a major paybox attraction in the States, thanks to imported hits, she was a great catch for Paramount, which gave her the full star treatment. This didn't set too well with the studio's reigning queen, Swanson, and the two ladies indulged in temperamental upstaging, matching cars, jewels, salaries, dressing-rooms and titled husbands, to the delight of the publicity department. In choosing Negri's first script, the studio was less than enterprising, trotting out Robert Hitchens's 1909 melo, **Bella Donna**, which Pauline Frederick had filmed in 1915. Claude King (left), Lois Wilson (2nd left), Conrad Nagel (centre) and Pola (right), plus Conway Tearle and Adolphe Menjou, emoted in

Ouida Bergere's rewrite, directed by George Fitz-maurice, about a lady with a past, enraptured by an Egyptian sheik who persuades her to poison her hus-band. Near death, hubby discovers her wickedness, denounces her, and she flees to the sheik's tent, to find him entangled with another woman. She totters, dazed, into a sandstorm. The End.

▷ Cecil B. DeMille made the first emergence on a major scale from his long preoccupation with glamor-ous infidelities and indiscretions in 1923, when **The Ten Commandments** arrived. Starting with a budget of $600,000, generous for its time, he had planned to precede a modern melodrama by Jeanie Macpherson with a biblical prologue showing Moses announcing to Israel the laws of God, the penalties for breaking which formed the main story. A rearrange-ment, in fact, of the DeMille formula of interrupting a wages-of-sin drama with a flashback to ancient times. But this 'prologue' gripped his imagination and was enlarged to include the death of Pharaoh's son, the adoration of the golden calf, the flight of the Israelites through the Red Sea, enormous crowd scenes, colos-sal sets and a doubled budget. Such wanton expendi-ture sent the Paramount board into a corporate swoon, from which it recovered only when the com-pany's costliest production rapidly proved to be also its biggest money-maker. It was the biblical spectacle that drew and thrilled vast audiences, though the much longer modern tale which followed certainly kept them enthralled. This contrasted a good brother (Richard Dix) with a bad one (Rod La Rocque) who cheated both his wife (Leatrice Joy) with an adven-turess (Nita Naldi), and his church with shoddy ma-terials used in constructing a cathedral. Little did Rod know, during his assorted commandment-breakings, that the voluptuous Nita had escaped from a leper colony; that he would kill her after discovering she has infected him; that his mother would perish in the col-lapsing cathedral; that he would die in a speedboat escape from the police, leaving brother Richard to enjoy the fade-out with Leatrice. DeMille propelled his players – including also Agnes Ayres, Theodore Roberts (seen here as Moses), Estelle Taylor, Charles de Roche and Julia Faye – through all this with such showmanlike gusto that nobody thought of laughing.

FOR THE OTHER PRODUCTIONS OF 1923 SEE PAGE 331.

1924

▽ **Singer Jim McKee** didn't rank high among William S. Hart's pictures, but it had historical importance in marking the end of one of the studio's longest star associations. It was his 28th film since he and his producer, Thomas Ince, had moved over to Paramount along with most of the other famous names from Triangle when that company collapsed. Hart (left) played McKee, an unsuccessful gold-miner whose partner (Gordon Russell, right) is killed when they hold up a stagecoach. He adopts the partner's child, supporting her by further outlawry until, by fade-out time, they realise they are in love. J. G. Hawks derived the rambling script from an original by Hart himself; Clifford Smith directed it, with Phyllis Haver, George Siegmann and Patsy Ruth Miller in the cast.

▽ Sidney Kent, the box-office-wise sales chief, found 'Manhandling is forbidden' in the Hays Office list of thou-shalt-nots. '**Manhandled** – a great title for a Swanson picture!' said he. Gloria and her director, Allan Dwan agreed. All they lacked now was that unavoidable detail, a story. Producer William Le Baron came up with a *Saturday Evening Post* yarn by Arthur Stringer about a department store salesgirl (Swanson, left) who, mad at her inventor boyfriend (Tom Moore, right), goes to a wild party where she attracts a rich couturier and other amoral types; eventually she returns to her boyfriend, manhandled, but chaste and chastened. Frank Morgan, Lilyan Tashman, Ian Keith, Paul McAllister, Arthur Houseman and Ann Pennington were also in the Frank Tuttle screenplay. The fans loved Gloria as a gum-chewing flapper: it was indeed one of her brightest performances, including a sharp impersonation of Chaplin in the party scene.

△ The rivalry between Gloria Swanson and Pola Negri – denied by both but not by Paramount publicists – took on additional piquancy early in 1924 when, within one month, Swanson in **The Humming Bird** and Negri in *Shadows Of Paris* were released, with both stars playing apache girls in Paris. Gloria was making all her films at the Astoria studio by this time, while Pola continued to reign on the West Coast; so did the company's right hand know what its left was doing? You bet it did; that 'feud' was box-office. Swanson won this particular confrontation, with a vivid performance in a strong script by Forrest Halsey from Maude Fulton's play about the leader of a Montmartre gang who abandoned her thieving for good works during World War I. Director Sidney Olcott gave Gloria's dramatic talent full reign in such scenes as this, her discovery of her American lover (Edmund Burns) wounded in hospital. Also cast: William Ricciardi, Adrienne d'Ambricourt, Cesare Gravina, Mario Majeroni.

△ Frederick Lonsdale's play *Spring Cleaning* came to the screen as a sex comedy-drama with an urbane sophistication rare in movies of the early twenties. **The Fast Set** related the matrimonial troubles of a novelist (Elliott Dexter) who enjoys the company of bookish friends, while his wife (Betty Compson, left) prefers the jazz and cocktail crowd. A playboy (Adolphe Menjou, right) begins an affair with her, arousing the husband to retaliate by bringing a prostitute (ZaSu Pitts) to one of their parties and telling the guests she is a professional in the game they play as amateurs. The playboy, wanting to keep his freedom, persuades the couple not to divorce. William C. de Mille adroitly directed a fine cast, including Grace Carlyle, Edgar Norton and little Dawn O'Day (who later mercifully changed her name to Anne Shirley), in the Clara Beranger screenplay.

▷ Trailing clouds of *Ten Commandments* glory, director Cecil B. DeMille and stars Rod La Rocque (left) and Leatrice Joy (right) gave an encore called **Triumph**. Its title proved over-optimistic. DeMille's usual scenarist, Jeanie Macpherson, provided him with less than the usual quota of sensations in her adaptation of May Edginton's novel about two brothers and a changeable girl. First Leatrice chose upright, wealthy, hard-working brother Victor Varconi, then she switched to disinherited brother Rod after he abandoned his prodigal life-style and made good at his father's factory. Eschewing biblical flashbacks this time, DeMille contented himself with an inserted scene from *Romeo And Juliet*. In the strong supporting cast were Theodore Kosloff, Robert Edeson, Julia Faye, George Fawcett, ZaSu Pitts, Raymond Hatton, Alma Bennett and Charles Ogle.

▽ The long association of Ernst Lubitsch with Paramount had begun in 1921, but it was not until three years later that he arrived at the Hollywood studio to make the first of his many triumphs there: **Forbidden Paradise**. In this delectable comedy Pola Negri (left) scintillated as the Czarina of a mid-European country who is rescued from revolutionaries by a young officer (Rod La Rocque, centre). Although he is betrothed to her lady-in-waiting, she annexes him as her lover. Disgusted to find he is one of many, he joins in a rebel plot, is caught, imprisoned, and pardoned by the Czarina, who has started a new affair with the French ambassador. Lubitsch's handling of the cast – also including Adolphe Menjou, Pauline Starke (right), Nick de Ruiz, Fred Malatesta – and the Hans Kraly-Agnes Christine Johnston script (from a Hungarian play by Lajos Biro and Melchior Lengyel which he produced again in 1945 as *A Royal Scandal* for Fox) had romantic sophistication and visual opulence. The latter (memorably, circular walls made of ornate curtains) owed much to Hans Dreier's work, the first in America of this former UFA designer. He remained to become chief art director of the studio's entire output until 1950, and was mainly responsible for the celebrated 'Paramount look' of elegance.

▽ **Monsieur Beaucaire** was a success more because it was an entertaining picture than because it was a Valentino picture. The legendary Rudy still had the bulk of his fan following, but it was beginning to dwindle. The reason why is apparent in this shot, from one of the film's lively duelling scenes: the man is sporting as many silks, satins, laces, jewels and beauty spots as the girl (Doris Kenyon) and even more sausage curls. The over-ornamentation, to the point of effeminacy, of the screen's sexiest male was the work of his second wife, designer Natacha Rambova, who drove the studio to distraction by supervising every detail of his costume and make-up. Rudy's bedizenment was partly responsible for the near flop of *The Young Rajah* and *A Sainted Devil*, his films bracketing *Beaucaire*, but this Booth Tarkington story, of a French duke posing as a barber to avoid marrying one of his lady loves, was strong enough to carry it, and anyway the Louis XV period called for extravagance. Madame Pompadour, Queen Marie, Beau Nash, Lord Chesterfield, Richelieu and Voltaire were among the historical characters in the roles played by Bebe Daniels, Lois Wilson, Lowell Sherman, John Davidson, Ian MacLaren, Paulette Duval and a huge cast in the Forrest Halsey script, under the direction of Sidney Olcott.

△ Broadway's biggest comedy hit of 1922 was **Merton Of The Movies** starring Glenn Hunter, whom Paramount already had under contract for pictures. He scored again in the film version, also a powerful crowd magnet, but his other movies didn't measure up and he soon returned to the theatre. The George S. Kaufman-Marc Connelly play, based on Harry Leon Wilson's novel, slung some satirical shafts at Hollywood as it told the tale of film fan Merton (Hunter, left) fired from his village store job and going to Tinseltown, where he is befriended by a slapstick comedienne (Viola Dana, right) who gets him into a studio. He wins a part in a burlesque of his idol, thinking it is serious drama; when his acting is laughed at he believes himself a failure, but is hailed as a new comedy star. James Cruze directed, with DeWitt Jennings, Charles Ogle, Charles Sellon,

Ethel Wales and Luke Cosgrave cast. It was remade in 1932 as *Make Me A Star* and in 1947 by MGM with the original title.

▽ Already a stage favourite for twenty years, J.M. Barrie's enchanting play was handled tenderly by its film-makers and the resulting screen version of **Peter Pan** got similar treatment from the critics. And, considering that the USA of the roaring twenties was hardly in tune with its gentle whimsicality, the public's response was gratifying; in British territories it drew even bigger crowds. Nevertheless, many felt that some of the magic in its live performance disappeared on screen. Betty Bronson, here putting on Peter's shadow, was chosen by Barrie himself from many screen tests and both she, and another elfin beauty as Wendy, Mary Brian, scored strongly. Ernest Torr-

ence, Esther Ralston, Cyril Chadwick, Anna May Wong and Philippe De Lacy were also directed by Herbert Brenon, whose fine production had the aid of photography by James Wong Howe and special effects by Roy Pomeroy, noted for parting DeMille's Red Sea in 1923 and for helping Paramount to break the sound barrier in 1928. Willis Goldbeck adapted Barrie's play and scripted it for the screen.

△ The wages of sin, Cecil B. DeMille's pet theme, was given another airing in **Feet Of Clay**, which opened with a dash of novelty as hero Rod La Rocque engaged in – and survived – a tussle with a shark. But the Bertram Millhauser-Beulah Marie Dix screenplay (from a novel by Margaretta Tuttle) quickly settled down to the maestro's usual formula: several reels of sinning followed by one reel of wages. The latter, pictured here, consisted of a suicide pact between Rod and wife Vera Reynolds. She had left him during the scandal that ensued when his shark wounds healed enough for him to respond to the approaches of vamp Julia Faye, later accidentally killed while evading her angry husband, Rod's doctor. Meanwhile Vera had become a fashion model, and we all knew what that meant; sure enough, a fling with Ricardo Cortez tempted her and she fell, then returned to Rod to find he had turned on the gas. The movie ended with its most imaginative scene, the couple's dreamlike journey towards death and back again. Robert Edeson, Theodore Kosloff and Victor Varconi were also in this vastly popular farrago.

FOR THE OTHER PRODUCTIONS OF 1924 SEE PAGE 332.

1925

▽ Ernie Adams (left) and Noah Beery (right) in one of the lighter of **The Light Of Western Stars** moments. Beery, the perennial villain, menaced hero Jack Holt and heroine Billie Dove in this rousing Western, one of the best that Paramount harvested from Zane Grey's abundant crop. Like most of the author's works, its story of ranchers fighting off cattle thieves was filmed several times; this version, scripted by George Hull and Lucien Hubbard (later a top producer) and directed by William K. Howard, was preceded by a 1918 silent and followed by 1930 and 1940 talkies, both from Paramount. Alma Bennett, William Scott, Eugene Pallette and George Nichols had supporting roles, and the outstandingly good photography was by Lucien Andriot.

▽ Somehow, D.W. Griffith's immense talent seemed to shrivel when he abandoned independent production for a big-studio contract. Like the other pictures in his 1925–6 Paramount period, **That Royle Girl** made the Master's great days look far away and long ago. Edwin Balmer's story, adapted by Paul Schofield, was a scrappy melodrama about a crook's daughter and a dance-band leader accused of murdering his (the latter's) wife. Gangsters, a roadhouse party and an abduction also figured in it, but the studio complained, after a dud preview, that there were too many close-ups of Griffith's protegée Carol Dempster (right) and not enough action. So he added a spectacular cyclone sequence costing $100,000 ... in vain. James Kirkwood, W.C. Fields (wasted), Harrison Ford (left) and Paul Everton were featured.

▽ Rudolph Valentino's eighth and final Paramount release, **Cobra**, came from a play by Martin Brown which flopped on Broadway. The screenplay by Anthony Coldeway, directed by Joseph Henabery, was no knockout either. Financed independently by P.A. Powers because the star (right) and his studio were mad at each other (thanks mainly to his wife's interference in production), it placed him in the unlikely setting of an antiques shop. There he was employed to charm the customers, but the lady he really aroused was the owner's wife (Nita Naldi, left), who eventually burned to death in a fire at their rendezvous hotel. Until then, Rudy and Nita smouldered with passion in another attempt to repeat their *Blood And Sand* sensation, but he was sliding at the box-office and Paramount didn't hinder his move to United Artists in 1925. A year later he suddenly died, aged 31 and America's women collapsed into grief. Although the span of his stardom was brief, the Valentino legend is everlasting: two major movies about him were made, 25 and 51 years after his death. His **Cobra** supporting cast included Gertrude Olmstead, Casson Ferguson, Hector Sarno and Eileen Percy.

△ Peter Pan became Miss Fix-it in **Are Parents People?** as Betty Bronson (centre) went to work on changing the minds of father Adolphe Menjou (left) and mother Florence Vidor (right) about getting a divorce. She pretended to run wild, was expelled from school, tried to flirt with a movie actor, and spent a night in a young doctor's flat. Talk about wickedness! Menjou and Vidor were more at home in this modern comedy than Betty, who never equalled her successes in Barrie fantasies; Lawrence Gray, Andre Beranger and Emily Fitzroy supported them in Frances Agnew's amusing screenplay, from a story by Alice Duer Miller. The unanimous praise for this picture resulted in a long-term contract for Malcolm St Clair, hitherto best known for directing *Rin-Tin-Tin* at Warners'. He became a prolific maker of Paramount-polished comedies.

▷ Queening it amid DeMille luxury, Lillian Rich (illustrated) played an aristocratic girl who was not above a rough-and-tumble on the chaise longue in the film that brought Cecil B. and Paramount to a parting of the ways. **The Golden Bed** brought to a head a series of budget disputes that began in 1923 over *The Ten Commandments*; now Zukor and Lasky tried to revise DeMille's contractual payment from a percentage of gross receipts to a percentage of the net profits, which were endangered by C.B.'s expensive methods. Insulted, the company's co-founder walked out, not to return until 1932. Jeanie Macpherson wrote the screenplay from a Wallace Irwin novel, with Rod La Rocque, Warner Baxter, Vera Reynolds, Theodore Kosloff, Henry B. Walthall and William Boyd supporting Miss Rich, whose impecunious heroine, having driven her husband to suicide, marries beneath her social class in order to become pecunious. Several reels, diamond bracelets, sable coats and DeMille orgies later, the money ran out and so did she. But could her new playboy lover keep her? Stop fidgeting, Junior, and watch the picture.

▽ By 1925 Gloria Swanson (illustrated) had been Paramount's glamour queen for six years (and off-screen was now the dazzling Marquise de la Falaise de la Coudraye), but she didn't baulk at playing a scruffy waitress in **Stage Struck**. Gloria knew a good part when she saw one. Allan Dwan directed her (for the seventh time) in her last big hit for the studio, a bubbling comedy about a working girl with boyfriend trouble. Her beau is hooked on everything theatrical, particularly actresses, so she decides to become one via mail-order acting lessons – with hilarious results. Lawrence Gray played the bf; Ford Sterling, Gertrude Astor, and an occasional splurge into Technicolor were also featured in the Forrest Halsey-Sylvia La Varre screenplay, produced by Dwan.

▽ A now forgotten star, Raymond Griffith (right) made several delightful comedies from the mid-twenties to the end of the silent era, when his inability to speak above a whisper forced him to retire. In the thirties he resurfaced as a major Hollywood producer. Probably his best acting vehicle was **Paths To Paradise**, in which Clarence Badger directed him and Betty Compson (centre) as a pair of jewel thieves eluding detectives during a weekend house party. Bert Woodruff (left), Tom Santschi and Fred Kelsey had parts in the script Keene Thompson derived from Paul Armstrong's play, *The Heart Of A Thief*, an entertaining blend of slapstick and wit, topped off with a breakneck car chase.

◁ Gloria Swanson returned to a red-carpet welcome in Hollywood from a sojourn in Paris, where she had acquired a titled husband and made a subtitled triumph: **Madame Sans-Gene**. This delightful comedy presented Gloria (left) as a laundress in revolutionary France; her customers include two soldiers, one of whom she marries when the revolution ends and he becomes a duke. The other becomes the emperor Napoleon whose sisters, offended by the new duchess' rough manners at court, urge him to order a divorce. Using her wiles – and a reminder of unpaid laundry bills – she persuades him not to comply. Warwick Ward (right), Charles De Roche, Madeleine Guitty and Emile Drain (as Napoleon) complemented a lively Swanson under Leonce Perret's direction. Forrest Halsey wrote the script from the Comédie Française hit of 1893 by Victorien Sardou and Emile Moreau. Much footage was shot in and around the Palace of Versailles.

△ **The Vanishing American** (GB: **The Vanishing Race**), a major 1925 hit, was plucked from the series of Zane Grey Westerns the studio was making on modest budgets and given an epic quality, particularly in its magnificent scenery and a powerful performance by Richard Dix (right), Paramount's most consistently popular male star of the twenties. It missed real greatness because commonplace fiction, involving a pretty schoolma'am (Lois Wilson, left) and a villainous government agent (Noah Beery, of course), was superimposed on its splendid theme of racial injustice, and the fine documentary material on Red Indian history. Lucien Hubbard produced and, with Ethel Doherty, wrote the screenplay, casting Malcolm McGregor, Guy Oliver, Charles Crockett and Bert Woodruff. It was the best of director George B. Seitz's enormous output of movies from 1916 to 1944.

◁ Betty Bronson's (illustrated) success as Peter Pan in 1924 encouraged Paramount to delve into its stock of J.M. Barrie properties for another vehicle for her gentle charm. The same director, Herbert Brenon, made **A Kiss For Cinderella** an even more delightful fantasy, filmed with delicacy and pictorial beauty, particularly in the dream sequence of Cinderella at the ball. Awake, the heroine was a London slavey who showed a light during World War I, attracting the attention of a policeman (Tom Moore) who fell in love with her. Esther Ralston, Henry Vibart, Dorothy Cumming and Ivan Simpson scored in supporting roles, the script by Willis Goldbeck and Townsend Martin made 108 minutes seem short, and there was unanimous praise for Julian Boone Fleming's art direction and J. Roy Hunt's photography. The critics raved; the exhibitors wept; the jazz-age crowds wanted no part of it.

◁ Pola Negri (right) made a rare excursion into comedy with **A Woman Of The World**, a romance between a glamorous cosmopolitan and a strait-laced councilman of a Middle West town she visits. Its unsophisticated inhabitants were cruelly caricatured by screenwriter Pierre Collings and director Malcolm St Clair, while Negri's vamp persona was more subtly mocked. Her method of arousing more than one passion in her staid beloved (Holmes Herbert) was to lash him with a bull-whip at a church bazaar when he was induced by the citizenry to order her out of town. The adaptation of Carl Van Vechten's best-selling novel *The Tattooed Countess* delighted Negri fans, and gave good roles to Charles Emmett Mack (left), Chester Conklin and Blanche Mehaffey.

FOR THE OTHER PRODUCTIONS OF 1925 SEE PAGE 332.

Revolution and Downfall
1926-1935

Fighting on all fronts to maintain Paramount's supremacy, Adolph Zukor paid particular attention to his theatre-buying campaign. Throughout the Twenties he steadily amassed properties ranging from single cinemas to entire circuits, often by outbidding other voracious chain-makers (Fox, Warner, Loew's-MGM, and United Artists, the latter formed in 1919 by Pickford, Fairbanks, Chaplin and Griffith), and sometimes by allowing the dubious methods of his notorious negotiator Stephen Lynch, the threat of whose wrecking crew backed up offers exhibitors couldn't refuse. Many of the acquisitions were partly paid for with Paramount stock – something Zukor bitterly regretted later.

Following a deal for control of the big Balaban and Katz circuit of Chicago, Sam Katz was put in charge of the theatre division, which grew to encompass nearly 2000 houses and was named Publix Theatres. The importance of this arm was such that the company's official title was changed in 1930 to Paramount-Publix. Its crowning glory was the Paramount in New York, a vast de luxe showplace at the base of a new Times Square skyscraper, the Paramount Building, opened in 1926. It was a good deal more palatial than the Warner Theatre, a short way farther up Broadway but, in August 1926, it was at the Warner that the first rumble of an industry-shaking earthquake was heard.

More precisely, a complete film programme with synchronized sound was heard as well as seen. John Barrymore's *Don Juan* was accompanied by music and sound effects, and preceded by an address by Will Hays, as well as orchestral, singing, dancing and comedy shorts, all recorded by Vitaphone. Perhaps because audible variety had been screened before (Paramount's Rivoli had presented some, made by DeForest Photophone, with Pola Negri's silent *Bella Donna* back in 1923), there was no box-office stampede. That came, however, in October 1927, when Warners opened *The Jazz Singer* with its brief sequences of Vitaphone singing – and dialogue. The magic was not so much in Al Jolson's songs (Eddie Cantor's had been heard on Photophone) as in his words, spoken in character during a feature film. The talkie revolution had begun.

It came in the nick of time: the crowds were showing signs of switching from silent movies to radio for their entertainment. All the studios, and a rapidly increasing number of exhibitors, hopped on the sound bandwagon. Fox countered the sound-on-disc Vitaphone with sound-on-film Movietone, easier to handle and more reliable technically. Paramount chose this system, and added synchronized effects and music to *Wings*, which had already opened to great acclaim (it later won the first 'best picture' Oscar). In 1928 a dozen other silents received the same treatment, while three more went back to the cameras for dialogue scenes to be inserted: *Beggars Of Life*, which offered the first spoken words in a Paramount picture, *Varsity* and *The Shopworn Angel*. In November *Interference* arrived as the company's first all-talkie. Aside from a few silents turned into sound-accompanied or part-talkie hybrids in 1929, all that year's releases had dialogue throughout.

Shortly before all this upheaval, Lasky supervised the construction of a new Hollywood studio on a 26-acre Marathon Street site costing $1 million. The old Vine Street lot had been popping at the seams; its original 'Barn' was transported to the new premises for sentiment's sake. Under Lasky and his lieutenant, Walter Wanger,

the old Famous Players publicity man B.P. Schulberg guided West Coast productions and William Le Baron headed the Eastern unit. The two studios had been jointly responsible for the biggest box-office hit of 1926, *Beau Geste*, but otherwise they were locked in such a deadly rivalry that it became a problem, and Astoria was closed down. Not for long: it came in very handy when the talkie rush started.

Talkies also led to the construction on the Marathon Street lot of a building containing four large sound stages equipped to meet the new technological challenge, but before a single clapper-board could be clapped on Scene 1 Take 1, the building burned to the ground. The tiny sound stage improvised by special effects wizard Roy Pomeroy (he had parted the Red Sea for DeMille's *Ten Commandments*) for *Interference* had to be reinstated, while on the old silent stages shooting had to be restricted to nights, when traffic noises were minimal. The Astoria studio was hastily renovated and reopened, proving convenient for Broadway stars, who knew how to bandy dialogue.

Early 30s splendour: the main administration building of the Marathon Street studios. But the Publix banner did not adorn the facade for long; in 1933, three years after assuming that name, the company was forced into receivership.

Zukor visiting another of Paramount's most prized assets, Mae West, on the I'm No Angel *set in 1933.*

great depression had dragged most of the movie giants down into a whirlpool of red ink. Net losses announced that year included: Universal $1,497,439; RKO $10,695,503; Warners $14,095,054; Fox $16,964,498. And Paramount slumped from a profit of $18,381,178 in 1930 to a deficit of $15,857,544 in 1932. The chief villain in this Paramount shocker was the Publix theatre chain. Many deals during its frantic growth had been swung by paying the theatres' sellers partly in stock, redeemable at a fixed date and price. After all, who had ever heard of Paramount shares going down? But too many redemption dates arrived after the stock market crash, thereby causing the guaranteed repurchase prices to appear astronomical.

Ironically, 1932 was a splendid year for the movies themselves. It boasted the return of Cecil DeMille (after six lean years as an independent and at MGM) with *The Sign Of The Cross*, and some dazzlers from Ernst Lubitsch (who had been the studio's most acclaimed director since 1928), Rouben Mamoulian (one of the talkie recruits from Broadway, along with George Cukor and John Cromwell among others), and the Von Sternberg-Dietrich team. New stars sparkled, among them Bing Crosby, George Raft, Sylvia Sidney, Charles Laughton and Cary Grant. Nevertheless, the studio could not escape suffering in the 1932 debacle: hundreds of employees, including Schulberg, made enforced exits, and the remainder took salary cuts.

It was the same sad story in New York, where the Paramount Building was rocked by boardroom battles which ousted sales chief Sidney Kent and – incredibly – Jesse Lasky. He followed Kent to Fox, and later became Mary Pickford's studio partner. In 1933 Paramount-Publix went into receivership.

When it emerged from bankruptcy in 1935, reorganized as Paramount Pictures Inc., an outside money-man, John Otterson, was made president; Emanuel Cohen, formerly with Paramount Newsreel (started in the mid-Twenties) and then Lasky's assistant, was studio head; and Adolph Zukor, the great survivor, was chairman of the board.

A director adored by players – he was once an actor himself – Ernst Lubitsch (left) sharing a studio lunch with Helen Mack, Jack Oakie and Mary Brian.

Fredric March, Claudette Colbert, Maurice Chevalier, Miriam Hopkins, Kay Francis, Walter Huston, Jeanette MacDonald, Helen Morgan, Charles Ruggles, Ruth Chatterton, Jeanne Eagels, Jack Oakie, Carol Lombard and the Marx Brothers all joined Paramount's contract list during 1929-30. Of the stars already there, Gary Cooper, Nancy Carroll, William Powell, Harold Lloyd, Clara Bow (who had arrived with Schulberg in 1925 and shot to superstardom in the 1927 *It*), Richard Dix, Charles 'Buddy' Rogers, Clive Brook, George Bancroft, Richard Arlen and W.C. Fields proved themselves microphone-worthy.

Pola Negri didn't. Neither did Emil Jannings, the great German star whose Hollywood career, capped by the first Academy Award to an actor, had resulted from Zukor's 1926 investment in the UFA company in Berlin, which in turn was inspired by the huge success of Jannings in UFA's *Variety*, a Paramount release in America. The UFA connection still lingered in 1930, when Josef von Sternberg went from Marathon Street to Berlin to direct Jannings in *The Blue Angel*, and brought back not only a triumphant film but also a sensational new star in its leading lady, Marlene Dietrich.

A year later Tallulah Bankhead arrived from London; a year after that, Mae West from Broadway – and what a goldmine she turned out to be! Paramount was again the glamour-queen castle it had been in the lush days of Swanson (who left in 1926 to go independent) and Negri. In the early Thirties, in fact, the studio was so loaded with stars that Myron Selznick, the agent of three of its biggest – Powell, Francis and Chatterton – caught it napping at contract-renewal time and whisked them over to Warner Bros. at much higher salaries.

The talkie boom kept Hollywood prosperous in the dark aftermath of Wall Street's crash in the autumn of 1929. But by 1932 the

1926

▽ There was a craze for the South Sea Islands in the mid-twenties. Radios vibrated with the swooning glissandos of Hawaiian guitars from coast to coast; no college sheik could serenade his sheba without a ukelele; vaudeville dancers swung enough grass skirts to feed America's stables; and a big 1925 Broadway hit was **Aloma Of The South Seas**. Paramount snapped up this play and made doubly sure of the box-office by casting Gilda Gray (right), the world-famous shimmy dancer, in the title role. She played a girl desired by two American visitors to her paradise isle; one gets lost forever in an overturned canoe during a storm, the other realises he belongs to the girl back home, so Aloma returns to her native lover. Maurice Tourneur wove the James Ashmore Creelman screenplay from the John Hymer-LeRoy Clemens play into scenes of beauty and drew good performances from Warner Baxter, Percy Marmont (left), William Powell and Julanne Johnston.

▽ The old impersonation formula was trotted out for Pola Negri (illustrated) in one of the less than adequate vehicles Hollywood gave her between good ones. **The Crown Of Lies** was made by Dimitri Buchowetzki, the star's favourite director after Lubitsch, but he seemed to have no more belief than the audience in Ernest Vajda's story, scripted by Hope Loring and Louis D. Lighton, about a New York boarding-house servant and aspiring actress who is spotted by a European envoy as the spitting image of the Queen of Sylvania. She is induced to go to that kingdom and pose as its monarch (missing in a *coup d'état*) long enough for rebels to be quelled, and for feature-length footage to be filled, before returning to bliss with her American boyfriend (Robert Ames). Noah Beery, Charles Post, Arthur Hoyt, Cissy Fitzgerald and Michael Vavitch also supported Pola through all this flummery.

△ Shot at Paramount's Astoria studio in suburban New York and at Atlantic City, mecca of beauty contests, **The American Venus** was dolled up with Technicolor in Ziegfeldian sequences like this one and given a slam-bang publicity campaign, both of which paid off at the box office. Under the razzle-dazzle lay a little comedy, scripted by Frederick Stowers from a Townsend Martin original, about rival cosmetics manufacturers and the daughter of one entering the Miss America contest. Frank Tuttle directed Esther Ralston (illustrated), Lawrence Gray, Ernest Torrence, Edna May Oliver, Ford Sterling, Kenneth MacKenna, George De Carlton, and three young hopefuls: Fay Lanphier, the actual Miss America of 1925, who didn't get far in movies; and Douglas Fairbanks Jr and Louise Brooks, who did.

△ Customers lured into cinemas by the fascinating title of **God Gave Me Twenty Cents** came out somewhat dazed by one of the more obscure screenplays of 1926. Dixie Willson's story was worked over by Elizabeth Meehan and John Russell, and directed by Herbert Brenon in an oblique, shadowy style designed to make much of little. It was set in New Orleans during the Mardi Gras; among the carousers are two sailors whose revels with an old flame of one of them are interrupted when he is distracted by a lovely (and pure) young waitress. William Collier Jr and Jack Mulhall played the tars, Lya de Putti (illustrated) the old flame of doubtful virtue, and Lois Moran the good one, whose discovery of twenty cents in the street had a symbolic meaning never clearly defined. The film served as the opening attraction on November 19th, 1926, at The Paramount Theatre, the showcase house on Broadway at Times Square, which was demolished three decades later.

△ The death of Beau – but he would live again and again in the many remakes of **Beau Geste**, which Paramount first filmed in 1926, a year after publication of Percival Wren's novel, an immediate bestseller. Ronald Colman (right) played Beau, Neil Hamilton (left) was Digby, and Ralph Forbes was John, who survived the brothers' exile in the French Foreign Legion, the Arab attacks on their fort and the cruelty of their sergeant – a gloriously villainous slice of ham from Noah Beery. Herbert Brenon directed his and John Russell's adaptation (scripted by Paul Schofield) with so sure a hand that he brought conviction even to the preposterous plot device of the stolen sapphire that motivated the Gestes' adventure. He had the advantage of a strong cast which also included William Powell, Victor McLaglen, Norman Trevor and, as the ladies back home in England, Alice Joyce and Mary Brian. In addition to being a fine example of film making, it was a commercial success rarely exceeded in the whole silent era; the most stupendous new super-cinemas of the mid-twenties were none too big for it.

▷ The biggest box-office surprise of 1926 was **Behind The Front**, an inexpensive knockabout comedy of which the studio expected little. What it got was big – even record – revenues from theatres all over the States and abroad. They say that no comedy about recruits in the armed forces, from Chaplin's *Shoulder Arms* on, has ever failed, and this one – about two friendly enemies conned into joining up by their mutual girlfriend (whom they find married to a profiteer after the war) and getting into riotous dilemmas in France – made stars of Raymond Hatton (left) and Wallace Beery (right), who had been character actors for over a dozen years. Beery, Noah's younger brother, later became a major MGM star, while Hatton returned to supporting roles in a 55-year-long screen career. They, and producer-director Edward Sutherland, won new Paramount contracts as a result of this hit, written by Monte Brice and Ethel Doherty from a story by Hugh Wiley, with Richard Arlen, Mary Brian, Tom Kennedy and Louise Lorraine also cast.

◁ **Fascinating Youth**, a lightweight romantic comedy, was designed to show off the 'graduating class' of Paramount's strongly ballyhooed School for Stars. These young hopefuls, all attractive performers, were led by Charles 'Buddy' Rogers (left), Iris Gray, Roland Drew, Jack Luden, Thelma Todd, Josephine Dunn and Ivy Harris (right). Their subsequent careers varied; only Rogers became a major star. Paul Schofield's script from a Byron Morgan original had Buddy promoting his father's resort hotel with an iceboat race, aided by his girlfriend, who brought in a galaxy of celebrities: Richard Dix, Percy Marmont, Lois Wilson, Thomas Meighan, Clara Bow, Adolphe Menjou, and directors Malcolm St Clair and Lewis Milestone. The director in charge, Sam Wood, did a bright, entertaining job.

▽ Two of the silent screen's most distinctive actresses shone in **Mannequin**: Alice Joyce (left) as the woman whose baby is stolen by a deranged nursemaid (ZaSu Pitts, right), and whose husband is the judge when the child, now grown into a fashion model, is on trial for murder. Fannie Hurst's credibility-stretching story, adapted by Walter Woods and Frances Agnew, gained in popular appeal from excellent direction by James Cruze and acting by Dolores Costello (as the daughter), Warner Baxter, Walter Pidgeon and the two ladies pictured. Alice, the serene beauty who had been a star for many years, was starting a five-picture contract with Paramount. She retired in 1930, but ZaSu still had a long way to go in a 47-year career ranging from Von Stroheim tragedies to the innumerable comedies which popularised her.

△ After 14 years in pictures Harold Lloyd was established, along with Chaplin, Langdon and Keaton, as one of the great comedy stars, and the switching of distribution of movies made by his own production company from Pathe to Paramount in 1926 was a major coup for the latter. First under the new set-up, **For Heaven's Sake**, maintained his high success rate, drawing massive crowds to a snappy, gag-packed story of a debonaire millionaire (Lloyd, left) who becomes the benefactor of a slum mission-house and falls for the missionary's daughter (Jobyna Ralston, right). The climax was a breathtaking chase through city streets on a double-deck bus. Sam Taylor directed the John Gay-Ted Wilde-Clyde Bruckman screenplay, with Noah Young, Paul Weigel and James Mason (not the future star) in the cast.

▽ Generally considered to be the personification of Gallic charm, but actually American born and bred, Adolphe Menjou (illustrated) was a Paramount star for seven years during a career that stretched from 1916 to 1960. His biggest silent success was **The Grand Duchess And The Waiter**, a debonaire comedy with a wafer-thin plot containing little not suggested by the title – that little being the infatuated waiter's true identity: a millionaire unable to approach his regal beloved (Florence Vidor) except in servant's disguise. Set in the studio's favourite city, Paris, it had delightful co-star performances and Lubitsch-like direction by Malcolm St Clair, who also produced. Andre Beranger, Lawrence Grant, Barbara Pierce, William Courtright and Dot Farley were also in Pierre Collings's screenplay, from John Lynch's adaptation of Alfred Savoir's play.

▽ The most exciting thing about **Love 'Em And Leave 'Em** was Louise Brooks as the gold-digging sister of Evelyn Brent (left). They worked in a department store, the staff of which provided the romantic permutations of Townsend Martin's lively screenplay. It had first seen light as a slangy novel – in verse, oddly enough – by John V.A. Weaver, who collaborated with George Abbott on its stage version, quite a hit in New York. The movie, directed by Frank Tuttle at the Astoria studio, was a good showcase for the dazzling Miss Brooks, but it was not until she made *Pandora's Box* and *Diary Of A Lost Girl* in Germany that real fame arrived, starting a cult which has lasted half a century. Lawrence Gray (right) and Osgood Perkins had the leads opposite Louise and Evelyn in the 1926 comedy.

▽ The serenely beautiful Alice Joyce (left), a star since 1910, had the best role of her career in **Dancing Mothers**, a sophisticated drama which Herbert Brenon directed in the same year as the whimsical *A Kiss For Cinderella* and the rugged *Beau Geste*, thus deserving the 1926 prize for versatility. Alice played a conventional matron who has an affair with the playboy lover (Conway Tearle) of her daughter (Clara Bow), shocking the girl and her philandering father (Norman Trevor) into reconsideration of their immoral ways. Standing out in the fine cast – which also included Donald Keith and Dorothy Cumming (right) – was the vibrant personality of Clara Bow, obviously a star in the making. Forrest Halsey's script, from a play by Edgar Selwyn and Edmund Goulding, won praise for its literacy and polish.

▽ Easy to see from Charles Lane's smirk and Louise Dresser's plethora of pearls that they were sinful sophisticates in **Padlocked**, a melodrama in which they brought an innocent girl close to the fate worse than death, but better than the life she'd led back home with her tyrannical father. The adventures of Lois Moran, from the moment she runs away to the big city and becomes a cabaret dancer, to her final close-up in the virile embrace of Richard Arlen, were watched by crowds of fans held enthralled by the strong script which James Hamilton and Becky Gardiner fashioned from Rex Beach's best-seller. Noah Beery, Helen Jerome Eddy and a teenage Douglas Fairbanks Jr were others well directed by Allan Dwan.

▷ Two stars on the way up, Clara Bow (right) and William Powell (left) were movie people playing movie people in **The Runaway**, she as an actress who flees from their Tennessee location site after accidentally shooting her fiancé (Powell); she finds refuge with a mountaineer and decides to stay with him even when the man she thought she'd killed turns up to take her back to Hollywood. William C. de Mille's directorial artistry was always evident in the telling of Charles Buck's story, adapted by Albert LeVino and featuring Warner Baxter, George Bancroft and Edythe Chapman. Bow's first starring role was more serious than most in her skyrocketing career, but at times her exciting ebullience broke through the backwoods drama. Powell's many years of stardom at Paramount, Warners and MGM were lying ahead, to end only in 1955.

◁ After Robert Flaherty made one of the greatest documentaries of all time in *Nanook Of The North*, Paramount regretted having rejected sponsorship of it, and commissioned **Moana** from him. 'Go to the South Seas, take as long as you need, and bring back another *Nanook*,' said Lasky. Both he and Zukor were well pleased with the outcome; not so the sales department. It was a lyrical, beautifully photographed study of the natives of Samoa, their traditions, customs, hunting, fishing, canoeing, dancing (see illustration) – but the nearest thing to drama that could be sold to the fans was the ceremony of a young man being tattooed. So they promoted it with bare-bosom artwork, headlined: 'The Love Life Of A South Seas Siren!'. But serious film lovers revered it (still do) and John Grierson coined the term 'documentary' in praising it.

△ Gloria Swanson's reign as queen of the Paramount studios came to an end with **Fine Manners** after eight years and 27 pictures, nearly all of them hits. (Her next for the company, and best of the lot, came 24 years later with *Sunset Boulevard*.) She was offered a new contract at $22,000 weekly plus a percentage – fabulous for those days – but was infatuated with the idea of producing her own movies for United Artists; later she wished she hadn't. This one was a light, bright comedy confection about a chorus girl with more dazzle than polish; her snobbish fiancé turns her over to his aunt for lessons in etiquette and demureness, which she learns so thoroughly that she loses her appeal. She wins back her beau by reverting to her real personality, to the relief of theatrefuls of romantic ladies. Eugene O'Brien (here with Swanson), Helen Dunbar, Walter Goss and John Miltern supported Gloria (illustrated) in the James Ashmore Creelman-Frank Vreeland screenplay, directed by Richard Rossen.

◁ British film-maker Herbert Wilcox was down to his last shilling when he completed his stylish production of **Nell Gwyn**, with Dorothy Gish (3rd right) as the vivacious mistress of Charles II (Rendle Ayrton, right). Rescue came from US tycoon J.D. Williams, who bought world distribution rights, forming British National Films to handle the picture, then sold American release rights to Paramount. Like the film itself, the less famous of the Gishes was lively and colourful, sexy and touching, and scored her biggest hit in Wilcox's screenplay from the Marjorie Bowen novel *Mistress Nell Gwyn*, with Juliette Compton, Sydney Fairbrother, Gibb McLaughlin and Forrester Harvey in the cast. It was just as strong a crowd-puller in the States as in its country of origin (where it opened the Plaza, built as Paramount's premier London theatre, which it still is), and Zukor promptly invested $1 million in another three British National pictures, to be directed by Wilcox and starring Dorothy Gish: *Limehouse* (re-titled *London* in America), *Tip Toes* (from a musical comedy, with its great Gershwin score silenced) and *Madame Pompadour*, all released in 1927. Anna Neagle played Nell Gwyn in Wilcox's 1934 remake.

▷ Thomas Meighan had been one of the most dependable actors and consistently popular stars at Paramount for a decade when he made **Tin Gods**. The William Anthony McGuire play (adapted by Paul Dickey, Howard Emmett Rogers and James Hamilton) gave him an absorbing story, but one which relied more on character development than on surface action, so restricting mass appeal. Good for the actors, though: Meighan, as an engineer who marries a wealthy woman, takes to drink after their baby dies in an accident, and goes to South America on a bridge-building job; Renee Adoree (borrowed from MGM), with him here, as a dancer whose love regenerates him and who, realising she can't replace his wife, kills herself; and Aileen Pringle as the wife with a better understanding of politics than of marriage. Allan Dwan directed, with a cast that also included William Powell, Hale Hamilton and John Harrington.

▽ Paramount has filmed **The Great Gatsby** three times, the first a year after its 1925 publication. Although hailed by the literati as F. Scott Fitzgerald's masterpiece, and despite his fame as the personification and chief chronicler of the frantic twenties, the novel had disappointing sales at the time, so no great public awaited the movie version. This, too, was less than a mass sensation, but the more sophisticated customers appreciated Herbert Brenon's deft handling of a fine cast: Warner Baxter (right) as the newly-rich Gatsby with a shady past; Lois Wilson (centre) as his old sweetheart, now married, still obsessing him; Hale Hamilton as her millionaire husband; William Powell as Gatsby's murderer; Neil Hamilton (left) as the all-observing 'I' of the novel; and Georgia Hale, Carmelita Geraghty, George Nash, Eric Blore. The Becky Gardiner-Elizabeth Meehan script indicated more care than inspiration.

△ **The Show-Off** has been the favourite part of many a comedy actor, and no wonder. This likeable braggart made his relatives (and audiences) alternately exasperated and delighted as his fortunes roller-coasted to a happy ending. Ford Sterling played him broadly in this, its first Paramount edition; Hal Skelly starred in the talking version three years later, *Men Are Like That*; then MGM remade it twice under the original title, with Spencer Tracy and Red Skelton. Lois Wilson (left) charmed as Sterling's long-suffering wife, and Louise Brooks (right), Gregory Kelly and Claire McDowell as his in-laws added to the fun. Malcolm St Clair directed from Pierre Collings' screenplay based on George Kelly's long-running 1924 New York stage hit, which in turn stemmed from a novel by William Wolff. Kelly, one of America's most successful playwrights, later had a beautiful blonde niece who became a famous movie star and Princess Grace of Monaco.

△ D.W. Griffith checked out of the Paramount lot and returned to United Artists after **The Sorrows Of Satan**, a picture unlike any of his others. Giving an impression of 'Faust' rewritten in purple ink, it originally came from the prolific pen of novelist Marie Corelli in 1895, when it created a sensation. It was subsequently filmed in England and in Denmark (*Leaves From Satan's Book*, 1920), then the author sold it to Famous Players-Lasky with the proviso that Cecil B. DeMille would not direct it. This strange ban expired with Corelli in 1924, and the company promptly assigned it to DeMille, but on the eve of production re-routed it to Griffith – one of the causes of the 1925–31 Paramount-DeMille divorce. Certainly, Cecil might have pepped up the tortoise-paced melodrama of a young man (Ricardo Cortez, left) losing himself in the fleshpots of modern society under the influence of a satanic *roué* (Adolphe Menjou) and a voluptuous temptress (Lya de Putti, right). Griffith and his writers, Forrest Halsey, John Russell and George Hull, handled it in heavy style with bizarre touches, drawing a dismal response from critics and public alike. However, Carol Dempster's performance as the heroine was called her best, and the picture itself an improvement on Griffith's last, *That Royle Girl*. Indeed, more recent viewers have considered it much under-rated.

▽ Danger: woman at work! Looking like a good little girl in gingham, Clara Bow (left) was actually a sophisticated flapper, bored with her marriage to a backwoods trader and planning to accompany a vacationing lawyer back to the big city, in **Mantrap**. A concurrent off-screen love affair with the movie's director, Victor Fleming, inspired one of Clara's best performances in a vehicle more dramatically substantial than her usual. Ernest Torrence, as her husband, and Percy Marmont (right) as her means of escape from him, also scored, with support from Eugene Pallette, William Orlamond, Tom Kennedy, Josephine Crowell, Kalla Pasha and Lon Poff (who should have been a comedy team but weren't). Ethel Doherty and Adelaide Heilbron adapted the Sinclair Lewis story for B.P. Schulberg's production, a box-office winner.

▽ Bebe Daniels, Ricardo Cortez, Wallace Beery, Arthur Edmund Carewe, Dale Fuller, Brandon Hurst and Eulalie Jensen made a capable cast, and William K. Howard was a highly regarded director, but their **Volcano** turned out to be just a 60-minute time filler. Bebe (illustrated) subdued her sense of humour and took a crack at romantic drama in this costume piece set in old Martinique. She arrives there to join her father and her fiancé (Cortez), only to find the former dead and the latter's family calling the wedding off. Why? Because the father's wife has revealed that the girl's real mother was that unspeakable thing, a native woman. However, love proves thicker than ancestry when Mont Pelee erupts, and Ricardo rushes to rescue Bebe from the lava flow. The last reel in Bernard McConville's script, from a play by Lawrence Eyre, was the best.

▷ Eddie Cantor (left) made his movie debut in **Kid Boots**, energetically playing a tailor's assistant from New York's East Side who becomes a caddy in a swank country club, where he falls for swimming instructor Clara Bow (right). A love triangle among the high-life set, and an inheritance of $3 million, figured in the plot that Tom Gibson adapted from the William Anthony McGuire-Otto Harbach-J.P. McCarthy musical comedy which, like Cantor himself, didn't really click without songs. Still, the star, fresh from two years in the Ziegfeld stage version, was a major attraction for the fans, and Miss Bow an even bigger one. Billie Dove, Lawrence Gray, Natalie Kingston and William Worthington were also in the B.P. Schulberg production, directed by Frank Tuttle.

△ A stronger story than usual buttressed the drolleries of W.C. Fields in **So's Your Old Man** (and the star used Julian Street's plot again for *You're Telling Me*, 1934). He also had an interesting supporting cast distinguished by a star in her own right, Alice Joyce, and a newcomer bound for stardom, Charles 'Buddy' Rogers. As a bibulous small-towner looked down upon by the wealthy family of his daughter's suitor (Rogers), Fields invents an unbreakable glass for cars, goes to Washington to demonstrate it and smashes up the wrong cars. On the homeward bound train, he wins the sympathy of a Spanish princess (Joyce, centre) whose friendship then makes the town snobs accept him, and his daughter gets her man. Gregory La Cava, who became an outstanding director of social comedies in the sound era, turned out a very funny silent one in this J. Clarkson Miller-Howard Emmett Rogers screenplay, with Marcia Harris, Frank Montgomery, Kittens Reichert and Julia Ralph in minor roles.

▽ Love blooms among nautical derring-do: Charles Farrell (left) and Esther Ralston (right) in **Old Ironsides**. This story by Lawrence Stallings, whose *What Price Glory* and *The Big Parade* were making small fortunes for Fox and MGM, respectively, was given an elaborate, big-budget production by B.P. Schulberg. It concerned early 19th-century sailing ships, the intrepid fighting men of the American merchant marines, and their battles with pirates in the Mediterranean. Loads of action, lots of comedy relief, no expense spared in spectacular effects, painstaking direction by James Cruze, and a cast including, besides the romantic leads, Wallace Beery, George Bancroft, Fred Kohler, Boris Karloff – but . . . Lack of surprises in the Walter Woods-Dorothy Arzner-Harry Carr screenplay was one of the buts that sank it at the box-office and in the critics' estimation, and the movie's 112 minutes in its mightily ballyhooed première runs (complete with Magnascope) were cut to 88 in general release 15 months later.

◁ Only a few years after 'German' was practically a dirty word, America's moviegoers developed a keen appetite for films from Germany, where they were being made with exciting new techniques and dramatic effects more potent than Hollywood offered. **Variety** (called **Vaudeville** in Britain, where vaudeville was called variety. Clear?) arrived in 1926, after a series of successful imports starring Emil Jannings and/or Pola Negri, and immediately became the biggest hit of all. Lya de Putti (illustrated) was the apex of a triangle story about a Berlin circus performer obsessed with jealousy over his wife and his trapeze partner, whom he kills. Jannings smouldered magnificently in the lead, strongly supported by Lya and Warwick Ward under E.A. Dupont's direction; Karl Freund's photography, replete with daring camera angles, was the outstanding feature of Erich Pommer's production. The film's triumph resulted in Paramount joining MGM in a 17-million reichsmark investment in UFA, which made it, and Hollywood careers for Jannings, de Putti, Dupont, Pommer and (the only one to last) Freund.

OTHER RELEASES OF 1926

The Ace Of Cads
Adolphe Menjou, Alice Joyce, Norman Trevor, Suzanne Fleming, Dir: Luther Reed. Michael Arlen's romantic drama of a widow, her profligate former lover, and her daughter, who falls in love with him.

The Blind Goddess
Louise Dresser, Jack Holt, Esther Ralston, Ernest Torrence. Dir: Victor Fleming. Pro: B.P. Schulberg. Woman accused of murder is defended by her daughter's fiancé, who proves the victim's partner is guilty.

Born To The West
Jack Holt, Margaret Morris, Arlette Marchal, Raymond Hatton. Dir: John Waters. A boyhood feud breaks out again when the rivals' families follow a mining boom to Nevada.

The Campus Flirt
Bebe Daniels, James Hall, Gilbert Roland, El Brendel. Dir: Clarence Badger. Heiress encounters antagonism at college, joins the reckless set, then achieves popularity as an athletics star.

The Canadian
Thomas Meighan, Mona Palma, Wyndham Standing. Dir: William Beaudine. Pro: William LeBaron. Somerset Maugham drama of an Englishwoman and a wheat farmer in Alberta. (Remake of *The Land Of Promise*, 1917)

The Cat's Pajamas
Betty Bronson, Ricardo Cortez, Arlette Marchal, Theodore Roberts. Dir: William Wellman. Pro: B.P. Schulberg. Romantic comedy of a little seamstress and an opera star, brought together by her pet cat.

Desert Gold
Neil Hamilton, Robert Frazer, William Powell, Shirley Mason. Dir: George B. Seitz. Pro: Hector Turnbull, B.P. Schulberg. An adventurous Easterner goes to the Mexican border to help his army friend capture a killer.

Diplomacy
Neil Hamilton, Blanche Sweet, Arlette Marchal, Matt Moore, Gustav von Seyffertitz. Dir: Marshall Neilan. Ambassadors and espionage agents juggle secret treaties and missing documents at a Deauville conference. (Remake of 1916 film)

The Eagle Of The Sea
Ricardo Cortez, Florence Vidor, Sam DeGrasse, Mitchell Lewis. Dir: Frank Lloyd. Pro: B.P. Schulberg. Pirate Jean Lafitte is involved in a plot to rescue Napoleon from St. Helena; a naval battle, and a love affair.

The Enchanted Hill
Jack Holt, Florence Vidor, George Bancroft, Mary Brian, Richard Arlen, Noah Beery. Dir: Irvin Willat. Western drama about a woman's ranch endangered by her treacherous foreman.

Everybody's Acting
Betty Bronson, Lawrence Gray, Louise Dresser, Ford Sterling. Dir: Marshall Neilan. Pro: Howard Hughes. Orphan girl, adopted by a theatrical troupe, falls in love with a taxi driver whose rich mother disapproves.

Forlorn River
Jack Holt, Arlette Marchal, Raymond Hatton, Edmund Burns. Dir: John Waters. Western by Zane Grey about ranchers versus rustlers.

Good And Naughty
Pola Negri, Tom Moore, Ford Sterling, Miss DuPont. Dir: Malcolm St. Clair. Comedy of an ugly duckling transformed into a man-magnet during a Florida yacht cruise.

Hands Up!
Raymond Griffith, Marian Nixon, Montagu Love, Virginia Lee Corbin. Dir: Clarence Badger. Western and Civil War satire in which the hero survives a spy plot, a firing squad and scalp-hunting Indians.

Hold That Lion
Douglas MacLean, Walter Hiers, Constance Howard, Cyril Chadwick. Dir: William Beaudine. Farce about a love-struck young man who follows his girl on an African safari and captures a lion by accident.

It's The Old Army Game
W.C. Fields, Blanche Ring, William Gaxton, Louise Brooks. Dir: Edward Sutherland. Village shopkeeper, bedevilled by customers and relatives, takes an accident-strewn motor trip to Florida.

Lady Of The Harem
Greta Nissen, William Collier Jr., Ernest Torrence, Louise Fazenda. Dir: Raoul Walsh. Adventure fantasy about a girl abducted by the Caliph and rescued by the leader of a rebel band. From stage hit, 'Hassan'.

Let's Get Married
Richard Dix, Lois Wilson, Edna May Oliver. Dir: Gregory La Cava. Pro: Townsend Martin. High spirited football star plays too rough in night clubs until tackled by the police. (Remake of *The Man From Mexico*, 1914)

London (GB Limehouse)
Dorothy Gish, John Manners, Elissa Landi. Dir: Herbert Wilcox. East End girl becomes a gentlewoman – of sorts. (British)

The Lucky Lady
Greta Nissen, Lionel Barrymore, William Collier Jr., Marc MacDermott. Dir & Pro: Raoul Walsh. American tourist falls in love with a European princess, promised in marriage to a rich count by her prime minister.

Man Of The Forest
Jack Holt, Georgia Hale, Warner Oland, El Brendel. Dir: John Waters. Zane Grey's tale of a man's courage conquering Western dangers.

Miss Brewster's Millions
Bebe Daniels, Warner Baxter, Ford Sterling. Dir: Clarence Badger. Hollywood extra's eccentric uncle offers her $5,000,000 if she can spend $1,000,000 fast. (Remake of *Brewster's Millions*, 1914 and 1921)

The New Klondike
Thomas Meighan, Lila Lee, Paul Kelly. Dir: Lewis Milestone. During the 20's boom in Florida land values a baseball player is double-crossed in a real estate scheme, but comes out a winner.

Paradise For Two
Richard Dix, Betty Bronson, Edmund Breese. Dir: Gregory La Cava. A man about town, told his income will be stopped if he doesn't marry and settle down, hires a young actress to play his wife.

Palm Beach Girl
Bebe Daniels, Lawrence Gray, John Patrick, Maude Turner Gordon. Dir: Erle Kenton. Country girl resists the efforts of her aunts and a millionaire to make her a debutante. (Remake of *Please Help Emily*, 1917)

The Quarterback
Richard Dix, Esther Ralston, Harry Beresford. Dir: Fred Newmeyer. Pro: Ralph Block. College football player, a part-time milkman, develops a forward-pass technique with bottles and wins the big game.

The Rainmaker
William Collier Jr., Georgia Hale, Ernest Torrence, Brandon Hurst. Dir: Clarence Badger. Prayers for rain are answered on the drought-stricken farm of an ex-jockey and his former nurse.

Say It Again
Richard Dix, Alyce Mills, Gunboat Smith, Chester Conklin. Dir: Gregory La Cava. Romantic comedy of a princess and an American who meet when he is a wartime soldier and later when he impersonates her royal fiancé.

Sea Horses
Jack Holt, Florence Vidor, William Powell, George Bancroft. Dir & Pro: Allan Dwan. Wife sails to East Africa seeking her husband, finds him a drunken derelict; the ship's captain comes to her rescue.

The Social Celebrity
Adolphe Menjou, Louise Brooks, Roger Davis, Elsie Lawson. Dir: Malcolm St. Clair. Small-town barber and manicurist go to New York, where he poses as a count and she, jealous of his new friends, exposes him.

The Song And Dance Man
Tom Moore, Bessie Love, Norman Trevor, Harrison Ford. Dir: Herbert Brenon. An entertainer fails on Broadway, goes on the road, returns to find his girl has become a star, engaged to another man.

Stranded In Paris
Bebe Daniels, James Hall, Ford Sterling. Dir: Arthur Rosson. American shopgirl has hectic adventures during a prize trip to Paris.

That's My Baby
Douglas MacLean, Margaret Morris, Claude Gillingwater. Dir: William Beaudine. A young man has a baby foisted on him by his rival in love, who tells the girl that the other is its father.

The Untamed Lady
Gloria Swanson, Lawrence Gray, Joseph Smiley. Dir: Frank Tuttle. Hot-tempered society girl is tamed by a yachtsman during a stormy trip.

We're In The Navy Now
Wallace Beery, Raymond Hatton, Donald Keith, Chester Conklin. Dir: Edward Sutherland. Pro: Joe Jackson. Farce about a boxer and his manager as unintentional navy recruits during the war.

Wet Paint
Raymond Griffith, Helene Costello, Bryant Washburn, Natalie Kingston. Dir: Arthur Rosson. The misadventures of a lovelorn bachelor, culminating in a wild ride in a driverless car.

You'd Be Surprised
Raymond Griffith, Dorothy Sebastian, Earle Williams. Dir: Arthur Rosson. Comedy-mystery in which the coroner, called in after a house-party murder, solves the case by accident.

You Never Know Women
Clive Brook, Florence Vidor, Lowell Sherman. Dir: William Wellman. Pro: B.P. Schulberg. Rich man pursues a vaudeville girl until her partner scares him off by pinning him to the wall in a knife-throwing stunt.

1927

▽ Esther Ralston (illustrated) was the lovely centrepiece of **Fashions For Women**, a romantic comedy expertly handled by Dorothy Arzner, making her debut as a director after creating a strong impression with her work on *Blood And Sand* and *The Covered Wagon* as film editor, and *Old Ironsides* as scenarist. She was one of the very few women in the whole history of Hollywood movies to have a successful directorial career, and her 17 pictures were mostly made for Paramount. Percy Heath, Jules Furthman and Herman Mankiewicz provided a well-written screenplay (derived from Gladys Unger's original) – one of those impersonation stories so popular at the time – in which Esther played a society queen retiring for a face-lift, and a cafe cigarette girl look-alike replacing her at a charity fashion show. Einar Hansen, Raymond Hatton, Edward Martindel and William Orlamond completed the cast.

△ Harold Lloyd buffs rate **The Kid Brother** very highly; some call it his best all-round performance. Instead of his usual urban go-getter, he played a country boy (right) in what was basically a male Cinderella story: treated with contempt by his father and two brawny brothers, he is a drudge until he meets a girl passing through with a medicine show. Then he becomes a man of action, outwitting both family and crooks in a series of gags and chases. Jobyna Ralston, Walter James, Eddie Boland and Constantine Romanoff took roles in the screenplay which required five writers to write – Ted Wilde, John Grey, Tom Crizer, Lex Neal, Howard Green – and two directors to direct – Wilde and the soon to be famous – over at Universal Studios for the classic *All Quiet On The Western Front* – Lewis Milestone.

▷ **The Potters** was successfully adapted from J.P. McEvoy's Broadway play, a comedy about an average family's ups and downs. Dad invests most of their savings in some apparently worthless oil stock which, when new wells start gushing, makes them rich with a suddenness that tests their characters. Their patience, as ever, is tested by Dad – not surprisingly, since he was played by W.C. Fields (illustrated), who added well-observed character acting to his usual clowning. Fred Newmeyer directed him, as well as Mary Alden, Ivy Harris, Jack Egan, Richard 'Skeets' Gallagher and Joseph Smiley in the J. Clarkson Miller-Sam Mintz-Ray Harris screenplay. It was one of the most enjoyable of the nine pictures Fields made at the Eastern studio (Astoria) before going to Hollywood in 1931 for good.

◁ In its dying years the silent screen reached heights that talking pictures didn't learn to equal for a long time. **Barbed Wire** was one of those memorable pre-sound achievements, and one of the two outstanding dramas in the generally disappointing Hollywood career of Pola Negri. Like the other, *Hotel Imperial*, it had a war background, and was prepared by the same producer-director combination, Erich Pommer and Mauritz Stiller. The latter (Garbo's distinguished Swedish mentor) was soon replaced by Rowland V. Lee, who brought out the full emotional intensity of his and Jules Furthman's screenplay, based on Hall Caine's 1923 novel *The Woman Of Knockaloe*, whose locale was shifted from the Isle of Man to France. It was the story of a girl (Negri, centre) falling in love with a German prisoner of war (Clive Brook, top) and defying her compatriots' blind hatred of all Germans. The book's double suicide ending was eliminated, but not its potent anti-war moral. Einar Hanson, Claude Gillingwater, Gustav von Seyffertitz, Clyde Cook and Charles Lane had supporting roles.

▽ **Soft Cushions** was an extraordinary Arabian Nights romp which might have got by as the libretto for a musical a couple of years later, but as a silent movie excited nobody over the age of ten. It was intended to provide a change of setting for the antics of Douglas MacLean (illustrated), a popular comedy star approaching the end of his Paramount contract (he would resurface in the thirties as a producer there). Similarly, his leading lady, Sue Carol, was soon to wind up her acting career and much later would be a familiar face around the studio as the wife and manager of Alan Ladd. The leads were supported by Richard Carle, Wade Boteler, Nigel De Brulier and Boris Karloff, directed by Edward Cline. G.R. Chester's story, adapted by Boteler and Fredric Chapin, had the star as a thief trying to buy a slave girl while harem guards, wazirs and sultans try to stop him. The celebrated Ben Carré designed gorgeous sets for this lame extravaganza.

▽ Spurred by the success of their *Grass*, Ernest B. Schoedsack and Merian C. Cooper took their cameras into the jungles of Siam and emerged with an even bigger hit: **Chang**. It was less purely documentary than its predecessor, some scenes having been rehearsed and staged for maximum dramatic effect, but all the flora and fauna on view were just as nature had made them. Authentic, too, was the slight story of a native family menaced by wild beasts, particularly the marauding tiger they called Chang (illustrated). The animal footage shot by the team ranged from the comical (a monkey comedian, destined to be copied endlessly in Tarzan pictures) to the awe-inspiring (a herd of elephants on a village-destroying rampage). This sequence was projected in Magnascope in major first-run theatres to overwhelming effect. The picture drew big crowds everywhere and returned its $70,000 cost many times over.

▽ Clara Bow pepped up a rather creaky comedy in **Get Your Man**, one of the many boulevard comedies Paramount translated into American during the twenties. The material that scripters Hope Loring and Agnes Brand Leahy derived from a play by Louis Verneuil couldn't have been flimsier without disappearing altogether, but Clara's verve and the smart pacing of the studio's new young director, Dorothy Arzner, made it watchable and even enjoyable, especially to the crowds of flappers it drew, along with their boyfriends. They could identify with either Clara or Charles 'Buddy' Rogers (both illustrated) as they met in a Paris museum and were locked in overnight; the ensuing romance was hindered by his fiancée (Josephine Dunn) and his family-proud marquis father (Josef Swickard) who didn't think Clara worthy of him. She was worth a bundle at the box-office, though.

▽ Long before Cagney or Robinson triggered a gat over at Warner Bros., George Bancroft was the first gangster star in **Underworld**, beginning a genre that was to reach its peak of popularity in the early talking era. It was also a double first for Ben Hecht, who had not written for the screen before, and who carried off the first Academy Award for best original story. A former Chicago newspaper reporter, he based it on first-hand observation of the hoodlums spawned by Prohibition, but the harsh reality of that time and place was softened by the artistic camera of director Josef von Sternberg. The combined narrative and visual excitements had extraordinary impact. Bancroft as the mobster, Evelyn Brent (right) as his moll, and Clive Brook (left) as the derelict lawyer he made his mouthpiece, played out their drama of romantic jealousy amid battles with the cops and a rival gang, culminating in Bancroft's violent death. Fred Kohler, Larry Semon (centre) and Helen Lynch also acted; Charles Furthman and Robert Lee scripted; the public poured in.

△ One of the most brilliant publicity campaigns in the history of the movies surrounded the making of Clara Bow's most famous vehicle. Elinor Glyn (right), author of heavy-breathing romances, announced that Miss Bow (left) had 'It', whereupon Paramount's propaganda department flooded the media with 'What Is It?' items, then B.P. Schulberg disclosed that Clara's next picture would be (surprise!) **IT**, written and co-produced by Mme Glyn. The whole gimmick was so effective that a little comedy about a shopgirl (Bow) chasing and captivating the store's owner (Antonio Moreno) became a smash hit and zoomed Clara to super-stardom. William Austin, Jacqueline Gadsden, Julia Swayne Gordon, Priscilla Bonner, Lloyd Corrigan and (briefly) Gary Cooper, as well as authoress Glyn herself, appeared in the Hope Loring-Louis Lighton adaptation, briskly directed by Clarence Badger. Josef von Sternberg also handled a few scenes. PS: 'It', of course, meant sex-appeal, with which Clara was endowed to an awesome degree.

▷ She was such an exciting bundle of energy and sex appeal that Clara Bow's audiences hardly cared whether her movies were good, bad or – like **Hula** – just adequate. She was at her flamboyant best as the daughter of a pineapple planter in Hawaii in the B.P. Schulberg production, directed by Victor Fleming with the straightforward vigour that was to stand him in good stead a dozen years later for *Gone With The Wind*. Clara's willing prey this time was Clive Brook (illustrated with her) as a reserved English engineer with a wife who doesn't stand a chance against such high-voltage competition. Arlette Marchal, Arnold Kent, Maude Truax and Albert Gran rounded out the cast. There was a current vogue for all things Hawaiian (no party was complete without a ukelele), so the Ethel Doherty-Doris Anderson screenplay (from a novel by Armine von Tempski) had a second box-office string to its Bow.

△ Paramount's bigwigs took a look at the lines of ticket buyers circling every first-run theatre where *Underworld* was being exhibited. 'Encore' they cried, and ordered another tough crime drama from the studio. Released five months later, **The City Gone Wild** proved to have little of the Von Sternberg classic's fascinating atmosphere. But there was enough of its potent action and narrative drive in the Jules and Charles Furthman screenplay to give the new movie box-office muscle. Thomas Meighan (right), Louise Brooks (left), Marietta Millner, Fred Kohler, Wyndham Standing and Duke Martin were guided by James Cruze through a tale of two men competing for a capitalist's daughter: one, a district attorney, was killed when he found that her father was the brain behind a crime gang; the other, a lawyer, involved himself with the chief mobster and his moll, to emerge triumphant from the climactic gun battle.

△ Another sensation from the UFA studios, **Metropolis** was one of several master works by Fritz Lang (*Dr Mabuse*, *Siegfried*, *M*) before he too was imported to Hollywood. He took almost two years to make this futuristic drama, so lavishly produced by Erich Pommer that it became the most expensive movie ever shot in Germany. The spectacular sets, dazzling camera effects (Karl Freund again) and imaginative production design were more impressive than the somewhat simplistic story, about slave workers rebelling against their robot masters, written by Thea von Harbou (Lang's wife). Gustav Froelich, Brigitte Helm (centre) and Alfred Abel headed the cast.

◁ John Monk Saunders, writer and ex-airman of World War I, took the idea for **Wings** to Jesse Lasky in 1926. He had in mind a story about young men in air training and combat which he thought would make a great movie. Lasky, eager for Paramount to have a war epic to match MGM's 1925 smash *The Big Parade*, agreed, providing they could get US government cooperation. This was forthcoming in a very big way: the studio eventually had the use of thousands of soldiers and pilots and hundreds of planes, plus the air-force schools near San Antonio, Texas, for location work. B.P. Schulberg, in charge of West Coast production, assigned writers Hope Loring and Louis D. Lighton; supervisor Lucien Hubbard and cinematographer Harry Perry, who had worked together on *The Vanishing American*; and director William Wellman. The last selection was risky: young Wellman had made only two pictures at Paramount (a flop, *The Cat's Pajamas* and, much better, *You Never Know Women*), but he burned with enthusiasm for the project and had the necessary aviation expertise, having been a much-medalled flyer in the war and a stunt pilot later. Casting was made with a shrewd eye on fan appeal, top roles going to handsome up-and-comers Charles 'Buddy' Rogers (left) and Richard Arlen (right) as airmen pals (the former shot down the latter by mistake in the climax) and the new sensation Clara Bow as, rather improbably, an ambulance nurse they vied for. Bit player Gary Cooper won a contract with his single scene, and others present were Jobyna Ralston, El Brendel, Henry B. Walthall, Roscoe Karns, Arlette Marchal, Richard Tucker, George Irving and Hedda Hopper. But it was the stunningly realistic flying sequences, all filmed without faking or process shots, that made its $2 million cost a hugely profitable investment. After a tumultuous premiere in August 1927, long key runs and a January 1929 general release with sound effects added, *Wings* became the first (and last non-talkie) winner of an Academy Award for best picture. That May 16th, 1929 birthday of 'Oscar' was quite an occasion for the company, which had four of the five nominated films, the others being *The Last Command*, *The Way Of All Flesh*, *The Racket* (produced by Howard Hughes for Paramount release) and Fox's *Seventh Heaven*.

▽ **Service For Ladies** needed dialogue for full effect, and that's what it would get in 1932, as *Reserved For Ladies*. Meanwhile, this comedy about a head-waiter in a ritzy Paris hotel who loses his professional cool over one of the guests, an American heiress, made a handsome follow-up to Adolphe Menjou's hit of the previous year, *The Grand Duchess And The Waiter*. Indeed, it was practically a reprise, so similar was Ernest Vajda's story (adapted by Chandler Sprague) to Alfred Savoir's preceding one. Kathryn Carver (Mrs Menjou at the time, and illustrated with him here) played the charmer the hero pursues and wins during winter sports at a Swiss resort; and Charles Lane and Lawrence Grant were prominent in support. The Benjamin Glazer production was the most popular of the Menjou gems that director Harry d'Abbadie d'Arrast polished to a high gloss.

△ The really up-to-date college girl of 1927 not only had to know how to drink bootleg booze from a flask, wield a cigarette holder, pet in the back seat and dance a mean Charleston; it was also a must that she complement her short skirt with bare knees and **Rolled Stockings**. That's how Louise Brooks (right) kept the boys on tenterhooks at the university explored in this B.P. Schulberg production, directed by Richard Rosson and screenwritten by Percy Heath (from a story by Frederica Sagor). The varsity lads most aroused by the luscious Louise were Richard Arlen and James Hall (left), who only paused in their rivalry for her long enough to vie for a place in the crew for the big boat race. Nancy Phillips waited for the leftover boyfriend, El Brendel supplied comic relief, and David Torrence headed the sorely-tried college faculty. Slightly sensational, wholly entertaining for the hot-diggity set.

▽ The year's most commercial title drew the consumers in, but they came out feeling vaguely undernourished by the entertainment sustenance purveyed by **The Popular Sin**. Its locale was Paramount's beloved Paris, where two men and two women of the *beau monde* change partners with bewildering frequency, tossing marriage and divorce around like jugglers. They were played in expert fashion by Clive Brook (right), Florence Vidor (left), Greta Nissen and Philip Strange, with Andre Beranger and Iris Gray in support. It was slickly directed by Malcolm St Clair, but he could have taken lessons in the nuances of French comedy from the lesser known d'Abbadie d'Arrast. His most successful scenes were in the Paris theatre for which the Brook character had written a play. Monta Bell's story was scripted by James Ashmore Creelman and produced by William Le Baron.

▽ The subtle talents of actor and director blended beautifully in **A Gentleman Of Paris**, starring Adolphe Menjou (whose success in Chaplin's *A Woman Of Paris* a few years before obviously inspired the title) and directed by Harry d'Abbadie d'Arrast. Critics greeted it with open arms, but the movie-going public gave it the cold shoulder. As a girl-chasing man-about-town, Menjou (left) tries to reform when his fiancée's parents take a poor view of him, but he finds one liaison hard to live down. It is with the wife of his valet, who gets revenge by setting him up for an accusation of card cheating, then grows remorseful and confesses so that his employer can begin a happy(?) married life. Nicholas Soussanin scored as the valet, his only leading role; others enacting the Chandler Sprague-Benjamin Glazer screenplay (from Roy Horniman's *Bellamy The Magnificent*) were Arlette Marchal, Shirley O'Hara, William B. Davidson, Lawrence Grant and Ivy Harris.

△ Essentially a singing comedian, Eddie Cantor didn't really connect as a movie star until he could be heard in talkies. **Special Delivery**, the second of his two silent films, couldn't equal the grosses of the first, *Kid Boots*, which had the additional box-office zing of Clara Bow, but Cantor was now a national favourite on radio, and his trip to Hollywood before dashing back to Broadway for the *Ziegfeld Follies* of 1927 was profitable all round. He himself wrote the story – of a postman in love with a waitress (Jobyna Ralston, here with Eddie) who has many other suitors, one of whom (William Powell) is a bad egg; after exposing the crook and winning a Black Bottom dance contest, he wins the waitress too. The cast, including Donald Keith, Paul Kelly, Jack Dougherty and Mary Carr, was well handled by William Goodrich, whose real name, Roscoe 'Fatty' Arbuckle, still bore the stigma of scandal, dating from his manslaughter trial in 1921.

▽ Spectators who caught on to the fact that **Senorita** was a send-up of *The Mark Of Zorro* story got more enjoyment from it than those who took it straight. Bebe Daniels (right), not too convincingly disguised as a man during much of this spoof swashbuckler, played a hard-riding, fast-shooting defender of her family's honour in a South American feud. After routing a villain from the rival hacienda, she duels with his cousin who wounds her and, discovering she is no caballero, woos her. James Hall, William Powell (left) and Josef Swickard supported Bebe in the John McDermott-Lloyd Corrigan yarn, directed by Clarence Badger for producer B.P. Schulberg. Good fun, but a tip-off on the company's estimation of its box-office power was its first-run New York advertising stunt: no title, names or stills, just a big question mark and 'Your money back if you don't enjoy this movie!'. In the event, few customers claimed a refund, but then not many paid in the first place.

▽ **New York** was a frantic drama of life and death among Manhattan's jazz and crime circles. Produced at the nearby Astoria studio by William Le Baron, it used some authentic street locales and an excellent cast to enhance an eventful, if unedifying, screenplay that gave audiences good value and Paramount a tidy profit. It centred on a songwriter (Ricardo Cortez) who is in love with a society girl (Lois Wilson), but gets into trouble with a visit from a gangster's mistress (Estelle Taylor, left) when her lover (William Powell, right) bursts in on them and kills her. Circumstantial evidence enmeshes Cortez; he is tried and convicted of murder, but the verdict is reversed when Powell is forced to confess. Luther Reed directed the Becky Gardiner-Barbara Chambers story, screenwritten by Forrest Halsey with minor roles for Norman Trevor, Margaret Quimby and a comedian who was to become a Paramount regular in the sound era, Richard 'Skeets' Gallagher (whose first name was dropped soon after).

△ **Madame Pompadour** was the fourth and last of the pictures Herbert Wilcox made in Britain with Dorothy Gish (right) starring and Paramount financing (later he imported the younger Gish sister again for an early British all-talkie, *Wolves*). Like the first, *Nell Gwyn*, it went to historical romance for its story, but it lacked the former film's down-to-earth charm and was less popular. A major production, nevertheless, as indicated by the employment of two more big Hollywood names: screenwriter Frances Marion to fashion the script from a play by Rudolph Schauzer and Ernst Wellisch; and Antonio Moreno (left) to co-star as the inn-keeper who fell in love with the mistress of Louis XV. The cast included Henri Bosc, Nelson Keys, Gibb McLaughlin, Marie Ault, Cyril McLaglen and Marcel Beauplan.

▷ **Hotel Imperial** was fascinating melodrama enlivened by wry comedy, both elements deftly handled by director Mauritz Stiller in his one complete Hollywood success. Stiller had been ousted from MGM after starting the first film there of his protégée, Garbo; his switch to Paramount yielded little more than this hit, which also proved to be the best American vehicle for Pola Negri's vivid, earthy personality. She is seen here as the chambermaid in a border town hotel, alternately occupied by Russians and Austro-Hungarians as the tide of war runs to and fro. A fugitive Austrian officer (James Hall) takes refuge there and falls in love with her, but she is desired by the commander of the resident Russians (George Siegmann) whose firing squad is an ever-present threat. Jules Furthman scripted Lajos Biro's novel and Erich Pommer, maker of several outstanding German hits, produced it as his first in America.

◁ A cold shoulder from the critics but a warm welcome from the public greeted **Children Of Divorce**, the trivial drama of two girls and a boy, friends who had grown up in luxury with loose-moralled parents. Clara Bow (right) vamped Gary Cooper (left) into marriage while Esther Ralston, in love with Gary, married and divorced another man; Clara conveniently died, and Gary and Esther got together at last. This Hope Loring-Louis D. Lighton script, from a novel by Owen Johnson, was too much (or not enough) for its credited director Frank Lloyd. 'I rescued the film from oblivion by remaking half of it in three days,' announced the ever-modest Josef von Sternberg. What really rescued it was the fans' adoration of Bow, and their awakening interest in Cooper (who had played a mere bit with her in *It* a few months before), not to mention the pair's much publicised off-screen affair. Einar Hanson, Norman Trevor and gossip columnist-to-be, Hedda Hopper, were others in director Lloyd's production.

▽ Here playing the proud father, happy in his home, and in his job as a bank cashier, Emil Jannings was about to meet his usual tragic fate in **The Way Of All Flesh**. This first Hollywood vehicle for Germany's greatest star borrowed (along with Samuel Butler's title) the theme of so many of his films: family man destroyed by lust. The screenplay which Jules Furthman and Lajos Biro based on Perley Poore Sheehan's story had Jannings taking bearer bonds for his bank to Chicago by train, on board which he is seduced and robbed by a luscious blonde (Phyllis Haver). Years later he returns, a derelict, catching secret glimpses of his family, to an accompaniment of sobs from very large and profitable audiences. Victor Fleming directed, with Belle Bennett, Donald Keith, Fred Kohler and Philippe De Lacy also featured in his cast.

▽ They don't come much odder than **Stark Love**. Karl Brown, a top cinematographer at the studio for many years (*The Covered Wagon* was one of his credits), realised a long-held ambition to direct when he took his cameras to North Carolina mountain country and shot the simple story of youthful romance versus family conflict among the region's primitive illiterates. The cast was filled by those very people, except for the leading couple, Forrest James (left) and Helen Mundy (right), both of whom Brown found in nearby Knoxville, Tennessee. Shooting his own script (from James Watt Raine's play *Luck Rides A Bold-Faced Nag*) in natural backgrounds, he spent very little on an extraordinary movie for glamorous Paramount to have sponsored. His venture into crude realism was a profitable one. Critics' praise helped. And that sexy title didn't hurt.

◁ Sure that he had a winner in *Old Ironsides*, B.P. Schulberg put another big-scale action 'special' into production before the first one's release. **The Rough Riders** was similarly given a heavy budget and, undaunted by the earlier disappointment, Paramount gave the completed film gala openings for extended runs at increased prices. But it failed to live up to its publicity and was soon cut from 134 to 105 minutes for general release. Victor Fleming's handling of the action sequences had pace and scope; between them, however, were too many conversations (via subtitles) and enough flag waving to over-satisfy the most chauvinistic customer. Herman Hagedorn's story, scripted by John Goodrich, Robert Lee and Keene Thompson, concerned the volunteers recruited by Theodore Roosevelt to fight in Cuba during the 1891 Spanish-American war. In the cast were Noah Beery (left), George Bancroft (centre), Frank Hopper, Mary Astor, Charles Emmett Mack and Fred Kohler. Charles Farrell, the romantic lead in both this and the other Schulberg epic, was dropped from the studio roster as a jinx; promptly signed by Fox, he went on to form one of the most popular teams in movie history with Janet Gaynor.

OTHER RELEASES OF 1927
(All silents)

Afraid To Love
Clive Brook, Florence Vidor, Norman Trevor, Jocelyn Lee. Dir: Edward H. Griffith. Pro: B.P. Schulberg. Farce about a man who will lose his inheritance unless he marries within 24 hours. (Remake of *The Marriage Of Kitty*, 1915)

Arizona Bound
Gary Cooper, Betty Jewel, Jack Dougherty, El Brendel. Dir: John Waters. Young cowboy accused of a stagecoach robbery escapes lynching, finds the loot and proves his innocence.

Blind Alleys
Thomas Meighan, Greta Nissen, Evelyn Brent. Dir: Frank Tuttle. Pro: William Le Baron. Man and bride are separated in New York when he is knocked down by a car and she is abducted by jewel thieves.

Blonde Or Brunette
Adolphe Menjou, Greta Nissen, Arlette Marchal. Dir: Richard Rosson. Parisian marries village girl, divorces her when she takes to wild city ways; married to a dull second wife, he yearns for the first.

The Cabaret
Gilda Gray, Tom Moore, Chester Conklin, Mona Palma. Dir: Robert Vignola. Night club dancer is courted by a detective and a gangster; the latter is killed by her brother, who successfully pleads self defence.

Casey At The Bat
Wallace Beery, ZaSu Pitts, Ford Sterling. Dir: Monte Brice. Pro: Hector Turnbull. Village junkman and baseballer home-runs to fame.

Drums Of The Desert
Warner Baxter, Marietta Millner, Ford Sterling. Dir: John Waters. Oil prospectors try to force the Navajos off their Arizona territory; their clash is subdued by the U.S. Cavalry.

Evening Clothes
Adolphe Menjou, Virginia Valli, Louise Brooks, Noah Beery. Dir: Luther Reed. Pro: B.P. Schulberg. A wealthy farmer follows his restless wife to Paris, where he falls for a cabaret girl, loses his money, but regains his wife.

Fireman, Save My Child
Wallace Beery, Raymond Hatton, Josephine Dunn. Dir: Edward Sutherland. Pro: B.P. Schulberg. Comic bunglers disrupt the fire brigade.

The Gay Defender
Richard Dix, Thelma Rodd, Fred Kohler. Dir: Gregory La Cava. In Spanish California an adventurer is unjustly accused of murder; as a fugitive, he gets revenge on the real culprit.

Honeymoon Hate
Florence Vidor, Tullio Carminati, William Austin. Dir: Luther Reed. Flirtatious American heiress on a European tour plays rival admirers off against each other and marries one of them.

Jesse James
Fred Thomson, Nora Lane, Montagu Love. Dir: Lloyd Ingraham. Pro: Alfred Werker. Between bouts of banditry, the notorious outlaw romances a Northern girl accused of spying in the South.

A Kiss In A Taxi
Bebe Daniels, Douglas Gilmore, Chester Conklin, Richard Tucker. Dir: Clarence Badger. French farce about a cafe waitress wooed by a poor artist and a rich boulevardier.

Knockout Riley
Richard Dix, Mary Brian, Osgood Perkins. Dir: Malcolm St. Clair. Steel worker becomes a prizefighter after knocking out a pro boxer in a cafe brawl. Jailed when the pro frames him, he trains on the rock-pile, emerges to win.

The Last Outlaw
Gary Cooper, Betty Jewel, Jack Luden. Dir: Arthur Rosson. New sheriff, riding Flash the Wonder Horse, tracks down the killer of his predecessor and finds it is his girl friend's brother.

The Last Waltz
Willy Fritsch, Kathe von Nagy. Dir: Arthur Robison. Pro: Charles Whittaker. Viennese romance from an Oscar Straus operetta. (German)

Let It Rain
Douglas MacLean, Shirley Mason, Wade Boteler. Dir: Edward Cline. Pro: MacLean. Action comedy involving sailors and marines – and a girl.

Love's Greatest Mistake
Josephine Dunn, James Hall, William Powell, Evelyn Brent, Frank Morgan. Dir: Edward Sutherland. Pro: William Le Baron. Girl wooed by a financier refuses to give his letters to her sister's lover, a blackmailer.

Manpower
Richard Dix, Mary Brian, Philip Strange, Charles Mailes. Dir: Clarence Badger. Ex-serviceman exposes the local tractor factory's manager as a crook, and uses a tractor to save the town from a flood disaster.

The Mysterious Rider
Jack Holt, Betty Jewel, Charles Sellon, David Torrence. Dir: John Waters. Westerner foils a double-crossing land owner who cheats California homesteaders.

Nevada
Gary Cooper, Thelma Todd, William Powell, Philip Strange. Dir: John Waters. Cowboy unmasks a rancher as the mastermind of a railway gang.

Now We're In The Air
Wallace Beery, Raymond Hatton, Louise Brooks. Dir: Frank Strayer. Dumb US airmen drift across battle lines in a balloon to the Germans, who send them back as spies; they're caught and almost shot.

One Woman To Another
Florence Vidor, Theodore Von Eltz, Hedda Hopper. Dir: Frank Tuttle. A couple's attempts to marry are frustrated by a vamp.

The Open Range
Lane Chandler, Betty Bronson, Fred Kohler. Dir: Clifford Smith. Cowboy rides Flash the Wonder Horse against cattle-rustling Indians.

Ritzy
Betty Bronson, James Hall, William Austin. Dir: Richard Rosson. Farce by Elinor Glyn, about a small-town flapper who sails to London determined to marry a duke, unaware that the young man chasing her is a duke incognito.

Rough-House Rosie
Clara Bow, Reed Howes, Arthur Houseman, Douglas Gilmore. Dir: Frank Strayer. Pro: B.P. Schulberg. A millionaire tries to turn a night club dancer into a lady, but she goes back to her former boyfriend, a boxer.

Rubber Heels
Ed Wynn, Thelma Todd, Chester Conklin, Robert Andrews. Dir: Victor Heerman. Pro: William Le Baron. Dotty detective, hired to guard a visiting princess's jewels, chases their thieves to Canada, goes over Niagara Falls on an ice floe.

Running Wild
W.C. Fields, Mary Brian, Claud Buchanan, Marie Shotwell. Dir: Gregory La Cava. Brow-beaten by his second wife, his daughter, his stepson and even his dog, Elmer is transformed by a stage hypnotist.

Serenade
Adolphe Menjou, Kathryn Carver, Lina Basquette, Lawrence Grant. Dir: H. d'Abbadie d'Arrast. Comedy of a composer and his wife, who hits a sour note when she is given competition by his operetta's leading lady.

She's A Sheik
Bebe Daniels, Richard Arlen, William Powell, Josephine Dunn. Dir: Clarence Badger. A spoof on desert melodramas, about an Arab chieftain's daughter who captures a handsome young man.

Shanghai Bound
Richard Dix, Mary Brian, George Irving, Jocelyn Lee. Dir: Luther Reed. Freighter captain on the China coast saves a group of Westerners from bandits. Attacked again at sea, they are rescued by a US warship.

Shootin' Irons
Jack Luden, Sally Blane, Fred Kohler. Dir: Richard Rosson. Cowboy survives a wild horse stampede and hunts down a stagecoach robber.

The Spotlight
Esther Ralston, Neil Hamilton, Arlette Marchal, Nicholas Soussanin. Dir: Frank Tuttle. A girl cons her way into a theatrical career by pretending to be a glamorous Russian actress. (Remake of *Footlights*, 1921)

Swim, Girl, Swim
Bebe Daniels, James Hall, Josephine Dunn, Gertrude Ederle. Dir: Clarence Badger. College wallflower finds popularity as a champion swimmer. Filmed to capitalise on the fame of Ederle, in 1926 the first woman to swim the Channel.

The Telephone Girl
Madge Bellamy, Warner Baxter, Holbrook Blinn, May Allison, Lawrence Gray. Dir & Pro: Herbert Brenon. Switchboard girl thwarts an election candidate's dirty political manoeuvre. (Remake of *The Woman*, 1915)

Tell It To Sweeney
George Bancroft, Chester Conklin, Jack Luden, Doris Hill. Dir: Gregory La Cava. Pro: B.P. Schulberg. Comedy of rival engine drivers, one of whom loves the other's daughter but loses her to their boss's son.

Ten Modern Commandments
Neil Hamilton, Esther Ralston, Maude Truax, El Brendel, Jocelyn Lee, Roscoe Karns. Dir: Dorothy Arzner. The maid in a theatrical boarding house helps a young song writer to crash Broadway.

Tip Toes
Dorothy Gish, Will Rogers, Nelson Keys, John Manners. Dir: Herbert Wilcox. Pro: J.D. Williams. American vaudeville girl and her two uncles, stranded in London, get out of trouble when she captures a rich suitor. (British)

Time To Love
Raymond Griffith, William Powell, Vera Veronina. Dir: Frank Tuttle. Pro: B.P. Schulberg. Farce about two men and a girl playing the love game in Paris.

Too Many Crooks
George Bancroft, Mildred Davis, Lloyd Hughes, El Brendel. Dir: Fred Newmeyer. Headstrong heiress, seeking material for a play, throws a house party for thieves, blackmailers and con-men.

Two Flaming Youths
W.C. Fields, Chester Conklin, Mary Brian, Jack Luden. Dir: John Waters. Slapstick comedy about a sheriff and a carnival showman who is mistaken for a fugitive from the police.

Wedding Bills
Raymond Griffith, Hallam Cooley, Anne Sheridan, Iris Stuart. Dir: Erle Kenton. Pro: B.P. Schulberg. Often a best man but never a groom, the hero finally gets his girl after adventures with a vamp and a stolen necklace.

We're All Gamblers
Thomas Meighan, Marietta Millner, Cullen Landis. Dir: James Cruze. Pro: Lucien Hubbard. Prizefighter injured by woman's car becomes nightclub owner, comes to her aid when she is involved in a shooting.

The Whirlwind Of Youth
Lois Moran, Donald Keith, Vera Veronina. Dir: Rowland V. Lee. Pro: B.P. Schulberg. English girl in Paris loves fellow art student; they part, and are reunited on the war front, where she drives an ambulance.

The Woman On Trial
Pola Negri, Einar Hanson, Arnold Kent, Andre Sarti. Dir: Mauritz Stiller. Pro: B.P. Schulberg. Cast out by her jealous husband, a woman kidnaps her own child, then kills the man hired to compromise her.

The World At Her Feet
Florence Vidor, Arnold Kent, Richard Tucker, Margaret Quimby. Dir: Luther Reed. Pro: B.P. Schulberg. Comedy of a lady lawyer and her neglected husband who get involved with a couple seeking divorce.

1928

▽ In 1925 when Anita Loos, already a veteran screenwriter at 32, wrote a book called **Gentlemen Prefer Blondes**, she presented herself with an annuity that was still paying rich dividends in 1981 when she died, aged 88. An immediate best-seller, the hilarious diary of a gold-digger was turned into a play by Miss Loos; it wowed Broadway in 1926, and so did its musical version in 1949. Tours, revivals, foreign rights, movie rights – all paid off in a big way. Paramount shared in the prosperity with its 1928 film, directed by Malcolm St Clair and featuring newcomer Ruth Taylor (illustrated) as dizzy blonde Lorelei Lee, Alice White as her worldly-wise friend Dorothy, and Ford Sterling, Holmes Herbert, Emily Fitzroy, Mack Swain, Trixie Friganza and Chester Conklin as their companions in New York, Paris, and luxury liner adventures. It was, however, the least entertaining of the many versions, with its broad silent clowning an inadequate substitute for the wit of the book and play. Twenty-five years later Fox filmed the musical edition, with more brass than class, but with Marilyn Monroe as Lorelei.

△ Josef von Sternberg followed his first major success, *Underworld*, with **The Last Command**, in which he directed Paramount's prestigious new import, Emil Jannings (right), for the first time. It was a fascinating study of a Czarist army commander who flees from the revolution to America – and poverty – winding up as a Hollywood extra. Ironically, he is chosen to play his past self, a Russian general, in a film whose director had been a revolutionary, and his rival in love, in Russia. Jannings, equally impressive in arrogance and humiliation, was supported by William Powell (left) as the sadistic director (said to personify Von Sternberg's view of the studio's ruthlessness), Evelyn Brent, Jack Raymond, Nicholas Soussanin and Michael Visaroff. Lajos Biro wrote the story from an idea by Ernst Lubitsch, and the screenplay was adapted by John F. Goodrich for producer B.P. Schulberg. The film, Jannings, and Biro were all nominated for the first Academy Awards, the actor winning an Oscar.

▷ **Ladies Of The Mob** provided a change of pace for Clara Bow, who subdued her usual effervescence for a strong underworld drama which scored at the box-office. She was surprisingly good as a girl brought up as a criminal by her mother who was embittered by the father's death in the electric chair. The girl saves her partner in crime from risking the same fate by keeping him away from a fatal bank robbery. Richard Arlen played opposite Clara (both illustrated); and they were supported by Helen Lynch, Mary Alden, Carl Gerrard and Bodil Rosing. The John Farrow-Oliver H.P. Garrett screenplay (from Ernest Booth's original) had plenty of tension, pulled tight by the direction of William Wellman.

▷ Rumours of Clara Bow's uninhibited life-style did more to enhance than to hurt her appeal as the screen's most enticing jazz baby in 1928. The lurid details would eventually turn public opinion against her but, meanwhile, **The Fleet's In** maintained the 'It' Girl's position as Paramount's biggest star. This whoop-it-up comedy showed the impact of the US Pacific fleet's shore leave on the Roseland dance-hall girls. Romance blooms between a sailor (James Hall, left) and the peppiest of the dime-a-dancers (Bow, right), but on his next leave he finds her wearing another guy's ring. The ensuing brawl wrecks the joint; he is arrested, she takes the blame; they clinch for the fade-out. Rubbish, but fun. Jack Oakie, starting on a busy career at the studio, stood out in a cast that included Eddie Dunn, Bodil Rosing and Richard Carle. Malcolm St Clair directed the Monte Brice-J. Walter Ruben screenplay.

△ It was no world-beater, but everybody liked **Easy Come, Easy Go**, a comedy that brought out Richard Dix's multitude of fans and made fresh ones for his new leading lady, Nancy Carroll (illustrated with him). As a play by the prolific Owen Davis, it had been a 1925 Broadway hit for Otto Kruger and Victor Moore in the roles filmed by Dix and Charles Sellon: a young man looking for a job, and a veteran thief. The former innocently becomes the latter's accomplice in the payroll robbery of a bank; then, realising what he has done, has a hectic time trying to return the loot undetected. Frank Currier, Arnold Kent and Guy Oliver were featured under Frank Tuttle's fast-paced direction of a lively script by Florence Ryerson.

△ **Doomsday** was a snooze-inducer about a girl who marries a wealthy landowner instead of the young farmer she loves. After discovering that money does not buy happiness, she returns to the farmer, hard work and true love. Fleshed out in Warwick Deeping's best-selling prose, this skeletal plot had proved popular as a novel, but neither Doris Anderson's adaptation nor Donald Lee's screenplay gave producer-director Rowland V. Lee much to work on. The average fan in the street took one look at the title and hurried on to the nearest Clara Bow whoop-up. Florence Vidor (left) delivered a winning performance in the lead and Gary Cooper (right), who had been an extra in her 1926 *The Enchanted Hill*, demonstrated that he was learning how to make love scenes convincing. Lawrence Grant and Charles Stevenson topped the supporting cast.

▽ **The Patriot** marked the start of Ernst Lubitsch's long contract with Paramount, where he had scored one brilliant success (*Forbidden Paradise*) four years earlier. The new one was his last silent picture (although sound effects and one or two lines of dialogue were added for an alternative version) and quite unlike all his other Hollywood works. No risqué gaiety here, but a drama of madness, conspiracy, and struggle for power in the court of Russia's Czar Paul I. Lewis Stone, whose performance won him an Academy Award nomination and a 25-year MGM con-tract, played the title role, the prime minister who put love for his country above loyalty to the deranged tyrant ruling it, and sponsored a plot to assassinate him. No one who saw Emil Jannings (left) as Paul, raging and cowering among Hans Dreier's vast marbled sets, could ever forget him. Lubitsch had directed Jannings many times in Germany, but never to such telling effect. Hans Kraly's adaptation of Alfred Neumann's play provided good parts, too, for Florence Vidor (right), Neil Hamilton, Vera Voronina and Harry Cording.

▽ Director William Wellman and writer John Monk Saunders drew on their experiences as wartime aviators in Europe to fashion **Legion Of The Condemned**, just as they had for *Wings*. The same rapturous reception, however, wasn't forthcoming for this one, although it did well enough financially and proved that Gary Cooper, who had had one scene in the earlier picture, was now a real star. The script, on which Jean De Limur collaborated with Saunders, featured Cooper (right), Barry Norton, Lane Chandler and Francis McDonald as young American volunteers in the Lafayette Escadrille, a sort of French Foreign Legion of the air formed in 1916. Cooper's assignment was to fly behind the German lines and drop a spy who, by a credulity-stretching coincidence, happened to be the girl whose apparent unfaithfulness had caused him to join up in the first place. Fay Wray (left) as the improbable jumper, Albert Conti and E.H. Calvert rounded out the cast, but all were upstaged by the thrilling air action, much of it left-over footage from *Wings*. Thirty years later Wellman had another go at the theme in Warner's *Lafayette Escadrille*, his last movie.

△ Clara Bow (left) bounced back into the lush world of Elinor Glyn romance in **Red Hair**. Another smash hit of *IT* proportions was the aim of the same director-producer combination of Clarence Badger and B.P. Schulberg, and they very nearly achieved it. Three scripters – Agnes Brand Leahy, Percy Heath and Lloyd Corrigan – toiled over a 1905 story dug out of Madame G.'s trunk in an effort to supply a showy part for the star. She played a manicurist on the make who captivates a rich young man (Lane Chandler) and gold-digs expensive clothes and jewels from his three guardians. The big scene was her engagement party at which, snubbed by her fiancé's friends, she throws a tantrum, strips to her lingerie, and plunges into the swimming pool. Lawrence Grant, William Austin (right), Claude King and Jacqueline Gadsdon were among those present. At one point the movie burst into Technicolor, only the old two-tone kind but enough to illustrate the title.

▽ **The Racket** was one of the earliest movies into which Howard Hughes, then only 23, poured his money and his eccentric talent as producer. Bartlett Cormack's play, which had excited Broadway with its tough realism, featured Edward G. Robinson as a Capone-like gang leader, a role made even more brutal by Louis Wolheim (left) in the movie. Like Ben Hecht's *Underworld*, it was written from the author's experience as a Chicago newspaperman, and its exposure of criminals thriving amid political corruption was so harsh that it was banned in that city as a play, and ran into censorship there (and elsewhere) as a film. Lewis Milestone's direction of the adaptation by Harry Behn and Del Andrews packed all the punch of the original, and then some. Strong performances by Thomas Meighan (centre), Marie Prevost (right), Skeets Gallagher, Sam de Grasse, George E. Stone and John Darrow. Its exhibitors prospered, and Hughes grew a little richer.

▽ Would **The Secret Hour** solve the Pola Negri problem facing the studio? Sidney Howard's sensational Broadway hit, *They Knew What They Wanted*, was bought for the star in an attempt to reverse the downward drift in her popularity. No dice. But she gave a strong performance under the direction of Rowland V. Lee, who also scripted, somewhat purifying the original story by having the mail order bride-to-be (Negri, left) of a middle-aged vineyard owner (Jean Hersholt) abandon herself to the passion of his younger foreman (Kenneth Thompson, right) only after their secret marriage. The would-be bridegroom had only himself to blame; he had attracted the girl in the first place by sending her the foreman's photograph instead of his own. Paramount sold the play to MGM for a talkie made a mere year later, *A Lady To Love*, with Vilma Banky and Edward G. Robinson; in 1940 a third studio, RKO, remade it under its original title, with Carole Lombard and Charles Laughton. It flopped every time.

▷ George Bancroft and Evelyn Brent (both illustrated) again submitted themselves to the moody genius of Josef von Sternberg for **The Drag Net**, which all concerned hoped would be another *Underworld*. It was not. Still, the plot, from a story by Oliver H.P. Garrett (*Nightstick*), showed off their talents – and those of William Powell, Leslie Fenton and Fred Kohler, to the approval of press and public alike. Bancroft glowered convincingly as an alcoholic ex-cop who thinks he has killed his friend and colleague in a gun battle with mobsters. When it is proved that one of the gangster's bullets was the fatal one, he snaps out of his boozy remorse and, aided by tough charmer Brent, hunts the killer down.

△ **The First Kiss** offered the public, with none too many takers, Gary Cooper (right) as a poor fisherman who, when not romancing the richest girl in town (Fay Wray, left), indulges in a little piracy in order to finance the training of his three layabout brothers for lucrative jobs. He is caught by the coastguard; the girl and the brothers help him through his trial, and he is paroled in the girl's custody. This totally incredible script did nothing to back up an advertising campaign for Cooper and Wray as 'Paramount's Glorious Young Lovers'. Rowland V. Lee produced, and directed a cast that also featured Lane Chandler, Leslie Fenton, Paul Fix, Monroe Owsley and Malcolm Williams in John Farrow's adaptation of Tristram Tupper's story *Four Brothers*.

△ With an old-fashioned plot and – much more of a handicap in this dying year of the silent film – no soundtrack, **A Night Of Mystery** created little box-office excitement and wound up on double-feature bills, despite two popular star names in Adolphe Menjou and Evelyn Brent (both illustrated). Ernest Vajda reached all the way back to an 1875 play by Victorien Sardou (*Ferreol*) for the basics of his screenplay, a melodrama about a French army officer who witnesses a murder of which his fiancée's brother is wrongly accused. To save him he makes a false confession, is tried and acquitted. Neither the cast, including William Collier Jr, Nora Lane, Raoul Paoli and Claude King, nor the direction by Lothar Mendes did anything to lubricate the story's arthritic joints.

▽ Moviemakers loved the story of **Forgotten Faces**; they used it over and over again. It started when Richard Washburn Child wrote *A Whiff Of Heliotrope* in 1918; two years later it was filmed as *Heliotrope* with Frederick Burton as Heliotrope Harry; in 1936 its talking version with Herbert Marshall was called *Forgotten Faces* for the second time, and in 1942 United Artists took it over from Paramount as *A Gentleman After Dark* with Brian Donlevy. But it was the 1928 edition that had the best cast, with Clive Brook (right) as Harry, supported by William Powell, Olga Baclanova (left), Mary Brian, Fred Kohler and Jack Luden; the best script, by Howard Estabrook and Oliver H.P. Garrett, and the best director-producer team in Victor Schertzinger and David O. Selznick. The story? Harry, on his way to jail, leaves his baby daughter on a rich family's doorstep. Fifteen years later he is the family's butler when his dissolute wife appears, claiming the girl, and he deliberately provokes her to kill him; she goes to prison charged with murder, and the girl is safe with her adoptive parents.

◁ A heavy-breather set in Mexican jungle country, **The Showdown** gave ticket buyers 84 minutes of impassioned melodrama. George Bancroft (centre) played a wildcat oil driller grappling with temptation when his boss's wife, driven to distraction by the heat of the climate and of three other men on the site, throws herself at him. But the noble chap keeps her at arm's length until her husband returns for the big showdown. Evelyn Brent (left), who was having a busy year, invested the central role with a kind of suppressed frenzy, very effective; Neil Hamilton, Leslie Fenton, Fred Kohler, Helen Lynch (right) and Arnold Kent were also prominent in a cast directed by Victor Schertzinger with emotional tension stressed. The Hope Loring-Ethel Doherty script stemmed from a play by Houston Branch.

△ Bebe Daniels (right), Richard Arlen and William Powell (left) made a strong heroine-hero-villain combination in **Feel My Pulse**, which had the additional advantage of a resourceful comedy director in Gregory La Cava, plus adept supporting performances by Melbourne MacDowell, George Irving and Charles Sellon. It was an up-tempo frolic with no pauses for audience *ennui*, concocted by Keene Thompson and Nick Burrows from an original by Howard Emmett Rogers. Bebe, a lifelong hypochondriac, inherits a sanitarium which is being used as a hide-out by a gang of rum-runners, one of whom is an undercover reporter. She helps him when they discover his identity and, now aware that they are not patients as she thought, silly thing, she traps them for the police.

△ B.P. Schulberg brought Emil Jannings and Josef von Sternberg together again for **The Street Of Sin** after a row in mid-production with Mauritz Stiller who, nevertheless, received sole director credit. Von Sternberg, the latter's replacement, had also collaborated on the original story with Benjamin Glazer, the producer under Schulberg, who had just been appointed head of all West Coast production. The screenplay by Chandler Sprague presented a gloomy London underworld drama about a prizefighter turned criminal (Jannings, left) who begins to reform under the influence of a Salvation Army lass (Fay Wray) when he is betrayed to the police by a jealous prostitute (Olga Baclanova, right). In spite of its star and title values, the picture had a disappointing reception. Stiller, leaving behind his protegée, Garbo, for Hollywood to remember him by, returned to Sweden where he died in November 1928.

△ Shot as a silent, **Beggars Of Life** had a few lines of dialogue added to its music and effects track to qualify it as Paramount's first feature with a spoken word. (The studio's first real talkie, *Interference*, arrived a few months later.) Otherwise, it was chiefly remarkable for the best Hollywood performance of Louise Brooks (right) before her German success for G.W. Pabst in *Pandora's Box*. She played a girl who, having killed her brutal father, dresses as a man and goes on the run with a young tramp (Richard Arlen, left). A hobo camp they join is raided by the police; its leader (Wallace Beery), attracted by her but realising his desire will never be reciprocated, helps the couple to flee to Canada. The raw power of hobo-author Jim Tully's best-selling book and its stage adaptation by Maxwell Anderson (*Outside Looking In*) came through in William Wellman's direction of the script by Tully and Benjamin Glazer, who also produced. Edgar Blue Washington, Roscoe Karns, Mike Donlin and Andy Clark were also in the cast.

△ The genius of director Erich von Stroheim was crippled by his chronic elephantiasis of footage, complicated by budget blindness. When he started shooting **The Wedding March** in June 1926 he had already created problems for Universal and MGM with his penchant for hugely inflated footage. By February 1927 his new picture was a half-million dollars over budget and ran for 33 hours. Entrepreneur P.A. Powers, who financed it because Von Stroheim's last completed work, *The Merry Widow*, had been a box-office hit, called a halt, and studio chief B.P. Schulberg assigned Josef von Sternberg and Julian Johnston to grapple with the six hours of film still remaining in October 1927 when Von Stroheim had finished editing. One year later it opened to great acclaim from the critics and (in big cities) the public, who actually saw only the first half of the story, written by the director and Harry Carr. Set in 1914 Vienna, it brilliantly contrasted the romance of a poor harpist (Fay Wray) and a prince (Von Stroheim, illustrated with Fay) with the latter's corrupt, money-hungry family, who force him to marry a dull heiress (ZaSu Pitts). With music-on-disc accompaniment and sequences in Technicolor, it ran two hours; the uncompleted second half, *The Honeymoon*, was shown (briefly) only in Europe. Prominent in **The Wedding March** cast were George Fawcett, Dale Fuller, Matthew Betz, Maude George, Cesare Gravina and George Nichols. Von Stroheim directed two more films, both unfinished, then prospered as an actor until 1955.

▽ With Chaplin's pictures becoming few and far between, Harold Lloyd was the star who attracted more people into more theatres than any other comedian, including Keaton. **Speedy**, his first release for over a year, delighted everybody. Directed by Ted Wilde at a snappy pace, it offered Harold (right) as a baseball-crazy taxi driver in love with a girl whose grandfather refuses to stop running the last horse-drawn trolley car in New York. When transport tycoons hire thugs to steal it, our hero rallies the neighbourhood to thwart them in a riot of comic action. Among the highlights shot in New York were a wild cab ride down 5th Avenue and a day at Coney Island. The script by a battery of authors and gag-men (John Grey, Lex Neal, Jay Howe, Howard Emmett Rogers) gave roles to Ann Christy (left), Bert Woodruff, Brooks Benedict, Byron Douglas and the king of home runs himself, Babe Ruth.

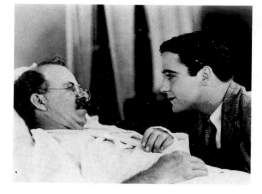

△ Excellent box-office receipts and matching audience response greeted **Varsity**, a college comedy-drama with a stronger script than most of its ilk. Charles 'Buddy' Rogers (right), whose fan following was on the rise, starred as a campus hero helped out of predicaments by the school's caretaker (Chester Conklin, left). The old boy, secretly his father, steers the lad away from drinking, gambling and wooing showgirls. Every now and then the mostly silent movie burst into dialogue and a theme song called, no kidding, 'My Varsity Girl, I'll Cling To You' (by Al Bryan and W. Franke Harling). Among the players were Mary Brian, Phillips Holmes (debut), Robert Ellis, John Westwood and undergraduates of Princeton University, where Frank Tuttle directed a lot of the Wells Root-Howard Estabrook screenplay.

▽ **Three Sinners**, moving slowly, followed Pola Negri (right) down the primrose path as she deserted her husband in Germany, was seduced en route to Vienna in a train which crashed, and took on a new identity when hubby presumed she had been killed. Years later he finds her hostessing in a gambling house and rejects her plea for forgiveness. Nettled, she leaves for America with a rich lover. Warner Baxter (left), Paul Lukas, Olga Baclanova, Tullio Carminati and Anders Randolph earned their salaries but few plaudits in this dreary drama. The title could have referred to the director Rowland V. Lee and writers Doris Anderson and Jean De Limur, who translated the Rudolph Bernauer-Rudolf Oesterreicher play to the screen. It was rewritten as a 1931 talkie for Ruth Chatterton, *Once A Lady*.

▷ In 1928 Pola Negri's popularity tide was at a really low ebb. Her talking test confirmed that her foreign accent would be a handicap, and her contract, which was up for renewal, was dropped. Thus, one of Hollywood's great names went into eclipse after only six years, during which time her exotic image had consistently been more successful in publicity than in mass appeal. Her last Paramount picture, **The Woman From Moscow**, directed at a funereal pace by Ludwig Berger, was a dismal drama about a princess (Negri, illustrated) in love with a revolutionary who kills her intended husband, then turns against her when his family is banished to Siberia, whereupon she commits suicide. Nobody suffered more than the audience. Paul Lukas and Norman Kerry had the male leads in John Farrow's screenplay, a rewrite of French playwright Victorien Sardou's *Fedora*, which had starred Pauline Frederick in 1918. Negri made several films in Germany and a few in Britain and America before going into a retirement that has lasted, at this writing, into her ninetieth year.

▷ Often called Josef von Sternberg's masterpiece by film historians, **The Docks Of New York** brought his remarkable visual artistry to full flower. Light and darkness, mists and shadows made the camerawork as compelling as the story, in which he again led George Bancroft through sleazy city streets to a drama of love and death in which the rough-hewn hero rescues a waterfront seeker of oblivion in suicide. He marries her, clears her from a murder charge and goes to jail for her. Betty Compson (here with Bancroft) gave a touching performance as the girl, with Olga Baclanova, Mitchell Lewis, Clyde Cook, Gustav von Seyffertitz and Guy Oliver in support. Jules Furthman wrote the script from a John Monk Saunders original for producer J.G. Bachmann. It was released only two months after the von Sternberg-Bancroft *The Drag Net*; silent movies were being cleared out of the way.

▽ An entertaining little melodrama called **Manhattan Cocktail** was the movie which showed the studio that it had important star material in Nancy Carroll (left), hitherto just a pretty ingenue. Her dramatic strength was brought to the fore by the sympathetic direction of Dorothy Arzner in Ernest Vajda's story about a young hopeful from a small town trying to get a break on Broadway where she, her brother and her boyfriend are caught up in the vortex of a hard-drinking circle dominated by a stage producer and his vampish wife. The latter steals the boyfriend, and the brother is killed while saving the girl from rape. She goes back home, sadder and wiser. Ethel Doherty's screenplay was trashy but gripping, and well acted also by Paul Lukas, Lilyan Tashman, Richard Arlen (right) and Danny O'Shea.

▷ No use calling **Abie's Irish Rose** crude claptrap. New York theatre critics tried that when Anne Nichols's play opened in 1922, and they were still saying it when it closed six years later. That run was then the longest in Broadway's history, and has since been exceeded only by two other straight plays (*Life With Father, Tobacco Road*). So Paramount willingly shelled out the highest price it had ever paid for screen rights: $500,000 against 50% of profits. The profits weren't all that great, as it turned out. Although it was a popular movie, efficiently adapted and directed by no less a team than Jules Furthman and Victor Fleming respectively, its comic 'Romeo and Juliet' theme of Irish bride and Jewish groom's families at loggerheads had been well milked by Universal's *The Cohens And The Kellys* comedies before it could be released. Nancy Carroll and Charles 'Buddy' Rogers, in the first of four pictures together, made a refreshing pair of young lovers (illustrated) amid the ethnic caricatures of J. Farrell MacDonald, Jean Hersholt, Bernard Gorcey (in his original Broadway role) and Ida Kramer. B.P. Schulberg produced.

△ Historically, the studio's most important event of 1928 was the making of **Interference**, its first all-dialogue feature. Commercially, it was money in the bank. Artistically, alas, it left something to be desired. Trapped in a tiny stage sound-proofed by inventive trouble-shooter Roy Pomeroy, the cast seemed to be immobilised by microphone paralysis. Clive Brook, Evelyn Brent, William Powell, Doris Kenyon, Brandon Hurst and Clyde Cook were, however, experienced professionals, and well equipped to keep audiences engrossed in the complications of the Roland Pertwee-Harold Dearden play. Above all, they could talk! Hardly ever letting them stop, Hope Loring's screenplay, with dialogue by Ernest Pascal, related the somewhat complicated mystery of a murdered adventuress (Brent). She, it would appear, has been blackmailing the wife (Kenyon) of her former lover (Powell). He was believed by his wife to have been killed in the war and she has remarried, but he is alive; both he and the wife are suspected of the murder; so is the wife's new husband (Brook). No director on the lot was eager to tackle the technical difficulties of the new invention, so Pomeroy directed it himself, with William C. de Mille sitting in to help and observe. Lothar Mendes, sometimes credited as director, actually handled a simultaneous silent version.

▷ Paramount's last 1928 picture was Ruth Chatterton's first ever (and her only silent one). Long a star on Broadway, and about to become a top name for the studio, she played opposite Emil Jannings (here with her) in **Sins Of The Fathers**, which otherwise was a pretty gruelling experience for its audiences. It was designed by writers Norman Burnstine and E. Lloyd Sheldon and director Ludwig Berger to fit the special Jannings talent for suffering. This time he was a restaurateur persuaded to become a bootlegger by a siren who then runs off with his money and another man. His wife dies heartbroken; his son goes blind from drinking dad's hooch; dad himself is jailed. The good cast included Jean Arthur, Barry Norton, ZaSu Pitts, Jack Luden, Matthew Betz, Harry Cording and Frank Reicher.

OTHER RELEASES OF 1928
(All silents)

Adventure Mad
Nils Asther, Eric Barclay, Nina Vanning, Paul Graetz. Dir: Lothar Mendes. Drama of conspiracy to rob English nobleman, set in Italy and Cairo. (UFA, German)

Avalanche
Jack Holt, Olga Baclanova, John Darrow, Doris Hill. Dir: Otto Brower. Gambler decides to take his son away from their sinful Western town, and breaks with his mistress. She and the son elope and are caught in an avalanche.

Beau Sabreur
Gary Cooper, Evelyn Brent, William Powell, Noah Beery. Dir: John Waters. Sequel to *Beau Geste* in which a young French officer fights an Arab uprising and loves an American writer gathering local colour in the Sahara.

The Big Killing
Wallace Beery, Raymond Hatton, Mary Brian, Lane Chandler. Dir & Pro: F. Richard Jones. Hired by one feuding mountain family to shoot up another, two gun-shy ex-circus men get them to bury the hatchet instead.

The Fifty-Fifty Girl
Bebe Daniels, James Hall, William Austin, Harry T. Morey. Dir: Clarence Badger. A girl bets the joint owner of her ranch that she can run it if he does the housework; the first to ask help gets the ranch. She wins.

Figures Don't Lie
Richard Arlen, Esther Ralston, Ford Sterling, Natalie Kingston, Doris Hill. Dir: Edward Sutherland. Pro: B.P. Schulberg. Comedy of office life concerning jealous young lovers and the boss's wife versus his secretary.

Fools For Luck
W.C. Fields, Chester Conklin, Sally Blane, Jack Luden. Dir: Charles Reisner. Con-man outwits himself when he unloads shares in a dry oilfield on a millionaire and it starts producing again.

Half A Bride
Gary Cooper, Esther Ralston, William Worthington, Mary Doran. Dir: Gregory La Cava. The honeymoon yacht of a girl and her middle-aged husband is wrecked, stranding its young captain with her on a desert island.

His Private Life
Adolphe Menjou, Kathryn Carver, Margaret Livingston, Eugene Pallette. Dir: Frank Tuttle. Farce about a Paris playboy, an American girl, his ex-mistress and her jealous husband.

His Tiger Lady
Adolphe Menjou, Evelyn Brent, Emil Chautard, Rose Dione. Dir: Hobart Henley. A duchess fascinated by tigers is drawn to a circus revue where she fascinates an elephant rider.

The Homecoming
Lars Hanson, Dita Parlo, Gustav Froelich. Dir: Joe May. Pro: Erich Pommer. Drama of a soldier, presumed killed, who comes home to find his former comrade-in-arms in the arms of his wife. (German)

Hot News
Bebe Daniels, Neil Hamilton, Paul Lukas. Dir: Clarence Badger. Camera girl, competing with a male photographer on a rival newspaper, gets them both kidnapped by a yachtsman she has exposed as a jewel thief.

Huntingtower
Harry Lauder, Vera Veronina, Pat Aherne, John Manners. Dir: George Pearson. A Russian princess is rescued from castle imprisonment. (British)

Just Married
Lila Lee, James Hall, Ruth Taylor, Harrison Ford, William Austin. Dir: Frank Strayer. Farce, centred on two fashion models trying to captivate the same man; set on a westbound transatlantic liner.

Kit Carson
Fred Thomson, Nora Lane, Dorothy Janis, William Courtright. Dir: Alfred Werker, Lloyd Ingraham. Government scout rescues an Indian girl from a bear, and later kills his fellow scout who attacks her.

The Legion Of Honor (aka **The Soul Of France**)
Jean Murat, Michele Verly, M. Desjardins. Dir: Alexander Ryder, A. Duges. Pro: Jacques Haik. Drama of brothers facing death on the battlefields of World War I. (French)

Love And Learn
Esther Ralston, Lane Chandler, Hedda Hopper, Claude King. Dir: Frank Tuttle. Comedy about a girl who keeps her parents from separating by getting herself into a series of scrapes.

Loves Of An Actress
Pola Negri, Nils Asther, Paul Lukas, Richard Tucker. Dir: Rowland V. Lee. In the 19th century, Rachel's fame spreads from the Comedie Francaise around the world. She discards other lovers for a young diplomat.

The Magnificent Flirt
Florence Vidor, Loretta Young, Albert Conti, Matty Kemp. Dir: H. d'Abbadie d'Arrast. Comedy of a mother who uses her charms to solve the problem of her daughter's unsuitable suitor.

The Mating Call
Thomas Meighan, Evelyn Brent, Renee Adoree. Dir: James Cruze. Pro: Howard Hughes. Soldier returns to his farm to find his wife, having annulled their marriage, has wed again, and he is involved in a murder.

The Model From Montmartre
Nita Naldi, Ivan Petrovich, Louise Lagrange. Dir: Leonce Perret. Parisian drama of artist who marries a model, has an affair with a countess, returns to his wife. (French)

Moran Of The Marines
Richard Dix, Ruth Elder, Roscoe Karns, E.H. Calvert. Dir: Frank Strayer. Young hell-raiser joins the marines and is sent to China, where he rescues a general's daughter from a bandit, is taken prisoner, and freed by the girl.

Partners In Crime
Wallace Beery, Raymond Hatton, Mary Brian, William Powell. Dir: Frank Strayer. Bumbling detective and nutty reporter aid a cafe cigarette girl by tracking down the robbers who kidnapped her boyfriend.

Peaks Of Destiny
Leni Riefenstahl, Luis Trenker, Ernst Peterson. Dir: Dr Arnold Fanck. Triangle drama, set in the Alps, of a dancer, a skiing expert and a youth. (UFA, German)

Pioneer Scout
Fred Thomson, Nora Lane, William Courtright. Dir: Lloyd Ingraham, Alfred Werker. Western scout helps a covered wagon train to withstand attacks by outlaws disguised as Indians.

Quicksands
Richard Dix, Helene Chadwick, Alan Hale, Noah Beery. Dir: Jack Conway. Pro: Howard Hawks. US Army officer breaks up a drug-smuggling gang on the Mexican border. (Filmed 1922 by Aggar Co.)

The Sawdust Paradise
Esther Ralston, Reed Howes, Hobart Bosworth. Dir: Luther Reed. Street carnival girl, jailed for crooked gambling, is paroled to an evangelist, who helps her partner when a rival carnival burns him out.

Someone To Love
Charles 'Buddy' Rogers, Mary Brian, Jack Oakie. Dir: F. Richard Jones. When taking charge of a girls' school, an heiress's suitor convinces her that he's not a fortune-hunter. (Remake of *The Charm School*, 1921)

Something Always Happens
Neil Hamilton, Esther Ralston, Sojin, Roscoe Karns. Dir: Frank Tuttle. American girl in England seeks excitement and finds it when her fiancé takes her to a haunted house, where a Chinese thief lurks.

Sporting Goods
Richard Dix, Gertrude Olmstead, Ford Sterling, Philip Strange. Dir: Malcolm St. Clair. Comedy of a salesman who makes good by inventing a new type of golf suit. (Remake of *The Traveling Salesman*, 1916 and 1921)

The Sunset Legion
Fred Thomson, Edna Murphy, William Courtright. Dir: Lloyd Ingraham, Alfred Werker. Texas Ranger adopts two disguises: as a masked stranger he captures an outlaw gang, and as a gun salesman he captivates a girl.

Take Me Home
Bebe Daniels, Neil Hamilton, Lilyan Tashman, Joe E. Brown. Dir: Marshall Neilan. Backstage comedy in which a chorus girl and a seductive star have a fight over the former's boy friend; she has to replace the star in the show.

Three Week-Ends
Clara Bow, Neil Hamilton, Harrison Ford, Lucille Powers. Dir: Clarence Badger. Elinor Glyn comedy about a chorus girl helping her insurance salesman boyfriend to sell a policy to a Broadway producer.

Tillie's Punctured Romance
W.C. Fields, Chester Conklin, Louise Fazenda. Dir: Edward Sutherland. Circus owner and ringmaster vie for a lady, and take their show overseas during the war, creating havoc behind the German lines.

Under The Tonto Rim
Richard Arlen, Mary Brian, Jack Luden, Harry T. Morey. Dir: Herman Raymaker. Zane Grey western about a young goldminer solving the mystery of a murder for which his girl's brother has been framed.

The Vanishing Pioneer
Jack Holt, William Powell, Sally Blane, Fred Kohler, Roscoe Karns. Dir: John Waters. After clashing with the nearby townsfolk over their water supply, new settlers move on in westbound covered wagons.

Warming Up
Richard Dix, Jean Arthur, Claude King, Philo McCullough, Roscoe Karns. Dir: Fred Newmeyer. Comedy-drama of life on the baseball circuit, and a star player who overcomes adversity and wins his girl.

The Water Hole
Jack Holt, Nancy Carroll, John Boles. Dir: & Pro: F. Richard Jones. Arizona rancher tries to tame a flighty girl by taking her to live rough in an Indian cave; her fiancé follows, but she chooses the rancher.

What A Night!
Bebe Daniels, Neil Hamilton, William Austin, Wheeler Oakman, Charles Sellon. Dir: Edward Sutherland. A girl reporter and her editor's son have a breezy romance while getting a big story on political corruption.

Wife Savers
Wallace Beery, Raymond Hatton, ZaSu Pitts, Sally Blane, Ford Sterling. Dir: Ralph Cedar. Pro: James Cruze. Two American soldiers, stationed in Switzerland after the war, are rivals for a girl also wooed by a general.

1929

▽ **Redskin** no speak with forked tongue – nor any other kind. It was one of Paramount's last silent pictures, and thereby handicapped at the box-office. Made as a result of the success of *The Vanishing American*, it actually surpassed the 1925 production artistically. Richard Dix (centre) again played (very well) a Red Indian in the strong Elizabeth Pickett screenplay about a Navajo boy who is accepted as Thorpe College's first Indian student, then comes up against racial prejudice. Back on the reservation, he is shunned for his white man's ways, becomes a drifter, discovers oil, and claims it for his people. Magnificent scenery was given the benefit of Technicolor (intended throughout, but director Victor Schertzinger ran out of budget and shot the non-Indian sequences in black and white). Gladys Belmont, Tully Marshall, Jane Novak, George Rigas and Noble Johnson offered reliable support to Dix.

▷ Paramount delightedly discovered in **The Shopworn Angel** that its pretty ingenue of the last year of silents had the makings of a major talkie star. Nancy Carroll (right) positively glowed with intelligence and sensitivity as a showgirl amused by an ingenuous soldier on leave in New York. He falls seriously in love with her, while she continues her affair with a rich man – until the boy's embarkation for war service makes her realise how wrong she has been. Gary Cooper (left) was exactly right as the soldier; Paul Lukas, Emmett King, Mildred Washington and Roscoe Karns were effective in support under Richard Wallace's direction. Near the end the otherwise silent movie disconcertingly broke into speech, and song ('A Precious Little Thing Called Love' by Lou Davis and J.F. Coots), which at least proved that Nancy sounded as good as she looked. The Louis D. Lighton production was scripted by Howard Estabrook and Albert LeVino from a Dana Burnett story filmed first in 1919 as *Pettigrew's Girl* with Ethel Clayton and Monte Blue. MGM bought it from Paramount for the 1938 *Shopworn Angel* with Margaret Sullavan and James Stewart, and sold it back again for 1956's *That Kind Of Woman* starring the rather unlikely duo of Sophia Loren and Tab Hunter.

△ Jeanne Eagels (left), after years of Broadway stardom and three silent pictures, brought her fragile beauty and feverish intensity to the Astoria studio for two 1929 talkies, and later that year died of a heroin overdose. **The Letter** gave her the role in which Gladys Cooper in London and Katherine Cornell in New York had scored on stage. From its famous start, with the married lady firing shots into her lover's body, to her climactic cry 'I still love the man I killed!', this drama of heady passions, and lives ruined by an indiscreet letter, set deep in the tropical plantations of Somerset Maughamland, made potent movie material. Herbert Marshall (right), Reginald Owen (as the husband), O.P. Heggie, Irene Browne and Lady Tsen Mei, all making their American film debuts, were fine in the Monta Bell production, directed by Jean De Limur. The screenplay was written by Garrett Fort, with dialogue by Bell and De Limur. Marshall played the husband opposite Bette Davis in the 1940 Warner Bros. remake.

▷ Sizzling with vivacity, and revealing a Brooklyn accent that suited her personality exactly, Clara Bow (2nd right) passed the microphone test in **The Wild Party**. She played a madcap collegian chasing a handsome professor (Fredric March, left) and catching him, after she has been expelled and he has been shot by a drunken rapist inflamed by Clara's 'It'. Director Dorothy Arzner gave speedy pace to the script E. Lloyd Sheldon wrote from a story by Warner Fabian (whose *Flaming Youth* was a jazz-age classic). Jack Oakie, Phillips Holmes, Marceline Day, Joyce Compton, Jack Luden, Adrienne Dore (left of Clara) and Shirley O'Hara were among Clara's fellow students. 'You've had an eyeful of *IT* . . . now get an earful!' urged the ads. 'This production is intended for dwarfed intellects', snapped the *New York Times*. 'A hot ticket-seller', retorted the exhibitors.

△ **The Canary Murder Case** was one of the movies caught in the middle of the talkie revolution. Completed as a silent by Malcolm St Clair in 1928, it was extensively re-shot by Frank Tuttle to make it a 1929 all-talkie. As the first of S.S. Van Dine's vastly popular whodunit novels to reach the screen, it commanded strong business and built a new following for William Powell. He played the ineffably cultured detective, Philo Vance, solving the mystery of a blackmailing Broadway beauty's murder; he outsmarts cop Eugene Pallette, saves wrongly-accused James Hall, and unmasks the latter's father. Charles Lane (as the killer), Jean Arthur (here with Powell), Gustav von Seyffertitz, Ned Sparks, E.H. Calvert and Lawrence Grant also populated the rather sluggish Florence Ryerson-Albert LeVino script, which had dialogue by Van Dine himself. Cast as the ill-fated canary, Louise Brooks, who had by now embarked on her illustrious European career, failed to turn up for the dialogue dubbing, so the studio had to substitute the voice of Margaret Livingston.

▷ Preceding the event with a flood of publicity, Paramount unveiled its first musical and uncorked a champagne personality in **Innocents Of Paris** – Maurice Chevalier (illustrated). Already famous as a Paris music hall singer, he had made occasional appearances in French films since 1908, and at the age of 40 was somewhat on the mature side for trying a Hollywood debut. But his bubbling charm, polished technique and well-developed showmanship had an immediate impact on the moviegoing masses which propelled him into another 40 years of international renown. The partnership with Jeanette MacDonald was yet to come, and this first picture for the company had little to offer beyond his charisma and his songs (including his enduring hit, 'Louise', by Richard A. Whiting and Leo Robin, as well as half a dozen others in English and/or French). It was whipped up by Ernest Vajda and Ethel Doherty from a story by Charles Andrews about a singing junk dealer who rescues a child from the Seine, romances the boy's aunt, wins the attention of a show's producers and becomes a star. David Durand was effective as the boy, Sylvia Beecher less so as the aunt; John Miljan, Margaret Livingston, Russell Simpson, Jack Luden and George Fawcett also performed for director Richard Wallace. As the Hollywood studio's first musical, it was the production most disrupted when a fire destroyed the new sound stages, and shooting had to be completed in makeshift style on sets heavily draped against outside noises.

▷ Nancy Carroll and Charles 'Buddy' Rogers (both illustrated), having passed the talkie test in one dialogue-added hybrid each, continued their very popular partnership with the all-talking **Close Harmony**, a strong ticket-seller. A story of vaudeville troupers (a subject of which co-author Elsie Janis had first-hand knowledge) performing in a palatial movie theatre, it cast Buddy as a dance band leader and Nancy as the song and dance girl he meets, loses and finally gets. They were surrounded by Jack Oakie, Skeets Gallagher, Harry Green – a lively trio of comedians – as well as Greta Granstedt and Wade Boteler. The Percy Heath-John V.A. Weaver screenplay, from a story by Gene Markey and Janis, was directed by John Cromwell and Edward Sutherland. The delectable Nancy sang the best of its Richard A. Whiting-Leo Robin songs, 'I Want To Go Places And Do Things' – and she certainly did so at Paramount.

▷ Richard Dix sounded every vowel and consonant to the full satisfaction of his fans in **Nothing But The Truth**, and so another silent star won his talkie diploma. It was a hit, but the studio did not renew his contract at the end of the year; it was said he had reached too high a salary bracket. This comedy, about a man who bet he could get through 24 hours without telling a fib, always was a hit, first as a novel by Frederic Isham, then adapted to the stage by James Montgomery in 1916, and to the screen by Metro in 1920 (starring Taylor Holmes, father of Phillips). Now, with dialogue restored in John McGowan's screenplay, it achieved its highest laugh score (topped by the Bob Hope version a dozen years later). Victor Schertzinger directed a cast including Wynne Gibson (standing centre, debut), Berton Churchill, Ned Sparks (who was in the original play), and Helen Kane (foreground centre), with a best-selling song, 'Do Something' (by Bud Green and Sammy Stept).

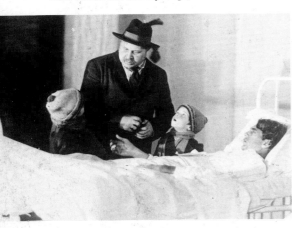

△ Following in the footsteps of his quondam co-star in German films, Pola Negri (strangely, they never acted together in Hollywood), through the Paramount door marked 'Exit', Emil Jannings left behind one 1929 release, **Betrayal**. And it was a dud. Even with the romantic attractions of Gary Cooper and Esther Ralston, direction by the usually potent Lewis Milestone and a handsome production by David O. Selznick, it drew sparse audiences whose word-of-mouth matched the critics' negative reviews. A director and an actor, Victor Schertzinger and Nicholas Soussanin, wrote the story about a Viennese artist (Cooper, right) who has a summer affair in Switzerland with a peasant girl (Ralston), returns the next year to find she has acquired a husband (Jannings, left) and dies with her in a toboggan crash, before and after which the husband puts in a lot of tragic emoting. Jada Weller, Douglas Haig and Bodil Rosing were also involved in the glum Hans Kraly screenplay.

▷ Now that the screen had found its voice, the studio was drawing more heavily than ever on material from Broadway, where the second half of the twenties brought the most prolific period in the history of world theatre, with one or more premieres almost every night. The incredible peak was reached when eleven plays opened on December 26, 1927. In August 1928, two comedy-dramas about newspapermen arrived: **Gentlemen Of The Press** and *The Front Page*. Paramount tried for both, was outbid by Howard Hughes for the rowdier, more successful latter, but got the former onto the screen first. Written by Ward Morehouse, theatre critic on the *New York Sun*, it marked the movie debuts of Walter Huston and Kay (then billed as Katherine) Francis (both illustrated), he as a reporter, she as his secretary – a wicked charmer he keeps as his mistress to save his daughter's fiancé from her clutches. Charles Ruggles, featured along with Betty Lawford and Norman Foster, also began a long Paramount contract. Millard Webb directed the Bartlett Cormack screenplay, produced by Monta Bell who had been appointed supervisor of the Astoria Studios where the film was shot.

▷ Olga Baclanova (centre), a striking blue-eyed blonde from the Moscow Art Theatre, had made an impression with several supporting performances in 1929 (notably opposite Jannings in *The Street Of Sin*) and was given a chance at stardom in **A Dangerous Woman**, the studio billing only her surname, Garbo fashion. In this John Farrow-E.E. Paramore adaptation of the best-selling novel *The Woman Who Needed Killing* (a title vetoed by Adolph Zukor as 'too rough') by an invader of Maugham territory, Margery Lawrence, Baclanova played the way-out-East wife who isn't getting enough of whatever it is she wants from her British colonist husband. After taking a lover, whom she drives to suicide, she makes a play for her young brother-in-law, who is about to succumb when she is bitten by a snake and dies. So did the picture, despite good performances by the star, Clive Brook (right), Neil Hamilton (left), Leslie Fenton and Clyde Cook, and all-stops-out direction by Rowland V. Lee. Louis D. Lighton produced.

▷ **The Four Feathers** was one of the few silent movies to succeed in a market dominated by the novelty of the talkies. It did have an abundance of synchronized sound effects, but the studio commendably refrained from post-production of chat scenes. This was the second of five pictures made from A.E.W. Mason's familiar story of a British army officer (Richard Arlen, right), branded as a coward. After receiving four symbolic white feathers from his comrades (William Powell, Clive Brook, Theodore von Eltz) and his wife (Fay Wray, left), he redeems his reputation in battle in the Sudan. The others, produced in 1921, 1939, 1955 (*Storm Over The Nile*) and 1977, were all British. Howard Estabrook's screenplay took the Merian Cooper-Ernest Schoedsack directorial team out of the documentary field and into fiction, although there was thrilling on-the-spot realism in their hippo stampede, bush fire and tribal warfare, shot in Africa. Lothar Mendes handled the bulk of the studio scenes, which also featured Noah Beery, Noble Johnson, George Fawcett and Philippe De Lacey.

▽ A new kind of movie comedy burst into view after the Marx Brothers took the short trip from Broadway, where they were starring in *Animal Crackers*, to the Astoria studio, which had never experienced anything like their hilarious anarchy. Neither had the cinema crowds watching **The Cocoanuts** and laughing up a storm at Groucho's (left) leering wisecracks, Harpo's (right) demented pantomime and Chico's (centre) Italianate clowning. The fourth brother, Zeppo, who eventually left the team, played straight man in a completely daffy story which more or less followed George S. Kaufman's original script. The stage show's songs by Irving Berlin were joined by one of his first written for the screen, 'When My Dreams Come True'. Robert Florey and Joseph Santley directed Mary Eaton, Oscar Shaw, Kay Francis, Basil Ruysdael, Cyril Ring and the statuesque Margaret Dumont, and with difficulty kept the Marxes on camera. A legend was born.

▷ **Dangerous Curves** was a circus drama with Richard Arlen as a daredevil on the high wire and a devil with women off it. The rival charms of bareback equestrienne Clara Bow (right) and the sleekly sophisticated Kay Francis (left) throw him into such a tizzy that he takes to the bottle. Not a good idea for a high-wire artist. At least Arlen had a better part than Clara, who seemed somewhat subdued by the problems of balancing on a horse while trying to remember her lines. Still, she got her man for the fade-out, and was responsible (along with those magic words 'All Talking!') for the excellent business the movie attracted. Lester Cohen's story, adapted by Donald Davis and Florence Ryerson, gave director Lothar Mendes a large cast to cope with, including David Newell, Anders Randolf, May Boley, Stuart Erwin, T. Roy Barnes, Joyce Compton, Jack Luden and Charles D. Brown.

▷ Josef von Sternberg's fourth and last outbreak of George Bancroft (foreground left) thuggery wasn't his best, but its melodrama had the director's distinctive, mesmerising atmosphere. More important, commercially: **Thunderbolt** talked! The burly star played a convict in death row who plots the murder of his girl's young lover, held in the same prison, on the eve of his own execution. Plenty of gangster violence and tough talk, with romantic interludes, exercised the talents of Richard Arlen, Fay Wray (2nd right), Fred Kohler, Tully Marshall (between the ladies), George Irving, Eugene Besserer (centre) and E.H. Calvert. Jules Furthman and Herman Mankiewicz wrote it for producer B.P. Fineman from an original by Furthman and his brother Charles.

▽ **Charming Sinners** was a splendid example of the early talkie period, when action was just a word the director used to start a take, dialogue was all-important, and the long chase was replaced by the *chaise-longue*. A scintillating cast, headed by Ruth Chatterton (centre – in the role that had given Ethel Barrymore an enormous 1926 stage success), Clive Brook (left), William Powell (right), Mary Nolan, Florence Eldridge, Laura Hope Crews, Montagu Love and Claude Allister, juggled with the assorted infidelities of Somerset Maugham's sophisticated comedy, *The Constant Wife*, written for the screen by Doris Anderson. Robert Milton, a director recruited from Broadway, kept the conversations flowing smoothly.

△ **The River Of Romance** was another version of Booth Tarkington's play *Magnolia*, first filmed as *The Fighting Coward* in 1924 and to be musicalised as *Mississippi* in 1935. Now much of the comedy had been deleted to concentrate on the romantic elements, making it a typical Charles 'Buddy' Rogers movie, and he pleased the fans as the peace-loving beau of the old South who refuses a duel, joins a river-boat crew and proves his gallantry by giving a villain his come-uppance. The screenplay by Ethel Doherty, Dan Totheroe and John V.A. Weaver was directed by Richard Wallace with, as dialogue director, George Cukor, starting a distinguished 53-year film career after 11 years in the theatre. It had a good cast – Rogers, Wallace Beery, Mary Brian (here with Rogers), June Collyer, Henry B. Walthall, Fred Kohler – and plenty of charm, mint-julep flavour.

▽ A successful successor to *The Canary Murder Case*, featuring several members of its cast once again directed by Frank Tuttle, **The Greene Murder Case** was generally rated as the best of S.S. Van Dine's top-selling mystery stories. William Powell (right) again did a beautifully professional job to make Philo Vance, the excruciatingly erudite amateur detective, a likeable person as he quizzes nine suspects after a slaying in the New York mansion of a millionaire. This time sweet little Jean Arthur was the killer (who doubtless agreed with Ogden Nash's immortal lines 'Philo Vance/needs a kick in the pants') and the denouement was followed by an exciting chase sequence. Eugene Pallette (left), Florence Eldridge, Ulrich Haupt, E.H. Calvert, Morgan Farley, Brandon Hurst and Gertrude Norman were also in it. The script was by Louise Long and Bartlett Cormack.

◁ Sax Rohmer's Chinese super-criminal, Fu Manchu, who kept millions of readers agog (probably still does) and was the central figure of a series of silent British shorts, arrived on the talking screen in all his insidious glory in **The Mysterious Dr Fu Manchu**. Mad with a lust for revenge, he sets out to kill the British officers he holds responsible for the death of his wife and child. He hypnotises his adopted daughter to aid his foul purpose, but two murders later she is told the truth about him by a young Englishman, and Fu turns his fury upon them. Trapped by police in time's nick, he commits suicide. Marvellously wild thriller; a box-office hit. Rowland V. Lee directed the Florence Ryerson-Lloyd Corrigan script with gusto, and it was acted the same way by Warner Oland (illustrated), the Swedish specialist in Oriental roles, as the eponymous villain, Jean Arthur, Neil Hamilton, O.P. Heggie, William Austin, Claude King, Tully Marshall and Evelyn Selbie.

▷ The assignment of two men to co-direct became fashionable in 1929, the team usually consisting of an established silent film director paired with one from the theatre, accustomed to handling dialogue. Edward Sutherland and Broadway's John Cromwell combined particularly well on **The Dance Of Life**, adapted by Benjamin Glazer and George M. Watters from the Watters-Arthur Hopkins stage success, *Burlesque*. Hal Skelly (right) repeated his original stage role of a bottle-scarred comedian whose long-suffering wife and partner takes him back after he has left her for the big time and another woman, and then hit the skids. In the part that made Barbara Stanwyck's name on Broadway, Nancy Carroll co-starred to moving effect, with Dorothy Revier, Ralph Theodore, May Boley, Oscar Levant (left), Charles D. Brown and George Irving in support. David O. Selznick gave it A production values, throwing in two-colour Technicolor for a flashy musical number. The score, by Sam Coslow, Richard A. Whiting and Leo Robin, included an enduring hit, 'True Blue Lou'. It was remade in 1937 as *Swing High, Swing Low* and in 1948 (by Fox) as *When My Baby Smiles At Me*.

△ **Welcome Danger** was completed as a silent under the direction of Malcolm St Clair then almost entirely re-shot, Clyde Bruckman directing, as Harold Lloyd's first talkie. The script, which somehow took four authors (Bruckman, Lex Neal, Felix Adler, Paul Gerard Smith) to concoct, had some holes in it and, although cut from three hours to two, seemed overlong. Nonetheless, it proved a popular and profitable release, in the Lloyd tradition. The story had him (left) failing to follow in his father's footsteps as a crook-catcher because he is preoccupied with botany, until a pretty girl's predicament embroils him in a San Francisco crime wave. Barbara Kent, Noah Young, Charles Middleton and Edgar Kennedy were in it too.

▷ Rouben Mamoulian, the celebrated stage director, revealed the potency of sound in heightening dramatic effect in **Applause**, a trail-blazing movie, years ahead of its time. Critics of dialogue as a stultifying influence on the motion picture were astonished by the mobility of the camera, as well as by the versatility of the soundtrack which Mamoulian demonstrated in this, his first film. What's more, it was accomplished on the Astoria lot, equipped with fewer technical resources than the West Coast studio. Helen Morgan (illustrated) extended the pathos of her performance as the original 'Julie' of *Show Boat* to the tragedy of her frowzy, gin-swilling burlesque queen here. Garrett Fort's script (from a Beth Brown novel) centred on her keeping her daughter in college and ignorant of her squalid life-style. At the end her fatal collapse is dismissed by a backstage cynic with 'Drunk again!' Joan Peers, Fuller Mellish Jr, Henry Wadsworth, Jack Cameron and Dorothy Cumming were featured in the Monta Bell production. It was a box-office failure which grew in prestige with the years.

▷ The third appearance together of Nancy Carroll (right) and Charles 'Buddy' Rogers (left) profited from their zooming popularity, but there was a deadly sameness about their material. **Illusion**, like *Close Harmony*, put them in the backstage world of vaudevillians, and, like *The Dance Of Life*, made Carroll take another partner when her man left her for better things. On the other hand, it had two fine Larry Spier songs in the ballad 'When The Real Thing Comes Your Way' and the up-tempo 'Revolutionary Rhythm', plus attractive performances by the stars, as well as June Collyer, Kay Francis, Regis Toomey, William Austin and peppy newcomer Lillian Roth. Lothar Mendes directed the tired Arthur Train story, scripted by E. Lloyd Sheldon.

△ 'Clara Bow flashing *IT* as she never flashed it before!' announced the ads, rather alarmingly, for **The Saturday Night Kid**, one of the redhead's more successful talking pictures. It was the second screen version of the George Abbott-John V.A. Weaver Broadway comedy that made a popular silent under its original title, *Love 'Em And Leave 'Em*. This one, re-written by Lloyd Corrigan, Ethel Doherty and E.E. Paramore Jr, had Clara (illustrated) and Jean Arthur as sisters after the same man with Jean, surprisingly, the naughtier of the two. They were department store employees, like most of the characters, selling a nice line in slangy repartee. Edward Sutherland directed them, together with James Hall, Edna May Oliver, Charles Sellon, Ethel Wales, Frank Ross and, in a bit part, Jean Harlow.

▽ **Sweetie** bounced along as a blithe frolic of flappers and their beaux in a college inherited by a chorus girl. It stemmed from the old play *The Charm School*, filmed silently only a year before as *Someone To Love* with Charles 'Buddy' Rogers, and in 1921 with Wallace Reid. In their 1929 rewrite, George Marion Jr and Lloyd Corrigan changed the main character's sex to suit Nancy Carroll (left). She was the chief drawcard, and shared the bright Marion Jr-Richard Whiting score's best song 'My Sweeter Than Sweet' with leading man Stanley Smith (right), but most of the footage went to comedians Jack Oakie (singing 'Alma Mammy'), Helen Kane (the 'Boob-a-doop Girl' of radio and record fame, booping the saucy hit 'He's So Unusual' by Al Lewis, Abner Silver and Al Sherman), Stuart Erwin and William Austin. Frank Tuttle directed. The success of this one spawned a seemingly endless series of collegiate musicals.

◁ Maurice Chevalier became the studio's biggest star and Ernst Lubitsch its most celebrated director when **The Love Parade** arrived, to a chorus of praise from the press and long lines at first-run cinema pay-boxes. It was something new in musicals. No back-stage show-must-go-on clichés here, no chorus cuties or wise-cracking comics, but a subtly sexy romance, light as a zephyr and floating on airs composed by Victor Schertzinger (better known as a director) with lyrics by Clifford Grey: 'My Love Parade', 'Nobody's Using It Now', 'Dream Lover', 'March Of The Grenadiers', 'Let's Be Common', 'Paris, Stay The Same'. It was astonishing how smoothly Lubitsch, in his first sound film, blended the songs with the action instead of staging them as interruptive 'numbers'. He also deftly guided vivacious soprano Jeanette MacDonald to stardom in her screen debut as the Queen of Sylvania, who, hearing gossip of her ambassador's skills as a boudoir diplomat in Paris, summons him home, tests his talents and marries him. She then tests his patience with her domineering ways, until he teaches her how to be a wife as well as a queen. Chevalier and Miss MacDonald (both illustrated, foreground) glowed for the first, but not the last, time under the Lubitsch touch; so did Britain's Lupino Lane and Broadway's Lillian Roth, with Eugene Pallette, Lionel Belmore and Edgar Norton in support. The Ernest Vajda-Guy Bolton screenplay, from a play by Leon Xanrof and Jules Chancel, was given a sumptuous production.

▽ Gertrude Lawrence may have been the toast of Broadway, but her talkie debut in **The Battle Of Paris** did nothing for her screen prestige (or Paramount's). The flung-together screenplay by Gene Markey was directed by Robert Florey, a Frenchman, as though he was disgusted with the Paris sets producer Monta Bell had provided on the Astoria lot, and you couldn't blame him. Charles Ruggles as a pickpocket (here with Gertie) and Walter Petrie as an American artist headed a supporting cast including Arthur Treacher, Gladys Du Bois and Joseph King, all of whom seemed flummoxed by Markey's dialogue. The picture's best asset was a couple of charming songs – 'They All Fall In Love', one of Cole Porter's earliest 'catalogue' numbers, and 'Housekeeping For You', contributed by Howard Dietz and Jay Gorney – both sung by the British star in the course of a role encompassing street singer, artist's model and war nurse. The triple approach, alas, didn't help.

▷ There's a built-in fascination that lends a theatrical thrill to all stories (from the melodrama of Bayard Veiller's *The Thirteenth Chair* to the comedy of Noel Coward's classic *Blithe Spirit*) which feature spiritualist seances. And it didn't fail **Darkened Rooms**, a low-budget, taut little drama which gave Neil Hamilton his best part since *Beau Geste* as a photographer who fakes spirit pictures for a phoney seeress, then goes into the seance business himself and, while pretending to bring a dead aviator's voice and spirit to the man's fiancée, is exposed by his own disapproving girlfriend. Evelyn Brent (illustrated with Hamilton), David Newell, E.H. Calvert, Doris Hill, Wallace MacDonald, Gale Henry and Blanche Craig figured in the screenplay by Melville Baker and Patrick Kearney (from a novel by Philip Gibbs), and it was directed by Louis Gasnier, who had made serials famous with *The Perils Of Pauline* fifteen years earlier.

▽ **Glorifying The American Girl** was Florenz Ziegfeld's catch-phrase for his Follies, and the maestro himself produced (or so the publicity would have us believe) this musical at the Astoria studio, to which the stars could commute from their Broadway shows. Millard Webb directed J.P. McEvoy's routine show-girl-makes-good story featuring stage beauty Mary Eaton (right), but this was ditched midway for what the customers really came to see, a big spectacular revue – the formula often used by Warner Bros. in years to come. Blossoming into Technicolor, it in-

cluded Eddie Cantor in a comedy sketch, Rudy Vallee singing his signature tune 'I'm Just A Vagabond Lover' (composed by him and Leon Zimmerman), and Helen Morgan reprising 'What Wouldn't I Do For That Man' (E.Y. Harburg, Jay Gorney) from her *Applause*. Also 'in person' were Adolph Zukor, mayor Jimmy Walker, banker Otto Kahn, writer Ring Lardner, Irving Berlin, Texas Guinan, Noah Beery, Johnny Weissmuller, and Ziegfeld himself, whose name later paid off in two MGM titles. Many alterations delayed production, and it showed.

▷ Gary Cooper loped into the topmost level of stardom, where he would remain for the next 31 years, in the 1929 version of **The Virginian**. It was his first all-talkie (nobody could deliver 'Yep' and 'Nope' like Gary) and one of the earliest sound westerns. The old story about the rancher whose best friend is caught and hanged by a posse while working for a rustler – the latter subsequently killed by the hero in a gun duel – began as a novel by Owen Wister, became a play by Kirk LaShelle, and was filmed twice before, in 1914 (directed by Cecil B. DeMille) and 1923, with a fourth movie to come in 1946. It was a winner every time, but Victor Fleming's direction of a script by Howard Estabrook and E.E. Paramore Jr made this one the biggest hit of all. Walter Huston portrayed a chilling villain in a cast including Richard Arlen, Mary Brian (here with Cooper), Chester Conklin, Eugene Pallette, E.H. Calvert and Helen Ware. Louis D. Lighton produced.

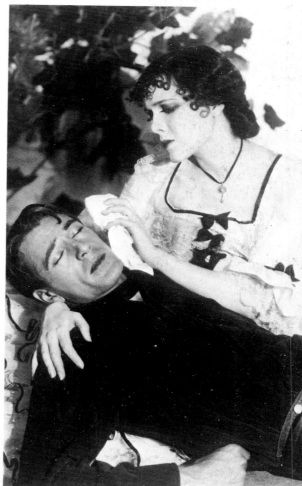

△ Ruth Chatterton and Clive Brook (both illustrated), stars whose restrained deportment and broad-A accents wowed metropolitan moviegoers but left small-towners nonplussed, teamed elegantly in **The Laughing Lady**. Victor Schertzinger directed this remake of *A Society Scandal*, a 1924 Gloria Swanson picture. The stylish Chatterton more closely matched the cool poise of its 1923 stage star, Ethel Barrymore, as an upper-crust lady in danger of getting burned. Divorced after an interlude with an amorous lifeguard, she winds up with her ex-husband's lawyer. The Bartlett Cormack-Arthur Richman adaptation of Alfred Sutro's play also employed Dan Healy, Nat Pendleton, Raymond Walburn and Nedda Harrigan.

△ An elegant filming of Edith Wharton's celebrated novel *The Children*, **The Marriage Playground** dealt with a group of American youngsters in Italy whose pleasure-chasing parents leave them in charge of the eldest (Mary Brian), and return from dancing around Europe to find she has fallen in love with an older man (Fredric March, left with Mary Brian). The romance was believably worked out in the sophisticated script by J. Walter Ruben and Doris Anderson, and directed with considerable style by Lothar Mendes, whose work in Germany, England and America has been largely ignored by film historians. His cast included Huntley Gordon and Lilyan Tashman (the parents), Kay Francis, William Austin, Seena Owen, Jocelyn Lee, David Newell and, as the children, Anita Louise (pointing), Mitzi Green (with purse, her debut) and Philippe De Lacey (in flecked suit).

△ William Powell got top billing for the first time in **Pointed Heels**, and kept it for the next quarter-century (before retiring into a prosperous and ripe old age). One of the better backstage musicals, it also started author Charles Brackett's Paramount association which developed into his great partnership with Billy Wilder. His story concerned a Broadway producer (Powell), a chorus girl (Fay Wray), and a songwriter (Phillips Holmes) whose romance with Miss Wray brings trouble from his family. A novel angle in the Florence Ryerson-John V.A. Weaver script, directed by Edward Sutherland, was the producer's saving his dull show by enlivening the cast with bootleg booze. A few ditties from Helen 'Boopadoop' Kane (including 'I Have To Have You' by Richard A. Whiting and Leo Robin), and a ballet in Technicolor, also caught attention. Skeets Gallagher (here with Kane), the ubiquitous Eugene Pallette, and Adrienne Dore supported.

OTHER RELEASES OF 1929
(All talkies unless indicated otherwise)

The Carnation Kid
Douglas MacLean, Frances Lee, Lorraine Eddy. Dir: E. Mason Hopper. Pro: Al Christie. A salesman is forced to change clothes with a gangster out to kill the District Attorney, then he saves the DA's life. (Part talkie)

The Case Of Lena Smith
Esther Ralston, James Hall, Gustav von Seyffertitz, Fred Kohler. Dir: Josef von Sternberg. Peasant girl is seduced by a young army officer in 1890s Austria; he commits suicide when his father takes their baby. (Silent)

Chinatown Nights
Florence Vidor, Wallace Beery, Warner Oland, Jack Oakie. Dir: William Wellman. Pro: David O. Selznick. Society woman takes up with a Tong leader in the Chinese quarter, narrowly escapes death and the fate worse than.

Divorce Made Easy
Douglas MacLean, Marie Prevost, Johnny Arthur, Frances Lee. Dir: Walter Graham. Pro: Al Christie. Husband threatened with disinheritance if he doesn't get rid of his wife tries to do so, in vain.

The Doctor's Secret
Ruth Chatterton, John Loder, H.B. Warner, Robert Edeson. Dir: William C. de Mille. A couple's dinner guests include a doctor who saw the wife with another man during a clandestine affair. (Remake of *Half An Hour*, 1920)

The Dummy
Ruth Chatterton, Fredric March, Mickey Bennett. Dir: Robert Milton. Pro: Hector Turnbull. Office boy feigns being deaf and dumb in order to trap kidnappers. (Remake of 1917 film)

Fashions In Love
Adolphe Menjou, Fay Compton, John Miljan, Miriam Seegar. Dir: Victor Schertzinger. Comedy of a famous concert pianist finding trouble while trying to maintain his reputation as a great lover.

Fast Company
Jack Oakie, Evelyn Brent, Skeets Gallagher. Dir: Edward Sutherland. Village baseball hero turns professional, defies crooks who try to bribe him, wins the big game and the actress he loves.

Halfway To Heaven
Charles 'Buddy' Rogers, Jean Arthur, Paul Lukas. Dir: George Abbott. Triangle drama of trapeze performers, the boy and girl flyers and their jealous catcher.

The Hole In The Wall
Edward G. Robinson, Claudette Colbert, David Newell. Dir: Robert Florey. Pro: Monta Bell. Melodrama about a bogus clairvoyant and her henchman, who kidnaps a child.

Hungarian Rhapsody
Willy Fritsch, Lil Dagover, Dita Parlo, Fritz Greiner. Dir: Hanns Schwarz. Pro: Erich Pommer. Caught with his general's flirtatious wife, a young officer is saved from disgrace by his girl. (German; silent)

Jealousy
Jeanne Eagels, Fredric March, Henry Daniell, Halliwell Hobbes. Dir: Jean de Limur. The wife of an artist, needing money, asks for it from her guardian, formerly her lover; in a jealous rage, the artist kills him.

The Kibitzer (GB **The Busybody**)
Harry Green, Mary Brian, Neil Hamilton. Dir: Edward Sloman. Comedy of a lovable nuisance who interferes with his daughter's love life, while gambling on horses and Wall Street.

The Lady Lies
Claudette Colbert, Walter Huston, Charles Ruggles, Tom Brown. Dir: Hobart Henley. A salesgirl has an affair with a widower and wins over his son and daughter from their snooty relatives.

Looping The Loop
Werner Krauss, Jenny Jugo, Warwick Ward, Gina Manes. Dir: Arthur Robison. Behind the scenes of a circus the triangle drama of a girl, a clown and an acrobat develops. (German; silent)

The Love Doctor
Richard Dix, June Collyer, Miriam Seegar. Dir: Melville Brown. A bachelor doctor is adored by his nurse and the girl loved by one of his patients. He brings the latter two together and marries the nurse.

The Man I Love
Richard Arlen, Mary Brian, Olga Baclanova, Jack Oakie. Dir: William Wellman. Pro: David O. Selznick. A young prizefighter's career and love for a girl are complicated by a predatory society beauty.

Marquis Preferred
Adolphe Menjou, Nora Lane, Chester Conklin. Dir & Pro: Frank Tuttle. The creditors of a spendthrift marquis make him into a limited company and marry him off to a wealthy woman. (Silent)

The Rainbow Man
Eddie Dowling, Marian Nixon, Frankie Darro. Dir: Fred Newmeyer. Drama with songs, about a song-and-dance man who adopts a little boy and falls in love with the latter's aunt.

The Return Of Sherlock Holmes
Clive Brook, H. Reeves-Smith, Harry T. Morey, Phillips Holmes, Betty Lawford. Dir: Basil Dean. Holmes wins a battle of wits with his arch-enemy, Moriarty, to protect a young couple on a transatlantic voyage.

Stairs Of Sand
Wallace Beery, Phillips Holmes, Jean Arthur. Dir: Otto Brower. Young Easterner runs into Western adventure via a good-bad bandit, a dance hall girl and a stagecoach robbery.

The Studio Murder Mystery
Neil Hamilton, Warner Oland, Fredric March, Florence Eldridge. Dir: Frank Tuttle. Hollywood writer probes the murder of an actor, committed by his director.

The Sunset Pass
Jack Holt, John Loder, Nora Lane. Dir: Otto Brower. Search for cattle rustlers leads to showdown between cowboy and rancher. (Silent)

The Wheel Of Life
Richard Dix, Esther Ralston, O.P. Heggie. Dir: Victor Schertzinger. In India a British officer's life is saved in battle by his colonel, with whose wife he has fallen in love.

Why Bring That Up?
George Moran, Charles Mack, Evelyn Brent. Dir: George Abbott. Comedy starring blackface team famous as The Two Black Crows; about their attempted fleecing by a shady lady.

The Wolf Of Wall Street
George Bancroft, Nancy Carroll, Paul Lukas, Olga Baclanova. Dir: Rowland V. Lee. Financier leaves his wife and ruins his partner when told of their affair by his maid, whose fiancé he had victimised.

Wolf Song
Gary Cooper, Lupe Velez, Louis Wolheim, Constantine Romanoff. Dir & Pro: Victor Fleming. Melodrama of a fur-trapper's conflict with a villainous rival and his stormy romance with a Mexican girl. (Part-talkie)

Woman Trap
Chester Morris, Evelyn Brent, Hal Skelly. Dir: William A. Wellman. Melodrama of estranged brothers, one a policeman, the other a criminal who commits suicide rather than be arrested by his brother.

1930

▽ **For The Defense** took just 15 days to shoot and turned out to be a surprise hit. When the plaudits and the profits rolled in, all concerned took bows: director John Cromwell, author Charles Furthman, screenwriter Oliver H.P. Garrett, producer David O. Selznick, and the cast: William Powell (illustrated), Kay Francis, Scott Kolk, William B. Davidson, Thomas Jackson and Jimmy Finlayson. Powell and Francis made a splendid combination of smooth sophistication several times at Paramount and later at Warners – almost as great as the legendary Powell-Myrna Loy team, later still, at MGM. Now he played a society lawyer who becomes the front man for gangsters, then is convicted of bribing a jury while getting his lady friend out of a jam. The central character was based on the headline-hitting New York attorney William Fallon, who also inspired Warner Bros.' *The Mouthpiece* in 1932.

▷ Popular novelist Katherine Brush turned out a pretty lightweight piece of fiction with **Young Man Of Manhattan** but, by the time producer-director Monta Bell and screenwriter Robert Presnell had finished working on it at the Astoria studio, it was a high-grade commercial property. Norman Foster and Claudette Colbert, then Mr and Mrs in private life too, played young married types; he is a sports writer and she is a movie columnist, and everything is just peachy until trouble arrives in the provocative shape of a Broadway blonde, whose approach is 'Cigarette me, big boy'. (This became a catchphrase among 1930 moviegoers.) Charles Ruggles (right) had an amusing part, and Ginger Rogers (left) made her feature-film debut as the blonde, giving voice to a number called 'I've Got It, But It Don't Do Me No Good'. Patience, Ginger!

△ The reason given for the abrupt departure of Emil Jannings after his sixth silent picture in Hollywood, *Betrayal*, was his inability to speak English. Clutching the first Oscar awarded to an actor (for *The Way Of All Flesh* and *The Last Command*), he returned to Berlin without waiting to attend the Academy ceremonies, and promptly made the first UFA all-talkie in perfectly adequate English as well as in a German version. It was **The Blue Angel**, his greatest international success. Josef von Sternberg went over to give the Erich Pommer production his unique atmospheric treatment and to extract a performance of tragic power from Jannings as a respectable schoolmaster fascinated, then humiliated, and finally ruined by a seductive music hall slut. But the star never forgave the director for making the latter's discovery, Marlene Dietrich (left), the most exciting thing in the film. As the coarse, disdainful temptress, strutting the stage and straddling a chair while singing 'Falling In Love Again' and 'Beware Of Blonde Women', Marlene created an unforgettable image of sensuality, overshadowing Jannings. They were supported by Kurt Gerron, Rosa Valetti and Hans Albers in the screenplay (from a Karl Vollmoeller-Carl Zuckmayer adaptation of Heinrich Mann's novel *Professor Unrath*), credited to Robert Liebman, but claimed by Von Sternberg as entirely his own work. No matter – it was a sensational hit.

◁ French charm spread like ripe camembert through an exceptionally silly story in **The Big Pond**, with Maurice Chevalier and Claudette Colbert (both illustrated) making tasty entertainment of it. A play by George Middleton and A.E. Thomas and a script by Robert Presnell and Garrett Fort (additional dialogue by Preston Sturges of whom much more would be heard) brought forth this: Venice guide falls for American tourist, her chewing-gum tycoon father disapproves, changes his mind when hero invents new product by spilling rum into his gum. Well, anyway, Chevalier had a great song in 'You Brought A New Kind Of Love To Me' (by Irving Kahal, Pierre Norman and Sammy Fain), a good one in 'Livin' In The Sunlight, Lovin' In The Moonlight' (Al Lewis, Al Sherman), and an old one in 'This Is My Lucky Day' (De Sylva, Brown, Henderson) from *George White's Scandals of 1926*. Hobart Henley directed it and Monta Bell produced at the Astoria studio, with George Barbier, Marion Ballou and Nat Pendleton featured. A French version was shot simultaneously.

◁ You had only to look at the title to know that **Dangerous Paradise** wasn't a serious attempt to film Joseph Conrad's *Victory*. Even more than Maurice Tourneur's 1919 version and the one that was to come from John Cromwell in 1940, this melodrama was directed by William Wellman strictly for blood-and-thunder. Probably just as well: Richard Arlen was not histrionically equipped for the complexities of the hero as written, but he was just right for the movie's rescuer of a girl (Nancy Carroll, illustrated) from the clutches of variously repulsive characters (Warner Oland, Gustav von Seyffertitz, Francis McDonald) in a steamy South Seas hotel. Entertaining rough stuff, no more. Grover Jones and William Slavens McNutt were credited with the screenplay 'suggested by Joseph Conrad's novel'.

△ Paramount bought the David Gray-Avery Hopwood play *The Best People* when it became a New York hit in 1924 and filmed it the following year, with mediocre results. It needed dialogue, and this it got in **Fast And Loose**; indeed, besides director Fred Newmeyer and screenwriters Doris Anderson and Jack Kirkland, its credits specified Bertram Harrison as 'dialogue director' and Preston Sturges for 'additional dialogue', so that department was well taken care of. Likewise the acting, with Miriam Hopkins, already established on Broadway, making her film debut as a rebellious girl defying her snobbish parents by pairing off with a mechanic (Charles Starrett, left), while her brother (Henry Wadsworth) falls for a chorus girl (Carole Lombard, right). Both outsiders refuse marriage until the parents get off their high horse; which they do, and a double wedding ensues. Frank Morgan, Ilka Chase, Winifred Harris and David Hutcheson also appeared in the Astoria studio production.

◁ A well-worn plot – the one about a gold-digging manicurist transformed by true love – was itself transformed into something special by the luminous performance of Nancy Carroll in **The Devil's Holiday**. In the part written by Edmund Goulding for Jeanne Eagels and vacated by her untimely death, Miss Carroll was nominated as best actress of the year and came a close second in the Academy voting to the winner, Norma Shearer (for *The Divorcee*, MGM). The air was thick with critics' bouquets, too, for the sensitive work of Phillips Holmes (here with Nancy) as the boy who wooed the girl from her mercenary pursuits, and for the warmth of Goulding's direction of his own material. Its basic similarity to *The Shopworn Angel* was obvious in the Carroll character, but this was an even more affecting love story, with a stronger supporting cast that included: James Kirkwood, Paul Lukas, ZaSu Pitts, Hobart Bosworth, Ned Sparks, Morgan Farley, Jed Prouty, Guy Oliver and radio's singing star Morton Downey.

▷ **Animal Crackers**, another adaptation from one of their Broadway shows, made a better Marx Brothers movie than their first screen effort. The George S. Kaufman-Morrie Ryskind story, tailored to celluloid by Ryskind and Pierre Collings – and frequently forgotten while the brothers ran riot – concerned the theft of a painting from Margaret Dumont (right), whose love-hate relationship with Groucho (centre) was becoming one of the greatest film affairs of all time. He gave voice to 'Hooray for Captain Spalding' (Bert Kalmar, Harry Ruby), later his radio signature song; Harpo (centre right) and Chico (left) did their musical specialties, Zeppo stooged and Lillian Roth soubretted, while Hal Thompson, Margaret Irving and Robert Greig merely acted under Victor Heerman's direction. The still-primitive microphone technique gave the Walter Wanger production a rather static look, but the Marxian one-liners, puns, non-sequiturs and miming scored repeatedly.

△ George Cukor was promoted to director for **Grumpy**, sharing the task with Cyril Gardner – although why the studio needed two directors to guide such an excellent actor as Cyril Maude (centre), who virtually carried the whole show, was a puzzle. Maude had been trouping the Horace Hodges-Thomas Percyval play through Britain and the US for years and had every nuance of the title role down pat. Grumpy was a veteran lawyer, irritable but lovable, who solves a minor mystery when a diamond, brought from South Africa to London by his daughter's sweetheart, is stolen, and suspicion falls upon one and all. Phillips Holmes (right), Paul Lukas, Frances Dade (left), Paul Cavanagh, Halliwell Hobbes and Olaf Hytten backed up the star ably in Doris Anderson's screenplay, a very talky talkie, shot in the Astoria studio, which was having its busiest year to date.

△ The best thing in **Safety In Numbers** was a delightful ballad, 'My Future Just Passed', by Richard Whiting and George Marion Jr, one of the six songs Charles 'Buddy' Rogers crooned in the course of an entertaining comedy by Percy Heath and Marion. Buddy played a handsome young heir to millions, and so sheer catnip to Manhattan gold-diggers. His uncle hires three wise Follies girls to guide and protect the boy (on the theory indicated by the title): Kathryn Crawford, Josephine Dunn and Carole Lombard and, of course, Buddy falls in love with one; it was Kathryn. The public picked Carole. Also in a cast kept bubbling by director Victor Schertzinger were Roscoe Karns, Francis MacDonald, Geneva Mitchell, Virginia Bruce, Richard Tucker, Lawrence Grant, and the fine black actress Louise Beavers. Script by Marion Dix. Illustrated from left: Dunn, Crawford, Rogers, Lombard, Mitchell, Bruce.

▽ Paramount bought a musical that had packed New York's 46th Street Theatre for a solid year: **Follow Thru**, put on by Lawrence Schwab and Frank Mandel, who could produce better than they could spell. The studio snapped up two of the cast, Jack Haley and Zelma O'Neal (left), to make their movie bows; also the tuneful De Sylva, Brown and Henderson score which included one of their biggest hits, 'Button Up Your Overcoat', plus 'I Want To Be Bad', 'Lucky Star', 'You Wouldn't Fool Me, Would You?' and 'A Peach Of A Pair'. To make box-officially sure, Nancy Carroll (centre) and Buddy Rogers (right) were cast as the golf professional's daughter and her handsome golf instructor whose links were romantic as well as sporting. Thelma Todd, as Nancy's rival in both fields, Eugene Pallette, Claude King, Albert Gran, Kathryn Givney and Frances Dee supported, with Schwab and Lloyd Corrigan co-directing and co-scripting. All in Technicolor, all talking, all singing, all golfing, all good fun.

▷ **The Mighty** wasn't. On the other hand, it had a lot to offer devotees of rough, tough cops-and-robbers stuff, and its star, George Bancroft, took second place to nobody in that line during the late silent and early sound period. He did a sturdy professional job as a criminal who is regenerated by his combat experiences in the Great War, and becomes a police chief – in which capacity he is as fearless as he has been in crime and on the battlefield. Director John Cromwell punched over the action sequences, and appeared briefly in a cast including Esther Ralston (here with Bancroft), Warner Oland, Raymond Hatton, Dorothy Revier, O.P. Heggie, Morgan Farley, Charles Sellon and E.H. Calvert. The script by Grover Jones, William Slavens McNutt and Nellie Revell was based on an original by Robert N. Lee.

▷ She had better pictures ahead, but **Honey** maintained the tempo of Nancy Carroll's rise, to the point of her receiving more fan mail than any other Paramount star in 1930. Scripter Herman Mankiewicz and director Wesley Ruggles refashioned as a musical comedy Ruth Chatterton's Broadway hit of 1916, *Come Out Of The Kitchen*, which the studio bought for a Marguerite Clark silent in 1919. Nancy, as the daughter of an impoverished Southern family leasing their mansion to a rich New Yorker, had a light-as-air romance with Stanley Smith, and delivered a few songs by Sam Coslow and Franke Harling. However, the sensational number was 'Sing You Sinners', slammed over with enormous gusto by Lillian Roth (left), later to be more famous for her autobiography about her alcoholism, *I'll Cry Tomorrow* (filmed with Susan Hayward as Lillian). Skeets Gallagher (right), Harry Green, ZaSu Pitts, Jobyna Howland, Mitzi Green and Charles Sellon also spread entertainment honey on the David O. Selznick production.

▽ Signed to a Paramount contract, and rushed from Berlin to Hollywood and through her first American picture while the excitement over *The Blue Angel* was still hot, Marlene Dietrich (centre) emerged as an absolute sensation in **Morocco**. Within a few months the studio beauticians had refined the German film's voluptuous trollop into a svelte creature of mysterious allure. Lovingly posed by director Josef von Sternberg and lusciously photographed by Lee Garmes in Hans Dreier's lavish sets (all three were Oscar-nominated, as was Dietrich herself), she gave the screen at last a glamour to rival Garbo. The fans went wild. Jules Furthman's script, from a novel by Benno Vigny, was the old chestnut about a cabaret singer torn between a soldier (Gary Cooper, left) and a moneybags (Adolphe Menjou, right), and it ended absurdly with the soignée heroine trailing love-struck into a desert. But who cared? It served to keep Marlene on camera for 97 minutes. Also cast: Juliette Compton, Ullrich Haupt, Francis McDonald, Albert Conti. Cooper, peeved by Von Sternberg's devoting all his attention to the lady, gave a moody performance, and all the more effective for that, as the Foreign Legionnaire.

▽ Helen Morgan (centre) was playing her former self, a nightclub singer, in **Roadhouse Nights**, a vehicle which gave her neither the outstanding songs she deserved nor scope for the extraordinary gift of pathos she displayed as the original stage 'Julie' in *Show Boat* and in her 1929 movie, *Applause*. Sadly, her career gradually got lost in a fog of alcoholism. In the new film it was Charles Ruggles (right) who was a tippler – at least he pretended to be while as a news reporter tracking down a mob of bootleggers to a rackety Chicago pleasure dome, where the melodramatic doings thought up by author Ben Hecht and scripter Garrett Fort were interspersed with cabaret diversions. The most stimulating of these came from a current New York rage, the comedy team of Lou Clayton, Eddie Jackson and Jimmy Durante (left). Whatever became of Lou and Eddie? Hobart Henley directing (at Astoria) a cast that included Fred Kohler, Fuller Mellish Jr and Joseph King, gave the movie considerable pace and power.

▽ What did **The Spoilers** have to make it worth filming five times? Well, aside from a sturdy plot by Rex Beach – always a reliable source – about conflicting mine claims in Alaska during the gold rush, it had a famous fight climax. The 1930 version, usually considered the best, had Gary Cooper (right) and William Boyd (and their doubles) slugging it out with set-wrecking gusto. Betty Compson and Kay Johnson supplied strong romantic angles; Harry Green and Slim Summerville (left) some so-so comedy relief; James Kirkwood and Oscar Apfel (the pioneer Lasky director who taught DeMille the ropes during the shooting of *The Squaw Man* in 1913) able work in support. The Bartlett Cormack-Agnes Brand Leahy screenplay was directed by David Burton and Edwin Carewe, and proved a powerful crowd magnet. The other four versions were in 1913 (Selig), 1923 (Goldwyn), 1942 and 1955 (both Universal). Note: William Boyd was not the actor of the same name, famous as Hopalong Cassidy, but a featured player from the theatre of the early thirties who became known (but not billed) as William 'Stage' Boyd.

▷ Paramount followed the vogue started by MGM with *The Hollywood Revue* and by Warner Bros. with *The Show Of Shows* and mounted a big, splashy, film revue. **Paramount On Parade**, loaded with songs, comedy sketches, production numbers and a star list big enough to choke a goat, gave the customers all the highlights of half-a-dozen scripted musicals without their having to sit through one of those plots. With (confusingly) credits to Albert Kaufman as producer and vaudeville veteran Elsie Janis as supervisor, it roped in all the available talent on the lot, including eleven directors – Dorothy Arzner, Otto Brower, Edmund Goulding, Victor Heerman, Edwin H. Knopf, Rowland V. Lee, Ernst Lubitsch, Lothar Mendes, Victor Schertzinger, Edward Sutherland, Frank Tuttle – and too many writers and composers to list. Its twenty items, seven of them in Technicolor, offered Jack Oakie, Skeets Gallagher and Leon Errol as compères, musical numbers performed by Maurice Chevalier (see illustration), Clara Bow, Charles 'Buddy' Rogers, Nancy Carroll, Dennis King, Ruth Chatterton, Nino Martini, Lillian Roth, Mitzi Green, Helen Kane, Harry Green, Zelma O'Neal, Mitzi Mayfair, Abe Lyman and His Band; and sketches with Gary Cooper, Fay Wray, Phillips Holmes, Virginia Bruce, Jean Arthur, Mary Brian, Richard Arlen, James Hall, Kay Francis, William Powell, Clive Brook, Warner Oland, Eugene Pallette, Evelyn Brent, Fredric March, George Bancroft, William Austin, Stuart Erwin – and then some! None of the songs became a best-seller, and the novelty of the revue format was pre-empted by the MGM and Warner studio bashes, as well as Universal's *The King Of Jazz* released a month before the Paramount offering. Nevertheless, a winner.

△ Sophisticated audiences got a kick out of **The Royal Family Of Broadway** (GB: **Theatre Royal**), while the big crowds hurried past to the nearest musical or action epic. Still, it paid its way and maintained Paramount's reputation for expertise in smart, polished entertainment. Enormously successful as a play by Edna Ferber and George S. Kaufman (it was one of the 17 that opened in New York in the last week of 1927), it caricatured the home life of the Barrymores in frolicsome style, thus incurring the wrath of the formidable Ethel B, but everybody else loved it. The movie had an even better cast, topped by Ina Claire (illustrated), the American theatre's queen of high comedy, and Fredric March, whose wicked impersonation of John B in the Los Angeles stage production had won him his Paramount contract. Henrietta Crosman, Mary Brian, Charles Starrett, Arnold Korff and Frank Conroy joined in the hilariously temperamental antics, directed by George Cukor and Cyril Gardner from a screenplay by Herman Mankiewicz and Gertrude Purcell.

▽ Harry d'Abbadie d'Arrast, whose films were even more distinctive than his name, went from Paris to Hollywood as assistant to Charlie Chaplin, and in 1927 directed three Adolphe Menjou pictures for Paramount. When he returned three years later for his first talkie, he really came into his own with **Laughter**. A romantic comedy of unusual charm, it was written by D'Arrast, Douglas Doty and Donald Ogden Stewart deftly enough to make them Academy Award nominees, and directed with a pace and sophistication worthy of no less a master of style than Lubitsch. The central figure was a Follies girl (Nancy Carroll at her most beguiling), married to a nice but dull millionaire (Frank Morgan, here with Nancy) and resuming an old affair with a composer (Fredric March) who brings her the gift of laughter. The situation was further complicated by her stepdaughter's fling with a sculptor. Glenn Anders, Diane Ellis and Leonard Carey ably supported the three leads. Seen again 50 years later, it looked as good as new.

▷ Ruth Chatterton did double duty in **The Right To Love**, playing both mother and daughter (illustrated), and was rewarded with an enthusiastic reception from crowded audiences. Women, especially, relished this celebration of their modern freedom, screenwritten by Zoe Akins from a 1928 best-seller, *Brook Evans*, by Susan Glaspell, one of America's most respected novelists of the time. The drama opened in a midwestern farming community, where a rancher and his wife live with her daughter by a secret lover. Learning that the harsh husband is not her father, the daughter turns against her mother and goes to China as a missionary. Later, urged by a letter from her mother to do so, she abandons duty to take a lover. Director Richard Wallace drew telling performances from his famous Broadway star, as well as from Paul Lukas, David Manners, Irving Pichel, George Baxter and Oscar Apfel.

◁ Definitely a three-handkerchief weepie, **Sarah And Son** proved to be one of the best productions from David O. Selznick during his three years at Paramount, and the most popular Ruth Chatterton vehicle to date. She suffered superbly as an Austrian woman married to a rotter who sells their baby to a rich couple. Leaving him, she spends the rest of the running-time finding her son and proving his identity, meanwhile rising from World War entertainer to opera star. Well written by Zoe Akins (from a Timothy Shea novel), and with its lachrymose elements made more telling by director Dorothy Arzner's restraint, it further gained artistically from a good cast (Fredric March (here with Ruth), Philippe De Lacey as the boy, Fuller Mellish Jr, Doris Lloyd, Gilbert Emery, William Stack) and commercially as the successor to Chatterton's hit, on loan to MGM, in *Madame X*. So, no sobs from exhibitors.

▷ Paramount remade its 1917 silent hit **Tom Sawyer** as a 1930 talkie, again hitting the box-office target. You'd have to be a pretty ham-fisted film-maker to score a miss with this story, and certainly neither director John Cromwell nor producer Louis D. Lighton was that. Aside from the charm and fun of Mark Twain's classic tale of childhood, the new movie had a particular attraction in the title role casting of Jackie Coogan (illustrated), the most important child star of the twenties, returning after three years off the screen, Now 15, and inevitably minus some of his former appeal, he did a good professional job and was ably supported by Junior Durkin (who was killed with Coogan's father in a car crash five years later) as Huckleberry Finn, Mitzi Green, Jackie Searl, Mary Jane Irving and Dick Winslow among the youngsters; Clara Blandick (illustrated), Tully Marshall, Lucien Littlefield, Jane Darwell, Ethel Wales and Charles Sellon their elders, and Charles Stevens as Injun Joe. Script by Grover Jones, William Slavens McNutt and Sam Mintz. The studio made the sequel, *Huckleberry Finn*, with the same principals in 1931, and a 'B' spin-off, *Tom Sawyer, Detective*, in 1938.

▽ **Manslaughter** popped up again, eight years after its silent success, with Claudette Colbert and Fredric March (both illustrated) in the parts originally played by Leatrice Joy and Thomas Meighan. That prolific writer and stager of New York hits, George Abbott, functioned in both capacities to update the Alice Duer Miller story about the District Attorney who falls in love with the wealthy girl he convicts of killing a traffic cop. After two years in jail, she spurns him, but eventually agrees that the law must apply equally to rich and poor. Colbert did her best dramatic work to date, particularly in the courtroom and prison scenes, demonstrating why her stardom lasted 15 years at Paramount and continued elsewhere; indeed, 50 years after this movie she was back on Broadway, still a star (and director Abbott in 1983 was still active on Broadway at the age of 95). Emma Dunn, Natalie Moorhead, Richard Tucker, Hilda Vaughn and Stanley Fields were also cast.

△ Jeanette MacDonald trilling 'Beyond The Blue Horizon' while leaning out of a train, accompanied by the wheels going clickety-clack and a chorus of railside wavers, remains one of the screen's immortal sequences. As an example of blissful integration of sight and sound it was unique in those early days of the talkie, and helped to make **Monte Carlo** another Ernst Lubitsch treat. Author Hans Mueller and scriptwriter Ernest Vajda supplied a gossamer plot, about high life among titled Europeans, which was spangled with Lubitsch comedy touches and starred Jack Buchanan (here with Jeanette) as a count posing as a coiffeur and Jeanette as the countess he pursued and eventually – er – coiffed. Another Richard Whiting-W. Franke Harling-Leo Robin hit, 'Give Me A Moment Please', and an operatic sequence based on *Monsieur Beaucaire* aided enjoyment, as did ZaSu Pitts, Claude Allister, Albert Conti, Lionel Belmore, Tyler Brooke, Edgar Norton and Donald Novis. The undeservedly disappointing grosses, except in Britain, were blamed on Buchanan, whose name meant little elsewhere.

◁ The best of three good pictures starring William Powell and Kay Francis during 1930, **Street Of Chance** took a penetrating look at the nervous, dangerous lives of Manhattan sharpshooters. Howard Estabrook won an Academy Award nomination for his script, based on a story by Oliver H.P. Garrett who, in turn, had been inspired by the career of New York's notorious gambler Arnold Rothstein. It traced a drama of brother against brother, the gambling king's younger sibling coming from California to challenge his supremacy. Their confrontation over the card table, followed by the older man's death, gave Powell (right) an acting showcase that made him a top star; Regis Toomey (left) as the brother, as well as Miss Francis and Jean Arthur as their mates, also registered strongly. John Cromwell directed the David O. Selznick production.

▷ **The Vagabond King** had already had a long reign when it won new box-office glory as Paramount's first all-Technicolor talkie. This was the musical version of *If I Were King*, which started life as a novel by R.H. Russell, became a stage hit in Justin McCarthy's dramatisation in 1901 and was filmed by Fox in 1920 and (as *The Beloved Rogue* with John Barrymore) in 1926 by United Artists. Producer Russell Janney, with William Post and Brian Hooker turned it into a musical with songs by Rudolph Friml and Hooker, a smash in New York in 1925 and in London in 1927 as *The Vagabond King*. Dennis King (illustrated) starred in the new movie, as he had on Broadway, giving splendid voice to 'Only A Rose', 'The Song Of The Vagabonds' and the other tunes decorating beggar-poet François Villon's swashbuckling adventures in Paris at the time of Louis XI. Jeanette MacDonald (illustrated) looked and sounded lovely in her second picture; Ludwig Berger directed them, as well as Warner Oland, singer Lillian Roth, O.P. Heggie and Arthur Stone in Herman Mankiewicz's screenplay. The studio filmed the story twice more, as *If I Were King* in 1938 and as *The Vagabond King* in 1956.

OTHER RELEASES OF 1930
(All talkies unless indicated otherwise)

Anybody's War
George Moran, Charles Mack, Neil Hamilton, Joan Peers. Dir: Richard Wallace. Comical adventures of the Two Black Crows as World War I volunteers in France.

Anybody's Woman
Ruth Chatterton, Clive Brook, Paul Lukas. Dir: Dorothy Arzner. Lawyer goes on a binge, wakes up married to a showgirl he has defended in court. She leaves him for another man, but returns.

Behind The Make-Up
William Powell, Kay Francis, Fay Wray, Hal Skelly. Dir: Robert Milton (also Dorothy Arzner, unbilled). Vaudeville partners both love a waitress; she marries the wrong one, who cheats on her and dies.

The Benson Murder Case
William Powell, Paul Lukas, Natalie Moorhead. Dir: Frank Tuttle. Amateur detective Philo Vance solves the mystery of a Wall Street financier's murder.

The Border Legion
Richard Arlen, Jack Holt, Fay Wray, Mary Brian. Dir: Otto Brower, Edwin H. Knopf. Zane Grey drama of the leader of a gang of rustlers who gives his life to save a pair of young lovers. (Remake of 1924 film.)

Burning Up
Richard Arlen, Mary Brian, Tully Marshall. Dir: Edward Sutherland. Car salesman becomes a speedway driver who wins the big race in which his friend is his most dangerous competitor.

Dangerous Nan McGrew
Helen Kane, Victor Moore, Stuart Erwin, James Hall. Dir: Malcolm St. Clair. The escapades, songs and romance of a sharpshooting girl with a medicine show in northern Canada.

Derelict
George Bancroft, Jessie Royce Landis, William Boyd. Dir: Rowland V. Lee. Freighter officers vie for captaincy and girl while bound for Rio.

Feet First
Harold Lloyd, Barbara Kent, Robert McWade, Lillian Leighton. Dir: Clyde Bruckman. Pro: Lloyd. A Honolulu shoe salesman survives a series of mishaps, including being flown to San Francisco in a mailbag, and dangling from a skyscraper.

Follow The Leader
Ed Wynn, Ginger Rogers, Stanley Smith, Ethel Merman. Dir: Norman Taurog. Nutty waiter accidentally knocks out a gangster, is acclaimed as the rival mob's leader, and helps his employer's daughter to score a hit on Broadway.

Heads Up!
Charles 'Buddy' Rogers, Helen Kane, Victor Moore, Margaret Breen. Dir: Victor Schertzinger. Musical with Rodgers & Hart songs, about a Coast Guard officer dealing with bootleggers who make use of his girl friend's yacht.

Her Wedding Night
Clara Bow, Ralph Forbes, Charles Ruggles. Dir: Frank Tuttle. Pro: E. Lloyd Sheldon. Movie star marries songwriter after a series of identity mix-ups on the Riviera. (Remake of *Miss Bluebeard*, 1925.)

Ladies Love Brutes
George Bancroft, Mary Astor, Fredric March, Margaret Quimby. Dir: Rowland V. Lee. A divorcing wife is romanced by a rough diamond who tries to be polished; he shows his true worth by foiling a kidnap plot.

Let's Go Native
Jeanette MacDonald, Jack Oakie, Kay Francis, James Hall, Skeets Gallagher. Dir: Leo McCarey. Musical variation on the 'Admirable Crichton' theme, with an assortment of shipwrecked characters beached on a tropical isle.

The Light Of Western Stars
Richard Arlen, Mary Brian, Regis Toomey. Dir: Otto Brower, Edwin H. Knopf. Zane Grey's western melodrama of ranchers versus rustlers. (Remake of 1925 film.)

Love Among The Millionaires
Clara Bow, Stanley Smith, Stuart Erwin. Dir: Frank Tuttle. Railroad owner's son, posing as a brakeman, woos a station cafe waitress; his father forbids marriage but love conquers.

The Man From Wyoming
Gary Cooper, June Collyer, Regis Toomey. Dir: Rowland V. Lee. Soldier in France marries ambulance girl who runs wild at parties; he returns to front; she follows. (Remake of *Civilian Clothes*, 1920.)

Men Are Like That
Hal Skelly, Doris Hill, Clara Blandick. Dir: Frank Tuttle. Second of four film versions of George Kelly's comedy about a big-talking non-achiever. (Remake of *The Show-Off*, 1926.)

Only Saps Work
Leon Errol, Richard Arlen, Mary Brian. Dir: Cyril Gardner, Edwin H. Knopf. Rich youth, trying to prove his independence, gets involved in an inept bank theft. (Remake of *Easy Come, Easy Go*, 1928.)

Only The Brave
Gary Cooper, Mary Brian, Phillips Holmes. Dir: Frank Tuttle. Rivals for a Southern Belle are a Confederate officer and a Union spy, who is caught, and saved from a firing squad by a Northern attack.

Playboy Of Paris
Maurice Chevalier, Frances Dee, O.P. Heggie, Stuart Erwin. Dir: Ludwig Berger. A waiter becomes a boulevardier after hours, causing a fight between his boss's daughter and a golddigger. (Remake of *Le Petit Café*, 1920.)

Queen High
Charles Ruggles, Frank Morgan, Stanley Smith, Ginger Rogers. Dir: Fred Newmeyer. Musical comedy about a garter manufacturer who, having lost a poker bet, has to become a servant to his partner.

The Return Of Dr. Fu Manchu
Warner Oland, Jean Arthur, Neil Hamilton. Dir: Rowland V. Lee. Sequel to *The Mysterious Dr. Fu Manchu* (1929) with the oriental fiend trying to wipe out the English family of his adopted daughters's fiancé.

The Santa Fe Trail
Richard Arlen, Rosita Moreno, Junior Durkin, Mitzi Green. Dir: Otto Brower, Edwin H. Knopf. Dramatic hindrances arise when a vast flock of sheep is being moved across the Western plains.

The Sap From Syracuse (GB The Sap From Abroad)
Jack Oakie, Ginger Rogers. Dir: Edward Sutherland. Stowaway in a transatlantic liner, mistaken for a mining engineer, romances a mine-owning girl.

The Sea God
Richard Arlen, Fay Wray, Eugene Pallette. Dir: George Abbott. Deep-sea diver rescues a girl from a lustful chieftain, fends off cannibals and pearl thieves in the South Seas.

Sea Legs
Jack Oakie, Lillian Roth, Harry Green, Eugene Pallette. Dir: Victor Heerman. Sailor, shanghaied into a foreign ship to take the place of a rich slacker, is accused of killing him when the substitution is revealed.

Seven Days' Leave (GB Medals)
Gary Cooper, Beryl Mercer. Dir: Richard Wallace. Pro: Louis D. Lighton. Barrie's 'The Old Lady Shows Her Medals'; tale of a London charwoman who adopts a soldier during the war.

Shadow Of The Law
William Powell, Regis Toomey, Natalie Moorhead. Dir: Louis Gasnier. Wrongly convicted prisoner escapes, finds a treacherous woman who could clear him. (Remake of *The City Of Silent Men*, 1921.)

The Silent Enemy
Documentary of Ojibwa Indians in Canada. Dir: H.P. Carver. Pro: W. Douglas Burdon, William Chanler. (Part-talkie.)

Slightly Scarlet
Clive Brook, Evelyn Brent, Paul Lukas. Dir: Louis Gasnier, Edwin H. Knopf. Gem thieves follow a rich American family from Paris to Nice, where romance hinders robbery. (Remake of *Blackbirds*, 1915.)

The Social Lion
Jack Oakie, Mary Brian, Olive Borden, Skeets Gallagher. Dir: Edward Sutherland. When taken up by a society gadabout, a prizefighter becomes a polo star, then goes back to his girl and the ring.

The Texan
Gary Cooper, Fay Wray, Oscar Apfel, Emma Dunn, Donald Reed. Dir: John Cromwell. Pro: David O. Selznick, Hector Turnbull. Bandit poses as the long lost son of a wealthy woman, until his past catches up with him.

True To The Navy
Clara Bow, Fredric March, Harry Green, Rex Bell. Dir: Frank Tuttle. A flirtatious soda-fountain girl in a drugstore near the San Diego naval base falls for the fleet's target-shooting champion.

The Virtuous Sin
Kay Francis, Walter Huston, Kenneth MacKenna. Dir: George Cukor, Louis Gasnier. Melodrama of Russian woman's love for two men, her husband and the general to whom she offers herself to save the husband.

With Byrd At The South Pole
Documentary of Comm. Richard E. Byrd's Antarctic expedition. Narration: Floyd Gibbons.

Young Eagles
Charles 'Buddy' Rogers, Jean Arthur, Paul Lukas, Stuart Erwin. Dir: William A. Wellman. Aviator in World War I regrets falling for a girl when he learns she is a spy; she turns out to be a US counterspy.

1931

▷ Maurice Chevalier was back at his irresistible best in **The Smiling Lieutenant** because, after a couple of vehicles less splendid than *The Love Parade*, he was back under the guidance of Ernst Lubitsch. *The Love Parade* and *Monte Carlo* had established the director's reputation so firmly that the new picture was able to buck a sudden public refusal to buy tickets for musical movies. Adapted from an operetta, *A Waltz Dream*, by Leopold Jacobson and Felix Doermann (based on a story by Hans Mueller) filmed silent in Germany in 1925, it now had its theatre music by Oscar Straus, with lyrics by Clifford Grey. The star (right) played a guards officer whose romance with a beautiful violinist is interrupted when, assigned to take care of a visiting king, he attracts the latter's dowdy daughter and is ordered to marry her. The violinist takes pity on the princess, shows her how to improve herself, and leaves her to the lieutenant. It was a delicious *soufflé*, served with the minimum of dialogue and maximum visual subtlety. Both leading ladies sparkled: Claudette Colbert was even more charming than when opposite Chevalier in *The Big Pond*, and Miriam Hopkins (left), still a newcomer from the stage, displayed a verve that made stardom inevitable. Also cast in the Ernest Vajda-Samson Raphaelson screenplay were Charles Ruggles, Hugh O'Connell, George Barbier and Elizabeth Patterson.

▽ You won't find **Twenty-Four Hours** (GB: **The Hours Between**) in any treatise on cinema art, but as an example of the efficient, entertaining, commercial movies the major studios were manufacturing by the dozen (none better than Paramount) it deserves attention. Louis Weitzenkorn based his hard, fast and somewhat sordid script on best-selling novelist Louis Bromfield's book about an alcoholic man-about-town (Clive Brook, right) involved with a nightclub dancer (Miriam Hopkins) and arrested when she is killed by her gangster husband (Regis Toomey). After his trial and acquittal, he reforms and returns to his adulterous wife (Kay Francis, left), who also mends her morals. Marion Gering directed the excellent stars and supporting players Charlotte Granville, George Barbier, Adrienne Ames, Minor Watson, Lucille LaVerne and Thomas Jackson.

▽ Only ladies who doted on magazine fiction got much of a buzz from **Honor Among Lovers** which strained credulity as it depicted, rather slowly, the dolours of a girl who marries the wrong man. The Austin Parker-Gertrude Purcell script's heroine, a secretary (Claudette Colbert, right), is wooed by her boss (Fredric March, left) but accepts his shifty colleague (Monroe Owsley), who loses a stock market gamble and resents his bride's appeal to the boss to rescue him. After a row, wife walks out, husband shoots and wounds boss, making wife realise she really loves boss. Talk about excitement. Dorothy Arzner's direction came to life only in the comedy relief scenes played by Charles Ruggles and Ginger Rogers, topping a supporting cast that included Pat O'Brien in one of his first movies, Ralph Morgan, Avonne Taylor, John Kearney and Leonard Carey.

▷ The mad Marxes (illustrated) rampaged through **Monkey Business** with as much abandon as in their earlier two frolics. It was the first of their pictures to be written especially for the screen, and their first to be made at the Hollywood studio. Not one of their classics, according to the critics, but theatre-rocking laughs erupted frequently as the brothers raced around a luxury liner chasing blondes, catching crooks and imitating Chevalier. Norman Z. McLeod directed the Arthur Sheekman screenplay, from a story by S.J. Perelman, Roland Pertwee and W.B. Johnstone which Thelma Todd, Rockliffe Fellowes, Ruth Hall, Tom Kennedy and Harry Woods did their best to get on with, between the zanies' gags. Alas, no Margaret Dumont this time.

▷ A Sergei Eisenstein production of Theodore Dreiser's masterpiece **An American Tragedy** is one of the great might-have-beens of the cinema. It seemed a probability when the Russian was invited to Hollywood by Jesse Lasky and, during several months at Paramount, wrote a treatment of the novel which Dreiser enthusiastically approved. The studio didn't. Eisenstein departed, others grappled with the script (finally credited to Samuel Hoffenstein) and the project was turned over to the company's current genius, Josef von Sternberg. His romantic, atmospheric style and the book's gritty realism cancelled each other out, resulting in disappointment to most critics and exhibitors. Seen again recently, it seems a flat, perfunctory, over-condensed recital of the story, culminating in an almost absurd courtroom sequence. Phillips Holmes (right), a fine young actor always handicapped by being too handsome, and the poignant Sylvia Sidney (left) were excellent as the ill-fated lovers; the rest – Frances Dee, Irving Pichel, Claire McDowell, Charles Middleton and Frederick Burton – had little to do. Dreiser was so enraged when he saw it that he had sued the company for damages, even though he had received the princely sum of at least $80,000 for the film rights. And it was banned in Britain, where censors ruled that making a girl pregnant was bad enough, but taking her out in a canoe to drown her was really going too far.

◁ Ruth Chatterton (illustrated) gloomed through 80 tear-stained minutes of **Once A Lady** as a kind of *Madame X* with a Russian accent. In fact, she had played the latter role with huge success while on loan to MGM, which is why Paramount disinterred a 1928 Pola Negri silent, *Three Sinners*, for Zoe Akins and Samuel Hoffenstein to rewrite with dialogue, and an extra dash of the 'X' ingredient: mother love. The celebrated stage director Guthrie McClintic left Broadway long enough to guide the star as a loose woman who abandons husband and daughter, letting them believe her dead, until her past catches up with her twenty years later. The British matinée idol Ivor Novello made his only Hollywood talkie appearance in a cast also including Jill Esmond, Theodore von Eltz, Bramwell Fletcher, Geoffrey Kerr, Doris Lloyd, Claude King, Ethel Griffies, Herbert Bunston and Lillian Rich. The story did no more for Ruth's career than it had done for Pola's.

△ Sylvia Sidney (illustrated), a new protegée of production chief B.P. Schulberg, replaced an old one, Clara Bow, in **City Streets**, and a greater contrast could hardly be imagined. The ebullient Clara, plagued by scandal, was having a nervous breakdown during her last Paramount year. The sad-eyed Sylvia, with her flower-like beauty and understated emotionalism, made a different kind of impact, and one that made her an immediate star. Gary Cooper (here with Sylvia), another master of underacting, played a carnival worker lured into crime by a racketeer's daughter in Dashiell Hammett's one and only original for the screen, adapted by Max Marcin and scripted by Oliver H.P. Garrett. It involved ten murders – 'none of them actually seen', noted director Rouben Mamoulian, who nevertheless gave it sizzling action, and hypnotic intensity enough to surpass his *Applause* triumph. Wynne Gibson, Paul Lukas, William 'Stage' Boyd, Guy Kibbee and Stanley Fields also scored in E. Lloyd Sheldon's production.

◁ A potboiler, but with the classy addition of Gary Cooper and Carole Lombard in the leads plus some name value in its best-selling author, Mary Roberts Rinehart, **I Take This Woman** simmered nicely on the box-office stove. Carole (right) made it bubble as a wild heiress whose father sends her to a Wyoming ranch to cool down; there she attracts cowhand Cooper (left) and, in a moment of caprice, marries him. Unable to stand the rugged life, she returns to New York for a divorce, while he joins a rodeo and is injured; she rushes back to him. Clinch. Marion Gering directed these far from startling events, scripted by Vincent Lawrence from the Rinehart novel *Lost Ecstasy*, and giving jobs to Lester Vail, Helen Ware, David Landau, Guy Oliver, Charles Trowbridge and Clara Blandick.

△ In **Dishonored**, spymaster Gustav von Seyffertitz publicly announces to all within earshot 'I am the head of the Secret Service!', picks up streetwalker Marlene Dietrich (left) and appoints her as Spy No X27. Immediately equipped with a palatial home and lavish costumes, she entraps enemy agent Warner Oland; then, disguised as a chambermaid, outwits foe Victor McLaglen (right). She captures him, loves him, allows him to escape, and is shot by a firing squad for her trouble. This ludicrous story, devoid of excitement or logic, not only managed to get by as entertainment, but attracted huge audiences as one of the year's biggest hits. Why? Dietrich. Everything else was subordinated to that hypnotic presence by director, writer (with Daniel Rubin) and (with Lee Garmes) lighting cameraman Josef von Sternberg.

▷ Back in 1915, millions lurched glassy-eyed from cinemas showing a DeMille movie called **The Cheat**. They had witnessed the ordeal of a woman selling herself to a rich Oriental who, when she wouldn't deliver the goods, branded her like cattle and was thereupon murdered. Fannie Ward was the scorched lady in this feverish melodrama; eight years later Pola Negri took the iron with similar public response. Now, in 1931 it was Tallulah Bankhead's turn, in Harry Hervey's new adaptation of the Hector Turnbull story. It was directed by George Abbott, with Irving Pichel (here with Tallulah), Harvey Stephens, Ann Andrews, Jay Fassett and Arthur Hohl in the supporting cast. But the old impact had largely disappeared: audiences confronted by the spectacle of Tallulah resisting the fate worse than death just didn't believe it.

▽ A 1929 smash on Broadway, **June Moon** lost none of its high-pressure hilarity, and only a little of its satirical bite, as Joseph Mankiewicz, Vincent Lawrence and Keene Thompson in their screen adaptation shifted some of the narrative attention to romance while retaining much of the play's dialogue by Ring Lardner and George S. Kaufman. Jack Oakie (left) scored strongly in his first starring role as an electrician short-circuited by his yearning to be a songwriter. The lovely Frances Dee (right) was his girlfriend, and Wynne Gibson, Harry Akst, June MacCloy and Sam Hardy were denizens of Tin Pan Alley, crisply rapping out the wisecracks. Edward Sutherland, the director, knew all about up-tempo comedy, in which a fast line is the shortest distance between laughs.

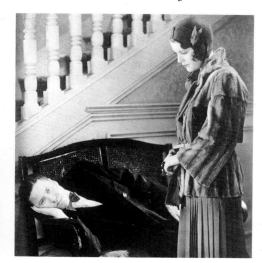

▷ Sophistication flourished in full flower when three of its most accomplished exponents – William Powell (right), Kay Francis and Carole Lombard (left) – starred in **Ladies' Man**. The heartless but fascinating script by Herman Mankiewicz, based on a novel by Rupert Hughes, offered Powell as a man-about-town who rejuvenates bored wives by taking them out (and in) while living on their gifts. This dubious profession proves dangerous not only to true love (Francis), but to life itself when the daughter (Lombard) of one of his infatuated matrons (Olive Tell) falls for him too, and their enraged husband and father (Gilbert Emery) knocks him through a window to his death. Although the tragic ending to what had been predominantly a worldly comedy was disconcerting, it was a popular movie, well directed by Lothar Mendes. It was Powell's fourth of six teamings with Francis and his second with Lombard (his wife from 1931 to 1933). By 1932 Powell, Francis and Ruth Chatterton had all moved over to Warner Bros. who, needing an injection of more 'classy' talent, had pulled off a raid on Paramount's star list. Lombard, who had been around in 'B' pictures and shorts for quite a while when Paramount signed her in 1930, stayed for seven years, becoming one of the studio's top names.

◁ The first of two similar stories screenwritten by the gifted Herman Mankiewicz (whose brother Joseph became more pominent later) for William Powell, **Man Of The World** immediately preceded *Ladies' Man*. Both had Powell playing a gigolo, with Carole Lombard (illustrated with him) as a romantic foil, and both made unappetizing material palatable through adroit treatment by all concerned. In this one the anti-hero blackmails the rich Americans he services in Paris, until he falls in love with one near-victim (Lombard); then his permanent amour (Wynne Gibson) threatens to betray him to the police if he leaves her. He stays, and Lombard goes back to the States with her fiancé (Lawrence Gray). Directed by Richard Wallace, Powell gave a fine performance, as did Gibson, who specialised in hard-boiled, soft-centred dames; Guy Kibbee, George Chandler, Tom Ricketts and Maude Truax also appeared.

△ Gary Cooper had a top-grade sagebrusher in **Fighting Caravans**, a Zane Grey yarn into which screenwriters E.E. Paramore Jr, Agnes Brand Leahy and Keene Thompson packed a lot of additional action and incident. There was a smattering of comedy, too, when the pals of a wagon train's leader, a wanted man, try to break up his romance with a caravan girl he has induced to pose as his wife in order to avoid arrest. The climax of their westward trek was the inevitable Indian attack, and it was a humdinger. Lily Damita, Ernest Torrence (right), Eugene Pallette, Charles Winninger, Fred Kohler, Tully Marshall (left), Eve Southern, James Farley, May Boley and Frank Campeau supported Cooper, co-directed by western specialist Otto Brower and David Burton, the latter experienced with dialogue. The splendid cinematography was also shared, by Lee Garmes and Henry Gerrard.

▽ **Scandal Sheet** had triple-star power going for it at the box-office, and the confident directorial touch of John Cromwell to make it a superior example of entertainment for the masses. Tough George Bancroft (illustrated), Kay Francis and Clive Brook were all assigned juicy roles in the Vincent Lawrence-Max Marcin screenplay, from an original by Oliver H.P. Garrett, about the ruthless editor (Bancroft) of a muck-raking newspaper who puts its exposure technique to personal use when his wife (Francis) announces that she is leaving him for another man (Brook). The lover gets the scandal-sheet treatment with dramatic results. Others involved were played by Regis Toomey, Gilbert Emery, Jackie Searl, Lucien Littlefield, Mary Foy and Harry Beresford.

◁ George Abbott, Broadway's most successful director and script doctor, took two years off from the theatre under a Paramount contract that yielded eight pictures between 1929 and 1931. One of the best was **Stolen Heaven**, for which Nancy Carroll stayed on the East Coast after completing *Laughter*. The studio gave her the leading man of her hit *The Devil's Holiday*, Phillips Holmes (here with her), and a story by the author of her star-making *The Shopworn Angel*, Dana Burnett, and if it didn't measure up to either of those, this romance of a girl of the streets and a young thief who takes her on an idyllic trip away from it all made a very popular movie. Whenever it teetered on the borderline between tender and mawkish, it was kept on the right side by the charm of its stars, adept work by Louis Calhern, Guy Kibbee and Joseph Crehan, and the skill of director Abbott, who also wrote the screenplay with George Hill.

▽ Not a football story as you may have thought, **Kick In** was an underworld drama, mildewed by time. Created as a one-acter for early-century vaudeville by Willard Mack, who developed it into a popular Broadway play for John Barrymore in 1914, it was filmed in 1917 (Pathe) and 1923, and by 1931 the only new thing about it was the cast. This was headed by Clara Bow (centre), looking overweight and subdued in her final movie for the company, and at the same time surprisingly effective in the serious role of a young wife struggling to help her ex-convict mate to reform. They are dragged back into a criminal milieu as the unwilling accomplices of an old pal of the husband, but finally manage to extricate themselves. Regis Toomey (left), Wynne Gibson, James Murray, Juliette Compton, Donald Crisp (right), Leslie Fenton, J. Carrol Naish and Paul Hurst supported strongly under Richard Wallace's direction. The script was dusted off by Bartlett Cormack.

▽ Edmund Goulding, who wrote and directed one of Nancy Carroll's best pictures, *The Devil's Holiday*, in 1930, performed the same chores (and they looked like chores) on one of her worst, **The Night Angel**, a year later. Intended as a prestige item with another fine talent, Fredric March, co-starred, it emerged as a major flop of 1931, which was a rather below-par year altogether. The heavy, slow-moving story, told with ersatz-Von Sternberg moodiness, began in a Prague brothel, whose keeper (Alison Skipworth) is sent to jail by the public prosecutor (March, right) while her daughter (Carroll, left) fends off lustful passes from the bordello's bouncer (Alan Hale, centre). Love blossoms between girl and lawyer, who accidentally kills the bouncer in a fight and is acquitted by the girl's testimony at his trial. All of which was something of a trial for everybody viewing it. Also in the cast: Phoebe Foster, Clarence Derwent, Herbert Druce and Katherine Emmett.

△ With such a wonderful Mark Twain story to work on, could **Huckleberry Finn** ever fail? A 1974 United Artists release finally managed to, but all the earlier versions had hearty welcomes: Paramount's in 1920 and 1931, MGM's in 1939 (with the best Huck, Mickey Rooney) and 1960. The 1931 version was made in response to the success of Twain's *Tom Sawyer* the year before, with the same producer, Louis D. Lighton, scenarists Grover Jones and William Slavens McNutt, and some of the same cast: Junior Durkin (centre) as Huck, Jackie Coogan (right) as Tom, Mitzi Green, Jackie Searl, Jane Darwell and Clara Blandick. Newcomers were Clarence Muse (left) as Jim, the absconding slave who sails down the river on a raft with the boys; Eugene Pallette, Charlotte Henry, Warner Richmond, Oscar Apfel and Guy Oliver. Norman Taurog took over from *Tom Sawyer's* John Cromwell as director and, as always, showed special skill in guiding youngsters.

▽ A romantic comedy as exuberant as its title, **Up Pops The Devil** came from a play by Frances Goodrich and Albert Hackett, still running in New York when Edward Sutherland started directing the movie. The husband-and-wife authors became one of Hollywood's most successful writing teams a few years later, starting with *The Thin Man*, and their witty style was retained in the Eve Unsell-Arthur Kober adaptation of this tale about bohemian inhabitants of Manhattan's Greenwich Village, played by Carole Lombard, Norman Foster, Stuart Erwin, Lilyan Tashman, Skeets Gallagher, Joyce Compton, Theodore von Eltz, Edward Nugent and Harry Beresford. It focused chiefly on a young writer (Foster, left) and an even younger dancer (Lombard, right), married, poor, and prone to outbreaks of jealousy. A minor hit—not surprisingly, given the ingredients.

▷ Five years after *Moana*, the great American documentary maker Robert Flaherty returned to the South Seas to film **Tabu** in collaboration with F.W. Murnau, the renowned German director. In the interim he had joined forces with W.S. Van Dyke in making *White Shadows In The South Seas* for MGM, but his intention to work in documentary style clashed with the studio's desire for a commercial romance, and he walked away from it. Exactly the same thing happened on the new production. Flaherty was interested exclusively in the natives' way of life, their customs and surroundings, while these aspects were subordinated to a melodrama of love and hate in the plans of Murnau, who bought out his collaborator and finished *Tabu* alone. A week before its premiere a car crash killed Murnau, aged 42; a loss to cinema art. The film was immensely successful, and won an Oscar for Floyd Crosby's photography.

△ The beauties in **Girls About Town** were euphemistically called gold-diggers or party girls; really they followed the oldest profession, providing diversion for visiting businessmen by the hour or the weekend. Zoe Akins wrote a dazzling comedy about them in *The Greeks Had A Word For It*, a Broadway stage hit which was filmed for United Artists release and was beaten to the screen by three months, Paramount having quickly grabbed a very similar Akins story. This one was rushed through the typewriters of scenarists Brian Marlow and ex-star Raymond Griffith, assigned to director George Cukor as his first at the Hollywood studio, and given a sparkling cast: Kay Francis (left), Lilyan Tashman, Joel McCrea (right), Eugene Pallette, Claire Dodd, Judith Wood, Adrienne Ames, Alan Dinehart, Lucille Gleason, George Barbier, Robert McWade and Louise Beavers. Out came a fast, rowdy movie, devoid of morals and loaded with entertainment.

▷ Unexpectedly, **Skippy** shot up from the mass of 1931 releases (Paramount alone had 62) not only as a money-making champion but as the recipient of a flock of Academy Award nominations: best picture, best actor (Jackie Cooper), best story adaptation (Joseph Mankiewicz and Sam Mintz), best direction (Norman Taurog – who actually won an Oscar). Jackie (illustrated), Taurog's nephew and a 9-year-old recruit from Hal Roach's *Our Gang* comedy shorts, was teamed with Robert Coogan (Jackie Coogan's younger brother) in a simple tale of two boys trying to make enough money to buy back their pet from the local dog catcher. It derived from that fruitful source of movie hits, the comic strips, this one by Percy Crosby. Moppets Mitzi Green and Jackie Searl, and adults Helen Jerome Eddy, Willard Robertson, Enid Bennett and Guy Oliver were cast in the Louis D. Lighton production. Everyone concerned came together again for a sequel, *Sooky*, a few months later, then the studio let Cooper slip away to MGM. The most popular child star since Jackie Coogan, he became a TV actor and producer as an adult and still makes occasional screen appearances.

▷ Sylvia Sidney (illustrated), so often on her way into or out of prison during her movie life, was right in there behind bars for much of **Ladies Of The Big House**. In this instance, star and movie were of equal merit: i.e. good, but not very. Ernest Booth's rather trashy melodrama about a young couple framed on a murder charge had the benefit of a hard-hitting script by Louis Weitzenkorn, who had sharpened his pen as a New York crime reporter and author of the hit *Five Star Final* (Warner Bros., 1931). Marion Gering, a recent Russian recruit to Paramount's contract list of directors, established a sympathetic working relationship with Miss Sidney (also of Russian descent) and went on to make five more of her pictures. In this one he drew colourful performances from Wynne Gibson, Esther Howard, Louise Beavers, Hilda Vaughn and Jane Darwell as big-house ladies, and Gene Raymond, Earle Foxe, Rockliffe Fellowes, Purnell Pratt and Theodore von Eltz as the men in the case. Star plus title attracted strong grosses.

◁ When Paramount signed her in 1931, Tallulah Bankhead (centre left) seemed a cinch for top stardom in the talkies. With that sinuous body, those heavy-lidded eyes, that air of cool chic barely restraining the devil-knew-what wickedness, and that voice – a mixture of Deep South drawl, Mayfair coo and whisky-sour contralto – how could she miss? Especially as she had just returned from seven years of stage stardom and widely publicised indiscretions as the toast, slightly burnt around the edges, of London. **Tarnished Lady**, however, disclosed the odd fact that her unique personality didn't come through the camera. She was just an efficient actress, capably handling Donald Ogden Stewart's witty dialogue as a Park Avenue girl who marries for money, gets bored, leaves her husband for a job and freedom, and goes back to him when he is ruined by the Wall Street crash. It was smartly directed by George Cukor and produced by Walter Wanger at the Astoria studio, with Clive Brook (left), Osgood Perkins, Phoebe Foster (centre right), Alexander Kirkland (right), Elizabeth Patterson, Eric Blore, Berton Churchill and Cora Witherspoon. Fine cast. Mixed reception.

OTHER RELEASES OF 1931
(All talkies)

Along Came Youth
Charles 'Buddy' Rogers, Frances Dee, Stuart Erwin. Dir: Lloyd Corrigan, Norman Z. McLeod. Stranded in London, a young American sportsman becomes a chef, then a steeplechase rider.

Beloved Bachelor
Paul Lukas, Dorothy Jordan, Charles Ruggles. Dir: Lloyd Corrigan. A great lover interrupts his philandering long enough to adopt a child; when grown up, she falls in love with him, ending his current affair.

Caught
Richard Arlen, Frances Dee, Louise Dresser. Dir: Edward Sloman. Calamity Jane, saloon keeper and cattle rustler, befriends a girl in love with the US Cavalry man sent to trap Calamity, who discovers he is her long-lost son.

Confessions Of A Co-Ed (GB **Her Dilemma**)
Sylvia Sidney, Phillips Holmes, Norman Foster. Dir: David Burton, Dudley Murphy. College girl has an affair with one student, marries another, has the first one's baby and returns to him.

The Conquering Horde
Richard Arlen, Fay Wray. Dir: Edward Sloman. Government agent in post-Civil War Texas helps a girl to get her herd to the Kansas cattle market despite Indian attack and white crooks. (Remake of *North of 36*, 1924)

Daughter Of The Dragon
Anna May Wong, Sessue Hayakawa, Warner Oland. Dir: Lloyd Corrigan. When Fu Manchu is killed in London, his daughter carries on his deadly pursuits until felled by her lover, an oriental detective.

Dude Ranch
Jack Oakie, June Collyer, Stuart Erwin, Mitzi Green. Dir: Frank Tuttle. Comical confusion at a western resort when entertainers hired to pose as desperate characters are confronted by real badmen.

The False Madonna (GB **The False Idol**)
Kay Francis, William Boyd, Conway Tearle. Dir: Stuart Walker. An adventuress claims to be the long-lost mother of a rich youth; when she developes a real affection for him, she admits her deception.

Finn And Hattie
Leon Errol, ZaSu Pitts, Regis Toomey, Lilyan Tashman. Dir: Norman Taurog, Norman Z. McLeod. Unsophisticated American family, on a Paris sight-seeing trip, running into trouble with a bogus princess.

The Gang Buster
Jack Oakie, Jean Arthur, Wynne Gibson. Dir: Edward Sutherland. Provincial insurance salesman in the big city gets caught up in the rivalry of two gang leaders.

The Girl Habit
Charles Ruggles, Sue Conroy, Tamara Geva. Dir: Edward Cline. Man-about-town settles down at last, but wedding plans are disrupted by an old flame, now a mobster's wife. (Remake of *Thirty Days*, 1922)

Gun Smoke
Richard Arlen, Mary Brian, William Boyd, Eugene Pallette. Dir: Edward Sloman. A hunter of wild horses ropes in a bunch of crooks disguised as rich businessmen touring the West.

His Woman
Gary Cooper, Claudette Colbert, Joseph Calleia. Dir: Edward Sloman. Ship's captain rescues a baby adrift in a boat, hires as nursemaid a girl on the run from a blackmail case. (Remake of *Sal of Singapore*, Pathe 1929)

Honeymoon Lane
Eddie Dowling, Ray Dooley, June Collyer. Dir: William James Craft. Pro: Sono-Art Productions. Musical comedy, about romantic complications in a honeymoon hotel, from Dowling's 1926 Broadway show.

Husband's Holiday
Clive Brook, Charles Ruggles, Vivienne Osborn, Juliette Compton. Dir: Robert Milton. Distracted by the emotional upheavals of his in-laws and attracted by another woman, a husband plans divorce, but repents.

It Pays To Advertise
Carole Lombard, Norman Foster, Eugene Pallette, Louise Brooks. Dir: Frank Tuttle. Soap manufacturer's son devises brilliant publicity campaign; father and competitor vie to get it. (Remake of 1919 film)

The Lawyer's Secret
Clive Brook, Charles 'Buddy' Rogers, Fay Wray, Richard Arlen, Jean Arthur. Dir: Louis Gasnier, Max Marcin. Lawyer who knows the truth about a murder can't disclose it without betraying his client.

The Mad Parade
Irene Rich, Evelyn Brent, Lilyan Tashman, Marceline Day, Louise Fazenda. Dir: William Beaudine. The stories of eight women brought together in uniform by World War I.

The Magnificent Lie
Ruth Chatterton, Ralph Bellamy, Charles Boyer. Dir: Berthold Viertel. Persuaded to lift a blind man's morale by impersonating a French star he idolises, a cafe entertainer falls in love with him.

Murder By The Clock
Regis Toomey, Lilyan Tashman, William Boyd. Dir: Edward Sloman. Rich family suffers killings until a daughter-in-law is revealed as the culprit.

My Sin
Tallulah Bankhead, Fredric March. Dir: George Abbott. About to marry money, a woman is confronted by the lawyer who defended her in her secret past.

Newly Rich (aka: **Forbidden Adventure**)
Mitzi Green, Jackie Searl, Edna May Oliver. Dir: Norman Taurog. Rival Hollywood child stars go to London and enjoy escapades with a young prince.

No Limit
Clara Bow, Norman Foster, Stuart Erwin, Harry Green. Dir: Frank Tuttle. Usherette in a New York movie palace falls for a handsome patron, gets involved with his robbery of a famous actress.

Personal Maid
Nancy Carroll, Pat O'Brien, Gene Raymond, Mary Boland. Dir: Monta Bell. Maid's romance with her employer's son is interrupted by the attentions of a rich man she meets during a holiday spree.

Rango
Documentary with slight story, filmed in Malaysian jungle. Dir & Pro: Ernest B. Schoedsack. A native family, their little boy and his pet orang-outang are menaced by a tiger, which is killed by a buffalo.

Rich Man's Folly
George Bancroft, Frances Dee, Robert Ames. Dir: John Cromwell. The family problems of a money-mad shipbuilder, in a modernized version of Dickens' 'Dombey and Son'.

The Road To Reno
Charles 'Buddy' Rogers, Peggy Shannon, Lilyan Tashman, William Boyd. Dir: Richard Wallace. A divorcing mother and her daughter have romances, the former with a cad really after the girl, whose brother kills him.

The Secret Call
Richard Arlen, Peggy Shannon. Dir: Stuart Walker. To avenge the death of her father, a telephone operator ruins the career of the man who caused it. (Remake of *The Woman*, 1915, and *The Telephone Girl*, 1927)

Secrets Of A Secretary
Claudette Colbert, Herbert Marshall, Georges Metaxa, Mary Boland. Dir: George Abbott. A social secretary saves her employer's daughter from blackmail by a gigolo and the charge of murdering him.

Silence
Clive Brook, Marjorie Rambeau, Peggy Shannon, Charles Starrett. Dir: Louis Gasnier, Max Marcin. Cockney crook in a condemned cell tells how he took the blame for his illegitimate daughter's murder of a blackmailer.

Sooky
Jackie Cooper, Robert Coogan, Jackie Searl. Dir: Norman Taurog. Pro: Louis D. Lighton. Sequel to *Skippy* (1931) in which the urchin pals get involved in Skippy's father's electioneering, and mourn Sooky's mother's death.

Touchdown (GB **Playing The Game**)
Richard Arlen, Jack Oakie, Peggy Shannon, Regis Toomey. Dir: Norman Z. McLeod. Pro: Louis D. Lighton. His girl convinces a football coach that he can't risk a player's life to win a game.

Unfaithful
Ruth Chatterton, Paul Lukas, Donald Cook, Juliette Compton. Dir: John Cromwell. Drama of a woman who, in order to save her brother's wife from scandal, sacrifices her own reputation.

Vice Squad
Kay Francis, Paul Lukas. Dir: John Cromwell. Foreign diplomat is trapped by a corrupt police squad into becoming an informer.

Women Love Once
Eleanor Boardman, Paul Lukas, Juliette Compton. Dir: Edward Goodman. The death of their child causes the reconciliation of a couple separated by bohemian life in Paris.

Working Girls
Charles 'Buddy' Rogers, Frances Dee, Paul Lukas, Stuart Erwin. Dir: Dorothy Arzner. Small-town girls arrive in New York in search of jobs and romantic men; they find both.

1932

▽ **Dancers In The Dark** took its audiences into the sleazy razzledazzle of the ten-cents-a-dance world. Unexpectedly strong in a fairly serious role for once, Jack Oakie played a bandleader on the make for taxi-dancer Miriam Hopkins (right); her steady boy-friend, saxophone tooter William Collier Jr, takes umbrage and, meanwhile, gangster George Raft (left) wants her to become his moll. Gosh, how they weighed her down. But the Hopkins verve glittered more brightly than the lights through this tawdry at-mosphere and made an unpleasant story acceptable, even enjoyable. Raft, no stranger to such surround-ings in his New York past, registered insinuating menace so vividly that he was promptly promoted to stardom. David Burton directed them, and Lyda Roberti, Eugene Pallette, Walter Hiers, Alberta Vaughn and Paul Fix in the James Ashmore Creel-man story, scripted by Herman Mankiewicz, Brian Marlow and Howard Emmett Rogers.

▷ Life and death in surburbia – a region not then often explored in movie drama – received intelligent writing and direction in **The Night Of June 13**, which focussed on four neighbouring households, es-pecially that of a man falsely accused of murdering his neurotic wife, actually a suicide. Clive Brook and Ad-rienne Allen (both illustrated) played these parts; Lila Lee was Gene Raymond's wife, who cannot give Brook a true alibi without ruining her marriage; Mary Boland and Charles Ruggles amused as a couple be-devilled by his father, Charley Grapewin, whose testi-mony frees Brook; Frances Dee, Helen Jerome Eddy, Helen Ware, Richard Carle and Arthur Hohl completed the gallery of characters, all portrayed with admirable precision. Stephen Roberts directed the Louis D. Lighton production, with a screenplay adapted from Vera Caspary's story by Agnes Brand Leahy, Brian Marlow and William Slavens McNutt.

△ Maurice Chevalier (centre) baulked at doing **One Hour With You** unless Kay Francis and Carole Lombard (towards both of whom he harboured romantic intentions) were cast as his leading ladies. Neatly averting the possibility of personal complica-tions during production, producer Ernst Lubitsch persuaded him to accept Jeanette MacDonald (left) and Genevieve Tobin (right) instead. So the delicious Chevalier-MacDonald partnership of *The Love Par-ade* was renewed, while Tobin, a deft comedienne, made an ideal collaborator in a decidedly *risqué* comedy of scrambled love affairs which also involved Roland Young, Charles Ruggles, George Barbier and

Josephine Dunn. With George Cukor directing the witty script Samson Raphaelson had wrought from a play by Lothar Schmidt (which Lubitsch had filmed for Warner Bros. in 1924 as *The Marriage Circle*), everything looked rosy. But after several weeks' work, Cukor found that producer Lubitsch was taking over more and more of the direction. He left the studio; Lubitsch re-shot much of his footage and got full director credit; Cukor was finally listed as 'dialogue director'. Although only one of its seven songs, the title number (by Richard Whiting and Leo Robin) beecame popular, the picture was nonetheless a joyous success.

▷ After a temporary eclipse, musicals were again in fashion by 1932. A hit partly responsible for their successful comeback, **The Big Broadcast** cashed in on the tremendous public adulation of radio stars. One of them was starting the longest career of any Paramount player: Bing Crosby (left). He had first appeared on screen in 1930 in *King Of Jazz* (Universal) as one of the Rhythm Boys trio, and subsequently in eight shorts, but it was his singing on radio and records that inspired the studio to give him the lead in this movie and a contract – the first of several which were to stretch over 24 years. He had three smash songs – 'Please', composed by Bing with Roy Turk and Fred Ahlert, which became his theme song; and two Rainger-Robin numbers, 'Here Lies Love', 'Where The Blue Of The Night' – and a role requiring him just to be himself: a happy-go-lucky crooner and top name in a broadcasting station, with Stuart Erwin as his rival for the affections of Leila Hyams (right). The script by George Marion Jr, from a William Ford Manley play, was directed by Frank Tuttle at a fast tempo to make room for such airwave celebrities as comedians George Burns and Gracie Allen, the Boswell Sisters, the Mills Brothers, Kate Smith, Arthur Tracy ('The Street Singer'), Donald Novis, scat-man Cab Calloway and his band, and Vincent Lopez and his orchestra.

◁ **The Devil And The Deep** had box-office insurance in a starry cast, and it needed it. The Harry Hervey story, adapted by Benn Levy, was a ripe melodrama which turned a submarine into an emotional pressure-cooker. Sub commander Charles Laughton (left) upped his jealousy periscope every time one of his men looked twice at his wife, Tallulah Bankhead. Gary Cooper (right) did more than look; Laughton got the guilty pair aboard the sub and sank it; they survived; he drowned. But he got the best notices. Marion Gering, a man, directed with an eye to the feminine trade, which received a bonus in the appearance of newcomer Cary Grant in a supporting cast featuring Juliette Compton, Henry Kolker, Paul Porcasi, Kent Taylor and Dorothy Christy.

▽ **Merrily We Go To Hell** is a title immortalised by the British censor, who insisted that the last word be replaced by a dash. Nothing in the movie itself could beat that for silliness, but the script made some good tries in that direction, always straining after modern sophistication which didn't often come off. Sylvia Sidney (right) and Fredric March gave it box-office clout and a pair of good performances as an heiress and a playwright whose marriage breaks up in a welter of party-going. His drinking and womanising drive her back to Papa, then a pregnancy threatens her life, bringing them together again. That's all Cleo Lucas's novel *I, Jerry, Take Thee, Joan*, gave Edwin Justus Mayer to make a script from, and it was hardly enough. However, there were passing pleasures in dialogue and incident, which were smoothly directed by Dorothy Arzner, whose cast included Adrienne Allen, Skeets Gallagher (left), Florence Britton, Kent Taylor, Esther Howard, George Irving and, in a bit part, Cary Grant.

◁ **Shanghai Express** starred Marlene Dietrich (centre) in the third of her six American pictures directed by Josef von Sternberg after *The Blue Angel*, and it proved the most popular with mass audiences. It made a profit of $3 million (in the days when a million *was* a million) because it had a strong story to support the mesmeric Dietrich beauty. As usual, Von Sternberg cast her as a glorified prostitute, this time Shanghai Lily, held by armed rebels while on a train journey with assorted passengers, including an ex-lover (Clive Brook), whose lives she saves by surrendering herself to a Chinese warlord (Warner Oland). Also on hand were Anna May Wong (left), Eugene Pallette, Louise Closser Hale, Lawrence Grant and Gustav von Seyffertitz. The luscious camerawork of Lee Garmes was rewarded with an Oscar. Harry Hervey's plot (which owed a lot to De Maupassant's 'Boule de Suif'), scripted by Jules Furthman, later gave rise to many remakes, rewrites and rip-offs.

▷ Rouben Mamoulian continued his run of successes with a brilliant version of **Dr Jekyll And Mr Hyde**. Whereas John Barrymore had played Hyde as a spidery fiend when it was filmed in 1920, Fredric March was now equally frightening as a grinning ape-man, emerging from handsome Dr Jekyll in graduated exposures of Karl Struss's camera. So impressive was March (right) all through his two-faced characterisation that he won the 'best actor' Oscar in 1932. (So did Wallace Beery in MGM's *The Champ* with one vote fewer, and the Academy altered its rules later to make such duplication of awards possible only on exactly tied voting). Miriam Hopkins (left) provided a provocative doxy for Hyde, Rose Hobart a touching fiancée for Jekyll, and Holmes Herbert, Halliwell Hobbes and Edgar Norton added British authenticity to the Samuel Hoffenstein-Percy Heath treatment of Robert Louis Stevenson's classic, which has survived ten movie adaptations. This remains the best.

△ The rowdy screen partnership of Victor McLaglen (2nd left) and Edmund Lowe (standing centre) which began in 1926 with *What Price Glory?* was superimposed on a murder story in **Guilty As Hell** (GB: **Guilty As Charged**). Not a whodunit, because you saw at the start who: a doctor strangling his unfaithful wife. The rest of the movie built up suspense as police captain McLaglen and reporter Lowe break down circumstantial evidence against the victim's lover (Richard Arlen) just in time to save him from the electric chair. Henry Stephenson (kneeling) as the guilty man, Adrienne Ames, Noel Francis, Ralph Ince, Elizabeth Patterson (left), Claire Dodd, Willard Robertson, Richard Tucker and William B. Davidson completed the strong acting team, coached by Erle Kenton in a clever Arthur Kober-Frank Partos script based on Daniel Rubin's novel *Riddle Me This*.

△ The familiar plot gimmick of twins – one good, one bad – was given another workout in **Strangers In Love**, with Fredric March (illustrated) doing double duty as the leading men. In William J. Locke's story, a popular novel as *The Shorn Lamb*, here screenwritten by Grover Jones and William Slavens McNutt, the bad twin forges his father's will to disinherit the good twin, who drifts into destitution; when he asks his brother for money the latter flies into a rage and dies of a heart attack. Good thereupon assumes Bad's identity, fooling even the dead man's secretary (Kay Francis) and they fall in love. The scripters, and director Lothar Mendes managed to work a nice strand of comedy into the dramatic pattern, and the picture pleased generally. In the cast: Stuart Erwin, Juliette Compton, George Barbier, Sidney Toler, Earle Foxe, Lucien Littlefield. Considering the studio's usual technical skill, the double shots of March were surprisingly poor.

▽ **If I Had A Million** crammed all the stars producer Louis D. Lighton could get his hands on into eight episodes, tied together by a Robert Andrews story about a dying millionaire (Richard Bennett) who thwarted his greedy relatives by picking his heirs at random from a telephone book. Gary Cooper, George Raft, Wynne Gibson, Charles Laughton, Frances Dee, Jack Oakie, W.C. Fields (right), Mary Boland, Charles Ruggles, Alison Skipworth (left), Gene Raymond, Roscoe Karns, May Robson, Lucien Littlefield, Grant Mitchell and Joyce Compton were directed by Ernst Lubitsch, Norman Taurog, Stephen Roberts, Norman Z. McLeod, James Cruze, William Seiter and H. Bruce Humberstone. No fewer than 18 scriptwriters were credited with the various segments, in which the most memorable of the windfall recipients were Miss Gibson as a pathetic prostitute and Laughton as a wage slave who celebrated by blowing his boss a magnificent razzberry.

△ Grey-bearded Marx Brothers addicts still cherish memories of **Horse Feathers**. This fourth eruption of the crazy-like-a-fox comics seemed to be happening at a university, where Groucho functioned as the crackpot president, Harpo (here, left, with Groucho) dashed in and out as the dog-catcher, Chico doubled as iceman and bootlegger and Zeppo, as Groucho's son, wooed the campus vamp. The priceless S.J. Perelman wrote the script with Bert Kalmar and Harry Ruby, who also contributed some forgettable songs; Thelma Todd, David Landau, Florine McKinney, Nat Pendleton, Reginald Barlow and Robert Greig suffered the slings and arrows of outrageous Marxes, and the whole shebang was held together with commendable aplomb by director Norman Z. McLeod.

◁ Family conflict between the generations kept interest alive through a superior 'B' production, **This Reckless Age**, a rewrite by Joseph Mankiewicz from Frank Tuttle's adaptation of *The Goose Hangs High*, Lewis Beach's play filmed silent in 1925. Two veteran Broadway stars, Richard Bennett and Frances Starr, expertly milked audience sympathy for the parents who sacrificed everything for the education of their children, while Charles 'Buddy' Rogers and Frances Dee (right) showed they weren't just pretty faces by making the selfish, pleasure-mad children convincing even when the script transformed them into dutiful supporters of Dad in a financial crisis. Tuttle directed the talented cast that also included Charles Ruggles (left), Peggy Shannon, Maude Eburne, David Landau, Mary Carlisle, Allen Vincent, Reginald Barlow and Grady Sutton.

◁ Marlene Dietrich's fourth film under Josef von Sternberg's bizarre direction had the advantage of his marvellous eye for atmospheric beguilement, but the handicap of his inability to strengthen a shaky script. The one S.K. Lauren and Jules Furthman wrote for **Blonde Venus** was downright decrepit. Marlene played a cabaret singer (emerging from a gorilla skin to render 'Hot Voodoo') whose poor but honest husband (Herbert Marshall) needs medical treatment abroad, for which she gets the wherewithal from a rich admirer (Cary Grant, here with her). Returning cured, husband discovers liaison and banishes wife; she wanders off into the Deep South and ever-deeper degradation as a prostitute, dragging her child (Dickie Moore) along with her until his father finds and claims him. Fade out. Fade in. Without explanation, she is now the toast of Paris, singing 'You Little So-and-So' to a nightclub crowd containing, to her – but not our – amazement, none other than Cary, who takes her back to Herbert and Dickie in America, where mother-love conquers all. This nonsense had Rita LaRoy, Sidney Toler and Robert Emmett O'Connor in minor roles, but small audiences. Marlene appeared to be losing her box-office grip.

△ W.C. Fields returned to Paramount after a four-year absence for **Million Dollar Legs**, a sort of Marx-mad comedy without the Brothers, but with the portly mutterer accompanied by a screenful of other good comedians: Jack Oakie (right), Lyda Roberti (left), Andy Clyde, Ben Turpin, Hugh Herbert, George Barbier, Billy Gilbert and Teddy Hart, plus pretty Susan Fleming (centre) and moppet Dickie Moore. Joseph Mankiewicz concocted an insane story set in Klopstokia, a country where everybody was sports crazy, children could jump six feet high and adults run a mile in a few seconds. Marshalling these talents they entered the Olympics, with wild results. Director Edward Cline took the fun at breakneck speed through a 64-minute spree treasured by *aficionados* as a classic of surreal comedy.

◁ Although she made three more there, the last of Nancy Carroll's pictures at Paramount that were worthy of her talent was **Hot Saturday**. It took a warm, sympathetic look at a girl made restless by small-town restrictions on her romantic nature, especially when she is attracted to a profligate young millionaire (Cary Grant). The gossip-mongers see to it that the few hours she spends in his home will cost her her job at the bank and her marriage to her virtuous fiancé (Randolph Scott, here with her), so she ups and leaves for New York and the high life with Cary. Harvey Ferguson's novel was screen-written by Seton I. Miller, Josephine Lovett and Joseph Moncure March and directed by William A. Seiter in refreshingly adult style. Miss Carroll was at her best; the two new leading men shone; Edward Woods, Lillian Bond, William Collier Sr, Jane Darwell, Rita LaRoy and Oscar Apfel supported sturdily. Resentful over several bad scripts, the high-tempered star gave the new studio regime a hard time, and they short-sightedly let her go when her contract expired in 1933.

▷ **Love Me Tonight** glided in as the best musical of 1932, and of many another year. Rouben Mamoulian, who had already set critics' enthusiasm alight during his brief movie career with a sentimental drama (*Applause*), a gangster story (*City Streets*) and a classic thriller (*Dr Jekyll And Mr Hyde*), now showed what he could do with a song-filled romance. He blended music and sound effects, dialogue and lyrics with pictorial pleasures, elaborating some of Lubitsch's innovations in the genre and adding some of his own. What a cast he had! Maurice Chevalier and Jeanette Mac-Donald (both illustrated) at their sparkling best; Charles Ruggles and Charles Butterworth, unobtrusively hilarious; the bewitching Myrna Loy; C. Aubrey Smith, Elizabeth Patterson, Ethel Griffies, Blanche Frederici, Joseph Cawthorn, Robert Greig and Herbert Mundin. And what songs! Nine of them written for the film by Richard Rodgers and Lorenz Hart, including the everlasting 'Lover', 'Isn't It Romantic?' and 'Mimi'. The vehicle was a Waldemar Young-Samuel Hoffenstein-George Marion Jr script, from a play by Leopold Marchand and Paul Armont, about a Parisian tailor who follows a noble customer home to get his bill paid, and is introduced at the chateau as a baron; there he is fascinated by a frosty princess, and soon makes her melt. The whole picture shimmered with charm.

△ Now making only one picture every two years, Harold Lloyd devoted even more care than usual to the production of **Movie Crazy**, his best sound film to date. He played a romantic scatterbrain who goes to Hollywood, is given a screen test, falls in love with an actress (Constance Cummings, left), and turns the studio sets into disaster areas. The funniest sequence in the Vincent Lawrence script (story by Agnes Christine Johnston, John Gray and Felix Adler) showed Harold (right) accidentally putting on a magician's jacket instead of his own at his boss's elegant party; eggs, rabbits and other paraphernalia popped out at the most embarrassing moments. Clyde Bruckman directed this money-spinner. Like Lloyd's leading lady in his silent two-reelers, Bebe Daniels, Miss Cummings went to England in the mid-thirties and enjoyed decades of stage and screen stardom there.

▽ Paramount found itself with another new star in George Raft (centre), who had commanded attention as a coin-flipping gangster in *Scarface* (UA, 1932) and as a menace to Miriam Hopkins in *Dancers In The Dark*. Producer William Le Baron assigned Vincent Lawrence and Kathryn Scola to tailor a Louis Bromfield story, **Night After Night**, to fit Raft's reptilian charm, and borrowed Archie Mayo from Warners to direct him as an ex-prizefighter running a swanky nightclub. Imagine Raft's chagrin when one of his supporting cast, just arrived from New York for her first film, made a bejewelled entrance, was greeted by a hat-check girl with 'Goodness, what diamonds!' replied 'Goodness has nothing to do with it, dearie', and walked away with the picture. 'Mae West stole everything but the cameras', said Raft later. The film caught the bold, pleasure-loving Prohibition era's atmosphere with style, and smart dialogue put over by an excellent cast that included Constance Cummings, Wynne Gibson, Alison Skipworth (left), Louis Calhern, Roscoe Karns and Bradley Page. Raft and West (right) did not appear together again until 1978, when he had a bit in her *Sextette*. They died within two days of each other in 1980; he was 85, she 87.

◁ *Merton Of The Movies* was always a hit, first as a novel by Harry Leon Wilson in 1922, then as a play by Marc Connelly and George S. Kaufman in 1923, and as a silent movie in 1924. Eight years later producer Louis D. Lighton gave it the talking treatment, which turned out to be a bright idea: re-titled **Make Me A Star** and re-scripted by Sam Mintz, Walter De Leon and Arthur Kober, it was not only louder but even managed to be funnier. This time Stuart Erwin was cast as the movie-struck country boy in Hollywood who becomes a comedy star in a burlesqued western that he thinks is serious drama. Erwin (right), playing more for laughs than the original Merton (Glenn Hunter), was fine, and so was Joan Blondell (borrowed from Warner Bros.) as the girl who shows him the Hollywood ropes. ZaSu Pitts, Ben Turpin, Charles Sellon, Helen Jerome Eddy, Sam Hardy, Ruth Donnelly (left) and Arthur Hoyt were also in William Beaudine's cast, and there were studio glimpses of Tallulah Bankhead, Clive Brook, Maurice Chevalier, Claudette Colbert, Gary Cooper, Phillips Holmes, Fredric March, Jack Oakie, Charles Ruggles and Sylvia Sidney. In 1947 MGM made yet another *Merton Of The Movies* with Red Skelton.

△ If Clara Bow had been cast as Lady Macbeth moviegoers couldn't have been more disconcerted than they were when their favourite purveyor of effervescent escapism, Ernst Lubitsch, offered them **The Man I Killed**, a grim drama, heavy with anti-war significance. They stayed away in droves, and the title was hastily changed to **Broken Lullaby**. But to no avail. The critics were much more welcoming than the public, for this was gripping stuff, expertly translated to film from a Maurice Rostand play by the director, and writers Ernest Vajda, Samson Raphaelson and Reginald Berkeley. It followed a young Frenchman as, nagged by conscience, he seeks out the family of a German soldier he had killed in the war, and tells them he had been a friend of the dead man in Paris. He confesses the truth to the latter's fiancée when they fall in love, and she persuades him not to reveal his guilt to the family. Phillips Holmes (left), Lionel Barrymore (right), and Nancy Carroll (centre right) gave affecting performances in the main roles, backed up by ZaSu Pitts, Tom Douglas, Lucien Littlefield, Tully Marshall, Louise Carter (centre left) and Emma Dunn. Its box-office failure ended the fine Carroll-Holmes team, and Lubitsch never made another drama.

▽ Nancy Carroll was getting a raw deal in some of the story assignments thrown at her towards the end of her Paramount contract. For instance, **Wayward**. This novelettish piece of fiction belonged to the pages between fashion layouts and household hints in a women's magazine; as a feature film it was a non-starter. The star (right) did what she could (which was quite a lot) with the role of a spirited girl marrying a good-looking but dull-living young man (Richard Arlen) who is dominated by his intolerant mother, played by Pauline Frederick (left) with silent-screen bravura. The Gladys Unger-William Day screenplay, from a novel by Matee Howe Farnham, tediously developed the wife-versus-mother conflict, a confrontation predictably intensified when the couple have a baby. Others performing under Edward Sloman's direction were Margalo Gillmore, John Litel, Dorothy Stickney and Gertrude Michael.

◁ **Madame Butterfly** minus Puccini's songs was like a bowl of cornflakes without milk: hard to swallow. It had been, of course, a story by John Luther Long in 1898 and a stage success by David Belasco in 1900, long before the opera came along, but by 1932 the drama of a Japanese girl won and deserted by an American naval officer looked merely quaint. Sylvia Sidney's (centre) delicate grace as the geisha, whose breaking heart is stilled by suicide, partly redeemed a long, slow tearjerker. However, Cary Grant (left, who had sky-rocketed in six months from a bit part in Sidney's *Merrily We Go To Hell*) was all at sea as Lieutenant Pinkerton, and director Marion Gering didn't get much out of Charles Ruggles (right), Irving Pichel, Helen Jerome Eddy, Edmund Breese, Louise Carter, Berton Churchill and Sheila Terry. Script by Josephine Lovett and Joseph Moncure March. A similarly ill-advised venture was Mary Pickford's silent version in 1915.

△ Ever anxious to remind the public of the dangers lurking in a big city for innocents tempted by its fleshpots, Hollywood once again presented New York in all its garish glamour in **Two Kinds Of Women**. The innocents this time were a straitlaced Senator (Irving Pichel) accompanied by his unsophisticated daughter (Miriam Hopkins, right, in a casting aberration), visiting Manhattan to launch a radio attack on its morals. Imagine his chagrin when she promptly takes up with a boozy Adonis (Phillips Holmes, left) and is caught with him in a police raid on a speakeasy. Worse still, she has to admit to having been shacked up with the playboy when his wife (Wynne Gibson, centre left) falls to her death from a window and he is accused of pushing her. Never a dull moment in Benjamin Glazer's script, from the Robert E. Sherwood play *This Is New York*, with Stuart Erwin, Claire Dodd, Vivienne Osborne, Stanley Fields, James Crane (centre right), Kent Taylor, Josepine Dunn and Adrienne Ames also cast. William C. de Mille returned to direct it.

◁ Jesse Lasky's last major achievement before being ousted from Paramount was to bring back to the fold his old partner, Cecil B. DeMille, whose productions elsewhere since 1925 (except *King Of Kings*, Pathe, 1927) were decidedly below par. The prodigal's return was approved by Adolph Zukor with the proviso that C.B. must not spend more than $650,000 on the remake of **The Sign Of The Cross**. First filmed in 1914 – and for many years before that a barnstormer around the country – Wilson Barrett's play was perfect DeMille material, floridly depicting the pure love of a Roman virgin (Elissa Landi) for Marcus Superbus (Fredric March, right) who is lusted after by the wicked Poppeia (Claudette Colbert, here with March), wife of Nero (Charles Laughton, seated). Spirit triumphed over flesh, once the latter had filled plenty of footage, and hero joined heroine and other Christians in an arena full of lions, etc. But the baddies were more fun: DeMille dipped the seductive Claudette into asses' milk for his biggest bathtub scene, and allowed Laughton, murmuring 'Delicious debauchery!' to overact gloriously. Ian Keith, Vivian Tobin, Harry Beresford, Ferdinand Gottschalk and Nat Pendleton had other roles in the Waldemar Young-Sidney Buchman screenplay. Completed in eight weeks and inside the budget, it was a spectacular, erotic, and financial success.

▷ Clark Gable (2nd left) was such a blazing new star in 1932 that acquiring him for **No Man Of Her Own** was considered a major coup. It came about when MGM wanted Fredric March to star with Norma Shearer in *Smilin' Through*, and an exchange was negotiated. Gable's potent magnetism had a responsive foil in Carole Lombard (centre), he as a crooked gambler on the run from detectives, she as a wise, big city girl, hiding out as a small town librarian who falls for his advances and marries him. He returns to New York for more easy money, but surrenders to the law when a jealous confederate (Dorothy Mackaill) threatens to expose him. This routine plot by Edmund Goulding and Benjamin Glazer, adapted by Maurine Watkins and Milton Gropper, caught fire from the Gable-Lombard spark, which also ignited a long off-screen fuse leading to marriage seven years later. Others in the Albert Lewis production, directed by Wesley Ruggles, were Grant Mitchell, Tommy Conlon (left), George Barbier (right), Elizabeth Patterson (2nd right) and J. Farrell MacDonald.

△ Seeming to have everything going for it – particularly the talking picture debut of Broadway's legendary star-playwright-producer-songwriter George M. Cohan (left) – **The Phantom President** turned out to be a disaster. Cohan hated Hollywood, his studio co-workers hated him, the public hated the finished film. Actually it wasn't at all bad and there was quite a smattering of praise from the critics, but it grossed less than it cost. In the Walter De Leon-Harlan Thompson screenplay, from a novel by George Worts, the star played a presidential candidate and his look-alike, a singing vendor of quack medicines, hired by political sharpies to impersonate the candidate. Having endured Cohan's bad temper during production, director Norman Taurog and fellow performers Claudette Colbert (centre), Jimmy Durante (right), George Barbier, Sidney Toler and Jameson Thomas weren't sorry that Durante's antics stole the picture. Richard Rodgers and Lorenz Hart provided songs, none of them hits. But five years later they and Cohan had a huge triumph on Broadway with *I'd Rather Be Right* – another presidential musical.

▷ Critics started raving over **Trouble In Paradise** in 1932 and they haven't stopped yet. In fact, its prestige as a masterpiece of sophisticated comedy has increased with the years: when it was released the box-office response was far from sensational, and at Academy Awards time it didn't receive a single nomination. The quintessence of Lubitsch, it displayed the director's talents for smooth narrative, delicate eroticism and visual wit, not to mention his knack of bringing out something special in his actors (he had been one himself, and delighted in acting out every scene on the set). Here they were, velvet-voiced Englishman Herbert Marshall (left) and Miriam Hopkins as a pair of jewel thieves, and Kay Francis (centre) as the wealthy charmer whose fleecing by them is complicated by the man falling in love with her, and his partner taking umbrage. Also given amusing roles: Charles Ruggles (right), Edward Everett Horton, C. Aubrey Smith, Robert Greig and Leonid Kinsky. Samson Raphaelson wrote the script from Grover Jones's adaptation of a play by Aladar Lazlo.

▽ A farce, first staged in Paris as *Pouche* by Rene Peter and Henri Falk, was adapted for Broadway as *Naughty Cinderella* by Avery Hopwood in 1925, and popped up again as a 1932 movie called **This Is The Night**. Lavishly Paramounted, it breezed through a fairly profitable release career, entertained a lot of people and was promptly forgotten by all, except Cary Grant fans: it gave him his first featured role. Billed below Lily Damita, Charles Ruggles, Roland Young and Thelma Todd, he played an Olympics javelin thrower (right) who throws a tantrum when he hears his wife (Todd) is having an affair with another chap (Young). All three men are fascinated by Damita (left) as the action shifts from Paris to Venice and compromising situations multiply madly. Claire Dodd and Irving Bacon were also involved in the script by George Marion Jr (who, with Ralph Rainger, wrote a couple of songs for it too) and Benjamin Glazer, directed by Frank Tuttle.

△ Philip Barry, the playwright whose high comedies (*Holiday*, *The Philadelphia Story*, etc.) made excellent screen material, was less fortunate with **Tomorrow And Tomorrow**, a curious drama which had had fair success on Broadway but was considered by movie fans as a must to avoid. It concerned a woman (Ruth Chatterton, right) whose happiness is impeded by her husband's (Robert Ames, left) unwillingness or inability – it was never clear which – to make her a mother. Becoming ill with emotional deprivation, she consults her doctor (Paul Lukas), whose treatment is more forthright than ethical, and in due course she produces his child. These proceedings, and the ensuing marital consequences, were worked out via exhausting bouts of dialogue in Josephine Lovett's script, enacted also by Tad Alexander, Harold Minjir, Walter Walker and Winter Hall, and directed at a snail's pace by Richard Wallace. Did the studio care if Chatterton had a flop when she was just leaving Paramount for Warners?

△ Paramount finished 1932 on a high note with **A Farewell To Arms.** Ernest Hemingway's bestseller, his first novel to be filmed, had the rich assets of direction by Frank Borzage, a specialist in love stories with a touch of tragedy (Fox's *Seventh Heaven*, 1927, *Three Comrades*, MGM, 1938), and performances of true star quality by Helen Hayes and Gary Cooper (both illustrated). Miss Hayes, one of the great ladies of the American theatre, made several screen appear-

ances during her 70-year career but none more impressive than this one as the English nurse in warswept Italy. Cooper, underacting with feeling, also found rewarding material in the role of an American ambulance officer caught up in a difficult love affair. The Oliver H.P. Garrett-Benjamin Glazer screenplay softened the book's ending, in which the nurse died with her unborn child; no improvement artistically, but pleasing to its big audiences. Adolphe

Menjou stood out in a supporting cast including Jack La Rue, Mary Phillips, Blanche Frederici, Henry Armetta, George Humbert, Mary Forbes and Gilbert Emery, while its technical excellence resulted in Academy Awards for cinematography (Charles B. Lang) and sound recording (Harold C. Lewis). Remakes in 1951, when Warner Bros. called it *Force Of Arms*, and 1957, when David O. Selznick restored its original title, were both failures.

OTHER RELEASES OF 1932

Aren't We All?
Gertrude Lawrence, Hugh Wakefield, Owen Nares. Dir: Harry Lachman. Frederick Lonsdale's comedy about the tangled affairs of an errant husband. (British; remake of *A Kiss In The Dark*, 1925)

The Broken Wing
Lupe Velez, Leo Carrillo, Melvyn Douglas. Dir: Lloyd Corrigan. Mexican village beauty falls for crashed American aviator, enraging the big-shot who loves her and who orders the intruder's execution, but is outwitted.

The Devil Is Driving
Edmund Lowe, Wynne Gibson, Lois Wilson. Dir: Benjamin Stoloff. Mechanic at a big garage discovers it is the centre of a car stealing racket; he avenges the death of his pal, caused by the mob's boss.

Evenings For Sale
Herbert Marshall, Sari Maritza, Charles Ruggles, Mary Boland. Dir: Stuart Walker. In order to make a living for himself and get the girl he loves, a nobleman becomes a gigolo in Vienna and attracts a rich American woman.

Forgotten Commandments
Sari Maritza, Gene Raymond, Marguerite Churchill. Dir: Louis Gasnier, William Schorr. Melodrama of loose morals at a Russian university, with religious motif illustrated by clips from DeMille's *Ten Commandments* (1923).

Lady And Gent
George Bancroft, Wynne Gibson, Charles Starrett, James Gleason. Dir: Stephen Roberts. When his manager is killed, a has-been boxer and his girl, a night club hostess, retire to a small town and rear the manager's son.

Lily Christine
Corinne Griffith, Colin Clive. Dir: Paul L. Stein. Hopelessly in love with a romantic writer, the wife of a dull husband kills herself. (British)

Madame Racketeer (GB The Sporting Widow)
Alison Skipworth, George Raft, Richard Bennett. Dir: Alexander Hall, Harry Wagstaff Gribble. Con-woman emerges from a prison term to sort out her family's problems.

Madison Square Garden
Jack Oakie, Marian Nixon, Thomas Meighan. Dir: Harry Joe Brown. Pro: Charles R. Rogers. Young prizefighter loses a big bout, but he and his friends crush a fight-fixing gang at the Garden.

The Man From Yesterday
Clive Brook, Claudette Colbert, Charles Boyer. Dir: Bethold Viertel. Reported missing, believed killed, a captain returns after the war to find his wife in love with another man; he gives her up.

The Miracle Man
Sylvia Sidney, Chester Morris, Irving Pichel. Dir: Norman Z. McLeod. A gang of grafters recruit an old faith healer, whose powers prove real and who regenerates the crooks. (Remake of 1919 film)

The Misleading Lady
Claudette Colbert, Edmund Lowe, Stuart Erwin. Dir: Stuart Walker. To win a role, an actress demonstrates her vamping technique on an unsuspecting bachelor; he abducts her and they fall in love.

No One Man
Carole Lombard, Ricardo Cortez, Paul Lukas. Dir: Lloyd Corrigan. In Palm Beach a young divorcée can't decide whether to choose a doctor or a playboy. She really loves the former but marries the latter, who dies.

Reserved For Ladies (GB Service For Ladies)
Leslie Howard, Benita Hume. Dir: Alexander Korda. A London waiter offers more than table service and finds true love on the menu. (British; remake of *Service For Ladies*, 1927)

70,000 Witnesses
Phillips Holmes, Dorothy Jordan, Charles Ruggles, John Mack Brown. Dir: Ralph Murphy. Murder mystery in which a football crowd watching a star player race to a touchdown see him tackled by death.

Sinners In The Sun
Carole Lombard, Chester Morris, Alison Skipworth, Cary Grant. Dir: Alexander Hall. Lovers learn that money won't buy happiness when they split up with the idle rich, so they get together again.

The Sky Bride
Richard Arlen, Jack Oakie, Virginia Bruce. Dir: Stephen Roberts. Daredevil in a flying circus loses his nerve after a crash, regains it when rescuing a child from the undercarriage of an airborne plane.

The Strange Case Of Clara Deane
Wynne Gibson, Pat O'Brien, Frances Dee. Dir: Louis Gasnier, Max Marcin. Adopted girl little knows that the dress shop lady who makes her wedding gown is really her mother, an ex-convict.

Thunder Below
Tallulah Bankhead, Charles Bickford, Paul Lukas. Dir: Richard Wallace. While blindness afflicts the boss of an oil crew in the tropics, his wife has an affair with his assistant. Remorseful, she commits suicide.

Undercover Man
George Raft, Nancy Carroll, Gregory Ratoff. Dir: James Flood. Vowing to track down his father's killer, a man becomes an undercover policeman.

The Vanishing Frontier
John Mack Brown, Evalyn Knapp, ZaSu Pitts, Raymond Hatton. Dir: Phil Rosen. Military outlaws plunder the pioneer homesteaders of California before government takes charge.

Wild Horse Mesa
Randolph Scott, Sally Blane, Fred Kohler. Dir: Henry Hathaway. A tamer of wild horses prevents a gang from capturing them with barbed wire. (Remake of 1925 film)

The Wiser Sex
Claudette Colbert, Melvyn Douglas, Lilyan Tashman, Franchot Tone. Dir: Berthold Viertel. Clash between a racketeer and a politician whose fiancée clears him of a framed murder charge. (Remake of *The Woman In The Case*, 1916, and *The Law And The Woman*, 1922)

The World And The Flesh
George Bancroft, Miriam Hopkins. Dir: John Cromwell. Melodrama of a rough seaman, promoted to commisar by the Russian revolution, trying to dominate a proud aristocratic beauty.

1933

▽ Jack Oakie, Jack Haley (left), Ginger Rogers (right), Thelma Todd, Gregory Ratoff, Lew Cody, Hale Hamilton, Jerry Tucker and Walter Walker seemed to be having such a whale of a good time performing in **Sitting Pretty** that the happiness spread to the audience. Directed by Harry Joe Brown, it was produced on the lavish side by Charles R. Rogers, who certainly didn't stint on the creative talent: Nina Wilcox Putnam authored; Jack McGowan, S.J. Perelman and Lou Breslow scripted; Mack Gordon and Harry Revel (who also played bits) wrote nine songs, including the chart-topping 'Did You Ever See A Dream Walking?'. The two Jacks, Oakie and Haley, played songsmiths hitch-hiking from New York to Hollywood and picking up a movie-crazy waitress on the way. The latter was Ginger, then on the verge of her Astaire era. The beautiful Thelma Todd, a 1926 graduate of Paramount's School for Stars, was soon to be the victim of suspected murder, never solved.

△ One or two French oaths must have escaped Maurice Chevalier's lips when he realised that chunks of **A Bedtime Story** were being stolen from him by a supporting actor about 44 years his junior. This was Baby LeRoy (left) who made his debut as an abandoned infant found by a Parisian *bon viveur*, whose fiancée (Gertrude Michael) takes a dim view of his hiring an unemployed showgirl as a live-in nurse-maid. She walks out on him, leaving him to wedding bells with nanny. The latter was charmingly played by Helen Twelvetrees (centre), who wasn't just a pretty name; and Edward Everett Horton, Adrienne Ames,

Earle Foxe, Leah Ray and Henry Kolker had their moments in support of the always entertaining Chevalier (right). His songs (by Ralph Rainger and Leo Robin) weren't up to much in the Emanuel Cohen production, and Norman Taurog's direction dragged a bit in spinning out the Benjamin Glazer-Waldemar Young-Nunnally Johnson treatment of Roy Horniman's *Bellamy The Magnificent*, a different version of which Paramount filmed in 1927 as *A Gentleman Of Paris*. But the main thing was Baby, goo-gooing to an accompaniment of millions of 'Aaahhs' from indulgent and happy customers.

△ If you're thinking of making a movie of **Alice In Wonderland**, don't. People have been aiming cameras at Lewis Carroll's classic time after time, from 1903 (a primitive one-reeler) to 1972 (a British spectacular in Eastmancolor), and always misfired. So don't be too critical of director Norman Z. McLeod, scripters Joseph Mankiewicz and William Cameron Menzies and producer Louis D. Lighton, who combined the 'Wonderland' adventures with a few from 'Through The Looking Glass', staged them in lavish sets, and cast every character with a well-known player. Unfortunately, somebody had the terrible idea of disguising the performers in elaborate masks to make them look like the books' famous Tenniel illustrations; so audiences attracted by the star names never saw the star faces. They resented it. Among those heard (along with a score by Dimitri Tiomkin) but scarcely seen: W.C. Fields, Gary Cooper, Jack Oakie, Edna May Oliver, Cary Grant, Richard Arlen, Louise Fazenda, Charles Ruggles (the March Hare, 2nd left), May Robson, Edward Everett Horton (the Mad Hatter, left), Alison Skipworth, Skeets Gallagher, Baby LeRoy, Polly Moran, Leon Errol, Ned Sparks, Raymond Hatton, and Charlotte Henry (right) as Alice. The spirit of Carroll's fantasy eluded Disney's artists, too, 18 years later.

◁ Bing Crosby followed his successful debut at the studio in *The Big Broadcast* with a cheerful romp through Paramount's second favourite locale, a college (the first: Paris). **College Humor**, named after a popular magazine of the time, provided him with one of his biggest song hits, 'Learn To Croon' by Sam Coslow and Arthur Johnston, and an easy role as a professor of music pursued by a pretty co-ed (Mary Carlisle) who, in turn, is being chased by the campus hero (Richard Arlen). Jack Oakie was on hand with his breezy pal act, while George Burns and Gracie Allen (both illustrated) ran a zany catering service, all three running up a good laugh score. Producer William Le Baron, director Wesley Ruggles and scriptwriters Claude Binyon and Frank Butler didn't forget the obligatory football game climax, either. The fans loved every one of its 80 minutes.

△ *Grand Hotel*, then making a fortune for MGM, inspired **From Hell To Heaven**, which placed its similarly multi-storied screenplay in a far from grand hotel near a racetrack. The interwoven dramas of the guests – horse owners, gamblers and assorted sinners – were held together by radio commentator Jack Oakie (illustrated), whose concluding line echoed the earlier film's: 'People come and go, but nothing ever happens'. Lots of things did happen, including Carole Lombard betting her virtue, such as it was, on a race result with Sidney Blackmer, and crook Bradley Page killing wife Shirley Grey. Also involved were Adrienne Ames, David Manners, Berton Churchill, Rita LaRoy, Verna Hillie, Walter Walker, Cecil Cunningham and, as the innkeepers, Donald Kerr and Nydia Westman. Erle Kenton briskly directed the Sidney Buchman-Percy Heath adaptation of Lawrence Hazard's story.

▽ 'Mae West, billed as a 'muscle dancer',' said *Variety* in 1912, 'sings while making interesting movements in a seated position.' In **She Done Him Wrong**, 21 years later, her gowns were often too tight for sitting, but those movements were still there while she rendered such deathless arias as Rainger and Robin's 'I Like A Guy What Takes His Time' and 'I Wonder Where My Easy Rider's Gone' (by Shelton Brooks). The double meanings in these songs and in the dialogue became single under Mae's outrageous technique, which infuriated blue-noses and sent most of the rest of the population rushing to the box-office.

Lowell Sherman directed this first West (right) starrer in 18 days at a cost of $200,000; it returned over $3 million. Adapted (and somewhat laundered) by Harvey Thew and John Bright from Mae's Broadway play, *Diamond Lil*, it was a fast and funny melodrama centred on an 1890's saloon owned by a crooked politician and dominated by his mistress, who desires the rescue mission man next door. He was the new fan rave, Cary Grant (left), cast with Gilbert Roland, Noah Beery, Rochelle Hudson, Owen Moore, Rafaela Ottiano, Louise Beavers and Fuzzy Knight. William Le Baron produced.

△ **Crime Of The Century** was hardly that, but it presented an ingenious little puzzler in which Jean Hersholt, as a doctor specialising in mental suggestion, confesses to a murder before it is committed – but is he really the guilty party? Both his wife, who has been indulging in extra-marital hankypanky, and one of his patients, a bank clerk who has stolen $100,000, breathe their last before reporter Stuart Erwin solves the mystery. Audiences were invited to beat him to it when the screen went blank for a minute near the end, a novelty which boosted popcorn and ice-cream sales, if nothing else. Wynne Gibson (illustrated), Frances Dee, Samuel S. Hinds, Gordon Westcott, David Landau and William Janney were in the Brian Marlow-Florence Ryerson screenplay, from Walter Espe's play, and William Beaudine directed it.

▷ A superior war aviation drama, **The Eagle And The Hawk** gave Fredric March (right) and Cary Grant (centre) gutsy roles, and Mitchell Leisen, formerly a costume and set designer for DeMille, a chance to cut his directorial teeth as Stuart Walker's associate. March, one of the most gifted actors in Hollywood, was particularly strong as an American ace in the Royal Flying Squadron who gradually becomes unhinged as he watches his comrades crash to their deaths. After flying too many sorties with whiskey as his fuel, he kills himself, but his reputation is saved from the disgrace of suicide by a fellow flyer (Grant) who takes his body up in a plane and crashes it. Carole Lombard (wasted in the brief role of a girl March meets while on leave in London), Jack Oakie, Sir Guy Standing (left), Forrester Harvey and Kenneth Howell were also in the John Monk Saunders story, adapted and given penetrating dialogue by Bogart Rogers and Seton I. Miller.

△ Paramount's latest import from Germany, Dorothea Wieck, had been elevated by *Maedchen In Uniform* to international stardom before she made her American debut in **Cradle Song**. Like the previous year's *Tomorrow And Tomorrow*, this drama dealt with frustration of the maternal instict, and added nothing to the company's prosperity, but otherwise it differed widely. Both the film and its star were sensitive, delicate and poignant. She played a nun (left), secretly longing for a child, delighted when a baby girl is left on the convent steps and, caring for her into adulthood, cherishes the hope that she too will take the veil. But the girl falls in love with a young man and chooses matrimony. Evelyn Venable as the girl (right), Louise Dresser as the prioress, Sir Guy Standing as a doctor and Kent Taylor as the suitor stood out in a fine cast including Gertrude Michael, Gail Patrick, Nydia Westman and Mischa Auer. The playwright Marc Connelly's adaptation of Gregorio Martinez Sierra's Spanish play was scripted by Robert Sparks and Frank Partos. This film established Mitchell Leisen as an important director.

▷ Paramount must be unique in the movie industry for buying a Noel Coward comedy and throwing out all the Coward dialogue. Without that, what is left? In **Design For Living** there remained a frail tale of two men and a girl, all loving each other and living together until she marries a conventional business man, gets bored, and returns to the other two. Even this plot, considered rather shocking in 1933, was altered in Ben Hecht's revision of the play to tone down the *ménage à trois* element. And one of the starring trio was miscast: sophisticated comedy was not Gary Cooper's (left) strong suit. In spite of all that, audiences got a lot of enjoyment out of it, because it had the inestimable asset of Ernst Lubitsch as director and producer, spinning a web of glamour and wit over the proceedings. Fredric March and Miriam Hopkins (right) had the right light touch and adroitly handled Hecht's new dialogue, which retained much of the gaiety if not the bejewelled words of the Master. Edward Everett Horton, Franklin Pangborn, Isabel Jewell, Wyndham Standing and Jane Darwell rounded out the cast.

▷ **Golden Harvest** was a rare attempt to deal, in film drama terms, with the great depression of the early thirties. Wheat was the specific subject; its harvesting maintained in spite of drought, low prices, strikes and stock market finagling. Nina Wilcox Putnam's story illustrating the theme was given solidly convincing treatment by screenwriter Casey Robinson and director Ralph Murphy, with rewarding response from actors Chester Morris, Richard Arlen (left), Julie Haydon (right), Genevieve Tobin, Lawrence Gray, Henry Kolker, Berton Churchill, Richard Carle and Roscoe Ates. The plot concerned two sons of a farmer. Morris goes to make a fortune on the Chicago grain exchange, while Arlen stays to run the farm, struggling to support his family and eventually leading a strike to raise the price of wheat, with disastrous results for Morris. Not a big movie, but one worth making and seeing.

▷ Mae West (illustrated) sashayed through **I'm No Angel**, her best picture, as Sister Honky Tonk, a carnival entertainer with intentions to climb the social ladder, 'wrong by wrong' if necessary. The William Le Baron production had her clearing herself of a murder charge, singing five songs, doing a turn as a lion tamer and setting her sights on Cary Grant. She didn't need a whip and chair to make him sit up and beg, but when it came to matrimony he backed off, so she slapped a million-dollar breach of promise suit on him. Meanwhile Mae was scattering around enough of her devastating one-liners to keep the audience convulsed much of the time, but some of the jokes and situations added fuel to the Legion of Decency's censorship drive. Grant, going West for the second time, and Edward Arnold, as the carnival owner, topped a strong supporting cast: Gertrude Michael, Kent Taylor, Gregory Ratoff, Irving Pichel, Dorothy Peterson, Ralf Harolde, William B. Davidson, Russell Hopton, Nat Pendleton. Wesley Ruggles directed the Lowell Brentano-Harlan Thompson screenplay for which Mae wrote a lot of her own material, as she usually did. Paramount, going through a financial crisis at the time, was grateful for the massive grosses generated by this one.

△ More than any of the other Hollywood giants, Paramount skimmed the cream of Germany's genius for movie making in the 20s and 30s. Besides importing some of the best stars, directors, writers and technicians from Berlin, it did very well with the American distribution of such pictures as *Metropolis*, *Variety*, *The Blue Angel* and **M**. This last, made in 1931, was already an international sensation when its 1933 release in the States held audiences spellbound by the drama of a psychotic child-killer terrorising a city while both the police and the underworld hunt him down. Based on an actual case in Dusseldorf, it combined documentary and expressionist techniques, cunningly woven by the master hand of Fritz Lang, who never did anything better in his 42 years as a director. The previously unknown Peter Lorre (illustrated) soared to stardom as M, the repulsive, frightening and yet pathetic psychopath, mass-murderer of children. He was supported by Ernest Stahl-Nachbaur, Ellen Widmann, Gustav Grundgens and Inge Landgut in the screenplay written by Thea von Harbou with the uncredited collaboration of Lang, her husband.

△ Sylvia Sidney (illustrated) was born to play Theodore Dreiser heroines. Her face, contoured to convey sorrow, was combined again with one of his doom-laden novels in **Jennie Gerhardt** and, as in *An American Tragedy*, she suffered beautifully as a girl beset by poverty and pregnancy. The father of her child having died in an accident before they could marry, she becomes a servant and falls in love with the son of the house (Donald Cook), but his family learn of her past and – but it was all too sad to bear thinking about. It took four scriptwriters – S.K. Lauren, Frank Partos, Josephine Lovett and Joseph Moncure March – to delete Dreiser's social commentaries and retain the tears, which were well and truly extracted by director Marion Gering, Sylvia, and supporting players Edward Arnold, Mary Astor, H.B. Warner, Louise Carter, Theodore von Eltz, Jane Darwell, Frank Reicher and Cora Sue Collins. It was a B.P. Schulberg production.

◁ With Groucho (right) as president, how could the banana republic of Freedonia avoid falling into anarchy? By plunging into war with a neighbouring state, that's how, thus allowing Harpo and Chico (left) the chance to do espionage duty. **Duck Soup** is usually cited as the best of the Marx Brothers comedies, but it was their last at Paramount, and a box-office flop. Their first real hit with mass audiences, *A Night At The Opera* (1935), was made when Irving Thalberg signed them (minus straight man Zeppo) to an MGM contract which yielded five films, equalling their Paramount total. Meanwhile, the 1933 riot, written by Bert Kalmar, Harry Ruby, Nat Perrin and Arthur Sheekman, threw satirical darts at war, politics and patriotism, finishing with a hilarious battle sequence. Kalmar and Ruby also contributed songs, but for once Harpo and Chico omitted their musical solos. On the other hand, Margaret Dumont was back again, inspiring a barrage of glorious insults. Leo McCarey directed, with Raquel Torres, Louis Calhern and Edwin Maxwell in the cast.

△ Resembling something the Marx Brothers forgot to pack when they moved out, the script of **International House** was a totally unhinged comedy which made up in exuberance what it lacked in sense. Top this: W.C. Fields (centre) as an air pilot and professor; George Burns and Gracie Allen as dotty doctor and nurse; Stuart Erwin breaking out in a rash whenever he proposed to luscious Sari Maritza; the much-married Peggy Hopkins Joyce luring Fields to her boudoir; Franklin Pangborn, Lumsden Hare and Bela Lugosi representing various nationalities . . . all let loose in a Chinese hotel, where ancient Oriental inventor Edmund Breese (left) demonstrates a new contraption that shows pictures by radio. Appearing on it were singer Rudy Vallee and bandleader Cab Calloway who, in reality, were still doing so decades later when it was called television. Moviegoers relished this comedy fricassee, garnished with songs and handsomely served by producer Albert Lewis, director Edward Sutherland and writers Lou Heifetz, Neil Brant, Francis Martin and Walter De Leon.

▽ For **The Woman Accused**, *Liberty Magazine* had the idea of commissioning ten well-known authors to write a chapter each of a serial story, without group consultation. The result of this elephantine game of consequences was snapped up by Paramount and assigned to the luckless Nancy Carroll (centre), as an actress whose affair with Cary Grant (right) during a pleasure cruise is interrupted by ex-lover Louis Calhern. He is brained with an Oscar in the ensuing row and his partner, John Halliday (left), accuses Nancy of murder, subjecting her to a shipboard mock trial. She survives this – and actual arrest later – to enjoy a fadeout clinch with Cary. Director Paul Sloane didn't seem to believe all this any more than anyone else, although scripter Bayard Veiller had ably cemented the jigsaw provided by Polan Banks, Rupert Hughes, Vicki Baum, Zane Grey, Vina Delmar, Irvin S. Cobb, Gertrude Atherton, J.P. McEvoy, Ursula Parrott and Sophie Kerr. In the cast: John Lodge, Jack La Rue, Irving Pichel.

◁ Ticket buyers attracted by the names of Claudette Colbert, Fredric March (both illustrated) and author Noel Coward to **Tonight Is Ours** must have wished they'd saved their money. It was a slow, verbose version of *The Queen Was In The Parlour*, always very minor Coward, and badly in need of a Lubitsch sparkle not forthcoming from its co-directors, Stuart Walker and Mitchell Leisen. An assembly of seasoned performers – Alison Skipworth, Paul Cavanagh, Arthur Byron, Ethel Griffies, Warburton Gamble and Clay Clement – spoke their lines nicely in support of the stars in the comedy of a princess (Colbert) who has fallen in love with a commoner (March) in Paris when she is recalled to take her throne. Her lover saves her from an assassin's bullet, and is approved by the revolutionaries as her consort. Edwin Justus Mayer wrote the lacklustre screenplay.

◁ **The Story Of Temple Drake** was credited (if that's the right word) with bringing to the boil a long-simmering campaign against movie violence and, especially, sex. By the following year the Legion of Decency, a censorship board set up by the Catholic church, was in operation, its threat of boycott by millions of the devout having a stronger effect on producers than the industry's old self-regulatory Production Code (the 'Hays Code') had exerted. Mae West's 1933 comedies further spurred the anti-spice enthusiasts, but *Temple Drake* was particularly condemned because its source novel, William Faulkner's *Sanctuary*, had sent waves of shock-horror through the Hays Office, which warned studios against filming it. The story told of a society girl on a roadhouse spree, raped by unnatural means and kidnapped by an impotent degenerate; then enjoying her life of degradation. Paramount got it passed with a toned-down (but still pretty steamy) script by Oliver H.P. Garrett, and was rewarded at the box-office. There was artistic merit, too, in the direction of Stephen Roberts and a stunning performance by Miriam Hopkins (centre), supported by Jack La Rue, William Gargan, Sir Guy Standing, Kent Taylor, Florence Eldridge, William Collier Jr (left), Elizabeth Patterson, Grady Sutton (right), Irving Pichel, Jobyna Howland and Hattie McDaniel. An inferior version was filmed by 20th Century-Fox in 1960 as *Sanctuary*.

▷ Maurice Chevalier (illustrated) followed the Marx Brothers, Nancy Carroll, Buddy Rogers, Clive Brook, Ruth Chatterton, William Powell, Kay Francis and Jeanette MacDonald (who moved over with Chevalier to MGM for *The Merry Widow*) on the 1932–33 list of expired Paramount contracts. He had been the studio's biggest star, but you'd never have guessed it from *The Way To Love*, a ramshackle affair with bits and pieces reminiscent of his earlier movies. As a sandwich-board man in Paris (of course), he found a dog (instead of Baby LeRoy), became a tourist guide, recued a carnival girl from her partner (a jealous knife thrower), fell in love and sang some fair Rainger-Robin songs. After two and a half weeks' shooting, Sylvia Sidney took a walk, and her heroine role went to Ann Dvorak (on loan from Warner Bros.), a fine dramatic actress, here wasted. Norman Taurog directed them, together with Edward Everett Horton, Minna Gombell, Douglass Dumbrille, John Miljan, Arthur Pierson, Nydia Westman, Sidney Toler and Blanche Frederici in the screenplay by producer Benjamin Glazer and Gene Fowler.

▽ B.G. 'Buddy' De Sylva was a triple-talented Mr Show Biz, achieving fame as one of the prolific songwriting team of De Sylva, Brown and Henderson (and portrayed as such by Gordon MacRae in 20th Century-Fox's *The Best Things In Life Are Free*, 1956); a movie-maker who became Paramount's production chief, and a producer of Broadway shows. Wearing the third hat, he presented **Take A Chance**, a 1932–3 hit, which moved straight over to the Astoria sound stages and celluloid, taking with it one of its stars, blonde June Knight, and many of its songs. Also, regrettably, its feeble story about small-timers struggling to rise from carnival to the big time. Monte Brice and Lawrence Schwab wrote it (with De Sylva) and directed it, with its other stage stars, Jack Haley and Ethel Merman, satisfactorily replaced by James Dunn (centre) and Lillian Roth – this was the latter's last movie for the company, her battle with the bottle having already begun. To give it a box-office lift, Buddy Rogers was added to a cast also containing Cliff Edwards, Lillian Bond, Lona Andre, Dorothy Lee and Robert Gleckler. The tuneful score's standouts were 'Eadie Was A Lady' (by B.G. DeSylva, Nacio Herb Brown and Richard A. Whiting) and 'It's Only A Paper Moon' (Harold Arlen, E.Y. Harburg, Billy Rose).

▷ Lots of laughs while **Three-Cornered Moon** was running through the projectors. This early example of the scatty comedies so popular in the thirties came from a play by Gertrude Tonkonogy about a family throwing themselves on the employment market (to their mutual dismay) after the Wall Street crash has eliminated their wealth. It was as delightfully different as the author's name. Claudette Colbert (centre), of the big brown eyes and deft acting technique, led the cast: Richard Arlen (centre with Colbert), Tom Brown (2nd right), Lyda Roberti, Hardie Albright, William Bakewell (right), Joan Marsh, Clara Blandick, Wallace Ford (2nd left), and, best of all, Mary Boland (left) as mother. After decades of Broadway stardom, and an occasional silent film, Miss Boland brightened dozens of movies with her unique comedy style until 1950. Elliott Nugent directed this B.P. Schulberg production, scripted by Ray Harris and S.K. Lauren.

▷ If **Song Of Songs** had a slightly shopworn feel about it, maybe it was because it had already been a novel (Hermann Sudermann), a play (Edward Sheldon), a 1918 movie (with Elsie Ferguson) and a 1924 movie (*Lily Of The Dust* starring Pola Negri). Disappointed with the returns on her last Von Sternberg picture, Paramount gave Marlene Dietrich (illustrated) a new director, the much garlanded Rouben Mamoulian, who lent the Leo Birinski-Samuel Hoffenstein script an elegant air. 'Poor Mr Mamoulian! I gave him a bad time,' said Dietrich later. Ticket-holders didn't have much fun either, as she developed from peasant girl to sculptor's model to cafe singer, and drifted from lover to lover. A woman's work is never done. Brian Aherne (here with Dietrich), Lionel Atwill, Alison Skipworth, Hardie Albright and Helen Freeman nobly supported the star.

◁ Cecil B. DeMille surprised everybody by following *The Sign Of The Cross*, not with one of his similar epics, but with a hard-hitting drama of contemporary American life. **This Day And Age** was a lot less spectacular yet more exciting than many a super-colossal, as it depicted a group of high school students putting their good citizenship lessons into action. Up in arms against crime and corruption, they zero in on a gangster mastermind and bring him to kangaroo court justice. Written by underworld drama specialist Bartlett Cormack, with young Richard Cromwell and bad guy Charles Bickford outstanding in a cast including Judith Allen (centre), Eddie Nugent, Ben Alexander (left), Harry Green, George Barbier, Louise Carter, Bradley Page (right) and Samuel S. Hinds, it was stirring stuff. The company's ad-men, nonplussed by the director's change of style, played safe with 'DeMille's First Great Spectacle of Modern Times!'

▽ **White Woman** didn't fool around with subtleties; it got right down to the nitty-gritty of melodrama from the outset and stayed there. A vagrant blonde plying her trade as an 'entertainer' (Carole Lombard, right) is faced with deportation from Malaya until she is rescued by a marriage proposal from the overseer of a rubber plantation (Charles Laughton). Her gratitude is tempered by repugnance, and he is soon cuckolded by a handsome hired hand (Kent Taylor). The husband relieves his chagrin by slave-driving the native workers, who murder him. Director Stuart Walker kept the cast (including Charles Bickford, left, Percy Kilbride, James Bell, Marc Lawrence, Charles Middleton, Claude King and Ethel Griffies) acting at fever pitch, although Lombard seemed to have costumiers and coiffeurs hidden in the jungle while the men toiled, sweated and forgot to shave. Authors Norman Reilly Raine and Frank Butler, and scripters Samuel Hoffenstein, Jane Loring and Gladys Lehman had evidently been impressed by the play *They Knew What They Wanted*: Laughton and Lombard virtually repeated their roles in its 1940 film version for RKO.

◁ Bing Crosby (centre left) was given full star-billing in his third picture, **Too Much Harmony**, but it was weaker stuff than *The Big Broadcast* and *College Humor*. The fans didn't care, as long as Bing was singing Sam Coslow-Arthur Johnston hits like 'Thanks' and 'Black Moonlight' (in which the chorus girls changed, skin and all, from white to black and back again), and the returns were fine. The story, which had him as a Broadway crooner stranded in the sticks where he discovers a great comedy team in Jack Oakie (right) and Skeets Gallagher (left), was dashed off in a weak moment by Joseph Mankiewicz with dialogue by Harry Ruskin. Judith Allen (centre right) and Lilyan Tashman leading-ladied, and Harry Green, Ned Sparks, Grace Bradley, Kitty Kelly and Billy Bevan supported. Edward Sutherland directed the well-appointed William Le Baron production.

◁ **One Sunday Afternoon** gave playwright James Hagan a Broadway success, and Gary Cooper (illustrated) a vehicle of charm, humour and sentiment in the Grover Jones-William Slavens McNutt screen adaptation. He played a dentist who fails to appreciate his gentle wife (Frances Fuller, here with him), while still dreaming of the belle (Fay Wray) he had once lost to a rival (Neil Hamilton); until the latter pair reappears and he realises he has the right girl after all. Roscoe Karns, Jane Darwell, Clara Blandick and Sam Hardy were other 1910 Brooklyn types in a time and place convincingly suggested by director Stephen Roberts for producer Louis D. Lighton. The rights were sold to Warner Bros. who made a bigger hit of it as *The Strawberry Blonde* in 1941 (James Cagney was better cast than Cooper as the aggressive hero), and a musical version that excited nobody in 1948.

△ The historic first encounter between W.C. Fields (illustrated) and Baby LeRoy occurred in **Tillie And Gus**, a bout in which the younger man won some points but the heavyweight scored a comedy knock-out. Actually, of course, the veteran star was in no danger of picture-stealing by the infant (it was a publicity 'feud') but his leading lady gave formidable competition: British actress Alison Skipworth (illustrated) then seventy, was very funny as a landlady from Alaska joining up with her husband (Fields), a card-sharper from China, to outwit a crook fleecing her niece. All was somehow resolved by a ferryboat race. Not much sense but lots of laughs in the Francis Martin-Walter De Leon screenplay from Rupert Hughes's story, directed by Martin and produced by ex-star Douglas MacLean, with Jacqueline Wells, Clifford Jones, Barton MacLane, George Barbier, Edgar Kennedy and Clarence Wilson in the cast.

▽ Like most of Paramount's ladies, Claudette Colbert (illustrated) had to take a turn as a mother who trips along the primrose path, then takes the road to redemption. In **Torch Singer** (GB: **Broadway Singer**) she negotiated an unlikely detour en route, swerving from nightclub queen to children's auntie on the radio. A resourceful actress, Colbert made you believe in her search for the child she abandons (played variously by one-year-old Baby LeRoy and six-year-old Cora Sue Collins), which occupied most of the soapy script Lenore Coffee and Lynn Starling wrung from Grace Perkins's play *Mike*. Alexander Hall and George Somnes shared directorial duties on the Albert Lewis production, with Ricardo Cortez (illustrated), David Manners, Lyda Roberti, Helen Jerome Eddy, Kathleen Burke, Charley Grapewin and Ethel Griffies in the cast. Of its Rainger-Robin songs, sung by Colbert herself, 'Give Me Liberty Or Give Me Love' was the torchiest.

△ Watching with green eyes the grosses rolling in for the first Johnny Weissmuller *Tarzan* movie, Paramount (which was suffering a bout of jealousy of MGM in 1933) signed up another Olympics swimming champion for **King Of The Jungle** and turned him and an assortment of animals loose in the African section of the backlot. Larry 'Buster' Crabbe (illustrated) went on to play Tarzan himself, Flash Gordon and other muscular types for the next thirty years, but none with more popular success than this hero, who is captured with his lion pals by a circus owner and taken to the States, where he earns enough to buy back his and the lions' freedom. Max Marcin, Philip Wylie and Fred Niblo Jr scripted author Charles Stoneham's work for Bruce Humberstone and Marcin to direct, with Frances Dee, Irving Pichel, Sidney Toler, Douglass Dumbrille, Robert Barrat, Nydia Westman and Warner Richmond in the cast.

OTHER RELEASES OF 1933

Big Executive
Ricardo Cortez, Elizabeth Young, Richard Bennett. Dir: Erle Kenton. When his wife is accidentally killed, a Wall Street broker is accused of murdering her; he is having an affair with another woman.

Billion Dollar Scandal
Robert Armstrong, Constance Cummings, Frank Morgan, Olga Baclanova. Dir: Harry Joe Brown. Pro: Charles R. Rogers. Paroled convict, employed as a financier's masseur, learns secrets of a giant oil stock swindle.

Disgraced
Helen Twelvetrees, Bruce Cabot, Adrienne Ames. Dir: Erle Kenton. Policeman's daughter discovers that her lover is marrying another girl and threatens to kill him, but her father beats her to it.

Gambling Ship
Cary Grant, Benita Hume, Glenda Farrell. Dir: Max Marcin, Louis Gasnier. Melodrama of a gambler getting caught up in the warfare of rival owners of floating casinos and falling for the mistress of one of them.

The Girl In 419
Gloria Stuart, David Manners, James Dunn. Dir: Alexander Hall, George Somnes. Pro: B.P. Schulberg. Two hospital doctors solve the riddle of a girl patient, beaten up by gangsters and refusing to say why.

Girl Without A Room
Marguerite Churchill, Charles Farrell, Charles Ruggles. Dir: Ralph Murphy. Pro: Charles R. Rogers. Comedy of a village lad from Tennessee studying art in Paris with a crowd of Left Bank eccentrics.

He Learned About Women
Stuart Erwin, Alison Skipworth, Susan Fleming. Dir: Lloyd Corrigan. Comedy about an unworldly bookworm who inherits $50,000,000 and is besieged by confidence tricksters of both sexes.

Hell And High Water (GB Cap'n Jericho)
Richard Arlen, Judith Allen, Sir Guy Standing. Dir: Grover Jones, William Slavens McNutt. Adventures of a garbage scow owner with his adopted baby and a girl he saves from drowning.

Hello, Everybody
Kate Smith, Randolph Scott, Sally Blane. Dir: William A. Seiter. By becoming a radio singing star, a farm girl earns enough to vanquish land-grabbers seeking the property of her and her neighbours.

Her Bodyguard
Edward Arnold, Wynne Gibson, Edmund Lowe. Dir: William Beaudine. Millionaire hires a detective to keep rival admirers away from a Broadway beauty; she falls in love with her bodyguard.

Heritage Of The Desert
Randolph Scott, Sally Blane. Dir: Henry Hathaway. Action drama by Zane Grey in which claim-jumping villains are outwitted by a range-rider. (Remake of 1924 film)

His Double Life
Lillian Gish, Roland Young. Dir: Arthur Hopkins, William C. de Mille. Comedy by Arnold Bennett about a reclusive man who enjoys life better as a valet when his own valet dies and is buried under the master's name.

I Love That Man
Nancy Carroll, Edmund Lowe, Robert Armstrong. Dir: Harry Joe Brown. Pro: Charles R. Rogers. Adventurous couple tour the country pulling off confidence tricks, go straight and run into trouble.

Island Of Lost Souls
Charles Laughton, Richard Arlen, Bela Lugosi, Leila Hyams. Dir: Erle Kenton. H.G. Wells's thriller about a shipwreck survivor on an island inhabited by a mad surgeon and the hybrid creatures he has made.

A Lady's Profession
Alison Skipworth, Roland Young, Kent Taylor, Sari Maritza. Dir: Norman Z. McLeod. Pro: Albert Lewis. Lively English dowager helps an impoverished nobleman out of trouble with racketeers.

Luxury Liner
George Brent, Zita Johann, Frank Morgan, Vivienne Osborne. Dir: Lothar Mendes. Triangle drama of wife, husband and other man is climaxed by the latter's murder on a transatlantic liner.

Mama Loves Papa
Mary Boland, Charles Ruggles, Lilyan Tashman. Dir: Norman Z. McLeod. Domestic comedy about an ambitious wife, a temptress, and a furniture salesman who becomes a park commissioner.

Man Of The Forest
Randolph Scott, Harry Carey, Buster Crabbe. Dir: Henry Hathaway. Outdoor melodrama climaxed by a fight between a crooked sheriff and a lion. (Remake of 1926 film)

Midnight Club
Clive Brook, George Raft, Helen Vinson, Alison Skipworth. Dir: Alexander Hall, George Somnes. An ingenious band of thieves set up alibis by planting their doubles at a swank London club while they go to work.

Murders In The Zoo
Randolph Scott, Charles Ruggles, Gail Patrick, Lionel Atwill. Dir: Edward Sutherland. Mad with jealousy, a zoologist kills his wife's lover with snake serum, pushes her into a crocodile pit, and is crushed by a python.

The Mysterious Rider
Kent Taylor, Gail Patrick, Irving Pichel. Dir: Fred Allen. Revised version of Zane Grey's story of homesteaders' struggle against a double-crossing land owner. (Remake of 1927 film)

Pick-Up
George Raft, Sylvia Sidney. Dir: Marion Gering. Pro: B.P. Schulberg. Jailed wife of a convict is released and falls in love with a taxi driver; husband escapes, menaces them.

Song Of The Eagle
Richard Arlen, Mary Brian, Louise Dresser, Charles Bickford. Dir: Ralph Murphy. Pro: Charles R. Rogers. Drama of the struggle between legitimate brewers and the bootlegging gangsters who take over during Prohibition.

Strictly Personal
Marjorie Rambeau, Eddie Quillan, Dorothy Jordan. Dir: Ralph Murphy. Pro: Charles R. Rogers. Crook takes over control of a respectable 'lonely hearts' club, degrades it into a scandalous rendezvous.

The Sunset Pass
Randolph Scott, Tom Keene, Kent Taylor. Dir: Henry Hathaway. Western melodrama about a government agent breaking up a gang; from Zane Grey's story. (Remake of 1929 film)

Supernatural
Carole Lombard, Randolph Scott, Vivienne Osborne. Dir: Victor Halperin. When on the point of killing a fake spiritualist, an heiress possessed by the spirit of an executed murderess comes to, and recovers.

Terror Aboard
Charles Ruggles, Neil Hamilton, Verree Teasdale. Dir: Paul Sloane. Pro: William Le Baron. Thriller about a cruise ship with a diminishing passenger list, which includes a busy killer.

To The Last Man
Randolph Scott, Esther Ralston, Jack La Rue, Noah Beery. Dir: Henry Hathaway. Family feud calmed by young love, after a climactic fight between the villain and the heroine. (Remake of 1923 film)

Under The Tonto Rim
Stuart Erwin, John Lodge, Verna Hillie. Dir: Henry Hathaway. A slow-witted cowboy rises to the challenge of danger, ousts the outlaws, wins the boss's daughter. (Remake of 1928 film)

1934

▷ The company got its 1934 release schedule off to an entertaining but, box-officially speaking, unpromising start with **Four Frightened People**. Again indulging in an uncharacteristically non-epic production, Cecil B. DeMille followed *This Day And Age* with an adventure drama from the novel by British film critic E. Arnot Robertson, adapted by Lenore Coffee and Bartlett Cormack. The four, played by Claudette Colbert, Herbert Marshall (both illustrated), Mary Boland and William Gargan, were frightened by an epidemic of bubonic plague that had broken out in a ship in which they were passengers. They took to a lifeboat, then had to face the terrors of the Malayan jungle before reaching safety. DeMille took his stars on a rugged location trip to one of the wilder Hawaiian islands, where he put them through an ordeal by undergrowth, rocks, water, insects and weather while shooting scenes of their trek — pretty hard on Marshall's artificial leg, Boland's plump middle age and Colbert's weakness from a recent appendectomy. All survived to get excellent reviews. Leo Carrillo, Tetsu Komai, Chris-Pin Martin, Nella Walker and Ethel Griffies filled the minor roles. After this one, DeMille went back to big-scale, big-budget spectaculars for his remaining 22 years.

▽ It had an accomplished cast and an out-of-the-rut story, but **The President Vanishes** (GB: **Strange Conspiracy**) couldn't buck moviegoers' apathy towards political subjects, and the critics were less impressed than they had been by a similar picture, *Gabriel Over The White House*, made the year before at MGM by the same producer, Walter Wanger. Its hero was an isolationist President of the US (Arthur Byron, illustrated) at loggerheads with his pro-war cabinet; he pretends to be kidnapped, to show by the ensuing media uproar how false propaganda can mislead the public. Director William Wellman gave surface force to an unconvincing script by Lynn Starling, Carey Wilson and Cedric Worth, from an anonymous novel generally credited to detective story writer Rex Stout. In the cast: Edward Arnold, Paul Kelly, Rosalind Russell (beginning her 37-year screen career), Charley Grapewin, Peggy Conklin, Osgood Perkins, Janet Beecher, Walter Kingsford, Sidney Blackmer and Edward Ellis.

△ The chief come-on in **Come On, Marines** was a newcomer to the Paramount roster named Ida Lupino. A fluffy 15-year-old with bleached hair and pencilled eyebrows, she had little besides an English accent to distinguish her from dozens of Hollywood blondes, and few could imagine that this descendant of many stage generations would become a powerful dramatic actress and an astute director. Meanwhile, she decorated comedies like this rowdy romp in which the marines rush to the rescue of shipwrecked children, who turn out to be a gaggle of glamour girls. Some fun, eh, boys? Especially as the censorious Production Code wasn't enforced until four months after the movie was released. Richard Arlen led the lads, Ida (left) the gals, including Grace Bradley, Clara Lou (later Ann) Sheridan, Lona Andre and Toby Wing (right). Roscoe Karns, Monte Blue, Colin Tapley, Virginia Hammond and Fuzzy Knight also impersonated a variety of characters in Philip Wylie's story, scripted by Byron Morgan and Joel Sayre, and directed by Henry Hathaway.

▷ More spectacular than Mae West's first two starrers, **Belle Of The Nineties** cost more than both combined, and still reaped a big profit. The story, written by Mae herself, was pretty weak, and the Hays Office had snapped its scissors on some of her best lines (even the original title, *It Ain't No Sin*, was forbidden), but that unique presence, and her command of innuendo which could raise laughs from the most innocuous remarks, kept the movie simmering. So did the superb Duke Ellington and his orchestra, helping Mae (illustrated) through four numbers, notably an Arthur Johnston-Sam Coslow hit, "My Old Flame", but the rest of the cast — Roger Pryor, John Mack Brown (there with Mae), John Miljan, Katherine De Mille, James Donlan, Warren Hymer, Libby Taylor, Benny Baker, Stuart Holmes, Edward Gargan — didn't get much of the spotlight in the tale of a New Orleans singer juggling romances with a boxer and a millionaire while her villainous boss lusts after her. Looking like an upholstered egg-timer, the star was kept on screen front and centre throughout by astute director Leo McCarey in the William Le Baron production.

△ There was a pun in the title of **Kiss And Make Up**: Cary Grant played a celebrated beautician to whom wealthy ladies in Paris flock. He gives extra-special treatment to one client (Genevieve Tobin, with him here) and marries her, only to find that she is really more interested in making herself up than in kissing, so he plays around with other beauties before realising that his plain-jane secretary (Helen Mack) is the right girl for him. Stephen Bekeffi's flimsy comedy was directed by Harlan Thompson, who worked with George Marion Jr and Jane Hinton on the script. Producer B.P. Schulberg swathed it in furs and satins, and drenched it in perfumes and cosmetics to attract the feminine trade, also casting Edward Everett Horton, Mona Maris, Lucien Littlefield, Katherine Williams, Rafael Storm, Doris Lloyd and Henry Armetta in support. The response was negligible.

▷ George Raft, in whose impassive face the eyes flashed danger signals, and Carole Lombard, the embodiment of sophisticated sparkle, blended like whisky and soda in **Bolero**, one of the year's most successful releases. It didn't rely entirely on the potent chemistry of the co-stars (illustrated): they, and director Wesley Ruggles, had a well constructed story (put together by Carey Wilson, Kubec Glasmon and Horace Jackson, from an idea by Ruth Ridenour) to work on. Raft played an ambitious music-hall hoofer who becomes the owner of a smart Paris *boîte*, and loses his dance partner (Lombard) when she snares a rich husband. Time lapse for World War, from which the dancer emerges with a weak heart. At the grand reopening of his club, his new partner turns up too drunk to perform the big number (Ravel's 'Bolero') with him — but who should be in the audience but Carole, ready and able to step in! The subsequent acclaim is so overwhelming that he collapses and dies in his dressing-room ...... Gertrude Michael, William Frawley, Frances Drake, Sally Rand (performing her famous fan dance) and Ray Milland filled out the cast, and crowds filled the theatres.

▷ Fredric March, completing his five-year contract with **Good Dame** (GB: **Good Girl**) got one of those knife-in-the-back farewells the studios often gave departing stars. He was completely miscast as a tough-talking cardsharp in a carnival sideshow, while Sylvia Sidney (illustrated with March) got the star spotlight as a chorus girl with a sophisticated surface and a heart of mush, loving him no matter what. They drifted through the sordid backgrounds and pretty crimes of the William Lipman-Vincent Lawrence-Frank Partos-Sam Hellman screenplay, encountering Jack La Rue, Noel Francis, Russell Hopton, Kathleen Burke, Bradley Page and Walter Brennan on the way, and finishing with an over-sentimental night court wedding scene in which silent star William Farnum (brother of the first Lasky-DeMille hero, Dustin) played the judge. Marion Gering directed the B.P. Schulberg production, a flop.

◁ An excursion into the supernatural took the company to an artistic high point in its 1934 programme. **Death Takes A Holiday** proved that Mitchell Leisen, wielding a strong dramatic sense together with a delicacy of touch, was a valuable addition to the studio's directors' list, on which he would remain for 18 years. The multi-awarded playwright Maxwell Anderson wrote the screenplay with Gladys Lehman and Walter Ferris, basing it on a play by Alberto Casella about the Angel of Death assuming human form. He visits a country house as a mysterious prince, fascinating but frightening all except a girl who falls in love with him, then leaves her family and fiancé in order to accompany him into the unknown. E. Lloyd Sheldon gave this a sumptuous production, and the acting throughout, especially by Fredric March (left) and Evelyn Venable (centre) in the leads, was immaculate. Also: Sir Guy Standing (right), Gail Patrick, Kent Taylor (centre right), Helen Westley, Katherine Alexander, Henry Travers, Kathleen Howard (2nd right), G.P. Huntley Jr.

▽ Cecil B. DeMille returned to the historical (well, sort of) and the spectacular with **Cleopatra**. Although it did not entirely escape the strange hex that has always afflicted pictures about the Queen of the Nile (it wasn't C.B.'s most popular epic by any means), at least it didn't cause financial panic like Rank's *Caesar And Cleopatra* (1945, Vivien Leigh) and 20th-Fox's *Cleopatra* (1963, Elizabeth Taylor). The grandiose, slow-moving pageant, an eyeful if not a mindful, was written by Waldemar Young, Bartlett Cormack and Vincent Lawrence, and staged with the great showman's customary panache. Claudette Colbert (centre), charming, talented and miscast, coped nobly with Caesar (Warren William), Antony (Henry Wilcoxon) and asp. Others on parade: Joseph Schildkraut, Gertrude Michael, C. Aubrey Smith (2nd left), Ian Keith (left), Irving Pichel (right), Claudia Dell, Arthur Hohl, Ian MacLaren.

△ Bing Crosby (illustrated) showed some improvement as an actor in **Here Is My Heart**, although hardly commanding the finesse of Adolphe Menjou in *The Grand Duchess And The Waiter*, of which it was a remake. On the other hand, could Menjou sing? Bing eased some great Ralph Rainger-Leo Robin songs through his velvet pipes, including two best-sellers, 'June In January' and 'With Every Breath I Take', while posing as a waiter to be close to princess Kitty Carlisle. She also sang beguilingly during the Monte Carlo romance produced by Louis D. Lighton and directed by Frank Tuttle in fine style. Roland Young, Alison Skipworth, Reginald Owen, Cecilia Parker, William Frawley and Akim Tamiroff were featured in the Edwin Justus Mayer-Harlan Thompson rewrite of Alfred Savoir's play, and a big public loved it.

◁ A high-octane cast – Fredric March (right), Miriam Hopkins (left), George Raft (centre right), Helen Mack (centre left), William Collier Jr, Nella Walker, Gilbert Emery, Kitty Kelly, Blanche Frederici – sparked some interest in **All Of Me**. They didn't get much help from James Flood's limp direction of a very talky screenplay by Sidney Buchman and actor Thomas Mitchell, from Rose Porter's play *Chrysalis*, which didn't click on stage either. The drama concerned a rich girl (Hopkins) hesitating to marry a teacher (March) while taking an interest as a social worker in a jailed thief (Raft) and his pregnant girlfriend (Mack). She helps the thief escape, but when he kills a cop and, cornered, jumps to his death, followed out of the window by his lover, she is somehow convinced that marrying the teacher is a good idea. Audiences could have told producer Louis D. Lighton that right at the start.

△ **Melody In Spring** was an amiable musical made to cash in on the radio fame of Lanny Ross (centre left). This rather bland young singer was handicapped by a lack of hit numbers (Harlan Thompson and Lewis Gensler composed), only one, 'Ending With A Kiss', measuring up to the standard of songs usually given to Bing Crosby, whose success as a movie star the studio was hoping to duplicate. No such luck. The picture was stolen by Charles Ruggles (left) as a dog-biscuit king determined to thwart Lanny's wooing of his daughter (delightfully played by the piquant Ann Sothern, centre right), and for once he overshadowed his perennial screen wife, Mary Boland (right). Playwright Benn Levy wrote the script, based on a fragile story by Frank Leon Smith, and director Norman Z. McLeod gave it enough charm to fill 75 minutes painlessly. George Meeker, Herman Bing, Norma Mitchell and Thomas Jackson rounded out the cast.

▷ A neat variation on that perpetual winner *Charley's Aunt* was worked by **She Loves Me Not**, in which Princeton undergrads Bing Crosby and Edward Nugent give refuge to nightclub girl Miriam Hopkins (here with Crosby), who is on the run after witnessing a murder. They dress her as a man to fool dean Henry Stephenson and his daughter Kitty Carlisle, who shared with Crosby the above-average songs punctuating the comedy; one of them, 'Love In Bloom' (Rainger and Robin again), became a tremendous disc seller for Bing. The Edward Hope story had been turned into a Broadway success by Howard Lindsay before Benjamin Glazer adapted and produced it as a movie. Like most hits, it was remade: by Paramount as *True To The Army* (1942) and by 20th Century-Fox as *How To Be Very Very Popular* (1955). This version, directed by Elliott Nugent with Lynne Overman, Judith Allen, Ralf Harolde, George Barbier and Henry Kolker cast, was the best.

△ Adapted from a play, *The Great Magoo*, which its authors, Ben Hecht and Gene Fowler, described as 'the romance of a flagpole sitter and his Coney Island doxy, something like 'Romeo and Juliet'' and which expired on Broadway after eleven performances, **Shoot The Works** (GB: **Thank Your Stars**) was not resuscitated by the pell-mell direction of Wesley Ruggles or the performances of Jack Oakie (illustrated), Ben Bernie (his film debut), Dorothy Dell, Arline Judge, Alison Skipworth (illustrated), Paul Cavanagh, Roscoe Karns, William Frawley and Lew Cody. Screenwriter Howard J. Green cleaned up the dialogue but couldn't do much with the ramshackle story of carnival grifters out to make a fast buck in the lower level of show biz, while pursuing their love lives, Oakie with Dell, Karns with Judge. Its one real virtue was 'With My Eyes Wide Open I'm Dreaming', a smash song by Mack Gordon and Harry Revel, sung by Miss Dell, a blonde beauty soon to be killed in a car crash. Cody, prominent on screen for two decades, also died just after the jinxed picture was finished. It was remade with Bob Hope in 1939 as *Some Like It Hot* (no relation to the Curtis-Lemmon hit of 1959).

▷ Critics and customers (who should have been more numerous) were dazzled and thrilled by **Crime Without Passion**, written, produced and directed by Ben Hecht and Charles MacArthur, collaborators on plays and films for many years. Having the Astoria, New York studio practically to themselves they, photographer Lee Garmes, and special effects director Slavko Vorkapich unveiled many striking technical innovations, later widely copied. The moody melodrama concerned an attorney who knows all the angles of criminal law, which comes in handy when, fired by jealousy, he kills his mistress – or so he thinks. Claude Rains (illustrated centre), seen by moviegoers for the first time (he was only heard in *The Invisible Man*), scored brilliantly in the lead, with Margo as his girl, Whitney Bourne, Stanley Ridges, Greta Granstedt and Esther Dale in support.

▷ Damon Runyon's guys and dolls were given a highly entertaining outing by veteran director Marshall Neilan in **The Lemon Drop Kid**, a superior 'B' release which reappeared in a more elaborate production seventeen years later as a Bob Hope vehicle. In this version Lee Tracy (right), who made up in fast-talking, ebullient personality what he may have lacked in conventional good looks, proved to be an ideal Runyon hero as the racetrack tipster getting tangled into trouble with both the underworld and the law before extricating himself for a fade-out embrace with Helen Mack, who was a winning performer herself. Others bringing the Howard J. Green-J.P. McEvoy screenplay to life included Minna Gombell, William Frawley (left), Robert McWade, Henry B. Walthall, Kitty Kelly, Del Henderson, Clarence Wilson and Baby LeRoy.

◁ Planned as a 'B' picture, **Six Of A Kind** developed in the writing, casting and shooting into a humdinger of comedy entertainment. The originally assigned stars, Mary Boland (centre right) and Charles Ruggles – popular as a team throughout the thirties – were joined first by George Burns (right) and Gracie Allen (left), then by W.C. Fields (centre left) and Alison Skipworth, who had teamed in *If I Had A Million* and *Tillie And Gus*. (Burns and Allen, of course, were a duo on stage, screen, radio and TV – and at home for four decades). The dizzy yarn by Keene Thompson and Douglas MacLean, scripted by Walter De Leon and Harry Ruskin, had Ruggles and Boland taking off by car for a California vacation, unaware that they are carrying $50,000 stolen from a bank by Charlie's colleague, who means to hold up the car. But they pick up an exasperating pair, the Burnses, who cause them to change their route, and they aren't stopped until Nevada sheriff Fields, aided by innkeeper Skipworth, arrests them. W.C.'s celebrated pool-table routine delighted audiences; so did the other five farceurs, all of them directed by Leo McCarey with considerable verve.

△ Paramount gave up on Dorothea Wieck after poor box-office returns on *Cradle Song* and **Miss Fane's Baby Is Stolen** (GB: **Kidnapped**) and the lovely actress, too gentle a personality for the time, returned to Germany. The new movie was expected to do well in view of the tremendous and prolonged public interest in the Lindbergh baby kidnap case, but the urgency of suspense somehow failed to communicate itself in Alexander Hall's direction of the Rupert Hughes story, adapted by Jane Storm and scripted by Adela Rogers St Johns. Wieck played a Hollywood star, distraught when her baby is snatched for ransom, and Alice Brady shared top-billing as a farm woman who stumbles on the kidnappers' hideout. William Frawley was a police captain; George Barbier the star's director; Alan Hale, Dorothy Burgess and Jack La Rue were the crooks, and the victim was enacted with panache by the studio's resident infant, Baby LeRoy (here with Wieck).

◁ **Little Miss Marker** (GB: **Girl In Pawn**) pleased the fans, the critics, and the head office accountants with a lively Damon Runyon comedy featuring Adolphe Menjou (left), Dorothy Dell, Charles Bickford, Shirley Temple (right) and Lynne Overman, directed by Alexander Hall. What made this yarn about Runyon's hard-shelled, marshmallow-centred gamblers a big attraction was the tot given fourth billing and destined for the most profitable child stardom of all time. But woe was Paramount! She was under contract to Fox. The studio's own girl getting a star build-up, Dorothy Dell, died in a traffic accident as the film went into release. The B.P. Schulberg production, scripted by William Lipman, Sam Hellman and Gladys Lehman, dealt with a cuteness-proof bookie landed with custody of a delinquent client's daughter, whose father fails to reclaim her. It was remade in 1949 as *Sorrowful Jones*, in 1963 by Universal as *40 Pounds Of Trouble*, and in 1980 (again by Universal) with its original title.

◁ **We're Not Dressing** was a distant descendant, through the *Male And Female* line, of Barrie's *The Admirable Crichton*. One hopes that seeing it did not hasten the onset of Sir James's final illness soon afterwards for, in truth, it was a vulgar, raucous distortion of the author's comedy of social reversal which must, at the very least, have made him wince. On the other hand, it made the average moviegoer (and exhibitor) beam with pleasure as it followed the original storyline – upper class survivors of a shipwreck having to take orders from an underling on a desert island – and gussied it up with gags and musical numbers. The latter scored best, with six Mack Gordon-Harry Revel songs giving Bing Crosby (left), in good voice as the take-charge sailor, one smash, 'Love Thy Neighbor', and two hits, 'May I?' and 'Good Night, Lovely Little Lady'. The comedy was sometimes diverting, sometimes leaden in the hands of Ethel Merman (right, who also sang), Leon Errol, George Burns and Gracie Allen, while Carole Lombard (centre) all disdainful allure, added romantic interest and box-office zip. Ray Milland still in the early days of his long and sometimes illustrious Paramount career, had a small part in the Benjamin Glazer story, scripted by Horace Jackson, Francis Martin and George Marion Jr, and directed by Norman Taurog.

▽ Broadway in the twenties was brightened by three series of lavish revues, Florenz Ziegfeld's 'Follies', George White's 'Scandals' and Earl Carroll's 'Vanities', all three subsequently used for their title values by Hollywood. The first and grandest went to MGM, the second to Fox and the third to Paramount, who benefited from the years of newspaper publicity which Earl Carroll had a remarkable knack for attracting. He was credited as co-author of Murder At The Vanities, with whodunit writer Rufus King supplying the murder element; Carey Wilson, Sam Hellman and Joseph Gollomb scripted, Mitchell Leisen directed and E. Lloyd Sheldon produced it. The plot's victim, Gertrude Michael, was killed while singing a number in celebration of marijuana (served her right, said Purity Coders), and everybody on- and back-stage went through the police wringer of Victor McLaglen (centre left). They included London's Danish star Carl Brisson (left) in the first of his three Paramount pictures, lark-voiced Kitty Carlisle, Jack Oakie (centre right), Dorothy Stickney, Charles Middleton, Jessie Ralph, Gail Patrick, Donald Meek and Clara Lou Sheridan (later to be better known as Ann). Frequently, and fortunately for the box-office, the investigation was interrupted by Duke Ellington and his orchestra, gorgeous gals, superbly staged production numbers, and lots of songs, the big one being 'Cocktails For Two' by Sam Coslow and Arthur Johnston, unmistakably inspired by Tchaikovsky.

▽ Total collapse into side-holding, knee-slapping, button-busting laughter could be observed in every audience watching W.C. Fields in It's A Gift. Devotees of the comedian called it his funniest picture. Jack Cunningham rewrote the story by J.P. McEvoy and Charles Bogle (a pseudonym for Fields), which the star had filmed silent as It's The Old Army Game in 1926, about a small town shopkeeper. Now, as then, it was really just a string of gags and situations perfected by Fields in his decades of vaudeville, Ziegfeld Follies and movie shorts, including the classic porch scene in which his sleep is frustrated by wife, telephone, neighbours and milk bottles. The rosy-nosed comic pulled off rare feats in (a) preventing Baby LeRoy (here with him) from stealing any scenes and (b) using a blind man as a laugh-raising character. Kathleen Howard (great as the wife), Jean Rouverol, Julian Madison, Tommy Bupp, Diana Lewis, T. Roy Barnes and Charles Sellon supported, and Norman Z. McLeod directed briskly. William Le Baron's low-budget production earned a useful profit.

△ Mrs Wiggs Of The Cabbage Patch dates right back to 1901, when Alice Hegan Rice's novel found an eager public. Three years later it again reached high popularity when playwright Anne Crawford Flexner put the smiling-through-tears Mrs W and her brood of shantytown children on the Broadway stage. Paramount, knowing a sure box-office bet when it saw one, bought it and eventually filmed it three times, in 1919, 1934 and 1942. The middle version was best because, after an hour of looking at poverty through rose-coloured glasses, the picture did an amazing switch to

△ W.C. Fields fans had a field day when The Old-Fashioned Way came around. Their bibulous hero was both author (under his nom de plume, Charles Bogle) and star of this saga of a pre-war theatrical troupe keeping one jump ahead of the sheriff while its leader, The Great McGonigle, worms his way out of unpaid bills, deals with his daughter's romance, placates his temperamental Thespians, takes a few sideswipes at Baby LeRoy (here with him), and juggles. Interpolated into the Jack Cunningham-Garnett Weston script were elements of the old Fields vehicle, Poppy, a scene from the famous barnstormer The Drunkard and a ballad called 'A Little Bit Of Heaven Known As Mother'. Judith Allen and Joe Morrison supplied love interest; Jan Duggan, Nora Cecil, Jack Mulhall, Del Henderson, Clarence Wilson, Richard Carle and Otis Harlan added character comedy to the William Le Baron production, directed by William Beaudine.

red-hot romance: the screen smouldered with the arrival of W.C. Fields (centre), the mere sight of whom caused ZaSu Pitts (right) to fling aside all maidenly reserve and begin a fervent wooing. Norman Taurog directed them, as well as Pauline Lord, a stage star doing fine work in the title role, Evelyn Venable, Kent Taylor, Donald Meek, and the kids: Edith Fellows (left), Jimmy Butler, George Breakston, Virginia Weidler. The pre-sound comedy star, Douglas MacLean, produced the screenplay by William Slavens McNutt and Jane Storm.

▽ One of the great curiosities of the screen: The Scarlet Empress, Josef von Sternberg's ultimate apotheosis of Marlene Dietrich (left) as a glamour goddess, swathed in furs and tulles, bathed in Sternbergian lighting and cosseted in Bert Glennon's soft-focus photography. The historical romance contrived by Manuel Komroff had Dietrich running around enormous rococo sets as the young Catherine of Russia, pursued by her demented bridegroom, the Grand Duke Peter (Sam Jaffe, looking disconcertingly like Harpo Marx); dominated by the formidable empress Elizabeth (Louise Dresser, 2nd right), and adored by the handsome Count Alexei (John Lodge—2nd left – who gave up movie stardom to become Governor of Connecticut and US Ambassador to Spain and Argentina). They – and C. Aubrey Smith, Olive Tell (kneeling), Gavin Gordon, Jameson Thomas, Jane Darwell, Edward Van Sloan and Maria Sieber (Dietrich's daughter) – were subordinated to the star, and to the decor (featuring astonishing gargoyles) of art director Hans Dreier and designers Peter Ballbusch and Richard Kollorsg. Having its release just preceded by that of Korda's Catherine The Great didn't help at the box-office, where activity kept strict tempo with the film's deadly slow narrative.

▽ **Now And Forever** brought Henry Hathaway to the big time after years of apprenticeship as assistant director, then director of Paramount westerns and a low-budget remake of *The Witching Hour*. He would be making pictures for the next forty years, generally with more inspiration than he displayed in this routine drama, which was boosted to importance by its cast: Gary Cooper, Carole Lombard, Shirley Temple (here with Cooper), Sir Guy Standing, Charlotte Granville, Gilbert Emery, Akim Tamiroff, Jameson Thomas and Henry Kolker. The Louis D. Lighton production had a workmanlike script by Sylvia Thalberg (Irving's sister) and Vincent Lawrence, from a Jack Kirkland-Melville Baker original, tailored to suit Cooper as a con-man who steals Granville's jewels and hides them in the teddy bear of Shirley, his daughter. She finds them; Dad's mistress, Lombard, takes the blame; he lets their rich owner adopt the kid. Neither Gary nor Carole sparkled, doubtless aware that the big attraction was 6-year-old Shirley, who went on from here to keep the wolf from Fox's door.

△ A melodrama of the old dark house variety, designed by playwright Elizabeth McFadden to make the customers shudder, **Double Door** had quite a healthy run on Broadway. So set on duplicating this 1933 success was Paramount that it promptly signed Mary Morris (right – not to be confused with the British actress of similar sinister roles) and Anne Revere (film debut) from its cast, and virtually photographed it as it stood. The theatrical contrivances piled up, and sometimes toppled into unintended comedy as its villainess (Morris) tyrannised her half-brother (Kent Taylor), a noble fellow but a bit of a drip, and his demure, long-suffering bride (Evelyn Venable, left) in a pre-Great War New York mansion equipped with a sound-proof torture chamber and decorated with urns containing the ashes of long-gone relatives. Sir Guy Standing, Colin Tapley and Halliwell Hobbes kept straight faces while acting out the Gladys Lehman-Jack Cunningham screenplay for director Charles Vidor.

▽ Fun at the expense of Puritan traditions in 18th-century New England had provided the Theatre Guild with an unexpected New York hit in **The Pursuit Of Happiness**, and its film version began the long Paramount contract of producer Arthur Hornblow Jr. He and director Alexander Hall dressed it charmingly in period and gave it a delightful cast, headed by Francis Lederer and Joan Bennett (both illustrated) but predictably dominated by Charles Ruggles and Mary Boland as Joan's parents, shocked when she is caught bundling with Lederer, a young deserter in the War of Independence. 'Bundling' was a quaint custom in which courting couples shared a bed equipped with a centre board keeping them apart. It was frustrating for the box-office too: the returns were most disappointing. Minor Watson, Walter Kingsford, Barbara Barondess, Henry Mowbray, Holmes Herbert and Colin Tapley were in the Jack Cunningham-J.P. McEvoy-Stephen M. Avery-Virginia Van Upp screen adaptation of the stage play by Lawrence Langner and Armina Marshall.

OTHER RELEASES OF 1934

College Rhythm
Jack Oakie, Lyda Roberti, Joe Penner, Lanny Ross, Helen Mack. Dir: Norman Taurog. Musical about rivalry between two collegians that continues after they graduate. Song hit: 'Stay As Sweet As You Are'.

Eight Girls In A Boat
Douglass Montgomery, Dorothy Wilson, Kay Johnson. Dir: Richard Wallace. Pro: Charles R. Rogers. At a continental finishing school, one of the girls becomes pregnant and attempts suicide.

Elmer And Elsie
George Bancroft, Frances Fuller. Dir: Gilbert Pratt. Comedy about a truck-driver who believes women must be subservient; but it's his wife's ideas that push him to success. (Remake of *To The Ladies*, 1923)

The Great Flirtation
Elissa Landi, Adolphe Menjou, David Manners. Dir: Ralph Murphy. The marital and professional vicissitudes of Viennese stage stars on Broadway culminate in separation when the wife falls for a playwright.

Here Comes The Groom
Jack Haley, Mary Boland, Neil Hamilton, Patricia Ellis. Dir: Edward Sedgwick. To help an heiress out of a romantic escapade, a goofy bachelor poses as her husband and gets involved in the theft of her mother's jewels.

Ladies Should Listen
Cary Grant, Frances Drake, Edward Everett Horton. Dir: Frank Tuttle. Pro: Douglas MacLean. The affairs of a young man about town are complicated by his switchboard operator, secretly in love with him.

The Last Round-Up
Randolph Scott, Barbara Fritchie, Fred Kohler. Dir: Henry Hathaway. The leader of a gang of cattle rustlers sacrifices his life to save a pair of young lovers. (Remake of *The Border Legion*, 1924, 1930)

Limehouse Blues
George Raft, Jean Parker, Anna May Wong, Kent Taylor. Dir: Alexander Hall. Half-caste gang leader in London falls in love with his underworld rival's daughter; a jealous Chinese girl betrays him to the police.

Lone Cowboy
Jackie Cooper, Lila Lee, John Wray, Addison Richards. Dir: Paul Sloane. An orphan from Chicago goes west to live with his uncle and gets caught up in the latter's search for his wife and the man she ran away with.

Many Happy Returns
George Burns, Gracie Allen, Guy Lombardo and His Orchestra. Dir: Norman Z. McLeod. Musical comedy in which George is bribed by her father to marry Gracie, whose dizzy ideas wreck a department store and a movie studio.

Menace
Gertrude Michael, Paul Cavanagh, Henrietta Crosman, John Lodge, Ray Milland. Dir: Ralph Murphy. Thriller about three people hounded by a maniac who wrongly holds them responsible for his brother's death.

No More Women
Edmund Lowe, Victor McLaglen, Sally Blane. Dir: Albert Rogell. Rowdy rivals over girls and under water, two deep-sea divers co-operate long enough to salvage $2 million in sunken gold.

The Notorious Sophie Lang
Gertrude Michael, Paul Cavanagh, Alison Skipworth, Leon Errol. Dir: Ralph Murphy. Police chief sets a visiting English crook to catch America's queen of jewel thieves, but they join forces and escape.

Private Scandal
Phillips Holmes, Mary Brian, ZaSu Pitts, Ned Sparks. Dir: Ralph Murphy. The office staff of an embezzling financier are thrown into a turmoil when he is found dead, apparently a suicide; but it is murder.

Ready For Love
Richard Arlen, Ida Lupino, Marjorie Rambeau. Dir: Marion Gering. An innocent girl's escapade gets her branded as a scarlet woman by small-town gossips; she is rescued from a vigilante attack by the local editor.

The Search For Beauty
Buster Crabbe, Ida Lupino, Robert Armstrong, Gertrude Michael. Dir: Erle Kenton. The male and female Olympic swimming champions are deluded into becoming fronts for get-rich-quick promoters.

She Made Her Bed
Richard Arlen, Sally Eilers, Robert Armstrong. Dir: Ralph Murphy. The lives of a fairground owner and his wife are complicated by romantic interlopers, a baby, an escaped tiger and a disastrous fire.

Thirty-Day Princess
Sylvia Sidney, Cary Grant, Edward Arnold. Dir: Marion Gering. Pro: B.P. Schulberg. Unsuccessful actress scores a hit with a young newspaper owner when she is hired to impersonate a visiting princess.

The Thundering Herd
Randolph Scott, Judith Allen, Noah Beery. Dir: Henry Hathaway. Drama of buffalo hunters versus Indians, climaxed by a stampede across a frozen lake. (Remake of 1925 film)

The Trumpet Blows
George Raft, Adolphe Menjou, Frances Drake. Dir: Stephen Roberts. Melodrama set in Mexico about two brothers, one a bandit, the other a bullfighter.

Wagon Wheels
Randolph Scott, Gail Patrick, Monte Blue. Dir: Charles Barton. Wagons heading westward, led by a fugitive from justice, are attacked by Indians. (Remake of *Fighting Caravans*, 1931)

Wharf Angel
Victor McLaglen, Dorothy Dell, Preston Foster, Alison Skipworth. Dir: William Cameron Menzies, George Somnes. Pro: Albert Lewis. A man evading the police finds love and friendship in the toughest joint on San Francisco's waterfront.

The Witching Hour
Sir Guy Standing, John Halliday, Judith Allen, Tom Brown. Dir: Henry Hathaway. Pro: Bayard Veiller. Young man on trial for murder is acquitted because he did it under hypnotism. (Remake of 1921 film)

You Belong To Me
Lee Tracy, Helen Morgan. Dir: Alfred Werker. The little son of a vaudeville couple is adopted by a comedian and a famous singer.

You're Telling Me
W.C. Fields, Joan Marsh, Buster Crabbe, Adrienne Ames. Dir: Erle Kenton. Comedy of an unsuccessful inventor who gains prestige among fellow small-towners when a glamorous visitor calls. (Remake of *So's Your Old Man*, 1926)

1935

▷ 1935 got off to a splendid start for Paramount with **Lives Of A Bengal Lancer**, a rousing action drama with Gary Cooper (left) as a seasoned officer in India taking two newcomers from England under his wing. One of them is the son of their commanding officer and, during their adventures in the tribal conflict on the Northwest Frontier, he is captured. Trying to rescue him, the other two are caught and all three tortured before making their escape. Richard Cromwell (2nd right) as the youth, Franchot Tone (right) and Cooper made a fine gung-ho trio, with Sir Guy Standing impressive as the father, and sturdy support from C. Aubrey Smith, Monte Blue, Kathleen Burke, Akim Tamiroff, J. Carrol Naish, Douglass Dumbrille and Colin Tapley. Director Henry Hathaway paced the big action sequences for maximum excitement and leavened them with humour, notably in a snake-charming scene; Ernest B. Schoedsack collaborated with some spectacular Indian footage. Producer Louis D. Lighton used writers in droves to picturize Francis Yeats-Brown's book, final credits going to Grover Jones, William Slavens McNutt, Achmed Abdullah, Waldemar Young and John Balderston. No problem with box-office credits – this became one of the company's biggest grossers to date.

▽ Not an unbitten nail in the house as the suspense mounted in **Four Hours To Kill**. Richard Barthelmess (left), back at Paramount after sixteen years and still a star, played a criminal who gets away from the cop taking him to jail, long enough to kill the man whose betrayal has convicted him. Charles Wilson as the cop and Noel Madison as the double-crosser matched the star's strong performance in this central story. Meanwhile, several sub-plots were involving Gertrude Michael, Ray Milland, Joe Morrison, Helen Mack (right), Dorothy Tree, Henry Travers, Roscoe Karns and Olive Tell in Norman Krasna's adaptation of his play, *Small Miracle*, which used the *Grand Hotel* formula of separate stories in one setting, this time the lobby and auditorium of a New York theatre. It was the first success of the director-producer team of Mitchell Leisen and Arthur Hornblow Jr.

△ The returns on *Bolero* were in, and so good that Paramount not only gave **Rumba** the same co-stars, George Raft and Carole Lombard (both illustrated), and a similar title, but some of the same plot. Naturally, it took two authors (Guy Endore, Seena Owen) and three screenwriters (Howard J. Green, Harry Ruskin, Frank Partos) to come up with the idea of dancer Raft meeting heiress Lombard when they win a Cuban lottery with duplicated tickets, and to have Raft's life supposedly threatened by New York gangsters. But they only needed good memories to make Raft's partner refuse to go on at the Broadway opening, whereupon Lombard could come to the rescue and step in to dance the big number with him as the climax. Numbed by a sense of *déja vu*, audiences gave an apathetic reception to William Le Baron's production, directed by Marion Gering, with Lynne Overman, Margo (centre with Raft), Monroe Owsley, Gail Patrick, Iris Adrian, Samuel S. Hinds, Akim Tamiroff and Virginia Hammond also cast.

▷ A major crowd-magnet of the year was the combination of Bing Crosby and W.C. Fields in **Mississippi**, a musical version of Booth Tarkington's *Magnolia*, one of the studio's favourite stories. First filmed silent in 1924 as *The Fighting Coward*, it was reworked in 1929 as *River Of Romance*, a Buddy Rogers talkie. Here Bing, as an avoider of duels and thus a social outcast in the Old South, joins a show boat skippered by W.C., redeems his reputation, and wins Joan Bennett (here with Bing). Along the way, he wrapped his velvet voice around a superb Rodgers and Hart score including "Soon", "Down By The River" and "It's Easy To Remember (So Hard To Forget)". The Fields high spot was a convulsing poker game during which he somehow drew five aces. Edward Sutherland directed Arthur Hornblow Jr's production, scripted by Claude Binyon, Herbert Fields, Jack Cunningham and Francis Martin, and featuring Gail Patrick, Queenie Smith, John Miljan, Fred Kohler and Claude Gillingwater.

△ Phyllis Bottome's then widely read novel **Private Worlds** became absorbing movie drama in the hands of expert professionals Gregory La Cava (director), Walter Wanger (producer), and Lynn Starling (screenwriter). Claudette Colbert and Charles Boyer (both illustrated) performed in compelling style as two of the doctors in a mental institution, where staff members strive to keep their own emotional entanglements from affecting their patients' problems. Intelligent, romantic and rather solemn, it scored on novelty as well as cast strength (Joel McCrea, Joan Bennett, Helen Vinson, Esther Dale, Samuel S. Hinds and Guinn Williams were also in it) at a time when hospitals and psychiatry had not yet become commonplace on screen and television.

▷ **Enter Madame**, a huge hit on Broadway back in 1920, resurfaced on the screen fifteen years later with the serenely composed Elissa Landi (right) somewhat oddly cast as its wildly temperamental opera-star heroine. Somewhat flummoxed by being required to sing (Nina Koshetz dubbed for her) and throw tantrums (for which she should have had another double), Elissa settled for looking lovely (which no one could have done better), while Cary Grant (left) suffered amusingly as the husband ranking third in importance to her, after her career and her mad entourage. Elliott Nugent directed at a fast pace, wasting no time on subtleties, but the Charles Brackett-Gladys Lehman screenplay still seemed too long. Benjamin Glazer produced this version, a box-office dud, off the play by Gilda Varesi (its star on the stage) and Dorothea Donn-Byrne. Lynne Overman, Frank Albertson, Paul Porcasi, Sharon Lynne and Cecilia Parker were featured.

◁ **Goin' To Town** didn't startle Mae West's fans by straying far from her usual story of an ambitious working girl rising from rhinestones to diamonds, and it took pains not to shock censorship groups too much. Of course, Mae could no more be separated from sexual insinuation than Donald Duck from his quack, but her shafts of wit were now toned down from the outrageous to the merely naughty, and the audience reaction to the film was similarly subdued. It made plenty of money, though, and so did Mae (centre). Her 1935 income reached $480,000 (which made her America's most highly paid woman), studio chief Emanuel Cohen having formed a separate West unit called Major Pictures. Later that year it was discovered that he had signed her and other Paramount stars to new contracts with himself instead of the company, which took a poor view of the idea. Meanwhile, theatres prospered with this William Le Baron production from a script West wrote (based on a story by Marion Morgan and George Dowell) about a saloon singer who inherits a ranch, strikes oil and crashes high society in pursuit of a husband and respectability. Mae extended her vocal range to the big aria, or an approximation thereof, from Saint-Saëns's "Samson and Delilah", but seemed more at home with "He's A Bad, Bad Man But He's Good Enough For Me" by Sammy Fain and Irving Kahal. Alexander Hall directed her, Paul Cavanagh, Ivan Lebedeff, Tito Coral, Marjorie Gateson, Fred Kohler, Gilbert Emery, Monroe Owsley, Grant Withers, Luis Alberni and Adrienne d'Ambricourt.

◁ Asked by an interviewer which of her films she liked best, Marlene Dietrich once said, "**The Devil Is A Woman**, because it made me look so beautiful". Either she was kidding, or proving again that beauty is in the eye of the beholder. Elaborately coiffed and loaded with enough make-up to clear out Max Factor's shelves, she was brought close to the edge of absurdity, her usual loveliness disguised by director Josef von Sternberg's exaggerated treatment. (This is a minority opinion among Dietrich addicts, many of whom rate the movie highly.) It was the star's last picture under Von Sternberg's guidance, and its box-office failure ended his eight-year stay at the studio. A remake of a 1920 breast-heaver starring Geraldine Farrar, *The Woman And The Puppet*, the Pierre Louÿs story was set in 1890 Seville, where a *femme fatale* drove one man after another mad with desire before she ruined them. The great American author of sociological and political novels, John Dos Passos, was selected to write the script, presumably because of his Spanish name. Not a good idea. The star's new leading man, Cesar Romero, had 40 film years ahead of him; Lionel Atwill (here with Dietrich), Alison Skipworth, Edward Everett Horton, Don Alvarado and Lawrence Grant were also featured; but the best credits were those of cinematographers Lucien Ballard and Von Sternberg and art director Hans Dreier for the atmospheric magnificence they achieved. Two more remakes, both French: *The Female* (1958; aka *A Woman Like Satan*), and *That Obscure Object Of Desire* (1977).

△ A fat budget was lavished on a handsome but unexciting picturization of Stark Young's novel, **So Red The Rose**, which dealt in mildly pleasing fashion with the romantic and domestic travails of a Southern family during the Civil War. (This film's commercial failure made Hollywood wiseacres refer to *Gone With The Wind*, while in production, as 'Selznick's Folly'; later they wished they hadn't.) A trio of eminent playwrights, Lawrence Stallings, Maxwell Anderson and Edwin Justus Mayer wrote the script, and it was directed by one of the screen's giants, King Vidor (who didn't mention it in his autobiography), but the only lasting impressions were made by Victor Milner's camera work and the tender performance (as a Dixie belle pining for her soldier's return) of Margaret Sullavan (left), borrowed from Universal, where her husky voice and quicksilver personality had made her famous. The Douglas MacLean production also featured Randolph Scott (right), Walter Connolly, Robert Cummings, Janet Beecher, Elizabeth Patterson, Dickie Moore (centre), Charles Starrett, Johnny Downs, Daniel Haynes and Clarence Muse. "So red the ink", muttered Paramount's put-upon and disgruntled bookkeepers.

▽ Paramount sent George Raft (right) out on two 1935 dance band gigs — in movies. The first, *Stolen Harmony*, wasn't anything to hit the cymbals about, but **Every Night At Eight** was a jolly affair with plenty of laughs and songs in the course of a totally forgettable story. Today, one dimly recalls something about three factory girls being turned into a famous singing trio by radio bandleader Raft. But still vivid in the memory are the creamy voices of Alice Faye (2nd left) and Frances Langford (left) singing, respectively, "I Feel A Song Coming On" (by Dorothy Fields, Jimmy McHugh and George Oppenheimer) and "I'm In The Mood For Love" (Fields, McHugh), both of which became enduring standards. Alice, borrowed from Fox for her only film on this lot, and Frances, making her screen debut, had both been band singers, but Patsy Kelly's (3rd left) presence in the trio had no musical reason; she was just a marvellous comedienne. Walter Catlett, Herman Bing, Harry Barris and The Three Radio Rogues were also in it, and it had off-screen man power in director Raoul Walsh, producer Walter Wanger, and writers Gene Towne and Graham Baker, who adapted Stanley Garvey's story *Three On A Mike*.

◁ Ranking high among her hard-done-by heroine performances, Sylvia Sidney's **Mary Burns, Fugitive** won her a flock of good reviews and increased box-office stature. The Walter Wanger production was a disturbing crime thriller, so strongly written (by Gene Towne, Graham Baker and Louis Stevens) and directed (by William K. Howard) that audiences shared Sylvia's anguish when, as a law-abiding cafe owner who becomes infatuated with a gangster, she (right) is dragged down to his criminal level, arrested and convicted; then escapes from prison to lead the police to her lethal lover. Melvyn Douglas co-starred as the girl's faithful friend, a blind chemist who had little to do but stand by, ready for the fade-out clinch; Pert Kelton, Brian Donlevy (left), Wallace Ford, Frank Sully and Charles Waldron supported. The most striking performer in the cast, however, even overshadowing Sylvia in their scenes together, was Alan Baxter as the public enemy, a memorable portrayal of understated menace – indeed, Paramount would have had a new star if George Raft had not already been on the payroll but, in the event, Baxter had to settle for 35 years of secondary Raft-like roles.

△ Sylvia Sidney took a holiday from her usual gloom in **Accent On Youth** with the part that had given Constance Cummings a Broadway hit in 1934: a young secretary deciding she prefers older men, particularly her employer, a successful playwright. Since he was played by Herbert Marshall (here with Sylvia), dictating in the most mellifluous voice in the business, you could understand her preference and see how it could complicate both their love lives. Although it occasionally reminded one of the all-talk, no-action movies of five or six years earlier when sound was the big attraction, Douglas MacLean's production did move smoothly and had a script by Claude Binyon neatly developing Samson Raphaelson's play. Phillip Reed, Catherine Doucet, Astrid Allwyn, Holmes Herbert, Ernest Cossart, Donald Meek, Dick Foran, Lon Chaney Jr and Samuel S. Hinds were in the cast directed by Wesley Ruggles. Paramount remade it twice, as *Mr Music* in 1950 and *But Not For Me* in 1959.

◁ George Raft returned to the underworld of big-city crime and corruption, in which he had first caught the public's attention, in **The Glass Key**. Dashiell Hammett's best-seller, written in his brisk, objective style with an abundance of plot, action and snappy dialogue, made perfect movie material for whodunit addicts. Raft (left) played the lieutenant of a political boss (Edward Arnold) who comes under suspicion, along with an assortment of shady types, when a senator's son (Ray Milland, right) is found murdered. Emerging from a series of attacks, tortures and confrontations with other suspects, Raft proves that the senator killed his son in a rage, which had no more to do with the rest of the story than its unexplained title. Director Frank Tuttle, producer E. Lloyd Sheldon, scripters Kubec Glasmon, Kathryn Scola and Harry Ruskin, and actors Charles Richman, Claire Dodd, Guinn Williams, Robert Gleckler and Emma Dunn contributed to a fluent money-maker.

◁ A fortune-hunting manicurist and a playboy on his uppers touched **Hands Across The Table**, and a hit was born. They were Carole Lombard and Fred MacMurray (both illustrated), a delightfully well-blended team in the Vina Delmar story, given a sparkling Norman Krasna-Vincent Lawrence-Herbert Fields screenplay in which the pair followed the manicure with a romantic fling and enjoyed it so much that they ditched their prospective spouses and stayed together forever. Ralph Bellamy and Astrid Allwyn played the wealthy but comparatively dull rejects, with Ruth Donnelly, Marie Prevost, William Demarest and Herman Bing also in a cast directed with style and sparkle by Mitchell Leisen. This highly praised and profitable picture established Leisen as a comedy director of distinction; although it was produced by E. Lloyd Sheldon, the influence of Ernst Lubitsch (studio head at the time) was clearly discernible. It also boosted Lombard to the top echelon of Paramount stars, and pointed the way to MacMurray's long and successful career.

▷ By 1935 only Jeanette MacDonald and Nelson Eddy could get away with the outmoded theatricalities of operetta. Carl Brisson and Mary Ellis (both illustrated) gave it a good try, but **All The King's Horses** and all Paramount's men couldn't put a winner together again from an old play by Max Giersberg and Lawrence Clark, turned into a stage musical by Frederick Herendeen and Edward Horan. Now it was rewritten by Frank Tuttle (who also directed) and Frederick Stephani, and recomposed by Sam Coslow, whose song 'A Little White Gardenia' was its single profitable item, although dance director Leroy Prinz did get an Oscar nomination for his big waltz number. The stars, charmers who never caught on in Hollywood, played out a Ruritanian romance about a movie actor impersonating a king which left audiences heavy-lidded with boredom. Edward Everett Horton, Katherine De Mille, Eugene Pallette, Edwin Maxwell and Arnold Korff were also in the William Le Baron production.

△ It looked like just another western, and a pretty small one at that, by Paramount standards – but what a goldmine **Hop-A-Long Cassidy** turned out to be! The character created by Clarence Mulford in 1912 and sustained through a couple of dozen novels was brought to the screen by producer Harry Sherman in 1935 with William Boyd featured. In pictures since 1919, often directed by Cecil B. DeMille, Boyd (illustrated) was no cowboy, but he learned fast and soon became permanently identified as Hopalong (the hyphens were removed after the first movie) by millions of fans. The good-natured, non-smoking, non-drinking hero's adventures, long on human interest, short on violence, were specially popular with family audiences. After 41 releases through Paramount, Sherman shifted to United Artists in 1942 for 25 more, the last 12 produced by Boyd who bought the TV rights and made a fortune. This first of the longest series of features ever made was scripted by Doris Schroeder and directed by Howard Bretherton, with James Ellison, George 'Gabby' Hayes, Paula Stone, Charles Middleton, Robert Warwick, Kenneth Thompson and Willie Fung in the cast.

▷ At his peak in the mid-thirties, W.C. Fields (right) returned from a triumphant loan-out to MGM and his classic Micawber in *David Copperfield* to make one of his more hilarious comedies: **The Man On The Flying Trapeze** (GB: **The Memory Expert**). The British title gives a better idea than the former of his role in the Charles Bogle (Fields)-Sam Hardy story, slaved over by scripters Ray Harris, Jack Cunningham, Bobby Vernon and Hardy, which really boiled down to the comedian's old theme of a worm turning against his tormentors, meaning everybody else in the world – except a sympathetic daughter, played by durable ingenue Mary Brian, just as she did in the 1927 silent *Running Wild*. Kathleen Howard (left) reprised her hen-pecking wife of *It's A Gift*, and other splendid character actors directed by Clyde Bruckman (veteran of Harold Lloyd gag-fests) were Grady Sutton, Lucien Littlefield, Vera Lewis, Oscar Apfel and Walter Brennan. Fields used his voice in both pompous orondity and *sotto-voce* mutterings better in this than in any other picture.

△ **Ruggles Of Red Gap** has never failed, least of all in Leo McCarey's admirably straightforward version with Charles Laughton (2nd left), in his finest comedy performance, as the gentleman's gentleman lost in a poker game by his English employer (Roland Young) to a rancher (Charles Ruggles, 2nd right). The latter's family and townsfolk in the Old West react in various laugh-stirring ways to his arrival, the funniest being Mary Boland's socially ambitious lady of the house, a tank-town grande dame. Two other superb comediennes – ZaSu Pitts (left) as the spinster with whom the valet settles down, and Maude Eburne (right) as a tough old-timer – graced a cast including Leila Hyams, Lucien Littlefield, James Burke, Del Henderson and Clarence Wilson. The Arthur Hornblow Jr production daringly interrupted the fun with a serious recitation of Lincoln's Gettysburg Address, a Laughton *tour de force*. Harry Leon Wilson's story had been filmed twice before this Walter De Leon-Harlan Thompson-Humphrey Pearson adaptation (1918, Essanay; 1923, Paramount) and had another airing in 1950 as *Fancy Pants*.

△ Myrna Loy (right) moved over from MGM (Paramount was on a borrowing spree in 1935) to play, of all things, a stunt flyer in **Wings In The Dark**. A test pilot (Cary Grant, left) falls in love with her and comes to her rescue, although blinded in an accident, when she is in danger of crashing during her Moscow-to-New York flight. A suspension of disbelief was required to enjoy this yarn, in which the strands of romance and suspense were efficiently intertwined by director James Flood, and the stars were convincing enough to keep the audience from thinking how great Loy and Grant would have been together in comedy. (That came 12 years later with RKO's *The Bachelor And The Bobby Soxer* and *Mr Blandings Builds His Dream House*). They were supported by Dean Jagger, Roscoe Karns, Hobart Cavanaugh and Russell Hopton in the Jack Kirkland-Frank Partos screenplay (story by Nell Shipman and Philip Hurn). It was produced by Arthur Hornblow Jr, who became Myrna's first husband in 1936. On completion of this movie she moved to London until MGM agreed with her salary ideas, then returned to resume her 50-year career as one of the most fascinating actresses in pictures.

▽ **Peter Ibbetson**, first filmed in 1921 as *Forever* with Wallace Reid and Elsie Ferguson, surfaced again as a vehicle for Gary Cooper and (on loan from RKO) Ann Harding (right, with Gary). Cooper and director Henry Hathaway were odd choices for George du Maurier's spiritual romance, faring best in the earlier scenes of a man meeting his childhood sweetheart again and killing her jealous husband. Later, imprisoned and delirious, he is reunited with her in dreams which make them lovers for eternity. This material was outside Cooper's range, and Harding, more patrician than ethereal, wasn't quite right either, but it was a splendidly produced film, very popular in Europe if not in the US. Ida Lupino, John Halliday (here with gun), Douglass Dumbrille, Donald Meek, Doris Lloyd, Gilbert Emery and moppets Dickie Moore and Virginia Weidler were in the Louis D. Lighton production, scripted by Waldemar Young and Vincent Lawrence (with additional scenes by Edwin Justus Mayer and John Meehan) from an adaptation by Constance Collier of the John Raphael stage version in which she had starred in 1917.

△ Informed that three writers (Walter De Leon, Francis Martin, Ralph Spence) worked on the story of **The Big Broadcast of 1936**, you could only conclude that they cancelled each other out. It was a nonsense featuring Jack Oakie (left) as a pop-singing heart-throb, Lyda Roberti as a man-mad countess who abducts him, George Burns (right) and Gracie Allen (centre) as television inventors, with Wendy Barrie, Akim Tamiroff, Henry Wadsworth, C. Henry Gordon and Benny Baker also involved. Once the plot was out of the way, the movie's *raison d'être* emerged: a super-vaudeville show with Bing Crosby (singing 'I Wished On The Moon', lyrics by, surprisingly, famed wit Dorothy Parker), Ethel Merman (singing 'It's The Animal In Me', cut – you could see why – from *We're Not Dressing*), Bill Robinson, The Nicholas Brothers, Amos 'n' Andy, Mary Boland and Charles Ruggles, Richard Tauber and The Vienna Boys' Choir, Ray Noble and His Band, Ina Ray Hutton and Her Melodears (!) and so on. Directed by Norman Taurog and produced by Benjamin Glazer so lavishly that it cost more than any of the Big Broadcast series, it was the only one to show a loss – which was blamed on the extravagance of Ernst Lubitsch's brief reign as head of all studio production.

△ Ben Hecht and Charles MacArthur followed their dazzling *Crime Without Passion* with another Astoria, New York, production which elicited even warmer enthusiasm among the smart set and left the fan-in-the-street even colder. The Scoundrel was Noel Coward's film debut, if you don't count a juvenile bit in D.W. Griffith's 1918 *Hearts Of The World*. He had evidently borne no grudge against Hecht for rewriting his *Design For Living*, and was in great clipped-consonant, plummy-vowel form as a deceased author, profligate in life, who returns to earth in search of true love. Julie Haydon, Stanley Ridges, Martha Sleeper (right), Ernest Cossart, Everly Gregg, Eduardo Ciannelli, Lionel Stander, O.Z. Whitehead, Harry Davenport, Hope Williams, Rosita Moreno (left), and rival wit Alexander Woollcott supported the Master (centre) in a movie attracting few beyond those who wanted to see what a brilliant writing-directing-producing pair could do with an even more brilliant writer-composer-lyricist-director-actor star.

△ A featherweight comedy kept floating airily by director Wesley Ruggles and a choice cast – Claudette Colbert (centre), Fred MacMurray (left), Ray Milland (right), C. Aubrey Smith, Luis Alberni, Donald Meek, Warren Hymer, Charles Wilson – **The Gilded Lily** gave both its audiences and its exhibitors a good time. Melville Baker and Jack Kirkland's story, scripted by Claude Binyon and produced by Albert Lewis, set a typist dithering between two men, an American reporter and an out-of-work Englishman. The latter turns out to be an aristocrat in disguise, and wealthy to boot, so of course she chooses the other guy. 'Colbert in the kind of role that made you rave about *It Happened One Night!*' said the ads, ignoring the absence of Gable in this one. However, it did show the studio it had much-needed male stars in MacMurray and Milland.

▷ **The Crusades** drew more than the usual barrage of sneers and jokes aimed at Cecil B. DeMille's works by the critics; what was worse, the public didn't seem to like it either. Probably his least popular epic, it jumbled historical facts about Richard the Lionheart's exploits during the Third Crusade, and lingered tediously over his romance with Berangaria of Navarre. Only in a tumultuous depiction of the Battle of Acre did DeMille's flair for spectacular action come to the fore in a welter of seething crowds, swords, arrows and catapults; the rest was alternately a richly dressed, carefully detailed pageant, and a Hollywooden idea of how people behaved and talked in the twelfth century. The central role needed the blithe swagger of Errol Flynn; what it got was Henry Wilcoxon (centre). 'Richard's queen', announced C.B. in a pre-casting manifesto, 'must have the acting ability of Helen Hayes and the vivacity of Miriam Hopkins'. He settled for Loretta Young (right). The stars fortunately had the support of Ian Keith (left), Katherine De Mille (an adopted daughter), C. Aubrey Smith, Joseph Schildkraut, Alan Hale, C. Henry Gordon, George Barbier, Montagu Love, William Farnum, Lumsden Hare, Hobart Bosworth, Pedro De Cordoba and Mischa Auer. The screenplay by Harold Lamb, Waldemar Young and Dudley Nichols had all the verve of a school essay.

OTHER RELEASES OF 1935

Annapolis Farewell
Richard Cromwell, Tom Brown, Sir Guy Standing. Dir: Alexander Hall. Pro: Louis D. Lighton. Drama of conflicts and friendships among students at the US Naval Academy.

Bar 20 Rides Again
William Boyd, James Ellison, George Hayes. Dir: Howard Bretherton. Pro: Harry Sherman. Third 'Hopalong Cassidy'.

Behold My Wife
Sylvia Sidney, Gene Raymond, Juliette Compton. Dir: Mitchell Leisen. Pro: B.P. Schulberg. To spite his snobbish family, a young man marries an Indian girl met during a western spree, and brings her home.

The Bride Comes Home
Claudette Colbert, Fred MacMurray, Robert Young. Dir & Pro: Wesley Ruggles. Comedy of a wilful girl who switches her matrimonial intentions back and forth between a millionaire and his bodyguard.

Car 99
Fred MacMurray, Ann Sheridan, Sir Guy Standing. Dir: Charles Barton. Pro: Bayard Veiller. After suspension from the police force for incompetence, a radio-car rookie rounds up a gang of bank robbers.

College Scandal (GB **The Clock Strikes 8**)
Kent Taylor, Arline Judge, Wendy Barrie. Dir: Elliot Nugent. Pro: Albert Lewis. Three male students infatuated by a college newcomer are attacked by a killer; a professor solves the mystery.

Coronado
Johnny Downs, Jack Haley, Leon Errol, Eddy Duchin and His Orchestra. Dir: Norman Z. McLeod. Pro: William LeBaron. A California beach resort is the scene of a musical about a rich lad, a sailor and two sisters.

The Eagle's Brood
William Boyd, James Ellison, George Hayes, Joan Woodbury. Dir: Howard Bretherton. Pro: Harry Sherman. Second 'Hopalong Cassidy'.

Father Brown, Detective
Walter Connolly, Paul Lukas, Gertrude Michael. Dir: Edward Sedgwick. Pro: Bayard Veiller. G.K. Chesterton's sleuthing priest tracks a diamond thief and induces him to surrender to Scotland Yard.

Here Comes Cookie (GB **The Plot Thickens**)
George Burns, Gracie Allen. Dir: Norman Z. McLeod. Pro: William LeBaron. Madcap heiress turns her father's palatial New York mansion into a clubhouse for unemployed entertainers.

Hold 'Em, Yale (GB **Uniform Lovers**)
Buster Crabbe, Patricia Ellis, Cesar Romero. Dir: Sidney Lanfield. Pro: Charles R. Rogers. Broadway con-men get nothing but headaches from an heiress, try to marry her off to a football hero.

Home On The Range
Jackie Coogan, Randolph Scott, Evelyn Brent. Dir: Arthur Jacobson. Pro: Harold Hurley. Young Westerner helps homesteaders in their struggle against land-grabbers. (Remake of *Code Of The West*, 1925).

The Last Outpost
Cary Grant, Claude Rains, Gertrude Michael. Dir: Louis Gasnier, Charles Barton. Pro: E. Lloyd Sheldon. War drama of two British officers in the Near East, aiding each other in battle but conflicting over a woman.

Little America
Documentary of Rear Admiral Richard E. Byrd's second exploratory and scientific expedition into Antarctica, photographed by John L. Herrmann and Carl O. Peterson.

Love In Bloom
George Burns, Gracie Allen, Joe Morrison, Dixie Lee. Dir: Elliott Nugent. Pro: Benjamin Glazer. Musical comedy about a girl going to New York from her father's decrepit carnival, and falling for a songwriter.

McFadden's Flats
Walter C. Kelly, Richard Cromwell, Jane Darwell, Andy Clyde. Dir: Ralph Murphy. Pro: Charles R. Rogers. Two old codgers alternate between friendship and feuding; their children fall in love.

Men Without Names
Fred MacMurray, Madge Evans, Lynne Overman. Dir: Ralph Murphy. Pro: Albert Lewis. Government investigator tracks down robbery gang from Brooklyn to Kansas, where they kill his partner before they are caught.

Millions In The Air
John Howard, Wendy Barrie, Willie Howard, Eleanore Whitney. Dir: Ray McCarey. Pro: Harold Hurley. Daughter of the radio Amateur Hour's sponsor enters the show incognito, teams up with a singing salesman and wins.

One Hour Late
Helen Twelvetrees, Joe Morrison, Conrad Nagel. Dir: Ralph Murphy. Pro: Albert Lewis. Trapped in an office building's stalled elevator are a secretary going to meet her boss, her jealous sweetheart, and the boss's eloping wife.

Paris In Spring (GB **Paris Love Song**)
Mary Ellis, Tullio Carminati, Ida Lupino. Dir: Lewis Milestone. Pro: Benjamin Glazer. Man and girl meet while intending Eiffel Tower suicide leaps, decide to arouse their spouses' jealousy instead.

People Will Talk
Mary Boland, Charles Ruggles, Leila Hyams. Dir: Alfred Santell. Pro: Douglas MacLean. The gossip-mongers get busy when a girl comes home to her family without her newly wed husband.

The Rocky Mountain Mystery
Randolph Scott, Kathleen Burke, Charles 'Chic' Sale. Dir: Charles Barton. Pro: Harold Hurley. Melodrama of new settlers versus townsfolk in the West. (Remake of *The Vanishing Pioneer*, 1928)

Scrooge
Sir Seymour Hicks, Donald Calthrop, Mary Glynne. Dir: Henry Edwards. Pro: Julius Hagen. The Dickens classic, 'A Christmas Carol', about a skinflint transformed. (British)

Shanghai
Loretta Young, Charles Boyer, Warner Oland. Dir: James Flood. Pro: Walter Wanger. The most powerful financier in Shanghai is ruined by the disclosure of his mixed-race parentage, but an American girl still loves him.

Ship Cafe
Carl Brisson, Mady Christians, Arline Judge. Dir: Robert Florey. Pro: Harold Hurley. Naughty countess, attracted by a ship's stoker, turns him into the singing star of a smart bistro.

Smart Girl
Ida Lupino, Kent Taylor, Gail Patrick. Dir: Aubrey Scotto. Pro: Walter Wanger. Lawyer, loved by two sisters, marries one, who leads him into a stock market swindle; the other one helps to extricate him.

Stolen Harmony
George Raft, Ben Bernie and His Band, Grace Bradley. Dir: Alfred Werker. Pro: Albert Lewis. Musical melodrama about an ex-convict touring with a dance band and helping police capture a crime gang.

This Woman Is Mine
Gregory Ratoff, John Loder, Benita Hume. Dir: Monty Banks. Drama of a lion tamer testing his theories about human and animal behaviour. (British)

Two-Fisted
Lee Tracy, Grace Bradley, Kent Taylor, Gail Patrick. Dir: James Cruze. Pro: Harold Hurley. Farce about a prizefighter and his manager who take jobs in a millionaire's home. (Remake of *Is Zat So?*, Fox 1927)

Two For Tonight
Bing Crosby, Joan Bennett, Mary Boland, Lynne Overman. Dir: Frank Tuttle. Pro: Douglas MacLean. Musical about a songwriter who takes on the job of creating a Broadway show score in seven days. Hit: 'Without a Word of Warning'.

The Virginia Judge
Walter C. Kelly, Robert Cummings, Marsha Hunt. Dir: Edward Sedgwick. Pro: Charles R. Rogers. A young lawbreaker's problems are solved by the treatment of an understanding judge.

Wanderer Of The Wasteland
Dean Jagger, Gail Patrick, Buster Crabbe. Dir: Otho Lovering. Pro: Harold Hurley. Western action drama from a novel by Zane Grey. (Remake of 1924 film)

Wings Over Ethiopia
Documentary of a journey through Ethiopia by airplane, automobile and mule, visiting savage tribesmen and the Emperor's palace. (Swiss)

Without Regret
Elissa Landi, Paul Cavanagh, Kent Taylor, Frances Drake. Dir: Harold Young. Pro: B.P. Fineman. Unintentionally a bigamist, a wife is blackmailed by a woman who is murdered. (Remake of *Interference*, 1928)

The Mountain Rises Again
1936-1957

In the mid-Thirties President Franklin D. Roosevelt's New Deal refloated the American economy out of the great depression, and by 1936 the movie trade winds were strong again. Paramount, after announcing over $3 million profit in its first post-receivership year, doubled that with its 1936 total, repeated the following year. It had been sustained during the dark days by Bing Crosby musicals, Cecil DeMille spectacles, and the outrageous sex comedies of Mae West. Her undulations having been only slightly modified by a powerful 1934 censorship upsurge (the church-led Legion of Decency), Mae still gave her every little movement a meaning of its own – and her dialogue at least two.

Although encouraged by Chairman Zukor, who went west to smooth out studio wrinkles, Ernst Lubitsch was miscast in the role of production chief to which he had been appointed in 1935 following the unsatisfactory tenure of Emanuel Cohen. After a year Lubitsch returned to making individual pictures and was replaced by William Le Baron, who lasted from 1936 to 1938, when Y. Frank Freeman took over. Meanwhile, at the New York head office, John Otterson also proved to be a one-year wonder as president. He handed the reins to Barney Balaban, once associated in the Balaban and Katz theatre chain with Sam Katz (the latter had vacated his post as Publix head man during the bankruptcy upheaval). A welcome atmosphere of permanency now settled on the peak of Paramount's mountain: Balaban remained president from 1936 to 1966, and Freeman vice-president in charge of production from 1938 to 1959.

However, a slump set in during 1938-9, when annual profits dropped below the $3 million mark as production costs escalated and radio competition boomed (Zukor regretted having to sell back the 50% of the Columbia Broadcasting System which he had bought for Paramount.) Threats to the industry loomed on several other fronts.

The US government filed suits against Paramount, Loew's-MGM, 20th Century-Fox, RKO and Warner Bros. charging them with violation of the Sherman Anti-Trust Act by their interlocking controls of film production and distribution, and theatre ownership. This new shock came in 1938, bringing with it the upheaval of a protracted series of legal battles between the major companies and the Department of Justice.

Television, already publicly available in London, reared its frightening head in several experimental transmissions in American cities. Eventually, Paramount became the first Hollywood company to participate actively in the television industry, both in transmission when Balaban bought a Chicago station, and production when the studio started making pictures for TV.

In 1939 the Nazi menace, long smouldering, erupted in the cataclysm of World War II, one commercial result of which was the loss of many overseas markets. Europe had about twice as many

left *Paramount was quick to exploit the amazing invention that eventually would bring the company vast revenue. As early as 1939 it released* Television Spy, *one of the first movies to feature the new entertainment medium.*
right *Grace Kelly won 1954's best actress Oscar with one of her four Paramount films,* The Country Girl.

Zukor and his wife in front of a bust commemorating his 80th birthday in 1953, when he had been Chairman of the Board for 28 years after 19 as President.

cinemas as America, and revenue from them had often made the difference between a movie's financial success and failure.

Then, in 1940, Congressman Martin Dies broke into front page headlines by charging that Hollywood was a seething hotbed of Communism. The House Un-American Activities Committee continued to take damaging potshots at the industry until, a decade later, they had become a witch-hunt, led by Parnell Thomas (later jailed) and the eventually detested Senator Joseph McCarthy, recklessly branding many talented liberals as traitors.

But in the Forties, Hollywood's headaches were responding to that infallible analgesic, money in the box-office. Unlike the first world conflict, World War II had an increasingly stimulating effect on movie attendances. The public's appetite for entertainment seemed limitless. Paramount concentrated on the escapist variety, and prospered to the tune of over $13 million profit in America's first year at war. In the last one, it climbed to over $15 million. Then, instead of subsiding to a normal peacetime level, the 1946 figure zoomed to a stratospheric $39 million – easily the biggest profit ever registered by any film company. Paramount's competitors also hit new highs that year (20th Century-Fox, Warner Bros. and MGM came in with $22, $19 and $18 millions, respectively). And exhibitors reported that 1946 moviegoers had munched their way through $10 million worth of popcorn.

The studio's contribution to this prosperity was not in accelerated productivity. On the contrary: its 1936 release list of 71 pictures gradually slowed down to a mere 19 in 1946. Studio chief Freeman and his production overseers, B.G. De Sylva (formerly part of the famous songwriting team of Buddy De Sylva, Lew Brown and Ray Henderson) and Henry Ginsberg, made 'fewer but better' their motto. The Thirties hits of Crosby, DeMille and West had provided good entertainment but were in no danger of winning any critics' awards. That approval did occasionally greet the elegant comedies directed by Lubitsch and Mitchell Leisen, and, from 1940, the brilliant iconoclasms of Preston Sturges.

It was not until 1944, however, that Paramount won a 'best picture' Oscar from the Academy of Motion Picture Arts and Sciences – the first since *Wings* 16 years before. Leo McCarey's *Going My Way* did it, also winning a flock of other awards and taking a fortune at the box-office. The very next year, one of Billy Wilder's superb movies, *The Lost Weekend*, got the supreme prize, plus several other 'bests'. Before these two, Paramount had rarely figured in the five annual Academy *nominations* for best picture, let alone winning the Oscar itself, but from 1949 to 1956 the studio crowded the nominee lists with *The Heiress, Sunset Boulevard, A Place In The Sun, The Greatest Show On Earth* (the 1952 winner), *Roman Holiday, Shane, The Country Girl, The Rose Tattoo* and DeMille's remake of *The Ten Commandments*.

In 1948 the sword of Damocles that the US government had been holding over the industry for ten years fell at last. The major companies were found guilty of anti-trust law violations and ordered to dispose of their theatre interests. Paramount was the first to comply, hiving off all the properties Zukor had so assiduously collected, and becoming once again simply a production-distribution organization at the end of 1949 (only the Famous Players circuit of Canada and some overseas theatres escaped the axe.) The immediate result was a drop in Paramount Pictures' profits from $20 million in 1949 to $6 million in 1950.

By this time, television had grown from a science-fiction marvel into a stronger counter-attraction than radio had ever been. The industry fought it with visual developments that the new medium couldn't match. Three-dimensional effects were briefly successful, but the public soon tired of looking through the tinted glasses they were required to wear. Cinerama's gigantic curved screen was a sensation in the largest cities, but needed too much expensive equipment for general use.

The real breakthrough in big-screen exhibition came in 1953 with the debut of CinemaScope, sponsored by 20th Century-Fox and subsequently adopted by every other company – with the sole exception of Paramount. The 'squeezed' film of CinemaScope, when stretched in projection, resulted in a picture two and a half times wider than its height, impressively panoramic but often artistically awkward. Paramount developed a much less extreme width/height ratio and a sharper photographic quality in attaining a jumbo-sized picture. Called VistaVision, it involved the use of 70mm instead of squeezed film, and it was generally acknowledged to be an improvement over previous big-screen systems. It was augmented, like the others, by stereophonic sound.

But, as against approximately 17,000 US theatre screens of all shapes and sizes, there were over 40 million of those little screens shining in the nation's living rooms by the end of 1957. Could Paramount continue to thrive in a branch of show business no longer paramount?

Studio chief Y. Frank Freeman (left) and Zukor indulging in a little showmanship to publicise Paramount's answer to the 1953 success of CinemaScope.

1936

▽ Now that Marlene Dietrich was no longer being directed by Josef von Sternberg, Gary Cooper was happy to co-star with her in **Desire**. The lady herself emerged as less of a glamourised puppet and more of an actress, adding sparkle to her legendary beauty, as a jewel thief who drops some pearls she has stolen in Paris into the pocket of an American stranger in order to get them past the Spanish customs. While trying to recover them she develops a romantic interest in her duped man, confesses, and returns the loot to its rightful owners. In their first work together for five years, the stars (both illustrated) were directed by Frank Borzage, a specialist in romantic pathos, but the light, bright screenplay (by Samuel Hoffenstein, Waldemar Young and Edwin Justus Mayer) also reflected the influence of Ernst Lubitsch, its producer, who had just gratefully shaken off the burden of studio production chief. John Halliday, William Frawley, Ernest Cossart, Akim Tamiroff, Alan Mowbray, Zeffie Tilbury and Marc Lawrence supported in the adaptation of a play by Hans Szekely and R.A. Stemmle.

▷ Bing Crosby's casual style seemed just right for an easygoing Western musical, as demonstrated by **Rhythm On The Range** which rounded up a huge herd of profitable grosses (curiously enough, he never made another sagebrusher until the non-musical *Stagecoach* remake, 30 years later). In Benjamin Glazer's production he delivered two lazy smash-hits, 'I'm An Old Cowhand' by Johnny Mercer and 'Empty Saddles' by Billy Hill, while coaxing a footloose heiress (Frances Farmer) into marriage; but if it was Bing's singing that drew the crowds in, it was Martha Raye's clowning that gave them something to talk about. Signed to a contract after a screen test in which she belted out a number Sam Coslow wrote for her, 'Mr Paganini' (reprised in this film), she (left) was starting the movie phase of her 60-year career. Norman Taurog directed, and the writers (Mervin Houser, John Moffitt, Francis Martin, Walter De Leon, Sidney Salkow) almost outnumbered the featured players, who included Bob Burns (right), Lucille Gleason, Samuel S. Hinds, Warren Hymer and George E. Stone.

◁ Jack Benny's long and mutually profitable association with Paramount began with **The Big Broadcast Of 1937**. Although he had made occasional appearances in movies ever since MGM's *Hollywood Revue* in 1929, he was primarily a radio star – surprisingly, since that medium gave limited scope to his unique talent for expressionless pauses which became funnier the longer he held them. Even surrounded by such popular comics as Martha Raye, Bob Burns and, in their third *Big Broadcast*, George Burns and Gracie Allen, Benny (illustrated) was outstanding in the Lewis Gensler production, directed in lively style by Mitchell Leisen. It had one of those virtually nonexistent stories that seem to emerge whenever a crowd of writers go to work: Erwin Gelsey, Arthur Kober, Barry Trivers, Walter De Leon and Francis Martin disgorged a trifle about a small-town broadcasting station and a romance between Shirley Ross and Ray Milland. More important were the musical trimmings, ranging from Leopold Stokowski conducting a symphony orchestra to Frank Forrest singing, and a sexy chorus sinuously dancing 'La Bomba', and including Benny Goodman's clarinet, Larry Adler's harmonica, and the hit song, 'Here's Love In Your Eye'. Ralph Rainger and Leo Robin wrote the songs.

△ Comedy with a sexy story idea, but a 99% pure script, was forthcoming in **College Holiday**. Beautiful young students of both genders were induced to spend their summer vacation at a hotel run by a female eugenics nut who thinks their mating will produce perfect physical specimens. Since she was played by Mary Boland, with Jack Benny, Martha Raye, George Burns and Gracie Allen as her cohorts, laughs were abundant. The screenplay that J.P. McEvoy, Harlan Ware, Jay Gorney and Henry Myers toiled over was given the heave-ho while musical numbers took over (the students clearly preferring show production to reproduction). Leif Erickson, Marsha Hunt, Johnny Downs, Eleanore Whitney, Olympe Bradna, Louis Da Pron, Ben Blue and Etienne Girardot (centre) performed for director Frank Tuttle in Harlan Thompson's modestly successful production.

▽ Paramount was doing fine with zippy modern musicals, but kept trying for the classier (and duller) kind MGM was making with MacDonald and Eddy, and Columbia with Grace Moore. The studio seemed to find its match for Miss Moore in Gladys Swarthout, a Metropolitan Opera mezzo-soprano, and even better looking. They handed her a contract, and the lead in **Rose Of The Rancho**, a William Le Baron production set in old New Mexico, or possibly new Old Mexico, where the queen of the fiesta moonlights as a masked bandit, with secret agent John Boles in hot pursuit. Both stars (illustrated) were good, in spite of having to dash about on horseback, singing repeatedly. Broadway comedy star Willie Howard (as a Jewish gaucho), Charles Bickford, Grace Bradley, H.B. Warner, Don Alvarado, Herb Williams, Charlotte Granville, Benny Baker and Minor Watson were good, too; so was the Leo Robin-Ralph Rainger song hit 'If I Should Lose You', but they were all outweighed by the mildewed melodrama of David Belasco's 1906 play, filmed by Lasky and Cecil B. DeMille in 1914 with Bessie Barriscale, and now scripted by Frank Partos, Charles Brackett, Arthur Sheekman and Nat Perrin. Marion Gering directed.

△ Ethel Merman (illustrated) did a transcontinental dash from New York to Hollywood to repeat on film the role in **Anything Goes** that made her the brightest star on Broadway. The show opened in 1934 and was still running a year later when Benjamin Glazer had the movie in production with Bing Crosby, Charlie Ruggles, Ida Lupino, Arthur Treacher, Grace Bradley, Margaret Dumont, Robert McWade, Richard Carle and Matt Moore under the direction of Lewis Milestone. Quite a galaxy of talent but the real genius behind its stage and screen success was composer-lyricist Cole Porter, who gave Ethel three show-stoppers, 'You're The Top', 'I Get A Kick Out Of You' and the title number, which she belted out with wall-shaking gusto. They're still often heard a half century later, as is the lovely ballad 'All Through The Night', heard only as background music in the film. New numbers from other songsmiths were brought in to give Crosby a fair crack at the microphone but they didn't measure up to Porter's quality. Bing played the wooer of an English heiress (Lupino), stowing away in an Atlantic liner to be near her. Discovered, he poses as the partner of Public Enemy No 13 (Ruggles) who is posing as a clergyman. An unbelievable number of writers produced these and subsequent developments in a story feeble even for a musical: original authors P.G. Wodehouse, Guy Bolton; revisers Howard Lindsay, Russel Crouse; scripters Walter De Leon, Sidney Salkow, John Moffitt, Francis Martin.

◁ Variously described in the press as 'the greatest female impersonator of all time' and 'a monster of lubricity, menacing the sacred institution of the American family', Mae West (left) didn't give a damn, just as long as they kept talking about her and the dollars kept rolling in – as they did when **Klondike Annie** was released. She was back in the brawling Nineties as a 'Frisco dame who stabs her Chinese lover (Harold Huber) to death and hops aboard an Alaska-bound freighter. The passion of the skipper (Victor McLaglen, right) was immediately ignited by this gorgeous creature, and the cop (Philip Reed) pursuing her was similarly aroused. Meanwhile, Mae switched identities with a defunct evangelist (Helen Jerome Eddy) and raised the Arctic temperature as a hot-gospeller before giving herself up to the law. Several songs were injected into the script (written by Mae herself from a story by Marion Morgan, George Dowell and Frank Dazey); they included, appropriately, 'I'm An Occidental Woman In An Oriental Mood For Love', by Gene Austin. It was directed by Raoul Walsh and produced by William Le Baron, with Conway Tearle, Harry Beresford, Lucille Gleason, Esther Howard, Soo Yung and Lawrence Grant also in the cast.

▽ After an encouraging reception for their team-work in a so-so crime drama, *Big Brown Eyes*, Cary Grant and Joan Bennett were co-starred in **Wedding Present** as a scatterbrained pair of reporters who fall in love and out again when he is promoted to editor and she (illustrated) decides to marry a more stable character. He disrupts her wedding with police cars, fire engines etc, and in the confusion kidnaps the bride. It was the sort of screwball comedy in which Grant became a major star, but not for Paramount. His five-year contract expired with this one; during the next two decades he would return on single-picture deals. George Bancroft headed the supporting cast, with Gene Lockhart, William Demarest, Inez Courtney, Edward Brophy and George Meeker, and it was good to see Conrad Nagel and Lois Wilson back again. Richard Wallace directed the B.P. Schulberg production, scripted by Joseph Anthony from a Paul Gallico story.

△ A stage veteran of three decades, Gladys George at 36 was still a beautiful blonde, and she could give comedy lines a whiplash sting. Paramount signed her up when it bought her biggest Broadway success, the satirical *Personal Appearance*, then in a fit of Hollywood illogic cast her in a dismal tear-milker, **Valiant Is The Word For Carrie**, while giving her play to Mae West and losing its title value by calling it *Go West, Young Man*. Miscast seemed to be the word for Gladys (centre), but she surprised with a strong performance (nominated for an Oscar) that put some backbone into the flab, produced and directed by Wesley Ruggles, about a small town's most scandalous tart, whose love for two orphaned tots makes her not only pure, but also the owner of a dry-cleaning business. John Howard (left), Arline Judge (right), Dudley Digges, Harry Carey, William Collier Sr, Isabel Jewell, Maude Eburne, John Wray and kids Jackie Moran and Charlene Wyatt were in Claude Binyon's screenplay, from Barry Benefield's best-seller, whose mostly female readers attended *en masse*.

▽ Another opera star was recruited to partner Gladys Swarthout (illustrated) in **Give Us This Night**: Jan Kiepura, a Polish tenor who had already achieved great popularity in continental movies. His first Hollywood picture was also his last. William Le Baron's production didn't skimp on the budget; the songs, for example, bore the prestigious names of Erich Wolfgang Korngold and Oscar Hammerstein II and included the first operatic sequence composed for a movie, a souped-up 'Romeo And Juliet' extravaganza. Jacques Bachrach's frail story, scripted by Edwin Justus Mayer and Lynn Starling (singing fisherman becomes overnight star when chosen to substitute for over-the-hill tenor), tottered under the weight of the trimmings, and Alexander Hall got amateur night performances from a cast that included Philip Merivale (illustrated), Alan Mowbray, Benny Baker, William Collier Sr, Sidney Toler and Michelette Burani. The fans steered clear of it.

◁ The company's best picture of the year, **The General Died At Dawn**, was basically no more than a blood-and-thunderer, but was continually lifted to a higher category by imaginative treatment. Lewis Milestone, whose work through the years ranged from the humdrum to the masterly, hit his top form in creating, together with cinematographer Victor Milner, a bizarre atmosphere, and in giving a fast pace to the interplay of some colourful characters: a bandit general (Akim Tamiroff, centre) plotting a takeover of northern China; an American soldier of fortune (Gary Cooper, left) trying to foil him, the general's aide (Dudley Digges, 2nd right), and a hireling (Porter Hall) whose daughter (Madeleine Carroll, 2nd left) lures the American and his arms money aboard a train which is captured. For the finish, see title. William Le Baron's exciting production was written in literate style (though sometimes too wordy for the medium) by playwright Clifford Odets from a novel by Charles Booth. Also in the cast: Philip Ahn, William Frawley, J.M. Kerrigan (right) and, briefly, as reporters, Milestone, Odets and John O'Hara. The movie was big box-office.

▽ The drama of an uproar created by a has-been movie star's memoirs was milked for more than it was worth in **Hollywood Boulevard**. Robert Florey's direction and Marguerite Roberts's script (from a novel by Faith Thomas) strove for importance as a fame-means-nothing treatise but came out as a middling 'B'. John Halliday was top-cast as the author whose attempted murder during a row with his former mistress (Frieda Inescort) formed the climax; Marsha Hunt and Robert Cummings (illustrated centre) supplied romance, and C. Henry Gordon, Esther Ralston and Esther Dale supported. But the chief interest for film buffs was in cameos by Gary Cooper, Betty Compson and silent stars Maurice Costello, Francis X. Bushman, Charles Ray, Mae Marsh, Bryant Washburn, Pat O'Malley, Jack Mulhall, Jane Novak and Roy D'Arcy. The film's headline content, 'Hollywood Diary Secrets Bared!', drew topicality from the Mary Astor scandal: her private confessions, revealed in a court case, were current headline news.

▽ **The Princess Comes Across** adroitly combined a whodunit by Philip MacDonald with a romantic comedy novel by Louis Lucien Rogger, to give Carole Lombard and Fred MacMurray (both illustrated) a delicious successor to their *Hands Across The Table*. The script by Walter De Leon, Francis Martin, Frank Butler, Don Hartman, Claude Binyon and J.B. Priestley (for once, too many cooks didn't make a hash) sent a Brooklyn showgirl on a third-class trip to Europe from which she returns first class, posing as a Swedish princess in the hope of being discovered as a new Garbo. On the way, a shipboard musician falls for her and vice-versa, while they get the suspects in a blackmailer's murder sorted out. William K. Howard directed Arthur Hornblow Jr's production and kept things skimming along at a fine rate of knots, with Douglass Dumbrille, Alison Skipworth, William Frawley, Sig Rumann, Mischa Auer, Porter Hall, George Barbier and Lumsden Hare aboard.

▽ For the first time, Mae West took on a role already made famous by another star. On the stage *Personal Appearance* had been one of Broadway's biggest hits of 1934, with Gladys George as the movie queen whose car breaks down in a hick town while she is on an in-person tour. You would have expected her impact on the unsophisticated folks, and her allurement of a handsome young farmer, to be even more amusing when screenwritten and enacted by the flamboyant Mae in **Go West, Young Man**. But no. Under the Legion of Decency's scrutiny, the star had become more statuesque and less outrageous; the Lawrence Riley play's pace slowed down as she struck glamorous poses, always kept front and centre by director Henry Hathaway despite the presence of three other star names – Randolph Scott, Alice Brady, Warren William (here with Mae) – in a supporting line-up containing Lyle Talbot, Elizabeth Patterson, Isabel Jewell, Jack La Rue, Margaret Perry, Etienne Girardot, and Xavier Cugat and his orchestra. Emanuel Cohen's production was 'Westful, zestful,' said *Variety*; but 'Slipshod, tedious,' riposted the *New York Herald Tribune*, a verdict with which potential box-office customers concurred.

▷ Cecil B. DeMille went back to his Hollywood beginnings for **The Plainsman**. A lot of tumbleweed had rolled past movie cameras since *The Squaw Man*, which his new Western dwarfed in scope and cost, using six acres of the Paramount ranch and thousands of Sioux and Cheyenne Indians in action-packed panoramas. Second unit director Arthur Rosson shot location scenes in Montana, but there was a surprising abundance of process shots and studio 'outdoors', while the script (Waldemar Young, Lynn Riggs, Harold Lamb; adapted by Jeanie Macpherson from one story by Frank Wilstach, and another by Courtney Riley Cooper and Grover Jones) paid scant heed to historical fact. Its vast audiences didn't mind that, or the entirely imaginary romance between Wild Bill Hickok and Calamity Jane, crude roughnecks in life, here beautified into Gary Cooper and Jean Arthur (both illustrated). Also on hand were James Ellison as Buffalo Bill, John Miljan as General Custer, Frank McGlynn as Abraham Lincoln, Charles Bickford as a villainous gun-runner, Helen Burgess, Victor Varconi, and Anthony Quinn making his Paramount debut as a redskin.

△ **Thirteen Hours By Air** spearheaded that long, long fly-past of hijacked airplanes which have kept cinema and television audiences agog for half a century. This one – the aircraft, not the movie – took thirteen hours to cross the American continent because long-distance commercial aviation was still in its infancy when the E. Lloyd Sheldon production's assortment of passengers fastened their seat belts. Their various dramatic crises, romantic interludes and comedy-relief bits were devised by Bogart Rogers and Frank Dazey (script by Rogers and Kenyon Nicholson) whose most fruitful invention was the desperate ex-convict bent on a plane-snatch. Director Mitchell Leisen took off with an excellent cast – Fred MacMurray, Joan Bennett (both illustrated), Alan Baxter, John Howard, ZaSu Pitts, Brian Donlevy, Dean Jagger, Ruth Donnelly, Bennie Bartlett, Grace Bradley, Fred Keating, Marie Prevost, Jack Mulhall – and touched down with a hit.

△ '*King Of The Jungle* did okay for a low-budgeter. How about a female version, boys? Maybe call it **The Jungle Princess**.' So producer E. Lloyd Sheldon, writers Cyril Hume, Gouverneur Morris and Gerald Geraghty, and director William Thiele went to work and came up with an unpretentious production, a pleasant entertainment, and a whopping profit-maker. Dorothy Lamour, hitherto a minor band and radio singer, wrapped some of her curves in a sarong and became an instant star as the child of nature, reared with a pet tiger by tropical natives, but wooed and won by a handsome visitor from Western civilisation. He was Ray Milland (centre right with Lamour), rising to stardom after three years at Paramount; he stayed for twelve more, as did Lamour. Akim Tamiroff, Lynne Overman, Molly Lamont and Mala (left) were featured in the Max Marcin story, along with a sultry song hit by Leo Robin and Frederick Hollander, 'Moonlight And Shadows'.

▽ A minor but very popular item in the 40-year catalogue of director King Vidor, **The Texas Rangers** presented an eventful, rather original yarn, put over with plenty of yippee, about two cowboy pals who switched from wasteland wandering to law enforcement. Meanwhile a third former buddy took the opposite path, becoming an outlaw whom they were obliged to hunt down. Fred MacMurray (right) and Jack Oakie (left) made real characters of the Ranger recruits and Lloyd Nolan went bad convincingly, under the expert guidance of Vidor, who also wrote the story with Elizabeth Hill and produced its Louis Stevens screenplay, from material in a book by Walter Prescott Webb. He should have rejected some of the script's flat dialogue. Others in the cast were Jean Parker (centre right), prettily providing MacMurray's romantic interest; Edward Ellis, Bennie Bartlett, Elena Martinez, Frank Shannon. It was remade in 1949 as *The Streets Of Laredo*.

▽ Time seemed to stand still for W.C. Fields (centre). Eleven years after the first filming (*Sally Of The Sawdust*, 1925) of his Broadway stage success, **Poppy**, he was playing the same role again. His unique delivery of lines, not to mention the muttered ad libs, made his Eustace McGonigle, carnival con-man extraordinaire, even funnier than he had been in the silent version. Rochelle Hudson as the daughter he tries to palm off as an heiress, Richard Cromwell as the boy she loves, Catherine Doucet (right) as a phoney countess, Lynne Overman, Maude Eburne, Granville Bates and Rosalind Keith were also in William Le Baron's production, revised from Dorothy Donnelly's play by Virginia Van Upp and Waldemar Young. Fields was ill during filming, and director Edward Sutherland had to shoot around him and use a double for long-shots.

▽ A comedy with more charm than substance, **The Moon's Our Home** chronicled the impulsive romance and marriage of a movie star and an author-explorer who fail to appreciate each other's fame. Margaret Sullavan and Henry Fonda (both illustrated) brought warmth as well as spirit to the pair's clashes of career and temperament, although her frequent tantrums grew a little tiresome before the finish. There was extra piquancy for the fans in the fact that the co-stars, who had first played together on stage in 1928, were actually married in 1931, and divorced in 1933 because of problems similar to those they solved in the film. The fine cast, directed by William Seiter, included Beulah Bondi, Charles Butterworth, Margaret Hamilton, Walter Brennan, Henrietta Crosman, Dorothy Stickney and Lucien Littlefield. Walter Wanger produced the Isabel Dawn-Boyce DeGaw screenplay (from a novel by Faith Baldwin), with some witty dialogue added by Dorothy Parker and Alan Campbell.

▷ **The Milky Way** won Harold Lloyd (left) some of his best reviews, and its big audiences agreed that it topped the 1932 hit *Movie Crazy* (he had made one for Fox release in the interim) as his most entertaining comedy. Only the star this time, and not his own producer as was his custom, he had a stronger supporting cast than usual, including Adolphe Menjou, Verree Teasdale (Mrs Menjou, right), Helen Mack, William Gargan, Lionel Stander, Dorothy Wilson, George Barbier and Marjorie Gateson. Director Leo McCarey set them a fast pace in a funny script by Grover Jones, Frank Butler and Richard Cornell about a timid milkman who accidentally knocks out a champion boxer and is ballyhooed into prizefighting fame. E. Lloyd Sheldon produced the adaptation of a Broadway play by Lynn Root and Harry Clork, of which another version was filmed in 1946 as *The Kid From Brooklyn* with Danny Kaye.

△ The studio ventured away from black-and-white features for the first time since 1930 with **The Trail Of The Lonesome Pine**. It had been waiting for an improved 3-colour Technicolor to be perfected, and the new process enhanced the Walter Wanger production's appeal enormously, both on the screen and at the box-office. This was the third filming of John Fox Jr's novel, and the best: the 1916 and 1923 versions had nothing like the pictorial scope and cast strength of the modernised screenplay, written by Grover Jones, Harvey Thew and Horace McCoy, and directed with straightforward drive by Henry Hathaway. Fred MacMurray played the city stranger getting caught up in the lives of a primitive Kentucky mountain family and their feud with a neighbouring clan; Sylvia Sidney was the girl he tried to educate and came to love, and Henry Fonda her disapproving brother (right), who is killed as the feud is being settled. Fred Stone, Robert Barrat, Alan Baxter, Nigel Bruce, Beulah Bondi (left) and Fuzzy Knight scored in support of the stars, who shared top honours with the full-hued great outdoors.

◁ The studio's favourite story property, Alice Duer Miller's *The Charm School*, was dusted off once again for **Collegiate** (its original title was used in Britain), this time as a vehicle for Jack Oakie (illustrated). He brought a brash skill to the role – which had served Wallace Reid in 1921, Buddy Rogers in 1928 (*Someone To Love*), Nancy Carroll in 1929 (*Sweetie*) – of an unexpected heir to a girls' school, with startling effects on both him and it. Louis D. Lighton's production, snappily directed by Ralph Murphy, also employed a popular but terrible radio comedian, Joe Penner, the lush voice of Frances Langford, the legs, etc, of Betty Grable, plus Ned Sparks, Lynne Overman, Betty Jane Cooper, Henry Kolker, Mack Gordon and Harry Revel, the latter pair contributing the score as well. It included two great songs, 'You Hit The Spot' and 'I Feel Like A Feather In The Breeze'. Walter De Leon and Francis Martin rewrote the script.

OTHER RELEASES OF 1936

The Accusing Finger
Robert Cummings, Marsha Hunt, Kent Taylor, Paul Kelly. Dir: James Hogan. Pro: A.M. Botsford. Tough prosecutor of killers is himself convicted of murdering his wife, then proved innocent by a colleague.

Along Came Love
Charles Starrett, Irene Hervey, Doris Kenyon. Dir: Bert Lytell. Pro: Richard A. Rowland. Romance of a shopgirl and a young doctor.

And Sudden Death
Randolph Scott, Frances Drake, Tom Brown. Dir: Charles Barton. Pro: A.M. Botsford. Fact-based fiction about the terrible results of driving after drinking.

The Arizona Raiders
Buster Crabbe, Marsha Hunt, Raymond Hatton, Johnny Downs. Dir: James Hogan. Pro: Dan Keefe. Western action drama from a story by Zane Grey.

Big Brown Eyes
Joan Bennett, Cary Grant, Walter Pidgeon, Lloyd Nolan. Dir: Raoul Walsh. Pro: Walter Wanger. A manicurist becomes a reporter and joins with a detective to solve a robbery case and expose an insurance racket.

Border Flight
Robert Cummings, Frances Farmer, John Howard. Dir: Otho Lovering. Pro: A.M. Botsford. A pilot at a US Coast Guard Air Base is captured with his girl by smugglers, whose boat is crash-dived on by his friend, saving them.

Call Of The Prairie
William Boyd, James Ellison, George Hayes, Muriel Evans. Dir: Howard Bretherton. Pro: Harry Sherman. Fourth 'Hopalong Cassidy'.

The Case Against Mrs Ames
Madeleine Carroll, George Brent, Alan Baxter. Dir: William A. Seiter. Pro: Walter Wanger. Courtroom drama of a woman accused of murdering her husband.

Desert Gold
Robert Cummings, Buster Crabbe, Marsha Hunt, Tom Keene. Dir: James Hogan. Pro: Harold Hurley. An Easterner goes west to help his army officer friend to capture a killer. (Remake of 1926 film)

Drift Fence
Buster Crabbe, Tom Keene, Katherine DeMille. Dir: Otho Lovering. Pro: Harold Hurley. Another Zane Grey tale about the good guys triumphing over Western law breakers.

Early To Bed
Mary Boland, Charles Ruggles, Gail Patrick. Dir: Norman Z. McLeod. Pro: Harlan Thompson. A husband and wife get into trouble with gangsters because of his sleep-walking.

Easy To Take
John Howard, Marsha Hunt, Eugene Pallette. Dir: Glenn Tryon. Pro: Jack Cunningham. Radio 'uncle' falls heir to the spoiled nephew of a supposedly rich woman; he supports the boy, tames him, and wins his older sister.

F-Man
Jack Haley, Grace Bradley, William Frawley. Dir: Edward Cline. Pro: Val Paul. A soda-jerker's efforts to become a G-Man are disastrous until he unwittingly captures a gang.

Fatal Lady
Mary Ellis, Walter Pidgeon, Norman Foster. Dir: Edward Ludwig. Pro: Walter Wanger. A singer is faced with a career disaster and love crisis when her shady past is resurrected.

Florida Special
Jack Oakie, Sally Eilers, Kent Taylor, Frances Drake. Dir: Ralph Murphy. Pro: Albert Lewis. Romance, comedy and music punctuate a murder mystery aboard a Florida-bound train.

Forgotten Faces
Herbert Marshall, Gertrude Michael, Robert Cummings. Dir: E.A. Dupont. Pro: A.M. Botsford. A father sacrifices his life to preserve his daughter's happiness. (Remake of 1928 film)

Girl Of The Ozarks
Virginia Weidler, Leif Erickson, Elizabeth Russell. Dir: William Shea. Pro: A.M. Botsford. Small-town editor helps a poor child out of various scrapes and, when her mother dies, he and his wife adopt her.

Heart Of The West
William Boyd, James Ellison, George Hayes. Dir: Howard Bretherton. Pro: Harry Sherman. Sixth 'Hopalong Cassidy'.

Her Master's Voice
Edward Everett Horton, Peggy Conklin, Laura Hope Crews. Dir: Joseph Santley. Pro: Walter Wanger. Husband's problems with his bossy in-laws are straightened out when he becomes a famous radio crooner.

Hopalong Cassidy Returns
William Boyd, James Ellison, George Hayes, Evelyn Brent. Dir: Nate Watt. Pro: Harry Sherman. Seventh 'Hopalong Cassidy'.

I'd Give My Life
Sir Guy Standing, Tom Brown, Frances Drake. Dir: Edwin L. Marin. Pro: Richard A. Rowland. Murder drama involving a state governor, his wife and her gangster son. (Remake of *The Noose*, First National, 1928)

It's A Great Life
Joe Morrison, Paul Kelly, Rosalind Keith. Dir: Edward Cline. Pro: Harold Hurley. Country boy enlists for national service in a logging camp and proves heroic during a forest blaze.

Lady Be Careful
Lew Ayres, Mary Carlisle, Buster Crabbe. Dir: Theodore Reed. A girl who never says 'Yes' is romanced by a sailor whose shipmates bet him he can't change her mind. He does.

Mind Your Own Business
Charles Ruggles, Alice Brady, Lyle Talbot, Jack LaRue. Dir: Norman Z. McLeod. Pro: Emanuel Cohen. Newspaper columnist and his wife are kidnapped by crooks, rescued by Boy Scouts.

Murder With Pictures
Lew Ayres, Gail Patrick, Paul Kelly. Dir: Charles Barton. Pro: A.M. Botsford. Newspaper reporter-photographer comes to the aid of a girl being framed for a murder.

My American Wife
Francis Lederer, Ann Sothern, Fred Stone, Billie Burke. Dir: Harold Young. Pro: Albert Lewis. Comedy of conflict in an Arizona family when the daughter brings home her new husband, a count. (Remake of 1923 film)

Nevada
Buster Crabbe, Kathleen Burke, Monte Blue. Dir: Charles Barton. Pro: Harold Hurley. Zane Grey western about a cowboy, accused of murder during a gold rush, hunting down the real killer. (Remake of 1927 film)

Once In A Blue Moon
Jimmy Savo, Nikita Balieff, Cecilia Loftus. Dir & Pro: Ben Hecht, Charles MacArthur. Russian aristocrats, refugees from the revolution, are given shelter in a clown's circus wagon.

Palm Springs (GB **Palm Springs Affair**)
Frances Langford, Smith Ballew, Sir Guy Standing. Dir: Aubrey Scotto. Pro: Walter Wanger. Musical about a gambler's daughter who needs a millionaire husband but chooses a cowboy.

Peg Of Old Drury
Anna Neagle, Sir Cedric Hardwicke. Dir & Pro: Herbert Wilcox. The romantic adventures of an actress in old London. (British)

The Preview Murder Mystery
Reginald Denny, Gail Patrick, Frances Drake, Rod La Rocque. Dir: Robert Florey. Pro: Harold Hurley. Professional and romantic rivalries among movie-makers result in the deaths of a star and a director.

The Return Of Sophie Lang
Gertrude Michael, Ray Milland, Sir Guy Standing. Dir: George Archainbaud. Pro: A.M. Botsford. Sequel to *The Notorious Sophie Lang* finds the jewel thief in trouble as she tries to go straight.

Rose Bowl
Tom Brown, Eleanore Whitney, Buster Crabbe, William Frawley. Dir: Charles Barton. Pro: A.M. Botsford. Tangled romances of three football heroes with a home-town girl and a Hollywood star are sorted out by the big game.

The Sky Parade
Jimmie Allen, William Gargan, Katherine DeMille, Kent Taylor. Dir: Otho Lovering. Pro: Harold Hurley. Flying aces enter commercial aviation after the war and invent an automatic pilot which criminals try to steal.

Soak The Rich
Walter Connolly, John Howard, Mary Taylor. Dir & Pro: Ben Hecht, Charles MacArthur. Comedy about the kidnapping of an heiress who is mixed up in radical politics at college.

A Son Comes Home
Mary Boland, Donald Woods, Julie Hayden, Wallace Ford. Dir: E.A. Dupont. Pro: Albert Lewis. A woman gives up her guilty son to justice when an innocent man (her adopted son) is accused of murder.

Spendthrift
Henry Fonda, Pat Paterson, Mary Brian. Dir: Raoul Walsh. Pro: Walter Wanger. Polo-playing playboy divorces his adventurous wife, who gets his money while he gets his true love.

Straight From The Shoulder
Ralph Bellamy, Katherine Locke, David Holt. Dir: Stuart Heisler. Pro: A.M. Botsford. Having witnessed a gang murder, a man and his son hide out in the country, where they find a new wife and mother.

Three Cheers For Love
Robert Cummings, Eleanore Whitney, John Halliday. Dir: Ray McCarey. Pro: A.M. Botsford. Girl majors in singing and dancing at her finishing school; her movie-producer father signs up its show's cast.

Three Married Men
Lynne Overman, William Frawley, Roscoe Karns, Mary Brian. Dir: Edward Buzzell. Pro: Arthur Hornblow Jr. Newlyweds are harassed by relatives, quarrel, separate, and are reunited by accident.

Three On The Trail
William Boyd, James Ellison, George Hayes, Muriel Evans. Dir: Howard Bretherton. Pro: Harry Sherman. Fifth 'Hopalong Cassidy'.

Till We Meet Again
Herbert Marshall, Gertrude Michael, Lionel Atwill, Rod La Rocque. Dir: Robert Florey. Pro: Albert Lewis. Lovers are separated by war and their assignments as spies for opposite sides.

Timothy's Quest
Tom Keene, Eleanore Whitney, Dickie Moore, Virginia Weidler. Dir: Charles Barton. Pro: Harold Hurley. The adventures of a little boy and girl who run away from an orphanage and find refuge on a spinster's farm.

Too Many Parents
Frances Farmer, Lester Matthews, Billy Lee. Dir: Robert McGowan. Pro: A.M. Botsford. Four boys lacking parental love are helped out of various scrapes by their military academy's janitor and its principal's daughter.

Trail Dust
William Boyd, James Ellison, George Hayes. Dir: Nate Watt. Pro: Harry Sherman. Eighth 'Hopalong Cassidy'.

Wives Never Know
Charles Ruggles, Mary Boland, Adolphe Menjou. Dir: Elliott Nugent. Pro: Harlan Thompson. Comedy of a long-wed couple trying to bring their love back to life by arousing each other's jealousy.

Woman Trap
George Murphy, Gertrude Michael, Akim Tamiroff. Dir: Harold Young. Pro: Harold Hurley. Reporter and senator's daughter are held for ransom by a New York mobster and a Mexican bandit, the latter actually a secret policeman.

Yours For The Asking
George Raft, Ida Lupino, Dolores Costello. Dir: Alexander Hall. Pro: Lewis Gensler. A roadhouse owner attracts a gold-digging adventuress, but he prefers a society beauty whose mansion he turns into a swank gambling hall.

1937

▽ Charles Ruggles (left) had a rare chance to show what he could do with a dramatic part in **Exclusive**, and it was enough to lift Benjamin Glazer's production out of the routine 'B' category. He was moving as a decent newspaper editor, dismayed when his wild daughter (Frances Farmer, right, also impressive) takes a job on the rival paper, a muck-raking tabloid owned by a racketeer (Lloyd Nolan). While rescuing her from her boss, the father is killed and she returns, chastened, to her editor fiancé (Fred Mac-Murray, centre). Best sequence in the John Moffitt-Rian James-Sidney Salkow script (from a story by James): the crash of a department store elevator. Ralph Morgan, Fay Holden, Willard Robertson and Horace MacMahon were also in director Alexander Hall's cast. Contributing to the film's air of authenticity was the first-hand experience of Glazer, Moffitt and James, all ex-newspapermen.

▽ In most scenes now, John Barrymore (centre) gazed into space rather than at the person he was talking to. His fellow players put up with it because they knew he was reading his lines from an off-camera blackboard. The memory had gone, along with much of the famous good looks. But – **Night Club Scandal** made clear – the inimitable style was still intact. It brought a touch of class and a fizz of excitement to a grade B whodunit, first filmed in 1932 as *Guilty As Hell*, which Lillie Hayward had rescripted to focus attention on Barrymore's role as a (literally) lady-killing doctor who terminated his wife and framed her lover for the deed. Lynne Overman, Louise Campbell (right), Charles Bickford, Evelyn Brent (left), Harvey Stephens, Elizabeth Patterson (who was in the original too) and J. Carrol Naish were in the cast, tautly directed by Ralph Murphy.

▽ The celebrated Lubitsch touch deserted Ernst in his handling of a routine triangle story called **Angel**. It looked a lot more brilliantly sophisticated than it sounded, with such *soigné* performers as Marlene Dietrich (left), Herbert Marshall (right), Melvyn Douglas, Edward Everett Horton, Ernest Cossart (centre), Laura Hope Crews and Ivan Lebedeff inhabiting high-life sets of typical Paramount elegance, but finding little in Samson Raphaelson's script to say with amusing effect. Coming off best were Horton and Cossart as valet and butler, tartly commenting on their betters, while the latter were concerned with the infidelity of a bored wife (Dietrich) of a London diplomat (Marshall) during a Paris fling with a stranger (Douglas) who later turns up at her home as a guest of the husband. The laughs were few and far between, the box-office drooped, and Dietrich left the studio after a seven-year reign, not to return until a decade had passed. Minor roles in Lubitsch's production of a Melchior Lengyel play were filled by Herbert Mundin, Dennie Moore, Leonard Carey and Michael Visaroff.

▽ **Swing High, Swing Low** turned out to be that well-remembered backstage drama, *The Dance Of Life*, in which Nancy Carroll and Hal Skelly uncorked the world's tear-ducts in 1929. Slanted more towards comedy in the Virginia Van Upp-Oscar Hammerstein II rewrite, it now starred Carole Lombard and Fred MacMurray (both illustrated) as entertainers, stranded in Panama, who marry, then part when he is offered a trumpeting job on Broadway. Jealous of a voluptuous singer (Dorothy Lamour), she divorces him; he goes on the skids, recovers, and wins her back. It was another success for the Mitchell Leisen-Arthur Hornblow Jr team, who gave it direction and production of the highest grade, as well as a strong supporting cast: Charles Butterworth, Jean Dixon, Harvey Stephens, Cecil Cunningham, Franklin Pangborn, Anthony Quinn. Originally a stage hit as *Burlesque*, the George Watters-Arthur Hopkins play was sold by Paramount to Fox for a third filming, as *When My Baby Smiles At Me*, in 1948.

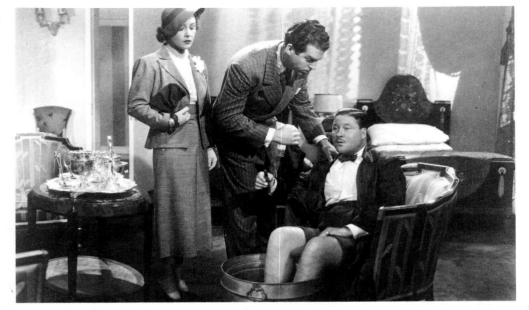

▽ Bing Crosby was the major magnet for **Double Or Nothing**'s box-office queues, and he kept his now phenomenal fan following happy with a nice bunch of songs, most popular of which was 'The Moon Got In My Eyes'. When it came to scene-stealing, however, Martha Raye (right) walked off with everything not nailed down. The cavern-mouthed comedienne was in great form as one of four recipients (Crosby, William Frawley, centre, and Andy Devine, left, were the others) of bankrolls from an eccentric millionaire which they had to double within thirty days. Author M. Coates Webster's inspiration seemed to have been *If I Had A Million*; scripters Charles Lederer, Edwin Gelsey, Duke Atterbury and John Moffitt added little of interest. Still, director Theodore Reed and producer Benjamin Glazer made it look good with gleaming sets, snappy editing (by Edward Dmytryk, whose directorial career was two years away) and an efficient supporting cast: Mary Carlisle, William Henry, Gilbert Emery, Walter Kingsford, Fay Holden, Benny Baker, Samuel S. Hinds and singer Frances Faye. Also present was Bing's partner from his old 'Rhythm Boys' days, Harry Barris.

▽ In a decade notable for its profusion of smart comedies, **Easy Living** shone among the brightest. Some devotees, indeed, class it as one of the most enjoyable fun films ever made, so inventive and perfectly paced were the script by Preston Sturges (from a Vera Caspary story) and the direction by Mitchell Leisen, who had some expert performers to work with. Jean Arthur played an office girl who, while riding on an open-top bus, has an expensive fur coat land on her. It has been thrown from a window by an irate millionaire (Edward Arnold) during a domestic fracas, and this eventuates in Miss Arthur (illustrated) being mistaken for Arnold's mistress by shopkeepers and hoteliers, who shower the bewildered girl with luxuries on credit. The hot-tempered tycoon's scenes with his long-suffering secretary (Esther Dale) and an excitable hotel manager (Luis Alberni) were hilarious, and the romance of his son (Ray Milland) with the girl had an airy charm. Mary Nash, Franklin Pangborn and William Demarest also scored in an Arthur Hornblow Jr production worth hornblowing about.

△ Billy Wilder, of all people, came up with a remarkably silly story, **Champagne Waltz**, which might have been more palatable with the dash of bitters his own direction and script would no doubt have given it five years later. Meanwhile, he and his collaborator Hy Kraft had to turn their yarn over to screenwriters Don Hartman and Frank Butler and director Edward Sutherland, none of whom was in sparkling mood. It concerned a pair of fun-loving American lads, Fred MacMurray (centre) – who should have been on double-time pay in 1936/7 – and Jack Oakie (right) opening a jazz café in Vienna, in direct competition with a waltz palace whose owner (Fritz Leiber) has a singing daughter (Gladys Swarthout, left). She has to choose between Fred's charm and Dad's business, a dilemma that didn't attract a lot of moviegoers. Several songs, Vivienne Osborne, Benny Baker, Maude Eburne, Herman Bing, Ernest Cossart and the dance team of Veloz & Yolanda were featured in Harlan Thompson's production. Adolph Zukor loved it, and put Wilder under contract. Now that *was* a good idea.

▽ The star of **Every Day's A Holiday** played Peaches O'Day, a confidence trickster, as a blonde and Mlle Fifi, a phoney French revue singer, as a brunette, but both were the same old Mae West, whose restricted range of expression and movement was at last beginning to pall on the public. Purity Leaguers still kept a corset on her screen dialogue, but she had just outraged church and press with a bawdy version of the Adam and Eve tale on the radio. This uproar, followed by mediocre returns on the new movie, prompted Paramount to let her go; she made four more pictures and many stage tours before she (but not her fame) died in 1980. This Emanuel Cohen production was actually one of her better vehicles, colourfully set in turn-of-the-century New York, where Mae sold the Brooklyn Bridge to easy mark Herman Bing, was run out of town by cop Edmund Lowe and brought back to trap corrupt police chief Lloyd Nolan (here with Mae as Fifi). The lively Jo Swerling plot was scripted by Mae as usual, and director Edward Sutherland got laughs via pros Charles Butterworth, Charles Winninger, Walter Catlett, Chester Conklin and the great Satchmo, Louis Armstrong. The West curves were – for the first and last time – adorned by Schiaparelli.

▽ **Thrill Of A Lifetime** featured a song, 'Keeno, Screeno And You', whose title referred to the prize-game gimmicks then being used to lure back crowds that were staying away because of too many dud movies like this one. The plot concocted by Grant Garrett, Seena Owen and Paul Gerard Smith displayed a breathtaking lack of novelty: a prim secretary's yearning for her playwright boss is unrequited until she takes off her glasses. (It was the boss, Leif Erickson, who needed them, considering she had been Betty Grable all along). Dorothy Lamour was prominently billed but made only a cameo appearance to sing the title song; also engaged were hayseed comedienne Judy Canova, Buster Crabbe (here, with Betty), Johnny Downs, Eleanore Whitney, Ben Blue, Franklin Pangborn, Tommy Wonder and The Yacht Club Boys. George Archainbaud directed, Fanchon Roger produced.

△ Encouraged by the success of *The Trail Of The Lonesome Pine*, Paramount shot another outdoor drama in Technicolor: **Ebb Tide**. It was less popular than its predecessor, with an even grimmer story and less attractive stars to sweeten it for the fans. However, Lucien Hubbard's production had guts, and the Bertram Millhauser script and James Hogan's direction caught the bitter strength of the Robert Louis Stevenson-Lloyd Osborne novel about a rum-swilling trio (Oscar Homolka, left, Ray Milland, and Barry Fitzgerald, right) taking a smallpox-infected boat across the Pacific, running into a typhoon and landing on an uncharted island, where they vie for a horde of pearls collected by a religious maniac (Lloyd Nolan). Milland, as the least brutal and the survivor of the three, Homolka, in his Hollywood debut, and Fitzgerald, also just starting in the States, were excellent, and well supported by Nolan, Frances Farmer, David Torrence, Lina Basquette and Charles Judels. It had been filmed silent in 1915, by Selig, and then in 1922 by Paramount. The studio remade it yet again in 1947 as *Adventure Island*.

▽ Leo McCarey defied all attempts to label his directorial style as it zigzagged from the comic anarchy of Marx Brothers and W.C. Fields farces to the unabashed tear-jerking of **Make Way For Tomorrow** and *Going My Way*. The latter film would get the Oscars and the paybox records; meanwhile the former won the respect of critics for not letting its sentimental story slop over. Vina Delmar's sensitive script stemmed from a Josephine Lawrence novel, by way of a Helen and Nolan Leary play, about the sadness of old age and the conflict between generations. Seasoned players Victor Moore (right), Beulah Bondi (left), Fay Bainter and Thomas Mitchell reached peaks of their careers, the first two as parents kept apart by lack of money, the other pair as their son and daughter-in-law unwilling to house them. Moore went to live with a reluctant daughter, Bondi to an old ladies' home, and audiences exited full of praise; but the subject was too melancholy for the box-office. Minna Gombell, Gene Lockhart, Louise Beavers, Elisabeth Risdon, Barbara Reed, Porter Hall and Maurice Moscovitch were other good actors employed.

▷ **Bulldog Drummond Escapes**, the ninth screen incarnation of the detective-adventurer created by 'Sapper' (H.C. McNeile), proved so popular that Paramount decided on a series, which stretched to eight features between 1937 and 1939. Running about an hour each and inexpensively made, with Edward T. Lowe or Stuart Walker producing and James Hogan or Louis King directing, they made for brisk entertainment. The first one was based on *Bulldog Drummond Saves A Lady*, co-authored by Gerard Fairlie and scripted by producer Lowe, with Ray Milland (left) as a light-hearted Drummond, Heather Angel (right) as his lady, Reginald Denny as his pal, E.E. Clive as his valet and Sir Guy Standing as the Scotland Yard chief. Standing died and was replaced in three films by John Barrymore, no less, who had a ball with extraordinary disguises; H.B. Warner then took over. Milland was too much in demand to be tied to a series, so John Howard ably Drummonded permanently; Angel gave way to Louise Campbell in three episodes; Denny and Clive remained throughout. Director Hogan's first cast also included Porter Hall, Fay Holden (who then became Andy Hardy's Ma in *that* series), Walter Kingsford and Clyde Cook.

▷ In the late thirties Paramount was notable for the best low-budget, fast-paced programme pictures in the business. **King Of Gamblers**, for instance, showed some of its more expensive brethren how to hold audience attention every minute, even if motivations were sometimes foggy and loose narrative ends left dangling. Robert Florey applied directorial zip to the Tiffany Thayer story about the czar of slot machines in the days before Las Vegas was built around them. Lots of high-octane acting by Akim Tamiroff (illustrated) as this shady character, until his reign was terminated by investigating reporter Lloyd Nolan and nightclub singer Claire Trevor. Other good performers of Doris Anderson's screenplay: Evelyn Brent, Harvey Stephens, Buster Crabbe, Porter Hall, Fay Holden, Cecil Cunningham, Colin Tapley and Helen Burgess.

△ Producer-director Frank Lloyd invested **Maid Of Salem** with considerable dignity and passion, but a sombre drama of witch-burning Puritans in 17th-century Massachusetts was not what the fans wanted from a Claudette Colbert-Fred MacMurray picture, and it was a financial flop. The miscast stars did their best with the roles of a New England girl and a Southern adventurer who fall in love, thereby shocking her townsfolk. She (illustrated) is accused of witchcraft, and he rescues her from death by fire after a tense trial sequence. The brooding atmosphere building up to mass hysteria was cleverly suggested, but it made the pace of the Bradley King-Walter Ferris-Durward Grinstead screenplay painfully slow at times. Good cast: Gale Sondergaard, Louise Dresser, Harvey Stephens, Beulah Bondi, Halliwell Hobbes, Edward Ellis, Donald Meek, E.E. Clive, and three exceptionally fine child performers, Bonita Granville, Virginia Weidler and Bennie Bartlett.

▽ The company scored a hit with **Internes Can't Take Money** (GB: **You Can't Take Money**) but it was like picking up a nugget and leaving the goldfield unmined. Why? Because its hero was Dr Kildare, and a year later MGM started making millions with the character in a long series of features and an even longer one on television, from which profits gushed even into the seventies. Joel McCrea played Max Brand's young doc (later made famous by Lew Ayres and then Richard Chamberlain) in an exciting Rian James-Theodore Reeves screenplay about his helping a gangster's widow to find her lost child. There was also a good deal of emergency surgery on underworld types along the way. Barbara Stanwyck (illustrated with McCrea) was compelling as the ex-convict mother; also cast, for producer Benjamin Glazer, and directed by Alfred Santell, were Lloyd Nolan, Stanley Ridges, Lee Bowman, Fay Holden, Pierre Watkin and Irving Bacon.

▽ Hundreds of grass skirts swung on swivel-hipped maidens, pineapple was the flavour of the week, and palm trees swayed to the swooning glissandos of 'Sweet Leilani' ... Hawaii, or a glorified facsimile thereof, was back on the screen; that song was being crooned to best-sellerdom by Bing Crosby; and **Waikiki Wedding** was a hit as big as the Pacific. The Frank Butler-Don Hartman story, scripted by them, Walter De Leon and Francis Martin, and shrewdly fashioned for the box-office by producer Arthur Hornblow Jr and director Frank Tuttle, had Bing as the pineapple growers' publicity whizz-kid who falls in love with the winner of his Pineapple Princess contest, Shirley Ross (illustrated with Bing). Meanwhile his side-kick, Bob Burns, had his hands full in more ways than one with Martha Raye, thus giving Bing the same comedy back-up that worked so well in *Rhythm On The Range*. Leif Erickson, George Barbier, Granville Bates, Anthony Quinn, Grady Sutton and Mitchell Lewis made up a solid supporting cast, and Harry Owens's Oscar-winning 'Leilani' had good companions in the Ralph Rainger-Leo Robin ditties 'Blue Hawaii', 'In A Little Hula Heaven', and 'Sweet Is The Word For You'.

△ **Souls At Sea** had plenty to offer action lovers, and they came in theatre-filling numbers to get it. Henry Hathaway's big-scale production concerned the US Navy's fight against 19th-century slave traders, with Gary Cooper caught in the middle. He was the accused in two court trials, first as an officer of a slave ship, then as the commander of an overloaded lifeboat, from which he had thrown men overboard. Such lack of ruth in our hero's conduct was explained by his being an intelligence man whose mission must not fail, shipwrecks and villainous cut-throats regardless. His pal through thick and thin was George Raft (illustrated right with Cooper), in a surprisingly lively excursion into character acting; Cooper, too, drew zest from the eventful Grover Jones-Dale Van Every script, based on Ted Lesser's story; and Frances Dee, Henry Wilcoxon, Harry Carey, Olympe Bradna, Robert Cummings, George Zucco, Porter Hall, Joseph Schildkraut, Virginia Weidler, Gilbert Emery, Fay Holden, Tully Marshall and Monte Blue all shone under Hathaway's direction. Once intended as a road-show special, it was switched to normal release and cut to 93 minutes, thereby gaining in narrative speed and tightness.

△ **I Met Him In Paris** (where else, if you were in a Paramount comedy?) wafted Claudette Colbert (centre) back, after the dolours of *Maid Of Salem*, to the kind of romantic fun that served her so often during her long career. The well-used Paris sets and their favourite occupant looked as good as new in this Wesley Ruggles diversion, presenting her as a work-weary fashion designer wooed by a cynical playwright (Melvyn Douglas, right) and a married novelist (Robert Young, left). The latter's wife (Mona Barrie) and the designer's fiancé (Lee Bowman) turned up, and the mild suspense of Claudette's choice of mate sustained Claude Binyon's screenplay, from a story by Helen Meinardi, until fade-out time. Douglas got top male billing, if you needed a clue. A jaunt to Switzerland for some skiing, skating and tobogganing made a nice change of scenery.

▽ Charles 'Buddy' Rogers came back for one last Paramount picture as Betty Grable arrived for her first as a star. It was **This Way, Please**, in which he played a Hollywood idol and she an usher in a theatre he visits. They looked each other over; they clicked. The movie didn't. Mel Shauer's production had a remember-the-budget look, and director Robert Florey seemed indifferent to the material supplied by the authors (Maxwell Shane, William Thomas) and the scripters (Seena Owen, Grant Garrett, Howard Green), and you couldn't blame him. Except for a remarkable mimic, Rufe Davis, the cast – Lee Bowman, Ned Sparks, Wally Vernon, Mary Livingstone, Porter Hall, Cecil Cunningham, Romo Vincent – was also on the droopy side. Off screen, the stars (illustrated) were linking Hollywood's past and present: Rogers had just married Mary Pickford (her third husband), and Grable was about to become Mrs Jackie Coogan (for a while).

▽ Cashing in on the current headlines about the Spanish Civil War, **The Last Train From Madrid** shirked arguments for or against either side. Strongly cast, with Dorothy Lamour, Lew Ayres (centre left on cart), Helen Mack, Lionel Atwill, Karen Morley, Gilbert Roland (centre right), Olympe Bradna, Lee Bowman, Robert Cummings, Evelyn Brent and Anthony Quinn, the George M. Arthur-Hugh Bennett production was otherwise deplorable. James Hogan's direction of an incredible script by Louis Stevens and Robert Wyler, from Elsie and Paul Harvey Fox's original, had a slapdash air, and for realism of time and place it might as well have been The Last Subway From The Bronx. Although slammed by the critics, it brought pretty good attendances, doubtless drawn by so many well-known players (of whom Ayres as a journalist and Bradna as a girl shot before the train reaches Valencia were best) enacting its sub-*Grand Hotel* batch of stories.

△ Five years before **High, Wide And Handsome**, director Rouben Mamoulian had dazzled everybody with new film musical techniques in *Love Me Tonight*. Five years before that, composer Jerome Kern and lyricist Oscar Hammerstein II had opened fresh vistas for the stage musical with *Show Boat*. Putting the three together seemed a remarkable coup for the studio, arousing expectations so high that disappointment with the result fell like a cloudburst on a picnic. Some critics and many customers liked it, and three of its songs ('The Folks Who Live On The Hill', 'Can I Forget You?', 'High, Wide And Handsome') are evergreens. But the returns were not exciting, and neither was Hammerstein's script about a circus girl (Irene Dunne, right) who marries a farmer (Randolph Scott, left) and, when he strikes oil and his men are attacked by railroaders, calls in her big-top friends to help him. The battle, involving acrobats and elephants, pepped up the picture considerably. Arthur Hornblow Jr produced, casting Dorothy Lamour, Alan Hale, Charles Bickford, Raymond Walburn, Akim Tamiroff, Elizabeth Patterson, William Frawley, Ben Blue and Irving Pichel.

▽ In 1937 Carole Lombard (centre) wound up her eight years with Paramount, during which time she had developed into a major attraction – and, for once, a departing star was given a good script. In fact, some buffs rate **True Confession**, written by Claude Binyon from a French play (*Mon Crime*) by Louis Verneuil and Georges Berr, as one of her best pictures. Fred MacMurray, opposite Lombard for the fourth time, played a struggling lawyer who wins fame by getting an acquittal, on a plea of self-defence, for his wife after she confesses to the murder of her boss. Actually she has done nothing of the kind; an uninhibited liar, she is now hounded by a screwball criminologist who knows the truth. All ended happily after much wild comedy, with broad satire in the courtroom sequence and funny performances by an often too shrill Lombard and John Barrymore as her zany nemesis. Wesley Ruggles directed; Albert Lewin produced (his first for the studio); Una Merkel (left), Lynne Overman, Edgar Kennedy (right), Porter Hall, Fritz Feld and Hattie McDaniel featured. Lombard made seven more films before her death in a 1942 plane crash during a War Bond selling tour.

▷ Exhaustingly thorough and determinedly epic, **Wells Fargo** alternated slabs of historical information with layers of domestic drama. The first ingredient gained from producer-director Frank Lloyd's sweeping style in depicting the development of the West's express service, with enough trail-blazing action to relieve the factual stodge. On the other hand, the lengthy footage allowed to the hero and heroine's love, marriage and conflict was a bit of a drag, although you couldn't help liking such nice, handsome people as Joel McCrea (centre right) and Frances Dee, who were Mr and Mrs off screen too (they celebrated their golden wedding in 1983). Lloyd Nolan, Robert Cummings, Bob Burns, John Mack Brown, Ralph Morgan, Henry O'Neill, Mary Nash, Frank Conroy, Harry Davenport, Porter Hall, Clarence Kolb and Stanley Fields (right) also figured in the Frederick Jackson-Paul Schofield-Gerald Geraghty screenplay, from a novel by Stuart Lake. Howard Estabrook was Lloyd's co-producer, as on *Maid Of Salem*, than which this one proved a sturdier paybox attraction.

OTHER RELEASES OF 1937

Arizona Mahoney
Robert Cummings, June Martel, Buster Crabbe. Dir: James Hogan. Pro: A.M. Botsford. Zane Grey story of a tenderfoot who gets tough when he tangles with western outlaws. (Remake of *Stairs Of Sand*, 1929)

Artists And Models
Jack Benny, Ida Lupino, Richard Arlen, Gail Patrick. Dir: Raoul Walsh. Pro: Lewis Gensler. Comedy of rivalries in the choice of queen of a charity ball, serving as a showcase for radio and record stars.

The Barrier
James Ellison, Jean Parker, Otto Kruger, Leo Carrillo. Dir: Lesley Selander. Pro: Harry Sherman. Melodrama of a father seeking to baulk his daughter's marriage by revealing a past stigma. (Remake of 1928 MGM film)

Blonde Trouble
Johnny Downs, Eleanore Whitney, Lynne Overman. Dir: George Archainbaud. Young songwriter crashes the crazy world of Tin Pan Alley and emerges with a hit. (Remake of *June Moon*, 1931)

Blossoms On Broadway
Edward Arnold, Shirley Ross, John Trent. Dir: Richard Wallace. Pro: B.P. Schulberg. Comedy-drama with songs, about a confidence man kidnapping a woman who owns a goldmine.

Borderland
William Boyd, James Ellison, George Hayes. Dir: Nate Watt. Pro: Harry Sherman, Eugene Strong. Ninth 'Hopalong Cassidy'.

Bulldog Drummond Comes Back
John Howard, John Barrymore, Louise Campbell. Dir: Louis King. Pro: Edward T. Lowe. From Sapper's 'Female Of The Species'. The heroine is kidnapped by a villain who leaves sound-recorded clues for Drummond.

Bulldog Drummond's Revenge
John Howard, John Barrymore, Louise Campbell. Dir: Louis King. Pro: Edward T. Lowe. From Sapper's 'The Return of Bulldog Drummond'. The killing of a scientist and theft of a secret formula are probed.

Clarence
Roscoe Karns, Johnny Downs, Eleanore Whitney, Eugene Pallette. Dir: George Archainbaud. Booth Tarkington's comedy about a young man who gets involved in a temperamental family's affairs. (Remake of 1922 film)

The Crime Nobody Saw
Lew Ayres, Vivienne Osborne, Eugene Pallette. Dir: Charles Barton. Three writers stumble on a plot for a new play when a neighbour is murdered; all the suspects confess for various reasons; one is guilty.

Daughter Of Shanghai
Anna May Wong, Charles Bickford, Evelyn Brent, J. Carrol Naish. Dir: Robert Florey. Pro: Harold Hurley. Lady detective and FBI man, both Chinese, solve a murder case concerning smugglers of illegal immigrants

A Doctor's Diary
George Bancroft, Helen Burgess, Molly Lamont, Sidney Blackmer. Dir: Charles Vidor. Pro: B.P. Schulberg. The owner of a fashionable hospital admits guilt after his house doctor is shot at a negligence trial by the patient's mother.

Forlorn River
Buster Crabbe, Ruth Warren, Harvey Stephens. Dir: Charles Barton. Zane Grey's melodrama of ranchers preyed upon by cattle rustlers. (Remake of 1926 film)

The Girl From Scotland Yard
Karen Morley, Robert Baldwin, Eduardo Ciannelli. Dir: Robert Vignola. Pro: Emanuel Cohen. The heroine survives a plane battle over Buckingham Palace and the fiendish villain's death ray.

The Great Gambini
Akim Tamiroff, Genevieve Tobin, Reginald Denny. Dir: Charles Vidor. Pro: B.P. Schulberg. Melodrama of a clairvoyant who predicts other peoples deaths and causes his own.

Her Husband Lies
Ricardo Cortez, Gail Patrick, Tom Brown, Akim Tamiroff. Dir: Edward Ludwig. Pro: B.P. Schulberg. Big-shot gambler is challenged for supremacy by a younger brother. (Remake of *Street Of Chance*, 1930)

Hideaway Girl
Martha Raye, Robert Cummings, Shirley Ross. Dir: George Archainbaud. Pro: A.M. Botsford. Girl fleeing from jewel robbery is hidden aboard his yacht by a playboy, whose fiancée is exposed as the real thief.

Hills Of Old Wyoming
William Boyd, Russell Hayden, George Hayes. Dir: Nate Watt. Pro: Harry Sherman. Tenth 'Hopalong Cassidy'.

Hold 'Em, Navy
Lew Ayres, John Howard, Mary Carlisle. Dir: Kurt Neumann. Drama of midshipmen's rivalry at Annapolis, with big football game climax.

Hopalong Rides Again
William Boyd, Russell Hayden, George Hayes. Dir: Lesley Selander. Pro: Harry Sherman. 13th 'Hopalong Cassidy'.

Hotel Haywire
Leo Carrillo, Mary Carlisle, Lynne Overman, Spring Byington. Dir: George Archainbaud. A doctor and his wife, their daughter, her fiance, a pair of detectives and a crooked astrologer in wild farce.

John Meade's Woman
Edward Arnold, George Bancroft, Francine Larrimore. Dir: Richard Wallace. Pro: B.P. Schulberg. Big businessman, rejected by the woman he loves, marries another and lives to regret it.

Let's Make A Million
Edward Everett Horton, Charlotte Wynters. Dir: Ray McCarey. Pro: Harold Hurley. Small-town shopkeeper is fleeced by con-men, gets his money back, buys land from his aunts and strikes oil.

Midnight Madonna
Warren William, Mady Correll. Dir: James Flood. Pro: Emanuel Cohen. In a battle for their daughter's custody, the mother is accused of immorality, and the father of greed for the child's inheritance.

Mountain Music
Martha Raye, Bob Burns, John Howard. Dir: Robert Florey. Pro: Benjamin Glazer. Comedy with songs, about a backwoods gal and a hillbilly who loves her only when having one of his crazy spells.

Murder Goes To College
Lynne Overman, Roscoe Karns, Marsha Hunt, Buster Crabbe. Dir: Charles Reisner. Pro: Harold Hurley. A private eye and a reporter team up to solve a campus killing puzzle.

A Night Of Mystery
Grant Richards, Roscoe Karns, Ruth Coleman, Helen Burgess. Dir: E.A. Dupont. Homicide in a wealthy New York family is investigated by erudite gumshoe Philo Vance. (Remake of *The Greene Murder Case*, 1930)

North Of Rio Grande
William Boyd, Russell Hayden, George Hayes, Lee J. Cobb. Dir: Nate Watt. Pro: Harry Sherman. Eleventh 'Hopalong Cassidy'.

On Such A Night
Karen Morley, Grant Richards, Roscoe Karns. Dir: E.A. Dupont. Pro: Emanuel Cohen. Flood waters maroon a houseful of people, including a Broadway star; her husband, wrongly accused of murder; and the real killer.

Outcast
Warren William, Karen Morley, Lewis Stone. Dir: Robert Florey. Pro: Emanuel Cohen. A lawyer and a girl come to the aid of an innocent doctor when he is accused of murder and threatened by mob violence.

Partners In Crime
Lynne Overman, Roscoe Karns, Anthony Quinn. Dir: Ralph Murphy. Pro: Harold Hurley. The investigators of *Murder Goes To College* get mixed up in politics and extortion.

Partners Of The Plains
William Boyd, Russell Hayden. Dir: Lesley Selander. Pro: Harry Sherman. 15th 'Hopalong Cassidy'.

Rustlers' Valley
William Boyd, Russell Hayden, George Hayes, Lee J. Cobb.. Dir: Nate Watt. Pro: Harry Sherman. 12th 'Hopalong Cassidy'.

She Asked For It
Vivienne Osborne, William Gargan, Roland Drew. Dir: Erle Kenton. Pro: B.P. Schulberg. Writer of best-selling mysteries assumes the identity of his fictional detective and discovers the murderers of his uncle.

She's No Lady
Ann Dvorak, John Trent. Dir: Charles Vidor. Pro: B.P. Schulberg. A bogus jewel robbery is exposed by an insurance investigator posing as an adventuress and a detective pretending to be a society playboy.

Sophie Lang Goes West
Gertrude Michael, Buster Crabbe. Dir: Charles Reisner. Pro: A.M. Botsford. Still trying to go straight, the international jewel thief finds danger on a California-bound train during her final adventure.

The Texas Trail
William Boyd, Russell Hayden, George Hayes, Judith Allen. Dir: David Selman. Pro: Harry Sherman. 14th 'Hopalong Cassidy'.

Thunder Trail
Gilbert Roland, Charles Bickford, Marsha Hunt, J. Carrol Naish. Dir: Charles Barton. Zane Grey western about a man missing for 15 years and returning to save his family from a villain's depradations

Turn Off The Moon
Charles Ruggles, Kenny Baker, Eleanore Whitney, Johnny Downs. Dir: Lewis Seiler. Pro: Fanchon Royer. Comedy with music, concerning assorted romances complicated by an astrologer's predictions.

Wild Money
Edward Everett Horton, Louise Campbell, Lynne Overman. Dir: Louis King. The penny-pinching auditor for a newspaper becomes a spendthrift while story-chasing.

1938

▽ **Artists And Models Abroad** (GB: **Stranded In Paris**) clocked up a high laugh score, as might be expected with Jack Benny (illustrated), Mary Boland, Monty Woolley, Charley Grapewin and Fritz Feld on hand, and it had loads of visual style, thanks to the directorial supervision of ex-designer Mitchell Leisen. Joan Bennett (illustrated) added her cool chic to the proceedings as an oil tycoon's daughter distracting Benny from his efforts to get a theatrical troupe out of hock when they were penniless in Paris. Songs and fashion parades took over from the Howard Lindsay-Russel Crouse-Ken Englund script at welcome intervals. Producer Arthur Hornblow Jr rounded out the cast with Phyllis Kennedy, Joyce Compton, G.P. Huntley Jr, Adrienne d'Ambricourt and the Yacht Club Boys. Like the previous year's *Artists And Models*, also starring Benny, it was mildly successful although it really had nothing to do with artists and models; the title was considered vaguely daring since its use on a series of Shubert revues on Broadway back in the 1920s.

▽ Erich Pommer, the most brilliant producer in Germany until he left it to the Nazis, joined with Charles Laughton to form Mayflower, a British production company which made three pictures with Paramount participation and American release. The first, **The Beachcomber** (GB: **Vessel Of Wrath**) was the most entertaining, and remarkable for having been directed by Pommer himself for once; also for giving Laughton and his wife, Elsa Lanchester (both illustrated), roles of equal importance. They attacked them with a histrionic relish wonderful to behold, he as an alcoholic derelict lazing through life in the Dutch East Indies, she as a missionary's spinster sister determined to reform him. Reacting variously to their clash of wills and eventual happiness together were Robert Newton, Tyrone Guthrie, Dolly Mollinger, Eliot Makeham, Rosita Garcia and Fred Groves. Bartlett Cormack adapted the W. Somerset Maugham story, which was remade 16 years later by Muriel and Sydney Box, as *The Beachcomber* with Robert Newton and Glynis Johns in the leads; *The African Queen*, however, was not a remake but a coincidence.

▽ A hefty budget and the luxury of all-Technicolor photography, still rare in 1938, were supposed to give **Men With Wings** importance, but the movie refused to become airborne. This was particularly disappointing because the same director and screenwriter, William Wellman and Robert Carson, had just had an Oscar-strewn triumph with *A Star Is Born* and their new one was expected to be in that category. And hadn't Wellman made the best of air epics in *Wings*? Yes, and it showed in some of the exciting action shots here; but the story kept getting bogged down in the old two-pals-and-a-gal formula, with Fred MacMurray (right) and Ray Milland vying for the love of Louise Campbell (left) when they should have been getting on with the more interesting subject of early aviation. Wellman also produced, casting Andy Devine, Walter Abel, Lynne Overman, Porter Hall, Willard Robertson, James Burke, and, playing the three leads as children, future star Donald O'Connor, Billy Cook and Virginia Weidler.

▷ Bob Hope (right) said '*Variety* is offering a $10,000 prize to anybody who can describe the plot'. He was talking about **The Big Broadcast Of 1938**, fourth and last of the musical series, and any attempt to win that prize would falter after saying it was an idiotic story about a transatlantic race by two super-liners, one staging an all-star radio show en route. For further information, consult writers Frederick H. Brennan, Howard Lindsay, Russel Crouse, Ken Englund, Walter De Leon and Francis Martin, or their spirits. Anyway, its chief claim to fame was Hope's film debut, after stage and radio successes. The start of his 30 Paramount years coincided with the end of W.C. Fields's 13; he (left) shifted to Universal after taking top-billing here over Dorothy Lamour, Martha Raye, Hope, Shirley Ross (centre), Lynne Overman, Leif Erickson, Ben Blue, Grace Bradley, singer Tito Guizar and diva Kirsten Flagstad. Mitchell Leisen directed; Harlan Thompson produced. Lots of songs, ranging from a Wagner aria for Flagstad to Leo Robin and Ralph Rainger's Oscar-winning hit, 'Thanks For The Memory', for Hope and Ross. Lots of box-office business, too.

△ **Prison Farm** was a brisk shocker about a girl thrust into a working institution for delinquents, manned (or womanned) by sadistic guards. J. Carrol Naish delivered the frightmare with special effectiveness as one of the official brutes, and Marjorie Main (left) was equally repellent as one of the female variety, while Shirley Ross (centre) suffered the heroine's torments convincingly. Stuart Walker's production was a sort of sex switch on Warner's *I Am A Fugitive From A Chain Gang* for the double bills, written by Robert Yost, Eddie Welch and Stuart Anthony, from an original by Edwin Westrate. Louis King directed a cast also including Lloyd Nolan (centre right), John Howard, Esther Dale, Porter Hall (2nd left), May Boley and silent star Anna Q. Nilsson.

△ **Dangerous To Know** offered a juicy chunk of melodrama, and found plenty of takers with sufficiently strong digestions. In the part that made Charles Laughton a star on the London stage in 1930's *On The Spot*, Akim Tamiroff was deliciously hammy. His luxury-loving, organ-playing, mistress-tormenting crime czar dominated Edgar Wallace's cunningly contrived play, screenwritten by Horace McCoy and William Lipman, produced by Edward T. Lowe and directed by Robert Florey. Anna May Wong, who had the same role in New York on stage, played the kept woman seeking revenge when the gangleader tries to discard her for a newcomer (Gail Patrick, right), and other effective acting jobs came from Lloyd Nolan, Anthony Quinn, Pierre Watkin (centre), Harvey Stephens, Roscoe Karns, Porter Hall, Hedda Hopper (left) and Hugh Sothern.

▽ Claudette Colbert and Gary Cooper in **Bluebeard's Eighth Wife**, directed by Ernst Lubitsch, sounded like sheer bliss to lovers of sophisticated comedy. And the opening scene – a shop in which Gary (left) is buying only pajama tops while Claudette (centre) requires only the bottoms – promised joys to come. They never did. The story, of a seven times married and divorced millionaire who meets his final match in an impoverished nobleman's daughter, grew steadily duller as this first collaboration of the later celebrated team, Charles Brackett and Billy Wilder (who called the hero/heroine introductions like the above his 'meet cutes'), ground on. The Lubitsch Touch became a heavy hand, and his dazzling Paramount decade was over; annoyingly, he went straight to MGM and scored a triumph with *Ninotchka*. His last Paramount cast included Edward Everett Horton, David Niven, Elizabeth Patterson, Herman Bing, Warren Hymer, Tyler Brooke (right) and Franklin Pangborn. The Alfred Savoir play, here adapted by Charlton Andrews, had been filmed silent in 1923 as a Gloria Swanson starrer.

▽ When **Romance In The Dark** flopped, Paramount gave up the struggle after three years of trying to make Gladys Swarthout an important movie name (the name itself didn't help), put her in one last non-musical 'B', *Ambush*, and said goodbye. The beauteous opera star with the gorgeous voice went back to stage and radio and did very well, thank you, but her last film musical was released with a dull thud and just lay there. Based on Hermann Bahr's old play *The Yellow Nightingale*, the Anne Morrison Chapin-Frank Partos script concerned a Hungarian miss getting caught up in the amorous dallyings of a tenor (John Boles) and his manager (John Barrymore, here with Gladys). H.C. Potter directed them and Claire Dodd, Fritz Feld, Curt Bois and Ferdinand Gottschalk in the Harlan Thompson production.

△ All-star action melodramas didn't come much better than **Spawn Of The North**, an eventful yarn of the war between Russian and American salmon-fishing fleets along the Alaskan coast. It was a winner for Paramount, which made several such big-scale mass entertainments in a period when other companies were scooping up all the Oscars and critics' awards. Even some of the reviewers enthused about the rugged vigour of Henry Hathaway's direction of this Barrett Willoughby story, scripted by Jules Furthman and Talbot Jennings. Performances pleased, too: Henry Fonda as the stalwart skipper; Dorothy Lamour as the gal who stands by him, defying the world, the fish and the devil; George Raft (here with Lamour), his pal who goes over to the bad guys but thinks better of it; John Barrymore, great fun as a grizzled, guzzling newspaperman; Akim Tamiroff, the Russian heavy; Louise Platt, Lynne Overman, Duncan Renaldo, Vladimir Sokoloff, Fuzzy Knight, John Wray. Charles Lang's photography, the exteriors shot mostly in Alaska, was an outstanding feature of the Albert Lewin production.

△ A super-colossal swashbuckler rolled off the Cecil B. DeMille assembly line, to be received with the usual shrugs from the critics and with open arms from the people who paid to get in. **The Buccaneer**, played with Fairbanks-like bravura by Fredric March, was a rip-roaring pirate called Jean Lafitte, summoned by President Andrew Jackson to help the United States against the wicked British in the War of 1812. His sea exploits were given the full C.B. treatment and his private life received a romantic once-over from the writers (Jeanie Macpherson, Edwin Justus Mayer, C. Gardner Sullivan, Harold Lamb, working from a story by Lyle Saxon), with Franciska Gaal (right) imported from Europe to play the Louisiana bayou girl who entrances him. Other principals in the customary 'Cast Of Thousands!' were Akim Tamiroff (left), Margot Grahame, Anthony Quinn, Walter Brennan, Ian Keith, Beulah Bondi, Douglass Dumbrille, Spring Byington, Robert Barrat, Gilbert Emery, Evelyn Keyes, Richard Denning and Holmes Herbert.

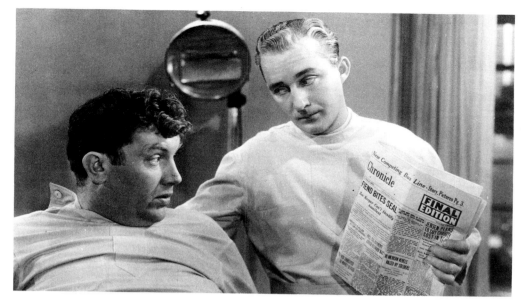

▽ With admirable directness and force **Hunted Men**, a 65-minute 'B', told much the same story as *The Desperate Hours* did at nearly twice the length 17 years later. A killer on the run from the cops takes refuge in an ordinary suburban home; he holds the family hostage but, gradually mellowing under their influence, he is finally induced by the head of the household to give himself up rather than expose them to a gun battle. Lloyd Nolan (left), always a splendid actor, gave a vivid performance in an above-average cast: J. Carrol Naish, Lynne Overman, Mary Carlisle (centre), Buster Crabbe (right), Anthony Quinn, Dorothy Peterson, Regis Toomey and Johnny Downs. Stuart Walker produced and Louis King directed the taut Horace McCoy-William Lipman screenplay, adapted from a story by Albert Duffy and Marion Grant.

▽ A good-natured comedy, **Thanks For The Memory** was designed to cash in on the huge hit Bob Hope and Shirley Ross (both illustrated) had scored with its title song in *Big Broadcast Of 1938*. And they were given another superb duet that spun a million discs: 'Two Sleepy People', by Hoagy Carmichael and Frank Loesser. Charles Butterworth, Otto Kruger, Laura Hope Crews, Hedda Hopper, Roscoe Karns, Patricia Wilder, William Collier Sr, Emma Dunn and Eddie 'Rochester' Anderson accompanied the two leads through Lynn Starling's screenplay – from the Albert Hackett-Frances Goodrich play *Up Pops The Devil*, first filmed in 1931 – about a bohemian couple's bumpy ride on the matrimonial highway. George Archainbaud directed and it was produced by Mel Shauer. Well received.

△ Bing Crosby's career went under a cloud called **Doctor Rhythm**, which had a silver lining called Beatrice Lillie. As always, Bea comported herself with a jaunty gentility that ever threatened to collapse into slapstick, while enacting the role of Lorelei Dodge-Blodgett, whose ward (Mary Carlisle) has Bing (right) for a bodyguard. He is really a doctor who has taken the job to help out his policeman pal (Andy Devine, left) and, would you believe it, he falls in love with the girl! The Jo Swerling-Richard Connell script was full of daring surprises like this. The audience found it more rewarding to concentrate on Bing's pleasant songs, among them: 'On The Sentimental Side', 'My Heart Is Taking Lessons', 'This Is My Night To Dream' by Johnny Burke and James V. Monaco. Emanuel Cohen's production, based on the O. Henry short story *The Badge Of Policeman O'Roon*, also cast Louis Armstrong, Laura Hope Crews, Fred Keating, Sterling Holloway, Rufe Davis, Franklin Pangborn and William Austin under the direction of Frank Tuttle. Business was below the Crosby average.

▽ That mellow voice, and special way with speeches that would sound too flowery from other actors, made Ronald Colman (illustrated) an ideal choice for François Villon in **If I Were King**, even though he was hardly the beggar-poet type. In Frank Lloyd's spacious production his whimsical romanticism had a great foil in Basil Rathbone's King Louis XI, the very picture of shrewd wit as he countered Villon's popularity with the poor and the Duke of Burgundy's plotting with the nobles. Given a literate script by Preston Sturges and smooth pacing by Lloyd, it was altogether the most satisfying movie version of Justin McCarthy's play. The others: starring William Farnum, by Fox, 1920 and, with music as *The Vagabond King*, Dennis King, 1930, and Orestes, 1956; both the latter by Paramount. This cast included Frances Dee, Ralph Forbes, Ellen Drew, C.V. France, Henry Wilcoxon, Heather Thatcher, Stanley Ridges, Sidney Toler, Colin Tapley, Montagu Love, John Miljan and Bruce Lester. Hans Dreier's and John Goodman's production design was an eyeful.

▷ Burns and Allen bounced back with a bird-brained but undeniably entertaining musical, **College Swing** (GB: **Swing, Teacher, Swing**) in which Gracie inherited a small-town school and George looked on sardonically as she reorganized the curriculum into delirium. For example, she hired vaudeville performers as professors, so both students and audiences enjoyed lessons from Martha Raye, Bob Hope, Ben Blue, Betty Grable and Jackie Coogan (both illustrated), Jerry Colonna, Skinny Ennis and the Slate Brothers. Also in Lewis Gensler's production, directed by Raoul Walsh, no less, were Edward Everett Horton, Florence George, John Payne, Cecil Cunningham, Robert Cummings, and a beautiful song by Frank Loesser, Manning Sherwin and Arthur Altman: 'I Fall In Love With You Every Day'. Two Loesser-Burton Lane contributions, 'Moments Like This' and 'How'dja Like To Love Me?' were also popular. The Walter De Leon-Francis Martin-Morrie Ryskind-Preston Sturges script grew from stories by Frederick Hazlitt Brennan and Ted Lesser – and we'd thought it was just another rewrite of the old *Charm School* inherited college formula, silly old us!

◁ The profits from *Jungle Princess* kept coming like the lava from its volcano, so Dorothy Lamour and Ray Milland (both illustrated) were ordered back to the studio tropics for **Her Jungle Love**. It had a bigger budget, which permitted Technicolor, extra crocodiles and an earthquake, but otherwise it stayed as close as possible to the first film's basics: lightly clad island beauty plus handsome male visitor plus the mating instinct, minus everything that might offend Aunt Agatha. While the stars got on with the mush (he gave her kissing lessons, etc.), her pet chimp and Lynne Overman, as Ray's co-survivor of their crash-landed plane, fought it out for comedy honours. Also involved were J. Carrol Naish, Jonathan Hale, Dorothy Howe, Archie Twitchell and Edward Earle, with George Archainbaud directing. The Gerald Geraghty-Kurt Siodmak story was scripted by Joseph Moncure March, Lillie Hayward and Eddie Welch, and produced by George M. Arthur. Box-office? Yes indeed it was.

▽ Bing Crosby (right) essayed his first semi-serious role in **Sing You Sinners**, and his success in it indicated that his career could indeed stretch beyond the bounds of musical comedy. In Claude Binyon's richly entertaining family story, he played the feckless brother of hard-working Fred MacMurray (centre); the money he loses on gambling keeps them broke even though they and kid brother Donald O'Connor (left) moonlight as a musical act. Finally he scrapes together enough to buy a horse which amazes everybody by winning a big race. Producer-director Wesley Ruggles punctuated the story with songs, three of them big hits: 'I've Got A Pocketful Of Dreams', 'Don't Let That Moon Get Away' (both by Johnny Burke and James V. Monaco) and the unforgettable 'Small Fry' (by Frank Loesser and Hoagy Carmichael) sung to 13-year-old O'Connor. Elizabeth Patterson, great as the boys' mother; Ellen Drew, a lovely heroine; John Gallaudet, William Haade and Irving Bacon completed the cast. A profit-maker.

▷ According to **The Texans**, there was a whole lot going on in the Lone Star state after the Civil War: the farmers and the cattlemen were struggling for the wide open spaces, new towns were springing up, the violent bigotry of the Ku Klux Klan was erupting and Joan Bennett (right) was choosing between Randolph Scott (left) and Robert Cummings. A well received and profitable release, it was a remake of the 1924 silent *North Of 36*, Emerson Hough's sequel to *The Covered Wagon*, now scripted by Bertram Millhauser, Paul Sloane and William Wister Haines. Lucien Hubbard produced, and James Hogan directed a cast that included May Robson, Walter Brennan, Harvey Stephens, Robert Barrat, Raymond Hatton, Francis Ford and Clarence Wilson.

△ Fritz Lang's third movie in America was an extraordinary one. The great German director seemed uncertain whether **You And Me** should be a drama of social significance or a comedy of romantic dilemma, and the critics were similarly flummoxed, giving it widely differing reviews. The public, noting that it starred Sylvia Sidney and George Raft (both illustrated), decided it was a sad tale about crooks in love, and most of them went to see something else. Norman Krasna's story, scripted by Virginia Van Upp, was set in a department store staffed mostly, thanks to its benevolent owner, by ex-convicts and parolees. Two of them fall in love, and into trouble because the rules do not permit them to marry. The stars were restrained and moving, but amusing scenes with Robert Cummings, Roscoe Karns, Barton MacLane, Harry Carey, George E. Stone, Warren Hymer, Guinn Williams, Bernadene Hayes and Joyce Compton sent the mood veering into comedy. There were even a few Kurt Weill songs thrown in to obfuscate Lang's intentions further.

▷ **King Of Alcatraz** was a fast, well written and directed thriller with unusually polished production values for an inexpensive programme picture. Significantly, just one writer provided both original story and script: Irving Reis. He put a bunch of escaped convicts, led by J. Carrol Naish (centre), aboard a passenger-carrying freighter; they took the tub over but met unexpected resistance from officers Lloyd Nolan (the patient here) and Robert Preston, who indulged in some amusing triangle stuff with Gail Patrick (right) whenever the action paused for breath, which wasn't often. Preston was making his screen bow in a cast also featuring Anthony Quinn, Harry Carey, Richard Denning, Dorothy Howe (left), Porter Hall, Gustav von Seyffertitz and Richard Stanley (who changed to his real name, Stanley Morner, when he went to MGM, then to Dennis Morgan at Warners, where stardom came at last). Robert Florey directed for breakneck pace. The title was a come-on: it was not a prison picture.

▽ Harold Gray's deathless creation, **Little Orphan Annie**, went from the funny papers to the movie cameras three times under its original title: in 1919 for Pioneer, in 1932 for RKO, and in 1938 for Paramount. And the mop-headed girl from the orphanage, her dog Sandy and her fairy godfather Daddy Warbucks had a golden era ahead in the record-breaking stage musical *Annie*, filmed in 1982 by Columbia. Meanwhile, not even the comic strip's most fervid fans could get wildly excited about this little picture. Ben Holmes directed for independent producer John Speaks, with Ann Gillis (right) a winning Annie, J. Farrell MacDonald (left) as an ex-fight manager, Robert Kent as a Golden Gloves hopeful, Ben Welden as a vicious loan shark, June Travis, J.M. Kerrigan, Sarah Padden, Harry Tyler, James Burke and Ian MacLaren. Script by Budd Schulberg, Samuel Ornitz and Endre Bohem.

△ The much publicised Hollywood spot where the stars came out at night gave its name to **Cocoanut Grove**, a mild musical starring Fred MacMurray (centre) as a bandleader (no strain on Fred's acting; he'd been a band musician for years when Paramount discovered him) and Harriet Hilliard as a singing schoolteacher. Giving them a few romantic scenes and getting the band from Chicago to Los Angeles was about the limit of the Sy Bartlett-Olive Cooper script's productivity; the rest was vaudeville, and entertaining enough while Eve Arden, Ben Blue, Rufe Davis, the Harry Owens orchestra and the comedy singing quartet, the Yacht Club Boys (illustrated), were on camera. Alfred Santell directed the George M. Arthur production, which was outlasted in popularity by two of the songs: 'You Leave Me Breathless' (Frederick Hollander, Ralph Freed) and 'Says My Heart' (Burton Lane, Frank Loesser).

△ Harold Lloyd (illustrated) had a lot of trouble with the script of **Professor Beware** and never did get it worked out to his satisfaction or anybody else's. The number of writers credited (authors Francis and Marion Cockrell, Crampton Harris, Jack Cunningham, Clyde Bruckman; screenwriter Delmer Daves) was a tip-off of long sessions in smoke-filled rooms, from which emerged a silly yarn about a professor of archaeology who imagines he is the reincarnation of an ancient Egyptian, gets in trouble with the police and goes on the run from LA to NY. The final 20 minutes came to life with a wild chase and fight sequence crammed with gags, but the preceding hour seemed awfully long. Elliott Nugent directed, with Phyllis Welch, William Frawley, Lionel Standing, Etienne Girardot, Raymond Walburn, Cora Witherspoon, Ward Bond, Thurston Hall, Montagu Love, Sterling Holloway, Spencer Charters and Guinn Williams in his cast. This was Lloyd's last via Paramount; he made only one more film before his death in 1971, at 77 a multi-millionaire.

OTHER RELEASES OF 1938

The Arkansas Traveler
Bob Burns, Fay Bainter, John Beal, Jean Parker. Dir: Alfred Santell. Pro: George M. Arthur. Itinerant printer helps a widow to run her local newspaper and successfully wages war on corrupt big shots.

Bar 20 Justice
William Boyd, Russell Hayden, George Hayes. Dir: Lesley Selander. Pro: Harry Sherman. 16th 'Hopalong Cassidy'.

Booloo
Colin Tapley, Jayne Regan. Dir & Pro: Clyde Elliott. White hunters in a Malayan jungle stalk a white tiger and bait their trap with a native girl.

Born To The West
John Wayne, Johnny Mack Brown, Marsha Hunt. Dir: Charles Barton. Zane Grey melodrama of a boyhood feud that breaks out again when the antagonists are grown up. (Remake of 1926 film)

Bulldog Drummond In Africa
John Howard, Heather Angel, Reginald Denny. Dir: Louis King. Pro: Edward T. Lowe. From Sapper's 'Challenge'. Heroes are menaced by both four-legged and human beasts in the wilds

Bulldog Drummond's Peril
John Howard, John Barrymore, Louise Campbell. Dir: James Hogan. Pro: Stuart Walker. From Sapper's 'The Third Round'. Drummond's pre-wedding party is interrupted by robbery and murder.

Campus Confessions
Betty Grable, William Henry, Eleanore Whitney. Dir: George Archainbaud. Pro: William Thomas. Comedy of sport versus studies, the former despised by the owner of a college where his son excels at basketball, wins Dad over.

Cassidy Of Bar 20
William Boyd, Russell Hayden, Nora Lane. Dir: Lesley Selander. Pro: Harry Sherman. 22nd 'Hopalong Cassidy'.

The Frontiersman
William Boyd, Evelyn Venable, Russell Hayden. Dir: Lesley Selander. Pro: Harry Sherman. 20th 'Hopalong Cassidy'.

Give Me A Sailor
Martha Raye, Bob Hope, Betty Grable. Dir: Elliott Nugent. Pro: Jeff Lazarus. Comedy with songs (including a hit, 'What Goes On Here In My Heart?') about a pair of sisters' romances with two sailors.

The Heart Of Arizona
William Boyd, Russell Hayden, Natalie Moorhead, George Hayes. Dir: Lesley Selander. Pro: Harry Sherman. 15th 'Hopalong Cassidy'.

Illegal Traffic
Robert Preston, Mary Carlisle, J. Carrol Naish. Dir: Louis King. Pro: William Thomas. G-Man breaks up the racket of a transport company which helps crooks make their getaway and shares the loot.

In Old Mexico
William Boyd, Russell Hayden, George Hayes, Jane Clayton. Dir: Edward Venturini. Pro: Harry Sherman. 18th 'Hopalong Cassidy'.

Love On Toast
John Payne, Stella Ardler, Benny Baker. Dir: E.A. Dupont. Pro: Emanuel Cohen. Soda-jerker in a New York drug store wins a Mr. Manhattan contest run by a publicity girl. Custard pie-throwing battles ensue.

The Mysterious Rider
Russell Hayden, Sidney Toler, Douglas Dumbrille. Dir: Lesley Selander. Pro: Harry Sherman. Action drama in the wide open spaces, from a Zane Grey story. (Remake of 1927 and 1933 films)

Pride Of The West
William Boyd, Russell Hayden, George Hayes. Dir: Lesley Selander. Pro: Harry Sherman. 17th 'Hopalong Cassidy'.

Ride A Crooked Mile
Akim Tamiroff, Frances Farmer, Leif Erickson. Dir: Alfred E. Green. Pro: Jeff Lazarus. Drama of a boy's efforts to help his father, a thief, to break out of Kansas State Penitentiary.

Say It In French
Ray Milland, Olympe Bradna, Irene Hervey, Mary Carlisle. Dir. & Pro: Andrew L. Stone. Golf champion comes home from France with a secret bride, to find his family has promised him to an heiress to avoid bankruptcy.

Scandal Street
Lew Ayres, Louise Campbell, Roscoe Karns. Dir: James Hogan. When an innocent girl is accused by small-town scandalmongers of immorality and murder, her fiancé comes to her rescue.

Sons Of The Legion
Lynne Overman, Evelyn Keyes, Donald O'Connor. Dir: James Hogan. Pro: Stuart Walker. War veteran under a cloud has his name cleared by his two boys while they try to join the junior American Legion.

Stolen Heaven
Gene Raymond, Olympe Bradna, Lewis Stone, Glenda Farrell. Dir. & Pro: Andrew L. Stone. After pulling off a jewel robbery, a young couple on the run pose as musicians and are reformed by a sympathetic maestro.

The Sunset Trail
William Boyd, Russell Hayden, George Hayes, Jane Clayton. Dir: Lesley Selander. Pro: Harry Sherman. 19th 'Hopalong Cassidy'.

Tip-Off Girls
Lloyd Nolan, Mary Carlisle, Evelyn Brent, J. Carrol Naish. Dir: Louis King. Pro: Edward T. Lowe. G-men wage war against the hijackers who prey on long-distance freight trucks.

Tom Sawyer, Detective
Donald O'Connor, Billy Cook, Robert Kent. Dir: Louis King. Pro: Edward T. Lowe. Mark Twain's Tom and Huck solve a rural murder mystery involving twin brothers.

Touchdown, Army!
John Howard, Robert Cummings, Mary Carlisle. Dir: Kurt Neumann. Pro: Edward T. Lowe. Two West Point men are rivals for a girl and on the football gridiron until the big Army-Navy game makes them friends

Tropic Holiday
Dorothy Lamour, Ray Milland, Martha Raye, Bob Burns. Dir: Theodore Reed. Pro: Arthur Hornblow Jr. Musical, set in Mexico, about a local beauty romanced by a visiting scriptwriter.

1939

▽ **Invitation To Happiness** concerned itself with romantic, career and class conflicts in the marriage of a prizefighter and a society lady. In other words, Scenario No 42A – the A indicating superior star casting and production accoutrements. Irene Dunne as the neglected wife and Fred MacMurray (right) as the ambitious slugger were attractive and efficient performers under the direction of Wesley Ruggles; the latter's brother Charles (left) added some welcome comedy at the head of the supporting line-up of Marion Martin (the boxer's inevitable blonde temptation), William Collier Sr, Oscar O'Shea and little Billy Cook. Claude Binyon's screenplay was based on an original (well, sort of) by Mark Jerome and produced by Ruggles. The critics shrugged it off, but the fans accepted its invitation with open wallets.

▷ **Midnight** was quintessential Paramount: verbal sparring and elegant adultery among *le beau monde*, wittily scripted by Charles Brackett and Billy Wilder, and smoothly directed by Mitchell Leisen in a Paris designed by Hans Dreier. Box-offices thrived on this delicious soufflé, and cinéastes have never stopped smacking their lips over it. The story by Franz Schulz and Edwin Justus Mayer concerned an American girl (Claudette Colbert), penniless in Paris, who is hired by a jealous husband (John Barrymore, here with Colbert) to use her charms on a gigolo (Francis Lederer) and so distract him from his wife (Mary Astor). This ruse is complicated by the girl's taxi-driver friend (Don Ameche), who has fallen in love with her, pretending to be her husband. Hedda Hopper, Rex O'Malley, Monty Woolley, Armand Kaliz and Elaine Barrie (the current Mrs Barrymore) filled minor roles in the Arthur Hornblow Jr production.

△ **The Great Victor Herbert** was an enjoyable musical with a less idiotic script than most composer biopics inflicted on their audiences. Walter Connolly looked and sounded convincing as the Irish-American conductor and songwriter who turned out an astonishing succession of Broadway operettas from the 1890s to the 1920s. Sixteen of his hits were given fullthroated treatment by Allan Jones, Mary Martin and Susanna Foster (right), and another dozen were featured in other ways. Also on view in Andrew L. Stone's production: Lee Bowman, Jerome Cowan, John Garrick (left), Pierre Watkin, Hal K. Dawson, Jimmy Finlayson, Judith Barrett, Richard Tucker. Stone, who also wrote the original with Robert Lively and directed the Lively-Russel Crouse screenplay, made biopics of Grieg and Johann Strauss many years later, with less success; he was really at his best with realistic thrillers. The Misses Martin (her greatest stage fame still to come) and Foster were both in their first leading roles. Best songs: 'Kiss Me Again', 'I'm Falling In Love With Someone', 'Ah, Sweet Mystery Of Life'.

1939

▽ **Persons In Hiding** was the first of four crime thrillers Paramount gleaned from one book, the factual best-seller purportedly written by FBI chief J. Edgar Hoover (actually ghosted by Courtney Riley Cooper). This one was based on the exploits of Bonnie and Clyde, whose movie heydey was yet to come. Its 70 minutes went like a bullet, with realistic production by Edward T. Lowe and sharp direction by Louis King making the most of a tight budget. Patricia Morison (illustrated, in her debut), Lynne Overman, Helen Twelvetrees, J. Carrol Naish (illustrated), Richard Denning, William Henry, William Collier Sr, William Frawley, Judith Barrett, John Eldredge, May Boley and Richard Carle were well cast in the Horace McCoy-William Lipman screenplay. It took the title of the book, and was followed by *Undercover Doctor*, *Parole Fixer* and *Queen Of The Mob*.

△ **Cafe Society** started something like a special unit in the studio, being the first of four pictures co-starring Fred MacMurray and Madeleine Carroll (both illustrated), written by Virginia Van Upp and directed by Edward H. Griffith. Well made, smoothly entertaining and forgettable, they were profitable releases from 1939 to 1941. This one was a light comedy about a rich, publicity loving girl who marries a reporter on a bet and is brought down to earth from the giddy glamour of her life to the reality of his. Shirley Ross, Allyn Joslyn, Jessie Ralph, Don Alvarado, Claude Gillingwater (the veteran actor's last appearance), Hilda Plowright, Paul Hurst and Mary Parker were also in the Jeff Lazarus production's cast.

▽ With popular appeal covering it like chocolate sauce on a sundae, **Disputed Passage** was relished by Paramount's sales department and exhibitors, and most of its audiences, but the critics found it a bit gooey. The styles of its author, Lloyd C. Douglas, the ex-doctor dispenser of best-selling tablets of sugar-coated drama (*Magnificent Obsession*, etc.), and its director, Frank Borzage, a specialist in high-class tear-jerkers for 40 years, blended nicely on the story of a great surgeon (Akim Tamiroff, right) urging his young protégé (John Howard) to forget about marrying his beautiful lover (Dorothy Lamour, left) and devote himself to science. Sheridan Gibney and Anthony Veiller adapted the Douglas novel, writing some effective dialogue for the leads and for Judith Barrett, Victor Varconi, William Collier Sr, Elisabeth Risdon, Keye Luke, Philip Ahn and Gordon Jones. Harlan Thompson produced.

◁ The first movie to be planned and produced as a Bob Hope vehicle, **The Cat And The Canary** established him as one of the industry's strongest crowd magnets. It was a lucky picture all round, winning Bob's leading lady, Paulette Goddard (here with him), a contract that made her a Paramount star for ten years. Always a hit on stage and in two previous screen versions (silent, 1927; talking, *The Cat Creeps*, 1930; both Universal) John Willard's old haunted house thriller got extra comedy life from Hope, Elliott Nugent's smartly paced direction and a bright script by Walter De Leon and Lynn Starling. The cast contained Douglass Montgomery, John Beal, Gale Sondergaard, Elizabeth Patterson, George Zucco, Nydia Westman and John Wray, one or more of whom were bent on terrifying the heroine into losing her inheritance by failing to last a night in a weird mansion. Hope was the radio comedian giving her dubious support. Arthur Hornblow Jr produced.

▽ A quick encore for *Cafe Society*'s stars, Fred Mac-Murray (centre) and Madeleine Carroll (right), director Edward H. Griffith, writer Virginia Van Upp and producer Jeff Lazarus, **Honeymoon In Bali** was not a musical, despite the title and the presence, as Mac-Murray's romantic rival, of Allan Jones (left), who had just moved over from a series of MGM song-fests. A light comedy, it was one for the ladies, who coaxed enough escorts along to make it a tidy moneymaker. The trite tale by Katherine Brush and Grace Mason of a cold career girl warmed up by Love was enlivened by the wit of Van Upp's script and a diverting cast which also included Helen Broderick, Akim Tamiroff, Osa Massen, Astrid Allwyn, John Qualen, Bennie Bartlett, Carolyn Lee, Georgia Caine and William B. Davidson.

△ **Jamaica Inn** positively bristled with famous names, all of whom preferred to forget it forever after. Look at these credits: producer Erich Pommer, director Alfred Hitchcock; author Daphne du Maurier, screenplay J.B. Priestley, Sidney Gilliat, Joan Harrison; camera Harry Stradling, Bernard Knowles; cast Charles Laughton (right), Maureen O'Hara, Leslie Banks (left), Robert Newton, Emlyn Williams, Marie Ney, Mervyn Johns, Wylie Watson, Morland Graham. How that lot managed to turn out an old-fashioned, unreal, creakily theatrical melodrama is beyond explanation. It was all highly coloured hugger-mugger (in black and white) about the exploits of smugglers, led by a squire (Laughton, hamming madly) and involving a beautiful orphan (O'Hara in her first lead) in early 19th-century Corn-

wall. After this third production, Mayflower Pictures closed down, and Laughton, Pommer and Stradling returned to Hollywood, accompanied by O'Hara. Hitchcock also left war-threatened Britain and began his American career with *Rebecca* – so triumph followed disaster, both from du Maurier novels.

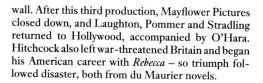

△ Inspired by President Franklin D. Roosevelt's declaration that a third of America's population was ill-housed, Arthur Arent wrote a play called ... **one third of a nation** ... which was produced by the Federal Theatre Project (itself created by F.D.R.'s New Deal) to considerable acclaim in 1938. The following year Dudley Murphy produced, directed and (with Oliver H.P. Garrett) adapted it for the screen, shooting in a New York tenement district for atmospheric accuracy. It was at once a social document and a touching love story about a girl trapped by poverty (Sylvia Sidney) and a young landlord (Leif Erickson). Others supporting Sidney in her last under Paramount contract (she returned to the stage, with occasional movie roles during the next 40 years) were Charles Dingle, Myron McCormick, Muriel Hutchison, Percy Waram, Hiram Sherman, Iris Adrian, Byron Russell and the future director Sidney Lumet (illustrated foreground), aged 14. The critics were respectful, but alas, for entertainment seekers slum clearance was Top Of The Unpops.

▽ The air was thick with Scottish burrs as **Rulers Of The Sea** unreeled its salty action. Some of the accents were genuine – notably that of Will Fyffe (left), in a rare excursion away from the British stage and screen – and the producer-director himself, Frank Lloyd, was Glasgow born. He made a rousing job of this splendid sea story about the planning, building and maiden voyage of the first steamship to cross the Atlantic in the days when sails were considered irreplaceable. Talbot Jennings wrote the script from an original by him, Frank Cavett and Richard Collins. It mixed excitement and factual history with just enough romantic interest, between Douglas Fairbanks Jr (right) and Margaret Lockwood (in one of two Hollywood movies she made in 1939), and with George Bancroft, Montagu Love, Lester Matthews, David Torrence, Ivan Simpson, Mary Gordon, Lawrence Grant and a young hopeful named Alan Ladd also cast. It was a box-office disappointment except in Britain, where Fyffe and Lockwood had marquee value.

▷ The old reliable, **Beau Geste**, hoisted the talented team of producer-director William Wellman and screenwriter Robert Carson out of the slight slump *Men With Wings* dropped them into, and gave the company a mammoth hit for the second time. They closely followed the 1926 movie's flashback format, with its memorable opening scene of a desert fort manned by corpses, but there was a greater feeling of size and excitement about the remake. Although they neither looked like brothers nor sounded English for the most part, Gary Cooper (left), Ray Milland (centre) and Robert Preston (right) made the Gestes believable as well as spirited; Brian Donlevy was a splendidly sadistic sergeant; J. Carrol Naish, Albert Dekker, Broderick Crawford, James Stephenson, Charles Barton, G.P. Huntley Jr and, as the ladies back in the stately home, Susan Hayward and Heather Thatcher, all supported valiantly. For some reason, Donlevy was detested by his fellow actors on location, but he had the last laugh, getting the only Oscar nomination among the actors. Hans Dreier and Robert Odell were nominated for their art direction. P.C. Wren's Foreign Legionnaires reappeared in Universal's minor 1966 version before being killed off finally (?) by the unfunny 1977 burlesque, *The Last Remake Of Beau Geste* starring Marty Feldman.

▽ Cecil B. DeMille had a big winner in **Union Pacific**. The great railroad-building era that opened up the West in the 19th century had been similarly covered by John Ford in *The Iron Horse* (1924); now C.B. added the colossal touch, with more actors, horses, sub-plots, scenery, train wrecks and running-time. Getting full co-operation from the Union Pacific Railroad, which provided historical data, early period trains and expert crews, he brought an air of authenticity (see illustration) to the sprawling melodrama of Ernest Haycox's novel, *Trouble Shooter*, adapted by Jack Cunningham for a screenplay by C. Gardner Sullivan, Walter De Leon and Jesse Lasky Jr (son of DeMille's old partner). Joel McCrea (borrowed from Samuel Goldwyn in exchange for Dorothy Lamour in *Hurricane*) and Barbara Stanwyck (whose skill and helpfulness amazed C.B., as it did all her other directors) co-starred in lively style, with Robert Preston, Brian Donlevy, Akim Tamiroff, Evelyn Keyes, Lynne Overman, Stanley Ridges, Anthony Quinn, Regis Toomey, Lon Chaney Jr, J.M. Kerrigan, Henry Kolker and Robert Barrat.

▽ One of the year's silliest offerings, **Paris Honeymoon** looked as though it had been whipped together in a hurry because the schedule called for another Bing Crosby release. Frank Butler and Don Hartman could have written musical comedy scripts in their sleep by this time, and possibly did while adapting Angela Sherwood's story about a Texas millionaire (Crosby, right) infatuated with a countess (Shirley Ross) whom he follows to Europe, where he rents a castle and falls in love with a village maiden (Francisca Gaal, centre). Edward Everett Horton (left), Akim Tamiroff, Ben Blue, Gregory Gaye, Rafaela Ottiano, Raymond Hatton and Victor Kilian scared up a few laughs in support, while Leo Robin and Ralph Rainger supplied Bing with a B-plus score: 'Joobelai', 'Funny Old Hills', 'I Have Eyes', 'Sweet Little Headache', the last sung to Miss Gaal, who was just that to the casting department; she returned to Budapest. Direction by Frank Tuttle was not exactly subtle.

△ A sluggish semi-remake of the silent Pola Negri success, **Hotel Imperial** had a disaster-strewn production history. In 1936 it was half finished by Henry Hathaway as *I Love A Soldier* with Marlene Dietrich starred; she bowed out and was replaced by Margaret Sullavan, who promptly broke her arm. The project was thrown into the drop-dead file, to be resuscitated when the studio signed Italian star Isa Miranda (centre), an arresting personality who made only one more Paramount film before resuming her illustrious European career. The Lajos Biro original was entirely rewritten by Robert Thoeren and Gilbert Gabriel to become a drama of a Balkan woman's 1916 search for the man who caused her sister's death. The public was not interested. Robert Florey directed a cast including Ray Milland (left), Reginald Owen (right), Albert Dekker, J. Carrol Naish, Gene Lockhart, Henry Victor and Curt Bois.

△ Another impressive achievement by director-producer William Wellman and screenwriter Robert Carson, following *A Star Is Born* and *Beau Geste*, brought **The Light That Failed** to the screen for the third time. It was more moving than the previous versions (Pathe, 1916, and Paramount, 1923), partly because Ronald Colman (illustrated) so perfectly fitted Rudyard Kipling's sad hero, the artist becoming blind from a war wound. Less predictably, Ida Lupino, as his Cockney model who splashes his masterpiece with turpentine in a fit of jealousy, came through with a powerful performance that started her on her career as a dramatic star. Walter Huston, Muriel Angelus (here with Colman), Dudley Digges, Ernest Cossart, Fay Helm, Halliwell Hobbes, Colin Tapley, Pedro De Cordoba and young Ronald Sinclair made notable contributions to an exceptionally well-acted film.

▷ Martha Raye and Bob Hope (billed in that order) looked as through they were enjoying themselves in **Never Say Die**, and their audiences certainly were. William Post's 1912 Broadway farce came up like new when modernised by Preston Sturges, Don Hartman and Frank Butler, and given Elliott Nugent's peppy directorial tempo. It started with a nutty millionaire (Hope, left) being given a month to live. While avoiding an adventuress (Gale Sondergaard) he meets a girl (Raye, right) who is avoiding a nasty prince (Alan Mowbray); Bob marries her so she can inherit his money and then wed her real sweetheart. But, reader – he didn't die, and they lived happily ever after! Andy Devine, Sig Rumann, Ernest Cossart, Frances Arms, Monty Woolley, Paul Harvey and Ivan Simpson added to the fun of Paul Jones's production.

△ Dorothy Lamour gently kidded herself in **St. Louis Blues** as a star who, fed up with her sarong-girl image and her slave-driving manager (Jerome Cowan), flees from Broadway and joins a Mississippi showboat troupe, becoming the toast of the South and the darling of the boat owner (Lloyd Nolan). Director Raoul Walsh's movie jes' moseyed along, pausing occasionally to refresh itself with a musical mint julep. Lamour had a hit in 'I Go For That' by Frank Loesser and Matty Malneck, whose band was much in evidence, while other numbers were sung by Tito Guizar, the Hall Johnson Choir and Maxine Sullavan (illustrated), whose swing version of 'Loch Lomond' became quite a vogue. The Jeff Lazarus production also featured Jessie Ralph, William Frawley, Mary Parker and Cliff Nazarro. Neither the authors, Eleanore Griffin and William Rankin, nor the scripters, Malcolm Stuart Boylan and John Moffitt, placed their creative powers under any strain.

▷ After four decades of success as a play, an opera and in two film versions (1915 with Pauline Frederick; 1923 with Gloria Swanson), **Zaza** was still a potent star vehicle. A spirited Claudette Colbert (illustrated) in the title role and an adroit George Cukor (back with the company which began his movie career) at the directorial helm refreshed its antiquated plot about a music hall singer becoming a great actress via an unhappy love affair with a married man. Albert Lewin's production was lavish, not least in the cast, which ranged from star comic Bert Lahr (illustrated – who went straight from this to the Cowardly Lion in *The Wizard Of Oz*), through Herbert Marshall, Genevieve Tobin, Ernest Cossart, Walter Catlett, Helen Westley, Rex O'Malley, Dorothy Tree and Monty Woolley, to Shakespearean star Constance Collier. The script, based on Pierre Berton's and Charles Simon's play, was by Zoe Akins, and there was an intriguing screen credit to 'Special advisor: Nazimova'. Another contributor was Fanny Brice, who coached Colbert for her songs (written by Frederick Hollander, Al Hoffman and Frank Loesser). Colbert replaced the accidentally injured Isa Miranda, who filmed *Zaza* in Italy four years later.

△ **Geronimo** scored ten out of ten for action, zero for social significance. Perpetuating the one-sided history of the Indian Wars as noble empire-builders versus redskins motivated by sheer blood-lust, this well-attended Western advertised its title character as 'the most feared Indian that ever ravaged the West . . . leading ten thousand yowling savages!'. Chief Thundercloud (illustrated) played this role with stony-faced authenticity, leaving the heavy emoting to Preston Foster, Ellen Drew, William Henry, Gene Lockhart, Ralph Morgan, Andy Devine, Marjorie Gateson, Monte Blue, Kitty Kelly and Addison Richards. Practically guaranteeing that it made a profit, Paul Sloane used *Lives Of A Bengal Lancer* as the basis for his script and, as director, lifted action highlights from other epics, notably *Wells Fargo*.

◁ Selling a lot of tickets on the strength of Jack Benny's radio popularity, plus the names of Dorothy Lamour and Edward Arnold (left), **Man About Town** was a middling musical that scored best while Benny and Eddie 'Rochester' Anderson were doing their inimitable master-and-manservant routines. Otherwise the tale of a Broadway producer in London, mixing with the high-falutin' set and pretending to be the dream man of two British wives (Binnie Barnes, right, and Isabel Jeans) to arouse the jealousy of his singing star (Lamour), was pretty yawn-making. Dorothy was a last-minute replacement for Betty Grable (who filmed one number before succumbing to appendicitis), and sang a swooner, 'Strange Enchantment', that caught on. The Matty Malneck band swung, the Merriel Abbott dancers terped, and Phil Harris, Monty Woolley and E.E. Clive acted in the Arthur Hornblow Jr production, directed by Mark Sandrich. It was written by Morrie Ryskind, Allan Scott and Zion Myers.

◁ Dipping another toe into the treacherous waters of character acting, Bing Crosby (centre left) tried a biographical role in **The Star Maker** and did all right as Gus Edwards, showman and songwriter. Careful to say it was 'suggested by' his career, the Arthur Caesar-Frank Butler-Don Hartman script (from an original by Caesar and William Pierce) didn't bother too much about accuracy as it traced Edwards's career from footloose singer to married man in a dull store job, and back to show business with the idea of discovering talented kids and touring them in vaudeville. When child labour laws intervened, he switched to radio with even greater success. His standard 'Schooldays' was a theme song, and Bing had a beauty in 'A Man And His Dream', plus a hit in 'An Apple For The Teacher', both by Johnny Burke and James V. Monaco. Louise Campbell, Linda Ware, Ned Sparks (left), Laura Hope Crews, Thurston Hall, Billy Gilbert (right), Darryl Hickman, Janet Waldo, and Walter Damrosch conducting the Los Angeles Philharmonic were in the Charles R. Rogers production, directed by Roy Del Ruth. 'Pleasant' was about the zenith of its praise from the critics.

OTHER RELEASES OF 1939

Ambush
Gladys Swarthout, Lloyd Nolan, Broderick Crawford, William Henry. Dir: Kurt Neumann. A secretary, her young brother and a friendly truck driver are caught up in the escape of an ill-fated gang of bank robbers.

Arrest Bulldog Drummond
John Howard, Heather Angel, Reginald Denny. Dir: James Hogan. Pro: Stuart Walker. From Sapper's 'The Final Count'; Drummond puts the quietus on a fiend who seeks to rule the world with a death-ray.

Back Door To Heaven
Wallace Ford, Stuart Erwin, Patricia Ellis, Aline MacMahon. Dir. & Pro: William K. Howard. Drama about the lives of Ohio schoolmates, one of whom becomes a gangster.

Boy Trouble
Mary Boland, Charles Ruggles, Donald O'Connor, Billy Lee. Dir: George Archainbaud. Department store clerk is harassed by two boys his wife makes him adopt, but his paternal feelings are aroused when scarlet fever breaks out.

Bulldog Drummond's Bride
John Howard, Heather Angel, Reginald Denny. Dir: James Hogan. Pro: Stuart Walker. From Sapper's 'Bulldog Drummond And The Oriental Mind'. Our hero's wedding is temporarily delayed by a villain in the series' finale.

Bulldog Drummond's Secret Police
John Howard, Heather Angel, Reginald Denny. Dir: James Hogan. Pro: Stuart Walker. From Sapper's 'Temple Tower'. Drummond fells a foe whose castle is equipped with torture devices.

Death Of A Champion
Lynne Overman, Virginia Dale, Donald O'Connor. Dir: Robert Florey. A memory expert investigates the killing of a champion great dane and assorted humans.

Disbarred
Robert Preston, Gail Patrick, Otto Kruger. Dir: Robert Florey. Pro: Stuart Walker. Brilliant female lawyer successfully defends criminal cases until she discovers that her sponsor is a murderer and she changes sides.

The Gracie Allen Murder Case
Gracie Allen, Warren William, Ellen Drew, Kent Taylor. Dir: Alfred E. Green. Pro: George M. Arthur. Detective Philo Vance untangles a mystery with dubious assistance from the comedienne.

Grand Jury Secrets
John Howard, Gail Patrick, Richard Denning. Dir: James Hogan. Pro: Samuel Engel. Reporter scores a news scoop by bugging the Grand Jury room and then clears up the fraud case under investigation.

Gulliver's Travels
Dir: Dave Fleischer. Pro: Max Fleischer. Cartoon feature, from the Swift classic, with songs by Leo Robin and Ralph Rainger.

Heritage Of The Desert
Donald Woods, Evelyn Venable, Russell Hayden. Dir: Lesley Selander. Pro: Harry Sherman. Zane Grey western about claim-jumpers meeting their match in upholders of the law. (Remake of 1924 and 1933 films)

I'm From Missouri
Bob Burns, Gladys George, Patricia Morison. Dir: Theodore Reed. Pro: Paul Jones. Small-towner takes a trip to England and causes comic uproar among peers and businessmen.

Island Of Lost Men
Anna May Wong, J. Carrol Naish, Anthony Quinn. Dir: Kurt Neumann. Pro: Eugene Zukor. Oriental girl seeks her father in Central America and finds him in the power of an evil gun-runner.

King Of Chinatown
Akim Tamiroff, Anna May Wong, J. Carrol Naish, Anthony Quinn. Dir: Nick Grinde. Pro: Harold Hurley. Melodrama of a gang czar and the underlings who seek to overthrow him.

The Lady's From Kentucky
George Raft, Ellen Drew, Hugh Herbert, ZaSu Pitts. Dir: Alexander Hall. Pro: Jeff Lazarus. A former bookie and an owner's daughter fall out when the former enters their horse in a big race; it wins; they reunite.

Law Of The Pampas
William Boyd, Russell Hayden, Steffi Duna, Sidney Blackmer. Dir: Nate Watt. Pro: Harry Sherman. 24th 'Hopalong Cassidy'.

The Llano Kid
Tito Guizar, Jan Clayton, Gale Sondergaard. Dir: Edward Venturini. Pro: Harry Sherman. Western drama of a bandit whose past catches up with him after he poses as a long-lost heir. (Remake of *The Texan*, 1930)

The Magnificent Fraud
Akim Tamiroff, Mary Boland, Lloyd Nolan, Patricia Morison. Dir: Robert Florey. Pro: Harlan Thompson. An actor assumes a dangerous off-stage role, impersonating a dictator who has been assassinated.

Million Dollar Legs
Betty Grable, Jackie Coogan, Buster Crabbe, Donald O'Connor. Dir: Nick Grinde. Fun-loving gals and guys come to the aid of the university by backing a rachorse, possessor of the title.

Night Work
Charles Ruggles, Mary Boland, Donald O'Connor. Dir: George Archainbaud. New manager of a de-luxe apartment house runs into comic troubles with his staff, his tenants and his family.

Our Leading Citizen
Bob Burns, Susan Hayward, Charles Bickford. Dir: Alfred Santell. Pro: George M. Arthur. A lawyer and his daughter are temporarily at odds with the former's junior partner, counsel for a ruthless industrialist.

Our Neighbors The Carters
Edmund Lowe, Genevieve Tobin, Fay Bainter, Frank Craven. Dir: Ralph Murphy. Pro: Charles R. Rogers. Comedy-drama of family life, upset when Dad's drug store is menaced by cut-price competition.

Range War
William Boyd, Russell Hayden, Pedro de Cordoba. Dir: Lesley Selander. Pro: Harry Sherman. 23rd 'Hopalong Cassidy'.

The Renegade Trail
William Boyd, Russell Hayden, George Hayes. Dir: Lesley Selander. Pro: Harry Sherman. 26th 'Hopalong Cassidy'.

Silver On The Sage
William Boyd, Russell Hayden, George Hayes, Ruth Rogers. Dir: Lesley Selander. Pro: Harry Sherman. 25th 'Hopalong Cassidy'.

Some Like It Hot
Bob Hope, Shirley Ross, Gene Krupa, Una Merkel. Dir: George Archainbaud. Pro: William Thomas. Comedy about a sideshow owner's ruses to raise money. Song: 'The Lady's In Love With You'. (Remake of *Shoot The Works*, 1934)

A Stolen Life
Elisabeth Bergner, Michael Redgrave. Dir: Paul Czinner. Pro: Anthony Havelock-Allan. (British) An identical twin takes over the identity (and husband) of her sister when the latter accidentally dies.

Sudden Money
Charles Ruggles, Marjorie Rambeau, Billy Lee. Dir: Nick Grinde. A salesman and his flighty family run wild when he wins a $90,000 sweepstake.

Television Spy
William Henry, Judith Barrett, Richard Denning, Anthony Quinn. Dir: Edward Dmytryk. Pro: Edward T. Lowe. Melodrama of a young man's invention of a television development which is stolen by foreign agents.

This Man Is News
Barry K. Barnes, Valerie Hobson, Alastair Sim. Dir: David MacDonald. Pro: Anthony Havelock-Allan. A reporter and his wife become amateur detectives, outwitting his editor and Scotland Yard as well as the villain. (British)

$1,000 Dollars A Touchdown
Joe E. Brown, Martha Raye, Susan Hayward. Dir: James Hogan. Pro: William Thomas. Comedy of show-biz couple inheriting a college and making it successful by building up its football team.

Undercover Doctor
Lloyd Nolan, Heather Angel, J. Carrol Naish, Broderick Crawford. Dir: Louis King. Pro: Edward T. Lowe. G-men crack down on a surgeon who patches up the bullet holes in public enemies.

Unmarried (GB Night Club Hostess)
Helen Twelvetrees, Buck Jones, Donald O'Connor. Dir: Kurt Neumann. Ex-prizefighter and his girl friend sponsor an orphan with boxing ambitions. (Remake of *Lady And Gent*, 1932)

What A Life!
Jackie Cooper, John Howard, Betty Field. Dir. & Pro: Theodore Reed. A small-town youth, his family and his high school observed in a comedy which developed into the Henry Aldrich series.

1940

▽ Paramount fielded one of its strongest teams for **Arise, My Love** – the same one, in fact, that had scored so strongly with *Midnight*: director Mitchell Leisen, producer Arthur Hornblow Jr, screenwriters Charles Brackett and Billy Wilder, cinematographer Charles Lang Jr, star Claudette Colbert (right). This one had more serious events to deal with (although laughter was never too far away) as Colbert played a Paris-based journalist reporting the Spanish Civil War, then World War II, with Ray Milland (centre) as an aviator whom she helped out of some tight corners. The script was being revised throughout production to keep pace with the war news – the leads were caught in an Atlantic torpedo attack and the fall of Paris – while a small war was waged on the set between Leisen and Wilder, who never could get on. But the finished product drew Oscars for authors Benjamin Glazer and John Toldy, and large, appreciative audiences. Rest of cast: Walter Abel, Dennis O'Keefe, George Zucco (left), Dick Purcell, Frank Puglia, Esther Dale, Nestor Paiva.

△ Paramount helped launch the new decade with one of its choicest releases, **Remember The Night**, written by Preston Sturges and produced and directed by Mitchell Leisen, who had collaborated so brilliantly on *Easy Living* three years earlier. Not a wild comedy this time, but a Capra-like mixture of sentiment and humour with the emphasis on character rather than plot. Barbara Stanwyck (illustrated), as a shoplifter whose trial was delayed by the court's Christmas recess, and Fred MacMurray (illustrated), as a district attorney who takes her home to his rural folks for the holidays, created a warm rapport that came across with irresistible charm. Beulah Bondi, Elizabeth Patterson, Sterling Holloway, Willard Robertson, John Wray, Paul Guilfoyle, Charles Waldron and Charles Arnt added grace notes to the stars' harmony, and both press and public responded with whole-hearted applause for all concerned.

⊲ The studio rewarded Preston Sturges for his splendid scripts (*Easy Living, Remember The Night*, etc.) by letting him take a crack at directing one of them, something he had long wanted to do. **The Great McGinty** (GB: **Down Went McGinty**) not only won him the 1940 Oscar for best original screenplay, but had the critics throwing their hats in the air to celebrate the arrival of a dazzling new film-maker. A broad satire on the way politics sometimes works in the USA, it detailed the rise of a dim-witted hobo (Brian Donlevy, left), pushed by a crooked wheeler-dealer (Akim Tamiroff, right) to the state governorship, and his eventual fall. It had the speed of a skyrocket and the sparkle of a catherine wheel as it fired off its hilarious barbs in a series of tightly edited scenes involving William Demarest, Muriel Angelus, Thurston Hall, Steffi Duna, Louis Jean Heydt, Esther Howard, Arthur Hoyt, Richard Carle and Libby Taylor. Paul Jones produced economically.

▷ Ernest B. Schoedsack, ten years after the memorable Paramount documentaries he filmed with Merian C. Cooper (they had since made movie history with *King Kong*), returned as the director of **Dr Cyclops**. No everyday pill-pusher, this doctor, but a marvel at treating people with a reducing problem: he made them 14 inches tall, just like that. Amazon country was the scene and unwary travellers the victims of the dotty scientist's experiments, until his power waned when he lost his magic spectacles. Albert Dekker (illustrated), eerily impressive as the doctor, was supported by Janice Logan, Thomas Coley, Victor Kilian, Frank Reicher, Charles Halton and Paul Fix in the Dale Van Every production. Technicolor enhanced the atmospheric camerawork of Henry Sharp and Winton Hoch, while Farciot Edouart and Gordon Jennings got an Academy nomination for their special effects.

△ Fans of their 1930s Warner Bros. musicals were bemused at finding Dick Powell and Joan Blondell (both illustrated) co-starred in a straight comedy-drama, **I Want A Divorce**. None too strong as either comedy or drama, the Adela Rogers St Johns story and Frank Butler script at least gave Powell (as a law student who marries, regrets it, but decides to stay with it after observing the misery divorce has caused other couples) a chance to show what an intelligent actor he was. The delightful Blondell was less well served by the George M. Arthur production, whose anti-divorce theme evidently didn't convince the stars; actually married since 1936, they were un-hitched in 1945. Their fictional problems here were directed by Ralph Murphy, with Frank Fay, Gloria Dickson, Jessie Ralph, Harry Davenport, Conrad Nagel, Dorothy Burgess, Sidney Blackmer and Louise Beavers in the cast.

⊲ Both script and songs had more zip in **Rhythm On The River** than in the average musical. No less a name than Billy Wilder appeared on the authors' credit line, along with Jacques Thery, and smart dialoguer Dwight Taylor wrote the screenplay. It was all about a famous songwriter (Basil Rathbone, right) whose inspiration has dried up, so he employs a couple of ghost writers, one for the music (Bing Crosby, centre) and one for the lyrics (Mary Martin, left). The two get together and decide they might as well get the acclaim and the royalties Rathbone will collect for their work, but there are no takers for their songs until he calls them back to share credit for a big Broadway show. The actual writers of this William Le Baron production's score, James V. Monaco and Johnny Burke, gave it three hits, 'That's For Me', 'Only Forever' and 'Ain't It A Shame About Mame?'. The stars were in sparkling form under Victor Schertzinger's direction, supported by the wry, piano-playing Oscar Levant, Oscar Shaw, Charley Grapewin, William Frawley, Lillian Cornell, Jeanne Cagney and Charles Lane. Business was strong.

▽ **The Biscuit Eater** popped up unheralded to become one of the surprise hits of the year. James Street's story, adeptly screenwritten by Lillie Hayward and Stuart Anthony, was an outstandingly effective boy-and-dog story, a legitimate tear-extractor. Stuart Heisler, just starting his directorial career after years as a film editor, drew a moving, natural performance from Billy Lee (left) as the lad whose bird-dog motivated such dramatic sequences as its rescue from a weird hermit, its competing in show-dog trials, and finally its death, leaving a litter of pups to soften the audience's throat lumps. The Jack Moss production used picturesque rural and swamp locations in Georgia for exterior shooting, and Snowflake (right), Cordell Hickman, Helene Millard, Lester Matthews, Richard Lane, William Russell and Earl Johnson for the supporting cast.

▽ Ray Milland and Ellen Drew (illustrated) were Hollywood exports to London for David E. Rose's Two Cities filming of **French Without Tears**. Director Anthony Asquith and his scriptwriters, Ian Dalrymple and Anatole de Grunwald, made a smooth, workmanlike job of transposing Terence Rattigan's first long-running stage hit to the screen. The effervescence and charm of its comedy about young Englishmen in France enjoying lessons in language and sex were retained, winning predominantly affirmative notices from the critics, as well as profitable returns. The fetching Janine Darcy and a group of British experts in light comedy – Roland Culver, David Tree, Guy Middleton, Kenneth Morgan, Margaret Yarde, Jim Gerald – supported the stars in Mario Zampi's production, one of the London studios' last before the Blitz temporarily halted them.

▷ Riotously depicting the dilemma of an impecunious clerk who, mistakenly thinking he's won $25,000 in a competition for a coffee slogan, goes on a spending spree on credit, **Christmas In July** confirmed Preston Sturges's reputation, established by *The Great McGinty*, as a phenomenal one-man hit maker. He was author, scripter and director, with Paul Jones again keeping reins on the budget as producer. This was Dick Powell's first picture after eight years as Warner Bros.' resident crooner, and he (centre) displayed a lively sense of comedy as the contestant. Ellen Drew (right) also pleased as his girlfriend, and they were surrounded by a colourful gaggle of Sturges characters played by Raymond Walburn, Ernest Truex, William Demarest, Franklin Pangborn, Rod Cameron, Alan Bridge, Georgia Caine, Ferike Boros and Harry Hayden.

△ The fourth and last of the crime stories based on the factual accounts in FBI chief J. Edgar Hoover's book, *Persons In Hiding*, **Queen Of The Mob** was the best of the lot. Moving like a bullet, it told a blood-spattered tale inspired by the career of Ma Baker, who raised her boys to be killers a mother could be proud of. The family's sexual kinks had to wait for a more permissive movie age and 1970's *Bloody Mama*; meanwhile Blanche Yurka (centre) ruled her deadly brood of robbers with cold ferocity, and her director, James Hogan, took bows for an outstanding B picture. Like the others, it was scripted by Horace McCoy and William Lipman and produced by Edward T. Lowe, who whipped them out in less than three weeks each. This one had Ralph Bellamy, Robert Ryan (debut), J. Carrol Naish (left), William Henry, Jeanne Cagney, Richard Denning (background), Paul Kelly, Jack Carson, Neil Hamilton, Hedda Hopper, John Miljan, Raymond Hatton (right) and Lloyd Corrigan in the cast.

▽ A close second to World War II as the hottest topic of 1939, *Gone With The Wind* and its new star, Vivien Leigh, were at their peak in January 1940 when **Sidewalks Of London** was released in America, looking like a brand new Leigh film. Actually she had made it just before becoming Scarlett O'Hara, and Paramount, no fools they, had held it back for over a year since its British release as **St Martin's Lane**. It was one of the Mayflower group produced by Erich Pommer and top-starring Charles Laughton (here with Leigh). He, Miss Leigh and Rex Harrison gave a spellbinding display of their special personalities and techniques, well blended by director Tim Whelan in command of a colourful cast: Tyrone Guthrie, Gus McNaughton, Maire O'Neill, Larry Adler, Helen Haye, screenwriter Bart Cormack, Phyllis Stanley, Jerry Verno, Edward Lexy. Clemence Dane's screenplay offered Laughton a Jannings-like role as a street entertainer who falls in love with a young dancer (Leigh) and gradually loses her to fame when she is taken up by a successful songwriter (Harrison). London's theatre world made a fascinating background, but the story lacked mass appeal.

△ Dorothy Lamour had helped Sam Goldwyn to blow up a box-office storm in *The Hurricane*; therefore starring her in **Typhoon** seemed a good idea to her home studio, and so it proved. She had a new hero in Robert Preston (left)—the publicity department didn't discourage rumours about an off-screen romance too—otherwise it was the usual tropical malarky, with not only the promised typhoon but a forest fire thrown in as a bonus. Lynne Overman (centre) and J. Carrol Naish (right), Paramount's busiest stock players, were featured for wry comedy and ripe villainy, respectively, with Chief Thundercloud, Jack Carson, Frank Reicher, Paul Harvey and Norma Nelson in support. Louis King directed the Allen Rivkin adaptation of Steve Fisher's story, and it was produced by Anthony Veiller in Technicolor, which was now being used more frequently.

▽ Produced as a one-off musical and with no great expectations of extraordinary success, **Road To Singapore** opened at key cities early in 1940, and *Variety*'s business reports immediately broke out in a rash of 'socko', 'boffo', 'smasheroo' and words to that effect. The names of Bing Crosby (centre), Bob Hope (right) and Dorothy Lamour (left) combined to exert powerful box-office suction, and their performances harmonised to perfection, although the coruscation of inside jokes and Crosby-Hope ad libs that made the subsequent *Road* movies so hilarious was a mere flicker in the script Don Hartman and Frank Butler wrought from Harry Hervey's original. It was, in fact,

▽ 'Deep in the heat of Africa … her hungry heart beat to tomtom rhythm!' announced a desperate adman to entice into **Safari** a public whose indifference – judging by the paybox figures – bordered on the cataleptic. It was difficult for prospective audiences to envisage jungle passions running riot in a couple of cool customers like Douglas Fairbanks Jr and Madeleine Carroll (both illustrated), who played the standard characters in dramas of this ilk: handsome white hunter and gentlewoman smitten by adulterous notions. The natives were restless, and the critics even more so, as the clichés trekked on inexorably. Edward H. Griffith directed and Anthony Veiller produced the Delmer Daves screenplay, adapted from Paul Hervey Fox's story and employing Lynne Overman, Tullio Carminati, Muriel Angelus, Billy Gilbert, Thomas Louden, Clinton Rosemond, Ben Carter and Madame Sul-Te-Wan.

pretty mild entertainment, sustained by Victor Schertzinger's nicely paced direction of the star trio, plus Charles Coburn, Judith Barrett, Anthony Quinn, Jerry Colonna, Pierre Watkin, Johnny Arthur and Miles Mander. There were good songs: 'Too Romantic' and 'Sweet Potato Piper' (James V. Monaco, Johnny Burke) and 'The Moon And The Willow Tree' (Schertzinger, Burke). Harlan Thompson produced. The story? Oh, yes: rich lad (Crosby) escapes father (Coburn) and fiancée (Barrett) for a vagabond trip with pal (Hope) to Singapore, where they rescue native girl (Lamour) from cabaret whipcracker (Quinn).

△ With a fat new contract resulting from the success of *Union Pacific*, Cecil B. DeMille splashed out with Technicolor for the first time in **Northwest Mounted Police**. This worked wonders for the exteriors but did nothing for a dull, scrappy script about heroic Mounties quelling Canadian uprisings in 1885, with derring-do by Gary Cooper (right) and Robert Preston (left), getting energetically derring-done despite the distractions of pure Madeleine Carroll and wildcat Paulette Goddard (centre). Many of the reviewers called it the showman's poorest Western, or Northwestern, but it rolled up Paramount's biggest grosses of the year. The studio had been worried by its outsize budget in wartime and cancelled C.B.'s planned location shooting in Canada, so he had to make do with Oregon and Hollywood. No restrictions on cast, however: Preston Foster, George Bancroft, Lynne Overman, Akim Tamiroff, Walter Hampden, Lon Chaney Jr, Montagu Love, Regis Toomey, Richard Denning and Robert Ryan, plus the four above, made quite a salary list. Alan Le May, Jesse Lasky Jr and C. Gardner Sullivan scripted from a book by R.C. Fetherstonhaugh.

▽ **Second Chorus** was in the second rank of Fred Astaire musicals, which still made it brighter than most. A nothing story by Frank Cavett related the exploits of two undergraduates (Astaire, right, and Burgess Meredith, at 41 and 32 respectively, were really stretching it there) who, seeking fame as trumpeters, acquire a band and a manager (Paulette Goddard, left) for whom they become romantic rivals. Several musical numbers later she says yes to Fred (in real life Paulette chose Meredith: they were married 1944–49), having survived dance routines with him that obviously didn't come as naturally as her dazzling personality. Artie Shaw provided his splendid band and, with Johnny Mercer, the best of a fair batch of songs, 'Love Of My Life'; while Charles Butterworth, Frank Melton, Jimmy Conlon and Adia Kuznetzoff also performed for director H.C. Potter. The Elaine Ryan-Ian McClennan Hunter screenplay was produced by Boris Morros.

▽ The nearest thing to a sequel to *The Cat And The Canary* that the studio could scare up without wasting time in writing one was **The Ghost Breakers**, which had practically the same story anyway. An even older haunted-house screamer (filmed in 1914 with H.B. Warner and 1922 with Wallace Reid), it gave Bob Hope (right) and Paulette Goddard (left) another highly profitable hit, he again playing the wise-cracking cowardly hero helping her to claim her inheritance and survive clutching hands, shrieks in the night, voodoo curses and his jokes in a Cuban mansion of horrors. Paul Lukas (centre), Richard Carlson, Anthony Quinn, Pedro De Cordoba, Willie Best, Virginia Brissac, Tom Dugan, Lloyd Corrigan, Noble Johnson and Paul Fix were also in Arthur Hornblow Jr's production, up-dated from Paul Dickey's and Charles Goddard's ancient play by Walter De Leon, and directed by George Marshall, who made it yet again in 1953 as *Scared Stiff*.

△ Despite evidence to the contrary, Paramount believed that there was a great movie to be mined from Joseph Conrad's **Victory**. Its third attempt to 'lick the script', as they say in the trade, was entrusted to producer Anthony Veiller, writer John Balderston, and director John Cromwell, who had been busy elsewhere for eight years, and who now tried to combine the pictorial romance of Maurice Tourneur's 1919 version and the flat-out melodrama of William Wellman in 1930 (*Dangerous Paradise*) with the intangibles of Conrad's moody style. Strangely, Cromwell blamed his failure on an inability to get a performance out of Cedric Hardwicke as the chief villain. Hardwicke, in fact, was singled out for critics' praise in a cast including Fredric March (left), Betty Field (right), Sig Rumann, Margaret Wycherly, Jerome Cowan, Fritz Feld and Rafaela Ottiano. Balderston wrote some trenchant dialogue for the story of a Dutch East Indies recluse (March) who is forced to grapple with life when a girl is menaced by cutthroats, and the atmosphere of evil invading a lotusland was compelling. However, the drama lost propulsion long before The End arrived.

▽ There were some interesting elements in **The Night Of Nights**, notably a convincing picture of the theatrical milieu and skilful acting by Pat O'Brien (on loan from Warners), Olympe Bradna, Roland Young (left), Reginald Gardiner, George E. Stone, Frank Sully, Murray Alper and two stars of the silents, Aileen Pringle and Pat O'Malley. But, considering the celebrated talents of its director, Lewis Milestone, and scriptwriter, Donald Ogden Stewart, it was a surprising flop. Made between two memorable Milestone hits, *The General Died At Dawn* and *Of Mice And Men*, it demonstrated the baffling variation in quality of his 40-year output. Evidently he just couldn't get interested in Stewart's sentimental story of a has-been playwright (O'Brien, right) inspired to make a comeback by his long-lost daughter (Bradna). George M. Arthur produced.

△ Jack Benny (right) and Fred Allen (left) carried on a long, carefully sustained 'feud' which did their radio ratings a power of good. Paramount, always the most alert of studios to popular trends on the airwaves, transferred the comedians' pingpong game of insults to the screen in **Love Thy Neighbor**, and the listening millions paid plenty to come out and watch them at it. More entertaining for the unenlightened were Mary Martin singing the number that made her name on Broadway, Cole Porter's 'My Heart Belongs To Daddy' (from 1938's *Leave It To Me* with Gene Kelly in her chorus), Eddie 'Rochester' Anderson, the Merry Macs and the Merriel Abbott Dancers. Producer-director Mark Sandrich used Verree Teasdale, Richard Denning, Jack Carson, Virginia Dale, Theresa Harris and Barnett Parker to help out in the acting department for the William Morrow-Edmund Beloin-Ernest Pagano-Zion Myers script about putting on a show.

▽ A memory piece that buttered up middle-aged moviegoers' nostalgia, **Those Were The Days** (aka **Good Old Siwash**) gave William Holden (left) his first star billing at Paramount, where he had started his career as one of the studio's publicity-touted 'Golden Circle' of young players in 1938 (others were Susan Hayward, Betty Field, Robert Preston, Patricia Morison, Ellen Drew, Louise Campbell, William Henry, Evelyn Keyes). Borrowed by Columbia for the title role in *Golden Boy*, he had come back famous, but the new picture gave no hint of the heights to be reached in his remaining 41 years. It was a simple tale, told in flashback, of a bumptious 1904 collegian who tones down his campus horseplay to woo a judge's daughter. She was played by Bonita Granville (right) who had been a wonderful rattlesnake of a child actress (*These Three*, etc.), but was now distressingly sugary – as was Don Hartman's script, produced and directed by Theodore Reed from stories by George Fitch, with Ezra Stone, Judith Barrett, William Frawley, Vaughn Glaser, Richard Denning, Phillip Terry, Tom Rutherford and Alan Ladd also cast.

OTHER RELEASES OF 1940

Adventure In Diamonds
George Brent, Isa Miranda, John Loder. Dir. & Pro: George Fitzmaurice. Lady jewel thief goes to South Africa in search of diamonds and finds romance with a British adventurer.

All Women Have Secrets
Virginia Dale, Joseph Allen Jr. Jeanne Cagney. Dir: Kurt Neumann. Comedy-drama about a young couple discovering that matrimony and university studies don't always mix.

Buck Benny Rides Again
Jack Benny, Ellen Drew, Phil Harris. Dir. & Pro: Mark Sandrich. Benny and his pals get into farcical tangles while trying to convince a girl that he's tough as any cowboy.

Cherokee Strip
Richard Dix, Florence Rice, William Henry, Victor Jory. Dir: Lesley Selander. Pro: Harry Sherman. A crook and his gang prey on a Western community until they get their comeuppance from a new marshal.

Comin' Round The Mountain
Bob Burns, Una Merkel, Jerry Colonna. Dir: George Archainbaud. Comedy of hillbilly family feuding with another, engaging in local politics and making music on the radio.

Emergency Squad
Louise Campbell, William Henry, Richard Denning, Anthony Quinn. Dir: Edward Dmytryk. Pro: Stuart Walker. Girl reporter rescued from cave-in of a tunnel she has accused crooks of sabotaging.

The Farmer's Daughter
Martha Raye, Charles Ruggles, Gertrude Michael, Richard Denning. Dir: James Hogan. Pro: William Thomas. Comic uproars ensue when rural gal invades the rehearsals of a Broadway musical.

Golden Gloves
Richard Denning, Jeanne Cagney, J. Carrol Naish, Robert Paige. Dir: Edward Dmytryk. Pro: William Thomas. Amateur boxing tournament is imperilled when a crooked promoter brings in a professional to fight the hero, who wins.

Hidden Gold
William Boyd, Russell Hayden, Ruth Rogers. Dir: Lesley Selander. Pro: Harry Sherman. 29th 'Hopalong Cassidy'.

Knights Of The Range
Russell Hayden, Jean Parker, Victor Jory. Dir: Lesley Selander. Pro: Harry Sherman. Bad men bite the dust again in a Zane Grey western.

The Light Of Western Stars
Russell Hayden, Jo Ann Sayers, Victor Jory. Dir: Lesley Selander. Pro: Harry Sherman. Zane Grey's durable Western melodrama of ranchers versus cattle thieves. (Remake of 1925 and 1930 films).

Moon Over Burma
Dorothy Lamour, Robert Preston, Preston Foster. Dir: Louis King. Pro: Anthony Veiller. A singer, stranded in Rangoon, arouses rivalry between two lumberjacks; all three are menaced by a forest fire.

Mystery Sea Raider
Henry Wilcoxon, Carole Landis, Onslow Stevens. Dir: Edward Dmytryk. Pro: Eugene Zukor. Unsuspecting American girl aids disguised Nazi captain's acquisition of a US freighter which then preys on Caribbean ships.

A Night At Earl Carroll's
Ken Murray, Rose Hobart, J. Carrol Naish. Dir: Kurt Neumann. Pro: Earl Carroll. When the night club impresario is kidnapped by racketeers, a new show is put together by his assistant and press agent.

Opened By Mistake
Charles Ruggles, Robert Paige, Janice Logan. Dir: George Archainbaud. Pro: Stuart Walker. Two newspapermen become involved with a mystery woman, an absconding banker and a body in a trunk.

Parole Fixer
William Henry, Robert Paige, Gertrude Michael, Anthony Quinn. Dir: Robert Florey. Pro: Edward T. Lowe. Lawyer gets gangsters paroled to help him to annex a society woman's fortune.

The Quarterback
Wayne Morris, Virginia Dale, William Frawley. Dir: H. Bruce Humberstone. Pro: Anthony Veiller. Shy student becomes college hero when his athletic twin brother replaces him on football team.

Quiet Wedding
Margaret Lockwood, Derek Farr, A.E. Matthews, Peggy Ashcroft. Dir: Anthony Asquith. Pro: Paul Soskin. A simple ceremony's preparations are enlarged and enlivened by eccentric relatives. (British)

Rangers Of Fortune
Fred MacMurray, Patricia Morison, Gilbert Roland, Albert Dekker. Dir: Sam Wood. Pro: Dale Van Every. Three Mexican gunslingers on the run pause to aid an old man and a girl.

Santa Fe Marshal
William Boyd, Russell Hayden, Marjorie Rambeau. Dir: Lesley Selander. Pro: Harry Sherman. 27th 'Hopalong Cassidy'.

Seventeen
Jackie Cooper, Betty Field, Otto Kruger. Dir: Louis King. Pro: Stuart Walker. Booth Tarkington's comedy of an adolescent youth finding out about love and other hazards of maturity. (Remake of 1916 film)

The Showdown
William Boyd, Russell Hayden, Jane Clayton. Dir: Howard Bretherton. Pro: Harry Sherman. 28th 'Hopalong Cassidy'.

Stagecoach War
William Boyd, Russell Hayden, Julie Carter, Harvey Stephens. Dir: Lesley Selander. Pro: Harry Sherman. 30th 'Hopalong Cassidy'.

Texas Rangers Ride Again
John Howard, Ellen Drew, Akim Tamiroff, May Robson. Dir: James Hogan. Pro: Edward T. Lowe. Contemporary Western in which the Rangers save an old lady's ranch from cattle rustlers.

Three Men From Texas
William Boyd, Russell Hayden, Andy Clyde. Dir: Lesley Selander. Pro: Harry Sherman. 31st 'Hopalong Cassidy'.

Untamed
Ray Milland, Patricia Morison, Akim Tamiroff. Dir: George Archainbaud. Pro: Paul Jones. Doctor on a hunting trip falls for wife of his guide, who dies when all three are trapped in a blizzard. (Remake of *Mantrap*, 1926)

The Way Of All Flesh
Akim Tamiroff, Gladys George, Muriel Angelus, William Henry. Dir: Louis King. Pro: Eugene Zukor. Bank messenger is fleeced of securities and becomes a derelict, believed dead by his family. (Remake of 1927 film)

Women Without Names
Ellen Drew, Robert Paige, Judith Barrett. Dir: Robert Florey. Pro: Eugene Zukor. Newlyweds, wrongly convicted of murder, are freed after the wife finds an eye-witness in prison. (Remake of *Ladies Of The Big House*, 1932)

The World In Flames
Pro: Albert J. Richard. Documentary feature from 1930s newsreels.

1941

▽ **Glamour Boy** (GB: *Hearts In Springtime*) showed how Hollywood could laugh at itself while using truth to inspire fiction, in this case a minor but enjoyable comedy. Jackie Cooper, again working at the studio which had made him a star ten years before in *Skippy*, played a former child actor (true) now a soda-jerk (false) but still remembered as Skippy (true). The Bradford Ropes-Val Burton script had him hired by the Marathon Studio (Paramount thinly disguised) to coach a boy with too-perfect diction (a wicked send-up of Freddie Bartholomew by Darryl Hickman, here being smacked by Jackie) to star in a remake of *Skippy*. Confusing? Yes, and it got more complicated as Cooper romanced a young singer (Susanna Foster) and supposedly kidnapped Hickman. Director Ralph Murphy neatly put over the satirical element in Colbert Clark's production, aided by Walter Abel, William Demarest, Maude Eburne, Jackie Searl, Ann Gillis, Norma Varden and Olive Blakeney.

△ Easing into the new year with a proven box-office combination, Paramount released **Virginia**, made in 1940 by the same co-stars, director and writer – Fred MacMurray and Madeleine Carroll (both illustrated), Edward H. Griffith and Virginia Van Upp – who had scored with 1939's *Cafe Society* and *Honeymoon In Bali*. This was a more solemn affair, and at times its 110 minutes seemed a lot too many as it examined the dilemma of a Southern girl who returns from an unsuccessful New York career to sell the old homestead, is urged not to by a Virginian she falls in love with, then is pulled the other way by a rich Northerner and his dissolute friends. MacMurray and Carroll again made a beguiling team as the lovers and were good to look at in Technicolor; so were the Southern scenery and a new find, Stirling Hayden (who married Miss Carroll in 1942), heading the supporting cast: Helen Broderick, Paul Hurst, Marie Wilson, Tom Rutherford, Louise Beavers, Leigh Whipper, and Carolyn Lee as a distressingly ubiquitous tot character-named 'Pretty' (illustrated). Director Griffith also functioned as producer and co-author.

▷ Nearly, but not quite, another *Wings* for Paramount, **I Wanted Wings** hit heights of excitement in its flying sequences and scored as a documentary of military air training, but was grounded when it came to romantic by-play. This element arrived when its trio of air cadets – Ray Milland, William Holden and Wayne Morris – was distracted by a seductive girl, played by Veronica Lake (here with Milland), whose role and whose performance of it were shot down by the critics. Nevertheless, the public hailed her as a sensational find; her long blonde hair hanging over one eye, the 'peekaboo' coiffure, became a national craze, and the studio quickly sealed her to a long-term contract. Brian Donlevy, Constance Moore, Harry Davenport, Hedda Hopper, Phil Brown, Hobart Cavanaugh, Richard Lane and Addison Richards were also in Arthur Hornblow Jr's production, directed by Mitchell Leisen, who was no William Wellman at this sort of thing. You could guess the script problems by the number of writers credited: Frank Wead, Eleanore Griffin, Beirne Lay Jr, Richard Maibaum, Sig Herzig.

△ Technicolor was a big plus for **Aloma Of The South Seas**, lavishly produced by Monta Bell and directed by Alfred Santell in sun-drenched exteriors. Dorothy Lamour (left) filled her sarong even more effectively than Gilda Gray had shaken her grass skirt silently 15 years before as Aloma. Jon Hall (centre) in half a sarong as Dorothy's lover, Philip Reed as his villainous rival, Katherine De Mille (right) as a native maiden, Lynne Overman as the only white man on the island, the wonderfuly pretty Scotty Beckett as an irritating tot, Fritz Leiber, Pedro De Cordoba and Esther Dale as elders, some refreshing underwater scenes and a volcano in stupendous eruption helped the alluring Dotty make it a big winner. Not exactly a remake, it kept the title and locale of the 1926 movie but junked the original story for another load of Polynesian claptrap, written by Seena Owen, Kurt Siodmak, Frank Butler and Lillie Hayward with a strange mixture of archaic dialogue and modern slang. Miss Owen was the only ex-star (1914–29) ever to make a successful career as a screenwriter.

▽ The company's most honoured picture of the year, receiving a flock of Academy Award nominations, was **Hold Back The Dawn**, a fascinating drama about refugees from Nazi-occupied Europe trying to enter the US via Mexico. In particular, it related the desperate ploy of a gigolo (Charles Boyer) who pretends to fall in love with a vulnerable American schoolteacher (Olivia de Havilland, right) in order to marry her and thus become a lawful immigrant. De Havilland, borrowed from Warners, was genuinely touching as the deceived bride and Boyer gave one of the best performances in his 55-year career. The picture began with him telling the story to director Mitchell Leisen on a Paramount set with the idea of selling it for a movie, one of several neat touches by scripters Billy Wilder and Charles Brackett, working from an original by Ketti Frings, and giving Leisen and producer Arthur Hornblow Jr another hit to rank with their *Midnight*. Strongly cast with Paulette Goddard (left), Walter Abel, Victor Francen, Rosemary DeCamp, Mikhail Rasumny and Billy Lee.

▽ A collector's item for connoisseurs of off-beat thrillers, **Among The Living** was a low-budget item, just 68 minutes long, which achieved quite a reputation in its day for unusual suspense elements. It came from the Sol Siegel unit (he became MGM's production head 17 years later) with Colbert Clark producing and Stuart Heisler directing a starless but able cast: Albert Dekker (left) in a dual role, Susan Hayward (right) showing vivid dramatic quality for the first time, Harry Carey, Frances Farmer, Maude Eburne, Gordon Jones, Dorothy Sebastian, Harlan Briggs, Frank M. Thomas. Dekker played a man accused of a murder committed by his twin brother, who has escaped from an asylum and is struggling to control new outbursts of violence. The Lester Cole-Brian Marlowe story was scripted with arresting tenseness by Cole and Garrett Fort.

▽ Fox's Jones Family had just bowed out and MGM was making a fortune with the Hardy Family so Paramount decided there was room for one more and turned the Aldriches into a series with **Henry Aldrich For President**. It received a warm welcome, and was followed by eight further adventures of the accident-prone Henry, his even dopier pal Dizzy, his family, and his high-school associates. This one involved them in an election of student president, with Henry winning against teenage political trickery. Like the rest, it was directed by Hugh Bennett for the Sol Siegel unit on a low budget, with Jimmy Lydon (left) as Henry, Charles Smith (right) as Dizzy and John Litel as Henry's father; Dorothy Peterson was his mother (replaced in the next eight by Olive Blakeney, who in real life became Lydon's mother-in-law!), with Kenneth Howell, June Preisser, Rod Cameron, Martha O'Driscoll, Vaughn Glaser, Helen Westcott, Lucien Littlefield and Mary Anderson. Val Burton's script stemmed from a radio series and a play by Clifford Goldsmith, both big hits, which had been adapted for *What A Life* (1939) and *Life With Henry* (1941) with Henry played by Jackie Cooper, at 20 considered too old for the subsequent series.

∇ Bob Hope (left) and Dorothy Lamour (centre), who were both kept rather busy during 1941, had another hit in **Caught In The Draft**. Harry Tugend's laugh-loaded screenplay gave Hope full rein as a Hollywood star who reluctantly joins the army and finds it a lot tougher than the movie version, even though his agent (Lynne Overman) and chauffeur (Eddie Bracken, right) are assigned to the same training camp as helpful buddies. His antics elicit a far better response from the colonel's daughter (Lamour) than from the colonel, and he marries her. Like Universal's current release on the same subject, Abbott and Costello in *Buck Privates*, it was very funny in spots and very profitable everywhere. Clarence Kolb, Paul Hurst, Irving Bacon and Ferike Boros supported in the B.G. De Sylva production, directed in broad comedy style by David Butler.

△ **The Monster And The Girl** offered ticket-buyers a mad surgeon's caprice: removing a gorilla's brain and replacing it with that of a wrongly executed gangster, which has the effect of sending the gorilla wildly lusting for revenge on the executioners. Meanwhile the dead man's sister has been forced into prostitution by his underworld associates. Just the thing to keep the kiddies quiet during a school holiday. And pretty mind-blowing for their elders too. Paul Lukas (left), Ellen Drew (right), George Zucco, Robert Paige, Joseph Calleia, Phillip Terry, Rod Cameron, Onslow Stevens, Marc Lawrence, Willard Robertson, Minor Watson and Cliff Edwards gave their histrionic all for direcor Stuart Heisler in this Jack Moss production, written by Stuart Anthony, and refused a seal of approval by the Society for Prevention of Cruelty to Gorillas.

∇ With praises for *The Great McGinty* and *Christmas In July* still coming in, the studio gave Preston Sturges his first A budget for **The Lady Eve**. Barbara Stanwyck's salary plus the fee Paramount had to pay Fox for Henry Fonda almost equalled the total cost of *McGinty*, but their box-office magnetism was worth it – not to mention their delectable performances as, respectively, a seductive card-sharp and the bashful millionaire she tries to fleece on an ocean liner (both illustrated). His outsmarting of her, her revenge, and

∇ He was a friendly street photographer; she was an out-of-town girl looking for a job and a home in the big city. Fred MacMurray and Mary Martin (both illustrated) in **New York Town** made an attractive, mildly diverting pair whose romance had the luck to be surrounded by colourful Manhattan types played by some of Hollywood's best character actors: Akim Tamiroff, Cecil Kellaway, Lynne Overman, Eric Blore, Iris Adrian, Fuzzy Knight, Margaret Hayes, Monte Blue. Robert Preston registered strongly as the second-best man in Mary's life. Charles Vidor, no relation to King, did his customary adept job of directing, although he let the tempo slacken enough to reveal the fragility of the Jo Swerling-Lewis Meltzer script from time to time. Anthony Veiller's production used a few songs, including the evergreen 'Love In Bloom' by – no surprise – Rainger and Robin.

their mutual attraction were detailed with comedy techniques ranging from subtle wit to physical slapstick in Sturges's screenplay (from a clever original by Monckton Hoffe) and direction. The Paul Jones production boasted a powerhouse of supporting players: Charles Coburn, Eugene Pallette, William Demarest, Eric Blore, Melville Cooper, Janet Beecher, Martha O'Driscoll, Robert Greig, Luis Alberni. Sturges had the gift of laughter, and he passed it on to grateful crowds.

△ With pretensions to documenting early jazz history indicated by its title, **Birth Of The Blues** actually blew a riff of entertaining fiction about street musicians becoming the toast of New Orleans as the Original Dixieland Jazz Band. They included Bing Crosby (left) as a hot clarinettist, Brian Donlevy (centre right) as an even hotter trumpeter, and a real jazz giant, trombonist Jack Teagarden, plus Mary Martin (centre left) as the group's vocalist. The last two joined Bing for a bouncy Johnny Mercer number, 'The Waiter, The Porter And The Upstairs Maid',

▽ John Van Druten's play *There's Always Juliet* underwent some drastic changes to become a comedy about an American airman in World War II discovering that the British beauty he loves is acting as a decoy for spies. **One Night In Lisbon** was the fourth product of the combined talents of Madeleine Carroll, Fred MacMurray (both illustrated), director Edward H. Griffith and scripter Virginia Van Upp, and it looked like one encore too many. It tried to blend sophisticated romance, whacky comedy and wartime topicality, and the mix fell pancake flat. Griffith, doubling as producer, gave it a highly polished look and an expensive supporting cast with such accomplished performers as Edmund Gwenn, Billie Burke, Dame May Whitty, Patricia Morison, John Loder, Reginald Denny, Marcel Dalio and Billy Gilbert. They, and the co-stars, gave it some box-office magnetism, but the audience reaction was mild.

but otherwise the score was a succession of great oldies, from the black classics, 'St Louis Blues', 'Memphis Blues' and 'St James Infirmary', to Tin Pan Alley evergreens like 'Melancholy Baby' and the marvellous title song by B.G. De Sylva (who produced the movie), Lew Brown and Ray Henderson. Eddie 'Rochester' Anderson, J. Carrol Naish, Cecil Kellaway, Warren Hymer, Horace MacMahon, Harry Barris, Ruby Elzy and little Carolyn Lee (right) were in the Harry Tugend-Walter De Leon screenplay, directed by Victor Schertzinger. A solid hit.

◁ **Louisiana Purchase** had no trouble finding a Hollywood purchaser after its 13-month run on Broadway. Its stage producer and co-author (with Morrie Ryskind) was none other than B.G. De Sylva, who had just been promoted to production chief of the Paramount studio. He imported Victor Moore (left), Vera Zorina and Irene Bordoni, three of the show's four stars, and replaced William Gaxton with the more box-officey (and more talented) Bob Hope (right) as the shady hero of the satire on the scandalous politics of Louisiana, then a headline topic. On behalf of New Orleans grafters, Bob framed Moore, a bumble-headed investigating senator from Washington, into some compromising escapades with Zorina and Bordoni. All four were in zestful form, aided by director Irving Cummings, producer Harold Wilson and a snappy Jerome Chodorov-Joseph Fields script in a movie that looked good in Technicolor and sounded tuneful in Irving Berlin's score. The latter included one hit, 'It's A Lovely Day Tomorrow', two other songs from the show's original twelve, and, to discourage any law suits that the inflammatory content of the script might have invited, an opening chorus – 'It's New To Us' – announcing the film as sheer fiction.

▽ A poorly motivated but ingratiating comedy-drama, **Reaching For The Sun** kept the Joel McCrea fans happy until his best picture came around later in the year (see *Sullivan's Travels*). This one rambled along at an erratic pace, opening with a clam-digger in the north woods going to Detroit to buy an outboard motor. If you went into the lobby long enough to buy popcorn, you came back to find him married to Ellen Drew (illustrated with Joel), expecting a baby, and tied to a job in a car factory. The rest of W.L. Rivers's script, from Wessel Smitter's novel *F.O.B. Detroit*, dealt with McCrea's longing for the woodlands while coping with his domestic problems and a bully at the plant who tries to kill him with a grappling iron. It added up to surprisingly little from a producer-director of William Wellman's importance, but the star and Miss Drew – as well as Eddie Bracken, Albert Dekker, Regis Toomey, Charles D. Brown, Billy Gilbert and James Burke – kept it watchable, and it pleased many.

▽ The studio's sequel machine switched into top gear when the *Road To Singapore*'s grosses were added up, and the result was **Road To Zanzibar**, regarded by some Bing Crosby-Bob Hope-Dorothy Lamour aficionados as the funniest of the trio's romps. The script, again by Don Hartman and Frank Butler (from a plot by Hartman and Sy Bartlett), and the direction, again by Victor Schertzinger, were frequently chucked overboard as the boys (Bing left, Bob right) let their sense of humour run riot. They played a couple of carnival con-men on a trek through Zanzibar in search of a diamond mine, with Lamour (for once not a native gal but a witty sophisticate) and Una Merkel tagging along. Aside from their free-wheeling ad-libs, the highlights were Crosby's singing and Hope's wrestling a gorilla. The Paul Jones production, a big money-maker, also employed Eric Blore, Iris Adrian, Douglass Dumbrille, Joan Marsh, Luis Alberni, Leo Gorcey, Lionel Royce and Leigh Whipper.

▽ Feeling herself outranked by her husband's job after five years of matrimony, a wife (Claudette Colbert) amuses herself with a romantic interloper (Brian Aherne, centre) before settling down again with hubby (Ray Milland, right). **Skylark** was a typical star vehicle of its time, light, bright and forgettable, with some of Hollywood's deftest supporting players: Walter Abel (left), Binnie Barnes, Mona Barrie, Ernest Cossart, Grant Mitchell, James Rennie, Armand Kaliz. Colbert fitted smoothly into the role that had given Gertrude Lawrence a Broadway success, Mark Sandrich's production and direction were in the studio's high-style tradition, and scripter Allan Scott's many alterations to the Samson Raphaelson play included a wildly funny scene in which Claudette tries to prepare a meal in a storm-tossed yacht. But **Skylark** never soared very high, either on the screen or at the box-office.

△ Madeleine Carroll (right) was directed by Edward H. Griffith in a Virginia Van Upp screenplay for the fifth time in **Bahama Passage**. This time Fred MacMurray bowed out and was replaced by Stirling Hayden (left) as a result of fan enthusiasm for his scenes with Carroll in *Virginia*. The new movie, from a novel by Nelson Hayes, was a curious drama set in a West Indies island supposed to have a deadly effect on white women's happiness. Determined to disprove this, a plantation overseer's sophisticated daughter decides to devote her energies and charms to attracting a handsome islander; when his loveless marriage conveniently collapses, she succeeds. There was little action and the romance didn't boast so much as one kiss, but it nonetheless generated an air of sexual tension that drew the crowds. Flora Robson, Cecil Kellaway, Leo G. Carroll (centre), Leigh Whipper (back to camera), Dorothy Dandridge, Mary Anderson and Technicolor were featured. Hayden, about six-and-a-half feet of tanned muscle and blond hair, threw lady customers for a loop (Carroll, too: she married him in 1942) and Paramount thought it had a new star. He thought otherwise and fled Hollywood for war-long Marines service.

△ The fourth and best picture from writer-director Preston Sturges, **Sullivan's Travels** went beyond his usual comedy field to explore dramatic realism in stark scenes on skid row and a prison farm. He wrote it specifically for Joel McCrea, who used hitherto untapped acting resources to play a comedy director, tired of Hollywood trivia, disguising himself as a hobo, and going out to seek the grassroots of America to get material for a serious movie. In the end he discovers that what the masses want and need most is laughter. They got plenty of that, along with the dramatic interludes, from Sturges here, and even some romantic interest in a waif accompanying McCrea, played by Veronica Lake (here with McCrea), whom the director found hard to handle and blamed for sending production nine days over schedule. William Demarest, Eric Blore, Margaret Hayes, Robert Warwick, Porter Hall, Esther Howard, Franklin Pangborn and Robert Greig were also in it; Paul Jones produced. Reviews were mixed and business disappointed, but it is now often cited as Sturges's masterpiece.

▽ The best thing in **Kiss The Boys Goodbye** was an incidental song, 'Sand In My Shoes', with music by Victor Schertzinger who also directed the movie, and words by Frank Loesser, throbbingly sung by Connee Boswell (who wasn't even featured in the billing). This must have irked its star, Mary Martin, who warbled several less exciting numbers in the course of a moderately successful amusement about a Broadway producer (Don Ameche, here with Mary) losing his marbles over a chorus girl. It was based on a 1938 play by Clare Booth which had kept New Yorkers laughing with its satire on that year's burning topic, 'Who will play Scarlett in *Gone With The Wind*?'. Now old hat, that factor gave way to traditional backstage musical elements in Dwight Taylor's and Harry Tugend's script, which had considerable wit of its own. Paul Jones produced, casting Raymond Walburn, Oscar Levant, Eddie 'Rochester' Anderson, Barbara Jo Allen (radio-famed as Vera Vague), Jerome Cowan, Elizabeth Patterson and Minor Watson.

△ For the third time producer Arthur Hornblow Jr led Bob Hope and Paulette Goddard (both illustrated) down memory lane, following *The Cat And The Canary* and *The Ghost Breakers* with **Nothing But The Truth**. This 1916 play (which, like Hope's other oldie, *Never Say Die*, had starred William Collier Sr on Broadway) had been filmed before in 1920 and 1929 and never misfired with its comedy about a man who bet $10,000 on his getting through a day without fibbing. Farcical embarrassments abounded in the Don Hartman-Ken Englund updated version of James Montgomery's stage hit, based in turn on Frederic Isham's novel, and now directed *con brio* by Elliott Nugent. The cast of seasoned comedy performers included Edward Arnold, Helen Vinson, Leif Erickson, Glenn Anders, Rose Hobart, Grant Mitchell, Catherine Doucet, Clarence Kolb, Willie Best and Mary Forbes.

OTHER RELEASES OF 1941

Border Vigilantes
William Boyd, Russell Hayden, Frances Gifford, Andy Clyde. Dir: Derwin Abrahams. Pro: Harry Sherman. 34th 'Hopalong Cassidy'.

Buy Me That Town
Lloyd Nolan, Constance Moore, Albert Dekker. Dir: Eugene Forde. Pro: Sol C. Siegel, Eugene Zukor. Comedy-drama of New York gangsters vying for control of a bankrupt Connecticut village.

Dancing On A Dime
Robert Paige, Grace MacDonald, Virginia Dale, Peter Hayes. Dir: Joseph Santley. Pro: A.M. Botsford. Stranded troupe puts together a hit show on a shoestring budget. Song hits: 'Manana', 'I Hear Music'.

Doomed Caravan
William Boyd, Russell Hayden, Minna Gombell, Andy Clyde. Dir: Lesley Selander. Pro: Harry Sherman. 32nd 'Hopalong Cassidy'.

Flying Blind
Richard Arlen, Jean Parker, Nils Asther, Roger Pryor. Dir: Frank McDonald. Pro: William Pine, William Thomas. Pilot of honeymoon air service tangles with enemy spies.

Forced Landing
Richard Arlen, Evelyn Brent, J. Carrol Naish, Nils Asther, Eva Gabor. Dir: Gordon Wiles. Pro: William Pine, William Thomas. US pilot, working in island republic, clashes with crooked air force chief.

In Old Colorado
William Boyd, Russell Hayden, Margaret Hayes, Andy Clyde. Dir: Howard Bretherton. Pro: Harry Sherman. 33rd 'Hopalong Cassidy'.

Las Vegas Nights
Tommy Dorsey and His Orchestra, Phil Regan, Constance Moore. Dir: Ralph Murphy. Pro: William Le Baron. Musical about entertainers making good in the casino capital. Screen debut of Frank Sinatra, singing 'Dolores'.

Life With Henry
Jackie Cooper, Eddie Bracken. Dir. & Pro: Jay Theodore Reed. Sequel to 'What A Life!' 1939. Henry Aldrich throws nearly everybody in town into tizzies with his efforts to win a trip to Alaska.

The Mad Doctor
Basil Rathbone, Ellen Drew, John Howard. Dir: Tim Whelan. Pro: George M. Arthur. A psychotic doctor marries and murders his patients, until the former fiancé of his latest bride comes to her rescue.

Mr. Bug Goes To Town (aka Hoppity Goes To Town)
Cartoon feature. Dir: Dave Fleischer. Pro: Max Fleischer. Songs by Hoagy Carmichael, Frank Loesser and Sammy Timberg.

The Night Of January 16th
Robert Preston, Ellen Drew, Cecil Kellaway, Nils Asther. Dir: William Clemens. Pro: Sol C. Siegel, Joseph Sistrom. A secretary is enmeshed in the embezzlement and murder committed by her boss.

No Hands On The Clock
Chester Morris, Jean Parker, Rose Hobart. Dir: Frank McDonald. Pro: William Pine, William Thomas. Action melodrama encompassing a bank robbery, murder, kidnapping and a climactic chase.

Outlaws Of The Desert
William Boyd, Brad King, Luli Deste, Andy Clyde. Dir: Howard Bretherton. Pro: Harry Sherman. 37th 'Hopalong Cassidy'.

Pacific Blackout (aka Midnight Angel)
Robert Preston, Martha O'Driscoll, Eva Gabor. Dir: Ralph Murphy. Pro: Sol C. Siegel. Escaped prisoner foils enemy agents' plot to destroy US city during mock air raid.

The Parson Of Panamint
Charles Ruggles, Ellen Drew. Dir: William McGann. Pro: Harry Sherman, Lewis Rachmil. Hard-hitting man of God assails the wicked ways of a gold-rush town. (Remake of 1916 film and *While Satan Sleeps* 1922)

Pirates On Horseback
William Boyd, Russell Hayden, Eleanor Stewart, Andy Clyde. Dir: Lesley Selander. Pro: Harry Sherman. 35th 'Hopalong Cassidy'.

Power Dive
Richard Arlen, Jean Parker, Roger Pryor, Helen Mack. Dir: James Hogan. Pro: William Pine, William Thomas. Newly designed plane is brought to success by a test pilot.

Riders Of The Timberline
William Boyd, Brad King, Eleanor Stewart, Andy Clyde, Anna Q. Nilsson. Dir: Lesley Selander. Pro: Harry Sherman. 38th 'Hopalong Cassidy'.

The Round-Up
Richard Dix, Patricia Morison, Preston Foster. Dir: Lesley Selander. Pro: Harry Sherman. Rancher overcomes dangerous deterrents while taking his cattle to market. (Remake of 1920 film)

Secrets Of The Wasteland
William Boyd, Brad King, Barbara Britton, Andy Clyde. Dir: Derwin Abrahams. Pro: Harry Sherman. 39th 'Hopalong Cassidy'.

The Shepherd Of The Hills
John Wayne, Betty Field, James Barton. Dir: Henry Hathaway. Pro: Jack Moss. Drama of conflict between mountain people of the Ozarks and outsiders trying to get their land.

Stick To Your Guns
William Boyd, Brad King, Andy Clyde, Jacqueline Holt. Dir: Lesley Selander. Pro: Harry Sherman. 40th 'Hopalong Cassidy'.

There's Magic In Music (aka The Hardboiled Canary)
Allan Jones, Susanna Foster, Margaret Lindsay, Lynne Overman. Dir. & Pro: Andrew L. Stone. Girl from a burlesque show is transformed into an opera singer at a music school camp.

Twilight On The Trail
William Boyd, Brad King, Wanda McKay, Andy Clyde. Dir: Howard Bretherton. Pro: Harry Sherman. 41st (and last for Paramount) 'Hopalong'.

West Point Widow
Anne Shirley, Richard Carlson, Cecil Kellaway. Dir: Robert Siodmak. Pro: Sol C. Siegel, Colbert Clark. Young mother has to strike out on her own when West Point's ban on wives takes effect.

Wide Open Town
William Boyd, Russell Hayden, Andy Clyde, Evelyn Brent. Dir: Lesley Selander. Pro: Harry Sherman. 36th 'Hopalong Cassidy'.

World Premiere
John Barrymore, Frances Farmer, Ricardo Cortez. Dir: Theodore Tetzlaff. Pro: Sol C. Siegel. Temperamental movie producer on a publicity tour encounters oddball characters, including a pair of Nazi spies.

You're The One
Bonnie Baker, Orrin Tucker, Albert Dekker, Jerry Colonna. Dir: Ralph Murphy. Pro: Gene Markey. Comedy of a talent agent's efforts to get his girl client a job as a band singer.

1942

▽ Dorothy Lamour climbed back into her sarong for another round of moonlit kisses and adventures amidst a Technicolored island's flora and fauna in **Beyond The Blue Horizon**. Its paybox figures proved that the public couldn't get too much of this kind of untrammelled escapism, even when the story was as addle-pated as E. Lloyd Sheldon's and Jack DeWitt's yarn about a white orphan, brought up as a native, turning out to be the heiress to millions. Scripter Frank Butler and director Alfred Santell gave the plot a once-over-lightly and garnished it with plenty of comedy by Jack Haley and Gogo the chimp, while Lamour romanced a new blond hero, Richard Denning (here with her), who was a bit player in her 1938 *Her Jungle Love*. Walter Abel, Patricia Morison, Frances Gifford, Elizabeth Patterson, Abner Biberman, Ann Doran, Frank Reicher, Gerald Oliver Smith and moppet Ann Todd were also in the Monta Bell production.

△ The tale unfolded by **This Gun For Hire**, of a professional killer getting involved with fifth columnists while falling for a cabaret blonde and seeking revenge for having been double-crossed, bore only vague resemblances to Graham Greene's novel *A Gun For Sale*. But Greene had called it 'an entertainment', and it was certainly still that when Albert Maltz and W.R. Burnett had finished Americanising, updating and rearranging it for producer Richard Blumenthal. It gripped from first shot to fade-out, thanks chiefly to Alan Ladd (left) as the laconic, passionless hit-man. Although billed below Veronica Lake (centre), Robert Preston and Laird Cregar (right), Ladd, who had been around for several years in minor roles, became an instant star when it was released. Director Frank Tuttle's handling of him, and of the whole film's mood of suppressed violence, was the triumph of a long career. His cast also included Tully Marshall, Mikhail Rasumny, Marc Lawrence, Pamela Blake and Bernadene Hayes; but the best acting came from villain Cregar, hugely overweight at 25 and fated to die at 28 after crash-dieting.

▷ A strong remake of Dashiell Hammett's murder mystery first filmed in 1935, **The Glass Key** top-billed Brian Donlevy, but it became a box-office howitzer because of the immediate popularity Alan Ladd and Veronica Lake (both illustrated) had triggered off in *This Gun For Hire*. They were a perfect match, both being short in stature and expressiveness – but what charisma! He played the side-kick of a slightly corrupt politician (Donlevy) accused of murder; ferreting out the real killer gets Ladd entangled with gangsters, the police and an enigmatic blonde (Lake). Stuart Heisler's direction and Jonathan Latimer's script worked up a heady froth of action and suspense while keeping Hammett's complicated plot clear and giving the cast – Bonita Granville, Richard Denning, Joseph Calleia, William Bendix (outstanding as a brutal bodyguard), Frances Gifford, Margaret Hayes, Moroni Olsen and Donald MacBride opportunities to impress. Fred Kohlmar produced.

△ Like Preston Sturges before him, Billy Wilder achieved his ambition to direct as well as write, and he too emerged as a superb film-maker. **The Major And The Minor**, scripted with his usual collaborator, Charles Brackett, from two stories (one by Edward Childs Carpenter, one by Fannie Kilbourne) had its big audiences laughing while Ginger Rogers (illustrated), posing as a 12-year-old to save train fare, was having a strange effect on the libido of a fellow passenger, officer Ray Milland, not to mention the boys at his military school when he, with ostensibly fatherly concern for the child, took her home. Rita Johnson, Robert Benchley, Diana Lynn, Edward Fielding, Norma Varden; also, Frank Thomas Jr, Raymond Roe, Charles Smith and Larry Nunn as the infatuated lads, and Lela Rogers, Ginger's real mother, as her mother, sparkled with the co-stars for producer Arthur Hornblow Jr. 'The censors didn't notice', said Wilder later, 'but we got away with situations sexier than *Lolita*.'

△ As was his wont, Cecil B. DeMille provided the Big One of the year in **Reap The Wild Wind** (and there was plenty of competition: the studio hit a high level in 1942). This was melodramatic adventure on the grand scale, over $2 million worth of storms and shipwrecks off the Florida coast, salvagers Ray Milland (left) and John Wayne (centre right) in combat for treasure and Paulette Goddard (centre left), and a climactic underwater fight with a giant squid, all in Technicolor. Anybody but DeMille would have been satisfied with a giant octopus, but a squid has two more arms; this one was made of red sponge rubber and operated electrically from a switchboard; some critics said it gave the best performance. Alan LeMay, Charles Bennett and Jesse Lasky Jr scripted from a novel by Thelma Strabel. Raymond Massey made a choice villain, Goddard and Susan Hayward (right) reprised their *Gone With The Wind* tests as 1840 Southern belles, and Robert Preston, Charles Bickford, Lynne Overman, Louise Beavers, Walter Hampden, Elisabeth Risdon and Hedda Hopper supported. Among the extras was George Melford, DeMille's fellow director in the old Lasky days.

▽ Bing Crosby (left) and Fred Astaire (2nd right) were dreaming of a White Christmas in **Holiday Inn**, and the crowds attracted by the screen's most popular singer and best dancer, as well as that song (certainly the biggest record seller of all time, and possibly the dreariest tune Irving Berlin ever wrote) were overwhelming. Berlin, who provided 12 other numbers, best of which were 'Lazy' and 'Be Careful, It's My Heart', won an Oscar for 'White Christmas' and was nominated, rather absurdly, for another as author of the story, adapted by no less a playwright than Elmer Rice and scripted by Claude Binyon. Aside from the novel idea of an inn open only on holidays (when it staged spectaculars that would have bankrupted any hotelier), the tale of two show-biz pals and their gals was strictly a time-filler between numbers. In their first teaming, the stars' easygoing styles meshed beautifully, and they were well backed up by Marjorie Reynolds (2nd left), Virginia Dale (right), Walter Abel, Louise Beavers, Harry Barris, and brother Bob Crosby's Bobcats. Producer-director Mark Sandrich, who had made five Astaire-Rogers pictures, harvested another walloping hit here.

▽ Having taken satirical swipes at Celluloid City in *Sullivan's Travels*, Preston Sturges made a typical Hollywood comedy in **The Palm Beach Story** and showed how it should be done. Claudette Colbert (right), at her sparkling best, played a restless wife who leaves her impecunious husband (Joel McCrea, left) to hunt for a rich admirer in Florida. There, she runs into a flock of zany characters, including a stuffed-shirt millionaire (Rudy Vallee, centre left) and his man-mad sister (Mary Astor, centre right). Before McCrea made her realise she couldn't improve on the man she had in the first place, the audience was treated to a succession of funny incidents and a barrage of lightning-fast dialogue. Ex-crooner Vallee, rather unexpectedly, almost stole the picture; also cast were William Demarest, Franklin Pangborn, Robert Dudley, Sig Arno, Jack Norton, Esther Howard, Jimmy Conlin, Harry Hayden, Monte Blue, Robert Warwick, Robert Greig and Roscoe Ates. Paul Jones produced it.

△ **The Lady Has Plans** teetered uncertainly between comedy and drama and never managed to achieve either with any impact. Set in that wartime happy hunting ground for spies and screenplay writers, Lisbon, it centred on Paulette Goddard as a news correspondent mistaken for a German espionage agent, and Ray Milland (here with Paulette) as an investigator unsure if she is or isn't; the proof lay in whether she had a tattoo in a certain place. Some fun, eh? Others embroiled were Roland Young, Albert Dekker, Cecil Kellaway, Margaret Hayes, Edward Norris, Addison Richards and Gerald Mohr; altogether a good cast, and there was some sparkle in Sidney Lanfield's direction of the Fred Kohlmar production, written by Harry Tugend from a Leo Birinski story. But not enough.

▽ Following three successful *Topper* movies based on Thorne Smith's comic ghost story, his similar novel *The Passionate Witch* was bought by Paramount and handed to the celebrated French director, Rene Clair, who turned it into **I Married A Witch**. It was the best film he made during his wartime sojourn in Hollywood; his deft way with fantasy blended neatly with the ghostly photographic effects and the bright Marc Connelly-Robert Pirosh script about a naughty 17th-century witch, reincarnated as a modern blonde (Veronica Lake, right), vamping an ambitious politician (Fredric March, left), descendant of the Puritans who'd burned her. Cecil Kellaway, cast as her father, another sprightly spirit, was a delight, and the three were supported by Robert Benchley, Elizabeth Patterson, Robert Warwick and Eily Malyon. In a deal unique in film history, this and two other features (*The Crystal Ball* and *Young And Willing* – see 1943) were produced by Paramount, which had plenty of completed product, and sold outright to United Artists, which hadn't enough and which released them as 'Screen Guild Productions'. A batch of new Hopalong Cassidys, made by Harry Sherman, was included in the deal whereby Paramount became a few millions richer.

△ A lively young cast and a rich crop of songs gave **The Fleet's In** customers their money's worth. Dorothy Lamour (left) and William Holden (2nd right), the co-stars, had sparkling support from Leif Erickson, Betty Jane Rhodes, Barbara Britton, comics Eddie Bracken (right) and Gil Lamb, Jimmy Dorsey's band with its smooth-as-silk vocalists Bob Eberly and Helen O'Connell, and two comediennes making their movie debuts, Betty Hutton (2nd left) and Cass Daley. Hutton, brought by stage and screen producer B.G. De Sylva from his Broadway hit *Panama Hattie*, made a sensational impact, belting out two smash songs, 'Arthur Murray Taught Me Dancing In A Hurry' and 'Build A Better Mousetrap'. Director Victor Schertzinger composed them, the title song, 'Tangerine' and 'I Remember You', all with lyrics by Johnny Mercer. When Schertzinger died, after turning out 88 films and countless tunes in 25 years, the picture was completed by his assistant, Hal Walker. The story, of a shy sailor whose pals make bets on his scoring with a man-proof nitery singer, was based by Walter De Leon, Sid Silvers and Ralph Spence partly on the Monte Brice-J. Walter Ruben *The Fleet's In* of 1928 and partly on the 1933 play *Sailor Beware* by Kenyon Nicholson and Charles Robinson. Paul Jones produced.

◁ Bing Crosby (centre left) and Bob Hope (centre right) were off on the **Road To Morocco**, and everybody was happy. Their third annual skylark started with them shipwrecked on a Mediterranean beach and finished with them on a raft floating into New York harbour with a couple of beauties picked up en route. In between was a wild spoof of all the Arab movies ever made, and an occasional respite from the boys' incessant clowning in Dorothy Lamour (left) as a Moroccan princess, to whom Bing warbled 'Moonlight Becomes You' (Johnny Burke, James Van Heusen) which gave him another best-seller. The Paul Jones production looked lavish, and director David Butler managed to keep the Oscar-nominated Don Hartman-Frank Butler (no relation to the director, but an Oxford-graduate Englishman specialising in Hollywood comedies) script on course while Bing and Bob gagged it up. In the cast: villain Anthony Quinn, Dona Drake (right), Vladimir Sokoloff, Mikhail Rasumny, George Givot, Andrew Tombes and the sultry Yvonne De Carlo, who became a star in the kind of films this one kidded. It was an even bigger hit than *Road To Zanzibar*.

◁ Alan Ladd's third leading role in eight months, and his first as a top-billed solo star, came in **Lucky Jordan**, the acid test for Paramount's new find. Could he carry a picture to box-office success on his own? Yes, indeed: Veronica Lake was absent this time, but the crowds were there, money in hand, for a moderate comedy-drama that didn't have any conspicuous attraction besides Ladd as killer-turned-patriot. The comedy element in the Darrell Ware-Karl Tunberg script (story by Charles Leonard) lay in the con-man hero's reactions to army service, the drama in his outwitting a Nazi spy gang. Frank Tuttle directed and Fred Kohlmar produced this confection, casting Helen Walker (illustrated with Ladd), a newcomer with a strong, pleasing personality, as an army welfare worker who catches Ladd's eye; Marie McDonald, Mabel Paige, Sheldon Leonard, John Wengraf, Lloyd Corrigan and Russell Hoyt.

△ A typical topical wartime musical, **Priorities On Parade** cost little and pleased many in those entertainment-hungry days. Its chief pleaser was Ann Miller (2nd left), always a zestful performer, dancing up a storm with a musical group who patriotically joined an aircraft factory. Although Frank Loesser wrote one of its songs (and, with Art Arthur, the practically plotless screenplay) none of them rose above the level of an immortal ditty called 'Co-operate With Your Air Raid Warden'. Propaganda gets everywhere when there's a war on! Sol C. Siegel produced, and Albert Rogell directed a cast who made up in enthusiasm whatever they lacked in class: Jerry Colonna (left), Johnnie Johnston (2nd left), Betty Rhodes (right), Barbara Jo Allen (Vera Vague), Rod Cameron, Eddie Quillan, Harry Barris and The Debonaires.

◁ Norman Panama and Melvin Frank, who had served in Bob Hope's army of radio gag writers, whipped up a nifty story for him in **My Favorite Blonde**, polished for the screen by Frank Butler and Don Hartman. It was a fast farce about a vaudevillian (Hope, left) who plays straight man for a trained penguin; during a train hop between dates he encounters a beautiful British spy (Madeleine Carroll, centre) and helps her to elude her Nazi enemies. Man, woman and bird were chased across the States by road, rail and plane at a rate of a hundred laughs an hour. Others involved were Gale Sondergaard and George Zucco (two of the most sinister heavies in the business), Victor Varconi, Erville Alderson (right), Lionel Royce and Walter Kingsford. Sidney Lanfield directed the Paul Jones production. Very funny, and very box-office.

▽ Exhibitors of **Star-Spangled Rhythm** only had to announce the cast and collect the money. Ingeniously, writer Harry Tugend, producer Joseph Sistrom and director George Marshall had put together a movie combining comedy, patriotic sentiments, spectacular song-and-dance and the Paramount studio. It was all about sailor Eddie Bracken who brings his shipmates to the studio where his father, Victor Moore, is egged on by telephonist Betty Hutton (here with Moore) to pose as the studio boss for their benefit; he is really the gateman, but everybody pitches in to put on a show for the boys. And *what* a show, with numbers and sketches from Bob Hope, Bing Crosby, Mary Martin, Ray Milland, Franchot Tone, Fred MacMurray, Dick Powell, Alan Ladd, Susan Hayward, Eddie 'Rochester' Anderson, Jerry Colonna, William Bendix, MacDonald Carey and Miss Hutton; directors Cecil B. DeMille, Preston Sturges and Ralph Murphy; Vera Zorina, choreographed by Balanchine; Paulette Goddard, Dorothy Lamour and Veronica Lake singing 'A Sweater, A Sarong And A Peekaboo Bang'. Two other Johnny Mercer-Harold Arlen songs, 'That Old Black Magic' and 'Hit The Road To Dreamland', were huge hits.

▽ The vitality of the British studios in the face of appalling wartime handicaps was demonstrated by **The Avengers**, which was titled **The Day Will Dawn** in its home country and had nothing to do with the much later *Avengers* TV series. Although made for its time with a good deal of flag-waving propaganda, the heroism it celebrated was genuine enough, and excitingly conveyed by director Harold French in a hard-hitting Terence Rattigan-Anatole de Grunwald-Patrick Kirwan screenplay (from a story by Frank Owen) about a British Commando raid on Nazi-occupied Norway in aid of freedom fighters who had blown up a U-boat base. Producer Paul Soskin gave it a magnificent cast: Hugh Williams (right), Deborah Kerr (centre), Ralph Richardson, Griffith Jones, Francis L. Sullivan, Roland Culver, Finlay Currie (left), Patricia Medina, Bernard Miles and Niall MacGinnis had the best roles.

▽ A fantasy about a smalltown idealist emerging victorious from a battle of wits with crooked politicians, **The Remarkable Andrew** looked like something Frank Capra had turned down. Its whimsies included helpful advice from the ghost of President Andrew Jackson, plus those of George Washington, Jesse James and others, seen only by the hero. Stuart Heisler, a talented director but no Capra, seemed flummoxed by the curious material provided by writer Dalton Trumbo, but he drew attractive performances from William Holden (right) as the young man enjoying hallucinations, Ellen Drew (centre) as his girl, and Brian Donlevy (left) as the shade of Jackson. Also in Richard Blumenthal's production were Rod Cameron, Frances Gifford, Porter Hall, Richard Webb, Montagu Love, Gilbert Emery, Minor Watson, Nydia Westman and Brandon Hurst. Remarkable wasn't the word for the grosses.

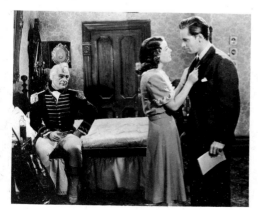

△ Third and best of three Westerns which brought Richard Dix (right) back to Paramount, where he had been a major star of the twenties, was **Tombstone, The Town Too Tough To Die**. Jut-jawed Dix was one of the most convincing of the many actors to play that ubiquitous character of Western legend, Wyatt Earp, here cleaning out the desperadoes from a brawling Arizona mining town. Plenty of action in the Dean Franklin-Charles Reisner script and William McGann's direction. Harry Sherman gave it unusually handsome production values for a B picture in this genre, and cast Kent Taylor, Frances Gifford, Edgar Buchanan (left), Victor Jory, Don Castle, Rex Bell and Clem Bevans. The intriguing title also helped at the box-office.

△ **Wake Island** had medals pinned on its chest by the critics, the public and the Academy (four nominations) as the first realistic movie about World War II in the Pacific. Writers W.R. Burnett and Frank Butler, using more fact than fiction, and director John Farrow, marshalling a highly skilled unit of artists and technicians, showed the US Marines desperately holding the little South Pacific island against stronger Japanese forces for two savage weeks soon after Pearl Harbor. In the end it was a defeat, but a glorious one. Joseph Sistrom's production recruited a virile cast including Robert Preston (centre), Brian Donlevy (right), William Bendix, Macdonald Carey (left), Albert Dekker, Walter Abel, Rod Cameron, Phillip Terry, Frank Albertson, Damian O'Flynn, Mikhail Rasumny and hundreds of extras, plus Barbara Britton for under-emphasised romantic interest. But it was the real-as-newsreel action in this uninhibited patriotism-rouser that made it one of the year's most potent successes.

◁ Rosalind Russell, a forthright actress with a scintillating sense of comedy, was in fine form in **Take A Letter, Darling** (GB: **Green-Eyed Woman**) as an advertising executive who hires a male secretary. He was tall, dark and Fred MacMurray, so the eventual outcome was predictable. But getting there was entertaining most of the way, with Robert Benchley – here with Russell – especially amusing as her partner, in a cast containing Macdonald Carey, Constance Moore, Cecil Kellaway, Dooley Wilson, Charles Arnt and Florine McKinney. Mitchell Leisen applied his usual directorial sheen to the flimsy material woven by Claude Binyon from George Beck's original, and Fred Kohlmar produced. However, once the central theme of a sex reversal in the conventional office relationship was established, the ideas department went out to lunch.

△ Following the success of *Reap The Wild Wind*, Paulette Goddard (centre) and Susan Hayward (right) were cast as rival leading ladies again in another story by Thelma Strabel, **The Forest Rangers**. When the double-barrelled onslaught of fiery femininity got too much for him, ranger Fred MacMurray (left) sought the comparative tranquility of forests crackling in red-hot Technicolor. In the climax of Harold Shumate's eventful screenplay, wealthy wife Goddard rescued rejected charmer Hayward from a particularly spectacular blaze; while Albert Dekker, Lynne Overman, Eugene Pallette, Regis Toomey, James Brown, Rod Cameron and Clem Bevans also had their moments. George Marshall directed the profitable Robert Sisk production. Surprisingly, it yielded a smash song hit, 'I've Got Spurs That Jingle, Jangle, Jingle' by Thomas Lilley.

△ If the hoydenish and energetic Judy Canova's role, as an entertainer on the run from a bunch of gangsters who finds refuge in an all-male institution, seemed vaguely familiar in **True To The Army**, it was because Miriam Hopkins had played it in *She Loves Me Not* back in 1934. Then the fugitive hid in a boys' college, now it was a military camp, where keeping her gender a secret caused farcical complications, some of them funny. Canova, a hillbilly comedienne and singer, was very popular in radio and movies with the down-home folks; more universal in appeal were the rich tenor of Allan Jones (left) and the dancing vitality of Ann Miller (right), who co-starred, with Jerry Colonna, William Demarest, Rod Cameron, Gordon Jones, Clarence Kolb and John Miljan in support. Sol C. Siegel produced and Albert Rogell directed the neat little musical, rewritten by Art Arthur and Bradford Ropes from the play Howard Lindsay derived from an Edward Hope story.

△ Like some of the script material in **The Great Man's Lady**, Barbara Stanwyck (centre left) was 109 years old as she reminisced about her pioneering past in the wide open spaces. Fortunately for the movie, she was her vivid, no-nonsense self in the main footage, ably partnered by Joel McCrea as the husband she both encourages and inspires in his efforts to find the West's richest treasure: oil. Brian Donlevy (left), as the other man in her life, topped the supporting cast, in which Thurston Hall (right), Lloyd Corrigan (centre right), Lucien Littlefield, George Irving, Katherine Stevens and Lillian Yarbo were also employed. The story compiled by Adela Rogers St Johns, Seena Owen and Vina Delmar, wide-ranging in space and time, held only intermittent interest, and W.L. Rivers's screenplay had longueurs which were reflected in the paybox receipts. The production values, particularly William Mellor's photography, were class A, but this only adequate saga lacked producer-director William Wellman's usual gusto.

▷ **Mrs Wiggs Of The Cabbage Patch**, who looked at poverty through rose-tinted glasses, reappeared yet again in 1942. She had sold a lot of books for author Alice Hegan Rice in 1901, and plenty of tickets for playwright Anne Crawford Flexner in 1904; Paramount filmed her and her shanty town brood of kids in 1919 and 1934 (a sequel, *Lovey Mary* was made in 1926 by MGM) and their popular appeal still seemed inexhaustible. Doris Anderson tinkered very little with the 1934 William Slavens McNutt-Jane Stern script; director Ralph Murphy and producer Sol C. Siegel also left well enough alone, giving it only a new cast: Fay Bainter, Hugh Herbert, Vera Vague (Barbara Jo Allen), John Archer, Barbara Britton, Moroni Olsen, Janet Beecher, Carolyn Lee, Carl 'Alfalfa' Switzer, Billy Lee, Betty Brewer and Harry Shannon. Bainter gave a touching performance as Mrs W., but Herbert and Vague (both illustrated) were no comedy match for W.C. Fields and ZaSu Pitts in the preceding version.

OTHER RELEASES OF 1942

Are Husbands Necessary?
Ray Milland, Betty Field, Patricia Morison. Dir: Norman Taurog. Pro: Fred Kohlmar. A happy marriage almost breaks up when a temptress from the husband's past reappears.

Dr. Broadway
Macdonald Carey, Jean Phillips, J. Carrol Naish. Dir: Anthony Mann. Pro: Sol C. Siegel. Doctor becomes a detective when Manhattan sharpies lead him into being charged with murder.

Fly By Night
Richard Carlson, Nancy Kelly, Albert Basserman. Dir: Robert Siodmak. Pro: Sol C. Siegel. Melodrama concerning a young hospital doctor who gets caught up in an espionage network.

Henry Aldrich, Editor
Jimmy Lydon, Charles Smith, Rita Quigley. Dir: Hugh Bennett. Pro: Sol C. Siegel. Henry Aldrich lands in hot water after being elected editor of his high school paper.

Henry And Dizzy
Jimmy Lydon, Charles Smith, Mary Anderson. Dir: Hugh Bennett. Pro: Sol C. Siegel. With his pal and girl friend, Henry Aldrich borrows a motor-boat which sinks; they have an adventurous time replacing it.

I Live On Danger
Chester Morris, Jean Parker, Roger Pryor. Dir: Sam White. Pro: William Pine, William Thomas. Radio reporter looking for a news item finds more than he expected when he stumbles on a murder plot.

My Heart Belongs To Daddy
Martha O'Driscoll, Richard Carlson, Cecil Kellaway. Dir: Robert Siodmak. Pro: Sol C. Siegel. College professor helps a bubble dancer to keep her baby's custody, which her in-laws try to grab.

Night In New Orleans
Preston Foster, Patricia Morison, Albert Dekker. Dir: William Clemens. Pro: Sol C. Siegel. Aided by his wife, a police lieutenant extricates himself from a murder charge and breaks up a gambling gang.

Street Of Chance
Burgess Meredith, Claire Trevor. Dir: Jack Hively. Pro: Sol C. Siegel. Amnesia victim, accused of a killing, probes into his past.

Sweater Girl
Eddie Bracken, June Preisser, Philip Terry, Nils Asther. Dir: William Clemens. Pro: Sol C. Siegel. Murders occur while collegians stage a revue. Song hit: 'I Don't Want To Walk Without You'. (Remake of *College Scandal*, 1935)

Torpedo Boat
Richard Arlen, Jean Parker, Dick Purcell, Phillip Terry. Dir: John Rawlins. Pro: William Pine, William Thomas. Adventures of the men who go down to the sea in lethal little PT boats.

Wildcat
Richard Arlen, Arline Judge, Buster Crabbe, William Frawley. Dir: Frank McDonald. Pro: William Pine, William Thomas. Rival prospectors challenge each other to bring in the first oil well.

The Wrecking Crew
Richard Arlen, Chester Morris, Jean Parker. Dir: Frank McDonald. Pro: William Pine, William Thomas. A man thought to bring bad luck to his fellow demolition workers proves it isn't so.

1943

▷ Silly but fun, **Happy Go Lucky** fitted neatly into the wartime escapism vogue for light musicals and got Paramount's 1943 release schedule off to a profitable start. Mary Martin (centre) and Dick Powell (left) were the singing leads, and very nice too, but Betty Hutton (right) walked off with the picture in an ear-splitting rendition of 'Murder He Says', which reaped a lot of radio and record royalties for Frank Loesser and Jimmy McHugh. Other diverting people were the original swoon-crooner Rudy Vallee, now typed in daffy millionaire roles, Eddie Bracken, Mabel Paige, Eric Blore and Clem Bevans. The Walter De Leon-Norman Panama-Melvin Frank script had Martin as a cigarette girl who saves enough tips to buy a Caribbean cruise in search of a rich husband; she finds Vallee but switches to beachcomber Powell when love dawns; meanwhile Hutton chases Bracken and catches him. Harold Wilson produced in Technicolor and, inexplicably, Warners' German expert in drama, Curtis Bernhardt, was borrowed to direct this very American frivolity.

△ An unpretentious, thoroughly ingratiating comedy came from one of the company's most prolific directors of the forties, George Marshall. **True To Life** told the tale of a radio scriptwriter who moves in on what he thinks is a typical middle-class family to glean material for a soap opera. He finds, in fact, a household of eccentrics and one romantically inclined girl, played by Mary Martin (right) in her most effective, least affected performance to date. Dick Powell (seated) as the scripter and Franchot Tone (left) as his rival shared laugh-making honours with veterans Victor Moore, Mabel Paige, William Demarest, Ernest Truex and Clarence Kolb, and youngsters Beverley Hudson and Raymond Roe. The Don Hartman-Harry Tugend screenplay, from a story by Ben and Sol Barzman and Bess Taffel, was produced by Paul Jones. Some fans of Powell and Martin, presuming it would be a musical, were disappointed; but it had an incidental song hit in Hoagy Carmichael's 'The Old Music Master'.

▽ Several Hollywood producers were shooting or preparing movies about women on the battlefronts (British studios had been full of girls in uniforms for years) when **So Proudly We Hail** was released as one of the first to pay tribute to American nurses in World War II. With three stars, Claudette Colbert (right), Paulette Goddard and Veronica Lake (left), a long (125 minutes), eventful script by Allan Scott and a hefty budget, director-producer Mark Sandrich delivered a popular success. Whether he, so adept with the artificialities of musicals, should have tackled the terrible realities of the Bataan siege, was a moot point. While the story's action, excitement and patriotic fervour swept you along, too often you were reminded that camera and make-up men stood by to gloss the dirt and gore. Still, it received four Oscar nominations, for screenplay, photography, special effects in the battle scenes, and Goddard's performance, her best dramatic work. Rest of cast: George Reeves, Barbara Britton, Walter Abel, Mary Servoss, John Litel, Sonny Tufts, Mary Treen, Kitty Kelly, Ann Doran, James Bell, Bill Goodwin.

▽ Billy Wilder and Charles Brackett had written many brilliant scripts together before **Five Graves To Cairo**, but this was the first for which they also functioned as a director-producer team. It was a superb spy story, vibrating with suspense, about a British agent (Franchot Tone) taking a job in a Sahara oasis hotel during the North African campaign of World War I, and trying to learn from its star guest, Field Marshal Rommel (Erich von Stroheim, right) the location of his arms dumps. As the beleaguered innkeepers, Anne Baxter (left) and Akim Tamiroff strongly supported Tone's fine performance, but you couldn't take your eyes off the charismatic Stroheim, whose career as an actor was longer (and less strife-torn) than as director. Fortunio Bonanova, Peter van Eyck and Miles Mander had briefer roles in this much acclaimed drama, a revised and updated version of Lajos Biro's *Hotel Imperial*.

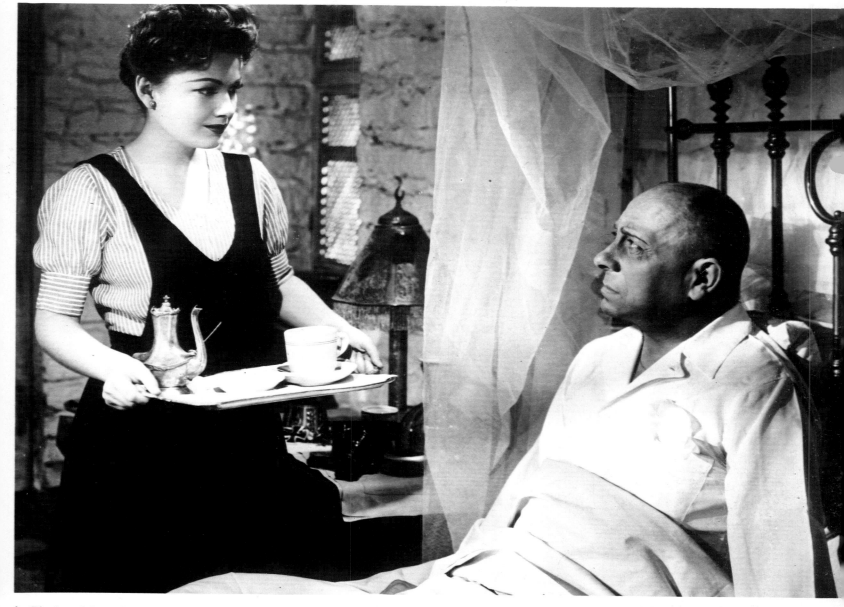

▷ The law of diminishing returns caught up with **Let's Face It**. The story of three matrons getting revenge on their unfaithful husbands by hiring three young men as 'escorts' was a slightly scandalous and highly successful Broadway comedy in 1925 as *The Cradle Snatchers*, and then a Fox film hit in 1927. With a Cole Porter score and Danny Kaye in his first star-ring role, it became the musical stage smash of 1941 as *Let's Face It*. Paramount's 1943 version, minus most of Porter's songs, made it bigger, brassier and once too often. Not well received despite the presence of Bob Hope (centre) and Betty Hutton (left), it offered more noise than wit and had too many characters running around: the wives (Eve Arden, ZaSu Pitts, right, Phyllis Povah), the gigolos, now soldiers (Hope, Dave Willock, Cully Richards), their girls (Hutton, Marjorie Weaver, Dona Drake), the husbands (Raymond Walburn, Andrew Tombes, Arthur Loft) and their three tootsies (uncredited but, for the record, one was Yvonne De Carlo). Sidney Lanfield directed and Fred Kohlmar produced the frenetic screenplay which Harry Tugend based on the Dorothy and Herbert Fields musical and the Norma Mitchell-Russell Medcraft play. Tempus fugit note: the Hope and Arden roles were played in 1925 by Humphrey Bogart and Mary Boland.

▽ 'Epic' was a word often used in the praise showered on Ernest Hemingway's novel **For Whom The Bell Tolls** on its publication in 1940, so when Paramount bought it for $150,000 the same year it was naturally assigned to Cecil B. DeMille. After many changes of command and script rewrites, it came under the producer-director control of C.B.'s 1915 assistant Sam Wood, who had risen high since his last movie at the studio in 1926. He turned out a big, impressive picture that reaped international honours and sold millions of tickets. But it was not entirely satisfactory, because the deletion of much of the book's Spanish Civil War detail by Dudley Nichols's screenplay left insufficient plot to sustain 170 minutes of screen time. The demolition of a bridge by partisans and the love of an American mercenary (Gary Cooper, centre) for a refugee (Ingrid Bergman, right) were stretched out to the limit of Wood's slow tempo; almost an hour was cut for its reissue. Cooper, whom Hemingway said he'd had in mind while writing, and Bergman, who replaced Vera Zorina after three weeks' shooting, were excellent; ditto Akim Tamiroff, Katina Paxinou (left) (Academy Award), Arturo de Cordova, Vladimir Sokoloff, Mikhail Rasumny, Victor Varconi, Joseph Calleia, Fortunio Bonanova. Fine production design by William Cameron Menzies and Technicolor photography by Ray Rennahan.

△ Claudette Colbert and Fred MacMurray (both illustrated) were back together again in **No Time For Love**, and the fans gave them a hearty welcome. She was a New York photographer; he a subway tunnel digger; both were attractive, high spirited, and well-equipped to deal with the snappy dialogue and romantic slapstick of a typical love-hate comedy. The complications that ensued when he became her assistant were given a fast workover in the Claude Binyon-Warren Duff script (from a story by Robert Lees and Fred Rinaldo) and director Mitchell Leisen's urbane touch added a sheen of sophistication. Fred Kohlmar's production, class A in all departments, featured Ilka Chase, June Havoc, Richard Haydn, Paul McGrath and Marjorie Gateson.

△ Producer Fred Kohlmar groped around in the old Famous Players file and plucked out a 1914 comedy by James Montgomery called *Ready Money*. Even with the cobwebs blown off, the script renovated by Art Arthur, Walter De Leon and Arthur Phillips, gussied up with Technicolor and spangled with songs, **Riding High** (GB: **Melody Inn**) looked pretty second-rate. But Dorothy Lamour didn't, as a burlesque stripper putting on a show back home at an Arizona dude ranch to help Dick Powell and Victor Moore (both illustrated) pay off the mortgage on a silver mine. No movie could be a total loss with those stars – plus Cass Daley (reprising 'He Loved Me Till The All-Clear Came' from *Star Spangled Rhythm*), Gil Lamb, Glen Langan, Rod Cameron, Bill Goodwin and Milt Britton's band – but this one came dangerously close. George Marshall directed it between good ones.

▷ **Dixie** took Bing Crosby (right) further back in pop music history than *Birth Of The Blues*, giving him an eye-filling but mind-emptying movie supposedly about the life of Dan Emmett, who wrote the title song in the mid-19th century. Dan, a minstrel man, intended it to be a ballad, but its tempo hotted up when a fire broke out backstage, making it just right to be the South's battle hymn, or so the Karl Tunberg-Darrell Ware script (from Claude Binyon's adaptation of William Rankin's original) would have you believe. While the minstrel sequences were enjoyable, especially in Bing's frequent solos – including a new hit, 'Sunday, Monday And Always' by Burke and Van Heusen – there was a tiresome triangle romance involving Dan's true love (Dorothy Lamour) and the polio-afflicted girl (Marjorie Reynolds) he marries out of pity. Billy De Wolfe (left), getting welcome laughs in his film debut, Lynne Overman, Eddie Foy Jr, Raymond Walburn, Grant Mitchell, Clara Blandick, Robert Warwick and Louis Da Pron were in it. Edward Sutherland directed and Paul Jones produced, giving it Technicolor, and lush period trappings designed by Raoul Pene Du Bois.

△ A grim story of Nazis versus underground fighters in Czechoslovakia, **Hostages** was too downbeat for wartime crowds. It was based on fact, but the effect was melodramatic in the Frank Butler-Lester Cole treatment of Stefan Heym's novel, and director Frank Tuttle allowed the players to indulge in some over-ripe acting. Sol C. Siegel's production featured Luise Rainer (centre), Arturo de Cordova (left), Paul Lukas (right), William Bendix, Katina Paxinou and Oscar Homolka, with Reinhold Schunzel, Roland Varno, Hans Conreid and Steven Geray. This was the farewell to films of Miss Rainer, who had been absent for five years after the fastest rise (two 'best actress' Academy Awards in her second and third movies, *The Great Ziegfeld* 1936 and *The Good Earth* 1937) and fall of any star.

▷ Surefire stuff for wartime crowds, **China** co-starred Loretta Young (left), but she was there strictly for name value and perfunctory romantic interest in a picture that was 90% Alan Ladd (centre). He played an American salesman in China who values profits over patriotism until Pearl Harbor turns him into a heroic guerilla, blowing up Japs by the thousand. John Farrow, having achieved battle realism in *Wake Island*, settled for box-office action this time in his direction of producer Richard Blumenthal's flag-wagger, written by Frank Butler from a novel by Archibald Forbes. William Bendix (2nd left) topped an otherwise Oriental supporting cast including Philip Ahn, Sen Yung (right) and Iris Wong. By the time it was released, Ladd was giving a more convincing real-life performance, having joined up in 1942.

OTHER RELEASES OF 1943

Aerial Gunner
Chester Morris, Richard Arlen, Jimmy Lydon. Dir: William Pine. Pro: Pine, William Thomas. Two airforce men, rivals for the same girl, become comrades during battles over the Pacific.

Alaska Highway
Richard Arlen, Jean Parker, William Henry. Dir: Frank McDonald. Pro: William Pine, William Thomas. Men overcome dangers and setbacks to push through an Alaskan-Canadian motorway.

The City That Stopped Hitler: Heroic Stalingrad
Russian documentary.

The Crystal Ball
Paulette Goddard, Ray Milland, Gladys George. Dir: Elliott Nugent. Pro: Richard Blumenthal. Texas gal loses a beauty contest but wins her man while working with a phoney fortune-teller. (United Artists release)

The Good Fellows
Cecil Kellaway, Mabel Paige, Helen Walker, James Brown. Dir: Jo Graham. Pro: Walter MacEwen. Comedy about a father who spends more time on his fraternal lodge meetings than on his business and family.

Henry Aldrich Gets Glamour
Jimmy Lydon, Charles Smith, Diana Lynn. Dir: Hugh Bennett. Pro: Walter MacEwen, Michel Kraike. Henry comes back from a prize trip to Hollywood to find himself the talk of his home town.

Henry Aldrich Haunts A House
Jimmy Lydon, Charles Smith, Olive Blakeney. Dir: Hugh Bennett. Pro: Walter MacEwen, Michel Kraike. Henry and friends are terrified in a mansion supposedly inhabited by ghosts, actually a counterfeiting gang.

Henry Aldrich Swings It
Jimmy Lydon, Charles Smith, Olive Blakeney. Dir: Hugh Bennett. Pro: Walter MacEwen, Michel Kraike. Having joined the school orchestra when a pretty music teacher arrived, Henry inadvertently steals a priceless violin.

High Explosive
Chester Morris, Jean Parker, Barry Sullivan. Dir: Frank McDonald. Pro: William Pine, William Thomas. Sudden death is inches away from the drivers transporting nitroglycerine.

Lady Bodyguard
Anne Shirley, Eddie Albert, Roger Pryor. Dir: William Clemens. Pro: Sol C. Siegel. Farce concerning a daredevil test pilot and the lady executive of an insurance company who gives him a million-dollar policy.

Minesweeper
Richard Arlen, Jean Parker, Russell Hayden. Dir: William Berke. Pro: William Pine, William Thomas. His name blackened by a past mistake, a naval officer takes on a dangerous assignment and redeems himself.

Night Plane From Chungking
Robert Preston, Ellen Drew, Otto Kruger. Dir: Ralph Murphy. Pro: Walter MacEwen, Michel Kraike. Wartime plane crash-lands in the jungle; passengers are at enemy's mercy. (Remake of *Shanghai Express*, 1932)

Salute For Three
Betty Rhodes, Macdonald Carey. Dir: Ralph Murphy. Pro: Walter MacEwen. Musical about a girl singer prompted by her press agent to start a publicity romance with a war hero that becomes genuine.

Submarine Alert
Richard Arlen, Wendy Barrie, Nils Asther. Dir: Frank McDonald. Pro: William Pine, William Thomas. So that he can work his way into a spy network, a government agent is publicly dishonoured.

Tornado
Chester Morris, Nancy Kelly, William Henry, Marie McDonald. Dir: William Berke. Pro: William Pine, William Thomas. A coal-miner is led along dangerous paths by his over-ambitious wife's desire for wealth.

Young And Willing
William Holden, Eddie Bracken, Susan Hayward. Dir. & Pro: Edward H. Griffith. Young hopefuls look for love in a New York theatrical boarding house, and jobs on Broadway. (United Artists release)

1944

▽ A musical had to be pretty terrible to flop during the war. **And The Angels Sing** wasn't and didn't. It had an entertaining cast and some good tunes by the surefire Jimmy Van Heusen-Johnny Burke team, but it was hobbled by a story theme that musicals had been using ever since *The Broadway Melody* in 1929: a sister act thrown out of harmony by a man. This time there were four girls: Dorothy Lamour (right), Betty Hutton (centre), Diana Lynn and Mimi Chandler, and the man was Fred MacMurray (left) as a bandleader who got the sisters their big break. Raymond Walburn as their father, Eddie Foy Jr, Frank Albertson, Mikhail Rasumny and Frank Faylen were others responding brightly to George Marshall's direction, in which author Claude Binyon had a hand. E.D. Leshin produced the Norman Panama-Melvin Frank screenplay. Best numbers: Lamour's 'It Could Happen To You' and Hutton's 'The Rocking Horse Ran Away'.

▽ **Our Hearts Were Young And Gay**, the memoirs of actress Cornelia Otis Skinner, daughter of stage star Otis Skinner, written in collaboration with her friend, Emily Kimbrough, made a popular book and an even more successful movie. The girls, played with *joie de vivre* by Gail Russell (left) and Diana Lynn (right), kicked up their heels decorously and delightfully in the Paris of 1923. Charles Ruggles and Dorothy Gish (in her first Paramount release for 17 years) as their parents; James Brown and Bill Edwards as their romantic escorts, and Beulah Bondi, Alma Kruger and Jean Heather in support, were all perfectly cast in a picture loaded with charm. The screenplay was written and produced by Sheridan Gibney and directed by Lewis Allen.

△ Cecil B. DeMille's contribution to the war effort, **The Story Of Dr Wassell**, was inspired by a radio talk by President Roosevelt about the US Navy doctor who rescued nine wounded men from the Japanese in Java and got them to Australia. A fictional story by James Hilton was based on the facts, and later published as a book, which Alan Le May and Charles Bennett shaped into the final screenplay; all the ten men involved in the perilous exploit gave first-hand accounts to the writers, Wassell with some reluctance. He may have had an inkling of the over-heroic unreality DeMille would spread over it, the clichés falling thick as the Japs' bombs, and feminine interest being dragged in, with Laraine Day as the hero's girl, Signe Hasso as a Dutch nurse, and Carol Thurston as a native beauty. Gary Cooper (illustrated), never more stalwart and straight-faced, starred convincingly, and was supported also by Dennis O'Keefe, Paul Kelly, Elliott Reid, Carl Esmond, Stanley Ridges, Minor Watson and Victor Varconi. There was plenty of spectacular action (even a volcano, which suddenly erupted when second unit director Arthur Rosson was shooting jungle war footage in Mexico, and which was hastily added to the script) and Victor Milner's Technicolor camerawork excelled. But it was below-par DeMille at the box-office.

▽ One of Somerset Maugham's minor novels, **The Hour Before The Dawn**, was up-dated to World War II by adapter Lesser Samuels, but down-dated by a creaky plot about a noble Englishman who discovers that the girl he has married is an enemy spy. He is so taken aback that he abandons his pacifist beliefs, joins the army, and strangles her, but not soon enough to conceal Veronica Lake's inadequate histrionic voltage for her role. Franchot Tone in the lead (illustrated with Lake) looked British enough, even if he didn't sound it, and had the support of seasoned professionals John Sutton, Binnie Barnes, Philip Merivale, Nils Asther, Henry Stephenson and Edmond Breon, who all seemed to be acting by numbers in this one. Frank Tuttle directed and William Dozier produced the Michael Hogan screenplay, and probably wished they hadn't.

▽ Espionage in wartime England was put to excellently effective cinematic use in another adaptation from an eminent British novelist. **Ministry Of Fear** underwent considerable rewriting by Seton I. Miller (who also produced) from one of Graham Greene's best 'entertainments'. But no harm done – it was a superior example of director Fritz Lang's distinctive style of thrillers which had been exciting audiences for a quarter-century, and it easily achieved places in both the company's profit column and the critics' Ten Best lists of 1944. Lang drew a riveting performance from Ray Milland as a man released from a mental hospital into the madness outside, which catches him up in a network of Nazi spies, fake spiritualists and microfilm thieves. Marjorie Reynolds (centre with Milland), Carl Esmond, Hillary Brooke, Dan Duryea, Percy Waram, Alan Napier, Erskine Sanford, Mary Field, Byron Foulger and Lester Matthews had their moments in a bewilderingly complex plot which left a few loose ends dangling, but was never dull.

▽ Fears that **The Hitler Gang** would be either a melodrama of hate-the-Hun propaganda or, with minor comedian Bobby Watson (right) cast as the Fuhrer, a mere burlesque, were groundless. It turned out to be a surprisingly serious history of the Nazis' rise to power, treated with as much restraint as the subject allowed (the facts were more incredibly lurid than fiction) by director John Farrow and writers Albert Hackett and Frances Goodrich. Watson's Hitler looked and sounded uncannily true to life, and he was surrounded by fine character actors – many of them German emigrés relishing the chance to debunk the idols who were holding their homeland in thrall – Martin Kosleck as Goebbels, Alexander Pope as Goering, Luis van Rooten as Himmler, Alexander Granach as Streicher, Victor Varconi (left) as Hess, Roman Bohnen, Ray Collins, Fritz Kortner, Ivan Triesault, Reinhold Schunzel, Lionel Royce, Ludwig Donath, and that superb villain and/or comedian of innumerable Hollywood films whose name shrank from Siegfried Rumann to Sig Rumann (and finally Ruman) as his reputation grew. This excellent movie was produced by Joseph Sistrom.

△ That one-man hit factory, Preston Sturges, having satirically disposed of politics, motherhood and other worthy subjects, turned his iconoclastic pen and camera on World War II flag-waving in **Hail The Conquering Hero**. It won loud laughs from large audiences and an Academy nomination for best original screenplay, but it had nearly got lost in the conflict between Sturges and studio boss Buddy De Sylva, who tried to re-cut the producer-director's completed movie. Eddie Bracken (centre foreground) had the part of his life as an asthmatic marine recruit, rejected and sent home; on the way he is taken up by a fun-loving bunch of marines who fit him with a fake story of gung-ho action, and he finds himself being feted as a hero by his home towners. How he got straightened out with his family and girlfriend (Ella Raines) involved a great gaggle of character actors, many of them Sturges regulars, including William Demarest, Raymond Walburn, Franklin Pangborn, Elizabeth Patterson, Jimmy Conlin, Georgia Caine, Esther Howard and Alan Bridge.

▽ Preston Sturges never made a funnier picture than **The Miracle Of Morgan's Creek**, and it scored his highest paybox results since *The Lady Eve*. Amazingly audacious for its time, it blew a resounding razz at American morals and ideals, with Betty Hutton (right) ascending heights of dizzy blondeness as one Trudy Kockenlocker. She enjoys herself no end at a wartime kiss-the-boys-goodbye party and nine months later gives birth to sextuplets; unable to recall who the father is, she gets her dopey 4-F suitor (Eddie Bracken) to take the credit, while her father (William Demarest, centre) fumes and the event becomes a national furore. The Kockenlocker household and its astonished small-town associates – enacted also by Diana Lynn (left), Porter Hall, Brian Donlevy, Akim Tamiroff, Esther Howard, Emory Parnell and Alan Bridge – were given 99 minutes of comic lines and hilarious incidents by Sturges, who wrote, directed and produced, and somehow avoided the scissors of the censors. Maybe they were laughing too hard to reach for them.

▷ Stricken ladies falling in love with their doctors have always been odds-on box-office bets. **And Now Tomorrow** (the year's most meaningless title) had Loretta Young (left) experiencing a relapse in the affliction – deafness – she had suffered five years earlier in *Alexander Graham Bell*. Now, instead of Don Ameche's telephone, Alan Ladd's new serum came to her aid; and when her fiancé (Barry Sullivan, right) dropped out, Dr Ladd dispensed heart-balm as well. As expected, it was a strong grosser, drawing the Young and Ladd fans, the latter celebrating his return from the army after over a year's absence. The marshmallow script by Frank Partos and (surprisingly) Raymond Chandler came from a Rachel Field novel; it was directed by Irving Pichel and produced by Fred Kohlmar, who also cast Susan Hayward (centre), Beulah Bondi, Helen Mack, Cecil Kellaway, Grant Mitchell, Darryl Hickman, Anthony Caruso and Jonathan Hale.

▷ **Double Indemnity** had all the suspense of a hand-grenade with the pin out. The fact that it still grips after several viewings, hooking attention from first scene to last, gives it a claim to rank as one of the most brilliant examples of storytelling in movie history. Billy Wilder (whose usual partner, Charles Brackett, thought the story disgusting and refused to collaborate) worked with Raymond Chandler on the script, based on James Cain's short novel, resembling his *Postman Always Rings Twice*, about an insurance salesman lured by a woman to murder her husband in such a way that they could collect on his accident policy. Their sex-charged plotting of the crime, the killing itself, the body's disposal, and the ever-increasing menace of the subsequent insurance investigation, had a cold-blooded fascination that no director but Wilder could command. He had to use much coaxing to make Fred MacMurray eschew his nice-guy persona for the woman-hungry murderer role; it was his best. Equally potent were Barbara Stanwyck (illustrated), in a symbolically phoney blonde wig as the amoral wife, and Edward G. Robinson as the investigator, while telling support came from Porter Hall, Jean Heather, Byron Barr, Richard Gaines, Fortunio Bonanova, and Tom Powers as the victim. The influence of Chandler was apparent in the trenchant dialogue and the seedy Los Angeles atmosphere of Joseph Sistrom's production. The Academy honoured it with seven nominations but the actual awards went to *Going My Way*; forty years on, it has won the Oscars of time.

△ If it hadn't been such a legendary Broadway hit, a 1941 triumph for Gertrude Lawrence and the then unknown Danny Kaye, **Lady In The Dark** might have had a better reception from movie critics. On its own values it had a lot to offer filmgoers, and they responded with very sizeable grosses. Just as well, because Paramount had unzipped its wallet for a lavish production by B.G. De Sylva, directed by Mitchell Leisen, photographed in Technicolor by the multi-awarded Ray Rennahan and gorgeously designed by Hans Dreier and New York's celebrated Raoul Pene du Bois. Furthermore, it was expensively cast, with Ginger Rogers (centre), Warner Baxter, Ray Milland, Jon Hall and Mischa Auer (in the roles originated by Lawrence, Bert Lytell, Macdonald Carey, Victor Mature and Kaye), plus Barry Sullivan, Phyllis Brooks, Gail Russell, Mary Phillips, Harvey Stephens, Fay Helm and Edward Fielding. Moss Hart's story, adapted by Frances Goodrich and Albert Hackett, had more novelty than most librettos, dealing with a fashion magazine editress who is going bananas because of three men in her life and the tensions of her job. She consults a psychiatrist and relives some entertaining dreams, the most spectacular being a circus extravaganza during which she sings the big number, 'The Saga Of Jenny'. Several other songs in the Kurt Weill-Ira Gershwin stage score were sorely missed; so was Kaye. Nevertheless, quite a show.

△ A deliciously unnerving ghost story took possession of the screen in **The Uninvited**. Director Lewis Allen's serious treatment of the tingling script which Dodie Smith and Frank Partos derived from a novel by Dorothy Macardle (*Uneasy Freehold*) was rather unusual for such movies, which usually indulged in comedy relief á là *Cat And The Canary*. None of that here, and no sliding panels or clutching hands, but loads of spectral atmosphere as a young couple (Ray Milland and Ruth Hussey) move into a rural English house, all sunshine and chintz, while a strange girl (Gail Russell, right) keeps visiting, bringing with her an intangible presence of evil. Gradually the three are drawn into a vortex of terror by the girl's dead mother, whose spirit is trying to reveal secrets of the past. It was a genuine thriller, and a credit to Allen, the British theatre director making his first film; producer Charles Brackett, working without Billy Wilder for once; and the cast, completed by Donald Crisp (left), Cornelia Otis Skinner, Dorothy Stickney, Barbara Everest and Alan Napier. Even its theme tune, Victor Young's 'Stella By Starlight', was a haunting hit which has become a durable standard.

∇ **The Great Moment** was the third Preston Sturges film released in 1944 and the single flop of his meteoric career as a Paramount director-producer which had started only four years before. A biographical story about a Boston dentist who pioneered in the use of ether as an anaesthetic in the 19th century, it was based on a book by Rene Fulop-Miller, *Triumph Over Pain*. Curious material for Sturges to choose, and his treatment of it was even odder, ranging from serious drama to slapstick comedy, and abounding with flashbacks. Considering the movie's erratic changes of mood, the cast (Joel McCrea and Betty Field – both illustrated – Harry Carey, William Demarest, Franklin Pangborn, Porter Hall, Louis Jean Heydt, Edwin Maxwell, Grady Sutton, Thurston Hall, J. Farrell MacDonald, Jimmy Conlin) performed well, and there were flashes of Sturges brilliance from time to time. He had shot it in 1942 and kept it on ice for two years while the company wondered what to do with it. This failure, and his frequent clashes with production chief B.G. De Sylva, cued Sturges's exit from Paramount; elsewhere he made only four more pictures, none of them hits.

∇ They were beginning to shoot some of the less important productions in Technicolor by 1944: **Rainbow Island**, for instance, with Dorothy Lamour (centre) in another palm-tree paradise. Aware that Dotty's sarong was getting pretty threadbare after being dipped in so many studio lagoons, they took a formula South Seas story by Seena Owen and laughed it up with comic sailors, singing and dancing cuties, and fairly diverting results. As a white girl brought up in native style Lamour had her costumes cut as far as they could go and her tongue in her pretty cheek, sending up her cliché role, while Barry Sullivan, Eddie Bracken (right) and Gil Lamb (left) played merchant marines escaping from the Japs and causing uproar among the islanders. Others directed by Ralph Murphy in E.D. Leshin's production: Anne Revere, Forrest Orr, Marc Lawrence, Reed Hadley, Olga San Juan, Elena Verdugo, Yvonne De Carlo. Four songs relieved the Walter De Leon-Arthur Phillips script.

◁ About halfway through **Practically Yours**, spectators started wondering what to have for supper. Norman Krasna's comedy started brightly enough, with an over-romantic girl (Claudette Colbert, right) intercepting a loving message sent to his dog by an Air Force pilot (Fred MacMurray, left) just before he crashed into the Pacific. Thinking herself to be his bereaved sweetheart, she and everyone else are thrown all of a heap when he turns up alive; then the script went AWOL. The co-stars, who always worked well together, lent some sparkle to the silly situations that ensued, and were helped by Cecil Kellaway, Robert Benchley, Gil Lamb (centre), Jane Frazee, Mikhail Rasumny, Rosemary DeCamp and Tom Powers and the skill of producer-director Mitchell Leisen. It was a feeble finish for Colbert's 16 years of Paramount success; she left the studio, but was still starring on screen in the 1960s and on Broadway in the 1980s.

△ Bing Crosby, Betty Hutton and a smash song, 'Accentuate The Positive' by Johnny Mercer and Harold Arlen, were the life-preservers that prevented **Here Come The Waves** from sinking into the flood of mediocre musical flag-wavers the studios poured out in the early forties. Bing played a singing idol joining the Navy in the hope of seeing action at sea, but winding up in charge of shows staged by the female sailors, two of whom were Betty Hutton (illustrated). Fortunately for the audience's nerves, one of the twins she played was comparatively demure, and this one got Bing after a lot of dashing about, misunderstandings, mistaken identities and musical interruptions, the latter coming as welcome relief from the slap-happy script Allan Scott, Ken Englund and Zion Myers wrote. The other sister wound up with Bing's pal, Sonny Tufts, cast with Ann Doran, Noel Neill, Gwen Crawford, Mae Clark, Catherine Craig, Harry Barris and Oscar O'Shea by producer-director Mark Sandrich. Best scene: Crosby sending up the current Sinatra craze by crooning 'That Old Black Magic' to swooning bobby-soxers.

▷ The stars circling the Paramount mountain blazed proudly on 15 March, 1945 as the company was presented with its first 'best picture' Oscar since *Wings* was honoured at the first Academy Awards ceremony 16 years earlier. **Going My Way** achieved not only that supreme accolade, but six other Academy Awards, to author-director-producer Leo McCarey, actors Bing Crosby (left) and Barry Fitzgerald (right), writers Frank Butler and Frank Cavett, and songsmiths James Van Heusen and Johnny Burke. The public voted for it too, with a landslide of dollars since its 1944 release: $6 million in USA and Canada rentals was big money in those days. The cause of all this excitement was no colossal epic, but a gentle, endearing comedy-drama about a young priest (Crosby) assigned to take over a New York church from its ageing incumbent (Fitzgerald), writing a song to aid the church funds, taming the local street lads, and winning the testy old priest's friendship. When the church burns down, a diva of the Metropolitan Opera (Risë Stevens) agrees to tour with its choir for its rebuilding. The obvious pitfalls of sloppy sentimentality and religious schmaltz in such a story were miraculously avoided, although at times McCarey came perilously close – and even closer in his RKO sequel, *The Bells Of St Mary's*, again with Crosby but not Fitzgerald. The latter had set a record with two Oscar nominations for *Going My Way* as best actor and best supporting actor (later rules prevented this). Also cast: Gene Lockhart, Frank McHugh, William Frawley, James Brown, Jean Heather, Stanley Clements, Porter Hall, Fortunio Bonanova, Eily Malyon.

∇ You either resisted the romantic melodrama of **Frenchman's Creek**, in which case you wasted your time and money, or you sat back and let its lush extravagance wash over you. A few million readers of Daphne du Maurier's best-seller took the latter course; most of them, and millions more, succumbed to this Talbot Jennings adaptation, filmed with style and magnificence by Mitchell Leisen. Joan Fontaine, lovely in Restoration costumes, played an English gentlewoman, and Arturo de Cordova, swashbuckling like mad, a French pirate she falls in love with after fleeing from a wicked nobleman to her home in Du Maurier country (Cornwall). Basil Rathbone (illustrated with Fontaine), Ralph Forbes, Nigel Bruce, Cecil Kellaway, Mary Field, Patricia Barker, David Clyde and Moyna MacGill hit the right note of elaborate make-believe set by Leisen, and the B.G. De Sylva-David Lewis Technicolor production boasted Oscar-winning art direction by Hans Dreier and Ernst Fegte, awarded in 1945.

◁ Exhibitors got less than the title promised from most bookings of **Standing Room Only**. It was an amusing comedy by Darrell Ware and Karl Tunberg, based on a story by Al Martin about crowded living conditions in wartime Washington, but unfortunately Columbia had an even funnier movie on the same subject (*The More The Merrier*) on release. However, this one took a different narrative course, when its heroine, secretary Paulette Goddard, got around the hotel room shortage by booking boss Fred MacMur- ray (left) and herself into a luxurious home as servants. Complications and embarrassments proliferated en- joyably before their ruse was discovered. Goddard, MacMurray, Edward Arnold (right) and Roland Young knew their way around laugh-raising lines and situations; Hillary Brooke, Anne Revere, Porter Hall, Clarence Kolb, Marie McDonald, Veda Ann Borg and Isabel Randolph were right behind them, with expert guidance from Sidney Lanfield. The producer of this diversion was Paul Jones.

OTHER RELEASES OF 1944

Dangerous Passage
Robert Lowery, Phyllis Brooks, Jack La Rue. Dir: William Berke. Pro: William Pine, William Thomas. To avoid all those who seek to relieve him of his fortune, a young heir boards a slow boat that's bound for danger.

Dark Mountain
Robert Lowery, Ellen Drew, Regis Toomey. Dir: William Berke. Pro: William Pine, William Thomas. Triangle melodrama about a forest ranger, his girl friend, and the crooked business man she marries.

Double Exposure
Chester Morris, Nancy Kelly, Phillip Terry. Dir: William Berke. Pro: William Pine, William Thomas. Hero rescues a girl photographer from a pursuing villain whom she has snap- ped in the act of killing.

Gambler's Choice
Chester Morris, Nancy Kelly, Russell Hayden. Dir: Frank McDonald. Pro: William Pine, William Thomas. Three children grow up; one to become a policeman, the other boy a gambler, the girl a singer.

Henry Aldrich, Boy Scout
Jimmy Lydon, Charles Smith, Olive Blakeney. Dir: Hugh Bennett. Pro: Walter MacEwen, Michel Kraike. Leading Scout Henry has his hands full with an obnoxious new boy in the troop, finally reforms him.

Henry Aldrich Plays Cupid
Jimmy Lydon, Charles Smith, Diana Lynn. Dir: Hugh Ben- nett. Pro: Walter MacEwen, Michel Kraike. Thinking his stern teacher might be softened by marriage, Henry takes disastrous steps to find him a wife.

Henry Aldrich's Little Secret
Jimmy Lydon, Charles Smith, Olive Blakeney. Dir: Hugh Bennett. Pro: Walter MacEwen, Michel Kraike. While its mother is out of town, Henry takes care of a baby and suffers hilarious embarrassments.

I Love A Soldier
Paulette Goddard, Sonny Tufts, Beulah Bondi, Barry Fitz- gerald. Dir. & Pro: Mark Sandrich. Wartime comedy about a female welder in a shipyard; she's supposed to be man-proof, but a GI on leave fixes that.

The Man In Half Moon Street
Nils Asther, Helen Walker, Paul Cavanagh. Dir: Ralph Murphy. Pro: Walter MacEwen. A young-looking scientist, actually ancient, resorts to killing young men for the glandu- lar extract he needs.

The Memphis Belle
Documentary of US bombing mission over Germany. Dir. & Pro: William Wyler.

The National Barn Dance
Jean Heather, Charles Quigley, Robert Benchley. Dir: Hugh Bennett. Pro: Walter MacEwen. An executive rejects a musi- cal troupe for his radio station; they take jobs in his home, put on an impromptu show, win a contract.

The Navy Way
Robert Lowery, Jean Parker, William Henry. Dir: William Berke. Pro: William Pine, William Thomas. Rivalries come to a head and friendships are forged among men being trained for the US Navy.

One Body Too Many
Jack Haley, Jean Parker, Bela Lugosi. Dir: Frank McDonald. Pro: William Pine, William Thomas. Mystery-farce in which a dim-witted insurance salesman becomes a detective by mistake.

Take It Big
Jack Haley, Harriet Hilliard, Ozzie Nelson and His Orches- tra. Dir: Frank McDonald. Pro: William Pine, William Thomas. Comedian reduced to playing the rear end of a horse inherits a rundown ranch; with his show pals he makes a go of it.

Till We Meet Again
Ray Milland, Barbara Britton, Walter Slezak. Dir: Frank Borzage. Pro: Borzage, David Lewis. Allied pilot is shot down over occupied France and a novice nun helps him elude the Gestapo by posing as his wife.

Timber Queen
Richard Arlen, Mary Beth Hughes, June Havoc. Dir: Frank McDonald. Pro: William Pine, William Thomas. An air force man on leave gets involved with a girl's problems in the logging industry.

You Can't Ration Love
Betty Rhodes, Johnnie Johnston, Marie Wilson. Dir: Lester Fuller. Pro: Walter MacEwen, Michel Kraike. Musical about college girls solving the wartime shortage of male stu- dents by rationing their dates.

1945

▽ What Spike Jones and His City Slickers did to that venerable torch song 'Chloe' was the hilarious high spot of **Bring On The Girls**. Aside from this melodic hatchet job, Fred Kohlmar's Technicolor musical was strictly for war-weary fans who weren't too choosy. The mechanical script by Darrell Ware and Karl Tunberg, based on a Pierre Wolff story, concerned a drippy millionaire (Eddie Bracken, right) who joins the navy to escape the blandishments of gold-diggers. He is pursued by a nightclub cigarette girl (Veronica Lake, left) intent on smoking out his bankroll, but he marries a socialite beauty (Marjorie Reynolds), while his buddy (Sonny Tufts) winds up with Veronica, his ex-girlfriend. Alan Mowbray, Grant Mitchell, Thurston Hall, Peter Whitney, Porter Hall, Joan Woodbury, Lloyd Corrigan, Frank Faylen, Sig Arno, Andrew Tombes, Huntz Hall and Norma Varden filled a supporting cast topped energetically by dancer Johnny Coy. Not much pezazz in the direction by Sidney Lanfield.

△ A dotty but likeable comedy, **Out Of This World** offered Eddie Bracken as a Western Union messenger who delivers singing telegrams with so much talent that he becomes a superstar crooner – and no wonder: he has Bing Crosby's voice. The dubbed-in dulcet tones coming out of Bracken's funny face was the novelty angle that made the picture talked about. It also gave cause for some satire on the phenomenon of screaming, swooning teenagers in Walter De Leon and Arthur Phillip's script, which was otherwise on the yawn-making side. Diana Lynn (here with Bracken) put in a refreshing appearance as a pianist who involves the hero with her all-girl orchestra (Miss Lynn was actually a concert pianist before Paramount discovered her), but Veronica Lake had little chance to shine in the dull role of an agent's secretary who helps Bracken hit the big time. Others performing for director Hal Walker were two great character actresses, Florence Bates and Mabel Paige; radio comic Parkyakarkus (also known as Harry Parke, born Harry Einstein), loud comedienne Cass Daley, Donald MacBride, Olga San Juan and bandleaders Ray Noble, Carmen Cavallaro and Ted Fiorito; Bing lent the venture his quartet of sons, Gary, Lin, Philip and Dennis, as well as his own voice. Sam Coslow's production (he also co-authored with Elizabeth Meehan) boasted two Johnny Mercer-Harold Arlen songs that became standards: the title number, and 'June Comes Around Every Year'.

▽ One for the ladies, **Love Letters** was the kind of heart-tug drama that in the television future would be known as soap opera. It made good use of that favourite old plot device, amnesia, beautifully suffered in this case by Jennifer Jones. Among other wartime traumas provided for the star was her discovery that the letters she treasured had been written, not by her loved one, but by another man. Since he was Joseph Cotten (with her here), you just knew that he would charm away her loss of memory and everything would turn out all right in the end. Meanwhile, you could enjoy the opulence of Hal B. Wallis's production, and some high-style acting by the stars, as well as Anita Louise, Ann Richards, Gladys Cooper, Cecil Kellaway, Reginald Denny, Ernest Cossart, Byron Barr and Robert Sully. Both Jones and Cotten were borrowed from David O. Selznick who, via his customary memos, bombarded Wallis and director William Dieterle with instructions on every detail concerning his beloved Jennifer. A lovely title theme composed by Victor Young helped the movie, which was scripted by one novelist, Ayn Rand (of *The Fountainhead* fame), from another's book, Chris Massie's *Pity My Simplicity*, to become a profitable release.

△ **Miss Susie Slagle's** wasn't just a pretty tongue-twister; it was an audience-pleaser too. The remarkable Lillian Gish (2nd right), 33 years after her film debut (with another four decades on stage and screen to go, the frail-looking lady has outlasted all other silent stars) played Miss Slagle, who ran a Baltimore boarding house for students of the famous John Hopkins Hospital medical school. Their assorted romances and career crises in the screenplay Anne Froelick and Hugo Butler worked up from Augusta Tucker's novel made a non-starter for fans wanting thrills, but a treat for those to whom charm, and a pleasing period atmosphere (1910), were enough. Producer John Houseman employed new director John Berry (his colleague in the old Mercury Theatre days with Orson Welles) and a cast that included Veronica Lake, Sonny Tufts (left), Joan Caulfield, Billy De Wolfe, Bill Edwards, Lloyd Bridges (right), Pat Phelan and Theodore Newton (the hospital hopefuls) and Ray Collins, Morris Carnovsky, Ludwig Stossel and Roman Bohnen (their elders). Mild box-office.

▽ A slick screenplay by Milton Holmes took Alan Ladd (right) back to the kind of good-bad character that he played best. **Salty O'Rourke** was a gambler involved in a crooked scheme with a bribable jockey. It blows up in his face, and he decides that the quieter life urged on him by his schoolteacher girlfriend is a better bet after all. No question about the box-office fate of this one; Ladd's popularity was at its zenith. And the vigorous style of director Raoul Walsh (borrowed from Warner Bros.) made sure that the entertainment didn't flag. His cast in E.D. Leshin's production contained dependable players – William Demarest (left), Gail Russell, Bruce Cabot, Spring Byington, Darryl Hickman, Lester Matthews, Marjorie Woodworth – but the memorable performance came from 18-year-old Stanley Clements (centre) as a jockey who wouldn't cooperate on a fixed race and was murdered by the fixers.

▷ A million-dollar cast struggling with ten cents' worth of material made a dispiriting spectacle in **Duffy's Tavern**, which combined two well-worn screen musical formulas: the radio show and the all-star revue. The former utilised Ed Gardner's series of the title, which had a big listening public, and inspired (if that's the word) the Norman Panama-Melvin Frank script about innkeeper Gardner and record studio boss Victor Moore enlisting the aid of Hollywood stars to stage a benefit for their enterprises. Marjorie Reynolds and Barry Sullivan conducted a mild romance, while most of the rest of Paramount's contract list went to work on some slapdash songs and sketches. Director Hal Walker and producer Danny Dare's ill-used gathering of talent included Bing Crosby (and his four sons, Gary, Dennis, Lin, Philip), Betty Hutton, Paulette Goddard (right), Alan Ladd, Dorothy Lamour, Eddie Bracken, Brian Donlevy (left), Sonny Tufts, Veronica Lake, Arturo de Cordova, Barry Fitzgerald, Cass Daley, Diana Lynn, Robert Benchley, William Demarest, Howard Da Silva, Billy De Wolfe, Walter Abel, Johnny Coy, Olga San Juan and Bobby Watson.

▷ The Cinderella department, Pygmalion section, was stocked with comic, romantic and dramatic goodies for **Kitty**, displayed with style by director Mitchell Leisen. Paulette Goddard (2nd right) reached the peak of her career as the 18th-century London guttersnipe transformed into a duchess by a fop (Ray Milland, centre) and a dowager (Constance Collier) who need the money their protégée can command as the wife of a nobleman (Reginald Owen). Rosamund Marshall's novel, as adapted by Karl Tunberg and Darrell Ware (who also co-produced), proved there was plenty of entertaining life left in the old plot, even to the expected fade-out with young love triumphant. The studio's technical experts captured the period atmosphere down to the last wig and wink, helped by a stalwart supporting cast that included Patric Knowles (right), Cecil Kellaway (left), Dennis Hoey, Sara Allgood, Eric Blore and Edgar Norton. It recouped every cent of its high cost, and then some.

△ Somewhere around reel three or four of a Betty Hutton picture, you begin to feel the need for earplugs and dark glasses. That certainly applied to **Incendiary Blonde**, a biographical (sort of) movie about Texas Guinan, one of the most famous figures of the cabaret-crazy twenties. A vaudeville singer in the century's first decade, she became a cowgirl movie star in the next, but really hit her stride in the Prohibition era as the 'Queen of the Night Clubs' (also the title of her one talkie, a 1929 Warner musical, grade Z). Whoopee-making crowds paid inflated prices to be greeted by her stentorian 'Hello Suckers!' and drink her bootleg hooch, while the tabloids front-paged her frequent police raids and trips to the clink. All this gave Betty (illustrated centre) the green light to accelerate her forceful style of acting and singing to new highs of razzle-dazzle, in which she was encouraged by director George Marshall, and assisted by Arturo de Cordova, Charles Ruggles, Barry Fitzgerald, Mary Phillips and Eduardo Ciannelli. The Claude Binyon-David Butler script prettied up the sleazier aspects of Tex's life, Joseph Sistrom's Technicolor production had a rhinestone glitter, and the soundtrack was loud with standard songs of the times, including the now evergreen 'It Had To Be You'. A hit.

△ Dorothy Lamour, with neither a song nor a sarong to help her, gave one of her best performances in **A Medal For Benny**, although she and everyone else were subordinated to J. Carrol Naish's rich role of a *paisano* in a Southern California town whose ne'er-do-well son, Benny (who never appeared) becomes a war hero. Naish, the Irish-American so good at playing Latin types, did it with much gusto and got an Academy nomination, as did the story by John Steinbeck and Jack Wagner. Satirical fun, reminiscent of *Hail The Conquering Hero*, arose from the posthumous adulation showered on the previously despised Benny by the town's publicity-hungry dignitaries, while romance bloomed between his sweetheart, Lamour, and Arturo de Cordova (here with her). Mikhail Rasumny, Frank McHugh, Rosita Moreno, Douglass Dumbrille, Grant Mitchell and Fernando Alvarado were others well directed by Irving Pichel in the Paul Jones production, another hit for veteran screenwriter Frank Butler.

▽ **Masquerade In Mexico** revealed that either the plot of *Midnight* or its director (or both) had gone stale after six years. Anyway, Mitchell Leisen was ill advised to remake one of his best comedies, to which musical trimmings were now added and practically every delight taken away. None of the new cast – Dorothy Lamour (on phone), Arturo de Cordova (right), Ann Dvorak (2nd left), Patric Knowles, George Rigaud (left), Mikhail Rasumny, Natalie Schafer (centre) and dancer Billy Daniels – could match the original's finesse. And Karl Tunberg's revised script (from Edwin Justus Mayer's and Franz Schultz's story) stumbled where the old Brackett-Wilder winner pranced. It now had Lamour as a showgirl stranded south of the border, hired by a husband to lure a bullfighter away from his infatuated wife. Producer Tunberg's budget didn't stretch to Technicolor, which the colourful locale needed, but he bought a couple of unmemorable songs that gave it no box-office assistance.

◁ Killingly funny, except to those who didn't think killing was funny, **Murder, He Says** delivered a surprise package of laughs at the same time as the similarly lethal farce *Arsenic And Old Lace* was scoring its expected movie hit for Warner Bros. Jolly murders were in vogue. Fred MacMurray (right), giving a terrific performance, starred as an insurance salesman out gathering statistics: a series of shocks is what he actually collects when he visits a family of homicidal hillbillies. Marjorie Main (2nd left) was a riot as their buzzsaw-voiced Maw, while Helen Walker (2nd right), Peter Whitney (left), Jean Heather, Mabel Paige, Porter Hall and Barbara Pepper threw themselves with spirit into the hilarious proceedings, which looked wild but were carefully calculated by author Jack Moffitt and scriptwriter Lou Breslow, and firmly controlled by director George Marshall. E.D. Leshin produced for the Sol C. Siegel unit.

▽ Incredible as it may seem, some of the company's top brass disliked **The Lost Weekend** so much, and the California preview's opinion cards were mostly so derogatory, that this work of art was almost withheld from public view permanently. Serious consideration was given to a $5 million offer from a syndicate of distilleries which believed that suppression of such a powerful anti-booze document was worth that much to their business. But rescue was at hand. A screening for the New York critics aroused overwhelming enthusiasm for Billy Wilder's direction of his and producer Charles Brackett's screenplay, and for Ray Milland's performance. Any idea of shelving the film was abandoned, and it was released to international acclaim as well as a shower of Academy Awards: best picture, best actor, best direction, best script. Jane Wyman (right), Phillip Terry, Howard Da Silva, Doris Dowling and Frank Faylen splendidly supported Milland (left), who was hardly ever off screen in his amazingly sensitive and moving portrait of an alcoholic on a three-day bender. Charles Jackson's novel underwent some alterations but lost none of its potency; in fact, it gained from the visual realism of John Seitz's camera in Manhattan streets (shot there), bars, pawnshops, theatre, hospital (a harrowing psychopathic ward sequence) and Milland's delirium-haunted apartment.

▷ Many surviving *Road* buffs still insist that **Road To Utopia** was the funniest of the Bing Crosby-Bob Hope-Dorothy Lamour series. It began with Bob and Dotty as married parents reminiscing about old times in the Klondike with their dear departed friend Bing (here, below, with Bob above) who, in the flashback taking up most of the running time (and we do mean running), was last seen on an ice-floe pursued by killers, after a hectic race between them and the starring trio to find an Alaskan goldmine. A drily hilarious commentary by Robert Benchley kept the audience more or less in touch with the story amid an avalanche of wisecracks, ad libs, inside jokes, sight gags, talking animals and songs, of which 'Personality' by Johnny Burke and Jimmy Van Heusen was the best. The flashback over, the movie ends with its most outrageous gag: Bing turns up alive and well, to find that the Hopes' son looks exactly like a Crosby! The Norman Panama-Melvin Frank script had a single goal: to get laughs. They got enormous paybox figures too. The cast also included Douglass Dumbrille, Hillary Brooke, Jack La Rue, Nestor Paiva and Robert Barrat. The studio was wisely spacing out the *Road* releases; this one finished shooting in March 1944 and was held back until December 1945.

△ The unlikely team of Betty Hutton and Barry Fitzgerald (both illustrated) had **The Stork Club** confected for them by B.G. (Buddy) De Sylva, who had traded in the onerous job of supervising Paramount's output for the producership of individual pictures. He also wrote, with John McGowan, this fable of a good samaritan (Hutton) rescuing a tattered derelict (Fitzgerald) from drowning. Needless to say, the hobo turns out to be a zillionaire, and she is transformed from a hat-check girl to a lady of luxury, whereupon her boyfriend (Don De Fore) returns from the wars suspecting The Worst. The tiresome misunderstandings were relieved by a brace of rousing Hutton songs, 'I'm A Square In The Social Circle' and 'Doctor, Lawyer, Indian Chief'; Betty, indeed, was practically the whole show, and her fans came out in force. Others assisting her under Hal Walker's direction were Robert Benchley, Bill Goodwin, Mikhail Rasumny and Iris Adrian, remembered for her slambang delivery of dialogue. How much (if anything) the Stork Club, New York's famous night-time oasis of the forties, contributed to the budget for this huge plug is still moot.

▷ Hal B. Wallis, Warner Bros.' production chief from 1933 to 1944, resigned to form his own company within Paramount, thus beginning a 25 year association with the studio. His first offering, **The Affairs Of Susan**, was a novel, amusing comedy, which gave Joan Fontaine (left) a gold-plated showcase for her talents in the role of an actress who was never off stage. Each of the four men she kept on romantic tenterhooks – George Brent (right), Dennis O'Keefe, Walter Abel, Don De Fore – knew a different Susan as she changed her personality to suit the man. The invention of this beautiful chameleon won authors Thomas Monroe and Laszlo Gorog an Oscar nomination, and Richard Flournoy joined them to develop the script, which William Seiter directed with *élan*. Rita Johnson, Byron Barr, Mary Field and Warren Hymer were other cast members helping the Wallis unit get off to a promising start.

OTHER RELEASES OF 1945

Follow That Woman
William Gargan, Nancy Kelly, Regis Toomey. Dir: Lew Landers. Pro: William Pine, William Thomas. Private detective joins the army, spends his 7-day leave clearing up a murder case involving his wife.

High-Powered
Robert Lowery, Phyllis Brooks, Roger Pryor. Dir: William Berke. Pro: William Pine, William Thomas. After an accident, a construction worker fights his fear of heights and gets back his nerve.

Hold That Blonde
Eddie Bracken, Veronica Lake, Albert Dekker. Dir: George Marshall. Pro: Paul Jones. Funny things happen when a kleptomaniac millionaire falls for a seductive jewel thief. (Remake of *Paths To Paradise*, 1925)

Midnight Manhunt (aka One Exciting Night)
William Gargan, Ann Savage, George Zucco. Dir: William Thomas. Pro: William Pine, Thomas. A corpse hidden in a wax museum starts reporters on a wild goose chase.

Scared Stiff (aka Treasure Of Fear)
Jack Haley, Ann Savage, Barton MacLane. Dir: Frank McDonald. Pro: William Pine, William Thomas. Reporter gets mixed up in frantic plot concerning priceless jade chessmen.

Tokyo Rose
Byron Barr, Osa Massen. Dir: Lew Landers. Pro: William Pine, William Thomas. Drama of the Japanese propaganda broadcaster to American troops, and her capture.

The Unseen
Joel McCrea, Gail Russell, Herbert Marshall. Dir: Lewis Allen. Pro: John Houseman. Thriller about a girl who takes a job as governess in a mysterious household and is haunted by the murder of her predecessor.

You Came Along
Robert Cummings, Lizabeth Scott, Don Defore. Dir: John Farrow. Pro: Hal B. Wallis. Girl conducts three airmen through War Bond selling tour, falls in love with one, learns he has a fatal disease, marries him.

1946

▽ The action highlight of **Monsieur Beaucaire** was Bob Hope (centre) out-Erroling Flynn as he clashed swords with villain Joseph Schildkraut in a sequence added by Frank Tashlin after the preview. Even without the spoof duel, the picture scored as a riotous burlesque of costume romances, with Hope and his gag-writers, led by scenarists Melvin Frank and Norman Panama, in great form. He played a barber to the court of Louis XV, getting more close shaves than he gives as he becomes embroiled in royal intrigues, is sentenced to the guillotine, and then reprieved in order to pose as the French ambassador to Spain. It was a supposedly fatal mission, but Hope sprang eternal. Rather surprisingly Technicolor was not used on Paul Jones's lavishly dressed production; otherwise nothing was stinted, certainly not good supporting players: Joan Caulfield (left), Patric Knowles, Marjorie Reynolds, Cecil Kellaway, Reginald Owen (as King Louis), Constance Collier, Douglass Dumbrille, Howard Freeman, Hillary Brooke, Fortunio Bonanova, Mary Nash, Leonid Kinskey. George Marshall directed, adding one more to his long list of box-office winners. It was hilarious entertainment, even for lovers of the Booth Tarkington novel and the old Valentino movie.

▽ Western gambling queen Barbara Stanwyck shot land baron George Coulouris just as he was about to kill wagonmaster Ray Milland (seated centre right, looking at Barbara); and that's how California was saved for Statehood. And this was only the finale of **California**, after an hour and a half of US Western history, movie version. The Frank Butler-Theodore Strauss screenplay, from a story by Boris Ingster, had resemblances to *The Covered Wagon* in earlier scenes but missed that film's epic sweep, throwing realism into the horse-trough and galloping away into riproaring melodrama. The name of the villain Coulouris played, Pharaoh Coffin, warned you that subtlety was not the watchword of producer Seton I. Miller and director John Farrow; but if you wanted old-style action, they had it in abundance, and in Technicolor. Portraying a regenerated army deserter and a heroine with a shady past didn't stretch the talents of Milland and Stanwyck, but they were a definite plus for the paybox, as was Barry Fitzgerald as an amusing old-timer. Eduardo Ciannelli, Albert Dekker, Frank Faylen, Gavin Muir, Roman Bohnen, James Burke, Julia Faye and Anthony Quinn combined to provide a solid supporting cast.

△ Jack Haley, after a nine-year absence from the studio during which he had become a movie immortal as the Tin Man in *The Wizard Of Oz*, returned for a bouncy little musical, **People Are Funny**. Like so many Paramount song-and-dance comedies, it was based on the theory that the millions who listened to the radio were potential cinema customers. The screenplay by David Lang and Maxwell Shane pretended to tell how John Guedel's radio show 'People Are Funny', enormously popular in American homes at the time, first got on the air. It happened when big-time producer Philip Reed took up small-station announcer Haley's idea and sold it to hard-to-please sponsor Rudy Vallee. Helen Walker provided charming romantic interest and Frances Langford (illustrated) guest-starred to sing 'I'm In The Mood for Love' (by Dorothy Fields and Jimmy McHugh) in the neat little comedy Sam White directed and produced for the William Pine-William Thomas unit. Also cast: Clara Blandick, Ozzie Nelson and Art Linkletter.

△ **Cross My Heart** was Carole Lombard's *True Confession* rewritten for Betty Hutton, whose fans were alone in thinking it an improvement. Substituting Sonny Tufts (here with Betty) and Michael Chekhov for the original's Fred MacMurray and John Barrymore accentuated its road company look, and John Berry's direction indicated that farce was not his forte. Nevertheless, the understructure of the Louis Verneuil-Georges Berr story about a compulsive liar who confessed to a murder she hadn't committed, so that her lawyer boyfriend could win fame by defending her, stood up well under the redecorating job of scripters Harry Tugend and Claude Binyon. Tugend, who also produced, gave the star five Burke-Van Heusen songs to which she applied her inimitably supercharged treatment, and he employed a supporting cast that included Ruth Donnelly, Rhys Williams, Iris Adrian, Howard Freeman and Alan Bridge. An irritating feature of Lombard's version – the heroine preceding each falsehood by thrusting tongue in cheek – was unfortunately retained.

▽ A Harvard student, Richard Henry Dana Jr became a sailor in order to investigate working conditions at sea in the 1830s, and subsequently published a book, **Two Years Before The Mast**, that shocked America. Many of its brutal facts were retained in Seton I. Miller's romanticised film version, which he wrote (with George Bruce) and produced, and which John Farrow directed in spirited style; however, the epic *Mutiny On The Bounty* effect they aimed for didn't quite come off. Brian Donlevy (here behind Howard Da Silva, 2nd left front) played Dana

and Alan Ladd (foreground right) starred as a shipowner's son shanghaied to serve under a sadistic captain (Da Silva) and flogged so cruelly that he starts a mutiny which results in a Boston trial and new laws to protect seamen's interests. The three leads put up convincingly virile performances, with good support from William Bendix (foreground left), Barry Fitzgerald (background centre), Albert Dekker, Ray Collins, Esther Fernandez, Darryl Hickman, Luis van Rooten and Roman Bohnen. The trade winds blew heartily on the box-office.

△ **The Perfect Marriage** took the trivial troubles of the overprivileged and blew them up into a comedy as flimsy as a soap bubble. Loretta Young (centre) and David Niven (right) played a young couple, charming, handsome, rich, and happily married for ten years, who have a spat and almost a divorce; after interference by friends, relatives and prospective lovers they kiss and make up, leaving the audience in a so-what mood. Such insubstantial material, depending almost entirely on dialogue, had got by in the early talkie days, but more movement and incident than director Lewis Allen or screenwriter Leonard Spiegelgass provided were needed now for box-office success. One essential that producer Hal Wallis did supply was a cast of expert professionals to support the rather wooden leads: Charles Ruggles, Eddie Albert (left), Virginia Field, Rita Johnson, ZaSu Pitts, Jerome Cowan, Nana Bryant, Louella Gear, Howard Freeman. The source play by Samson Raphaelson had a modest Broadway run in the 1944-5 season with Miriam Hopkins and Victor Jory starring.

▽ John Houseman, the producer of **The Blue Dahlia**, experienced as much suspense during its making as its audiences eventually did. Raymond Chandler had started writing it as one of his Philip Marlowe novels, couldn't finish it, and sold it to Paramount with himself as screenplay writer. When its end-of-production date (fixed and unalterable) loomed near, he still couldn't finish the story. This brilliant writer's muse needed booze to function properly, so he went home, locked himself incommunicado to the studio, with a well-stocked cellar, and lo! pages of script emerged day by day to be rushed to the eager hands of Houseman, director George Marshall and the cast, which included Alan Ladd

(left), Veronica Lake, William Bendix (right), Howard Da Silva, Doris Dowling, Tom Powers, Will Wright, Hugh Beaumont, Howard Freeman, Don Costello and Frank Faylen. They just beat the deadline, and their movie beat most of its competitors at the box-office. While lacking Chandler's usual fascinating interplay of characters, it satisfied as a tense whodunnit, with Ladd as an ex-serviceman returning to find his promiscuous wife murdered. He and his war-shocked buddy (Bendix) are the chief suspects, among several less likely ones, until he sleuths out the least likely (Wright as a house detective the wife had spurned) in a confusing denouement the author must have found at the bottom of a bottle.

△ Another 1944 Broadway play, Lillian Hellman's **The Searching Wind**, was brought to the 1946 screen by Hal Wallis. This one had no time for frivolity; its subject matter was serious indeed – nothing less than war and peace, right and wong, international diplomacy and career opportunism. So, of course, it was advertised as a husband-wife-other-woman drama. That fooled few, but the film failed, ironically enough, because it was too serious and had too much material to cope with cinematically; while disdaining shallow waters, it never went quite deep enough. The clash of European ideologies and the pre-echo of war guns in the thirties went on off-screen as they were discussed by the cast, particularly Robert Young (centre) as an American diplomat who couldn't stand firm on anything, and Sylvia Sidney (left) as a tough-minded, high-principled journalist, during their spasmodic romance in several countries and over many years. William Dieterle directed them; also: Ann Richards (right) as Young's wife, Dudley Digges (outstanding in the role he played on the stage), Douglas Dick, Albert Bassermann, Ian Wolfe, Dan Seymour and Marietta Canty. The script, by Hellman herself, had more talk than grip.

▷ World War II was already last year's news when the cryptically titled O.S.S. (standing for America's Office of Strategic Services) came out, so the Richard Maibaum production had to be good to win the public's attention. It was. The heroics expected of an Alan Ladd combat drama – he joins a team of secret service operators parachuted into occupied France, where they blow up a vital tunnel and he escapes from the Nazis after being captured – were all there, but so was an unexpected realism. The customary happy ending was eschewed with the hero (left) breaking down and weeping when the heroine, a member of the team (Geraldine Fitzgerald, right, excellent) is taken by the Gestapo. Sharp direction by ex-actor Irving Pichel drew effective performances from Patric Knowles (centre), Onslow Stevens, John Hoyt, Richard Benedict, Don Beddoe, Gavin Muir, Richard Webb, Harold Vermilyea and Bobby Driscoll in roles written by Maibaum. Ladd returned to make it after four months of staying at home until the studio came up with a suitably lucrative new contract.

△ Paramount won its first 'best actress' Oscar with **To Each His Own**, thanks to a moving performance by Olivia de Havilland. Charles Brackett's drama – he was the producer, author and, with Jacques Thery, screenwriter – belonged to the *Stella Dallas* school, with much of the slush removed. It covered 27 years, World Wars I and II, and the sorrows of an unwed mother who gives her son for adoption and regrets it. After making a fortune in the cosmetics business between the wars, she encounters him in London where, as an American serviceman wanting to marry, he is assisted by a lord whom she had rescued during an air raid and who brings them together at last. John Lund (here with de Havilland, in his film debut) as the son – and his father in earlier scenes – and Roland Culver as the nobleman headed the supporting cast, with Mary Anderson, Phillip Terry, Virginia Welles, Bill Goodwin, Victoria Horne, Frank Faylen and Willard Robertson. The good taste and professional polish of Brackett and director Mitchell Leisen removed any disparagement in the terms 'a woman's picture' and 'a tear jerker' from this successful movie. The star made it after two years' absence from the screen during which she sued Warner Bros. for release from a contract they extended to include periods of suspension which they could impose at will. To the relief of all Hollywood actors, she won, and the law limiting contracts to seven years, regardless of suspensions, is officially known as 'The de Havilland Decision'.

▽ Barbara Stanwyck, even better than Bette at being bad, won the Davis Cup for wicked women in **The Strange Love Of Martha Ivers**. Director Lewis Milestone gave her the green light for an emotional display in a ripe melodrama which started with teenage Martha killing her autocratic aunt (Judith Anderson), and finished with her meeting a violent death as the wife of an alcoholic district attorney (Kirk Douglas). An innocent man is hanged for the aunt's murder, but Martha keeps quiet and so does the (very) young lover with whom she intends to elope. Having then disappeared, he grows up into Van Heflin (here with Stanwyck) and reappears as a professional gambler and a possible blackmailer after Martha's marriage. She soon makes plans to polish off husband and/or lover, but the latter ends in the comparatively safe arms of an ex-convict girlfriend (Lizabeth Scott). John Patrick's story and Robert Rossen's script were utter tosh, but nobody in this movie's large and profitable audiences got a wink of sleep, or, indeed, wanted to. Producer Hal Wallis gave Douglas his first screen part (he was excellent) and Scott her second in a cast including Roman Bohnen, Janis Wilson, Darryl Hickman, Ann Doran and James Flavin.

◁ Joel McCrea (left), a good actor and a fine looking outdoor hero as **The Virginian**, couldn't match the fans' memory of Gary Cooper telling the villain 'When you call me that, smile' – still a popular catchphrase 17 years after the first talking version of Owen Wister's novel and Kirk La Shelle's play. (It had also been filmed silent twice, in 1914 and 1923.) Paul Jones's new production had a slightly faded look altogether, in spite of the vivifying effect of Technicolor; the lack of punch in Stuart Gilmore's direction allowed viewers to reflect that too many ranchers had made too many rustlers bite the dust since movies began. But it was still a classic Western story, tampered with very little by ace scripters Frances Goodrich and Albert Hackett, about a cattle man (McCrea) whose best friend (Sonny Tufts, 2nd left) goes over to his arch-enemy (Brian Donlevy), the leader of a stock-stealing gang. Both the renegade and the crook pay the ultimate penalty, one by a posse's rope, the other by an exciting shoot-out at the climax. Barbara Britton (2nd right), Fay Bainter, Henry O'Neill, Tom Tully, Willard Robertson (right), William Frawley, Marc Lawrence, Paul Guilfoyle and Vince Barnett filled the cast round-up.

▽ The success of *Our Hearts Were Young And Gay* in 1944 made a sequel seem a good idea, so Gail Russell (left) and Diana Lynn (right) put on their flappers' short skirts and cloche hats of the twenties again for **Our Hearts Were Growing Up**. The girls, now at college, get into a scandalous tangle with bootleggers, led by Brian Donlevy. They should have stayed in Paris, said disgruntled exhibitors as business slumped. It was an endearing little picture, though, with most of the nostalgic appeal of the first Cornelia Otis Skinner-Emily Kimbrough memoir of their youth. Norman Panama and Melvin Frank developed the script from an original story by Frank Waldman; William Russell directed and Daniel Dare produced, retaining James Brown and Bill Edwards from the first cast as the girls' boys. Besides Donlevy, newcomers were Billy De Wolfe (centre), William Demarest, Sara Haden, Mikhail Rasumny, Mary Hatcher, Frank Faylen and Sharon Douglas.

▷ Employing three of the greatest names and talents of modern show business, **Blue Skies** reunited Bing Crosby (left) and Fred Astaire (right) in their second Irving Berlin musical (this time in Technicolor) to score Paramount's biggest hit of 1946. With a budget in the $3,000,000 bracket, it harvested more than three times as much in world-wide rentals. And it deserved to: both stars were in dazzling form, and Berlin contributed 20 splendid numbers, the best of four new ones being 'You Keep Coming Back Like A Song' (Crosby) and 'A Couple Of Song And Dance Men' (Astaire and Crosby) and the stand-out of the oldies a sensational 'Puttin On The Ritz' routine (Astaire) choreographed by Hermes Pan. Berlin was also credited with the 'idea' for the story, which was something else again. A meandering yarn covering a quarter of a century, it concerned a chorus girl (the lovely Joan Caulfield) who marries a nightclub owner (Bing), divorces him, gets engaged to a dancer (Fred) and breaks that off; the dancer takes to the bottle and is cripped by falling off the scenery during the 'Heat Wave' number; singer and dancer decide they are well rid of her. Allan Scott adapted this stuff for scripter Arthur Sheekman, and Stuart Heisler directed it for producer Sol Siegel, casting Billy De Wolfe, Olga San Juan, Frank Faylen, Victoria Horne and moppet Karolyn Grimes. Producer-director Mark Sandrich, who made the first Astaire-Crosby-Berlin hit, *Holiday Inn*, collapsed soon after starting this one and died of a heart ailment.

OTHER RELEASES OF 1946

The Bride Wore Boots
Barbara Stanwyck, Robert Cummings, Diana Lynn, Patric Knowles. Dir: Irving Pichel. Pro: Seton I. Miller. Wife loves horses, husband hates them; separation ensues, then he wins her back by forcing himself to ride a race.

Hot Cargo
William Gargan, Jean Rogers, Philip Reed. Dir: Lew Landers. Pro: William Pine, William Thomas. Two ex-servicemen pay a visit to their dead buddy's home and stay to put his endangered business back on its feet.

Swamp Fire
Johnny Weissmuller, Virginia Grey, Buster Crabbe. Dir: William Pine. Pro: Pine, William Thomas. Navy man returns from the war with nerves shattered, and rehabilitates himself as a freighter pilot.

They Made Me A Killer
Robert Lowery, Barbara Britton, Lola Lane. Dir: William Thomas. Pro: William Pine, Thomas. A girl saves an innocent man accused of committing murder during a bank robbery.

The Well-Groomed Bride
Olivia de Havilland, Ray Milland, Sonny Tufts. Dir: Sidney Lanfield. Pro: Fred Kohlmar. Complications over a bottle of champagne, wanted by a navy officer for a launching and a bride for her wedding, bring them into conflict.

1947

▽ **My Favorite Brunette** was the first production of Hope Enterprises, a set-up which made Bob Hope (left) an entrepreneur as well as the star of his pictures, and helped towards making him a multi-millionaire (some say the richest entertainer ever). The comedy opened in San Quentin, where Hope, awaiting execution, goes into a flashback account of how he was mistaken for a private eye (the real one was Alan Ladd in an unbilled bit) and tries to become one in order to aid a mystery woman (Dorothy Lamour, right) menaced by gangsters, who get rid of him by framing him as a killer. After the flashback he receives a last minute reprieve, much to the disappointment of the executioner (Bing Crosby in another guest spot). It was a laugh-loaded burlesque of the Hammett-Chandler school of thrillers, and very popular. Elliott Nugent directed the Daniel Dare production, written by Jack Rose and Edmund Beloin, with Peter Lorre, Lon Chaney Jr, Charles Dingle, Reginald Denny, Jack La Rue, John Hoyt, Ann Doran, Frank Puglia and Willard Robertson in the cast.

▽ **Golden Earrings** was so ridiculous you couldn't help liking it. What's more, the production by Harry Tugend and the direction by Mitchell Leisen had such panache that they made the Yolanda Foldes novel's screenplay (by Abraham Polonsky, Frank Butler and Helen Deutsch, a strong team) look better than it really was. And it brought back the legendary Marlene Dietrich after 10 years away from Paramount during which her career had been interrupted by distinguished services in combat-zone shows and anti-Nazi broadcasts to Germany. In baubles, bangles and dark make-up she now whispered and slunk alluringly as a gypsy wench whose caravan makes a romantic refuge for a British agent (Ray Milland, here with Marlene) while he is on a secret mission to purloin Hitler's poison gas formula. Despite Dietrich's fame she was given second billing, in a cast also containing Murvyn Vye, Bruce Lester, Dennis Hoey, Reinhold Schunzel, Ivan Triesault, and news commentator Quentin Reynolds as himself, given the hopeless task of making the trumpery seem authentic. Vye, as a male gypsy, sang the title number.

△ The critics jabbed **Desert Fury** with barbs sharper than the cactus in its Technicolored landscape. The moviegoing masses however, sat agog as this hybrid of old-fashioned melodrama and modern horse-opera bloomed in all its preposterous glory. Lewis Allen directed the events that were triggered off by wilful Lizabeth Scott running away from her finishing school to her home in the West. She promptly meets and falls for slightly psycho gambler John Hodiak (here with her), whose wife has died mysteriously and who is only too well known by the girl's mother, gambling-hall proprietor Mary Astor. She bribes cop Burt Lancaster to redirect her daughter's libido, which he is well equipped to do, and Lizabeth is further put off Hodiak by the revelations of his henchman, Wendell Corey. A few passion-packed reels later, Lancaster kills Hodiak in a car chase climax and rides off into the sunset with Lizabeth, and what more could you want for the price of a ticket? Hal Wallis produced the screenplay by Robert Rossen, A. I. Bezzerides and Ramona Stewart, from the latter's novel, and effectively showcased three of his new contractees: Lancaster, who had made a stunning debut the year before in *The Killers* (Universal); Corey in his first film role; and Scott, the blonde with a dark brown voice, who looked spectacular in a gorgeous wardrobe. The performance you remembered, though, was Astor's.

△ Paramount had been suffering from a manpower shortage in the handsome hero department and was delighted to welcome two young stars back from the wars for **Blaze Of Noon**. Six years after his hit in *I Wanted Wings* and four years after leaving the studio for the real Air Force, William Holden (2nd left) played one member of a flying circus family switching to air mail work in the 1920s. Another was Sterling Hayden (whose name had hitherto been spelt Stirling), absent for over five years while serving in the Marines. They, and Anne Baxter (2nd right), William Bendix (left), Sonny Tufts (right), Howard Da Silva, Jean Wallace, Lloyd Corrigan, Johnny Sands and Will Wright responded convincingly to John Farrow's direction; stunt work in the air by Paul Mantz was exciting, and the period detail was accurate. The whole production, in fact, was a credit to Robert Fellows's technical team. However, the script by Arthur Sheekman and Frank Wead, from Ernest K. Gann's novel, flew into thick cloud when depicting at inordinate length the romance and marriage of Holden and Baxter, ever threatened by the obsession with flying which kills him in the end.

△ Even if it wasn't the most original plot line in the world, this one served very well to make **Dear Ruth** a laugh hit: After an exchange of increasingly impassioned pen-pal letters with a girl he has never met, an airman on leave presents himself at her home, only to find that the letters were written by her over-romantic, under-age sister. Bringing the kid's secret to light and reacting to its repercussions kept director William Russell's well paced cast busy throughout, with funny dialogue and situations left practically intact by scriptwriter Arthur Sheekman from Norman Krasna's play, which had made a small fortune in 20 months on Broadway. It made another with this Paul Jones production; the movie public loved it. William Holden (left) as the bewildered airman, Joan Caulfield (centre) as Ruth, cold to him at first but soon getting warmer, Edward Arnold (right) as her outraged father, Billy De Wolfe as her indignant suitor, Mona Freeman as the troublesome sister and Mary Phillips as the placatory mother didn't miss a trick. According to Krasna, he based most of the characters on the household of Groucho Marx.

▽ The year's longest running time (146 minutes), most extensive shooting schedule (102 days) and fattest budget (about $5 million) were lavished on **Unconquered**. It was Cecil B. DeMille at his most prodigal and preposterous, but it made a profit and gave millions of people escape from humdrum reality, so who cared about the critics? Set in America's 18th-century colonial days, it traced the romance of a Virginia militiaman (Gary Cooper) with an English immigrant (Paulette Goddard) while all hell is breaking loose in Indian attacks, fires, explosions, and unbridled performances from the stars (both illustrated), and from Howard Da Silva as a villainous trader, Katherine De Mille as his Indian wife, Boris Karloff as a redskin chief, Cecil Kellaway, Henry Wilcoxon, Ward Bond, Sir Aubrey Smith, Victor Varconi, Virginia Grey, Porter Hall, Gavin Muir, Alan Napier and Marc Lawrence. The Charles Bennett-Fredric Frank-Jesse Lasky Jr screenplay, from Neil Swanson's novel *The Judas Tree*, climaxed in the siege of Fort Pitt by flaming arrows and fireballs, so realistically staged that 30 extras landed in hospital and Goddard was on the receiving end of DeMille's rage for refusing to participate. You could hardly blame her: she had already endured so much (shooting the rapids in a canoe, being sold at a slave auction, escaping a torture stake, and taking a bath in a barrel) that Hollywood wits called the movie 'The Perils of Paulette'. Ray Rennahan's Technicolor camera work was outstanding. This film marked Cooper's 20th anniversary at Paramount and was his last there; he starred elsewhere during his remaining 17 years.

△ Big audiences responded enthusiastically when Betty Hutton (left) let 'em have it with both barrels in **The Perils Of Pauline**, a perfect vehicle for her unsubtle but stimulating talents. As Pearl White, who between 1914 and 1920 was one of the biggest of all movie stars, Betty turned on the energy full force, not to mention the tear ducts, and belted out some excellent Frank Loesser songs ('I Wish I Didn't Love You So', an Oscar nominee; 'Poppa Don't Preach to Me', and 'The Sewing Machine', a Hutton classic). These and a lot of energetic gags, plus entertaining scenes of how films were shot in the rowdy days of silent serials, of which Pearl was queen, practically buried the thin story by P. J. Wolfson and Frank Butler ('With a salute to the original *Perils Of Pauline* serial author Charles Goddard,' said a screen credit) which didn't bother too much about the facts of her career. Producer Sol Siegel and director George Marshall made it a fast-moving show, save for the soggy romance between Betty and John Lund (centre), and cleverly used veterans of the White era – Chester Conklin, William Farnum, Snub Pollard, James Finlayson, Creighton Hale, Hank Mann, Heinie Conklin, Bert Roach, Francis McDonald – and Pearl's villain in the 'Pauline' serial, Paul Panzer - in the cast with William Demarest, Constance Collier, Billy De Wolfe and Frank Faylen as other Hollywood types. Technicolor detracted from period authenticity.

▽ Claude Binyon had been writing bright scripts at Paramount for 15 years when he assumed producer's chores for **Suddenly It's Spring** – and suddenly he, Paulette Goddard, Fred MacMurray and director Mitchell Leisen lost their sparkle. Oddly enough, it was his (and P. J. Wolfson's) script that let the movie down; his production looked spanking fresh and technically efficient. Miss Goddard (left) played an army officer who returns from World War II service to find that her lawyer husband (MacMurray, centre) wants a divorce; she refuses, and prospective future spouses complicate the couple's situation until the inevitable reconciliation. The switch in sexes did nothing to revive a well-worn formula, and the off-form director and stars had little help from a supporting cast lacking in comedy verve: Macdonald Carey (right), Arleen Whelan, Lillian Fontaine, Frank Faylen, Frances Robinson, Victoria Horne. The light touch, alas, was evident only at the box-office.

▽ In **Calcutta** Alan Ladd and William Bendix, playing pals for the umpteenth time, sought the killer of a third buddy, and tangled with jewel smugglers in the exotic bazaars and sinister alleys of the Paramount lot. Gail Russell (here with Ladd), miscast as the victim's girlfriend, was unmasked as the moll of one of the criminals in Seton I. Miller's screenplay, which contained few other surprises. Also scurrying about under John Farrow's direction, either helping, or in conflict with, the heroic chums, were Lowell Gilmore, June Duprez, Gavin Muir, Edith King, John Whitney and Benson Fong. Miller produced this cheap and cheerful action melodrama, made profitable by the ever-faithful Ladd addicts.

▷ Passions ripened in the Texas wheat fields of **Wild Harvest** when a hip-swinging gal sashayed among the virile grain gatherers. She was Dorothy Lamour (right), who turned buddies Alan Ladd (centre left) and Robert Preston (left) into rivals, and thereby switched what had started as an unusual picture of farmer workers to just another triangle movie. The always forceful direction of Tay Garnett, who had just made *The Postman Always Rings Twice* (MGM), instilled something of its sensual heat into this one, and the three stars did a good job of acting teamwork with Lloyd Nolan (centre right), Richard Erdman, Allen Jenkins, Anthony Caruso, Will Wright, Walter Sande and Frank Sully. But the screenplay by John Monks Jr didn't have enough dramatic impetus to push Robert Fellows's production into success with non-members of the Ladd and Lamour fan clubs.

△ **Road To Rio**, the fifth trip to the Bing Crosby-Bob Hope-Dorothy Lamour well, drew up more buckets of profits; the source seemed inexhaustible, but Paramount let it alone for five years after this one. It was more of a straight comedy with music than any of its predecessors since the first, and comic anarchy that had been approaching Marx Brothers madness broke loose only rarely in the Bing and Bob let's-gag-it-up style. A funny show, nonetheless, with a serviceable if unoriginal script (by Edmund Beloin and Jack Rose) about a pair of musicians avoiding an arson rap – the fire was an accident – by hopping a boat to Rio de Janeiro. On board they are fascinated by a gorgeous girl (Lamour, who else?) whose reaction to them ranges mysteriously from warm to freezing, because she (centre) is being hypnotised by her wicked aunt (Gale Sondergaard as yet another female baddie) so that she will marry a Brazilian she dislikes. After a lot of laugh-raising action, the boys rescue her, and she chooses Bob (left) to wed. But Bing (right) got the best songs, by Johnny Burke and Jimmy Van Heusen, topped by 'But Beautiful'. Norman Z. McLeod, who had been directing at other studios for a decade, started a new contract with this Daniel Dare production; his cast included Frank Faylen, Joseph Vitale, Nestor Paiva, Robert Barrat, Jerry Colonna, the Wiere Brothers and the Andrews Sisters.

△ The studio flung itself into another all-star musical jamboree in **Variety Girl**, and vast crowds of ticket buyers joined in. It was great propaganda for the Variety Club (show business's international charity for children) as well as Paramount, whose Hollywood lot has been exposed to public gaze in films more than any other. Mary Hatcher and Olga San Juan went to the studio in search of movie glory, as the heroines of the wisp of a story it took the combined efforts of Edmund Hartmann, Frank Tashlin, Robert Walsh and Monte Brice to create. They encountered everybody producer Daniel Dare and director George Marshall could rope in for sketches, songs (not Frank Loesser's best), or just a few kind words: Bing Crosby and Bob Hope in a hilarious golfing scene, Gary Cooper, Ray Milland (left), Alan Ladd, Barbara Stanwyck, Paulette Goddard, Dorothy Lamour, Sonny Tufts, Joan Caulfield, William Holden (right), Lizabeth Scott, Burt Lancaster, Gail Russell, Diana Lynn, Sterling Hayden, Robert Preston, Veronica Lake, John Lund, William Bendix, Barry Fitzgerald, Cass Daley, Howard Da Silva, Macdonald Carey, Billy De Wolfe, Patric Knowles, William Demarest, Mona Freeman, Cecil Kellaway, Virginia Field, Richard Webb, Frank Faylen, De Forest Kelley, Pearl Bailey, Spike Jones and his City Slickers, directors Cecil DeMille, Mitchell Leisen and Marshall himself, writer Frank Butler and, in Technicolor, George Pal's Puppetoons. Only the pregnant Betty Hutton was absent; so were critics' praises – but paybox queues were very much present.

▽ Hal Wallis put his four contract stars, Burt Lancaster (right), Lizabeth Scott (left), Kirk Douglas and Wendell Corey (centre) to work in **I Walk Alone**, a piece which must have reminded him of his old days at the Warner Bros. gang-thriller factory. Lancaster had the Cagney-like role of a convict finishing a stretch, and looking for revenge and a pay-off from his doublecrossing ex-leader (Douglas), now a nightclub boss who has taken over his former girlfriend (Scott). The bitter Lancaster suffers a brutal beating, sees his pal (Corey) killed, and trades bullets in a darkened room with Douglas before the latter is finished off by the cops. Charles Schnee wrote the script from a play by Theodore Reeves, *Beggars Are Coming To Town*, which flopped; Byron Haskin directed a cast including Marc Lawrence, Kristine Miller, George Rigaud, Mike Mazurki and Mickey Knox. The ultimate effect of its clenched-teeth melodrama was more depressing than stimulating.

△ Having lost Bing Crosby's *Going My Way* sequel, *The Bells Of St. Mary's*, to the studio next door (RKO), Paramount took its time before reuniting the stars of its 1944 record-breaker in **Welcome Stranger**. Crosby (right) and Barry Fitzgerald (left) played virtually the same roles again, the latter as a heart-of-gold curmudgeon resenting the arrival of the former, a new assistant with a penchant for breaking into song. Author Frank Butler and scripter Arthur Sheekman just changed the scene from church to clinic, the leads from priests to doctors, the extras from congregation to patients, and Bing's best deed from saving Barry's church to saving his life via an appendectomy. Along the way several new Crosby hits filled the soundtrack – 'Country Style', 'As Long As I'm Dreaming', 'My Heart Is A Hobo', by Burke and Van Heusen – while the young medico romanced a lovely clinic aide. She was Joan Caulfield, heading the supporting cast (although billed over Fitzgerald), with Wanda Hendrix, Frank Faylen, Elizabeth Patterson, Robert Shayne, Percy Kilbride, Charles Dingle, Mary Field and Don Beddoe. Producer Sol C. Siegel and director Elliott Nugent had a winner in this one, but it was all pretty mechanical.

OTHER RELEASES OF 1947

Adventure Island
Rory Calhoun, Rhonda Fleming, Paul Kelly. Dir: Peter Stewart. Pro: William Pine, William Thomas. Beachcombers sail to a tropical island where a criminal holds power. (Remake of *Ebb Tide*, 1922 and 1937)

Big Town (aka Guilty Assignment)
Philip Reed, Hillary Brooke, Robert Lowery. Dir: William Thomas. Pro: William Pine, Thomas. Through his newspaper articles, an editor traps the killer terrorising a town.

Big Town After Dark (aka Underworld After Dark)
Philip Reed, Hillary Brooke, Richard Travis. Dir: William Thomas. Pro: William Pine, Thomas. The 'Big Town' editor and his girl reporter bring a mob of gangsters to justice.

Danger Street
Jane Withers, Robert Lowery, Bill Edwards. Dir: Lew Landers. Pro: William Pine, William Thomas. After buying a magazine publishing company, two young men find themselves enmeshed in a murder.

Easy Come, Easy Go
Barry Fitzgerald, Diana Lynn, Sonny Tufts. Dir: John Farrow. Pro: Kenneth MacGowan. Habitual gambler is unlucky with horses, gets his daughter's taxi-driver fiance into trouble while she runs their boarding house.

Fear In The Night
Paul Kelly, Kay Scott, DeForrest Kelley. Dir: Maxwell Shane. Pro: William Pine, William Thomas. Put under hypnosis by a killer, a man wakes up to find what he thought was a nightmare has really happened.

I Cover Big Town (aka I Cover The Underworld)
Philip Reed, Hillary Brooke, Robert Lowery, Mona Barrie. Dir: William Thomas. Pro: Wiliam Pine, Thomas. Newspaper girl proves herself an ace crime reporter when she solves a murder case.

The Imperfect Lady (GB Mrs. Loring's Secret)
Ray Milland, Teresa Wright, Sir Cedric Hardwicke. Dir: Lewis Allen. Pro: Karl Tunberg. English aristocrat falls for music hall girl who becomes the missing witness in a murder case.

Jungle Flight
Robert Lowery, Ann Savage, Barton MacLane. Dir: Peter Stewart. Pro: William Pine, William Thomas. Two airplane pilots are caught up in conflict beteen contenders for ownership of a Latin American mine.

Ladies' Man
Eddie Bracken, Cass Daley. Dir: William Russell. Pro: Daniel Dare. Having struck oil, a hayseed comes to town, mixes with entertainers and golddiggers.

Seven Were Saved
Richard Denning, Catherine Craig, Russell Hayden. Dir: William Pine. Pro: Pine, William Thomas. When an army plane makes a forced landing in the Pacific the survivors, including a Japanese prisoner, fight for life.

The Trouble With Women
Ray Milland, Teresa Wright, Brian Donlevy. Dir: Sidney Lanfield. Pro: Harry Tugend. A psychology professor with fixed theories about women is made to revise them by an enterprising girl reporter.

Where There's Life
Bob Hope, Signe Hasso, William Bendix. Dir: Sidney Lanfield. Pro: Paul Jones. International uproar over a New York disc jockey identified as the long-lost heir of a dying European monarch.

1948

▽ Billy Wilder directing a Viennese operetta sounds like pouring vinegar over a chocolate sundae. However, there was not a trace of his acidulated cynicism in **The Emperor Waltz**, a sugary confection for Bing Crosby which was either a delectable musical treat or a foolish waste of directorial genius, depending on your taste. It could hardly have been better done, allowing for its inane story about a turn of the century phonograph salesman (Crosby) who unsuccessfully tries to interest the Emperor Franz Joseph (Richard Haydn) in his wares, while applying a more romantic approach to a royal niece (Joan Fontaine, here with Bing). The break-through in both cases results from a flirtation between his pet mongrel and the girl's pampered poodle. It was all just the cutest thing you ever saw. The writing of Wilder and Charles Brackett had its felicities, the production by Brackett was Technicolorfully lush in sumptuous sets and period costumes, and Bing's singing caressed the ear with 'I Kiss Your Hand, Madame', 'Friendly Mountains', 'The Kiss In Your Eyes', and the Strauss title tune plus lyrics. Roland Culver, Lucile Watson, Sig Rumann, Harold Vermilyea and Roberta Jonay also performed well. So did the box-office.

△ Back into the cold, cruel world after his trip to never-never land in *The Emperor Waltz* went Billy Wilder, to cast a sardonic eye over post-war Berlin in **A Foreign Affair** and resume his characteristic mood of cynicism. It was not one of his best directorial efforts; some critics deplored the use of a ruined city for comedy entertainment, and ticket buyers were unprofitably scarce. On the other hand, Charles Brackett's production was impeccable, the script he, Wilder and Richard Breen wrote from a story by David Shaw had many distinctive touches, and it was never dull. Jean Arthur (right), in one of her by then rare appearances, was irresistible as a prim Congresswoman in a delegation visiting American forces of occupation; unofficial meetings with captain John Lund (centre) thaw her out. But Lund is already more than fraternising with a local charmer, none other than Marlene Dietrich (left), hypnotically glamorous as ever but displaying new resources in characterisation. Her sultry renditions of 'Black Market', 'Illusions', and 'Ruins Of Berlin' (by Frederick Hollander, composer of Dietrich's *Blue Angel* songs), however, eventually proved less beguiling to the captain's ears than Jean's 'Iowa Corn Song'. Among those present: Millard Mitchell, Peter von Zerneck, William Murphy, Stanley Prager, Gordon Jones.

△ **Whispering Smith** was Alan Ladd's first Western, his first movie in Technicolor, and a commercial hit. It was really more of a detective story than a horse opera, presenting the star as an agent assigned to smoke out a gang of train wreckers and looters, and dismayed to find that his best friend (Robert Preston) is implicated in their crimes. Frank Spearman's story, adapted by Frank Butler and Karl Lamb, moved fast under Leslie Fenton's direction to a climax of frantic action with our hero triumphant. Ex-actor Fenton knew what made performers tick, and got good results from Ladd (illustrated), Preston, Brenda Marshall, Donald Crisp, William Demarest, Fay Holden, John Eldredge, Frank Faylen, Murvyn Vye and J. Farrell MacDonald. Mel Epstein produced. Spearman's central character, said to be based on a real railroad dick, figured in other pictures made in 1916, 1926, 1935 and 1952, none as good as this.

▽ Location filming at West Point gave **Beyond Glory** an appearance of verisimilitude which the contrivances of an unconvincing plot soon dispersed. It did well commercially, thanks to the presence of Alan Ladd (left), but even his fans had to admit that at 35 he was a little over-ripe for the role of a military cadet, albeit a senior one who has seen active service. The screenplay by Jonathan Latimer, Charles Marquis Warren and William Wister Haines put Ladd on trial at the Academy for victimising a junior cadet; meanwhile he is haunted by guilt over the wartime death of an officer. He is, need you ask, innocent on both counts, and after several flashbacks, court evidence by his guardian, the officer's widow (Donna Reed, right) and a friendly shrink, plus a speech by General Eisenhower, it becomes clear that there is nothing really wrong with Ladd, West Point or the USA. Robert Fellows produced and John Farrow directed a cast containing George Macready, George Coulouris, Henry Travers, Harold Vermilyea, Conrad Janis, Tom Neal, Geraldine Wall, Luis van Rooten and Audie Murphy (centre), America's most decorated World War II soldier, in the first of his many screen roles, generally as a soldier or a cowboy.

▽ Loretta Young, a thirty-year screen veteran at the age of 35, often seemed to depend more on her wide-eyed beauty than on acting strength to maintain her stardom. Occasionally, though, she flashed with a real gem of a performance, like her frightened lady in **The Accused**, a college teacher who accidentally kills a student and is hounded by a detective (Wendell Corey) suspecting murder. Eventually arrested and tried, she is defended by an admirer (Robert Cummings, with her here), formerly the guardian of the victim (Douglas Dick), claiming self-defence. Since the undergraduate had been majoring in rape at the moment of his demise, the jury's verdict came as no surprise to the audience. It was good, tense melodrama, well directed by the very experienced William Dieterle for the Hal Wallis unit. Other actors in the taut screenplay Ketti Frings derived from a novel by June Truesdell were Sam Jaffe, Sara Allgood, Mickey Knox and Suzanne Dalbert.

▽ As a correspondence-school dentist who switched from wide open faces to wide open spaces, Bob Hope went West in **The Paleface**, married sharp-shooting Calamity Jane and helped her to capture some dirty dogs who were selling arms to the Indians. This slapstick classic, held from release for a year in a product backlog, a frequent Paramount procedure at the time, turned out to be Hope's biggest box-office hit. Meanwhile its song, 'Buttons And Bows' by Jay Livingston and Ray Evans, had become a best-seller; later it won an Oscar. Another outstanding asset was Howard Hughes's lavishly endowed and much publicised star Jane Russell as Calamity (here with Hope), in a cast including Robert Armstrong, Iris Adrian, Bobby Watson, Jack (once Jackie) Searl, Joseph Vitale, Clem Bevans, Charles Trowbridge and Stanley Andrews. The fast, gag-loaded screenplay by Edmund Hartmann and Frank Tashlin was directed by Norman Z. McLeod. Robert Welch's production looked good in Technicolor, apart from some obvious back-projection effects. It was remade in 1967 as *The Shakiest Gun In The West*, a Universal low-budgeter.

▷ Kept on ice for seven years after its release in Britain where it was made, **Hatter's Castle** looked ready for American distribution by 1948, when Deborah Kerr and James Mason had become internationally famous names. The continually increasing popularity of its author, A.J. Cronin, was another factor in its resuscitation. On its own merits as a strong drama with a Dickensian narrative grip, only slightly weakened by a loss of 12 minutes' running time en route from London, it was a sturdy entertainment for all but the most frivolous moviegoers. Rodney Ackland's adaptation, meticulously filmed by director Lance Comfort and producer Isidore Goldsmith, had a worthy cast led by Robert Newton as the poor hatter whose fortunes flourish while his family withers under his tyranny; Kerr was his restless daughter, Emlyn Williams her seducer, Mason the sympathetic doctor, Beatrice Varley the long-suffering wife, and Enid Stamp-Taylor the 'other woman'. Above all, it was Newton (illustrated), attacking his role with controlled bravura, who gave the picture its punch.

▽ An 89-minute nerve-wracker called **Sorry, Wrong Number** gave Barbara Stanwyck (illustrated) one of the juiciest roles in her long career, and she squeezed every drop of drama out of it. The screenplay by Lucille Fletcher was an unusual one, expanded from her award-winning radio play with a single main character (read by Agnes Moorehead in the broadcast), a neurotic invalid, dependent on her bedside telephone, who overhears a conversation that discloses a plot to kill her. Her mounting hysteria and frantic efforts to get help occupy most of the footage, with suspense cleverly sustained by director Anatole Litvak and the star, who holds the screen alone for long stretches. Burt Lancaster was chilling as the murderous husband, while Ann Richards, Wendell Corey, Harold Vermilyea, Leif Erickson, Ed Begley, William Conrad and John Bromfield registered in briefer parts. It proved to be a profitable attraction from Hal Wallis, who co-produced with Litvak. Stanwyck's nomination for an Academy prize was applauded by all her co-workers over the years; but, like Garbo's *Camille* and Garland's Vicki Lester, this was one of those eminently Oscar-worthy performances left unaccountably unawarded.

▽ **Isn't It Romantic?** asked Daniel Dare's production hopefully. Well, yes, in a mild, forgettable sort of way, with the romance mostly occurring when Veronica Lake (centre) dumped fiancé Billy De Wolfe in favour of handsome con-man Patric Knowles (left). Veronica, Mona Freeman, and Mary Hatcher (right) were the daughters of ex-colonel Roland Culver in this comedy adapted by Theodore Strauss, Joseph Mischel and Richard Breen from a story by Jeanette Nolan; Pearl Bailey, Kathryn Givney, Richard Webb and Larry Olsen rounded out the cast, directed by Norman Z. McLeod. Songs cropped up from time to time, the best still being the one Rodgers and Hart wrote in 1932 for *Love Me Tonight* and now reprised as a title theme; and De Wolfe got laughs with 'At The Nickelodeon', a number burlesquing silent movies – anachronistically, in view of the story's post-Civil War Indiana setting. Lake, who had often been hard to handle, did not have her seven-year contract renewed, and this poor man's *Meet Me In St Louis* was her last Paramount picture.

▽ Hal Wallis sent Ray Milland and director Lewis Allen back to their native Britain to make **So Evil My Love**, and they returned with a Victorian melodrama giving off a pungent whiff of sulphur and greasepaint. Ostensibly an artist but devoting more time to being a seducer, thief and murderer, Milland's character entices a young widow (Ann Todd, here with him) into stealing rare paintings, robbing her alcoholic best friend (Geraldine Fitzgerald) and even killing the latter's husband. She is so besotted with the cad that she is willing to let the friend be hanged for the murder, but she catches him out with another woman, stabs him and gives herself up to the police. Allen directed this depravity and old lace with more finesse than the synopsis might indicate, and Milland as the handsome rotter, Todd as the gullible widow and Fitzgerald as the genteel wino were excellent. They were surrounded by a selection of gems from London's acting treasury: Raymond Lovell, Leo G. Carroll, Martita Hunt, Hugh Griffith, Raymond Huntley, Moira Lister, Finlay Currie, Muriel Aked. The Ronald Millar-Leonard Spiegelgass screenplay came from a novel by Joseph Shearing.

◁ Another of Alan Ladd's frequent trips to the Orient occurred in **Saigon** ('The Paris of the East' instructed the ads, for backward geographers), a thick-ear drama about ex-airforce pals taking on a flying job for a crooked importer that is interrupted by a forced landing in a rice paddy, a river boat trip with a blonde both pals fall for, and a run-in with the police during which one pal is killed. Ladd (right) survived for the fade-out with Veronica Lake (left), rather cheeseparingly billed as 'a half-million dollar blonde'; in their final movie together they maintained a deadpan sangfroid unmatched since Buster Keaton. Douglas Dick played Ladd's side-kick, Morris Carnovsky the crook and Luther Adler the police chief; Wally Cassell, Mikhail Rasumny and Luis van Rooten were also in director Leslie Fenton's cast. P.J. Wolfson produced and, with Arthur Sheekman, wrote the script from Julian Zimet's story. Nothing here to engage the attention of anybody except the most action-mad customers.

△ Wacky comedian Richard Haydn made a wacky comedy as the first of this three directorial efforts for Paramount, and very amusing **Miss Tatlock's Millions** was too. He was fortunate in having the expert guidance of producer Charles Brackett, who also collaborated with Richard Breen on the screenplay from a Jacques Deval story. It concerned a Hollywood stunt man (John Lund, seated centre) who agrees to help an embattled young heiress (Wanda Hendrix, left) stave off predators by pretending to be her nutty relative. Others involved were Robert Stack, Leif Erickson, and some of the screen's most accomplished offbeats: Barry Fitzgerald (right), Monty Woolley (standing centre), Ilka Chase, Dorothy Stickney, Elizabeth Patterson, Dan Tobin, Hilo Hattie and Haydn himself. Aside from Lund's miscasting in a role needing the verve of an Errol Flynn, it was an excellent 'B' attraction.

▷ A melodramatic dazzler, **The Big Clock** was cunningly plotted by novelist Kenneth Fearing and tightly screenwritten by another author of mysteries, Jonathan Latimer. It was set mainly in the headquarters of a huge publishing firm, whose boss (Charles Laughton, illustrated – doing Nero in modern dress) was a psychotic tyrant. When he kills his discarded mistress, he becomes aware of a shadowy witness, whose identity he must discover. He assigns the detective work to his most trusted editor (Ray Milland) who is too fearful of the consequences to reveal that the witness was himself. After several reels of nail-biting suspense their climactic confrontation ends with the boss hurtling down an elevator shaft. A stylish thriller and a profitable attraction, the Richard Maibaum production was handled expertly by the studio's busy Australian director, John Farrow (father of actress Mia), whose cast was grade A: Maureen O'Sullivan (Mrs Farrow) as Milland's helpmate; Elsa Lanchester (Mrs Laughton) as a dotty artist; George Macready, Rita Johnson (left), Harold Vermilyea, Dan Tobin, Henry Morgan, Luis van Rooten and Lloyd Corrigan.

▷ A major success of the 1945–6 Broadway season was scored by **Dream Girl**, written by one of America's foremost playwrights, Elmer Rice, as a vehicle for his wife, Betty Field. Expected to recreate her role of a female Walter Mitty when Paramount bought the screen rights, she was unfortunately replaced by Betty Hutton (illustrated), who had more box-office power but was totally miscast. The Cinderella-like dreamer of the original gentle comedy became a wealthy blonde and her romantic imaginings acquired a brassy glitter in director Mitchell Leisen's treatment of Arthur Sheekman's rewrite. When movie money came in at the door, charm flew out of the window, leaving many viewers wondering why producer P.J. Wolfson didn't go the whole hog and turn it into a musical. Featured in its often unrelated episodes were Macdonald Carey, Patric Knowles, Virginia Field, Peggy Wood and Walter Abel, with Lowell Gilmore, Carolyn Butler, Frank Puglia and Zamah Cunningham. Its reception from the public was lukewarm; from the critics, scathing.

OTHER RELEASES OF 1948

Albuquerque
Randolph Scott, Barbara Britton, Lon Chaney Jr. Dir: Ray Enright. Pro: William Pine, William Thomas. Western drama about a young man's rebellion against his domineering uncle.

Big Town Scandal (aka Underworld Scandal)
Philip Reed, Hillary Brooke, Stanley Clements. Dir: William Thomas. Pro: William Pine, William Thomas. Editor and girl reporter clear up a racket in which basketball games are fixed.

Caged Fury
Richmond Denning, Sheila Ryan, Buster Crabbe. Dir: William Berke. Pro: William Pine, William Thomas. Circus people are terrified by a homicidal maniac in their midst; he makes lions do the killing.

Disaster
Richard Denning, Trudy Marshall. Dir: William Pine. Pro: Pine, William Thomas. Melodrama of an innocent man's struggle to prove he was framed for murder.

Hazard
Paulette Goddard, Macdonald Carey. Dir: George Marshall. Pro: Mel Epstein. Gambling girl loses a bet, runs away, falls in love with detective sent to bring her back.

Mr. Reckless
William Eythe, Barbara Britton. Dir: Frank MacDonald. Pro: William Pine, William Thomas. Roughneck drillers help each other when things get tough in the oilfield, but fall out when a pretty girl comes along.

My Own True Love
Melvyn Douglas, Phyllis Calvert, Wanda Hendrix. Dir: Compton Bennett. Pro: Val Lewton. English widower is about to remarry when his son comes home from a prisoner-of-war camp and falls in love with his father's fiancée.

Night Has A Thousand Eyes
Edward G. Robinson, Gail Russell, John Lund. Dir: John Farrow. Pro: Endre Bohem. Melodrama about a vaudeville mentalist who proves that he really has the power to foretell the future.

The Sainted Sisters
Veronica Lake, Joan Caulfield, Barry Fitzgerald. Dir: William D. Russell. Pro: Richard Maibaum. Turn-of-the-century adventuresses run from the city to a small town, where they learn to live within the law.

Sealed Verdict
Ray Milland, Florence Marly, Broderick Crawford. Dir: Lewis Allen. Pro: Robert Fellows. Romance of an American officer in post-war Germany and the ex-mistress of a Nazi on trial for his crimes.

Shaggy
Brenda Joyce, George Nokes. Dir: Robert E. Tansey. Pro: William Pine, William Thomas. The happy life of a father, a boy and a dog is disrupted by the man's new wife.

Speed To Spare
Richard Arlen, Jean Rogers, Richard Travis. Dir: William Berke. Pro: Wiliam Pine, William Thomas. A daredevil on wheels gives up his stunt-driving career, takes a job in his friend's trucking firm and an interest in his girl.

Waterfront At Midnight
William Gargan, Mary Beth Hughes, Richard Travis. Dir: William Berke. Pro: William Pine, William Thomas. While investigating a racket on the docks, a cop discovers that his brother is implicated.

1949

▽ Greed, blood and guts were the main ingredients in **Rope Of Sand**, an adventure thriller served up by writer Walter Doniger for fans who liked raw meat on their entertainment menu. And there were plenty of them, as the returns indicated. Burt Lancaster's presence was also a reason for its commercial strength – he played a thief who has hidden a fortune in diamonds and is trying to reach their South African cache ahead of several other stop-at-nothing characters, including a bent police chief, an unscrupulous gem dealer and a shady lady. Producer Hal Wallis and director William Dieterle put over this tough stuff in the sock-it-to-'em style they had developed in their old Warner Bros. days. Lancaster's potent performance was matched by those of Paul Henreid, Claude Rains, Corinne Calvet (her Hollywood debut), Peter Lorre (right with Lancaster), Sam Jaffe, John Bromfield and Mike Mazurki.

▽ **Sorrowful Jones** was an entertaining remake of the 1934 hit, *Little Miss Marker*, and notable as Bob Hope's first semi-serious vehicle. Dropping his usual cowardly comic persona, he handled the sentiment and the wisecracks with equal ease as a bookie obliged to play guardian to a gambler's little daughter while getting involved with race-fixers, racketeers and a nightclub singer. Casting Lucille Ball in that role scored a plus for the Robert Welch production, but the absence of Shirley Temple as the adopted moppet was a definite minus; Mary Jane Saunders (illustrated with Hope) was cute and took Sidney Lanfield's direction well enough, but who could replace Shirley? The Damon Runyon story had a new script smartly tailored for Hope by Jack Rose, Edmund Hartmann and Melville Shavelson, with parts for William Demarest, Thomas Gomez, Bruce Cabot, Houseley Stevenson, Ben Welden and Tom Pedi.

▽ Every quarter-century or so, Paramount has felt the need to make another stab at filming F. Scott Fitzgerald's masterpiece, **The Great Gatsby**, but never quite gets it right. The attempts to capture the novel's elusive fascination have become longer and more expensive – Herbert Brenon's version ran 81 minutes in 1926, Elliott Nugent's 92 in 1949, and Jack Clayton's 146 in 1974 – while being stubbornly resisted by the mass public (a stage adaptation also failed). Some critics rate the 1949 try highest, and Alan Ladd (centre) the most believable Gatsby, indicating either that he was a better actor than he has been given credit for, or that the enigmatic character of the millionaire with a mysterious past fitted his personality with ease. Less fortunate was the casting of Betty Field (left) as the girl who obsesses him, and whose accidental killing of her husband's mistress causes Gatsby's murder by the dead girl's husband. (Fitzgerald provided plenty of plot; it was his style that eluded.) Although a talented actress, Miss Field simply wasn't glamorous enough to motivate Gatsby. Right in their roles, though, were Macdonald Carey, Barry Sullivan (right), Ruth Hussey, Shelley Winters, Howard Da Silva, Elisha Cook Jr, Henry Hull, Ed Begley, Carole Matthews and Nicholas Joy. Richard Maibaum produced, and collaborated with Cyril Hume on the script.

△ Bing Crosby (left) added another hit to his collection with **A Connecticut Yankee In King Arthur's Court** (Connecticut was omitted from the title overseas). Mark Twain's social satire had been delighting readers for sixty years and audiences for almost thirty; it was filmed by Fox in 1920 with Harry C. Myers and in 1931 with Will Rogers. The latter had a dry wit less evident in this latest version, which compensated with a dazzling production (the sets and costumes made you glad Technicolor had been invented) and a lilting score by Burke and Van Heusen that allowed Bing to prove he was in good voice. But it yielded only one best-seller: 'Busy Doing Nothing', sung as a trio by Sir Cedric Hardwicke (right), William Bendix (foreground) and Crosby, respectively playing King Arthur, one of his Knights, and the blacksmith who dreams himself back through the centuries to Camelot, where his modern knowledge makes him hailed as a wizard. They were accompanied in director Tay Garnett's cast by Rhonda Fleming (centre), a luscious heroine; Henry Wilcoxon, Murvyn Vye, Virginia Field, Alan Napier, Julia Faye, Joseph Vitale and Richard Webb. Edmund Beloin wrote the screenplay for Robert Fellows's costly but profitable production.

▷ For sheer mass magnetism, never mind artistic subtleties, there was nothing in 1949 to touch **Samson And Delilah**. In fact, with approximately $12 million in rentals coming from North American theatres alone, it was by far the biggest money-maker in Paramount's history to date. This record resulted from a lavish application of the patented Cecil B. DeMille formula: biblical spectacle plus sex, personified in the title roles by Victor Mature and Hedy Lamarr (both illustrated), who may not have been Old Testament types exactly, or even persuasive actors, but they could certainly put on the old zingaroo. While they were occupied by seduction, hair-cutting and toppling the Philistine temple, George Sanders stole the performance honours as the Saran of Gaza in a cast also including Angela Lansbury, Henry Wilcoxon, Fay Holden, Russ Tamblyn, Julia Faye, William Farnum, Olive Deering, Lane Chandler, Victor Varconi, John Miljan, Moroni Olsen and countless extras. DeMille had problems with a Samson who suffered from various phobias, necessitating the use of a double, which C.B. abhorred; and a Delilah whose beautiful face determinedly resisted dramatic expression. A studio strike during production didn't help either. The Jesse Lasky Jr-Fredric Frank script, from an original, based on the Bible story, by Harold Lamb, and a novel by Vladimir Jabotinsky, climaxed with the fall of the temple, which took five months to build and eight days to knock down for a thrilling and eye-boggling sequence.

△ Received with indifference at the time, but now a collector's piece of Hollywood kitsch, **Bride Of Vengeance** purported to tell the history of the feud between Cesare Borgia and the Duke of Ferrara in 16th-century Italy. The efforts of director Mitchell Leisen, who seemed to be more interested in his designers than in his players, to make the elaborate production look authentic were negated by the script's stagey dialogue and the performances of Paulette Goddard (illustrated), John Lund, Macdonald Carey (illustrated), Raymond Burr, Albert Dekker, John Sutton, Rose Hobart, Donald Randolph, Anthony Caruso, Nicholas Joy and Fritz Leiber, almost all of whom were wildly miscast and trying not to show it. According to Michael Hogan and Cyril Hume, the writers of Richard Maibaum's production, the Duke (Lund) is plotted against by Cesare (Carey), who forces his sister Lucretia (Goddard) to marry him, having cleared the way by murdering her husband. Carey attacks Lund's territory, Goddard poisons Lund, he survives, she realises she loves him, repents, and helps him defend his city with a huge cannon built by Dekker. Bang. The End.

▽ Ray Milland descended further from his villainy in *So Evil My Love*, right down to the Devil himself in **Alias Nick Beal** (GB: **The Contact Man**), an interesting excursion into fantasy which got an affirmative response from the critics but not much business. Mindret Lord's story, screenwritten persuasively by Jonathan Latimer, was virtually the Faust legend in modern dress, with Milland appearing out of thin air to sidetrack an honest politician from his anti-crime campaign by offering him wealth, power and a voluptuous blonde. The victim, well played by Thomas Mitchell, accepts corruption and lives to regret it. Always a good actor, the star was splendidly insinuating as the prince of tempters, Audrey Totter (here with Milland) made an effective seductress, and George Macready, Fred Clark, Darryl Hickman, Geraldine Wall, Henry O'Neill and Nestor Paiva filled out the cast. Endre Bohem's production was astutely directed by John Farrow.

△ An out-of-the-rut drama, **Chicago Deadline** was one of the better Alan Ladd starrers. He played a reporter delving into the life and death of a lady of easy virtue, using her diary to trace people she had known, including mobsters and their molls, evil magnates, a boxer and his manager. A call-girl friend helps him to piece together the jigsaw of the mystery woman's life, and the investigation uncovers two murders and a suicide before a gangster is revealed as the man who brought her to destitution. Warren Duff fashioned the script (from a 1933 best-seller, *One Woman* by Tiffany Thayer) whose many flashbacks gave Donna Reed a stronger part than Ladd's – they were never seen together. Arthur Kennedy as her brother, June Havoc (here with Ladd) as the call-girl and Berry Kroeger as the villain expertly led the supporting cast: Irene Hervey, John Beal, Shepperd Strudwick, Harold Vermilyea, Tom Powers, Dave Willock. Lewis Allen directed the Robert Fellows production.

△ The third teaming of Bing Crosby (right) and Barry Fitzgerald (left), in **Top O' The Morning**, was one too many. Awash with enough stage-Irish whimsy to make audiences gag even (or especially) in the Emerald Isle itself, this Edmund Beloin-Richard Breen screenplay had Crosby arriving from America to the old country to investigate the theft of the Blarney Stone for his insurance company, with the dubious assistance of local policeman Fitzgerald. The latter, sporting an Oirish accent so thick that subtitles would have been welcome, has a crusty exterior, a heart of gold, and a daughter (Ann Blyth) for Bing to sing to. Hume Cronyn, Eileen Crowe, John McIntire, Tudor Owen, John Eldredge and Jimmy Hunt also performed under David Miller's slow-paced direction, and the score included some fair new songs by Johnny Burke and Jimmy Van Heusen – plus, inevitably, 'When Irish Eyes Are Smiling'. While technically efficient, Robert Welch's production had nothing like the crowd magnetism of *Going My Way* or even *Welcome Stranger*.

△ The story of *Dear Ruth*, not to mention its box-office prosperity, left it wide open for a sequel, which arrived a little late (three years after) to reap the full benefit. Nonetheless, **Dear Wife** won a hearty public reception for the lively activities newly invented for Norman Krasna's characters by Arthur Sheekman and N. Richard Nash. William Holden and Joan Caulfield (both illustrated) were now married and obliged by the housing shortage to live with her family; inevitable antagonisms eventuate, and they are intensified by Caulfield's mischief-making sister, Mona Freeman, whose machinations to set Holden up as a rival candidate to father Edward Arnold in the state senate election cause domestic chaos. Also plenty of laughs, mostly sparked by Arnold's hilariously apoplectic performance. Billy De Wolfe and Mary Phillips also scored again in Richard Maibaum's production, with Arleen Whelan, Raymond Roe, Elizabeth Fraser and Harry Von Zell, all directed with a sure comedy sense by Richard Haydn.

△ Unquestionably the company's finest artistic achievement of the year, **The Heiress** received nominations for eight Academy Awards (winning in four categories) and many foreign honours. Paramount was Olivia de Havilland's lucky studio; she won her second Oscar there with a superbly modulated performance as the dewy-eyed heroine (2nd left), dominated by her stern father, who thinks she has found love with a forbidden suitor, then becomes a hardened spinster when this fortune-hunter jilts her. Years later, now wealthy in her own right, she repulses his abject return, with a memorable line: 'Yes, I can be cruel; I have been taught by masters.' Like its source, Henry James's 1881 novel, *Washington Square*, the screenplay was beautifully written by Ruth and Augustus Goetz from their successful stage version, and its filming by producer-director William Wyler was meticulous in all departments. De Havilland's work was lent impeccable support by Ralph Richardson (left), repeating his London theatre performance as the father; Montgomery Clift (2nd right), believably attractive as the suitor; Miriam Hopkins (right) as the heroine's confidante; and, in minor roles, Vanessa Brown, Mona Freeman, Ray Collins and Selena Royle.

▽ Little did producer Hal Wallis and director George Marshall know when they made a little comedy called **My Friend Irma** that they were uncapping a box-office oil well for Paramount that would keep gushing for 16 years. It was Jerry Lewis (right). With his partner, Dean Martin (centre right), who stayed for half that time until they became solo stars, Lewis had a supporting spot that made an immediate impact on the fans. John Lund, Diana Lynn (centre left), Marie Wilson (left) and Don De Fore were the principals in the slapsticky saga which, like *Gentlemen Prefer Blondes*, was related by a comparatively bright brunette (Lynn) dishing the dirt about her dumb blonde chum, Irma (Wilson). This dizzy character first became famous in a popular radio series, and even more so on screen as she swapped her larcenous lover (Lund) for a singing soda-jerk (De Fore) in Cy Howard's story which he co-adapted with Parke Levy. Hans Conreid, Kathryn Givney and Percy Helton were also in it.

◁ That plot gimmick so well loved by scenario writers – the dilemma of friends who go their separate ways and later face each other on opposite sides of the law – was given its umpteenth airing in **Streets Of Laredo**. William Holden (right) as the reformed outlaw and MacDonald Carey (left) as his ex-pal, still up to no good, were the antagonists in the final showdown, resolved when Carey is shot by Holden's girl, Mona Freeman, after 90 minutes of conventional horse-and-holster action had rolled through the projectors. In the role Fred MacMurray had played in *The Texas Rangers*, of which this was a remake, Holden gave a sturdy performance, well backed up by Carey, Freeman, William Bendix (centre), Stanley Ridges, Clem Bevans, James Bell and Alfonso Bedoya, but Leslie Fenton's direction of Charles Marquis Warren's new script didn't have the sweep of King Vidor's original treatment. Assets added by producer Robert Fellows were Technicolor and a Ray Evans-Jay Livingston title song that became a hit.

◁ Barbara Stanwyck (illustrated) played her third heartless murderess for Paramount in **The File On Thelma Jordon** (sometimes shortened to *Thelma Jordon*), a workmanlike shocker ranking well below *Double Indemnity* but with many similarities to *The Strange Love Of Martha Ivers*. Like Martha, Thelma is a lethal niece, and a district attorney finds that aiding her proves disastrous for him. The unhappily married DA (Wendell Corey) has to prosecute when she is tried for murder and, so seductive are her charms, he deliberately loses the case, thus ruining his career. The brazen hussy is freed, but fate and the Production Code polish her off in a car crash. Hal B. Wallis produced again, using a script by Ketti Frings based on a Marty Holland story, and Robert Siodmak directed in his best *film noir* style. From the star down to the bit players, it was convincingly acted; Paul Kelly (right), Joan Tetzel, Stanley Ridges, Richard Rober, Minor Watson, Laura Elliot, Barry Kelly, Basil Ruysdael and Jane Novak were present. So were ticket buyers in profitable numbers.

▽ Taking a sharp detour from the jolly Roads she had travelled with Crosby and Hope, Dorothy Lamour found herself embroiled in a jewel robbery and suspected of murder while working as a secretary to a crooked psychiatrist in **Manhandled**. 'You've never seen a Lamour like this!' announced the advertising with misguided enthusiasm: the fans were perfectly satisfied with the Lamour they'd been seeing, and passed this one up. The Whitman Chambers-Lewis Foster script, adapted from L.S. Goldsmith's novel *The Man Who Stole A Dream*, was a pretty stodgy affair, straining for suspense but getting bogged down in writer Foster's slow direction. A cast also comprising Dan Duryea, Sterling Hayden (here with Lamour), Irene Hervey, Alan Napier, Philip Reed, Harold Vermilyea, Art Smith and Irving Bacon was the best asset of the low-budget William Pine-William Thomas production, which was no relation to Gloria Swanson's same-titled 1924 hit.

△ Something for the students of the art of Betty Hutton: **Red, Hot And Blue**, a mixture of backstage musical, murder mystery and Cinderella story. John Farrow returned to screenwriting to collaborate with Hagar Wilde on the script (adapted from Charles Lederer's original) as well as directing it and keeping the star front and centre in as many scenes as possible. Betty responded with a characteristic performance, pausing just this side of exhaustion in her exuberance, as a Broadway hopeful pitching woo with stage director Victor Mature (with Betty here) and, when his backer is killed, coping with both the underworld and the police who have her tabbed as the murderer. She had plenty of breath left to wham out four songs (the best: 'Where Are You, Now That I Need You?') by Frank Loesser, who also appeared in the cast, along with William Demarest, June Havoc, Raymond Walburn, Onslow Stevens, Joseph Vitale, Jane Nigh, William Talman and Art Smith. Slick, fast and noisy, the Robert Fellows production was a popular release. A 1936 Broadway musical with the same title had a Cole Porter score and co-starred Bob Hope – both, alas, absent here.

△ Laughter seldom subsided in the crowds that flocked to see Bob Hope in **The Great Lover**. The commonplace title gave no hint of the inventive screenplay whipped up by Edmund Beloin, Jack Rose and Melville Shavelson for Beloin's production. It was about dark doings on a transatlantic liner, where scoutmaster Hope (left) gets into more trouble than his gang of kids when he encounters a card-sharper and a penniless duke with a beautiful daughter, and tops off his adventures by capturing a murderer. Rhonda Fleming (right) played the decorative object of Bob's wooing, Roland Young was the man no one would suspect of being a strangler, Roland Culver made a believable nobleman, Richard Lyon and Gary Gray led the youngsters, Jim Backus, George Reeves and Sig Arno supported, and there was a funny walk-on bit by Jack Benny. Director Alexander Hall kept the action skipping along.

OTHER RELEASES OF 1949

Captain China
John Payne, Gail Russell, Jeffrey Lynn. Dir: Lewis Foster. Pro: William Pine, William Thomas. Captain gets revenge on the conspirators who made him lose his ship.

Dynamite
William Gargan, Virginia Welles, Richard Crane. Dir: William Pine. Pro: Pine, William Thomas. Expert professional in the explosive field clashes with a younger colleague over a girl, causing danger at work.

El Paso
John Payne, Gail Russell, Sterling Hayden. Dir: Lewis Foster. Pro: William Pine, William Thomas. Lawyer finds that guns speak louder than words when he rids a Western town of its criminal element.

Song Of Surrender
Wanda Hendrix, Claude Rains, Macdonald Carey. Dir: Mitchell Leisen. Pro: Richard Maibaum. Farm girl marries a middle-aged museum curator in a small town, circa 1900; she regrets it when a younger one visits.

Special Agent
William Eythe, Laura Elliot. Dir: William Thomas. Pro: William Pine, Thomas. Government agent assigned to a cattle town where nothing ever happens has his boredom jolted by a crime wave.

1950

▷ A revised version of Samson Raphaelson's play, *Accent On Youth*, first filmed in 1935, **Mr Music** was tailored by Arthur Sheekman to suit Bing Crosby. But it was cut too long (113 minutes) to fit a small story, and audiences gave it a cooler reception than the star usually received. He played a golf-crazy songwriter whose secretary (Nancy Olson) tries to get him back to work, and whose producer (Charles Coburn) is waiting for the score of his new show. Evidently aware that this flimsy stuff needed bolstering, director Richard Haydn and producer Robert Welch threw in famous guests from time to time; opera star Dorothy Kirsten and pop stars Peggy Lee (here with Bing) and the Merry Macs sang, Marge (right of Bing) and Gower Champion danced, Groucho Marx leered. The cast proper also had plenty of talent; besides Olson, Coburn, and Crosby, whose Burke-Van Heusen songs included 'Life Is So Peculiar', 'Accidents Will Happen', 'High On The List', and 'Wouldn't It Be Funny?', there were Robert Stack, Ruth Hussey, Tom Ewell, Donald Woods, Ida Moore, Charles Kemper, and Haydn himself doing a Hitchcock.

▷ Just when you thought **Paid In Full** had scraped the bottom of the soap-opera barrel, it plunged a little deeper. During this glum drama everybody suffered – especially the heroine (Lizabeth Scott, illustrated) who knows she will die if she has a baby, but deliberately gets pregnant in order to replace her sister's child, for whose death she feels responsible. Both she and the unsympathetic sister (Diana Lynn) are in love with the same man (Robert Cummings), who married the sister. And so forth. The acidulous Eve Arden failed for once to pierce the glucose; Ray Collins, Stanley Ridges, John Bromfield, Frank McHugh, Laura Elliot, Louis Jean Heydt and Kristine Miller were also on hand. William Dieterle solemnly directed the Hal Wallis production, scripted by Robert Blees and Charles Schnee from a Frederic Loomis story. It seemed to have been made for female audiences by misogynists.

▽ How to make a successful movie, in one easy lesson: get a comedian or two and a script about idiots in the army, navy or air force, assign a competent director, and you're there. It never misses. **At War With The Army** certainly didn't; it catapulted Dean Martin (left) and Jerry Lewis (right) to the top box-office echelon, and had audiences falling about when Sergeant Martin unwisely enlists rattle-brained Private Lewis to help him out of girlfriend trouble. Writer-producer Fred Finklehoffe, working from a play by James Allardice, and director Hal Walker spaced out the slapstick gags to fit the over-generous running time (93 minutes) and enlivened some of the pauses between with some Mack David-Jerry Livingston songs, ranging from 'You And Your Beautiful Eyes' to 'The Navy Gets The Gravy But The Army Gets The Beans'. In the cast: Polly Bergen, Angela Green, Mike Kellin, Tommy Farrell, Jimmy Dundee, Dick Stabile, Dewey Robinson.

▽ As a result of the hefty grosses for his *Whispering Smith*, Alan Ladd (right) was back in boots and saddle for **Branded**, another commercial winner. Arizona and New Mexico, photogenic in Technicolor, were the background for some well-worn dramatic situations in Mel Epstein's production, written by Cyril Hume and Sydney Boehm from a story by Evan Evans. It was the old wheeze about an adventurer posing as a family's long lost heir – this one the son of a rancher – falling in love with his 'sister', getting conscience stricken, confessing the impersonation, and riding off to find the real son. Ladd, Mona Freeman (left), Charles Bickford (centre), Robert Keith, Joseph Calleia, Selena Royle, Tom Tully and Peter Hanson performed convincingly and Rudolph Maté's direction kept interest loping along.

▽ Chewers swallowed their gum and back-row couples forgot to pet when **Union Station** reached its frantic climax with William Holden (right) cornering Lyle Bettger (left), who had kidnapped a blind girl for ransom. Thomas Walsh's violent thriller, adapted from his novel *Nightmare In Manhattan* by Sydney Boehm, had a familiar plot which derived vitality and urgency from its setting: a big rail terminus where the girl's rich father is instructed to make the pay-off and where bustling crowds get in the way of the manhunt. Rudolph Maté, the top cinematographer turned director, filled the background with realistic touches while keeping suspense at a feverish pitch. Jules Schirmer's production cast Nancy Olson opposite Holden, as in *Sunset Boulevard*; also Barry Fitzgerald, Jan Sterling, Allene Roberts (the blind victim), Ralph Sanford and Herbert Heyes. Plenty of action at the payboxes too.

△ Like the recent *Streets Of Laredo*, Alan Ladd's **Captain Carey, USA** (GB: **After Midnight**) had an ace up its sleeve in an unexpectedly popular piece of music. 'Mona Lisa', by Jay Livingston and Ray Evans not only won them their second Academy Award for best song (first: 'Buttons And Bows') but sold a million or so records for Nat King Cole, while serving to publicise the movie. The latter was otherwise strictly dramatic, and only fitfully interesting as scripted from a Martha Albrand novel by Robert Thoeren and directed by Mitchell Leisen. Producer Richard Maibaum gave Ladd plenty of cast support in Wanda Hendrix (here with Ladd), Francis Lederer, Joseph Calleia, Celia Lovsky, Angela Clarke, Roland Winters, Luis Alberni and Russ Tamblyn. As the captain sent to Italy on a post-war assignment to track down the Nazi collaborators who had betrayed their fellow townsfolk during the war, Ladd appeared more inscrutable than ever; doubtless he was as baffled by Albrand's multi-knotted plot as the audience.

△ No mean star-spotter, Hal Wallis gave a young stage actor named Charlton Heston (right) his Hollywood start with the leading role in **Dark City**. The camera took an immediate liking to the strong new face, and so did the public, although the picture was nothing to throw hats in the air about. The script by Larry Marcus and John Meredyth Lucas, based on the former's novel *No Escape*, followed an ex-serviceman, now a bookie, down the neon-flashing streets of underworld melodrama as he tries to escape death at the hands of a mentally unbalanced gangster who bears him a grudge. Director William Dieterle caught the atmosphere of the gambling and crime infested milieu, and guided Heston, Jack Webb as the vengeful nut, and Lizabeth Scott (left – an earlier Wallis discovery) and Viveca Lindfors as the women in the case, through effective performances; also Dean Jagger, Don De Fore, Henry Morgan, Ed Begley, Walter Sande and Mike Mazurki. But this dark city had been visited too often before.

▽ Optimistically advertised as 'the biggest Technicolor musical of all time,' **Let's Dance** stumbled over a tired script and the incongruous casting of its co-stars. Betty Hutton and Fred Astaire (billed in that order) were a pair whose personalities tended to cancel each other out, and they were further handicapped by having to play the hackneyed roles of a song-and-dance team splitting up and getting together again. Author Maurice Zolotow and screenwriter Allan Scott tried to vary the formula by making the girl a widowed mother with a problem about custody of the children, but it wasn't very interesting, so

the entertainment burden fell on the musical numbers, put over with professional verve by the stars. However, Frank Loesser's songs fell below their usual high standard, Norman Z. McLeod directed the cast, featuring Roland Young, Ruth Warwick, Lucile Watson, Barton MacLane, Shepperd Strudwick, Melville Cooper and George Zucco, in routine style, and the Robert Fellows production was altogether a disappointment. Hutton and Astaire (illustrated), at the peak of popularity after big MGM hits (hers in *Annie Get Your Gun*, his in *Three Little Words*), kept it out of the red.

▽ The studio wasted no time in getting a sequel to the 1949 surprise hit *My Friend Irma* to the cameras. In response to the immediate public enthusiasm for Dean Martin and Jerry Lewis, **My Friend Irma Goes West** put the emphasis on the pair (illustrated, right and left) in a practically plotless script by Cy Howard (who doubled as associate producer) and Parke Levy, which took them on a trip to Hollywood in search of fame and fortune, visiting Las Vegas en route. Marie Wilson (centre left), John Lund and Diana Lynn (centre right), in their original roles, accompanied them, along with Corinne Calvet, Don Porter, Harold Huber, Joseph Vitale and Lloyd Corrigan in what was little more than a succession of gags strung together, plus a few Livingston-Evans songs for Martin ('Baby Obey Me', 'Querida Mia'). To celebrate the discovery of a new star team, Hal B. Wallis was on the set as director of his production, just this once. He should have stayed in the office: it was a pretty cheesy picture.

△ After ten years of stardom elsewhere, Glenn Ford made an overdue Paramount debut in **The Redhead And The Cowboy**. He played a cowpuncher mistaken for a Confederate agent by a beauty who carries Civil War secrets, in this uneasy mixture of Western and espionage drama whipped together by Jonathan Latimer and Liam O'Brien from a yarn by Charles Marquis Warren. Ford, often an underrated actor, gave one of his quietly powerful performances as the cowboy, and Rhonda Fleming (here with him) made a gorgeous looking courier as the redhead (you had to take the title's word for that; the budget didn't run to Technicolor), with Edmond O'Brien, Alan Reed, Morris Ankrum, Edith Evanson and Ray Teal in support. Also in it, silent star Tom Moore in his last film. Leslie Fenton directed the Irving Asher production. This was no ordinary Western; but loading an outdoor movie with dialogue at the expense of action was asking for box-office trouble.

▽ **Riding High** wasn't a remake of the 1943 musical with that title, but a musical remake by Frank Capra of his 1934 movie *Broadway Bill*. Capra (if you're still with us) kept very close to the original Robert Riskin screenplay of Mark Hellinger's racehorse story, even re-using a few of the old long shots, while adding some new dialogue by Melville Shavelson and Jack Rose, and songs by Johnny Burke and Jimmy Van Heusen ('Sunshine Cake' scored most strongly) for Bing Crosby (seated centre). The latter was more easy-going and enjoyable than *Bill*'s Warner Baxter as the business man with greater interest in raising horses than making money; he did both with a no-hoper which finally repaid his devotion by winning the big race, but died in the attempt. The girl providing consolation was Coleen Gray (standing), while Raymond Walburn (left), Douglass Dumbrille, Clarence Muse (background), Paul Harvey, and Ward Bond repeated their old roles and were joined by Charles Bickford, William Demarest (right), Frances Gifford, James Gleason, Max Baer, Frankie Darro, Margaret Hamilton, Percy Kilbride, Gene Lockhart, Charles Lane and, in a rare non-Laurel bit, Oliver Hardy. It was, despite a descent into sentimental glop during the horse's funeral, pleasing entertainment with double box-office insurance in Crosby and Capra, one of the handful of director's names that meant something to the crowds.

△ In **Fancy Pants** an English actor on his uppers is brought home by a newly rich American girl to function as the family butler; the small town bigwigs think him to be at least an earl; the girl's mother basks in social one-upmanship; her father and boyfriend consider him expendable. This comedy hadn't been un-reeling for long before a sense of *déjà vu* was followed by the realisation that our old friend *Ruggles Of Red Gap* was back for yet another movie outing – his fourth. But Bob Hope, although having trouble with the accent of his native country (and failing to supplant Charles Laughton as the best Ruggles), made the old Harry Leon Wilson story – considerably rewritten by Edmund Hartmann and Robert O'Brien – come up like new, with hilarious assistance from Lucille Ball as the girl (with Bob here), plus Bruce Cabot, John Alexander, Norma Varden, Jack Kirkwood, Lea Penman, Hugh French, Eric Blore, Colin Keith-Johnston and Joseph Vitale. Director George Marshall gave Robert Welch's handsome Technicolor production the required farcical dash, and the box-office figures were fancy indeed.

△ For sheer audacity, **Sunset Boulevard** has rarely been equalled. Its 'hero' was a reluctant live-in gigolo (William Holden) for an older woman, its 'heroine' an egomaniacal ex-movie queen. Unconventional enough, but the real daring lay in the extraordinary mixture of fact and fiction applied to the ex-star as thickly as her make-up. In her first appearance for nine years, Gloria Swanson (here with Holden) played Norma Desmond, in some ways a parody of herself. Gloria was still vivid, famous, professionally active on stage and television; Norma was absurdly grandiose, pathetically neurotic, a has-been. Yet the line between the real and the imaginary was continually blurred by writer-director Billy Wilder in his most diabolically clever mood. When Norma visited the studio where she once reigned, it was Gloria's former realm, Paramount. There Norma was greeted by her director of silent days – Cecil B. DeMille, who made Gloria a star. At home Norma played bridge with H.B. Warner, Anna Q. Nilsson and Buster Keaton, Gloria's old Hollywood contemporaries. Most confusing of all: Erich von Stroheim, playing Norma's mysterious butler-guardian, was revealed as an erst-while director of hers – and when he ran a film on her home screen we saw an excerpt from *Queen Kelly*, in which Von Stroheim had actually directed Gloria. Even more deliciously mind-boggling was Wilder's statement that he had offered the Norma role to Mae West (who wanted to rewrite it), Mary Pickford (who wanted to control the production), Pola Negri (who was insulted), and Mae Murray (who was positively outraged). He was fortunate to get Swanson and, indeed, William Holden, when Montgomery Clift rejected the part written for him, that of the penniless writer taken in by Norma and eventually killed by her in a frenzy of jealousy and madness. The sordid but fascinating story, worked on for years by Wilder and producer Charles Brackett (this was the last of their superb collaborations) also gave roles to Nancy Olson, Fred Clark, Jack Webb and Hedda Hopper. Co-writer D.M. Marshman Jr shared the Oscar for best story and screenplay, and the film received nominations in every other major category.

◁ A grandiose Western, **The Furies** reached almost operatic heights of emotionalism as the irresistible force of a rebellious daughter met the immovable objections of her cattle-baron father. With such accomplished performers as Barbara Stanwyck (illustrated) and Walter Huston playing those roles, there was no danger of unwanted laughs breaking the mood, but the Niven Busch story, adapted by Charles Schnee, went almost over the top at times. Some heavy-going direction by Anthony Mann and the Freudian undertones in the star characters' relationship put the picture in danger of being dubbed 'Out West with The Barretts of Wimpole Street'; however, Mann (who had just scored a smash with *Winchester .73*, Universal) was particularly adept at giving outdoor drama a ring of reality and his tempo picked up here whenever he got out of the soundstage into the open. Wendell Corey and Gilbert Roland gave Stanwyck romantic complications in a grade A cast including Judith Anderson (in mirror with Huston), Thomas Gomez, Beulah Bondi, Albert Dekker, John Bromfield, Wallace Ford, Blanche Yurka and Louis Jean Heydt. Hal Wallis produced. This was the veteran Huston's last appearance; the stage and screen star died later in the year at the age of sixty-six.

▽ Warm and cosy, **September Affair** wrapped its audiences in an eiderdown of romantic fiction while keeping them awake with a tremor of suspense ... Could Joseph Cotten (centre) and Joan Fontaine (left) get away with their stolen happiness? They were fellow passengers who miss their plane while sightseeing in Naples; when it crashes their names are on the list of fatalities, and they seize the opportunity for an idyll in Capri, until conscience sends them back to family (his, in America) and career (hers, as a concert pianist). Hal Wallis's production looked luscious; William Dieterle's handling avoided any over-sentimental pitfalls that might have marred a less alert director of Robert Thoeren's screenplay, and the soundtrack throbbed with Walter Huston's old recording of 'September Song', which became a hit all over again. Françoise Rosay, Jessica Tandy, Robert Arthur, Fortunio Bonanova, Anna Demetrio (right), Jimmy Lydon and Jimmy Lawrence supported Cotten and Fontaine, who were at their most attractive.

▽ A fair-to-middling Western given a patina of importance by two famous star names and Technicolor photography (still exceptional in 1950, but during the decade colour gradually overtook black-and-white), **Copper Canyon** had an unusual hero: a gunslinger who helps ex-servicemen and their families to become homesteaders after the Civil War. Ray Milland was unable to counteract blatant miscasting in this role, and Hedy Lamarr as his beloved looked even less at home in the wide open spaces. Faring more convincingly in John Farrow's cast were Macdonald Carey (illustrated, with Hedy), Mona Freeman, Harry Carey Jr, Frank Faylen, Hope Emerson, Ian Wolfe, James Burke, Francis Pierlot, Taylor Holmes, Peggy Knudsen and Percy Helton, most of them as pioneers seeking land and mineral riches. The Mel Epstein production, adapted by Jonathan Latimer from Richard English's original, had a sluggish air, reflected in the rental returns.

◁ Even if they were aware of being manipulated by scenario contrivances, viewers sat goggled-eyed, wondering what would happen next to the heroine of **No Man Of Her Own**. The professional expertise of director Mitchell Leisen and star Barbara Stanwyck (centre) saw to that. A William Irish novel, *I Married A Dead Man* formed the basis for the screenplay written by Sally Benson, Catherine Turney and Leisen with an eye to mass-appeal melodrama. Richard Maibaum's production was well cast, with the celebrated stage actress Jane Cowl, John Lund (right), Phyllis Thaxter, Lyle Bettger (left), Richard Denning, Esther Dale, Henry O'Neill, Carole Matthews and Milburn Stone helping Stanwyck through 98 minutes of travail. Her lady adrift was in trouble from the start, being pregnant, unmarried and caught in a train wreck. Having collected enough information about a male passenger who died in the smash, she passes herself off as his widow, recently wed, but after his wealthy family accept this false identity, she is confronted by her ex-lover, bent on blackmail. How shall she dispose of him? . . . Don't tell your friends the amazing climax.

OTHER RELEASES OF 1950

Cassino To Korea
War documentary. Dir: Edward Genock. Pro: A.J. Richards. Commentary: Quentin Reynolds.

The Eagle And The Hawk
John Payne, Rhonda Fleming, Dennis O'Keefe. Dir: Lewis Foster. Pro: William Pine, William Thomas. In 1863 two US law enforcers discover a plot to overthrow Mexico's ruler and invade Texas.

The Great Missouri Raid
Wendell Corey, Macdonald Carey, Ellen Drew. Dir: Gordon Douglas. Pro: Nat Holt. Melodrama tracing the lawbreaking exploits of Frank and Jesse James until they are brought down.

The Lawless
Macdonald Carey, Gail Russell, Lee Patrick. Dir: Joseph Losey. Pro: William Pine, William Thomas. Newspaper editor defends a Mexican boy against small-town bigotry in California.

Molly (aka The Goldbergs)
Gertrude Berg, Philip Loeb, Eduard Franz. Dir: Walter Hart. Pro: Mel Epstein. Mama's Jewish family is thrown into a tizzy by the visit of her old sweetheart, now rich, to her Bronx home.

Trio
Jean Simmons, Michael Rennie, Nigel Patrick. Dir: Ken Annakin, Harold French. Pro: Antony Darnborough. A collection of three short stories by Somerset Maugham: 'The Verger', 'Mr Knowall' and 'Sanatorium'. (British)

Tripoli
John Payne, Maureen O'Hara, Howard da Silva, Philip Reed. Dir: Will Price. Pro: William Pine, William Thomas. American marine forces clear out the pirates infesting coastal waters in 1805.

1951

▽ In **Submarine Command** an officer in the underwater force, who had been obliged by an enemy attack to save his ship and crew by submerging, leaving his captain to drown, is tortured by conscience until a sea battle off Korea proves his heroism. Nothing new in all this, but the cliches were offset by stirring action and crisp performances under John Farrow's direction, plus expert work by the technical team. The fans gave Joseph Sistrom's production a warmer reception than it got from the critics, who nevertheless still had a good word for William Holden's convincingly earnest hero (left), and for Nancy Olson and William Bendix (right), in the customary best gal, best pal assignments; Don Taylor, Darryl Hickman, Arthur Franz, Jack Kelly, Moroni Olsen and Peggy Webber took care of the other characters populating Jonathan Latimer's screenplay.

▽ Western author Luke Short wove such a densely plotted web in his novel **Silver City** that screenwriter Frank Gruber had a tough job untangling it to fit 90 minutes' running time. A mining engineer (Edmond O'Brien, left), having master-minded a hold-up of his company's office, is barred from the mining industry. With a new identity in a new town, he sets up shop as an assayer and schemes to wrest a rich silver lease from its operators (Edgar Buchanan, Yvonne De Carlo), but his conscience and Yvonne's allure change his mind, so he outwits hoodlums hired by their landlord (Barry Fitzgerald) to drive them out. His wooing and mining, however, are interrupted by the arrival of an old flame (Gladys George, right), and – wait, there's lots more..... Well, anyway, its audiences went home satisfied, and a modestly successful release was chalked up by director Byron Haskin and producer Nat Holt, with Richard Arlen, Laura Elliot and Technicolor.

▽ **Peking Express** turned out to be Paramount's third trip aboard *Shanghai Express* with another new destination but the same old plot. Although no more than a potboiler from the industrious director-producer team of William Dieterle and Hal B. Wallis, it was at least an improvement on 1943's *Night Plane From Chungking*, and held interest in the fate of passengers in a train halted by a gang of Oriental outlaws. Joseph Cotten (centre), Corinne Calvet (right), Edmund Gwenn, Marvin Miller, Benson Fong, Soo Yung, Gregory Gaye, Robert W. Lee and Victor Sen Yung enacted John Meredyth Lucas's rewrite of the Harry Hervey-Jules Furthman original well enough, although, as the glamorous prostitute, Calvet was no Dietrich. Technical excellence was keynoted by Charles Lang Jr's photography.

△ Thelma Ritter (right) established a record for supporting actresses by being nominated for Academy Awards six times, the second for her performance in **The Mating Season**. In this case 'supporting' was hardly the word; she was virtually the whole show as the outspoken mother of a wage-earner who moves up the social ladder by marrying an ambassador's daughter. Ma preserves her son's new status by pretending to be a servant and joining the couple's household, but after some amusing situations involving the bride's rich relatives, class barriers were happily hurdled. Although failing to extract much fizz from the lovely Gene Tierney (centre left; borrowed from 20th Century-Fox) and John Lund (centre right) as the newly-weds, director Mitchell Leisen gave Ritter her head and guided Miriam Hopkins, Cora Witherspoon, Jan Sterling, Larry Keating (left), Malcolm Keen, James Lorimar, Ellen Corby and Gladys Hurlbut through entertaining scenes written by producer Charles Brackett with Walter Reisch and Richard Breen.

△ Long the studio's producers of 'B' quickies, William Pine and William Thomas were known as the Dollar Bills because they never wasted a buck or failed to make a profit with their bread-and-butter output. **The Last Outpost**, a Western set in Civil War days with Confederate brother against Unionist brother and Indians against everybody, was the Bills' highest grossing release to date. It was their first of three starring Ronald Reagan (left) and Rhonda Fleming (right), and they opened the wallet wide enough to afford Technicolor and well-known supporting players, Bruce Bennett, Bill Williams, Noah Beery Jr, Peter Hanson, Hugh Beaumont, John Ridgely and Lloyd Corrigan. Lewis Foster directed the Geoffrey Homes-George W. Yates-Winston Miller story. Reagan, very good as the hero, had already been a leading man for a dozen years and was thirty away from becoming America's leading man.

△ Made with brisk efficiency and no more inspiration than the need to fill a release date (and enough seats to show a profit) **Appointment With Danger** offered Alan Ladd (left) as a flying postal inspector investigating airmail robberies. While he is infiltrating the suspected mob, it becomes a murder case, in which the only eye-witness is a nun. British star Phyllis Calvert (centre) played this, one of her few Hollywood assignments, with charm but was overshadowed on the distaff side by Jan Sterling as a sharp-tongued gang moll, while Paul Stewart, Jack Webb, Henry Morgan, Harry Antrim, Stacy Harris and Geraldine Wall showed up well in support. Producer Robert Fellows and director Lewis Allen finished shooting the Richard Breen-Warren Duff screenplay in 1949: Paramount was building a stockpile of Ladd pictures because he made no secret of intending to leave when his contract expired.

△ There should have been some sort of devotion to duty medal struck for Ray Milland (left) while the performer of the title role in **Rhubarb** strutted off with all the Best Animal Acting awards of the year. This was a ginger cat who, in H. Allen Smith's celebrated story, ingeniously expanded by the script of Dorothy Reid and Francis Cockrell, inherits the estate of an eccentric millionaire, thereby becoming the owner as well as the mascot of a baseball team. This seems to be a heaven-sent gift to publicist Milland until the furry heir's madcap temperament nearly drives the poor man around the bend; however, the team is eventually meowed to triumph. The two-legged star gave his usual good performance, never betraying his awareness that scene after scene was being stolen from him by a stunning histrionic exhibition of whisker-twitching, tail-lashing emotions and a vocal range running the gamut from hiss to purr. Jan Sterling (right), Gene Lockhart, William Frawley, Taylor Holmes, Elsie Holmes, Willard Waterman, Leonard Nimoy and Strother Martin were others hopelessly out-acted in the William Perlberg-George Seaton production, directed with what must have been tireless patience by Arthur Lubin, who had trained for the task by making Universal's series about Francis the talking mule.

▽ The company's prestige picture of the year, **A Place In The Sun**, proved to be also a highly profitable one, with co-stars Montgomery Clift and Elizabeth Taylor (both illustrated) – and rave reviews – exerting potent crowd magnetism. This was George Stevens's version of the Theodore Dreiser masterpiece, *An American Tragedy*, made with more detailed care and technical polish than Von Sternberg's 1931 effort, but ultimately again missing the book's tragic force. The novel's sociological study of class conflicts was side-tracked and the romantic interest emphasised, so one's abiding memory of the film was not of a factory worker's ambition cheated by fate, but of enormous, luscious close-ups of Taylor and Clift kissing. The Michael Wilson-Harry Brown script flowed as smoothly as Stevens's direction, although, as in the first movie, the climactic courtroom scene in which Clift is convicted of murdering his pregnant workmate (Shelley Winters, made to look excessively drab, but giving a splendid performance) didn't come off. All production elements were so superb that the Academy garlanded it with award nominations in nine categories, of which it won Oscars in six. Also cast: Ann Revere, Keefe Brasselle, Fred Clark.

◁ Confederate officer Alan Ladd (left) found himself in bad company when he joined Quantrill's Raiders, a bloodthirsty band of guerillas who rampaged through the North-South border states during the Civil War, killing and pillaging. **Red Mountain** stirred up a whole heap of action before Ladd, working from within, was instrumental in making Quantrill bite the dust under the guns of Federal troops. Produced in Technicolor by Hal B. Wallis and directed with typical William Dieterle attention to detail, it won enough profit to land on the right side of the ledger; Ladd's box-office magnetism, however, wasn't what it used to be. Lizabeth Scott, too modern a type for 19th-century heroine duty, John Ireland, Arthur Kennedy (right), Neville Brand, Jeff Corey, James Bell, Carleton Young, Walter Sande and Whit Bissell filled other roles written by George W. George, George Slavin and John Meredyth Lucas.

▽ The 'isn't-life-wonderful' effulgence of Frank Capra's great days had dimmed a little by the time he made **Here Comes The Groom**, his first of two Bing Crosby starrers in a row. It was an enjoyable trifle, though, and those two names, a strong supporting cast (Jane Wyman, here with Bing; Franchot Tone, Alexis Smith, James Barton, Robert Keith, Anna Maria Alberghetti, Walter Catlett, Connie Gilchrist, Minna Gombell, H.B. Warner and a scene-stealing kid, Jacques Gencel; guest stars Dorothy Lamour, Cass Daley, Louis Armstrong, and Phil Harris) and songs including the Johnny Mercer-Hoagy Carmichael Oscar winner, 'In The Cool Cool Cool Of The Evening', pushed it to the top flight of 1951 money-makers. Liam O'Brien collaborated with Robert Riskin, long Capra's writer, on the story, and with Virginia Van Upp and Myles Connolly on the script – all about a singing journalist who has to find a wife quickly so that he can bring two war orphans into the States. Jane, his ex-fiancee, is about to marry rich Franchot but can't resist the charms of Bing and the orphans, so Franchot has to make do with Alexis Smith. Nice make-do if you can get it.

▷ In 1925 a man named Floyd Collins was trapped in an abandoned mine shaft, and all America held its breath as the efforts to free him became front-page news. Billy Wilder used this incident for **Ace In The Hole** (aka **The Big Carnival**) which he wrote (with Lesser Samuels and Walter Newman), directed and produced as the most trenchant and least popular drama of his career. It was a marvel of realism and suspense, but its story was too harrowing, its leading character too despicable and its cynicism too biting for mass audiences to take. Kirk Douglas (left) scored an acting triumph as a has-been star reporter, job hunting in New Mexico, who sees a local accident – the owner of a last-chance desert cafe was the Collins of the screenplay – as his way back to the big time. He floods newspapers with human interest stories and whips up a national furore; thrilled crowds gather as he crawls in to comfort the trapped man, whose rescue he deliberately prolongs until it is too late. Wilder's dagger-thrusts at greed, ballyhoo and mob hysteria found their mark in settings of newsreel-like vividness. Robert Arthur as Douglas's young assistant, Richard Benedict (right) as the victim, and Jan Sterling as his tarty wife (asked to pray for him, she snaps 'Kneeling bags my nylons') stood out in a cast including Porter Hall, Frank Cady, Lewis Martin, Ray Teal, Geraldine Wall and Richard Gaines.

△ Bob Hope, who seemed to have a penchant for remaking old racetrack movies, counted the profits on *Sorrowful Jones* and reunited with its director and producer, Sidney Lanfield and Robert Welch, for another Damon Runyon story, **The Lemon Drop Kid**, which Paramount had filmed in 1934. He played a racing tipster with a knack for picking losers and an urgent problem with a gangster client who demands $10,000 worth of pacifying, or else. Aside from a laugh-loaded sequence in which Hope was disguised as an old lady (illustrated, with Cheerio Meredith) while involved in a retirement home racket, and an equally funny Santa Claus scene, the sparkle was a bit dimmed this time, but not at the box-office. Marilyn Maxwell, Lloyd Nolan, Andrea King, Jane Darwell, Fred Clark, William Frawley, Jay C. Flippen and Harry Bellaver were among the Runyon guys and dolls in the Edmund Hartmann-Robert O'Brien screenplay, and three songs by Ray Evans and Jay Livingston included one hit, 'Silver Bells'. Writer Frank Tashlin shot several added scenes in his directorial debut.

▽ Judging by **Darling, How Could You!** (GB: **Rendezvous**) which ended his long association with the studio, Mitchell Leisen was losing interest in directing. Momentary glimpses of his former brilliance weren't enough to illuminate this gas-lit comedy about a woman whose domestic life is disarranged by her daughter's flights of fancy, especially one about the mother having a clandestine love affair. The ghost of Sir James Barrie must have been grateful that the silly title (changed in Britain) disguised the fact that his play *Alice Sit-By-The-Fire* was its source. Theatre audiences had applauded two great actresses in the lead, Ethel Barrymore (1905) and Laurette Taylor (1932). Joan Fontaine (right) seemed to find it a strain, and didn't get much help from John Lund (left) who, like Leisen, was finishing his contract; Mona Freeman (centre), Peter Hanson, David Stollery, Gertrude Michael, Lowell Gilmore, Robert Barrat and Angela Clarke. Neither Harry Tugend's production of the Dodie Smith–Lesser Samuels screenplay, nor the cast, were able to attract the paying customers.

▽ Bob Hope's ever-faithful fans and ever-profiting exhibitors welcomed his third *My Favorite* romp, this time with Hedy Lamarr (left) as his seductive cohort in **My Favorite Spy**. Norman Z. McLeod directed them through a far-fetched adventure in which a United States espionage chief (who needs his head examined) decides that small-time burlesque comedian Hope is just the man to replace a murdered agent in a dangerous mission to Tangier. There Bob (right) converts a beautiful counter-spy and, together, they make a hash of enemy conspirators' plans before escaping in a wild Keystone chase aboard a fire engine. Occasionally hitting a slow spot but more often loaded with laughs and/or action, the script by Edmund Hartmann and Jack Sher from a Lou Breslow-Edmund Beloin original was smartly produced by Paul Jones, with Francis L. Sullivan, Arnold Moss, Marc Lawrence, Morris Ankrum, John Archer and Stephen Chase in the cast. RKO made a flop comedy with the same title and a similar story in 1942.

▽ These days, when astronomical budgets are poured into science-fiction rubbish which fills theatres (not to mention television screens) and returns profits of mind-blowing proportions, **When Worlds Collide** would look like a quickie from poverty row. In 1951 it was an 'exploitation special' from prestigious Paramount and a popular attraction. Sydney Boehm scripted and Rudolph Maté directed the Edwin Balmer-Philip Wylie story about terrified citizens planning to escape by rocket from the impact of a maverick planet heading towards Earth. The cataclysm promised by the the title finally arrived and it was a whopper for its day, straining the studio's special effects department to its limit and winning producer George Pal an Oscar. Until then, Richard Derr (centre), Barbara Rush (left), Peter Hanson (right), John Hoyt, Stephen Chase, Judith Ames, Frank Cady, Hayden Rorke and Mary Murphy coped with long stretches of dull dialogue, giving viewers ample time for a chat, a grope or a bag of popcorn.

△ William Wyler shot **Detective Story** in five weeks, very fast for him, and the speed was reflected in the picture's tempo. It was sensationally good filming of the Broadway smash by Sidney Kingsley, a mixture of realism and theatricality that kept a grip on its crowded audiences from beginning to end. Against a background of hectic activity in a New York police station – quite novel at the time, now a television and paperback commonplace – it unrolled the story of a detective with rigid principles, and his wife with a guilty secret. Vibrantly acted by Kirk Douglas (right) and Eleanor Parker (left), they reach emotional cli-

maxes that change their lives, while around them the business of the precinct rattles on in a succession of sordid and funny vignettes, especially well played by original New York cast members Lee Grant as a shop-lifter and Joseph Wiseman as a burglar. William Bendix, Horace MacMahon (background; also from the stage cast), Bert Freed, Frank Faylen, Bill Phillips, Grandon Rhodes, Cathy O'Donnell, Luis van Rooten, Michael Strong, Warner Anderson and George Macready registered vividly in the Philip Yordan-Robert Wyler screenplay. It won a place on practically every critic's list of the year's best movies.

OTHER RELEASES OF 1951

Crosswinds
John Payne, Rhonda Fleming, Forrest Tucker. Dir: Lewis Foster. Pro: William Pine, William Thomas. Trying to recover gold from a crashed plane in New Guinea, a captain encounters thieves and native head-hunters.

Dear Brat
Mona Freeman, Edward Arnold, Billy DeWolfe. Dir: William A. Seiter. Pro: Mel Epstein. Sequel to *Dear Ruth* and *Dear Wife* in which her young sister causes family ructions when she befriends a criminal.

The Flaming Feather
Sterling Hayden, Forrest Tucker, Barbara Rush, Arleen Whelan, Richard Arlen. Dir: Ray Enright. Pro: Nat Holt. Ranchers and US Cavalrymen rescue a girl abducted by renegade Indians.

Hong Kong
Ronald Reagan, Rhonda Fleming, Nigel Bruce. Dir: Lewis Foster. Pro: William Pine, William Thomas. The theft of a jeweled treasure is within an adventurer's grasp; he is restrained by his love of a good woman.

Passage West
John Payne, Dennis O'Keefe, Arleen Whelan. Dir: Lewis Foster. Pro: William Pine, William Thomas. Religious pioneers heading west are forced to accompany six escaped convicts.

Quebec
John Barrymore Jr, Corinne Calvet, Barbara Rush, Patric Knowles. Dir: George Templeton. Pro: Alan LeMay. In 1837 Canada the wife of a British general indulges in espionage and romance with a rebel leader.

Sailor Beware
Dean Martin, Jerry Lewis, Corinne Calvet. Dir: Hal Walker. Pro: Hal B. Wallis. Comic misadventures on a submarine cruise to Honolulu, where Dean romances a movie star. (Remake of *Lady Be Careful*, 1936; *The Fleet's In*, 1941)

That's My Boy
Dean Martin, Jerry Lewis, Ruth Hussey. Dir: Hal Walker. Pro: Hal B. Wallis. Pushed by his athletic father, hypochondriac Jerry joins his college football team, assisted by roommate Dean.

Warpath
Edmond O'Brien, Dean Jagger, Polly Bergen, Forrest Tucker. Dir: Byron Haskin. Pro: Nat Holt. After the Civil War, a lawyer becomes a revenge-hunting gunman when his fiancée has been killed by bandits.

1952

▽ **Just For You** was as mild as a milkshake, a comedy-drama-musical which surprisingly rolled up one of the company's biggest grosses of the year – a tribute to Bing Crosby's enduring popularity. He gave voice to a flock of so-so Harry Warren-Leo Robin songs (best: 'I'll Si-Si Ya In Bahia' and 'Zing A Little Zong') in the course of Robert Carson's screenplay, from Stephen Vincent Benet's *Famous*, about a Broadway producer making up for neglect of his teenage children (Robert Arthur, Natalie Wood) by taking them to a holiday resort along with his fiancee (Jane Wyman), with whom the son falls in love. Ethel Barrymore (right, with Natalie), doyenne of the American theatre, was wasted in a nothing role, her sole Paramount appearance in an intermittent film career stretching from 1914 to 1957. Regis Toomey and Cora Witherspoon were featured in the Pat Duggan production directed by Elliott Nugent.

▽ One of the popular team's better comedies, **Jumping Jacks** offered Jerry Lewis (foreground) as a song-and-dance man visiting his old stage partner Dean Martin (behind) at the Fort Benning, Georgia, training school for paratroopers. Jerry is there just to put on a show for the lads, but a mistaken identity mix-up forces him to emulate his hot-shot pal as a jumper. Meanwhile, Dean is crooning some fair songs to Mona Freeman (clinging to him here). Don De Fore, Robert Strauss, Marcy McGuire and Richard Erdman had parts in the script dreamed up by Robert Lees, Fred Rinaldo and Herbert Baker, produced by Hal Wallis and briskly directed by Norman Taurog. But it was the sight gags involving Jerry, parachutes and acrophobia that paid off.

△ Brushing the laurel leaves bestowed for *A Place In The Sun* from his hair, George Stevens turned to **Something To Live For**, a less ambitious undertaking which, while carrying considerable dramatic impact, aroused little enthusiasm among the buyers or sellers of tickets. Writer Dwight Taylor provided a quadrangle story of husband, wife, other woman and demon drink, the latter afflicting both the husband (Ray Milland, left), an advertising artist and a member of Alcoholics Anonymous, and the other woman (Joan Fontaine, right), a free-swilling member of Actors Equity. While they fought and won their battle with the bottle, the wife (Teresa Wright) and the audience suffered in silence. A great boost for AA if not for its excellent stars, who were supported by Douglas Dick, Richard Derr, Paul Valentine, Harry Bellaver, Frank Orth and Ruby Dee, the Stevens production glowed with his usual directorial polish.

▷ Cecil B. DeMille added to his long list of records with **The Greatest Show On Earth**, which grossed more money than any Paramount picture had ever done. And it won the Oscar for the best picture of 1952, which pleased him even more. Preparations for this world-wide smash started in 1949, when the company paid Ringling Brothers-Barnum and Bailey $250,000 for facilities and rights to the title, which had long been that circus's slogan (the payment should have been reversed, for the fabulous publicity), and DeMille toured with the big top before finalising the Fredric Frank-Barre Lyndon-Theodore St John script, from a Frank-St John-Frank Cavett story. He cast Charlton Heston (left) as the circus manager, James Stewart as a clown hiding from the police, Betty Hutton (right) as a dare-devil trapeze artist, Dorothy Lamour as an aerialist hanging by her teeth, Cornel Wilde as a high-wire walker and Gloria Grahame as a girl stunting with elephants; also Lyle Bettger, Laurence Tierney, John Kellogg and Henry Wilcoxon, the latter doubling as associate producer. Their scrambled dramas came to a head in a climactic train wreck with wild animals breaking loose. Garish in Technicolor, ear-numbing with noise, it may not have been the greatest show on earth, but it was a three-ring knockout for kids of all ages.

◁ The part and the player were attuned to perfection in **Come Back, Little Sheba**. Shirley Booth's extraordinary character study of a well-meaning but exasperating woman had won raves during the Broadway run of William Inge's play, and in the same role for her screen debut she walked off with the 'best actress' awards of the Academy, the New York Film Critics and the Cannes Festival. In other hands, this housewife's over-emotional sentimentality might have been as maddening to audiences as to her alcoholic husband, but Booth (right) made her truly moving, with the sensitive guidance of director Daniel Mann, also repeating his stage assignment. The off-casting of Burt Lancaster (left) was another triumph: his study of drab frustration as the husband finally driven to violence couldn't have been better done. Terry Moore as the couple's sexy young tenant whose presence disturbed him, Richard Jaeckel as her boyfriend, and Philip Ober, Walter Kelley and Lisa Golm in minor roles, fitted nicely into the Hal B. Wallis production of Ketti Frings's screenplay. The title came from the wife's plaintively repeated cry for her long-lost dog, symbol of happier days.

△ Four years after *The Paleface*, the inevitable arrived: **Son Of Paleface**. Bob Hope (right), Jane Russell (left) and producer Robert Welch were in good shape again and, with the added attraction of Roy Rogers and his famous horse Trigger, the sequel was a box-office dazzler only slightly paler than the original. Frank Tashlin moved up from co-writer of the first to director, giving a galloping pace to the script, constructed by Joseph Quillan, Welch and himself, about a tenderfoot arriving in the West to collect the fortune supposed to have been left by his father. He is helped by a government agent (Rogers) on the trail of a bandit (Russell) who turns out to be the owner of the Dirty Shame saloon; ridin', shootin', slapstick and laugh lines proliferated until Hope got the girl and Rogers got Trigger. All three stars sang new Livingston-Evans numbers, none of them as enormous a hit as the original's 'Buttons And Bows', which was reprised; Bill Williams, Lloyd Corrigan, Paul Burns, Douglas Dumbrille, Harry Von Zell and Iron Eyes Cody acted; and the whole shebang was brightened by Technicolor. Rogers, who had been the biggest name in 'B' westerns for ten years, did little on screen after this, switching to business interests and reputed to be almost as wealthy as Hope.

△ Bing Crosby (left), Bob Hope (right) and Dorothy Lamour (centre) hit the road again after a five-year lapse. **Road To Bali**, their sixth excursion together and the only one in Technicolor, looked remarkably like the roads to Singapore, Zanzibar, Morocco, Utopia and Rio; the careless rapture of the male stars' comic anarchy and ad libs (were they ever impromptu?) now had a well rehearsed air, and Dorothy's sarong surely had changed not a stitch (now *there* was a girl who knew how to keep her figure). The script by Frank Butler, Hal Kanter and William Morrow (something about a couple of song-and-dance men in the South Seas seeking a treasure and getting chummy with an island princess) and the Burke-Van Heusen songs (except for a swoony Lamour number, 'Moonflowers') came from the remainder counter. The movie, however, was disappointing only in comparison with its predecessors: there was a generous quota of laughs, director Hal Walker drew bright performances from his cast, who included Murvyn Vye, Carolyn Jones and Peter Coe, and Harry Tugend's production had plenty of flash. But the series was now twelve years old, and the law of diminishing returns was raising its dismal head. Paramount put up a Road Closed sign; a misguided final instalment, *Road To Hong Kong*, was made for United Artists ten years later.

▽ After making **Somebody Loves Me**, Betty Hutton (illustrated) had a row with the studio and walked out. The temperamental star's skyrocketing career came to earth with a bump and, except for a minor 1957 film and sporadic stage appearances, she has not been seen again. At her explosive best in her Paramount finale, with quieter dramatic interludes well handled, she played Blossom Seeley, a singer who headlined in big-time vaudeville for many years before retiring as the wife of her partner, Benny Fields. Seeley's catalogue of songs ranged from 'Way Down Yonder In New Orleans', in her early-century days when she was known as a 'coon-shouter' in San Francisco, to the Gershwin title number which became her theme song in later years; others put over with the well-known Hutton élan included 'I Cried For You', 'Smiles', 'Teasing Rag', 'Rose Room', and 'Jealous'. There were golden oldies in the script situations too, written and directed by Irving Brecher, and the slick George Seaton-William Perlberg production (in Technicolor) was no better or worse than most show-biz biopics. Ralph Meeker as Fields, Adele Jergens, Robert Keith, Henry Slate, Sid Tomack, Billie Bird and an unbilled bit by Jack Benny helped it along.

▷ Theodore Dreiser's first novel, *Sister Carrie*, was printed in 1900 and suppressed for twelve years by its publishers, who feared it was 'too immoral' to issue. In 1950 it was filmed as **Carrie** – and shelved for two McCarthy-ridden years in case it might be branded 'un-American'. Neither opinion bears much scrutiny today, but the movie certainly does: a superb achievement by director-producer William Wyler and scripters Ruth and Augustus Goetz, softening Dreiser's realism, perhaps, but preserving his dramatic power. Jennifer Jones was at her best as the country girl learning big city ways and becoming a successful actress; Eddie Albert was brilliant as her first lover; Laurence Olivier (with her here), as the richer second one whose infatuation leads to his ruin, surpassed them both in a towering performance. Miriam Hopkins (as his vengeful wife), William Reynolds, Mary Murphy, Basil Ruysdael and Barry Kelley supported ably in a period Chicago atmosphere exactly captured.

△ **The Atomic City** was something of a surprise package in that the cast, director and title indicated nothing more than a routine 'B' programme-filler. In fact it was an exceptionally well-handled thriller, using authentic locations inside the Los Alamos atomic energy plant and telling a suspenseful story of a young boy kidnapped by Russian agents, who demand secret documents on the hydrogen bomb as ransom. The author-screenwriter Sydney Boehm's taut fiction was treated in documentary style by Jerry Hopper in his first feature as director, and Joseph Sistrom produced on a low, well spent budget. Lee Acker as the boy, Gene Barry as the father who rescues him with help from the FBI; Nancy Gates (right), Michael Moore, Milburn Stone, Lydia Clarke (left), Leonard Strong, Frank Cady and Bert Freed performed efficiently.

◁ Written, produced and directed by Leo McCarey, with Myles Connolly collaborating on the script, **My Son John** was astoundingly nominated for the 'best story' Academy Award. A ludicrously overdrawn piece of claptrap, it concerned the Communist son of flag-waving, bible-thumping parents who, stricken to the core by their discovery of his political persuasion, treat him like the sinning daughter in a Victorian melodrama. Greater than their grief when he dies is their pride in his recanting just in time to save his soul and his Americanism. Helen Hayes (centre) returned from Broadway to play the mother after a long screen absence, and Robert Walker (left) ended his too short career as the son: he died while the picture was still in production, and footage of him from *Strangers On A Train* was used to complete it. Van Heflin, Dean Jagger (right), Richard Jaeckel, Frank McHugh, Minor Watson and Todd Karns were also prominent. The only excuse for this distressing waste of talents could be that it was made while the country's anti-Red hysteria, the Un-American Activities Committee's witch-hunt and the Hollywood black-listing were at their height.

▽ **The Turning Point** was a satisfying melodrama inspired by an actual Senate investigation into organised crime which had made headlines in 1951. The forceful script, developed by Warren Duff from a story by Horace McCoy, followed a young lawyer appointed by the state governor to head the probe while his reporter friend digs up some sensational evidence against one of the syndicate bosses, pointing to corruption within the Senate Committee itself. The pal (William Holden, illustrated) is killed, leaving the lawyer (Edmond O'Brien) to finish the job and get his girl (Alexis Smith). All three convinced with forthright performances, supported by Neville Brand, Ed Begley, Ted de Corsia, Tom Tully, Howard Freeman, Adele Longmire and Ray Teal. William Dieterle's direction kept a tight hold on the dramatic tension, and the Irving Asher production did very nicely at the ticket wickets.

OTHER RELEASES OF 1952

Aaron Slick From Punkin Crick (GB **Marshmallow Moon**)
Dinah Shore, Alan Young, Robert Merrill. Dir: Claude Binyon. Pro: George Seaton, William Perlberg. Musical comedy, about a rural widow whom a city slicker is trying to fleece.

Anything Can Happen
Jose Ferrer, Kim Hunter, Kurt Kasznar. Dir: George Seaton. Pro: William Seaton, William Perlberg. Comedy of a Russian immigrant family, particularly the son getting used to American ways and finding a bride.

The Blazing Forest
John Payne, Richard Arlen, Lynne Roberts, Agnes Moorehead. Dir: Edward Ludwig. Pro: William Pine, William Thomas. Logger falls for girl and fells trees on her aunt's property, until interrupted by a fire.

Caribbean
John Payne, Arlene Dahl, Sir Cedric Hardwicke. Dir: Edward Ludwig. Pro: William Pine, William Thomas. Pirates are beaten back after they try to take possession of a Caribbean island in the 18th century.

The Denver And The Rio Grande
Sterling Hayden, Dean Jagger, Edmond O'Brien. Dir: Byron Haskin. Pro: Nat Holt. Rival railroad builders fight against time and each other to push the iron horse though the West.

Encore
Nigel Patrick, Roland Culver, Kay Walsh, Glynis Johns. Dir: Harold French, Anthony Pelissier, Pat Jackson. Three Somerset Maugham stories introduced by the author: 'The Ant And The Grasshopper', 'Winter Cruise', 'Gigolo And Gigolette'. (British)

Hurricane Smith
John Ireland, Yvonne De Carlo, Richard Arlen, Forrest Tucker. Dir: Jerry Hopper. Pro: Nat Holt. Melodrama of conflict between a charter boat's skipper and the fortune hunter who hires him in the south seas.

The Savage
Charlton Heston, Susan Morrow, Ted de Corsia. Dir: George Marshall. Pro: Mel Epstein. Drama of heredity versus environment in which a man, born white and raised as a red Indian, has problems with both races.

The Stooge
Dean Martin, Jerry Lewis, Polly Bergen. Dir: Norman Taurog. Pro: Hal B. Wallis. A song-and-dance man in 1930s vaudeville has a stooge whose comedy antics become the big attraction; they split up.

1953

▽ Any Western displaying Charlton Heston (left), Jack Palance (right) and Technicolor in all their rugged grandeur should be worth the ticket price. A good number of customers thought so, and **Arrowhead** rewarded them with an above-average sagebrusher, handsomely produced by Nat Holt from W.R. Burnett's novel *Adobe Walls*. The story, set in desert country of the south-west, was about a US Cavalry officer (Heston) leading a unit assigned to make peace with the Apaches but forced into battle, which narrowed down into head-to-head conflict between the officer and the Indians' chief (Palance). Nothing new here, but Charles Marquis Warren, directing from his own script, kept the action stirring and the characters interesting. Besides the leads, Katy Jurado, Brian Keith, Mary Sinclair, Milburn Stone, Richard Shannon, Lewis Martin and Frank DeKova played with spirit. Western specialist Warren went on to greater success in television with *Gunsmoke*, *Rawhide* and other series.

▷ Notable on several counts, **Roman Holiday** proved that William Wyler's brilliance wasn't restricted to drama. His first comedy since 1935 became the top collector of international awards for the company in 1953, including three from the Academy out of a remarkable total of ten nominations. Like Shirley Booth the year before, Audrey Hepburn (left) turned the rare trick of winning the 'best actress' Oscar with her first Hollywood role; the studio had signed her as a result of her Broadway stage hit in *Gigi* after minor British film appearances. She was a refreshing young charmer as a princess who plays truant from royal duties while on an official visit to Rome, and goes on a sight-seeing tour with a newspaper reporter (Gregory Peck, right) and a photographer (Eddie Albert), the former falling in love with her in vain. In his first (and, to date, only) Paramount picture, Peck showed why he was one of the most celebrated actors in the business, while Hartley Power, Margaret Rawlings, Tullio Carminati and Harcourt Williams ably supported. Wyler shot Ian McClelland Hunter's modern fairy tale (scripted with John Dighton) in Rome, a city whose beauty was enhanced by the cameras of Franz Planer and Henri Alekan – surprisingly, in black and white. Strong box-office.

▽ By the end of 1953 Paramount was still eking out its backlog of Alan Ladd pictures, while other companies had already released some he'd made since his departure two years before. In comparison with those, **Botany Bay** looked good. Ladd (left) and James Mason co-starred in this 18th-century sea melodrama, the former as a student unjustly sentenced to deportation to Australia, the latter as the captain of the convict ship, flogging and keel-hauling his cargo of prisoners with sadistic abandon. This road company *Mutiny On The Bounty* by the same authors, Charles Nordhoff and James Norman Hall, was scripted by Jonathan Latimer and directed by John Farrow in flamboyant style, winning few plaudits from the press but giving full satisfaction to exhibitors and their action-loving patrons. As a beauty improbably aboard the hell-ship, Patricia Medina was lusted after by Mason before a happy ending with Ladd, while Sir Cedric Hardwicke (right), Murray Matheson, John Hardy, Dorothy Patten and Anita Bolster took care of other roles. The Technicolor production was supervised by Joseph Sistrom.

△ Heaped helpings of vocal music provided sorely needed nourishment to an underweight Cinderella story in **The Stars Are Singing**. Anna Maria Alberghetti, as a Polish refugee who had entered the United States illegally, sang; Rosemary Clooney (left), in her screen debut as a show-business hopeful who befriended the girl, sang (most enjoyably, her famous hit 'Come On-A-My House'); Lauritz Melchior, veteran of the Metropolitan Opera and MGM musicals, sang, while helping Anna Maria to start an operatic career. Dancer Tom Morton (right) and comedian Bob Williams, with his hilariously disobedient dog, Red Dust, varied the entertainment as they joined Fred Clark, Mikhail Rasumny, John Archer, Lloyd Corrigan and Don Wilson. Liam O'Brien's screenplay, based on a story by Paul Hervey Fox, was produced in Technicolor by Irving Asher and directed by Norman Taurog. Not much box-office, but those who came in seemed glad they did.

▽ Bob Hope's stock characterisation of comical coward became tiresome before the end of **Here Come The Girls**, because the Edmund Hartmann-Hal Kanter script (from an original by Hartmann and Martin Rackin) gave him no scope for any variation. He (centre left) was a stumble-footed chorus dancer whose producer orders him to go on for the show's leading man every time the latter is warned that he'll be killed on stage by a gangster. This happened with monotonous frequency. So did a succession of production numbers, staged in splendiferous 1950's style, although the story for some reason was set about 40 years earlier. Hope did all he could with his below-par material, Rosemary Clooney brought a fresh note to her chorine role, Tony Martin was in good voice as the show's star, Arlene Dahl (right) played his girlfriend and Robert Strauss her gangster admirer. Millard Mitchell, William Demarest (left), Fred Clark (centre right), Zamah Cunningham and the four Step Brothers also appeared in Paul Jones's Technicolor production, directed by Claude Binyon. Undistinguished, but it yielded good returns.

▷ All this kicking towards the camera by (left to right) Dean Martin, Marjie Millar, Pat Crowley and Jerry Lewis was supposed to illustrate that **Money From Home** was in 3-D, a popular gimmick for a while in the early fifties. And, dear reader, did this comedy need it! Unfortunately the 3-D register was so inaccurate that the film had to be generally released flat. One of the weakest Martin and Lewis vehicles, it attempted a mix of the stars' formula characters with the gambling fraternity of Damon Runyon, whose original story was unimproved by screenwriter Hal Kanter. Richard Haydn, Robert Strauss, Sheldon Leonard, Jack Kruschen and Romo Vincent were in the Hal Wallis production, directed by George Marshall.

△ Producers William Pine and William Thomas made a try for big-time box-office with **Sangaree** by giving it not only Technicolor but the latest marvel, 3-D. Stereoptical films had actually been experimented with for many decades, and in the early fifties they suddenly caught the public's fancy, but the 3-dimension illusion was never satisfactory, the necessary wearing of coloured glasses was a nuisance, and it soon proved a passing craze. This movie, which quickly subsided into 2-D bookings, was an 18th-century melodrama with Fernando Lamas (left), Arlene Dahl (later Mrs Lamas), Patricia Medina, John Sutton, Francis L. Sullivan (right), Tom Drake, Charles Korvin, Lester Matthews and Willard Parker, directed by Edward Ludwig. David Duncan and Frank Moss adapted Frank Slaughter's novel about family conflicts stirred by a plantation owner making a slave's son his heir; impassioned romance and pirates' exploits also jostled for the audience's attention, and it all happened way down south in the land of cotton..... Look away, look away, said the bloodless and unmoved critics.

▷ One of the small minority of Westerns with a valid claim to be works of art, **Shane** had a classic shape: stranger on horseback arriving from nowhere, helping a family to save their homestead from ruthless cattlemen, then riding out to nowhere again. It was meticulously directed by George Stevens, excellently performed by Alan Ladd as the mysterious Shane, Jean Arthur and Van Heflin as the homesteaders; also Jack Palance as the worst of the bad guys; Elisha Cook Jr as his victim in one of the most shocking murder scenes on film; Ben Johnson, Edgar Buchanan, and Brandon De Wilde (here with Ladd) as the hero-worshipping child whose 'Come back, Shane!' echoed through the poignant fade-out. The Stevens production, written by A.B. Guthrie Jr from Jack Schaeffer's novel, earned Paramount $9 million in America alone, and six Academy Award nominations. Ironically, the one that won an Oscar – photography by Loyal Griggs – lost much of its beautiful composition during an unusually long post-production period (16 months) when wide-screen became the rage and **Shane** was cut to fit the new format.

△ Bob Hope (left) and Mickey Rooney (right) made a great new team of laugh-raisers in **Off Limits** (GB: **Military Policemen**). Although not always in top gear, Hal Kanter's and Jack Sher's ingenious screenplay was kept moving snappily enough by director George Marshall to give mass audiences a fast, funny show. It concerned a prize-fighter's manager who has no sooner joined the army to look after his drafted boxer than the boy is rejected from the service. The manager (Hope) is assigned to the military police force, where he discovers a new boxer (Rooney), falls in love with the latter's aunt (Marilyn Maxwell) and afoul of the sergeant (Eddie Mayehoff) while making a shambles of army regulations. The cast – which also included Stanley Clements, John Ridgely, Marvin Miller and, for a touch of authentic prizefight atmosphere, Jack Dempsey – was a lively bunch, and the lushly blonde Maxwell, as a nightclub singer, threw in a bit of vocal entertainment. Harry Tugend produced.

◁ Hal Wallis rushed Dean Martin (right) and Jerry Lewis (left) from one picture to another while his new discoveries were hot. Who knew whether the crowds' enthusiasm would cool as fast as it had ignited? (It didn't.) **Scared Stiff** was the first of many remakes the team was to do; its source was the durable Paul Dickey-Charles Goddard play *The Ghost Breaker*, with the thriller element now almost entirely abandoned in favour of the comedy by scripters Herbert Baker and Walter De Leon. The story – which, if you count in the virtually indistinguishable *Cat And The Canary*, had already been filmed eight times – concerned an apparently haunted mansion inherited by a girl who visits it and survives its terrors with the aid of a young admirer, in this case Martin, while Lewis overdoes the scared-stiff mugging and yowling. Lizabeth Scott played the heiress, and Carmen Miranda (centre) was a bright spot in a cast including Dorothy Malone, Tom Powers, George Dolenz, William Ching and, in an unbilled bit, Bing Crosby and Bob Hope. George Marshall, again directing, had done a better job on Hope's *Ghost Breakers* in 1940, and the songs (also mostly second hand) did little to improve a ramshackle entertainment. But awfully profitable.

▽ George Pal's productions were invariably lively entertainment and commercially rewarding for their various studios. **The War Of The Worlds** was one of the Hungarian merchant of fantasy's better efforts, working up to a succession of action climaxes as violent aliens from outer space invaded the Earth. Although the H.G. Wells novel on which Barre Lyndon based his screenplay had been a popular seller since 1898, this kind of story had novelty value in 1953 cinemas, especially when depicted with such sensational visual and aural effects as the Paramount illusion experts devised here. Their efforts were worthy of an Oscar (and got one), but the same could hardly be said for the script, the directing of Byron Haskin or the acting of Gene Barry (right), Ann Robinson (left), Les Tremayne, Robert Cornthwaite, Sandro Giglio, Lewis Martin and Jack Kruschen, all handicapped by a shortage of plot and a plethora of dialogue until the war began. This property had been gathering dust since 1924, when Jesse Lasky bought it from Wells.

△ 'Let's let the boys loose on a golf course!' said producer Paul Jones or director Norman Taurog or writer Edmund Hartmann or co-writer Danny Arnold in the smoke-filled room where the next Martin and Lewis was being cooked up. Whoever did have the idea, it was a good one, but – nobody came up with much of a story for **The Caddy**, a ramshackle vehicle for a pair then at their box-office peak. Jerry Lewis (left) played a crowd-shy golfer who coaxes his pal (Dean Martin) to use him as coach and club-carrier in a big tournament; catastrophic in both jobs, he gets them banned from the pro circuit, so they go into show business. Donna Reed and Barbara Bates were their girlfriends; others cast included Joseph Calleia, Fred Clark (right), Marshall Thompson, Frank Puglia, Argentina Brunetti, Clinton Sundberg, and golf champs Sam Snead and Ben Hogan. Martin had a smash-hit in the Harry Warren-Jack Brooks song, 'That's Amore'.

▽ 'Tear-jerker' was the dismissive epithet used by most critics in their **Little Boy Lost** reviews. But this was a persuasive exercise in movie sentiment, astutely crafted by director-writer George Seaton from a story by Marghanita Laski, and it opened up an unexpected development in Bing Crosby's career. In his first completely dramatic role Crosby (left) played, very convincingly, an American news reporter who returns to France after the war to find a son he has never seen: the child has disappeared in an air raid, his mother has been killed, and now the father is led to an orphanage where his hopes and doubts are aroused by a likely boy, who, he finally realises, is not his; but he adopts him anyway. Claude Dauphin, Nicole Maurey, Gabrielle Dorziat, Peter Baldwin, Colette Dereal and especially, Christian Fourcade (right) as the boy supported the star with skill. The William Perlberg production, made in France, may not have drawn such crowds as Crosby's musicals did, but it pleased a lot of people.

◁ Excitement and realism as sharp as barbed-wire made Billy Wilder's version of a Broadway theatre hit, **Stalag 17**, one of the year's most potent movies. Wilder's direction, production and (with Edwin Blum) script pointed up the comedy and suspense of the Donald Bevan-Edmund Trzcinski play, set in a German prisoner-of-war camp where a hut's American inmates are dominated by a gambling con-man whom they suspect of tipping off their frustrated escape attempts to the Germans. He proves them wrong by unmasking the real culprit. The effect of action maintained in a restricted, monotonous locale throughout two hours' running time was an achievement of the true film-making art. The acting couldn't have been better, with William Holden (centre right) giving an impeccable performance in the lead, which won him an Oscar. Robert Strauss (left) and Harvey Lembeck amusingly relieved the anxiety-ridden atmosphere at times; Don Taylor, Neville Brand, Richard Erdman (right), Peter Graves and Michael Moore stood out as their fellow prisoners, and co-author Trzcinski had a small part. Otto Preminger was in his element as the camp commandant, and Sig Rumann walked off with several scenes as a pompous but gullible guard.

▽ Once upon a time (in 1945, to be exact) there were three English girls living with their father on a Pacific island. They were lively, pretty, innocent young ladies. Then 1500 United States marines landed. **The Girls Of Pleasure Island**, having established this provocative situation, spent an hour and a half looking for a story worth telling, gave up, and settled for whatever entertainment value there lay in the handsome young people and scenery. Not enough, said moviegoers led by the title to expect a musical or a sexploitation piece. Dorothy Bromiley, Audrey Dalton and Joan Elan were the girls; Don Taylor,

Gene Barry, Peter Baldwin, Philip Ober and Richard Shannon were among the invaders, and Leo Genn (left) and Elsa Lanchester (right) did the best acting. F. Hugh Herbert (not to be confused with comedian Hugh Herbert, who was confused enough) adapted William Maier's original and, with Alvin Ganzer, co-directed Paul Jones's Technicolor production. In the same year Herbert's *The Moon Is Blue* became a hit because calling its heroine 'a virgin', right out loud, created a notorious censorship brouhaha. No such shocking language occurred in this one, nor anything else of much interest.

◁ It was **Thunder In The East** on the billboards but a cold drizzle on the screen, Everett Riskin's production being one of the rare instances of an ambitious, expensive Paramount picture failing to arouse public or critical interest, let alone enthusiasm. Underpopulated audiences sat prostrated with tedium as the cast talked their way through interminable pages of dialogue in a script that eliminated any excitement from Alan Moorehead's novel, *Rage Of The Vulture*. It was about an American adventurer (Alan Ladd) selling war material to a pacifist Indian prince (Charles Boyer) during the newly independent country's upheavals in 1947, and meanwhile falling in love with the blind daughter (Deborah Kerr, left) of a British missionary (Cecil Kellaway, right). The credits bristled with top names, not only in the cast, which also featured Corinne Calvet and John Williams, but in all departments: direction, Charles Vidor; photography, Lee Garmes; screenplay, Jo Swerling; and so on. Their work finished in 1951 and the result was shelved for over a year.

△ Something out of the ordinary in movie biographies arrived with **Houdini**, a 106-minute run-through of the extraordinary life of America's world-famous escape artist. Philip Yordan's screenplay, from a story by Harold Kellock, was about as factually accurate as most biopics, meaning not very, but it entertainingly followed its subject from his conjuring in 1890s fairgrounds to amazing millions by delivering himself from locked chains, handcuffs, straitjackets, sealed chests underwater, etc, until he attempted one stunt too many in 1926. Tony Curtis (left) made a lively Harry Houdini, with likeable support from Janet Leigh (right; then Mrs Curtis) as his wife, Torin Thatcher as his assistant, Angela Clarke, Sig Rumann, Stefan Schnabel, Ian Wolfe, Connie Gilchrist and Michael Pate. George Pal produced, for once without special effects, and George Marshall's direction had good pace except in a few over-extended romantic scenes. Houdini made a couple of early silent features for Paramount but, looking nothing like Curtis, didn't click as a movie star.

▷ **Forever Female** was, believe it or not, a movie version of Sir James Barrie's 40-year-old playlet *Rosalind*, the last of the long shelf of manuscripts he had sold to Paramount, the industry's most assiduous devotee (and most ruthless re-titler) of his works. After it had been tarted up, modernised and expanded by Philip and Julius Epstein, this was not so much Barrie's charming little comedy as an attempt to recapture the campy brilliance of *All About Eve*. Backstage bitchiness abounded as an over-the-hill Broadway star (Ginger Rogers, right) vied with an ambitious ingenue (Patricia Crowley) for the lead in a new play and for its author (William Holden, centre); she lost both, but kept her producer husband (Paul Douglas, left) as her better nature took over. The principals, put through their paces smartly by Irving Rapper, handled their frequently witty lines with skill, and had able support from James Gleason, Marjorie Rambeau, Jesse White, King Donovan, George Reeves and Richard Shannon. Considering its star power and considerable entertainment value, it was strange that the crowds decided to give this production (in the charge of Pat Duggan) the cold shoulder.

OTHER RELEASES OF 1953

Cease Fire
Korean war semi-documentary. Dir: Owen Crump. Pro: Hal B. Wallis. Members of a US infantry company in real-life roles, filmed in Korea.

Flight To Tangier
Joan Fontaine, Jack Palance, Corinne Calvet. Dir: Charles Marquis Warren. Pro: Nat Holt. International spies and fortune hunters search across the North African desert for a crashed plane containing a cargo of gold.

Jamaica Run
Ray Milland, Arlene Dahl, Wendell Corey, Patric Knowles. Dir: Lewis Foster. Pro: William Pine, William Thomas. Clashes among six contenders for a family estate culminate in a murder.

Pony Express
Charlton Heston, Forrest Tucker, Rhonda Fleming, Jan Sterling. Dir: Jerry Hopper. Pro: Nat Holt. Buffalo Bill Cody and Wild Bill Hickok battle against stagecoach station owners and Sioux Indians to establish the pony express.

Those Redheads From Seattle
Rhonda Fleming, Gene Barry, Agnes Moorehead. Dir: Lewis Foster. Pro: William Pine, William Thomas. Woman takes her daughters to Alaska during the gold rush, finds her husband murdered, tracks the killer.

Tropic Zone
Ronald Reagan, Rhonda Fleming, Estelita, Noah Beery Jr. Dir: Lewis Foster. Pro: William Pine, William Thomas. Banana plantation owners struggle against shipping magnates lusting for monopoly.

The Vanquished
John Payne, Jan Sterling. Dir: Edward Ludwig. Pro: William Pine, William Thomas. Southern officer in the Civil War comes homes to investigate civic corruption.

1954

⊲ Producer Paul Jones shot the works in lavish costumes, spectacular sets and luscious Technicolor for **Casanova's Big Night**, but this effort to duplicate Bob Hope's 1946 success, *Monsieur Beaucaire*, failed to come off. As a tailor's assistant masquerading as Casanova, induced by a nobleman to test his fiancee's faithfulness, and becoming enmeshed in Venetian court intrigues, Hope (right) skilfully mixed the moods of great lover and scared rabbit. The climax, a slapstick riot, had him dressed as a dowager while fighting a duel with Basil Rathbone. Too often, though, the pace of Norman Z. McLeod's direction slackened and the inventiveness of the Hal Kanter-Edmund Hartmann script (based on a story by Audrey Wisberg) flagged. The cast ranged from beauty Joan Fontaine (left) to boxing giant Primo Carnera; in between, Audrey Dalton, Frieda Inescort, Hope Emerson, Hugh Marlowe, John Carradine, John Hoyt, Robert Hutton, Arnold Moss, Lon Chaney Jr and Raymond Burr. Box-office returns were healthy, but nowhere near Hope's strongest.

⊲ Title: **Elephant Walk**. Scene: a tea plantation in Ceylon. Cast: the oddball owner of the plantation, his dewy bride from England, the handsome estate manager, guests, servants, natives. Plot: triangle, romance, domestic discord – plus. The plus was a magnificent herd of elephants going spectacularly berserk and making matchsticks of the palatial sets. The customers thoroughly enjoyed this climactic sequence, as well as the game of spotting long-shots of Vivien Leigh, the movie's original star, who suffered one of her emotional breakdowns during the production and had to be replaced. The studio borrowed Elizabeth Taylor (left) from MGM again, so that William Dieterle could re-shoot most of Leigh's scenes and finish the picture, which co-starred her with Peter Finch as the husband and Dana Andrews (right) as the overseer, all three doing their professional best with their stock characters. Abraham Sofaer, Abner Biberman, Noel Drayton, Rosalind Ivan, Philip Tonge and Edward Ashley had other roles in the script John Lee Mahin shaped from Robert Standish's novel for producer Irving Asher. Seen through the Technicolor cameras of Loyal Griggs, Liz and the scenery looked gorgeous.

△ Shirley Booth and Robert Ryan (both illustrated) gave romance a middle-aged glow which, predictably, failed to light up the box-office for **About Mrs Leslie**, but many who saw it remember it with affection. Shirley played a boarding-house keeper whose past is revealed, via flashback, when a millionaire's will makes her a beneficiary: they had enjoyed a blissful backstreet affair. This material was deftly handled by the director of the preceding Booth success, *Come Back, Little Sheba*, Daniel Mann, as well as by Ketti Frings and Hal Kanter, who adapted a story by Vina Delmar. The Hal Wallis production's cast included Alex Nicol, Marjie Ryan, Philip Ober, James Bell and Henry Morgan.

⊲ Remarkably similar to (and in production simultaneously with) *Elephant Walk*, **The Naked Jungle** was also a drama about a bride arriving at a tropical plantation to find conflict with her groom, the plantation's owner, and her marital troubles eventually dwarfed by a natural catastrophe demolishing their mansion. This time the scene was South America, the crop was cocoa instead of tea, and the calamity was caused by smaller but even more frightening invaders than elephants: an army of voracious soldier ants, eating everything and everyone in their path until stopped by a conflagration. This climax packed a thrilling punch, and the preceding reels also held excitement in the full-bloodied performances of Eleanor Parker (left) as the wife refusing to knuckle under and Charlton Heston (right) as the husband who regarded her as a necessary nuisance. Byron Haskin directed them and Abraham Sofaer, William Conrad, Douglas Fowley, Romo Vincent and John Dierkes in the Ranald MacDougall-Philip Yordan screenplay, adapted from Carl Stephenson's story, *Leiningen Versus The Ants*. The producer, as the extraspecial effects might suggest, was George Pal, and it was in eye-catching Technicolor.

▽ Writer-director George Seaton topped all his other achievements with **The Country Girl**, while helping Bing Crosby (centre) to reveal new facets of his acting talent, and guiding Grace Kelly (left) to win, although miscast, the Oscar as the year's best actress. William Holden (right) also brought total conviction to his performance in the least demanding of the three main roles, a stage director who takes a chance on giving a once great star (Crosby) the lead in a new play in spite of his dipsomania. At first he believes the actor's excuse for his drinking bouts – the strain of his unstable wife's dependence on him – but gradually he realises the lush is also a liar, and would collapse without the vigilant support of the wife (Kelly). When the star pulls himself together for an opening night triumph, his wife rejects a romantic approach from the director. The Clifford Odets stage hit (a much more powerful drama than its bland title suggested) had its play-within-a-play changed to a musical so that Crosby could sing a couple of Harold Arlen-Ira Gershwin numbers, but it was his tragic portrait of a weakling that did so much to make the film memorable. Anthony Ross, Gene Reynolds, Jacqueline Fontaine and Robert Kent were also in the William Perlberg production, which won high praise from most reviewers, did good business, and garnered a second Oscar, for Seaton's screenplay.

1954

▷ While it was a somewhat mild and conventional romantic comedy to have come from Billy Wilder, **Sabrina** (GB: **Sabrina Fair**) was nevertheless – or, perhaps, therefore – one of his most popular movies. Samuel Taylor's amusing play, about the stir created in a wealthy household by the arrival of the lovely daughter (Audrey Hepburn, right) of the chauffeur (John Williams), was adapted by director-producer Wilder with Taylor and Ernest Lehman, and with typical injections of astringent wit. There was a lot of fun in the girl's wooing by the family's playboy son (William Holden) and the efforts of his unromantic elder brother (Humphrey Bogart, left) to break up the unsuitable affair; in the process, he too falls in love with, and finally wins, her. Hepburn was a delight but the male stars were less happily cast, Holden a touch too serious and Bogart, making his Paramount debut after 24 film years, downright surly (perhaps because Wilder hated him, and vice-versa). Others on hand were Martha Hyer, Walter Hampden, Marcel Dalio, Joan Vohs, Nella Walker, Ellen Corby and a superstar of the silents, Francis X. Bushman. The picture made most of the critics' best-of-the-year lists, not to mention a handsome profit.

◁ Star comedian Danny Kaye (left) had good luck with **Knock On Wood**. Making his first Paramount appearance after ten years as a major Hollywood name, he played a vaudeville ventriloquist in whose dummy secret papers of international importance have been hidden – only he doesn't know it. Eastern and Western espionage agents made him the bewildered focal point of their activities in a comedy that benefitted from a concentration of creative efforts: writing, directing and producing (in Technicolor) were all done by the team of Norman Panama and Melvin Frank. Kaye moved through the complicated plot with the ease of an electric eel, giving off sparks of zany humour, while Mai Zetterling (right), Torin Thatcher, David Burns, Abner Biberman, Gavin Gordon, Steve Geray, Diana Adams and Leon Askin played more or less straight. Also helpful were a couple of numbers written by Sylvia Fine (Mrs Kaye) and choreographed by Michael Kidd. A special 1954 Oscar was awarded to the star 'for his unique talents, his service to the Academy, the motion picture industry and the American people'. That seemed to cover just about everything.

△ The studio's directorial strength was given a great boost by the arrival of Alfred Hitchcock, whose first of six pictures there (including some of his finest) was **Rear Window**. Hitch loved to handicap himself – as in the isolation of *Lifeboat*, the long takes of *Rope*, etc – and in this movie achieved an astonishing amount of action and suspense with a hero confined by a broken leg to one room. From its window, he, a press photographer, watches the people in opposite windows through a telephoto lens, and sees some strange goings-on, including a murder, whose perpetrator finds him out... The exciting climax came like a slug of brandy after a feast of frissons for voyeurs. James Stewart (left) was excellent as the wheelchaired spy, Grace Kelly (who spent more time at Paramount than at her home studio, MGM) acted as well as she looked in Technicolor as his fiancee (right), Thelma Ritter added her own particular brand of refreshing comedy as his masseuse, and Wendell Corey, Raymond Burr and Judith Evelyn supplied strong support. John Michael Hayes based his ingenious screenplay on a story by Cornell Woolrich. Both artistically and commercially, an outstanding success.

◁ One of the best pictures dealing with the Korean war, **The Bridges At Toko-Ri** scored with the critics and the crowds mainly on its stirring sea and air action, filmed in Technicolor with US Navy co-operation. James Michener's novel, adapted by Valentine Davies, centred on a bomber pilot (William Holden, left) and his crew, part of an aircraft carrier force assigned to destroy vital North Korean bridges, an exploit which costs them their lives. Mark Robson, directing William Perlberg and George Seaton's impressive production, held the gung-ho heroics and flag-waving down to reasonable proportions while concentrating on character interest via some excellent performances by Holden, Grace Kelly in the brief role of his anxious wife, Fredric March as an admiral conscience-stricken about sending men to their death, and Mickey Rooney (right) as a crew member; also Charles McGraw, Earl Holliman, Robert Strauss, Willis Bouchey, Keiko Awaji, and Gene Reynolds.

▷ The biggest hit of the year, **White Christmas** swelled Paramount's bank balance by $12 million from American theatres plus almost as much from the rest of the world. The names and talents of Bing Crosby (right), Danny Kaye (left) and Irving Berlin did the trick. With sparkling assistance from Rosemary Clooney and Vera-Ellen (centre) in the song-and-dance department they made a thoroughly entertaining musical out of a dull, hackneyed story from the usually bright pens of Norman Panama, Melvin Frank and Norman Krasna, indifferently directed by Michael Curtiz, who had just finished 27 years with Warner Bros. Resembling *Holiday Inn* but not as good, it was about a couple of entertainers, who, aided by their sister-act girlfriends, put on a show at a winter resort hotel to make it a success for their old Army officer. With few facilities, they stage numbers elaborate enough to tax the resources of Radio City Music Hall. Robert Emmett Dolan's production in Technicolor, the first movie to be made in VistaVision, the company's answer to CinemaScope, boasted 15 Berlin songs: new hits like 'Count Your Blessings', 'The Best Things Happen When You're Dancing', 'Love, You Didn't Do Right By Me', and 'Sisters', and old ones like 'Blue Skies', 'Heat Wave' and the inevitable title dirge. Also cast: Dean Jagger, Mary Wickes, Sig Rumann and dancer John Brascia.

△ The public wasn't ready for a send-up of musical Westerns, judging by the cool reception it gave **Red Garters**, while a non-satirical example of the genre, *Seven Brides For Seven Brothers* broke records for MGM in the same year. But Paramount, and particularly producer Pat Duggan, director George Marshall and writer Michael Fessier deserved applause for daring to be different. That aim was most strikingly achieved in the deliberately artificial scenery of art directors Hal Pereira and Roland Anderson, the stylised set dressing of Sam Comer and Ray Moyer, and the bold use of Technicolor by them and photographer Arthur Arling. The action went lickety-split, gun-totin' hero Guy Mitchell and saloon gal Rosemary Clooney (centre) sang some mighty purty numbers by Jay Livingston and Ray Evans (no hits, though), and the other lively folks in a town called Paradise Lost were played by Jack Carson (left), Patricia Crowley, Gene Barry, Cass Daley, Reginald Owen, Buddy Ebsen, Joanne Gilbert and Frank Faylen. Not much gallop in the story about a cowboy seeking revenge for his brother's death; it turned horse-opera clichés upside down, but ultimately wore out its own joke.

▷ Say what you like, Jerry Lewis had a vitality and an individual style that made him a consistent box-office attraction for Paramount all the way from 1950 to 1965, applauded by slapstick-loving masses and, latterly, revered by highbrow French critics. Nevertheless, in **Living It Up** his dopey hero with sinus trouble, mistaken for radiation disease as he was ballyhooed into nationwide celebrity, did coarsen the character played so wittily by Carole Lombard in 1937's *Nothing Sacred*, Hollywood's brightest satire on the power of publicity. The Norman Taurog remake, written by Jack Rose and Melville Shavelson, produced by Paul Jones, with Dean Martin as Jerry's doctor, Janet Leigh, Sheree North (his dancing partner here), Edward Arnold, Fred Clark and Sig Rumann, was louder but not funnier. Between the two movies it became a Broadway musical, *Hazel Flagg*, which also fell short of the original.

OTHER RELEASES OF 1954

Alaska Seas
Robert Ryan, Jan Sterling, Brian Keith. Dir: Jerry Hopper. Pro: Mel Epstein. Conflict between fishermen and the salmon cannery. (Remake of *Spawn Of The North*, 1938)

Jivaro (GB **Lost Treasure Of The Amazon**)
Fernando Lamas, Rhonda Fleming, Brian Keith. Dir: Edward Ludwig. Pro: William Pine, William Thomas. The Brazilian jungle and head-hunting Indians hamper three men and a woman searching for gold.

Secret Of The Incas
Charlton Heston, Robert Young, Thomas Mitchell, Nicole Maurey. Dir: Jerry Hopper. Pro: Mel Epstein. Adventurer follows a map to an ancient treasure and finds archaeologists already digging on the site.

Three-Ring Circus
Dean Martin, Jerry Lewis, Joanne Dru, Zsa Zsa Gabor. Dir: Joseph Pevney. Pro: Hal B. Wallis. Army buddies join a circus; Jerry has his troubles as a lion-tamer's assistant; Dean has his with two beautiful girls.

1955

▽ Anna Magnani (right), an international star after many Italian successes, made her American debut in **The Rose Tattoo** and blew up a storm of praise. It was a delayed triumph: Tennessee Williams had written the play for her five years earlier, but, unable to speak English, she was unwilling to tackle the Broadway stage. Now, with a fair grasp of the language and retakes as a safety net, she swung with volcanic emotionalism into the role of a Sicilian dressmaker obsessed by the memory of her late husband and by the purity of her daughter. These were taken care of by, respectively, a muscular truck-driver and an innocent sailor. Producer Hal Wallis, while ensuring that the background of a town on America's Gulf coast was expanded for the screen, played safe by assigning the script and direction to their creators in the theatre, Williams and Daniel Mann. As the stranger recognised by the widow as possessing her husband's rose tattoo (symbolising sexual prowess), Burt Lancaster (left) made a perfect match for his forceful co-star; Marisa Pavan and Ben Cooper gave conviction to their young romance; Jo Van Fleet and Virginia Grey scored as town scandal-mongers. Magnani, cinematographer James Wong Howe, and Hal Pereira and his art department team all won well-deserved Oscars, and the film also achieved nomination in several other Academy categories.

▷ Having wowed Broadway as a musical comedy star (in *Wonderful Town*), Rosalind Russell (centre) thought the time was ripe for a song-and-dance show on film. But **The Girl Rush**, the one she and her producer husband Frederick Brisson chose, was a rather rattle-trap vehicle for an actress with Rolls-Royce style. In Phoebe and Henry Ephron's story she arrives in Las Vegas thinking she has inherited a half ownership of the famous Flamingo hotel-casino, when what her father has actually left her is a tumbledown dump; the rest of the movie's 85 minutes was spent in ironing out misunderstandings, a romance with Flamingo boss Fernando Lamas, and some secondary smooching between Eddie Albert and Gloria de Haven, plus a generous batch of Hugh Martin-Ralph Blane songs, best of which was 'An Occasional Man' put over by the fetching de Haven. Director Robert Pirosh co-scripted with Jerome Davis, and choreographer Robert Alton co-produced with Brisson, featuring James Gleason, Marion Lorne and that gaudy money machine, Las Vegas, which in all its Technicolor and VistaVision glory out-dazzled even Roz. When your background is more exciting than what your cast is doing in front of it, boys, you're in trouble.

△ Hitchcock sprang a surprise – and a disappointment to thriller addicts – by turning to romantic comedy for much of **To Catch A Thief**. Shocks and suspense were held to a minimum as the maestro applied a light, Lubitschian touch to a crime story so mild it could have served as the libretto for a musical. Based on a novel by David Dodge, the John Michael Hayes script was about a notorious cat burglar (Cary Grant, left) who, although now reformed, is the chief suspect when a wave of jewel robberies sweeps Cannes. He tracks down the real thief by using an insurance company's list of potential victims, one of whom has a daughter (Grace Kelly, right) even more attractive than her mother's jewels. The dalliance of ex-thief and rich girl progressed amid splendid backgrounds of the Riviera, a visual treat in Technicolor and VistaVision which alone was worth the price of admission paid by profitable crowds. They were also rewarded by delightful performances from the co-stars, and Jessie Royce Landis as the mother, John Williams as the insurance investigator, Charles Vanel, Brigitte Auber and Jean Martinelli. During production in the south of France, Miss Kelly met Prince Rainier of Monaco. . . . . . but that's another story.

▽ Still in a merry mood after *To Catch A Thief*, Alfred Hitchcock again made comedy the chief ingredient of his second 1955 movie, **The Trouble With Harry**. It was black comedy this time, with a strong dash of the macabre and, as its central figure, a man's corpse discovered deep in the woods of Vermont by various eccentric characters, who bury, disinter, and rebury it. Their activities and motives become progressively funnier – or just bewildering – depending on your mood. There was pleasure for all, though, in the locale of autumnal New England, seen through Robert Burks's wide-screen colour cameras, and in the off-beat performances of Edmund Gwenn (left), John Forsythe, Shirley MacLaine (right), Mildred Natwick and Mildred Dunnock. This was the film debut of MacLaine, who had actually lived the formula fiction of a chorus girl replacing an ailing Broadway star in a performance (of *The Pajama Game*) seen by a Hollywood producer (Hal Wallis) who signed her up. The movie, scripted by John Michael Hayes from a novel by Jack Trevor Story, was a personal favourite of Hitchcock, but that didn't prevent it from becoming one of his few box-office flops.

▽ Dean Martin (left) and Jerry Lewis (right) clowned through another box-office winner in **Artists And Models**, which had nothing to do with Jack Benny's movie of the 1930s; Paramount had a bad habit of putting its pet titles on different stories. This one chronicled the experience of a comic-strip artist and his sleep-talking pal; the former gets his ideas from the latter's dreams, and when these start to include top-secret information (the dreamer is telepathic as well as wacky) the boys are in trouble with East and West agents. Technicolor, VistaVision and several musical numbers dressed up this foolery, which was put over in the style relished by Martin and Lewis's vast public, and the team had exceptionally strong feminine support in Shirley MacLaine (2nd right) displaying her Broadway song-and-dance talents for the first time in her second film), Dorothy Malone (2nd left), Eva Gabor and Anita Ekberg. Also effective under Frank Tashlin's direction were Eddie Mayehoff, Jack Elam and George Winslow. Tashlin, Hal Kanter and Herbert Baker worked the Don McGuire adaptation of a play by Michael Davidson and Norman Lessing into an amusing script for producer Hal B. Wallis, but at 109 minutes the fun ran out before the running-time did.

▽ **The Far Horizons** made an ambitious attempt to depict the historic Lewis and Clark Expedition which, sponsored by the US government, trekked from St Louis to the northwest until it reached the Pacific, having explored regions then (1803–6) unseen by any Americans except the Indians. Unfortunately, the William Pine-William Thomas production was not based on history but on a novel by Della Emmons, adapted by Winston Miller and Edmund North to look like movie fiction, complete with a romance between one of the expedition's leaders and an Indian maiden. Plus factors were a good deal of rugged action and magnificent scenery caught by director Rudolph Mate, formerly an ace cameraman, and cinematographer Daniel Fapp in VistaVision and Technicolor. The strongest paybox assets, though, were Charlton Heston (left) and Fred MacMurray (back at Paramount after eight years), vigorously convincing as Lewis and Clark, and backed by a large and suitably adequate cast including Donna Reed (right), William Demarest, Barbara Hale, Herbert Heyes, Ralph Moody and Argentina Brunetti.

◁ Reviews and audiences response varied from hurrah to ho-hum for **We're No Angels**, with adverse opinions predominant. There was too much pointless dialogue and too little action in Albert Husson's character comedy, which may have played better on the stage than in Ranald MacDougall's screenplay, directed by Michael Curtiz with the pace of a tortoise in winter. However, no movie with a cast containing Humphrey Bogart (left), Peter Ustinov (right), Joan Bennett, Basil Rathbone, Aldo Ray (centre) and Leo G. Carroll could be watched without enjoyment. They brought entertaining teamwork to a story about three soft-boiled villains (Bogart, Ustinov, Ray), escaped from Devil's Island, who are sheltered by a shopkeeper and his wife (Carroll, Bennett) and who repay them by killing their ruthless, property-snatching relative (Rathbone) with a snake. This bit of excitement, alas, occurred off-screen. The family's eviction prevented and a romance of young lovers (nicely played by John Smith and Gloria Talbott) saved, the trio depart, leaving the audience to think that what had sent them to Devil's Island in the first place might have made a better picture.

▽ A familiar thriller situation – criminals on the run forcing a family to make its home a hide-out for them – was still fairly novel when **The Desperate Hours** scored its successes as a book, a play and a movie. And certainly it has never been done better, before or since, than by Joseph Hayes, who wrote all three. William Wyler, producing and directing with his usual meticulous care for detail, maximised the suspense all its characters (and all its audiences) went through when three escaped convicts, two brothers (Humphrey Bogart, right, and Dewey Martin) and a psychotic confederate (Robert Middleton), hold in terror a suburban family (Fredric March left, Martha Scott, Richard Eyer and Mary Murphy) until the police close in on them. It was exceptional among such films in probing behind the surface tension to show unexpected strengths and weaknesses in the people involved. The cast, which also had Arthur Kennedy, Gig Young and Ray Collins, was dominated by superb performances by Bogart, in his next to last role, and especially March, in a marvellous study of a brave man not ashamed to admit fear to his hero-worshipping son, played by the remarkable child actor, Eyer. The father role was originally intended for Spencer Tracy, but neither he nor Bogart would accept second billing.

▽ In **Strategic Air Command**, as in *The Stratton Story* (MGM 1949), James Stewart (right) and June Allyson (left) played a baseball player and his loved one, and as in *The Glenn Miller Story* (Universal, 1954), they had a box-office smash. But what made this the company's biggest money magnet of 1955 was not so much the co-stars' domestic sequences, which in fact were a bit of a drag, but the airborne footage caught by the Technicolor-VistaVision cameras of William Daniels. This was often breathtaking as it depicted Stewart, having given up his baseball career to join the air force, training to fly America's latest atomic bomb-carrying jets. Playing with his usual deceptively unassuming skill, Stewart was surrounded by stalwart performances from Barry Sullivan, Frank Lovejoy, Alex Nicol, Bruce Bennett, Jay C. Flippen, James Bell and James Millican, with director Anthony Mann seeming more at ease with the all-male scenes, while letting the romantic ones become too soft. Samuel Briskin's production of the Beirne Lay Jr-Valentine Davies screenplay from Lay's Oscar-nominated story had spectacular size and scope.

△ Bob Hope (2nd left) dropped most of his trade-marked mugging and wise-cracking for some admirable character acting in **The Seven Little Foys** as the Irish-American entertainer, Eddie Foy. Although in no danger of winning any Oscars, it had a less phoney ring than the average show business biopic, and gave a lot of ticket buyers a good time. Melville Shavelson directed and Jack Rose produced, both collaborating on the screenplay about Foy's eventually successful efforts, after the death of his wife, to form their seven children into a top of the bill vaudeville act. (Two of them later became well known, Bryan as a Hollywood producer, Eddie Jr as a comedian. The latter spoke this film's off-screen narration). It was dressed up with Technicolor, VistaVision and nostalgic musical numbers, the memorable high spot being a song-and-dance sequence with Hope and James Cagney, who made his guest appearance as a favour, without payment, reprising his famous impersonation of George M. Cohan in Warner's *Yankee Doodle Dandy*. Milly Vitale, George Tobias, Angela Clarke and Herbert Heyes supported.

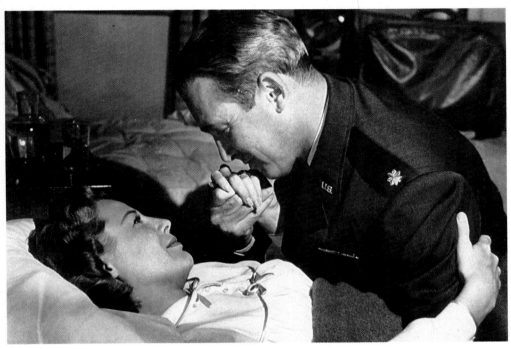

▽ James Cagney (right) never seemed quite right in a Western: the face and movements had a big-city look, there was no trace of a drawl in that rapid-fire whisper, and the figure was not designed by nature to sit tall in the saddle. Still, **Run For Cover** was one of the better sagebrush dramas among the few he made, and he was too good an actor and too strong a personality to be less than riveting, miscast or not. In this, his only full-length role at Paramount in thirty years of stardom, he played an ex-convict so thoroughly reformed that he becomes a sheriff; not so regenerated is his young side-kick (John Derek, left) who gets him involved in a train robbery. Beautiful Swedish actress Viveca Lindfors, also an unusual type for a Western, was the romantic interest, and Ernest Borgnine, Jean Hersholt (in his farewell after four decades on screen), Grant Withers and Jack Lambert made their presence felt. William Pine and William Thomas produced the Winston Miller screenplay in VistaVision and Technicolor. Considering the highly regarded talents utilised – Nicholas Ray was the director, Irving Ravetch and Harriet Frank Jr the authors – its overall effect was surprisingly mild.

▽ Whatever Homer may have left out of his *Odyssey* was added by Ben Hecht, Irwin Shaw, Hugh Gray, Franco Brusati, Ennio de Concini, Ivo Perelli and Mario Camerini for **Ulysses**, produced by Dino De Laurentiis and Carlo Ponti, who didn't mind shelling out the lire for writing talent. Or any other kind: it was a lavish production even by Italian epic standards, spectacular in Technicolor as it kept its audiences agog with a 104-minute rundown on the legendary adventures of the King of Ithaca, taking in encounters with Circe, Cassandra and the Cyclops. Kirk Douglas made a vigorous Ulysses, and Silvana Mangano, Anthony Quinn (illustrated), Rosanna Podesta and Sylvie were among a huge cast directed by Camerini with DeMillean gusto. Harold Rosson's camera work enhanced the eye-filling fantasy.

△ Can a career woman live without love? was the question posed by **Lucy Gallant**. Of course not, said the ladies in the audience, admiring the spirited independence and impeccable coiffure of Jane Wyman (right), but at the same time being thrown into pulsating transports by virile Charlton Heston (left). Male customers, if they stayed awake during the dressmaker-heroine's travails, noted that professional scene-stealers Claire Trevor and Thelma Ritter were in good form. Robert Parrish, last at the studio as a teenage extra in *This Day And Age* (1933), was now in the director's chair and didn't let them pinch too much from the stars, who did well enough with the Winston Miller-John Lee Mahin script (from a novel by Margaret Cousins) in which Wyman rises to a fashion-house fortune and Heston strikes oil in Texas, while their love life runs into trouble. The William Pine-William Thomas production, chic in VistaVision and Technicolor, also cast Wallace Ford, William Demarest, Tom Helmore, Mary Field, Roscoe Ates, and costume designer Edith Head in a rare screen appearance.

OTHER RELEASES OF 1955

Conquest Of Space
Walter Brooke, Eric Fleming, William Hopper. Dir: Byron Haskin. Pro: George Pal. Father and son at loggerheads aboard a space craft on an exploratory mission to Mars.

Hell's Island
John Payne, Mary Murphy, Francis L. Sullivan. Dir: Phil Karlson. Pro: William Pine, William Thomas. Double-crossing and blood-letting ensue when a group of adventurers is lured to a Caribbean island by a priceless ruby.

Mambo
Silvana Mangano, Vittorio Gassman, Shelley Winters. Dir: Robert Rossen. Pro: Carlo Ponti, Dino De Laurentiis. Working girl is launched into fame and fortune by a nobleman who sees her dancing the mambo at a party.

You're Never Too Young
Jerry Lewis, Dean Martin, Diana Lynn, Nina Foch. Dir: Norman Taurog. Pro: Paul Jones. Batty barber, chased from his job by a murderous thief, boards a train disguised as a 12-year-old boy.

1 9 5 6

▽ Wading knee-deep in soap-opera suds, **The Proud And The Profane** never reached its goal of becoming another *From Here To Eternity*, which its mixture of military and romantic elements resembled from time to time. Set in a Pacific island during World War II, it offered William Holden as an ultra-tough Marine officer encountering a war widow who arrives with a Red Cross contingent. Since she was Deborah Kerr (illustrated), the lady was hardly the type to fall straight into his rough arms; she hated him for a reel or two before deciding she loved him, whereupon she got pregnant; his wife conveniently died back home; meanwhile, guns thundered. What all this would have been like without the skill of director-writer George Seaton (working from a novel, *The Magnificent Bastards*, by Lucy Herndon Crockett), producer William Perlberg, and Holden, Kerr, Thelma Ritter, Dewey Martin, William Redfield, Marion Ross, Theodore Newton, Adam Williams, Ross Bagdasarian and Peter Hanson in the cast, one shudders to imagine. As it was, a goodly number of customers were attracted and seemed well satisfied.

▽ Bing Crosby's fabulous career with Paramount ended after 23 years with a remake of his 1936 hit, **Anything Goes**. The first thing to go was the original's story: while still set aboard a luxury liner, the Sidney Sheldon rewrite concerned a couple of Broadway stars looking for a leading lady for their new show. One (Crosby) gets more than interested in a French dancer (Jeanmaire) and promises her the role; meanwhile his partner (Donald O'Connor, left) does exactly the same with an American entertainer (Mitzi Gaynor, right); sorting out the duplicate booking then served to string the movie's musical numbers together. Always one of Cole Porter's best scores, comprising 'All Through The Night', 'You're The Top', 'I Get A Kick Out Of You', 'Blow, Gabriel, Blow', 'Anything Goes', the old songs were joined by 'It's De-Lovely' from Porter's *Red, Hot And Blue* and three excellent new ones by Jimmy Van Heusen and Sammy Cahn. Crosby was in great voice, and Jeanmaire danced an effective dream-ballet choreographed by her husband Roland Petit, but they were outshone by the singing, dancing and youthful zest of O'Connor and Gaynor. Robert Lewis's cast also included Phil Harris, Kurt Kasznar, Walter Sande and Richard Erdman. The Robert Emmett Dolan production was a dazzler in Technicolor and VistaVision.

▷ **Three Violent People** was a Western which, while not coming anywhere near epic or classic stature, at least steered clear of formula. James Edward Grant's script, based on a Leonard Praskins-Barney Slater original, grabbed audience interest from the start, when a rancher (Charlton Heston, left) comes home with a bride (Anne Baxter, right) after the Civil War. He runs into plenty of trouble, both indoors and out, what with the girl causing fraternal rivalry and her honky-tonk past catching up with her, and the carpet-baggers from the north threatening to snatch his land. Gripping stuff, resourcefully handled by director Rudolph Mate and colourfully photographed in VistaVision by Loyal Griggs. Producer Hugh Brown didn't stint on the cast either; supporting Heston and Baxter were Gilbert Roland, Tom Tryon, Forrest Tucker, Bruce Bennett, Elaine Stritch, Barton MacLane, Bobby Blake, Peter Hanson and Robert Arthur. It roped in a good profit.

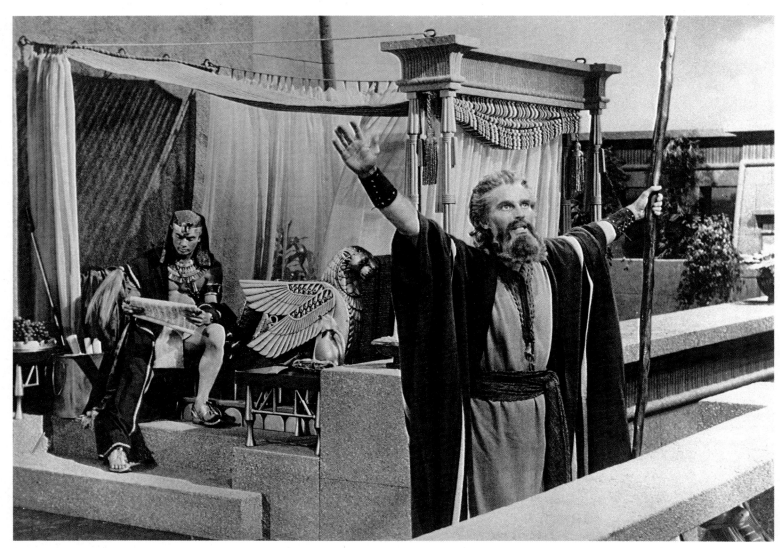

△ Cecil B. DeMille's second crack at **The Ten Commandments** was so festooned with publicity superlatives and money records that its audiences expected to be not so much entertained as stupefied. It was the longest (3 hours, 39 minutes), most expensive (over $13 million) picture in Paramount's history, and it returned more than three times the company's previous record receipts (with DeMille's *Greatest Show On Earth*) to top $80 million world-wide and beat all other pictures except *Gone With The Wind*. Production began in October 1954, when DeMille headed an immense location troupe at Mount Sinai, south of Cairo, where cinematographer Loyal Griggs trained four Technicolor-VistaVision cameras on 12,000 people for the Exodus sequence. Shooting continued into 1955 on 12 sound stages in Paris and 18 in Hollywood, spilling over from Paramount to the RKO studio next door, and in 1956 DeMille's perennial film editor, Anne Bauchens (now 76) completed nine months' work on it. The story of Moses, which in the producer-director's 1923 *Ten Commandments* was little more than a prologue for a modern tale, had been expanded by Aeneas MacKenzie, Jesse Lasky Jr, Jack Garris and Frederic Frank, whose script was 'based on the Holy Scriptures and other ancient and modern writings'. (The credits were as grandiose as everything else.) Charlton Heston (right), unsurpassed among Hollywood actors in giving biblical epics credibility, led the Israelites and a cast including Yul Brynner (left), Anne Baxter, Edward G. Robinson, Yvonne De Carlo, John Derek, Debra Paget, Sir Cedric Hardwicke, Nina Foch, Judith Anderson, Vincent Price, Henry Wilcoxon (also associate producer), Martha Scott, John Carradine, H.B. Warner, Ian Keith, Douglass Dumbrille and John Miljan. The film itself? Undeniably impressive, even though there were moments when the story seemed to be lasting as long as it took Moses to live it.

▽ **The Rainmaker** was written for television by N. Richard Nash, who then extended it into a successful New York play. Following the procedure that worked well for *The Rose Tattoo*, Hal B. Wallis assigned the author to write the screen treatment, and the play's director, Joseph Anthony, to handle the film (later he repeated the job for its Broadway musical version, *110 In The Shade*). Burt Lancaster (centre) blustered convincingly in the title role, an itinerant salesman/conman/he-man whose arrival with claims to being a rainmaker has an impact on a drought-stricken farming community, particularly a spinster (Katharine Hepburn, left) withering on the vine as she keeps house for her father and brothers. Her emotional flowering under the rain of the newcomer's romantic ideas, and her realisation that he is a fake while her family's needs are real, gave Hepburn a chance to show the range of her extraordinary talent. Wendell Corey, Lloyd Bridges (centre left), Earl Holliman (right), Cameron Prud'homme (centre right) and Wallace Ford provided stalwart support. With its abundance of dialogue and limited action, it often smacked of the theatre rather than the cinema, but it was good theatre.

▷ To a year notable for important remakes (*Ten Commandments*, *Anything Goes*) Alfred Hitchcock contributed **The Man Who Knew Too Much**, a new version in Technicolor and VistaVision of the British thriller which in 1934 established his reputation internationally as the master of suspense. Now rewritten by Angus McPhail and Hitch's regular scripter, John Michael Hayes, the story of a couple searching for their child, kidnapped in order to keep their mouths shut about an assassination plot they had stumbled upon, was considerably longer than in the original film; opinions differed on whether it was an improvement. 'The first version was the work of a talented amateur; the second was made by a professional,' said Hitch, never troubled with false modesty. The D.B. Wyndham Lewis-Charles Bennett yarn had all its old thrills (though more widely spaced) including the famous Albert Hall concert climax, and box-office success was ensured by its first-rate co-stars, James Stewart (right) and Doris Day, who were supported by Bernard Miles, Brenda de Banzie, Ralph Truman, Daniel Gelin (left), Mogens Wieth, Alan Mowbray, Hillary Brooke, Richard Wattis, Noel Willman and Carolyn Jones. It's theme song, an insidious waltz called 'Que Sera, Sera (Whatever Will Be, Will Be)' became a best seller, Day's signature tune and an Academy Award winner.

△ In the 26 years since the studio had made **The Vagabond King** as its first all-colour all-talkie, such enormous strides had been made in both Technicolor and sound techniques that the 1956 remake couldn't fail to be better entertainment. As François Villon, the poet of the people in Louis XI's France, and the aristocratic beauty he loved, Oreste (left; shorn of his surname, Kirkop, and touted as a star find) and Kathryn Grayson (right; fresh from her hit in MGM's *Kiss Me Kate*) brought fine voices to Rudolf Friml's score, including 'Only A Rose', 'Song Of The Vagabonds' and 'Some Day', which had stood time's test since 1925, when Justin McCarthy's play *If I Were King* was turned into a Broadway musical. Friml's last work before his death at 92 was composing additional songs (with lyrics by Johnny Burke) for the new screenplay by Ken Englund and Noel Langley, produced by Pat Duggan and directed with a heavy hand by Michael Curtiz. Rita Moreno as a tavern maid and Walter Hampden as the king stood out in a cast with Sir Cedric Hardwicke, Leslie Nielsen, William Prince, Jack Lord, Gavin Gordon and Florence Sundstrom. Both its stars disappeared from the screen after its box-office returns came in. Such an old-fashioned type of operetta was a dead duck to the fifties public, and VistaVision and all the other technical innovations of the modern cinema merely served to make it look embalmed.

▽ Only moviegoers totally allergic to Danny Kaye's style of clowning could resist **The Court Jester**, and the returns indicated that there weren't many of those. Norman Panama and Melvin Frank scored a three-way hit, even bigger than their *Knock On Wood* for Kaye in 1954, with their writing, directing and producing – the latter very lavish in the now *de rigueur* VistaVision and Technicolor. Their story was an uproarious spoof on medieval adventure yarns, taking Danny (centre) through a series of crackpot incidents as one of a Robin Hoodish band who works his way into the English court and becomes jester to the wicked King (Basil Rathbone), whom he then helps to dethrone. Of course he finds time for a bit of romancing, with Glynis Johns (right), and a few songs (by his wife, Sylvia Fine, and Sammy Cahn), but the high spots in a picture with practically no lows were a riotous jousting match and a hilarious gag about the pellet with the poison, the vessel with the pestle and the chalice from the palace. Rathbone was rich in a role he used to play straight in Errol Flynn epics, and Angela Lansbury, Cecil Parker (left), Mildred Natwick, John Carradine, Robert Middleton, Michael Pate, Alan Napier, Edward Ashley, Herbert Rudley and Noel Drayton helped the fun to sparkle.

△ Spencer Tracy (left), aged 56, and Robert Wagner (right), 26, were oddly cast as brothers in **The Mountain**, a tall story about a luxury liner, crashed on an Alp, that Bob wants to loot. Spence wants to stop him. A lot of climbing and snarling ensued. Tracy's first picture as a free-lance after twenty years of MGM stardom was a hard slog for actors and audiences alike. Ranald MacDougall wrote it from a novel by Henri Troyat, and producer-director Edward Dmytryk shot much of it in the French Alps, which looked handsome in VistaVision and Technicolor. Also cast: Claire Trevor, Richard Arlen, E.G. Marshall, William Demarest, Anna Kashfi and Barbara Darrow.

▽ Dean Martin (standing) and Jerry Lewis (crouching) made fun of the classic Western showdown scene in **Pardners**, a burlesque which spared none of the genre's sacred cows or cowboys. Like many of the Martin and Lewis movies of this period, it was a remake – this time of Bing Crosby's 1936 *Rhythm On The Range* – with Dean as a stalwart ranch foreman foiling raiders with the dubious aid of Jerry as a tenderfoot from the East. Some of the gags in Sidney Sheldon's screenplay were threadbare, but the picture roped in plenty of customers. Agnes Moorehead, Lon Chaney Jr, Lori Nelson, Jackie Loughery, Lee Van Cleef, Jack Elam, John Baragrey and Jeff Morrow were others directed by Norman Taurog in the Paul Jones production.

▽ **Hollywood Or Bust** meant bust for Dean Martin and Jerry Lewis. After their seven years on the screen together, Martin departed for a broader range of roles at various studios, while Lewis stayed as Paramount's resident comic for another decade. There was nothing in this picture to suggest any urgent need for their further collaboration. One (Lewis, right) did his squawking insanity act and the other (Martin, centre) his singing romance routine in the same old alternation, applied to a script by Erna Lazarus about a movie-mad nitwit driving across the States to his Mecca (see title) and joined by a gambler who is wont to break into song when they pick up a pretty girl (Patricia Crowley, front) en route. Once in Hollywood, the nitwit meets his dream goddess (Anita Ekberg, left, for whom the title's 'or' should have been changed to 'and') and the 95-minute Technicolor-VistaVision romp ended not a second too soon. Hal B. Wallis's production, directed brightly enough by Frank Tashlin, also cast Maxie Rosenbloom, Willard Waterman, Kathryn Card and Jack McElroy.

△ With **War And Peace** weighing in at only 11 minutes under *The Ten Commandments* the company had both contenders for the super-colossal championship of 1956: in this corner, Tolstoy, trained by King Vidor; in the other, the Bible, under the management of DeMille. The latter was the easy winner on box-office points, but the former's artistic style scored with many observers. Produced by Carlo Ponti and Dino De Laurentiis in Italy for $6 million, about half what it would have cost in Hollywood (but it still had a struggle to earn a profit), Vidor's epic was a praiseworthy attempt to compress the huge novel into three and half hours of film, but it was seriously marred by eccentric casting and an illusion-shattering diversity of English, American and Continental accents. However, the acting of Audrey Hepburn (right) as Natasha, Henry Fonda as Pierre, Mel Ferrer (left) as Prince Andrei and Herbert Lom as Napoleon was often impressive, and even more so were the battle scenes directed by Mario Soldati, while Jack Cardiff's and Aldo Tonti's camera work brought Technicolor and VistaVision to their zenith. John Mills, Vittorio Gassman, Oscar Homolka, Helmut Dantine, Anita Ekberg, Barry Jones, Milly Vitale, Jeremy Brett, Wilfrid Lawson, Tullio Carminati and May Britt ably filled roles in the Vidor-Bridget Boland-Robert Westerby-Mario Camerini-Ennio de Concini-Ivo Perelli script (one occasion when an army of writers didn't lose the war). Spectacular in battle, opulent in peace, this version was to be dwarfed by the 6-hour Russian one of 1968, not least in critics' acclaim.

▽ A controversial best-seller which was published as a factual account, then discredited, **The Search For Bridey Murphy** arrived on screen just ahead of a gaggle of split-personality females (*Three Faces Of Eve*, *Lizzie*, etc) and so had novelty value going for it. Teresa Wright (centre) had an actress's field day as an American housewife thrown by an amateur hypnotist (Louis Hayward, left) into a previous incarnation as an Irish peasant. The material had a built-in fascination and the frantic climax, when the woman cannot be brought back to the present, was carried off in exciting style by the star and director Noel Langley, who also adapted the Morey Bernstein book. Up till then monotony threatened as flashback followed flashback, and the total effect was far from exhilarating. Nancy Gates, Kenneth Tobey, Richard Anderson (right) and Walter Kingsford had subsidiary roles in the Pat Duggan production.

1957

▽ Jerry Lewis (right) was back in that never-failing comedy situation, a screwball recruit coping with army life, in **The Sad Sack**. This was slightly the more successful of his two 1957 movies (*The Delicate Delinquent* was the other) immediately after he and Dean Martin were divorced by mutual consent. Inspired by the title character created by cartoonist George Baker, long a favourite in the funny papers, the Edmund Beloin-Nate Monaster script got the star mixed up with espionage agents and an Arab plot as well as the usual military misfit's disasters, some of which were very funny. The studio gave him a stronger than average supporting cast – Peter Lorre, David Wayne (left), Phyllis Kirk, Shepperd Strudwick, Gene Evans, George Dolenz, Joe Mantell and the luscious Liliane Montevecchi – and a director, George Marshall, who had been delivering money-makers for 40 years. Hal Wallis produced.

▽ Elvis Presley burst upon the Paramount scene with **Loving You**, the first of seven pictures he made for the company over a ten-year period after Hal B. Wallis signed him to a non-exclusive contract. His being discovered and given a contract was what the Hal Kanter-Herbert Baker screenplay was all about: he played a country boy whose singing is heard by publicity woman Lizabeth Scott, wife of bandleader Wendell Corey, and – quick as a flash – he becomes the band's biggest attraction. Elvis (left) had little to do under Kanter's careful direction but to appear ill at ease in his sudden success, and he conveyed this without trying; but when he went into singing action it was like turning on a high-voltage switch. The atmosphere on screen and in the audience fairly crackled and the reason for the Presley furore became clear with his special delivery of seven songs, best of which was the title number by Jerry Lieber and Mike Stoller. Dolores Hart (right; debut), James Gleason, Technicolor and VistaVision were featured in this very profitable movie. It was the star's second, but his film career really took off a few months later with the release of MGM's *Jailhouse Rock*.

△ **Fear Strikes Out** attracted attention as riveting drama about an insecure youth driven to the edge of insanity by the obsessive desire of his father to make him a baseball star. Twenty-four-year-old Anthony Perkins's portrayal of a nervous breakdown victim (right) exteriorised inward turmoil so poignantly that it was almost painful to watch; it established him as an important actor, but at the same time typed him into too many twitchy roles in the following decades. As his father, Karl Malden matched him in controlled intensity, and Norma Moore (left), Perry Wilson and Adam Williams stood out in support. All were directed fluently by Robert Mulligan, noted for his television work and making his big-screen debut with this Ted Berkman-Raphael Blau screenplay, produced by Alan Pakula (another first), later better known as a director. It was a true story – based on Jim Piersall's autobiography – and looked it.

△ Bob Hope (centre) rounded out his 20 years at Paramount with **Beau James** and left the studio. His screen career continued for another 15 years, but they didn't bring him anything better than this biography of the most famous mayor since Dick Whittington – the colorful, hedonistic Jimmy Walker, who reigned over New York in its dizziest days and nights of the twenties. Rarely out of the headlines or the gossip columns, he had a jaunty charm which Hope caught perfectly. The portrait's darker tones, however, betrayed the star's limitations as a dramatic actor. Also, writer-director Melville Shavelson and writer-producer Jack Rose, who based their script on Gene Fowler's book, could have probed Walker's civic corruption and marital infidelity with a more candid camera, and so scored a hit instead of a near-miss. Assets included evocative atmosphere and songs of the period, Alexis Smith, Vera Miles (left), Paul Douglas, Darren McGavin, Walter Catlett, Horace MacMahon, cameos by Jack Benny, Jimmy Durante (right), George Jessel, and narration by Walter Winchell (replaced for Britain by Alastair Cooke).

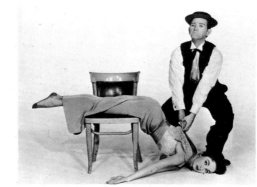

△ As Westerns go, **The Lonely Man** was interesting rather than exciting. It offered two actors specialising in suppressed emotions, Jack Palance and Anthony Perkins, resulting in a contest to out-smoulder each other as father and son. Perkins won by a twitch as the unwelcoming offspring of Palance, a gunfighter who returns home, bent on reformation, 17 years after deserting his family. Henry Levin directed from a Harry Essex-Robert Smith screenplay, and the Pat Duggan production also featured Neville Brand, Robert Middleton, Lee Van Cleef, Elisha Cook Jr and (here with Palance) Elaine Aiken.

▽ The irresistible combination of two such high-powered stars as Burt Lancaster (right) and Kirk Douglas (left) and a title as stimulating as **Gunfight At The O.K. Corral** had all but Western haters lining up at box-offices around the world. And the ticket price brought plenty of excitement. The oft-told tale of intrepid Marshal Wyatt Earp and tubercular gambler Doc Holliday joining forces against the wicked Clanton gang has not oft been told as well as this. Producer Hal Wallis surrounded Lancaster as Earp and Douglas as Holliday (both actors he had helped to

▽ **The Joker Is Wild** took us on another biographical ride on the merry-go-round of showbiz fortunes, this time in the company of comedian Joe E. Lewis, played by Frank Sinatra, here getting a girl rush. A singer who lost his voice when thugs roughed him up, Joe became a night club star as a stand-up comic, then a fall-down drunk. Sinatra's charisma and acting skill sustained the sleazy story, as well as the box-office. Several period songs, plus an Oscar-winning new one, 'All The Way', dotted Oscar Saul's screenplay (from Art Cohn's book), produced and directed by Charles Vidor with a strong supporting cast: Mitzi Gaynor, Jeanne Crain, Eddie Albert, Beverly Garland, Ted de Corsia and Jackie Coogan.

nudge starwards in the 40s) with equally strong talents: John Sturges, who had recently scored with *Bad Day At Black Rock*, directed; best-selling novelist Leon Uris wrote the script; and Oscar-winning Jo Van Fleet was memorable as the woman who had a hard time with Doc. Rhonda Fleming, John Ireland, Earl Holliman, Lyle Bettger, Frank Faylen and Kenneth Tobey were others on hand. The big showdown promised by the title was a lulu, the Clantons needing enough bullets and blood-letting for a small war before they bit the dust – in Technicolor and VistaVision of course.

△ Valentino, Harlow, Crawford, Flynn, Fields, Chaney, Raft, Gable, Lombard... Add Buster Keaton to the list of stars whose movie biographies should never have been made. **The Buster Keaton Story** distorted much of the comedy and tragedy that abounded in his life, and junked true drama to make room for a soapy script about a star shattered by unrequited love for a glamour queen, then deserted by his long-suffering wife. His alcoholism and the early Hollywood atmosphere were handled well enough by Sidney Sheldon who directed and, with Robert Smith, wrote and produced, but the same impassable block that tripped up the other biopics couldn't be avoided: the subject's face and personality were unique, and too familiar for any impersonator to be fully convincing. That aside, Donald O'Connor (illustrated) did a praiseworthy job, especially in the acrobatic gags re-staged by Keaton himself, while Ann Blyth (here being manhandled), Rhonda Fleming, Peter Lorre, Larry Keating, Richard Anderson and Dave Willock supplied lacklustre support.

△ George Cukor, busy at other studios for 19 years, returned to hold Anna Magnani's tempestuous temperament within bounds long enough for her to give another spellbinding performance in **Wild Is The Wind**. This tale of an Italian brought to Nevada as a rancher's bride because she reminded him so much of his late wife, her sister, developed along *They Knew What They Wanted* lines when she had an affair with his adopted son; actually it was derived from a 1946 Italian film, *Furia*, written by Vittorio Novarese and Goffredo Alessandrini. Anthony Quinn as the husband and Anthony Franciosa (here with Magnani) as the lover were towers of strength in a cast including Dolores Hart, Joseph Calleia, Lily Valenti, James Flavin and Joseph Vitale. The VistaVision production of Hal Wallis and Paul Nathan was handsome, and Arnold Schulman's screenplay kept the drama taut – aided histrionically during location filming by the Magnani-Franciosa affair overflowing from fiction into fact. The speedy arrival from Hollywood of Shelley Winters, Franciosa's fiancée, got the picture yards of ticket-selling publicity in the gossip columns, which it was too good to need.

△ After directing **Omar Khayyam**, William Dieterle understandably discontinued his 27-year Hollywood career and returned to Europe. This was hardly material worthy of the prestigious maker of *Pasteur, Zola* and suchlike biopics: often resembling a glorified school pageant photographed in VistaVision and Technicolor, it was well mounted, decently acted and stunningly solemn. Cornel Wilde (centre) played the 11th-century Persian astronomer-poet whose adventures while defending his country and his Shah from the onslaughts of assassins occupied the bulk of Frank Freeman Jr's production. Raymond Massey, Michael Rennie, John Derek, Debra Paget, Sebastian Cabot and Margaret Hayes also enacted Barre Lyndon's script, while Yma Sumac's phenomenal singing suggested that the whole thing would have been better as a musical. But to quote Omar's 'Rubaiyat', ''Tis nothing but a magic shadow show.... Ah, take the cash in hand and waive the rest!'

△ A forerunner of the disaster epics which would batter audiences' sensibilities in the 70s, **Zero Hour!** had an airliner's pilots and some of its passengers floored by food poisoning caused by the in-flight catering (this was the most plausible part of the story), whereupon an ex-airman on board, unnerved by wartime traumas, pulls himself together and the plane to a safe landing. Hall Bartlett's direction cleverly sustained all the tension developed by screenwriters Arthur Hailey, Bartlett and John Champion, who was also the producer. Dana Andrews (right) did a commendable job of conveying fear and suspense, and was well assisted by Linda Darnell (left), so beautiful you didn't worry about her acting; Sterling Hayden, Jerry Paris, Peggy King and Elroy Hirsch were in it too. The storyline, which originated in the acclaimed TV play *Flight Into Danger*, was used again with variations by many scriptwriters (including its author, Hailey) and 23 years later was the acknowledged basis for glorious burlesque in *Airplane!*.

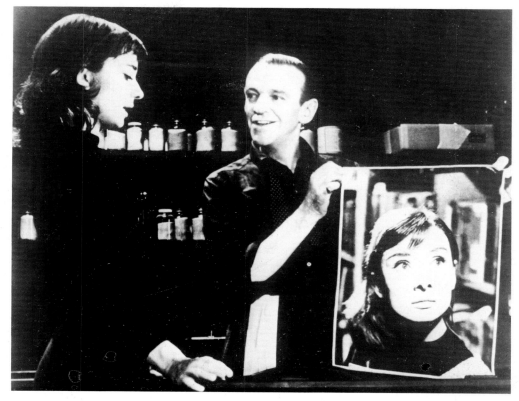

△ **Funny Face** was pure joy from start to finish. Ravishing to the eye, its production design by photographer Richard Avedon and cinematography by Ray June made you glad that Technicolor and Vista-Vision had been invented; while the ear was beguiled by a succession of superb songs. In performances of elegance and wit, Audrey Hepburn (left) played a bookshop salesgirl, Fred Astaire (right) a photographer who sees in her a fresh type for his pictures, and Kay Thompson a magazine editor who flies them to Paris for a whirlwind spree of fashion photos, sightseeing and romance. Astaire and Hepburn shimmered with charm and talent, but the revelation was Thompson, with a presence so magnetic that she even stole a song and dance from Astaire. This was 'Clap Yo' Hands' (from *Oh Kay*) which, like 'How Long Has This Been Going On?' (from *Rosalie*), was added from another Gershwin show to the songs George and Ira wrote – 'Funny Face', 'S'wonderful', 'He Loves And She Loves', 'Let's Kiss And Make Up' – for the 1927–9 stage hit starring ageless Fred and his sister Adele. The original's great 'My One And Only' and silly story were dropped in this Roger Edens production, directed by Stanley Donen, and three new numbers by its author, Leonard Gershe, and Edens were used; their 'Bonjour, Paris' was a knockout. The film was prepared by the Arthur Freed unit at MGM, who sold it to Paramount and sent over the superbly talented team of Edens, Donen, Gershe, June, Thompson, choreographer Eugene Loring and music arrangers Adolph Deutsch and Conrad Salinger to make it. Lucky Paramount!

△ An unpretentious Western, **The Tin Star** was made absorbing by a literate script, sympathetic direction, and vivid character drawing by Henry Fonda (centre) as a former sheriff who becomes a bounty hunter and Anthony Perkins (right) as a green, newly-appointed sheriff whom he teaches how to play the law-and-order game. Director Anthony Mann had a distinctive way with the kind of sagebrusher that went deeper than just surface action to probe into motives and personalities, and this Barney Slater-Joel Kane story offered him ample scope for it. Producers George Seaton and William Perlberg gave it some gilt-edged talents in screenwriter Dudley Nichols, cinematographer Loyal Griggs and no less a music composer than Leonard Bernstein; the supporting roles, too, were in good hands: Neville Brand, John McIntire, Lee Van Cleef, Betsy Palmer, Michael Ray, James Bell, and Peter Baldwin.

OTHER RELEASES OF 1957

The Delicate Delinquent
Jerry Lewis, Martha Hyer, Darren McGiven. Dir: Don McGuire. Pro: Jerry Lewis. Tenement janitor is arrested with slum hoodlums, then a friendly policeman gives him a chance to become a rookie cop.

The Devil's Hairpin
Cornel Wilde, Jean Wallace, Mary Astor. Dir. & Pro: Cornel Wilde. Drama of a champion racing driver's disgrace and downfall, the redemption of his character and his eventual comeback.

Hear Me Good
Hal March, Merry Anders, Joe E. Ross. Dir. & Pro: Don McGuire. Con-man tries to fix a beauty contest and arouses the mobster boy friend of one of the girls.

Mr. Rock And Roll
Alan Freed, Rocky Graziano, Lois O'Brien. Dir: Charles Dubin. Pro: Ralph Serpe, Howard Kreitsek. Ace disc jockey Freed stages a jamboree of real rock stars to make the wild new music respectable in the 50s.

Short Cut To Hell
Robert Ivers, Georgeann Johnson, Murvyn Vye. Dir: James Cagney. Pro: A.C. Lyles. Twisted young killer seeks revenge when he finds the syndicate is double-crossing him. (Remake of *This Gun For Hire*, 1942)

Stowaway Girl (GB Manuela)
Trevor Howard, Elsa Martinelli, Pedro Armendariz. Dir: Guy Hamilton. Pro: Ivan Foxwell. The captain falls for a half-caste beauty smuggled aboard his ship; he is made to regret it. (British)

The Big Money
1958-1984

In his 1958 report to stockholders, president Barney Balaban was able to announce the company's largest annual profit since 1949. At $12.5 million it was well ahead of all rivals' results, and seemed to promise a general upturn in the industry's fortunes, which had been on the downgrade for a dozen years. However, a long time of struggle was to elapse before that promise became a reality. Paramount, along with the others, suffered from a steady decline in theatre attendances through the Sixties, a trend reflected in a decrease in gross income until the middle of the decade, when inflated ticket prices began to mask the erosion.

At that point, upheavals in the top echelon of Paramount executives were reaching a crisis. In 1965 the management, headed by executive vice-president George Weltner who had assumed day-to-day control the year before when Balaban became chairman of the board, was assailed by a dissident group of directors led by Broadway producers Ernest Martin and Cy Feuer and chemicals mogul Herbert Siegel. While this group was making plans for a proxy battle to unseat the management, Gulf & Western Industries made an offer of $83 a share (almost $10 over the market price), which was accepted at the company's annual meeting, and the deal went into effect on 19 October 1966. Thus Paramount became the first major film organisation to be owned by a conglomerate.

Gulf & Western, encompassing financial, manufacturing and mining companies, created a 'Leisure Time' group containing Paramount (most importantly), as well as book publisher Simon & Schuster and New York's Madison Square Garden (both acquired during the Seventies); this formed 14% of the conglomerate which entrepreneur Charles Bluhdorn had founded in 1957. Paramount proved to be a major contributor to the parent's income – especially when the 25-year drift in the film industry's attendance figures

came to an end at last. In 1972 the number of tickets sold in the domestic region (USA and Canada), which had dropped from 4 billion in 1946 to 820 million in 1971, rose to 954 million and thenceforth the annual average approximated 1 billion. Bluhdorn's management made sure that Paramount shared fully in the upturn; he maintained a very active interest in the company even after relinquishing the presidency in 1969 and appointing, successively, Stanley Jaffe, Frank Yablans, David Picker and Michael Eisner, who took up the reins in 1977. In 1974 Bluhdorn also relinquished the chairmanship of the Paramount board to Barry Diller. While on a jet flight from Gulf & Western's properties in the Dominican Republic in February 1983, Charles Bluhdorn suffered a heart attack and died, aged 56. In 1984 his successor as head of Gulf & Western, Martin S. Davis, announced an executive reorganisation: Diller and Eisner resigned; Arthur Barron and Frank Mancuso were promoted to president of the Gulf & Western Entertainment and Communications (formerly 'Leisure Time') Group, and chairman of Paramount, respectively.

Both before and after the take-over by Gulf & Western, Paramount Television was an increasingly vital factor in the organisation's prosperity. The little home screen, villain of the box-office slump, had developed into a hero of the recovery. The company continued to demonstrate the value of the 'if you can't beat 'em, join 'em' theory by creating a vast quantity of material for television, as well as supplying feature films released from 1950 onwards. Para-

left *Charles Bluhdorn, who made Paramount part of his conglomerate, Gulf & Western Industries, in 1966.*
right *After a long Oscar drought, the studio won three major awards for* Hud *at the Academy's 1964 gala.*

left *Zukor (here with Ali MacGraw and Ryan O'Neil on the* Love Story *set in 1970) was entitled Chairman Emeritus from 1964 to 1976, when he died, aged 103.*
right *George Lucas (left) and Steven Spielberg, the teaming that brought* Raiders Of The Lost Ark *(1981) and* Indiana Jones And The Temple Of Doom *(1984) to the screen, personify the big money era – especially in box-office success.*

mount features which had appeared between 1929 and 1949 were sold in 1958 to MCA, the conglomerate which acquired Universal Pictures in 1962; thus the pre-1950 Paramount talkies are now under Universal control.

Another deal involving Paramount and Universal was of far-reaching significance and one of the most important achievements of Bluhdorn's tenure. In 1970 he and Lew Wasserman, the chairman of MCA, agreed on a combined distribution outlet for the two companies in all regions except the domestic. This firm, Cinema International Corporation, was enlarged in 1981 when MGM, which had just taken over United Artists, became a joint owner, with the result that the foreign territories once covered by four separate distribution networks were henceforth served by one, now called United International Pictures.

While obviously making economic sense, this development, together with the steady diminution in the number of theatres operating, would seem to confirm that the movie business was in decline. Financial figures told a different story. In the Sixties, Paramount had only one release (*The Odd Couple*, 1968) reaching $20 million in domestic rentals. In the Seventies there were fifteen ranging from that sum to a phenomenal $96 million (*Grease*, 1978). The latter contributed to the year's domestic rentals total of $290 million, the highest ever scored by any company; and the 1979 world-wide rentals soared to $551 million, another all-time record.

These were numbers that were beyond the dreams of avarice in earlier decades – and they were not simply a result of inflation. The show business bible, *Variety*, published a list of the industry's biggest money-makers, adjusted to allow for year-by-year inflation; though the list was topped by 1939's *Gone With The Wind* (MGM), eight of the first ten were released between 1972 and 1982.

On the Hollywood front, the old-style 'dream factory' system disappeared at Paramount as at the other studios. Gone were the days when you could tell from a picture's star billing which company made it; by 1958 only Jerry Lewis remained from Paramount's formerly well populated roster of big names under exclusive contract. Fewer pictures were being shot at the studio; more were being acquired from outside sources. Although the general average in the Sixties was nothing to be ashamed of, there were few (*Psycho, Breakfast At Tiffany's, Hud, Becket, Seven Days In May,* among others) outstandingly good pictures. And at the end of the

decade the big-money concept flourished as costs escalated alarmingly. $86 million went into the making of five pictures (*Paint Your Wagon, Waterloo, The Molly Maguires, Catch 22* and *Darling Lili*) whose domestic rentals totalled only $33 million.

Fortunately, these expensive losers were balanced by such 1968-70 hits as *True Grit, The Odd Couple*, the Zeffirelli *Romeo And Juliet, Love Story* (a $50 million winner), *Rosemary's Baby* and *Goodbye Columbus*, plus many profitable bread-and-butter releases. In 1972 the studio had a double triumph in *The Godfather*, which brought Paramount its first 'best picture' Academy Award for 20 years – and more dollars (over 86 million of them) than one film had ever delivered to any company.

Two years later the Academy's prize-giving function was something of a Paramount festival, heaping a record 39 nominations on the star-crowned mountain. Virtually all the categories (for each of which five nominations are made) had between one and five Paramount entries, including three for 'best picture': *The Conversation, Chinatown* and *The Godfather Part II* which set a precedent for sequels by winning the top Oscar. The company won an impressive ten awards altogether.

Robert Evans, who had followed Jacob Karp and Martin Rackin (1960-64) and Howard W. Koch (1965-66) as production head, had a lot of good movies to brag about, as did his successors, David Picker (1975-77), Donald Simpson (1978-82) and Jeffrey Katzenberg. Quality remained high from the mid-Seventies onwards, both in the studio's own output and in pictures financed or collaborated on or simply picked up for release. From *Nashville* in 1975 to *Terms Of Endearment* in 1983, memorable releases crowded in: *The Day Of The Locust, Face To Face, Three Days Of The Condor, Days Of Heaven, 1900, Saturday Night Fever, Pretty Baby, Gallipoli, Heaven Can Wait, The Elephant Man, Airplane, Ordinary People,* (the 1980 Oscar winner), *Atlantic City, Reds, Trading Places,* etc. Many of these attracted not only critics' praise but also box-office profits – and none greater than the new champion, *Raiders Of The Lost Ark* (1981) whose world-wide rentals totalled nearly $200 million. This was indeed the big money era.

When the young Adolph Zukor established a new prestige in the art and the business of motion pictures seven decades ago, he made it to last. There are still many chapters and volumes to be written in the Paramount story.

1958

▽ Tom Tryon and Gloria Talbott were the young couple (illustrated) caught in an unusual domestic dilemma in **I Married A Monster From Outer Space**. All those who found the title enticing loved the film, even though the latter didn't exactly deliver what the former promised: the husband is actually being used by outer-spacelings to conquer the world, and after a lot of low-budget science-fiction action both he and it are saved. Producer-director Gene Fowler Jr and author-scripter Louis Vittes made this look better than it sounds, but not much. Ken Lynch, Jean Carson, Valerie Allen, John Eldredge, Maxie Rosenbloom and Alan Dexter were others on view. Made by the director who also gave you the still fondly regarded *I Was A Teenage Werewolf*.

▽ A typical Jerry Lewis farce, noisy and nutty, **Rock-abye Baby** continued the series of his solo starrers that kept critics sharpening their fangs and exhibitors counting their blessings for year after profitable year. This one made Jerry (left) the bachelor fan of movie siren Marilyn Maxwell, who allows him to take care of her triplets while both they and her marriage are kept shrouded in secrecy lest they spoil her glamour-queen image. There were not-so-faint echoes of *The Miracle Of Morgan's Creek*, a much better comedy, in Frank Tashlin's screenplay, produced by Lewis, but Tashlin's direction had snap and he injected a lot of laugh-raising new material into scenes involving the production of a DeMillean religious epic and the operatic rages of Baccaloni (the former Metropolitan star) as the father of Jerry's girlfriend, Connie Stevens (right). Reginald Gardiner, Hans Conreid, Isobel Elsom and Alex Gerry added to the fun. In Technicolor and VistaVision.

△ After a quarter of a century of matinée-idolatry, Clark Gable (right) looked a bit jaded in **Teacher's Pet** as a hardboiled newspaper editor softened by a lady instructor of journalism. He visits her class, stays to study the teacher more closely, and becomes her star pupil. Since she was played by Doris Day (centre) in daisy-bright form and he was no mean comedy actor, the screenplay by Fay and Michael Kanin, short on plot but full of diverting incidents, kept audiences as happy as they were large. Gable was still potent box-office and Day was the most popular female star in the business. William Perlberg's production also cast Gig Young (left) as the teacher's boyfriend, highbrow but lowered by strong drink; Mamie Van Doren, Nick Adams, Jack Albertson, Marion Ross, Peter Baldwin, Florenz Ames and Charles Lane were on hand to support, and George Seaton's direction went with an appropriate swing. The Kanins' script and Young's performance, which almost stole the picture, were nominated for Academy Awards.

△ Lana Turner (centre) interrupted her long Hollywood career to star in a British production, **Another Time, Another Place**, as an American newspaper-woman in London during World War II. There she embarks on an ill-fated love affair with a married man (Sean Connery, right) whose death in action solves their romantic problem but plunges her into a nervous breakdown. (It also removed from the cast its most vital personality, which would develop into full bloom four years later as James Bond.) The remainder of Stanley Mann's script, adapted from a novel by veteran screenwriter Lenore Coffee, dealt slowly and slushily with the press woman's relationships with her lover's widow (Glynis Johns) and her own fiancé (Barry Sullivan). Terence Longdon, Sidney James, Doris Hare, Bill Fraser (left) and an excellent boy actor, Martin Stephens, also performed for Lewis Allen, directing in his native Britain again. The Joseph Kaufman production was staged mostly in a Cornish village. Lana seemed preoccupied through it all, no doubt because she was being harassed by a disreputable lover who had followed her from Hollywood and who, on their return, was stabbed to death by her protective daughter.

▽ In **King Creole**, an Elvis Presley role with more dramatic substance than most inspired surprising glimmers of acting talent in the rock star. The formula of male Cinderella making good was integrated with a sturdy underworld story that would have held up even bereft of an electrifying singer at its centre; with Elvis (illustrated) flashing a viable screen personality that didn't often come through in his movies, and exercising that billion-dollar vocal style at frequent intervals, the Hal Wallis-Paul Nathan production came home a winner. This was the only Presley film directed by Michael Curtiz (his intimidating methods were not relished by the star); a pity, in view of the performance Curtiz extracted from him as the hero in this much-revised – by Herbert Baker and Michael V. Gazzo – version of Harold Robbins's best seller *A Stone For Danny Fisher*. His rise from manual work in a honky-tonk to singing stardom on the main stem of New Orleans was complicated by the machinations of a ruthless boss and his frightened moll, marvellously played by Walter Matthau and Carolyn Jones (illustrated). Dolores Hart as Elvis's true love, Dean Jagger as his abject father, Liliane Montevecchi and Paul Stewart also registered. A few years later, Hart abandoned her leading-lady career to become a nun, Mother Dolores of the Benedictine order.

◁ How to turn a scorching play into a tepid movie was demonstrated by **Desire Under The Elms**. One of the most powerful works of America's great playwright, Eugene O'Neill, it was a sensational 1924 stage hit, bringing acclaim to Walter Huston as a septuagenarian farmer in 1850 New England who makes his family live by the rule 'God is hard'. The emotional explosion that rocks the puritan household, when his young wife and his son mate and she kills their illegitimate baby, is the stuff of tragedy – and of a censorship problem that kept it off the screen for 34 years. Then it was entrusted to Don Hartman, writer of Danny Kaye musicals, to produce; ultra-modern author Irwin Shaw to script, and TV emigré Delbert Mann to direct. Their brief: make it a vehicle for Sophia Loren (illustrated), and never mind about the miscasting. All the styles clashed, O'Neill's stark drama became a turgid triangle story, and Loren's hugely publicised Hollywood debut was a dud. As father and son – here with Loren – Burl Ives (although his key role was subordinated to the star's) and Anthony Perkins (on ground) kept closer to the author's mood; Anne Seymour, Frank Overton, Jean Wills, Roy Fant and Rebecca Welles sufficed in support.

▽ Sophia Loren (left) threw off the dolours of *Desire Under The Elms* for the romantic gaiety of **Houseboat**, the second and one of the best of the movies she made during three Paramount years. Cary Grant (centre) came back to his original studio to co-star as a man trying to be a good father to his three small children after the death of their mother; with the help of a woman who enters their floating home as housekeeper, he wins their love, and hers too. The stars blended beautifully; Harry Guardino (right; outstanding as the houseboat's handyman), Martha Hyer, Eduardo Ciannelli, Murray Hamilton, John Litel, Madge Kennedy, Mary Forbes and Werner Klemperer also showed up well in the Jack Rose production. A highlight of the screenplay (by Rose and director Melville Shavelson) was a scene in which the father talked about life and death to his elder son; Grant did it perfectly. Shavelson's handling of the kids (Paul Peterson, Mimi Gibson, Charles Herbert) was particularly adept throughout. The picture looked good in VistaVision, Technicolor and the box-office reports.

△ **St Louis Blues** had no connection with the 1939 Dorothy Lamour picture of the same title, and not much, either, with the life story of W.C. Handy which it purported to relate. Having begun his long career at the end of the last century as a minstrel show performer, Handy became known as the Father of The Blues; he was the first to set down the folk tunes of the Negro and turn them into a universally popular form of modern music. He composed many of the most familiar blues, wrote several books on the subject, and died world famous. But according to this Robert Smith production, he was a dull character (played stiffly by Nat King Cole, left, one of the finest artists in popular song America ever produced), turned this way and that by romances with two women (Eartha Kitt, centre, and Ruby Dee) and the influence of his Bible-loving, show business-hating father (Juano Hernandez). Allen Reisner's direction did nothing for the actors or for the limp script by Ted Sherdeman and producer Smith. The thing to do was just ignore the narrative interruptions and enjoy the concert of some great black stars: Cole, Kitt, Pearl Bailey, Ella Fitzgerald, Cab Calloway (right) and Mahalia Jackson, among others. 'Beale Street Blues', 'Careless Love', 'Way Down South Where The Blues Began', 'Memphis Blues', 'Morning Star' and of course the title song were sound-track treats.

◁ According to the movies, a favourite Nazi ploy during the war was infiltrating Allied lines with English-speaking German soldiers in American uniforms. **When Hell Broke Loose** was among the films which made use of this gambit, thus giving its otherwise unremarkable drama an exciting lift. The story, by Oscar Brodney (who also co-produced with Sol Dolgin), traced the exploits of a racketeer (Charles Bronson, left) in the US Army who is informed by a friendly fraulein (Violet Rensing, right) of a plot to assassinate General Eisenhower. If it hadn't been for the hoodlum-hero's quick thinking and fast action, Ike could have been killed, we might be heiling Hitler to this very day, and nobody would have seen this far-fetched B picture. Kenneth Crane efficiently directed a cast also containing Richard Jaeckel, Arvid Nelson, Robert Easton, Kathy Carlyle, Ann Wakefield, Dennis McCarthy and Eddie Foy III. This was one of Bronson's first top-billed appearances; he had been around in minor parts for some time as Charles Buchinsky (his real name) and had to wait another ten years for international super-stardom.

▽ Spectacular footage of a blazing oil field and divertingly unfamiliar Venezuelan backgrounds gave value for ticket money in **Maracaibo**, an otherwise unremarkable movie about a fire-fighter, a mute oil tycoon, a good gal and a bad one. Ted Sherdeman's screenplay, based on a novel by Stirling Silliphant, packed a satisfying amount of action into 88 minutes, while leaving room for a romantic triangle well played by Cornel Wilde as the fire-dousing hero, Abbe Lane as his seductive old flame and Jean Wallace (Mrs Wilde, with him here) as her blonde rival. Francis Lederer, Michael Landon, colour and VistaVision were also featured under Wilde's producer-director aegis. This was one of the earliest of his triple-duty enterprises, all of which he filmed in far-flung locations during twenty years.

▽ Many an Alfred Hitchcock buff will tell you that the master's masterpiece is **Vertigo**, which has been dissected and analysed to a fare-thee-well in biographical studies and critics' tomes. It has, however, never been his most popular movie, because of its plot: teasing, often obscure and finally downright incredible. James Stewart (left) played a San Francisco detective hired to shadow a friend's wife (Kim Novak, right) with whom he becomes infatuated; witnessing her apparent suicide throws him into a state of shock, intensified by his morbid fear of high places. Then he begins to catch glimpses of the girl, still alive . . . His nerves, and the audience's, are thoroughly wrung out by the time he realises he has been used in an elaborate stratagem to dispose of the wife. It made little sense, but Hitchcock's treatment of the Samuel Taylor-Alec Coppel script (from a novel by Pierre Boileau and Thomas Narcejac) constantly enthralled, and its fascination was enhanced by Robert Burks's Technicolor-VistaVision photography, Bernard Herrmann's music score, and the acting of Stewart, Novak, Tom Helmore, Lee Patrick, Raymond Bailey, Konstantin Shayne and Ellen Corby.

◁ Mark Damon is seen here giving Connie Stevens the tough-guy treatment in **The Party Crashers**, a drama of teenage violence about a gang who get their kicks by breaking up other people's good times. Things start getting really rough when one of the lads catches his mother in the wrong bedroom and goes berserk. So intolerant, these delinquents. Bobby Driscoll, Frances Farmer (an unsuccessful comeback after 16 tragic years away), Onslow Stevens, Doris Dowling, Gary Gray and Denver Pyle were also in writer-director Bernard Girard's nasty picture, produced by William Alland who had previously plumbed depths and come up with *The Creature From The Black Lagoon*. The new one was the last film of both the ill-fated Miss Farmer and of Driscoll, the once-gorgeous former child star who was found dead in 1968, a drug-addicted vagrant.

▽ An amusing turn-of-the-century romp, **The Matchmaker** earned moviegoers' gratitude by bringing back from Broadway the delightful Shirley Booth (right) in her only comic film role. As the busy-body trying to find a wife for the risibly pompous, very rich owner of a store near New York and finally snaring him for herself, she shared acting honours with Paul Ford as the merchant. A sub-plot concerned his young assistants, who seize the chance for a spree when the older pair go to the big city; they follow them and find romance. Anthony Perkins (background) and Shirley MacLaine (centre) scored here, and there was lively support from Robert Morse, Wallace Ford (left), Rex Evans, Russell Collins, Perry Wilson and Gavin Gordon. The John Michael Hayes script had everybody talking too much (sometimes directly to the audience) and Joseph Anthony's direction needed a faster pace, but in the main it was a happy finale for producer Don Hartman, who died soon after making it. Few stories have had such a complex history; under its present title it had been a 1955 London and New York hit by Thornton Wilder, who had revised his unsuccessful 1938 version of it, *The Merchant Of Yonkers*; this he had based on a century-old Viennese comedy by Johann Nestroy, whose inspiration was the ancient English farce, *A Day Well Spent* by John Oxenford. And in 1964 it became the record-breaking musical *Hello Dolly*, filmed in 1969.

▽ **Hot Spell** reunited producer Hal Wallis, director Daniel Mann and star Shirley Booth (right) in what was virtually a repeat performance of their *Come Back, Little Sheba*. Again a housewife at her wits' end, Booth struggles to keep the domestic reins on a wayward husband while dreaming of happier days in the past, and again she copes with the problems of the household's younger generation. The earlier picture's intensity was missing, though, and this was a box-office failure; the star thenceforth devoted her exceptional talent to the stage and television. The James Poe screenplay, derived from *Next Of Kin*, a play by Lonnie Coleman, had a Deep South town for its setting and a sultry emotionalism for its mood; in short, Tennessee Williams *manqué*. It did offer another good chance for a forceful player, grasped by Anthony Quinn (left) as the macho husband ready to abandon his family for an enticing young girl; and Shirley MacLaine, Earl Holliman, Eileen Heckart, Warren Stevens, Clint Kimbrough, Jody Lawrance, Harlan Warde, and Valerie Allen made their presence felt. MacLaine showed herself ready for stardom, which she promptly got.

△ Sadly, the greatest success of Cecil B. DeMille's career, the 1956 *Ten Commandments*, was followed by a disastrous flop, **The Buccaneer**, and a month after its opening in December 1958 he died, aged 77. He had originally intended it to be a musical version of the swashbuckler he had made twenty years before under the same title, but his creative drive waned like his health; he turned the project over to his son-in-law, Anthony Quinn, to direct, and his protégé, Henry Wilcoxon, to produce ('under the personal supervision of Cecil B. DeMille'). As film-makers the two actors left much to be desired. A straight remake of the original with a new script by Jesse Lasky Jr and Berenice Mosk, it was an unexciting account of the pirate Lafitte coming to the aid of commander Andrew Jackson during the war of 1812, and its public and critical reception was icy, in spite of $5 million worth of VistaVision-Technicolor lavishness and an illustrious cast: Yul Brynner (right) as Lafitte, Charlton Heston as Jackson, Charles Boyer, Claire Bloom (left), Inger Stevens, Henry Hull, Lorne Greene, E.G. Marshall, Robert Warwick, John Hubbard, Douglass Dumbrille, Onslow Stevens, Jack Kruschen, Iris Adrian, Barry Kelley, Woody Strode.

OTHER RELEASES OF 1958

As Young As We Are
Robert Harland, Pippa Scott, Linda Watkins. Dir: Bernard Girard. Pro: William Alland. A romance between a young teacher and a male student develops into a school scandal and the talk of a small town.

The Blob
Steve McQueen, John Benson. Dir: Irvin Yeaworth Jr. Pro: Jack H. Harris. A thing dropped from outer space grows into an all-devouring mass that can't be stopped.

The Colossus Of New York
John Baragrey, Ross Martin, Mala Powers, Otto Kruger. Dir: Eugene Lourie. Pro: William Alland. When a scientist dies, his brain is implanted in an automaton to continue his work, but it runs lethally amok.

Country Music Holiday
Ferlin Husky, Zsa Zsa Gabor, Patty Duke. Dir: Alvin Ganzer. Pro: Ralph Serpe, Howard Kreitsek. Small-town singer takes a shot at big-time TV and learns to survive the hazards of metropolitan show business.

Geisha Boy
Jerry Lewis, Suzanne Pleshette, Marie McDonald, Sessue Hayakawa. Dir: Frank Tashlin. Pro: Jerry Lewis. A ham-handed magician entertaining the troops in Japan and Korea teams up with a little oriental boy.

High Hell
John Derek, Elaine Stewart, Patrick Allen. Dir: Burt Balaban. Pro: Balaban, Arthur Mayer. A thrill-seeking beauty and five gold prospectors are marooned, weather-bound for the winter, in a cabin on the Jungfrau.

The Hot Angel
Edward Kemmer, Jackie Loughery, Lyle Talbot, Mason Alan Dinehart. Dir: Joseph Parker. Pro: Stanley Kallis. On a surveying flight over uranium territory, an aviator is attacked by criminals.

The Space Children
Adam Williams, Michel Ray, Peggy Webber. Dir: Jack Arnold. Pro: William Alland. Children of rocket experts at a West Coast base come under the influence of a thing from outer space, preventing the launch of a huge missile.

The Spanish Affair
Richard Kiley, Carmen Sevilla. Dir: Don Siegel. Pro: Bruce Odlum. Triangle drama of an American architect travelling in Spain, his beautiful interpreter, and her lover who pursues them.

1959

▽ Neither **But Not For Me** nor its star, Clark Gable, was exactly fresh as the morning dew. The story, written 25 years before as a play, *Accent On Youth*, by Samson Raphaelson to great acclaim on Broadway, was a favourite at Paramount, where it was filmed in 1935 under its original title and in 1950 as *Mr Music*. The star was more than twice as old, and nearing the end of one of the most successful careers in Hollywood's history. Fortunately the picture's plot revolved around the hero's ripe age: Gable (left) played a veteran stage producer who takes on a young drama student as his secretary; she adores him; he feels a paternal affection developing into something more, and takes refuge in the sophisticated maturity of an old flame. Carroll Baker (right) was the girl, Lilli Palmer the woman. Attractive and skilful, they contrasted effectively opposite Gable's assured performance, with Lee J. Cobb, Barry Coe, Thomas Gomez, Charles Lane, Wendell Holmes and Tom Duggan in support. The George Seaton-William Perlberg production was screenwritten by John Michael Hayes and directed by Walter Lang.

▷ One of the least likely pairs of lovers in the annals of motion pictures: Sophia Loren and Tab Hunter (both illustrated) in **That Kind Of Woman**. Tab's awe-struck demeanour as he surveyed the superabundant charms of Sophia put one in mind of a hill-climbing novice suddenly finding himself on Mount Vesuvius. Incongruity aside, the wide-eyed Hunter and the volcanic Loren had individual attractiveness, and she was well able to take care of the dramatic demands of Walter Bernstein's script about a sophisticated woman discovering true love with an ingenuous soldier while considering marriage with a millionaire. This sounds exactly like the 1929 Nancy Carroll-Gary Cooper hit, *The Shopworn Angel*, but the credits attribute it to another author, Robert Lowry, and Sidney Lumet's direction put a new polish on shopworn material. George Sanders had the old Paul Lukas role of the girl's rich protector; Jack Warden, Keenan Wynn and Barbara Nichols applied assured comedy technique to the other significant parts. Carlo Ponti and Marcello Girosi co-produced, giving New York exteriors the realism only location shooting can offer; photographer Boris Kaufmann made the most of it. Loren and Ponti, long closely associated, had just married: they could have marked the occasion with a more important picture.

△ Anthony Franciosa (right), alert and sinewy as a greyhound, has always seemed ready to be a winner if given a fat acting part to go for. **Career** unleashed him on his best one since *A Hatful Of Rain*, which had taken him from Broadway to Hollywood in 1957, and he enjoyably sank his teeth into the role of an actor refusing to be discouraged by failure. Much of James Lee's screenplay was related in flashbacks when the actor is on the brink of success at last, and it also provided strong scenes for Shirley MacLaine (left) as Franciosa's alcoholic wife, Dean Martin (top-billed) as a stage director, and Carolyn Jones as a talent agent. They all performed in realistic style under Joseph Anthony's direction, as did supporting players Joan Blackman, Robert Middleton, Donna Douglas and Frank McHugh. The theatre atmosphere, too, came across: you could almost smell the dust and greasepaint. But like Lee's original Broadway play, the Hal Wallis production had only moderate impact at the box-office.

▽ Paramount at last got into the Tarzan act that had been swelling the profits of other companies since 1918, four years after Edgar Rice Burroughs published his first jungle story. **Tarzan's Greatest Adventure**, 25th in the series since the advent of sound, very nearly lived up to its title; diligent Tarzan watchers ranked it higher than all predecessors except MGM's Johnny Weissmuller vine-swingers of the thirties. Gordon Scott (left), who had a pleasing personality to go with his spectacular muscles, played the everlasting hero (for the fourth time) in Berne Giler and John Guillermin's action-loaded script, from an original by Les Crutchfield, in which he overcomes a murderous foe seeking a diamond mine in brightest Africa. Scott had been retained by independent producer Sy Weintraub when the latter took over the Burroughs estate's franchise from veteran Tarzan-filmer Sol Lesser; Weintraub switched the distribution from RKO to Paramount for this and the next one, *Tarzan The Magnificent*. Both were in colour, with exteriors shot in Africa and studio work completed in England. John Guillermin's smoothly directed cast featured Anthony Quayle, Sara Shane (right), Sean Connery, Scilla Gabel and Niall MacGinnis.

▽ No power in heaven or on earth was going to stop jut-jawed sheriff Kirk Douglas (illustrated) from wreaking revenge on the man who raped and murdered his wife – even when he turned out to be the son of his best friend, cattle king Anthony Quinn. **Last Train From Gun Hill** developed this strong basic situation in a steadily accelerating tempo, from a plethora of talk in the early reels to an eruption of action later on and a *High Noon*-like finish. There are few more satisfying cinema experiences than seeing two good actors of high-powered intensity turning it on full blast in conflict, and no pair could do it better than Douglas and Quinn, who had struck sparks off each other before in *Lust For Life*. They brought in the crowds and sent them out satisfied; competent assistance came from Earl Holliman, Carolyn Jones, Brad Dexter, Brian Hutton, Ziva Rodann and Walter Sande. The behind-the-camera credits bulged with grade A names: director John Sturges, producer Hal B. Wallis (in association with Douglas's Bryna Productions), screenwriter James Poe (working from a story by Les Crutchfield), composer Dimitri Tiomkin, and VistaVision-Technicolor photographer Charles Lang Jr.

◁ A strong character study by Van Heflin (right) as Pugachev, who led an 18th-century revolt against Russian serfdom, headed the asset column of **Tempest**. On the debit side were flat dialogue and formula love interest, although the latter was personably conveyed by Geoffrey Horne (centre left) and Silvana Mangano (centre right) in a name-laden cast including Helmut Dantine (left), Oscar Homolka, Agnes Moorehead, Vittorio Gassman, Robert Keith, Finlay Currie, Laurence Naismith, and Viveca Lindfors as the Empress Catherine II, whose throne was almost toppled by the uprising. Directed and, with Louis Peterson, written by Alberto Lattuada from Alexander Pushkin's *The Captain's Daughter*, it was spectacularly produced in Italy, France, Yugoslavia, Technicolor and Technirama by Dino De Laurentiis.

▽ Switching their attention for the first time to a Western, the versatile team of Norman Panama and Melvin Frank made **The Jayhawkers**, which steered clear of the wagonwheel ruts. The title referred to an unlawful band of militants who try to take control of one of the disunited states in the Civil War era, and the story concentrated on one homestead's defiance of the marauders. Although there were gaps in the narrative tension (it looked as if its four credited scripters – Frank, A.I. Bezzerides, Joseph Petracca and Frank Fenton – had contributed separate slabs of screenplay), effective outdoor footage, period atmosphere, and sturdy acting by Jeff Chandler (on floor), Fess Parker (standing), Henry Silva, Nicole Maurey, Herbert Rudley, Leo Gordon and Jimmy Carter (no, not that one) saw it through to popular approval. The Technicolor-VistaVision photography of Loyal Griggs was a decided asset; so was the dramatic score of Jerome Moross. This movie was more Frank than Panama, the former having directed as well as co-produced and co-written it.

◁ On the other hand, **The Trap** (GB: **The Baited Trap**) was more of a Norman Panama project. He directed this tense thriller, collaborated with Richard Alan Simmons on the script and co-produced with Melvin Frank. It was notable for a brace of compelling performances by Richard Widmark (left) and Lee J. Cobb (centre left), both simmering with so much repressed violence that the audience was held on tenterhooks waiting for the lid to blow off. It did so very satisfactorily after a gang leader's escape from the US to Mexico, planned by his lawyer, runs into trouble and they hole up in a small desert community, terrorising its inhabitants. Held to a tight 84-minute running time by Panama and editor Everett Douglas, it had no room for dull spots. Daniel Fapp's Technicolor camera gave the California desert a look of brooding malevolence, and the acting of Earl Holliman (centre right), Tina Louise, Carl Benton Reid, Lorne Greene and Peter Baldwin (right) fitted the mood. A profitable release.

▷ Red Nichols blew up a storm on the soundtrack while Danny Kaye (illustrated), impersonating him on screen, showed what a good straight actor he could be in **The Five Pennies**. This enjoyable biopic of the cornet virtuoso had some icky stretches when Red's young daughter came down with polio and he went into temporary eclipse, but the bulk of it was good fun, smartly directed by Melville Shavelson, who also scripted (with producer Jack Rose) from Robert Smith's original. Jazzmen Louis Armstrong (in tremendous form), Shelly Manne (as drummer Dave Tough), Bobby Troup, Ray Daley (as Glenn Miller), Bob Crosby and Ray Anthony (as Jimmy Dorsey) were cast, together with actors Tuesday Weld, in her first dramatic role at 15, Harry Guardino, and Barbara Bel Geddes, already a stage and screen star for two decades and with TV fame in *Dallas* another 20 years ahead. There were 25 musical numbers, including three by Sylvia Fine, the film's associate producer and Danny's wife. Hoynigen-Huene supervised the splendid colour photography.

△ The Technicolorful sets and costumes of **Li'l Abner** had all the exuberance of a children's bumper crayon book. So had its characters, who had originated in the famous comic strip by Al Capp and who, in 1956, were brought to life by writers Norman Panama and Melvin Frank and set to music by Gene De Paul and Johnny Mercer. Their show, a Broadway smash for 87 weeks, was choreographed by Michael Kidd, whose work was adapted to film by Dee Dee Wood; the other four men worked on the movie version, Panama producing, Frank directing, and the songwriters whipping up a few new ones to augment the show's best. Of the original cast, the aptly named Stubby Kaye (slamming over the audience-rouser, 'Jubilation T. Cornpone'), Peter Palmer (left, a handsome hunk as Abner), Julie Newmar, Carmen Alvarez and Howard St John made the stage-to-screen trip and were joined by Leslie Parrish (right, heroine Daisy Mae), Stella Stevens (as Appassionata von Climax!), Robert Strauss, Alan Carney, Joe E. Marks, Bern Hoffman and Billie Hayes. When not leapin', struttin' and stampin' around in the musical numbers, these inhabitants of Dogpatch were defying the government's decision that their town is America's most expendable spot and therefore ideal for atom-bomb testing. But they are really more interested in Sadie Hawkins Day, when the gals chase the guys and get to keep the ones they catch.

▷ Sophia Loren won the 1958 Venice Film Festival award for best actress with her work in **The Black Orchid**. Apart from that, plaudits (and profits) were sparse for Joseph Stefano's expanded television play, the noisy romance of a widower – well played by Anthony Quinn – and a widow who has her husband's criminal reputation to live down. Their marriage is delayed by the dramatics of their neurotic children, but happy ending time finally rolled around. Ina Balin, Sophia, Mark Richman and Quinn (left to right) were directed by Martin Ritt in the Carlo Ponti-Marcello Girosi production, along with Jimmie Baird, Naomi Stevens, Virginia Vincent, Frank Puglia and Whit Bissell.

OTHER RELEASES OF 1959

Don't Give Up The Ship
Jerry Lewis, Dina Merrill. Dir: Norman Taurog. Pro: Hal B. Wallis. Washington bigwigs want to know what Jerry did with a destroyer escort missing since World War II; he can't remember, sets out to find it.

The Hangman
Robert Taylor, Fess Parker, Tina Louise, Jack Lord. Dir: Michael Curtiz. Pro: Frank Freeman Jr. Rigid lawman learns from a humane sheriff how to temper justice with mercy, helped by a woman they both love.

The Man Who Could Cheat Death
Anton Diffring, Christopher Lee, Hazel Court. Dir: Terence Fisher. Pro: Michael Carreras. Thriller about a man, still youthful at the age of 104, thanks to gland operations, who becomes a murderer. (British; remake of *The Man In Half Moon Street*, 1944)

Thunder In The Sun
Susan Hayward, Jeff Chandler. Dir: Russell Rouse. Pro: Clarence Greene. A wagon-master, and the group of Basque immigrants he is guiding to California in 1847, ambush Indians planning to raid them.

Tokyo After Dark
Richard Long, Michi Kobi. Dir: Norman T. Herman. Pro: Herman, Marvin Segal. American military policeman who has accidentally killed a Japanese boy plans an escape from Tokyo, but decides to face his trial.

The Young Captives
Steven Mario, Luana Patten. Dir: Irvin Kirshner. Pro: Andrew Fenady. Thriller about a homicidal maniac holding as prisoners a young couple eloping to Mexico.

1960

▽ **The Savage Innocents** was an extraordinary film even for the mercurial Nicholas Ray, a cult figure to director buffs, who shot it in Canada, Greenland and England's Pinewood Studios. His screenplay, from a German novel, *Top Of The World* by Hans Reusch, concerned the struggles of an Eskimo family to make frozen ends meet, and the impact of civilisation on their primitive way of life. A slow and cumulatively impressive drama, more compelling visually than in its awkward dialogue, it got a mixed reception: the critics were mostly respectful, the public utterly indifferent. Having been sponsored by Italian, French and British interests, this must be one of the most international movies ever, with an American director-scripter, a German author, an Italian producer (Maleno Malenotti), and a Mexican-Japanese-Irish-Italian-British-Chinese-American cast including Anthony Quinn (illustrated), Yoko Tani, Peter O'Toole (first film), Marie Yang, Carlo Guistini, Lee Montague, Anna May Wong (last film), Marco Guglielmi and Kaida Horiuchi. The splendid snowscapes were photographed by Aldo Tonti in something called Technirama 70.

▽ The good news was Elvis Presley's return from army service. The bad news: **G.I. Blues** wasn't new. Watered down and uncredited, the 1933 Kenyon Nicholson-Charles Robinson play *Sailor Beware* was filmed yet again as the welcome-back movie for the most publicised American soldier since General MacArthur, and the story, about a serviceman breaking down the resistance of a hard-to-get beauty, now showed its age. Paramount had used it for Lew Ayres in *Lady Be Careful* (1936), William Holden in *The Fleet's In* (1942) and Dean Martin in *Sailor Beware* (1951). As before, the hero was egged on by buddies taking bets on his success; this time there was a sub-plot about forming a music group, cueing in a generous batch of Presley songs, the best being 'Wooden Heart', 'Tonight Is So Right For Love' and his classic 'Blue Suede Shoes'. As the niterie dancer who couldn't be had, Juliet Prowse (left) was a knockout, and Elvis (right), looking trim in khaki, short haircut and Technicolor, responded brightly to Norman Taurog, who directed him for the first of nine times. Robert Ivers, Leticia Roman, James Douglas, Sigrid Maier and Arch Johnson were also in Hal Wallis's production, which was scripted by Edmund Beloin and Henry Garson.

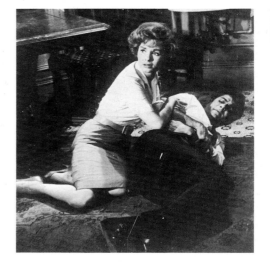

△ Robert Mulligan, who had made such an impressive directorial debut with *Fear Strikes Out* in 1957, returned from television work for his second feature, **The Rat Race**, again a winner but in a lighter vein than the first. Tony Curtis (right) played a jazz musician and Debbie Reynolds (left) a dance-hall girl; both of them are poor in a rich city, but are struggling to rise above the multitudes of other New York success-chasers, and share a flat together – platonically at first. Aside from their developing romance, there was practically no plot in the script Garson Kanin adapted from his own play: a series of incidents and character sketches of Manhattan types kept the movie flowing with so much quirky charm that the lack of solid story went unnoticed. Cameos by Jack Oakie and Kay Medford stood out among those of Don Rickles, Joe Bushkin, Gerry Mulligan, Sam Butera, Marjorie Bennett and Lisa Drake surrounding the excellent co-stars. The William Perlberg-George Seaton production, with its jazzy Elmer Bernstein score and Robert Burks's deft Technicolor camerawork, caught the real big-city atmosphere.

△ War movie watchers, accustomed to a patriotic slant or even outright propaganda, were nonplussed to find that **Under Ten Flags** told its World War II sea story from the German point of view. In the battle of wits between the commander (Van Heflin) of a Nazi raider, disguised as a merchant ship, and a British admiral (Charles Laughton) trying to keep his sea lanes open, the German was presented as the more intelligent and resourceful. Who won the war anyway? muttered some exiting customers. Most of them, though, enjoyed the action and the acting: a star-splashed cast comprised Laughton, Heflin, Mylene Demongeot (left), John Ericson (right), Alex Nicol, Eleanora Rossi-Drago, Cecil Parker, Liam Redmond, Gregoire Aslan, Folco Lulli and Ralph Truman. It was directed in Italy by Duilio Coletti, who collaborated on the adaptation of Admiral Bernhardt Rogge's diaries with Vittoriano Petrilli and Ulrich Mohr, with additional dialogue by William Douglas Home. Dino De Laurentiis produced lavishly, but the big crowds it was aimed at failed to arrive.

△ It was quite a year for Sophia Loren, who had three 1960 releases, thus completing her Paramount contract, made one film in England (*The Millionairess*), and started another in Italy (*Two Women*) which was to win her an Oscar. **Heller In Pink Tights**, the first release, matched its title in oddness. A mixture of soft-centre *bon-bons* making tasty but ultimately unsatisfying entertainment, it combined Western action, backstage comedy, period burlesque and an extraordinary essay in colourful design by the celebrated photographer Hoyningen-Huene, cinematographer Harold Lipstein and art director Gene Allen. They were given their head by director George Cukor in the Carlo Ponti-Marcello Girosi production, which let Loren and Anthony Quinn (both illustrated) loose in the wide open spaces with a barn-storming 1880 theatrical troupe, fending off creditors, sheriffs and Indians. Steve Forrest, Eileen Heckart and three former stars – the amazing child actress Margaret O'Brien, now grown up, and ex-matinée idols Ramon Novarro and Edmund Lowe – were featured in the Dudley Nichols-Walter Bernstein screenplay from a novel by Louis L'Amour, whose books have sold 130 million copies. It was inspired by the legendary career of Adah Isaacs Menken, who enthralled America for years with her equestrienne performance in *Mazeppa* (reproduced in the film) and her off-stage loves.

◁ Clark Gable and Sophia Loren, superstars when that term really meant something, exerted potent magnetism in **It Started In Naples**, both on the screen and at the paybox. Back in her native land after a few disappointing Hollywood years, Loren (illustrated) uncorked her former sparkle, laughing, shouting, singing and dancing through a breezy comedy by Michael Pertwee and Jack Davies, adapted by Melville Shavelson, Jack Rose and Suso Cecchi d'Amico, produced by Rose and directed by Shavelson. (Oddly enough, Rose and Shavelson took over from the Italian producers she had in Hollywood, Ponti and Girosi.) The story, never more than an excuse for displaying the stars' personalities, presented Gable as an American in Naples to settle the custody of his 10-year-old nephew, who wants to go to the States with him; the boy's aunt is determined to keep him in Italy; under the southern sun, conflict between aunt and uncle melts into, who'd have guessed it, love. US cameraman Robert Surtees caught some gorgeous Naples and Capri scenery in Technicolor and Vista-Vision, but most of the technicians and cast (Vittorio de Sica, Marietto, Paolo Carlini, Claudio Ermelli, Giovanni Filidoro) were working on home ground. Gable's death occurred three months after the movie's August 1960 release.

◁ 'Psycho Socko' was the headline studding Variety's pages of box-office reports when Alfred Hitchcock's most outrageous shocker broke out. For, although many of the critics were strangely cool, the public took to Psycho immediately and shot it up to the fifth biggest American gross (over $11 million) Paramount had ever reaped. Critical reassessment since then has placed it high in the Hitchcock canon, recognising the sheer technical brilliance that unnerved audiences pleasurably and made them believe a totally incredible story about a motel owner (Anthony Perkins, illustrated) switching identities with his dead mother and murdering a guest (Janet Leigh) who was absconding with her firm's money. Scenes of the ferocious stabbing in a shower – said by some to have been devised by Saul Bass, not Hitch – and the later killing of an investigator (Martin Balsam) are still regarded as classics in the genre. John Gavin, Vera Miles, John McIntire, Frank Albertson, Simon Oakland, Pat Hitchcock, Vaughn Taylor and Lurene Tuttle were also in the screenplay Joseph Stefano wrote from a story by Robert Bloch, and Bernard Herrmann's music score was a thriller in itself. 'No admission after the film has started' was a clever advertising gimmick that paid off. Three years after Hitchcock's death in 1980, Universal made a sequel, Pyscho II, again with Perkins and Miles.

△ Long before his involvement with orientals in TV's seemingly endless Hawaii Five-O, Jack Lord starred in an odd never-the-twain-shall-meet drama called Walk Like A Dragon. Here enjoying a cockroach race with Lilyan Chauvin, he was a cowboy visiting San Francisco, where he rescued a Chinese girl (Nobu McCarthy) from slavery, and took her back home to a frosty reception from his folks. Director, producer and (with Daniel Mainwaring) writer James Clavell set his unlikely goings-on in the 1870s, which didn't make any of it likelier, least of all Mel Torme as a gunslinger given to quoting the Bible and singing the title song. James Shigeta, Josephine Hutchinson, Michael Pate, Benson Fong and Donald Barry were in it too.

▽ The red light district of Hong Kong was The World Of Suzie Wong. Plying her trade in the oldest profession, Suzie nevertheless exuded more sweetness and light than any ingenue since Mary Miles Minter as she accepted William Holden's offer of a job as his model. An expatriate architect-turned-artist while sampling oriental fleshpots, Holden (left) promptly falls in love with the girl, disregarding taboos of race and class, not to mention the dismay of his friends. Despite the John Patrick screenplay's shortcomings – much too long at 129 minutes, incredible heroine, stilted dialogue – compounded by Richard Quine's slow direction, the movie was a box-office hit. Something about the East-West romance caught mass interest, just as it had as a play (by Paul Osborn) and novel (by Richard Mason). As Suzie, Hong Kong-born Nancy Kwan (right) became an international star; the rest of the principals were British: the delectable Sylvia Syms, Michael Wilding, Laurence Naismith, Bernard Cribbins, Lionel Blair. Ray Stark produced, in London and Hong Kong, the latter's special atmosphere coming vividly through Geoffrey Unsworth's Technicolor cameras.

◁ Somebody (producer Hal Wallis? Jerry Lewis himself?) had the eccentric idea of injecting Jerry Lewis slapstick into Gore Vidal's play Visit To A Small Planet and thereby giving the subject a transfusion of box-office zest. The operation was cleverly performed, but the patient died. Most of the satirical points Vidal made in the successful Broadway stage version were blunted in the screenplay by Edmund Beloin and Henry Garson, and overwhelmed by the star's noisy cut-ups as a cute creature (upside down here) from outer space observing the strange ways of the inhabitants of this small planet. It became just another Lewis movie, a treat for his fans, only fitfully amusing for non-believers. Needless to say, the galactic explorer fell in love: the lucky girl was Joan Blackman, heading a talented supporting cast including Fred Clark (right), Lee Patrick (left), Earl Holliman, John Williams, Ellen Corby, Gale Gordon, and Jerome Cowan. Norman Taurog directed.

△ Sophia Loren's last picture under her Paramount contract, A Breath Of Scandal, made both star and company glad to say goodbye. An ill-advised attempt at high-style romantic comedy, it suited neither the glamorous Italian Loren nor the veteran Austrian director Michael Curtiz, who in his seventies had lost his creative verve. Elaborately produced in Italy and Austria by Carlo Ponti and Marcello Girosi, the story concerned a princess whose father disagrees with her mother's plan to marry her off to a prince, and encourages her romance with a visiting American mining engineer, while Franz Joseph's court buzzes with gossip. Loren and John Gavin looked splendid in Technicolor but seemed to be acting by numbers; Maurice Chevalier, back at Paramount after 27 years, was the father and, with Angela Lansbury and Isabel Jeans, was much more in the right style; Tullio Carminati, Milly Vitale, Roberto Risso and Carlo Hintermann supported. Originally a minor Ferenc Molnar comedy staged on Broadway as Olympia in 1928, it was filmed a year later as John Gilbert's disastrous first talkie, His Glorious Night; undeterred, MGM had an adaptation written by Sidney Howard in 1938, and twenty years later sold it to Ponti, who got Walter Bernstein to do this script. Why any of them bothered remains moot. Illustrated left to right: Carminati, Lansbury, Jeans, Loren, Chevalier.

OTHER RELEASES OF 1960

The Bellboy
Jerry Lewis, Alex Gerry. Dir. & Pro: Jerry Lewis. Plotless series of gags about a bungling bellboy creating havoc in a Miami luxury hotel.

The Big Night
Randy Sparks, Venetia Stevenson, Dick Foran. Dir: Sidney Salkow. Pro: Vern Alves. Poor boy thinks fate has smiled on him when he finds a briefcase containing $200,000; but a thief and a crooked cop will kill to get hold of it.

The Boy Who Stole A Million
Maurice Reyna, Vergilio Textara, Marianne Benet. Dir: Charles Crichton. Pro: George H. Brown. Errand boy in a Valencia bank 'borrows' a million pesetas to help his father out; hectic chase follows. (British)

Chance Meeting (GB Blind Date)
Hardy Kruger, Micheline Presle, Stanley Baker. Dir: Joseph Losey. Pro: David Deutsch. The mistress of a Dutch artist in London is murdered; he is exonerated by a chance airport encounter. (British)

Cinderfella
Jerry Lewis, Ed Wynn, Judith Anderson, Anna Maria Alberghetti. Dir: Frank Tashlin. Pro: Jerry Lewis. Musical fantasy tailored from the fairy tale to suit the comedian.

Circus Stars
Documentary of Moscow Circus School. Dir: L. Kristy. (Russian)

Conspiracy Of Hearts
Lilli Palmer, Sylvia Syms, Yvonne Mitchell. Dir: Ralph Thomas. Pro: Betty E. Box. Jewish children are helped by a group of nuns to escape from a Nazi camp in Northern Italy. (British)

Five Branded Women
Van Heflin, Silvana Mangano, Vera Miles, Jeanne Moreau, Barbara Bel Geddes. Dir: Martin Ritt. Pro: Dino De Laurentiis. Disgraced for consorting with German troops, Yugoslavian girls become loyal underground fighters.

In The Wake Of A Stranger
Tony Wright, Shirley Eaton. Dir: David Eady. Pro: John Penington. Seaman, accused of murder after recovering from a drunken spree, gets deeper into trouble when seeking help from the real killers. (British)

Jack The Ripper
Lee Patterson, Eddie Byrne, Betty McDowall. Dir. & Pro: Robert Baker, Monty Berman. A mad surgeon is identified as the dreaded murderer of women in Victorian London. (British)

Prisoner Of The Volga
John Derek, Elsa Martinelli, Dawn Addams. Dir: Victor Tourjansky. A soldier survives dangerous hazards in his quest for revenge on the general who seduced his wife. (Italian/French)

Tarzan The Magnificent
Gordon Scott, Betta St John, John Carradine. Dir: Robert Day. Pro: Sy Weintraub. The jungle hero captures a policeman who has killed; then has to contend with the cop's vengeful family.

A Touch Of Larceny
James Mason, George Sanders, Vera Miles. Dir: Guy Hamilton. Pro: Ivan Foxwell. Admiralty man concocts a hoax disappearance, seeming to be a spy, in order to sue reporting newspapers for libel. (British)

1961

▽ The most interesting element in **Man-Trap** for film buffs was its director, Edmond O'Brien. The veteran actor, who had co-directed a picture (*Shield For Murder*, United Artists) seven years before, now took on the job single-handed, and co-produced (with Stanley Frazen) as well. He displayed a brisk narrative style and an ability to get strong performances from his featured players – Jeffrey Hunter, David Janssen (left), Stella Stevens (right) and Hugh Sanders – although their combined efforts added up to routine melodrama of the kind that keeps television screens alight between commercials. Hunter, who had just finished the title role in *King Of Kings* and seemed glad to switch from holier-than-thou to nerve-wracked, was impressive as a law-abiding man led by his ex-marine buddy (Janssen) to recover $3.5 million from a Central American syndicate; this ends in disaster, especially for his wife (Stevens), whose alcoholic nymphomania has marked her as a cert for sudden death right from reel one. The screenplay, written by Ed Waters from John D. MacDonald's novel *Taint Of The Tiger*, had nothing to do with Clara Bow's silent hit, *Mantrap*. Paramount just liked the title.

△ It was a case of third time not so lucky for Shirley MacLaine (left) when she made **All In A Night's Work** just after scoring resounding hits in two other sex-and-business comedies, *Ask Any Girl* and *The Apartment*. The new one missed the light touch of the first and the cynical *brio* of the second, but those comparisons aside, it was a pretty enjoyable way to spend an hour and a half with some amusing people: MacLaine, Dean Martin (centre), Cliff Robertson, Charles Ruggles (still chirpy at 75), Norma Crane, Jerome Cowan, Gale Gordon (right), Jack Weston.

The story concocted by Sidney Sheldon, Edmund Beloin and Maurice Richlin hinged on the questions: Is Shirley the secret mistress of publishing tycoon Ruggles? Will she blackmail his family, threatening scandal when he dies? Can his nephew and heir to his vast company (Martin) keep from falling in love with her? The answers were in the negative, while the box-office response was on the positive side. Joseph Anthony directed for producer Hal B. Wallis, who gave it Technicolor and a bright background score by future classical conductor Andre Previn.

△ An enterprise of monumental triviality when considered simply as a picture, Jack Sher's **Love In A Goldfish Bowl** took on a marginal historical significance when it was followed by a flood of similar films: it had been a forerunner of that phenomenon of the sixties, the beach-party movie. Girls in bikinis, muscular youths, surfboards, campfire roasts, ball games, love games, rock-and-roll . . . the mixture drew teenagers by the million, and sometimes was put over with enough verve to entertain people who had tottered past the twenty mark. This one only hinted at the delights in store, mostly confining itself to parties in a beach house, and the rivalry between two young men (played by singing pop-idols Tommy Sands, centre, and Fabian, left) for cute little Toby Michaels (right), while parents disapprove and try vainly to dampen the sparks of flaming youth. The Martin Jurow-Richard Shepherd production in Technicolor was written and directed by Sher, with Jan Sterling, Edward Andrews, John McGiver and Elizabeth MacRae in the cast.

▷ Although he would remain prominent on television and stage, and in charitable activities, Danny Kaye's screen career was tapering off after 17 dazzling years when he made **On The Double**. This 1961 movie was nowhere near his best, its promising plot situation having been developed with more care than flair by director Melville Shavelson and producer Jack Rose, who collaborated on the script. Like Kaye's *On The Riviera* a decade earlier, it revolved around the exact duplication in appearance of two unrelated men, a coincidence tough for audiences to swallow unless it's put over with more dash than it was given here. Still, Kaye (seen here in both roles) put up a good entertaining show as a GI, in London during World War II, who is the image of a British general and is used as his double for espionage work. Romance with Dana Wynter relieves his danger-ridden exploits against nasty Nazis, one of which involves his impersonating Marlene Dietrich. Assistant laugh-raisers included Diana Dors, Margaret Rutherford, Wilfrid Hyde White (right), Alan Cuthbertson and Jesse White. The handsome camerawork by Harry Stradling and Geoffrey Unsworth was in Technicolor and Panavision; VistaVision was being phased out.

▽ **Blue Hawaii** was utter bliss for Elvis Presley fans. It had El in uniform, El in swimsuit, El in love, El singing more songs than in any previous El film: fourteen. A slender story about a soldier returning home to Honolulu, where he insists on working as a tourist guide rather than in his father's pineapple company, now and then interrupted his singing. Otherwise the picture was chiefly notable for the one and only bad performance in Angela Lansbury's long and varied career: as the hero's addle-pated mother, she overacted quite alarmingly. Joan Blackman (with Elvis here) listened prettily as his girl, Roland Winters harrumphed adequately as his father; Nancy Walters, John Archer, Howard McNear, Gregory Gaye and Iris Adrian also performed for director Norman Taurog in Hal Wallis's production. Hal Kanter's script came from a story by Allan Weiss, and the title song from Bing Crosby's 1937 *Waikiki Wedding*; other songs wafting through the Technicolored palm trees included 'Beach Boy Blues', 'Hawaiian Sunset', 'Moonlight Swim' and 'I Can't Help Falling In Love'.

◁ Various critics found various faults in it, but **Breakfast At Tiffany's** had undeniable charm, personified by Audrey Hepburn (illustrated) as an impulsive minx who might have become sick-making in a less talented actress's hands. She was nominated for an Oscar, and her song 'Moon River' won statuettes for Henry Mancini and Johnny Mercer. The script by George Axelrod omitted some of the characters in Truman Capote's novella about a call girl and a writer in a Manhattan rooming house, and added one, a rich patroness (Patricia Neal) for the writer (George Peppard). The casting ranged from excellent (the heroine's cat, named Cat) to bizarre (Mickey Rooney as a Japanese photographer) and included Buddy Ebsen, Martin Balsam and John McGiver. Director Blake Edwards gave the Richard Shepherd-Martin Jurow production a modern fairytale glamour which made it hugely popular.

△ **The Pleasure Of His Company** was an anachronism in the swinging sixties. But a treat for moviegoers nostalgic for the days when talkies were young, stage plays were filmed as is, and you could hardly hear the dialogue above the rattle of cocktail shakers and teacups. The light, mild, conversational comedy Samuel Taylor and Cornelia Otis Skinner wrote for the theatre broke no Broadway or West End records but is still a favourite with rep and amateur troupes, and it made a pleasant 114 minutes in the cinema with its frequently witty dialogue and a cast loaded with charm. In only the second non-musical appearance (first: *On The Beach*, 1959) in his 55 years on stage and screen, Fred Astaire (2nd right) proved what we'd known all along, that he was a fine actor as well as the supreme song-and-dance man. He played a profligate who pops up after long absence to attend the wedding of his daughter (Debbie Reynolds, 2nd left), to her delight but to the consternation of his ex-wife (Lilli Palmer, centre) and her new husband (Gary Merrill, right). The bewilderment of bridegroom Tab Hunter (left) and the wry comments of Charlie Ruggles added to the fun in Taylor's straight adaptation of his play, elegantly produced in Technicolor by the William Perlberg and George Seaton partnership, and directed by Seaton.

△ When Marlon Brando directed **One-Eyed Jacks** (he's illustrated here doing so), the only picture he made for his own company, Pennebaker Productions, he experienced a rush of Von Stroheim to the head. Not even the spendthrift Erich (see *The Wedding March*, 1928) had driven Paramount executives closer to nervous prostration than Marlon, who stretched a $1.8 million budget to $6 million, a six-week production schedule to six months, and exposed more than a million feet of film, the all-time record. His final cut ran 4 hours 42 minutes, which was re-edited to exactly one-half by the studio. Although differing considerably from Brando's intention, the outcome was an absorbing Western, giving evidence of meticulous direction (the originally assigned Stanley Kubrick might have given it brisker pace), splendidly shot in Technicolor and VistaVision by Charles Lang Jr, and impressively acted in method style by Brando and Karl Malden, with Pina Pellicer, Katy Jurado, Ben Johnson, Slim Pickens, Timothy Carey, Elisha Cook Jr, Sam Gilman and Larry Duran. The Guy Trosper-Calder Willingham script, from a novel by Charles Neider, followed Brando's quest for revenge on his fellow outlaw, Malden, who has double-crossed him, leaving him to pay for their crimes, and has become an apparently respectable sheriff by the time Brando tracks him down for a violent climax. Frank P. Rosenberg produced.

▽ Metropolitan Opera star Helen Traubel (right) made one of her rare screen appearances in **The Ladies' Man** as the proprietress of a Hollywood hotel for girls, where in a rash moment she employed Jerry Lewis (left) as houseboy. He was a woman-hating bachelor, and bubble-brained to boot, but one of the girls (Pat Stanley) managed to love him, and he stumbled through various accidents to a happy ending. Lewis produced, directed and, with Bill Richmond, wrote the screenplay, some of it funny, some not. Stars of yesteryear – George Raft, Gloria Jean, Harry James and His Band – made brief but diverting appearances. It was Paramount's third otherwise unrelated movie with the same title.

OTHER RELEASES OF 1961

Blood And Roses
Mel Ferrer, Elsa Martinelli, Annette Stroyberg. Dir: Roger Vadim. Pro: Raymond Eger. In a modern Roman family with a history of vampirism, a girl becomes possessed by bloodlust. (French/Italian)

Blueprint For Robbery
Jay Barney, J. Pat O'Malley. Dir: Jerry Hopper. Pro: Bryan Foy. Gang plans and executes an $8,000,000 armoured truck robbery; three years later they fall out over the share-out.

Foxhole In Cairo
James Robertson Justice, Albert Lieven, Peter Van Eyck. Dir: John Moxey. Pro: Steven Pallos, Donald Taylor. Spy versus counterspy in North Africa, where a Nazi agent is fed false information by the British. (British)

Hey, Let's Twist
Joey Dee & The Starliters, Jo Ann Campbell, Kay Armen. Dir: Greg Garrison. Pro: Harry Romm. Musical showing how the twist developed into America's biggest dance craze since the Charleston.

1962

▽ A three-tiered Viennese pastry called *Sissi*, comprising three feature films produced in Austria, enjoyed enormous popularity in German-speaking countries during the late fifties. **Forever My Love** was the result of a scissors-and-paste job bringing them down to a single 147-minute picture for Paramount release in 1962, by which time its two young actors, Romy Schneider and Karl Boehm (together here), had become internationally known. Not as scrappy as might be feared after such treatment, the episodic story followed the 19th-century romance of Princess Elizabeth of Bavaria, who fascinates Franz Joseph of Austria when he is supposed to marry her sister. She becomes his Empress, much admired by their people for her beauty and charm, but less popular with the court because of her disregard for protocol, a passing romance with a count, and her frequent trips abroad with the Emperor, who loves her to the end. Most of the actual sorrows in their lives were omitted and too much romantic goo left in; still, it was a pretty movie to look at in Bruno Mondi's colour photography, well produced and directed by Ernst Marischka, who also wrote it (the story was previously staged as a Fritz Kreisler operetta 'Sissi', which was adapted for a 1936 Columbia film, *The King Steps Out*, directed by Von Sternberg). Magda Schneider, Romy's mother, played just that in a cast including Vilma Degischer, Gunter Knuth, Josef Meinrad and Uta Franz.

△ The characters in **The Counterfeit Traitor** were not the usual puppets of espionage fiction. Director and screenplay writer George Seaton had ways of making them talk – convincingly. You could believe in William Holden (right) as a Swedish-American businessman bluffing his way through the secret service networks of World War II Europe after he has been induced by the British to pose as a Nazi sympathiser. At the head of an interesting polyglot cast (Lilli Palmer, Hugh Griffith, Ernst Schroder, Eva Dahlbeck, Klaus Kinsky, Werner Peters, Stefan Schnabel,

Ulf Palme, Phil Brown, Erica Beer), Holden's performance was strong throughout, and particularly in a scene behind bars from which he watches the confederate he loves facing a firing squad. William Perlberg's Technicolor production gained from authenticity of story and backgrounds: based on a book by Alexander Klein recounting the true exploits of a Swedish agent, it was filmed on locations in Berlin, Hamburg, Copenhagen and Stockholm. It drew respectable business but, like other serious spy movies, couldn't compete with the flashy James Bond variety.

◁ Best known for his successful Bob Hope and Danny Kaye comedies, Melville Shavelson got Charlton Heston, of all people, to lead the frantic fun in **The Pigeon That Took Rome**. Italian shouting and American wisecracking assailed the ear throughout as Donald Downes's story, scripted, produced and directed by Shavelson, unfolded the tale of two US Army men who were smuggled into occupied Rome in 1944 to send back Nazi defence details by carrier pigeon, then became sidetracked by a couple of more alluring birds. Here, left to right: Elsa Martinelli, Heston, Gabriella Pallotta, Harry Guardino and ex-opera star Baccaloni; Brian Donlevy was also featured. This wasn't really Heston's cup of tea, nor, judging by the box-office returns, the average ticket-buyer's plate of spaghetti.

△ Jerry Lewis had one of his most entertaining offerings in **It's Only Money**, mainly because it contained a more substantial plot than his usual. The perennial goof played a television repair mechanic who teams up with his pal, a private eye, to track down a wealthy dowager's mysteriously missing nephew, to whom she is leaving her fortune. Jerry falls in love with her nurse, exposes her crooked lawyer, and discovers that her missing nephew is himself. This John Fenton Murray scenario was briskly put over, along with some well staged action gags, by director Frank Tashlin and the star (right), who had assistance from Zachary Scott as the double-dealing lawyer (his last role before his death at 51), Joan O'Brien (left) as the romantic nurse, Jesse White as the detective, Mae Questel as the dowager, and Jack Weston as a sinister butler. It was the fourth of six Lewis comedies produced by Paul Jones.

▷ A World War II drama that remains vivid in the memory twenty years after seeing it, **Hell Is For Heroes** was made by newcomers to Paramount: director Don Siegel and producer Henry Blanke. Although a small-scale production as war films go, it gave full rein to Siegel's special skill in conveying urgency and tension, and it was a final success in the long career of Blanke, who came to it from 35 years at Warner Bros., where he was a close associate of Hal Wallis and produced many of their biggest hits. Steve McQueen took a long stride towards stardom with his pungent performance as the leader of a reluctant handful of GIs, storming a seemingly impregnable German pillbox whose defenders are made to believe they are outnumbered. This single action was made to pack more dramatic punch than whole armies in battle. Bobby Darin (centre), James Coburn, Nick Adams, Fess Parker, Harry Guardino (left), Bob Newhart (right) and Mike Kellin backed up McQueen in acting strength as well as in the taut Robert Pirosh-Richard Carr screenplay.

▽ Shirley MacLaine (centre) and her husband, Japanese-based producer Steve Parker, joined to make **My Geisha**, along with several other internationally celebrated talents; co-star Yves Montand (left), Edward G. Robinson, Robert Cummings (right) and Yoko Tani, director Jack Cardiff, writer Norman Krasna, photographer Shunichuro Nakao and music director Franz Waxman. In spite of MacLaine's refreshingly offhand personality, and all the other clever people involved, the spark of life was never struck in this comedy of a movie director's actress wife disguising herself as a geisha girl to overcome his objections to starring her as Madame Butterfly in his forthcoming film. The beautiful Nipponese scenery was the movie's most beguiling feature, and Nakao and Cardiff, the British director who was even more renowned as a cinematographer, made the most of it via Technicolor's wide-screen process, Technirama. However, the thin story was stretched much too long, and before the two-hour mark was reached many in the audience had succumbed to the Japanese Sandman.

◁ Paramount's biggest money magnet in a rather lacklustre year was **Hatari!** which collected $7 million from North American theatres and a like amount from the international market. With John Wayne (centre) starring and Howard Hawks directing, that was to be expected. In his remarkable 40-year career Hawks made virtually every type of movie: this was his nature-in-the-raw animal picture, a series of exciting sequences shot in the wilds of Tanganyika (as it was then called) and held together by a loose yarn by Leigh Brackett about big game hunters. Wayne lurched around in dominating style as the leader of a group including Red Buttons, Hardy Kruger (right), Gerard Blain and Bruce Cabot in pursuit of four-legged merchandise for sale to zoos around the world. Elsa Martinelli was the beauty amid the beasts. Russell Harlan's photography in Technicolor and Henry Mancini's music score were decided assets, but a drawback was too little narrative interest for too much running time. Two and half hours of it had a wearying effect, especially for those not partial to watching terrified animals being chased and trapped.

△ Adventure story addicts who were attracted by the title of **Escape From Zahrain** got less than they bargained for. After a promising start in which the captured leader of a rebel movement in an Arab oil country makes his getaway, accompanied by four fellow prisoners, their long trek across a desert to the border went on and on, getting slower and slower. The charismatic presence of Yul Brynner (foreground centre) in the lead, supported by Sal Mineo (left), Jack Warden, Madlyn Rhue (kneeling right), Jay Novello and (wasted in a bit) James Mason, kept interest alive until the long chase ended. As director, Ronald Neame had often been more effective than his handling of this Robin Estridge script suggested; as producer, he picked some spectacular desert locations and assigned a fine cinematographer, Elsworth Fredericks, to film them in Technicolor. A pity the sand got into the script.

△ Never one of Tennessee Williams's most successful plays, **Summer And Smoke** flourished his usual high passions in the deep South along with his poetic imagery, but the dramatic tension wasn't there. Neither were the ticket-buying crowds. Best thing in it was the performance of Geraldine Page, repeating her off-Broadway stage role of the repressed spinster heroine, here in conflict with her straitlaced parents, Una Merkel (right) and Malcolm Atterbury. Laurence Harvey was the medical student who aroused her dormant desires, Rita Moreno the wilder type of gal who gratified his. They, and John McIntire, Pamela Tiffin, Earl Holliman, Lee Patrick and Thomas Gomez were directed by England's Peter Glenville (primarily a theatre director) in the Hal Wallis production, scripted by James Poe and Meade Roberts.

▽ One of John Ford's last and most popular pictures was **The Man Who Shot Liberty Valance**. Most of the critics received it with pernickety ifs and buts; the paying customers, with two star heroes to root for and the West's most violent villain to hate, gave it a much warmer welcome. Unusual in its contrast of old-style Westerners, exemplified by gun-slinger John Wayne, and new, in the person of lawyer-politician James Stewart (foreground), it told a simple story in a tricky way. Starting with a scene of Stewart, in successful maturity, being publicly acclaimed, it flashed back to his early days in the West as a poor tenderfoot, bullied by vicious outlaw Lee Marvin (standing) and be- friended by sharpshooter Wayne. The inevitable showdown between good and evil, fought in the classic quick-on-the-draw way, leaves Marvin breathing his last and Stewart victorious, hailed as a hero by the townsfolk. What they (and the audience, until another flashback reveals it) don't know is that Wayne, hidden nearby, had fired the fatal shot to protect his friend. Vera Miles played the girl Stewart wins, with Edmond O'Brien, John Carradine, Andy Devine, Lee Van Cleef, Ken Murray, Woody Strode and John Qualen also cast in the Willis Goldbeck production, screenwritten from a Dorothy Johnson story by Goldbeck and James Warner Bellah.

OTHER RELEASES OF 1962

Brushfire
John Ireland, Everett Sloane, Carl Esmond, Jo Morrow. Dir. & Pro: Jack Warner Jr. Melodrama of western residents in southeast Asia. Friends rescue a planter and his wife, held for ransom by guerrillas.

The Errand Boy
Jerry Lewis, Brian Donlevy, Sig Rumann, Iris Adrian. Dir. & Pro: Jerry Lewis, Ernest D. Glucksman. Hollywood studio head assigns addle-pated errand boy to check up on time-wasting employees; bedlam breaks loose.

Girls! Girls! Girls!
Elvis Presley, Stella Stevens. Dir: Norman Taurog. Pro: Hal B. Wallis. The admirer of a fishing-boat captain fails to captivate him with the offer of a new boat, but succeeds by arousing his jealousy.

The Siege Of Syracuse
Rossano Brazzi, Tina Louise, Sylva Koscina. Dir: Pietro Francisci. Pro: Galatea-Glomer-Lyre. Warrior chief, in love with one girl, promised to another, is kept from both by battles against the Romans. (Italian)

Too Late Blues
Stella Stevens, Bobby Darin, Vince Edwards. Dir. & Pro: John Cassavetes. Jazz musician and girl vocalist fall in love and out again; he is taken up by a rich woman, while the girl becomes a prostitute.

Where The Truth Lies
Juliette Greco, Jean Marc Bory, Liselotte Pulver. Dir: Henri Decoin. Pro: Alain Poiret, Michel Bernheim. A mysterious beauty is suspected of casting voodoo spells on her lover's wife. (French)

Wonderful To Be Young (GB **The Young Ones**)
Cliff Richard, Robert Morley, Carole Grey. Dir: Sidney J. Furie. Pro: Kenneth Harper. Musical about a rich man's son who produces a show to finance his youth club. (British)

1963

▽ How many moviegoers read the critics? Not a lot, if the returns on **All The Way Home** were any guide. Business stayed in the so-so category while the reviewers, almost without exception, went in for superlatives – and not because its author, James Agee, was a fellow film critic. It originated with his autobiographical, posthumously published novel *A Death In The Family*, which won the Pulitzer Prize and was called 'One of the most deeply worked out expressions of human feeling I have ever read' by critic Alfred Kazin. Similar raves greeted the stage adaptation by Tad Mosel, and Philip Reisman's screenplay retained the poignancy of book and play in showing the impact of a father's untimely death on his family and their gradual recovery. Rewarding roles were excellently performed by Jean Simmons (right), Robert Preston, Pat Hingle, Michael Kearney, John Cullum, Thomas Chalmers, and the remarkable Aline MacMahon (left) in her last screen appearance before she retired. The David Susskind production was one of only four pictures directed by Alex Segal, and the best.

△ Papa Jackie Gleason is saying something unfit for baby Linda Bruhl's ears, thinks mama Glynis Johns in this scene from **Papa's Delicate Condition**. The title referred to his lapses into booze in an amusing comedy written by producer Jack Rose from Corinne Griffith's memoir of her small town childhood in 1900s Texas. Charles Ruggles, Elisha Cook Jr, Laurel Goodwin, Charles Lane, Benny Baker, Murray Hamilton and Juanita Moore were others in director George Marshall's cast. It was charming but unremarkable – except for two things. Its song, 'Call Me Irresponsible', won Sammy Cahn and James Van Heusen an Academy Award and is still heard today. And its author had an amazing career. Throughout the twenties she was a major star, a fragile lovely called the Orchid Lady of The Screen, but talkies revealed Corinne's thin voice and Warners dropped her contract. 'Beautiful but dumb' said Hollywood. She turned to writing and had a dozen books published; then to real estate and finance, so astutely that by 1979, when she died at 83, she was one of America's richest women.

△ An early Broadway winner by Neil Simon (reputed to be the most financially successful writer in the history of the American theatre), **Come Blow Your Horn** became the first of seven of his comedies filmed by Paramount. Screen writer Norman Lear and director Bud Yorkin (they also produced) made it a bit too long and stage-bound for movie excellence. Nevertheless, it scored a high laugh total when Frank Sinatra found his swinging bachelorhood hampered by his young brother's efforts to copy it. The head-shaking and tongue-clicking over their life-style by their staid Jewish parents, Molly Picon and Lee J. Cobb (seated) added to the fun. Standing: Sinatra, girl friend Jill St John and brother Tony Bill. Here making his screen debut, Bill struck it rich as the co-producer of *The Sting* ten years later.

△ Middle-aged macho pervaded **Donovan's Reef**, a mercilessly hearty comedy about a bunch of American ex-service buddies living it up on a South Sea island. The unexpected arrival in their midst of a girl, in whose mouth butter wouldn't melt, throws a crimp into their highjinks; she is the proper Bostonian daughter of a prodigal father, one of the lotus-eating gang. They rally round him, their ringleader (John Wayne, left) tries to turn her father-recovery into a romantic spree, and the script, by Frank Nugent and James Edward Grant, rapidly ran out of ideas as producer-director John Ford settled for inconsequential bouts of slapstick and roughhouse. It was all good, more or less clean fun, but hardly worthy of one of the greatest film-makers, whose 50-year career was faltering through ill health. Lee Marvin (right), Jack Warden (the father) and Mike Mazurki played Wayne's fellow rounders, Elizabeth Allen was the girl, and fans were glad to see Dorothy Lamour and Cesar Romero back again. The scenery seen through William Clothier's Technicolor cameras was a treat, but the general effect was that of a boisterous and over-prolonged beer commercial.

◁ Laughs in stock on all floors when Jerry Lewis (left), adoring swain of elevator girl Jill St John (centre), gets a job in the same department store, unaware that her mother owns it and has hired him to show the girl what a lame-brain he is. **Who's Minding The Store?** zipped along with a succession of sight gags in the style of Harold Lloyd and Buster Keaton, smartly handled by Lewis and his usual collaborator in this period, director Frank Tashlin (who also wrote it with Harry Tugend). They reached their peak in a riotous scene in which Jerry tried to fit size five shoes on the size ten feet of a lady wrestler. Agnes Moorehead (mother), John McGiver (right), Ray Walston and Nancy Kulp were also featured in this lively Paul Jones production.

△ You couldn't help liking Paul Newman (right) in **A New Kind Of Love** – even in such a silly story, and such a boorish role as the wolf in columnist's clothing who changes a strictly-business couturiere's mind about men. She (Joanne Woodward, left) avoids him while on a Paris trip for the fashion shows, until a vision of St Catherine, patron saint of spinsters, advises her to get glamour and a man. Maurice Chevalier guest-starred to sing 'Mimi' and 'Louise' in a cast including Thelma Ritter, Eva Gabor and George Tobias. The Paris, New York and Hollywood production was lavish, but the press and paybox verdict was thumbs down. Melville Shavelson, its writer, director and producer, forgot to consult the patron saint of film-makers.

△ Still looking great after a quarter-century in the glamour girl business, Lana Turner (centre) popped up as the co-star of Dean Martin (right) in one of his better comedies, **Who's Got The Action?** He was a compulsive gambler with a genius for picking also-rans; she was his wife, so tired of watching their bank account dwindle that she set herself up as his bookie without telling him... whereupon all his horses started winning. There was a touch of Damon Runyon zest in the script, written and produced by Jack Rose from Alexander Rose's novel *Four Horse Players Are Missing*, and directed by Daniel Mann. Eddie Albert (second from right), Margo (Mrs Albert off-screen), Paul Ford, Nita Talbot (left), John McGiver, and Walter Matthau in a picture-stealing performance as an underworld biggie, were featured.

△ Rome wasn't built in 90 minutes, but **Duel Of The Titans** had no longer to spare for telling the tale of Romulus and Remus, as imagined by Sergio Corbucci, who wrote and directed this unhistorical spectacular. Steve Reeves (foreground right), a former Mr Universe, played Romulus and Gordon Scott (foreground left), a former Tarzan, was Remus; neither was in any danger of winning acting prizes, but a display of their awe-inspiring physiques was all their fans required. Both of these American muscle-ripplers had left Hollywood to strip down to essentials for the wave of flesh epics flooding from Italian studios; the men, and the movies, enjoyed international popularity. This story, like most of the others, substituted for a sensible plot a series of chases, physical conflicts and amorous episodes. These last involved the beauteous Virni Lisi as a Sabine princess; she and featured actors Massimo Girotti and Jacques Sernas were not far behind the stars in skin exposure, and all matched in decorative values the colourful scenery of Alessandro Jacovini's CinemaScope production.

△ Gower Champion, who was with Debbie Reynolds in the 1954 musical *Give A Girl A Break*, should have remembered that title when, nine years later, he starred her in his first directorial effort, **My Six Loves**. Instead, he and producer Gant Gaither were responsible for a glutinous concoction, written by John Fante, Joseph Calvelli and William Wood, which had Debbie (left) as a Broadway star vacationing at her Connecticut farm, where she finds six stray children. Captivated by their roguish ways, she is urged to adopt them by the local parson (Cliff Robertson, right) who also pitches a little woo on his own behalf. After hovering between love and career for a few reels, she takes on all seven of them, and – well, it was all just too adorable for words. David Janssen, Eileen Heckart, Jim Backus and Hans Conreid were others awash in the prevailing cuteness.

▷ **Hud** took Paramount into the Academy Award lists in a big way. It snapped up seven nominations, three of them getting enough votes to win Oscars for Patricia Neal (right) as best actress, Melvyn Douglas as best supporting actor and James Wong Howe as best cinematographer. All richly deserved, but it was hard luck on the two nominees chiefly responsible for the picture's success: Paul Newman (left), superb in the title role of an insensitive, amoral young Texan; and Martin Ritt, who directed with a keen regard for character and atmosphere. The locale was a dusty ranch containing a ramshackle house, Hud, his high-principled father (Douglas) and hero-worshipping nephew (Brandon De Wilde), their overworked housekeeper (Neal), and a lot of cattle which catch something and, in a distressing scene, have to be destroyed. While the others become aware of Hud's worthlessness, the household breaks up: it was a downbeat story that Irving Ravetch (who co-produced with Ritt) and Harriet Frank Jr adapted from Larry McMurty's novel *Horseman Pass By*. But the high standard of professionalism reached in all departments of its making made the picture not only a popular hit but a memorable item for connoisseurs.

▽ It seemed only yesterday that Van Johnson had been the big matinee idol over at MGM and Janet Leigh was chosen to play opposite him in her very first movie, *The Romance Of Rosy Ridge*. But 16 years had now flown by, Van was plumper, Janet was leaner, and the romance in **Wives And Lovers** was none too rosy. It was all brittle sophistication when its married couple – deftly played by the stars, seen here – were temporarily sundered by the husband's success as a writer, his agent (female) wanting more than ten per cent of him, and the wife being pursued by an amorous actor. As directed by John Rich, produced by Hal Wallis and adapted by Edward Anhalt from Jay Presson Allen's play *The First Wife*, the movie made for light, superficial, but sometimes witty entertainment. Shelley Winters, Martha Hyer, Jeremy Slate and Ray Walston sketched in some amusing Broadway and Hollywood types.

OTHER RELEASES OF 1963

Fun In Acapulco
Elvis Presley, Ursula Andress, Paul Lukas. Dir: Richard Thorpe. Pro: Hal B. Wallis. A part-time lifeguard in the Mexican resort is also a trapeze artist, a night club entertainer, and the love of a lady bullfighter.

A Girl Named Tamiko
Laurence Harvey, France Nuyen, Martha Hyer, Michael Wilding. Dir: John Sturges. Pro: Hal B. Wallis. Eurasian photographer uses his charm on women to help him get an American entry visa.

The Nutty Professor
Jerry Lewis, Stella Stevens. Dir: Jerry Lewis Pro: Lewis, Ernest Glucksman. Timid chemistry teacher concocts a potion that transforms him into a debonair swinger: a comedy Jekyll and Hyde.

1964

▽ Olivia de Havilland (illustrated) projected hysterical terror during most of **Lady In A Cage** with all the expertise and power expected of a star with two 'best actress' Oscars to her credit. Her emoting in writer-producer Luther Davis's grisly thriller did much to rivet attention on the plight of a rich widow, trapped in the elevator of her otherwise unoccupied home, being taunted and menaced by three vicious intruders (James Caan, Ann Sothern and Jeff Corey) while they enjoy an orgy of robbery and vandalism. Director Walter Grauman maintained an unrelenting pressure on the audience, among whom a really good time was had only by sado-masochists.

△ John Frankenheimer made a scorching political thriller in *The Manchurian Candidate* and an even better one in his next picture, **Seven Days In May**, two years later. Cunningly adapted for maximum suspense by Rod Serling from a best-selling novel by Fletcher Knebel and Charles Bailey II, the drama involved the aide (Kirk Douglas) of an ambitious, ultra-right-wing general (Burt Lancaster, here on TV) who is, the aide suspects, planning to overthrow the US government because the President (Fredric March) has signed a peace treaty with Russia. Evidence of an imminent military coup comes from the general's mistress (Ava Gardner) and a senator (Edmond O'Brien) sent by the President to an army base in Texas, where he is captured by the general's men and escapes with damning facts of the plot, which is quashed. March (right) took the acting honours, as he had a habit of doing against strong opposition, but all the stars scored effectively; good, too, were Martin Balsam, George Macready, John Houseman, Whit Bissell, Hugh Marlowe and Richard Anderson. Director Frankenheimer and his co-producer Edward Lewis delivered a movie that satisfied both the critics and the crowds.

▷ A tremendous hit in Britain, its production source, **Zulu** also drew all lovers of gung-ho excitement in America and elsewhere. It was a rip-roaring, hell-for-leather battle picture, its action pausing only long enough for some good actors to act. They were led by Stanley Baker (left) as a hard-bitten commanding officer, Michael Caine (right) as his seemingly effete right-hand man, and Jack Hawkins as an itinerant missionary, devoted to the Bible and the bottle. Ulla Jacobson played Hawkins's daughter, and James Booth, Nigel Green, Paul Daneman and Ivor Emmanuel four of the hundred men of the South Wales Borderers who, in 1879, faced thousands of attacking Zulu warriors in the heroic defence of Rorke's Drift. Climax after climax mounted to fever pitch as the long, bloody battle was depicted in meticulous detail and (except for the mysterious disappearance of Baker's crippling wound mid-way) with unerring realism by director Cy Endfield, a refugee from the disgraceful Hollywood blacklisting of so-called Communists. He co-produced with Baker and co-scripted with John Prebble, and the authentic atmosphere was captured by cinematographer Stephen Dade via South African locations, Technicolor and Technirama.

▽ Producer Samuel Bronston astonished the industry in the early sixties by turning out a series of huge epics, of which the last two were released by Paramount in the same year, 1964. **Circus World** (GB: **The Magnificent Showman**), made like the others at the vast studio he established near Madrid, challenged comparison with DeMille's *The Greatest Show On Earth* but failed to match it in either entertainment or box-office strength. A story by Philip Yordan and Nicholas Ray, and a cumbersome script worked on by Ben Hecht (his last), James Edward Grant and Julian Halevy, stifled this wide-screen spectacular, inviting viewers to become enthralled by a showman's domestic problems when what they really wanted to watch were his wild-west circus performers. These supplied some excitement (as did a big-top fire) but were too often shoved aside while their boss (John Wayne, left) searched for his old love (Rita Hayworth), who had left him and their daughter after her husband, distracted by jealousy, fell from a trapeze. Claudia Cardinale (right), Lloyd Nolan, Richard Conte, Wanda Rotha, Kay Walsh and John Smith were also involved, directed with fitful efficiency by Henry Hathaway. Filmed in Super-Technirama and exhibited in Cinerama in first-run situations.

▽ Flamboyant, lurid, eventful and trashy, **The Carpetbaggers** was expertly aimed at the box-office by producer Joseph E. Levine, and hit it with a bang. Director Edward Dmytryk guided George Peppard in the main role, Carroll Baker (illustrated, with Peppard) as a Hollywood sexpot, Alan Ladd as a Western star, Robert Cummings, Martha Hyer, Lew Ayres, Martin Balsam, Leif Erickson, Audrey Totter, Ralph Taeger, Elizabeth Ashley and Archie Moore through the 150-minute saga of a ruthless young tycoon's exploits in the aircraft and movie industries (not to mention the bedroom). The script, by John Michael Hayes, was based on the best-seller by Harold Robbins who drew his inspiration from the life of Howard Hughes. Alan Ladd's first appearance at Paramount in twelve years was also his last: before the film was released, he died, aged 50.

△ Bronston out-colossalled all his previous spectaculars (*King Of Kings, El Cid,* etc) with **The Fall Of The Roman Empire**, on which he lavished about $20 million, a fat budget even today; then, it was a real eye-popper. When the returns came in, adding up to a mere fraction of that cost and swelling previous losses, he had to throw in the towel and shut down his Spanish epic factory for good. Reviews of the new picture varied sharply: some called it a three-hour bore; others praised its literate script, its action highlights – including a chariot race and an abundance of deaths by spear, fire, poison and plague – and an undeniable magnificence of production. The screenplay by Philip Yordan, Ben Barzman and Basilio Franchino mixed romantic fiction with fact about the Romans' golden age under Marcus Aurelius, and the start of their decline under his degenerate son, Emperor Commodus. Director Anthony Mann kept it all under control, with the aid of many expert technicians; every dollar showed on the screen – in Technicolor and Ultra-Panavision 70, no less. And who could complain about a cast containing Alec Guinness, James Mason, Sophia Loren (left), Stephen Boyd (right), Omar Sharif, Mel Ferrer, Anthony Quayle, Christopher Plummer, Eric Porter and John Ireland, even if some of them did seem uneasy in their togas?

△ With prestige stamped all over it, **Becket** was the kind of picture that achieves Academy nominations, and it received no fewer than twelve of them. Only one actual Oscar winner emerged (the voters were mad about *My Fair Lady* that year): Edward Anhalt for his screenplay, deftly fashioned from Jean Anouilh's play. It was sumptuously produced by Hal B. Wallis, directed with dramatic flourish by Peter Glenville and acted by a gilt-edged cast: Richard Burton, Peter O'Toole, John Gielgud, Donald Wolfit, Pamela Brown, Martita Hunt, Sian Phillips, Paolo Stoppa, Felix Aylmer. The story of King Henry II (O'Toole, right) versus Thomas á Becket (Burton, left) – once his friend and eventually, as Archbishop of Canterbury, his ill-fated adversary – made a marvellous clash for strong, high-style actors, and both stars took their opportunities eloquently. Particularly notable among the Oscar-nominated contributions were Geoffrey Unsworth's photography, Margaret Furse's costumes and the John Bryan-Maurice Carter art direction, all combining to make the Technicolor film (shot in 70 mm in Britain) a visual pleasure. It was also big, important, impressive, and – sad to relate – just a little tedious on occasion.

▽ **Robinson Crusoe On Mars** sounded ominously like a load of Poverty Row junk. Actually the title exactly described a well-made version of the Defoe classic, imaginatively transported into the future. Winton Hoch's Technicolor cameras brilliantly used Death Valley, the forbidding California-Nevada desert territory, to portray Mars, where a stranded astronaut lives alone with a pet monkey until he encounters Man Friday, the survivor of an interplanetary war. Director Byron Haskin, producer Aubrey Schenck, screenwriters Ib Melchior and John Higgins, special effects expert Lawrence Butler, music director Van Cleave, art directors Hal Pereira and Arthur Lonergan, and actors Adam West (better known as TV's 'Batman') and Paul Mantee (illustrated) combined their talents in a low-budget adventure as entertaining as any multi-million-dollar star-war epic yet to come.

▽ Elvis Presley stepped up his output to three pictures a year in the sixties, the majority for MGM. His Paramount offering for 1964, **Roustabout**, was no better or worse than most of them, which suffered from carelessly developed scripts and depended (successfully) on the custom of an army of fans so huge that it bought an estimated total of 600 million Presley records – and they're still selling. Elvis got lucky with this movie when Barbara Stanwyck was persuaded by producer Hal B. Wallis, an old friend, to co-star as the owner of a carnival who hires vagabond Elvis (illustrated) as a handyman. He proves more valuable as an entertainer, wowing the crowds and attracting an offer from a rival outfit; the appeal of a girlfriend (Joan Freeman) brings him back to Stanwyck's show. Enthralling was hardly the word for the Anthony Lawrence-Allan Weiss screenplay, but there were compensations in the vocal score – the star had eleven songs – and the bright Technicolor-Techniscope production. John Rich's cast included Leif Erickson, Sue Ane Langdon, Dabs Greer, Steve Brodie and Pat Buttram; Raquel Welch made her debut in an unbilled bit, and Stanwyck her next to last appearance (except on television) before retirement.

▽ A story-line that might have become distastefully squalid in other hands was deftly manipulated into warm and enjoyable entertainment in **Love With The Proper Stranger**. At the same time, writer Arnold Schulman and director Robert Mulligan avoided the other danger of slipping into syrupy cuteness in telling the tale of a Manhattan shopgirl who meets and mates with a young man struggling to make a career as a jazz musician. They are in love, she is pregnant, and he prizes independence too much for marriage; but that's what they decide on after she flees from an arranged abortion. The environment of New York's seedier sections was precisely depicted, with the dismal elements relieved by colourful touches; in this and other respects the movie was similar to Mulligan's 1960 hit, *The Rat Race*. Natalie Wood and Steve McQueen (together here) exercised charm and skill as the worried lovers (she received her third 'best actress' Academy nomination) and lively character sketches came from Edie Adams – very funny as a quick-witted stripper – Tom Bosley and Herschel Bernardi. The producer was Alan J. Pakula, who teamed frequently with Mulligan after their 1957 feature debut with *Fear Strikes Out*.

◁ There's a whole lot of acting going on in this shot from **Where Love Has Gone**, a purple drama from the novel by Harold Robbins, evidently inspired by the Lana Turner case of 1958 (her daughter killed Lana's lover) as well as the desire to make plenty of money. The latter ambition was fully achieved by both the book and the movie wrung from it by writer John Michael Hayes, director Edward Dmytryk and producer Joseph E. Levine, who had all just worked on Robbins's *The Carpetbaggers* to even greater box-office effect. Right to left here: Susan Hayward as a well-born but loose living sculptress; Joey Heatherton as her daughter accused of stabbing mother's boy friend to death; George Macready and Bette Davis as formidably proper family elders shocked by the scandal. Mike Connors, Jane Greer, DeForrest Kelley, Anne Seymour and Anthony Caruso were others cast. The mother-daughter hatred depicted with the characteristic fire of Davis and Hayward kept the film alive (they were not exactly bosom pals off-camera either). Hate also motivated the critics.

△ **Paris When It Sizzles** (the title came from Cole Porter's song 'I Love Paris') was a dreadful remake of a 1955 French comedy which itself was nothing to set the Seine on fire, but at least had charm, as directed by Julien Duvivier. That quality disappeared under the leaden treatment of director-producer Richard Quine and writer-producer George Axelrod, who adapted the original screenplay (*Holiday For Henriette*) by Duvivier and Henri Jeanson. Its subject was the preparation of a script by a screenwriter (William Holden, uncharacteristically heavy and dull) and his secretary (Audrey Hepburn, illustrated, irritatingly arch) who act out in fantasy various movie genres with themselves as hero and heroine. They were all supposed to be romantic or funny or both. Support by Noel Coward, Gregoire Aslan and Raymond Bussieres, with cameos by Marlene Dietrich, Tony Curtis and (on the soundtrack) Fred Astaire and Frank Sinatra, plus a good-looking Technicolor production shot in Paris, failed to save it, and the Paramount contracts of Holden and Hepburn also expired. The best laugh came in the screen credit for Miss Hepburn's perfume by Hubert De Givenchy.

OTHER RELEASES OF 1964

The Disorderly Orderly
Jerry Lewis, Glenda Farrell, Susan Oliver. Dir: Frank Tashlin. Pro: Paul Jones. A medical school reject gets a job as an orderly and turns a hospital into a disaster area.

Law Of The Lawless
Dale Robertson, Yvonne De Carlo, William Bendix. Dir: William Claxton. Pro: A.C. Lyles. The son of a Western town's big shot is on trial for murder, while the judge is beset by his criminal enemies.

The Patsy
Jerry Lewis, Ina Ballin, Peter Lorre, Everett Sloane. Dir: Jerry Lewis Pro: Ernest Glucksman. When a comedy star dies suddenly, his studio signs up a knuckle-headed bellboy in a Hollywood hotel as his replacement.

Ring Of Treason (GB Ring Of Spies)
Bernard Lee, Margaret Tyzack. Dir: Robert Tronson. Pro: Leslie Gilliat. Drama based on the Portland spy case, in which a suburban English home housed a ring of Communist agents. (British)

Son Of Captain Blood
Sean Flynn, Ann Todd, Alessandra Panaro. Dir: Tullio Demichelli. Pro: Harry Joe Brown. Pirates' attack on a group of students at sea is foiled by a swashbuckling adventurer (played by the son of Errol Flynn). (Italian)

Stage To Thunder Rock
Barry Sullivan, Marilyn Maxwell, Scott Brady. Dir: William Claxton. Pro: A.C. Lyles. Sheriff tries to keep a captured bank robber under guard in a stagecoach station full of people eager to snatch the loot.

Walk A Tightrope
Dan Duryea, Patricia Owens, Terrence Cooper. Dir: Frank Nesbitt. Pro: Jack Parsons. Rich man is killed by a sinister stranger who has been shadowing the victim's bride and who accuses her of instigating the plot. (British)

Who's Been Sleeping In My Bed?
Dean Martin, Elizabeth Montgomery, Carol Burnett. Dir: Daniel Mann. Pro: Jack Rose. Television star keeps up a hectic round of love affairs with his friends' wives; finally settles down.

1965

▽ As a refreshing change from journeys to or from outer space, **Crack In The World** offered customers a group of scientists seeking a new energy source at the core of the earth. With more zeal than caution, one of them fires a nuclear missile down there, causing widespread consternation – and the title. Dana Andrews (front), Janette Scott (behind him), Kieron Moore and Alexander Knox headed director Andrew Marton's cast in the intriguing, if too talky, screenplay, which was eclipsed by the sheer physical excitement of earth-shattering special effects (by John Douglas) at the climax. The writers were Jon Manchip White and Julian Halevy, working for producers, Bernard Glasser and Lester Sansom.

△ Aficionados of horse-and-holster epics quickly guessed that the mild title of **The Sons Of Katie Elder** was hiding a brawling, rip-roaring Western when they noted that its top star was John Wayne and its director was Henry Hathaway, both guarantees of rough action. Once the early sequence of Katie's funeral was disposed of, Wayne (left), Dean Martin (right), Earl Holliman and Michael Anderson Jr, as her four vagabond sons gathered together for the obsequies, got to work with thudding fists and blazing guns to eliminate the varmints who have cast a shadow over their family's name and property rights. The Hal B. Wallis production in Technicolor was good rowdy fun, received with more enthusiasm by the ticket-buyers than by the reviewers, who wondered why it took four credited writers (author Talbot Jennings, scripters Allan Weiss, William H. Wright and Harry Essex) to concoct such undemanding stuff. The large cast included Martha Hyer (who became Mrs Wallis the following year), George Kennedy, James Gregory, Dennis Hopper, Jeremy Slate, Paul Fix, John Litel, Rhys Williams and John Qualen.

△ *Zulu* had brought Cy Endfield and Stanley Baker plenty of praise and money, so they went back to an African locale for **Sands Of The Kalahari**, another drama of gruelling adventure, but on a smaller scale. Endfield directed and wrote the script (from a novel by William Mulvihill) while co-producing with Baker (right), who didn't have the most prominent role this time. That went to Stuart Whitman (behind), who worked up a compelling portrait of an arrogant, super-macho professional hunter, one of a group of survivors stranded in the desert when their plane crash-lands. All of them – Baker, Susannah York (left), Harry Andrews, Nigel Davenport, Theodore Bikel, Barry Lowe – go through horrendous conflicts with natural dangers and each other as they trek across the torrid wastes, some of them succumbing altogether, and none more spectacularly than Whitman, who is polished off by a tribe of ferocious baboons. For the audience, it was a two-hour ordeal but in an enjoyable sort of way, with the heat, blood and sand coming realistically through the Technicolor cameras of Erwin Hillier. Soft-drink counters in the lobbies did a roaring trade.

◁ Car racing is a big thrill for some people, a noisy way to waste fuel for others. The former kept **Red Line 7000** in the black, but this low-budget actioner held interest also as a study of men caught up in crises created by their ambitions and rivalries. Their love lives figured prominently in George Kirgo's screenplay too, jealousy causing James Caan (centre) to attempt the killing of another driver on the track. Caan gave a star-making performance under the direction of Howard Hawks, who also produced, using actual speedway locations. Others cast: Norman Alden (left), George Takei (right), Laura Devon, Charlene Holt, Marianna Hill, Gail Hire, John Robert Crawford and James Ward.

▽ The company buttressed its release lists in the sixties with thirteen Westerns produced by A.C. Lyles, who knew how to make them efficiently, economically and entertainingly enough to keep the kids and their action-loving elders absorbed. **Black Spurs**, a typical example, had a complicated screenplay by Steve Fisher about a rancher who turns into a bounty-hunter, then becomes a gun-slinger, and finally goes back to being a good guy. Rory Calhoun (left), well seasoned in this sort of thing, switched his expressions around to fit the various segments of his role, while making the real villains bite the dust and bringing the love-light into the eyes of heroine Terry Moore. The cast included one of the producer's customary collections of faces from the past: Richard Arlen, Scott Brady (right), Linda Darnell (in her first film for years and her last: a month before its release she was killed by an accidental fire), Bruce Cabot, and Lon Chaney Jr. The Technicolor production was directed by R.G. Springsteen.

△ In 1965 Jean Harlow, like Oscar Wilde five years before, was given two biograpical treatments in simultaneously produced movies. Unlike the Wilde biopics, neither was worth a second look. Paramount's **Harlow**, with Carroll Baker (here with Raf Vallone as her stepfather) playing the platinum blonde dazzler, was commercially more successful than the other (with Carol Lynley in the title role), thanks to Joseph E. Levine's superior production values and the company's selling power. But the star's short, excitingly scandalous, and finally pathetic life had been turned into a long and tedious film with only casual resemblance to the true story. John Michael Hayes wrote it, with parts for Martin Balsam, Angela Lansbury, Peter Lawford, Mike Connors and Red Buttons in Gordon Douglas's cast. This failure proved again that Hollywood shouldn't attempt biographies of its old stars – Valentino, Chaney, Keaton, Gable and Lombard, now Harlow, later Crawford – whose faces and personalities are too well remembered to be convincingly portrayed.

◁ In the spy story spectrum whose rainbow has led to so many pots of gold for authors, publishers and movie-makers, **The Spy Who Came In From The Cold** was a long way from James Bond. No glamour or gadgets (and therefore, no such box-office records) for this agent, whose dark world of desperation and treachery was superbly depicted by producer-director Martin Ritt, writers Paul Dehn and Guy Trosper, and photographer Oswald Morris. They exactly caught the harsh mood of John Le Carre's novel in one of the best British films of the year – and a high point in the career of Richard Burton. He was to the life the weary, embittered player of the Cold War game, sent to trap an old adversary in East Germany and involved in the ensuing complexities with Claire Bloom (sharing his escape here), Oskar Werner, Peter Van Eyck, Sam Wanamaker, Cyril Cusack, Michael Hordern, Rupert Davies, Beatrix Lehmann, Robert Hardy, George Voskovec and Bernard Lee.

△ More notable for its stars (many of them in cameo roles) than its script, **In Harm's Way** was a World War II naval drama loaded to the gunwales with cliches and resembling a television series squeezed into one 165-minute instalment. Pearl Harbor formed the backdrop for an assortment of stories, fitfully exciting – like this battle sequence with John Wayne (left) and Kirk Douglas (right) – but lacking overall impact. Otto Preminger gave the Wendell Mayes screenplay (from James Bassett's original) an expensive production, and directed a cast also boasting Henry Fonda, Patricia Neal, Tom Tryon, Paula Prentiss, Brandon De Wilde, Dana Andrews, Burgess Meredith, Franchot Tone, Patrick O'Neal, Stanley Holloway, Jill Haworth, George Kennedy, Carroll O'Connor and Bruce Cabot. Paying customers liked it better than the press did.

△ Faint glimmers of super-stardom ahead were discernible in the good looks and easy style of Robert Redford (right) in **Situation Hopeless But Not Serious**. He and Michael Connors (left) played American airmen captured in 1944 by a dim-witted German air raid warden (Alec Guinness) who hides them in his cellar and likes having them around so much that seven years go by before he tells them the war is over. Produced and directed by Gottfried Reinhardt, son of the great Max, and scripted by Silvia Reinhardt from actor Robert Shaw's novel *The Hiding Place*, the film seemed as tediously hemmed in as its heroes, until they emerged at last to encounter a group of SS-uniformed men, who were really extras making a movie – a better one, no doubt.

▽ Happy ending for Telly Savalas (left) and Sidney Poitier (centre) as social workers in a Seattle 'crisis clinic' in **The Slender Thread**. Sydney Pollack's film worked up quite a head of steam in the suspense of 'will she, won't she' when a distraught woman telephones that she is about to succumb to an overdose of pills, taken with suicide in mind. Unable to elicit her address, Poitier has to keep her talking so that the call can be traced before she conks out. An even trickier task was to keep the audience absorbed by that single situation for an hour and a half. Writer Stirling Silliphant, producer Stephen Alexander and director Pollack did it, helped enormously by a bravura portrayal of the desperate lady by Anne Bancroft.

▽ In a frank attempt to duplicate the 1963 success of *Tom Jones*, the makers of **The Amorous Adventures Of Moll Flanders** reached even farther back into the 18th century and came up with a lavishly produced adaptation of Daniel Defoe's novel. Although by no means unentertaining in a light-hearted, light-headed way, it fell short of its goal both artistically and commercially. While edging beyond the wink-and-nudge technique of old sex comedies, Terence Young's direction of the Dennis Cannan-Roland Kibbee screenplay – a bawdy account of a servant girl's vertical rise in society while in horizontal positions, and her final romance with an outlaw – was restricted by censorship which had not yet reached its present acceptance of full nudity and explicit dialogue. It was also handicapped by Kim Novak's rather stolid performance in a role needing the dash of, say, a young Paulette Goddard. Game efforts by supporting players George Sanders (with Kim here), Richard Johnson (who made Kim Mrs Johnson, briefly), Angela Lansbury, Lilli Palmer, Vittorio de Sica, Daniel Massey, Leo McKern and Cecil Parker injected some life into the proceedings, but as its two hours-plus wore on, the more beds Moll hopped into, the less amusing it became. Marcel Hellman produced it in England and Technicolor.

▽ Carroll Baker, here deciding whether to climb into bed with George Maharis in **Sylvia**, played the title role with all the allure that had made her a star in *Baby Doll* nine years before, plus a surer acting technique that confirmed her as the best of the the many blondes touted as new Marilyn Monroes. Sylvia fascinates a millionaire (Peter Lawford), who pauses on the brink of matrimony to check on her mysterious past; he hires a private detective (Maharis) and sends him gumshoeing through sleazy spots in USA and Mexico, until.... The Sidney Boehm screenplay, from E.V. Cunningham's novel, went on and on, ever deeper into unlikelihood, but entertaining withal. Gordon Douglas directed for producer Joseph E. Levine, featuring Joanne Dru, Edmond O'Brien, Viveca Lindfors, Aldo Ray, and Ann Sothern in a brilliant cameo demonstrating that the vintage star may have lost her waistline but none of her talent.

◁ After seventeen years the long association of Jerry Lewis (left) and Paramount came to an end with **Boeing Boeing**. He was the last survivor from the studio's lengthy star-studded roster of the forties: such contract lists had now become part of Hollywood's past. He surprised his fans with a straight comedy performance, minus yowling and mugging, and was billed second to Tony Curtis (right) as the latter's pal, caught up in the frantic developments ensuing when Curtis, a journalist in Paris, conducts three separate love affairs simultaneously with three air hostesses in the same flat. He does it by timing their occupancy according to their flight schedules – until the inevitable snarl-up occurs. The three girls were decoratively played by Dany Saval, Suzanna Leigh and Christiane Schmidtmer, but the most diverting lady was Thelma Ritter as the sardonic housekeeper. Edward Anhalt adapted the play by Marc Camoletti, a fast farce that had whipped up a storm of laughs and phenomenal business on the London stage. It didn't have the same zip under John Rich's direction in this Hal Wallis production in Technicolor, and the box-office results disappointed.

△ The tiny plot of **The Girls On The Beach** – three college girls put on a show to pay off the mortgage on their Santa Monica sorority house – served to give the customers several eyefuls of well proportioned young people frolicking in the sun. The girl's boyfriends promised them the Beatles as the star attraction for the jamboree, but could only deliver the Beach Boys, the Crickets and Lesley Gore (illustrated), who were pretty good entertainers at that. Noreen Corcoran, Linda Marshall and Anna Capri played the co-eds drumming up the necessary for their sorority house; Martin West, Lana Wood, Steve Rogers and Peter Brooks were also prominent in the Harvey Jacobson production, directed by William Witney, who kept the David Malcolm screenplay moving brightly; but it made mature fans hanker for the old let's-put-on-a-show-kids days of Judy and Mickey. This Paramount pick-up from independent producers the Lebin Brothers would have been the beach-party masterpiece of 1965, if it hadn't been the year of *How To Stuff A Wild Bikini*.

OTHER RELEASES OF 1965

Beach Ball
Edd Byrnes, Chris Noel, Diana Ross & The Supremes. Dir: Lennie Weinrib. Pro: Bart Patton. Manager of college-boy musical group keeps them one step ahead of their creditors.

A Boy Ten Feet Tall (GB **Sammy Going South**)
Fergus McClelland, Edward G. Robinson, Constance Cummings. Dir: Alexander Mackendrick. Pro: Hal Mason. Adventures of a 10-year-old orphan during a journey from Suez to South Africa. (British)

Dr. Terror's House Of Horrors
Peter Cushing, Christopher Lee, Donald Sutherland, Ursula Howells. Dir: Freddie Francis. Pro: Milton Subotsky. The stories of five men foretold by a mystery man aboard their train: he is Death. (British)

The Family Jewels
Jerry Lewis, Donna Butterworth, Sebastian Cabot. Dir. & Pro: Jerry Lewis. A little girl has a chauffeur-bodyguard, and six uncles who want to adopt her – and her $30,000,000. (All seven male roles played by Lewis).

Revenge Of The Gladiators
Roger Browne, Scilla Gabel, Gordon Mitchell. Dir: Michele Lupo. Pro: Elio Scardamaglia. A rebel Roman slave leaves the army of Spartacus to track down the murderers of his parents. (Italian)

The Skull
Peter Cushing, Christopher Lee, Patrick Wymark, Jill Bennett. Dir: Freddie Francis. Pro: Milton Subotsky. The skull of the Marquis de Sade has an evil influence over its possessors, causing murder and other crimes. (British)

Town Tamer
Dana Andrews, Pat O'Brien, Terry Moore, Lon Chaney Jr. Dir: Lesley Selander. Pro: A.C. Lyles. His wife having been killed by a bullet meant for him, a Westerner declares war on lawbreakers.

Young Fury
Rory Calhoun, Virginia Mayo, William Bendix, Richard Arlen. Dir: Christian Nyby. Pro: A.C. Lyles. Fugitive comes home to find his son has grown into a hell-raiser who hates him. Outlaws' guns cauterise the filial wound.

1966

▽ Why Frank Sinatra, a very astute showman, allowed himself to be embroiled in an inflated B-minus picture like **Assault On A Queen** remains a puzzle. Usually a fine actor, he didn't appear to believe a word of his role as the leader of a gang raising a sunken U-boat and turning it into a pirate ship in order to plunder the 'Queen Mary'. Neither Rod Serling's script nor Jack Donahue's direction brought any conviction to the incredible plot of Jack Finney's novel, and even the special effects looked as if they had been shot in a bathtub. William Goetz produced, with a cast including (left to right) Alf Kjellin as an ex-Nazi who reverted to ruthless type when the action got hot, Sinatra, and Virna Lisi as the blonde in the torpedo bay; also Anthony Franciosa, Richard Conte, Errol John and Reginald Denny.

△ 'What's it all about, Alfie?' asked the song which became as popular as **Alfie** itself. The answer: sex. Its outspoken treatment of the subject shocked some, delighted many and attracted millions around the world, making it the most successful movie of the Swinging London era, and bringing major stardom to Michael Caine (right) as the amorous Cockney (the actor was the genuine article) for whom women – Millicent Martin, Shelley Winters, Vivien Merchant, Shirley Anne Field, Julia Foster (left), Jane Asher, Eleanor Bron – fell like ripe fruit. His sleepy-eyed (no wonder) confidences to the audience obviated any disgust his lechery might have aroused; this aside-to-the-camera trick was often used by Lubitsch, now by producer-director Lewis Gilbert. He and writer Bill Naughton (adapting his own successful stage play) effected several such ingratiating touches to make a deplorable tale a pleasure to watch.

▽ Taking a leaf from the Disney live-action book, Paramount released a good example of that endangered species, family entertainment, in **The Night Of The Grizzly**. It starred big Clint Walker (left) as an ex-sheriff turned rancher, here contemplating his discarded badge while wife Martha Hyer bottles a batch of kumquats – or somesuch. Their Wyoming peace is threatened not only by neighbours who covet their property, but also by an outlaw Clint had sent to jail, and – worst of all – a ferocious bear he has to confront in the climactic fight sequence. Keenan Wynn, Jack Elam, Nancy Culp, Kevin Brodie, Ellen Corby, Leo Gordon and Ron Ely were others in Burt Dunne's production, written by Warren Douglas and directed by Joseph Pevney.

◁ Lawrence Durrell's story, **Judith**, was filmed by Daniel Mann in a Kurt Unger production with a screenplay by John Michael Hayes from a script by J.P. Miller. Sophia Loren (right) played an Austrian woman who, tormented by her concentration camp memories, tracks her Nazi husband to Israel, intent on making him pay for his crimes. She is aided by a Jewish freedom fighter (Peter Finch, left) and a British officer (Jack Hawkins). Andre Morell and Hans Verner were others supporting Sophia, who appeared to have had a beautician on hand throughout her travails; however, her natural fervour kept breaking through the *maquillage*. The film was dismal.

△ The three most important people on a set are here lining up a scene for **Seconds**: left to right, star Rock Hudson, photographer James Wong Howe and director John Frankenheimer, each in the top rank of his profession. Howe, at 66 the most famous of cinematographers, had started at Paramount a half-century before as DeMille's slate boy, and shot his first film there in 1923. As autocratic as he was talented, he was wont to take over complete control unless curbed by a strong director like Frankenheimer. Hudson was one of Hollywood's five biggest box-office draws for eight straight years from 1957 to 1964. Paradoxically, he dropped below the top ten just as he gave his best performance in this fascinating drama, about a burntout man who bought youth and a new identity from a sinister organisation which later demanded a grisly penalty. David Ely's novel, a modern variation on the Faust theme, was scripted by Lewis John Carlino and given a fine production by Edward Lewis, particularly memorable for Howe's distorted camera effects at climactic points. Salome Jens, Will Geer, John Randolph and Jeff Corey were featured.

◁ Elvis Presley (illustrated) might have turned green with envy right down to his blue suede shoes if he had ever compared his own movie career with Crosby's or Sinatra's. They, too, went to Hollywood as the pop-singing idols of swooning multitudes; they, too, were called inept actors in their early films. But, while they had been given big-budget musicals and then Oscar-winning dramas, Elvis was forever stalled in vehicles like **Paradise, Hawaiian Style**. This, his second Hal Wallis production set in the Pacific islands, was no better – if anything, worse – than the first (*Blue Hawaii*) five years before, and a feeble celebration of his tenth anniversary on screen. Michael Murphy directed him with Suzanna Leigh, James Shigeta, Marianna Hill, Donna Butterworth, Philip Ahn, John Doucette, Mary Treen and Grady Sutton. So-so songs, bevies of cuties and a witless Allan Weiss-Anthony Lawrence script about a helicopter pilot added up to mush, Presley style.

△ The name of Tennessee Williams is good for quite a chunk of ticket sales, but Paramount's use of it as the author of **This Property Is Condemned** was cheating a bit. Tennessee's brief one-act play with this title consisted of a conversation between two children on a railroad track, and it formed merely a prologue for the script which Francis Ford Coppola, Fred Coe and Edith Sommer wrote: a drama, at once provocative and dismal, it was about a tubercular girl who escapes from her mother's broken-down Mississippi boarding house by marrying a brute – her mother's lover – while still meeting her true love. After a disastrous showdown caused by mother, she returns home and becomes the town slut. A vivid performance by Natalie Wood (right) was given strong support by Robert Redford (left), Kate Reid, Charles Bronson, Alan Baxter, Robert Blake and Mary Badham under Sydney Pollack's direction. John Houseman was the producer.

▽ Warren Beatty (right), Leslie Caron (centre) and Robert Cummings (left) applied enough charm and varying amounts of comedy finesse to make **Promise Her Anything** an enjoyable 98 minutes. Set in New York, but for some obscure financial reason shot in England, Stanley Rubin's production for Seven Arts was directed at farce tempo by Arthur Hiller who, like Beatty, had his real successes yet to come. William Peter Blatty's script concerned a widow (Caron) seeking security in the shape of a baby-hating baby doctor (Cummings). She prepares for his visits by stashing her own baby in the next flat, unaware that its tenant (Beatty), who also woos her, is filming blue movies there. Other offbeat Greenwich Village types came and went, as did the movie's effectiveness. Good support by Hermione Gingold, Lionel Stander, Keenan Wynn and Cathleen Nesbitt, and an authentic Manhattan atmosphere helped.

▽ Quite a remarkable fellow, this Cornel Wilde. After the lure of the Broadway stage caused him to abandon both a brilliant medical school career and a selection by the US fencing team for the 1936 Olympics, he took up acting, won a movie contract in 1940 and had 15 years of success as a handsome hero. Finding that less than satisfying, he became that rare Hollywood all-rounder, the producer, director, star and sometimes writer of his own pictures. Best of them was **The Naked Prey**. In this harrowing essay in suspense he was a white hunter whose safari was broken up by savage natives; stripped and defenceless, he could save his life only by outrunning them through the wilderness, pursued day and night. Wilde (foreground) had brilliant assistance from his writers, Clint Johnston and Don Peters, and I.A.R. Thompson's Technicolor photography of the African scenery, in making a little masterpiece.

△ The glittering talents before and behind the cameras, the best-selling book source and the massive budget all seemed to guarantee success in a big way for **Is Paris Burning?** But in the roller-coaster fortunes of the movies, nothing is certain. When the returns came in, it was Paramount and producer Paul Graetz who were burning, and there was no consolation in the indifferent reaction of its meagre audiences to the screenplay treatment (by Francis Ford Coppola, Gore Vidal, Jean Aurenche, Pierre Bost and Claude Brule) of the Larry Collins-Dominique Lapierre novel, a kind of *Grand Hotel* of the Paris liberation in WWII. Rene Clement directed the multi-threaded yarn woven around a Nazi plot to leave the city in flames. Leslie Caron and Orson Welles (both in the foreground), Glenn Ford, Kirk Douglas, Alain Delon, Charles Boyer, Anthony Perkins, Jean-Paul Belmondo, Simone Signoret, Yves Montand, George Chakiris, Robert Stack, Gert Frobe, Claude Dauphin and Daniel Gelin top-lined the huge, famous and international cast. The reviews could hardly have been worse if Hitler himself had written them.

△ It got a bit out of hand towards the finish, what with all the shouting and running around, but **Arrivederci, Baby** (GB: **Drop Dead, Darling**) was enjoyable most of the way. That is, unless one was repelled by its black-comedy 'hero', a ladies' man whose motto was love 'em and leave 'em dead, in order to inherit their estates. Tony Curtis and Rosanna Schiaffino, seen here, played the lady killer and the bride who outwitted him, supported by Nancy Kwan, Zsa Zsa Gabor, Lionel Jeffries and Fenella Fielding. Ken Hughes directed, produced and, with Ronald Harwood, wrote the British picture, giving it lush backgrounds in England and the South of France.

▽ **The Psychopath** was a British shock-and-shudder item with aspirations, indicated by title and author (Robert Bloch wrote both stories) to being another *Psycho*. Hitchcock was busy elsewhere, unfortunately. Several murders occurred, a doll was found near each corpse, and the police trail led to a German matron (Margaret Johnston, left) living surrounded by her friends – all dolls. Patrick Wymark, Alexander Knox, Judy Huxtable (right), John Standing and Thorley Walters were also in Freddie Francis's cast whose members, not content with roles they could sink their teeth into, did some scenery-chewing as well. Milton Subotsky produced.

OTHER RELEASES OF 1966

Apache Uprising
Rory Calhoun, Corinne Calvet, John Russell, Lon Chaney Jr. Dir: R.G. Springsteen. Pro: A.C. Lyles. Good folks of the West contend with stagecoach robbers, a crooked sheriff, and Indians on the warpath.

Bolshoi Ballet 67
Documentary of the Bolshoi Theatre School. Dir: Leonid Lavrosky, Aleksander Shelenkov. (Russian)

Johnny Reno
Dana Andrews, Jane Russell, Lon Chaney Jr, Richard Arlen. Dir: R.G. Springsteen. Pro: A.C. Lyles. Tough marshal arrives in town to see a glamorous saloon owner, stays to clear up a murder case.

Kid Rodelo
Don Murray, Janet Leigh, Broderick Crawford, Richard Carlson. Dir: Richard Carlson. Pro: Jack Lamont, James Storrow Jr. Drifter seeking a cache of gold finds that a bunch of killers has the same idea.

The Last Of The Secret Agents?
Marty Allen, Steve Rossi, Nancy Sinatra. Dir. & Pro: Norman Abbott. Spies and thieves meet their match in a crazy pair of amateur investigators who save the Venus de Milo.

Nevada Smith
Steve McQueen, Karl Malden, Suzanne Pleshette, Brian Keith, Arthur Kennedy. Dir. & Pro: Henry Hathaway. The earlier adventures of *The Carpetbaggers* (1964) cowboy character during California gold rush days.

The Swinger
Ann-Margret, Anthony Franciosa. Dir. & Pro: George Sidney. Respectable girl fakes a scorching autobiography to break into the magazine world.

Waco
Howard Keel, Jane Russell, Wendell Corey, Brian Donlevy. Dir: R.G. Springsteen. Pro: A.C. Lyles. Western town's citizens release a gunslinger from jail to get rid of the lawbreaking gang terrorising them; he does so.

1967

▽ Jane Fonda, producer-director Otto Preminger and Michael Caine in a happy moment during the shooting of **Hurry Sundown**. You might almost say *the* happy moment: this movie bristled with production problems. Citizens of the small Louisiana town where the bulk of filming occurred resented the Hollywood intrusion and made life especially tough for black principals Diahann Carroll, Robert Hooks and Rex Ingram; Preminger, not the easiest taskmaster in the world at the best of times, had noisy rows with his players; schedules and budgets went overboard. The outcome was a 146-minute mess, scrappily scripted by Thomas Ryan and Horton Foote from K.B. Gilden's best-seller about dissolute whites versus noble blacks. Silliest scene: Miss Fonda enticing Caine with a phallic saxophone. The strong cast, which helped it to gross a little more than its $4 million cost, included Faye Dunaway, John Phillip Law, Burgess Meredith and George Kennedy.

▽ Hitchcock worked wonders with a buried body as a source of black comedy in *The Trouble With Harry* – so wouldn't several disinterred corpses multiply the laughs? 'No' was the verdict from the underpopulated audiences of **The Busy Body**. Director-producer William Castle and writer Ben Starr took one of Donald Westlake's comic crime novels and overloaded the plot (gangster buried with a million dollars sewn in his suit, bodies transplanted, collector from the mob baffled, widow in a tizzy, etc) with slapstick and jokey dialogue. Sid Caesar (right), who seemed unable to repeat on film his success as a television comedian, was aided by an expert cast: Anne Baxter (left), Robert Ryan, Kay Medford, Richard Pryor, Jan Murray, Dom de Luise, Godfrey Cambridge, George Jessel, Arlene Golonka and Ben Blue.

△ A veteran gunfighter (John Wayne, left) and a whisky-soaked sheriff (Robert Mitchum, right) joined forces to wipe out the bad guys in **El Dorado**, a typical and very popular Howard Hawks brew of violent action and rowdy comedy, written by Leigh Brackett from Harry Brown's novel, *The Stars In Their Courses*. If you thought you'd seen it before, maybe you had. In 1959 Hawks made *Rio Bravo* for Warner Bros. with practically the same story, also starring Wayne and scripted by Brackett. The new one came just fifty years after Hawks first entered the industry (as a prop boy for Famous Players-Lasky), and he made only one more movie before his death in 1977: *Rio Lobo*, again with Wayne, script by Brackett, and that good old basic plot. His present cast included James Caan, Christopher George, Michele Carey (centre), Charlene Holt, Arthur Hunnicutt and Edward Asner.

▽ The domestic problems of a daffy young couple kept audiences beaming throughout the 106 minutes of **Barefoot In The Park**. Filmed while it was still a crowd magnet on Broadway, where it ran for nearly fours years, this second of playwright Neil Simon's many hits took two of its original leads – Robert Redford and Mildred Natwick – onto the screen and opened out the play's one-set confinement to become even better entertainment. Chief source of the fun, however, was still that one set (there were excursions into a New York restaurant and park), a fourth-floor flat in a walk-up apartment house into which the couple have just moved and which has hilariously dismaying drawbacks. It was amazing how many genuine laughs Simon managed to get from the ordeal of stair-climbing. There was no plot, just incidents, and they were enough when performed so beautifully by Jane Fonda (left), Redford (right) and Natwick, who got an Academy nomination for her funny portrait of the visiting mother attracted to an eccentric neighbour, played by Charles Boyer, charming as ever at 70. Mabel Albertson, Herbert Edelman and Fritz Feld had amusing bits in Hal B. Wallis's Technicolor production, directed by Gene Saks as his first for the screen. It drew a walloping $9 million from bookings in USA and Canada alone.

◁ Wild animals and wild Westerners are the most popular outdoor movie subjects, so why not combine the two? Get Hugh O'Brian, who was terrific as Wyatt Earp all those TV years, and make him a cowboy roping big game in Africa. Get Andrew Marton to direct; he made *King Solomon's Mines* there.... And so it came to pass: **Africa – Texas Style** (GB: **Cowboy In Africa**) was shot in Kenya, efficiently and colourfully, with a script by Andy White, a cast including Adrienne Corri (here with O'Brian and a scene-stealer), John Mills, Ronald Howard, Nigel Green and Tom Nardini, and an outstanding rhinoceros sequence. Marton's production had a good idea for a movie; an even better one for the subsequent television series, *Cowboy in Africa*.

△ **The Stranger** resulted from Luchino Visconti's attempt, mostly successful, at the difficult task of translating Albert Camus's novel, *L'Etranger*, into film language. Criticised by some for missing the spirit of the great existentialist work by giving it too literal a treatment, it was nevertheless a picture to haunt the mind as well as to charm the eye with Visconti felicities. Marcello Mastroianni (right) provided a moving study of the doomed man who rejects society's hypocrisies and commits a senseless murder. Anna Karina (left), Bernard Blier and George Wilson were also featured in the screenplay by Visconti, Suso Cecchi D'Amico, Georges Conchon and Emmanuel Robles, produced by Dino De Laurentiis.

△ **The Last Safari** was the final adventure of a white hunter who has become disillusioned by innumerable trips through the African wilds. The jaded mood was all too convincingly conveyed to depressed audiences by director-producer Henry Hathaway and star Stewart Granger (illustrated), both with long, successful careers behind them. The animals, hungrier, put on a more spirited show in John Gay's adaptation of *Gilligan's Last Elephant*, a novel by Gerald Hanley, which takes the hunter, accompanied by a rich young American (Kaz Garas) who irritates him, on safari to shoot the rogue elephant that has killed the hunter's best friend. When he finds the beast at last, he lets it go. The British-based production used a good deal of location footage, and the dark continent looked big, bright and beautiful for the Technicolor cameras of Ted Moore. Gabriella Licudi, Liam Redmond, Johnny Sekka and Eugene Deckers filled the supporting parts with efficiency, but unfortunately not many customers were there to see it.

▽ Suzy Kendall (right) was given a hard time when Norman Rodway (left) and Tony Beckley (centre) invaded **The Penthouse** where she had been enjoying an illicit rendezvous with a married man (Terence Morgan) in an apartment house still under construction. They were interrupted by the intruders, who proceeded to indulge their every kinky whim on the terrified lovers. An essay in sadism from the British studios, written and directed by Peter Collinson, and produced by Harry Fine from a play, *The Meter Man*, by C. Scott Forbes. The permissive era managed to survive this tasteless shocker, but it made some viewers wonder if the time hadn't come for censorship to make a comeback.

▽ One of the most resounding flops of all time was registered by **Oh Dad, Poor Dad, Mama's Hung You In The Closet And I'm Feeling So Sad**. In spite of the feverish efforts of a cast including Rosalind Russell as a smothering mother and Robert Morse as her dimwit son, plus Barbara Harris, Jonathan Winters and Lionel Jeffries, every make-'em-laugh sequence fell flat on its back and just lay there, like Hugh Griffith in this one with Roz. Ian Bernard scripted the indescribable story from Arthur Kopit's New York play (which was no great shakes to begin with), and Richard Quine directed the Ray Stark-Stanley Rubin production for Seven Arts. Additional scenes handled by Alexander Mackendrick were in vain and, after a year on the shelf, it was not so much released as allowed to escape.

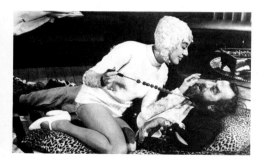

▷ Nathaniel Benchley's amusing novel *The Visitors* went through the typewriter of Ben Starr and the camera of producer-director William Castle and emerged as **The Spirit Is Willing**, to a critics' chorus of 'but the film is weak.' Vera Miles (left), Sid Caesar (right), Barry Gordon, John McGiver, Cass Daley, Mary Wickes and Jay C. Flippen did their best with the haunted-house inanities occurring after a couple rent a holiday home on the New England coast and find spectres from an old killing already in residence. But there were few takers for an offering billed as 'The first picture to face the biggest problem of our time: the sex life of ghosts!'

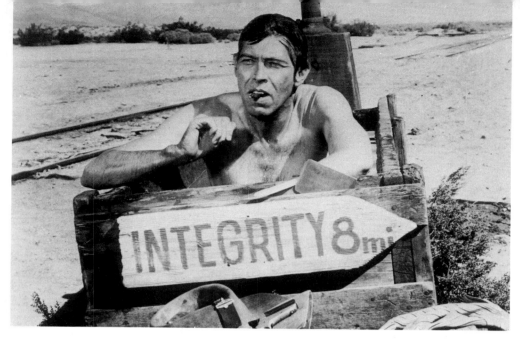

△ James Coburn had a whale of a time in **Waterhole No 3** playing a 'hero' who didn't draw the line at rape or murder. The movie's viewers (who should have been more numerous) enjoyed themselves, too, as soon as they got the hang of its racy, tongue-in-cheek treatment of the Western formula, notable for the outspoken dialogue and off-beat characters Joseph Steck and Robert R. Young worked into their screenplay. Coburn (illustrated) showed star quality as a gambler trying to find the proceeds, hidden in a waterhole somewhere in the desert, of a gold robbery;

△ There was colourful drama a-plenty in **Hostile Guns**, even if the wagon wheels creaked a bit in the screenplay (by Steve Fisher and Sloan Nibley) about a government marshal trekking across Texas with a coachload of prisoners bound for the state hoosegow. He is temporarily hindered by a disloyal deputy and a temperamental dance-hall dame, but iron-jawed determination and a fast draw on his six-shooter gets him through to a safe delivery in the end. This was an A.C. Lyles production, which meant that movie buffs could enjoy renewing acquaintance with several whatever-became-ofs among the cast, which was headed by George Montgomery (right) as the marshal and Yvonne De Carlo (left) as the lady of easy virtue, and included Tab Hunter, Brian Donlevy, Don Barry, Fuzzy Knight and Richard Arlen – the latter celebrating the fortieth anniversary of his Paramount stardom's start in *Wings*. The new picture, eye-filling in Technicolor and Techniscope, was directed by Western veteran R.G. Springsteen.

a lot of other low-life types have the same idea. Joan Blondell as the blowsy, breezy madam of a thriving bordello, and Carroll O'Connor as the sheriff with unlawful tendencies were outstanding in a good cast containing Bruce Dern, Margaret Blye, James Whitmore, Claude Akins and Timothy Carey. Producer Steck stretched the budget for Technicolor/Techniscope and his team, headed by director William Graham and cinematographer Robert Burks, created a town called Integrity, Arizona, that looked as if it might have existed – well, almost.

△ An absolutely first-class police thriller, **Warning Shot** gripped from start to finish. Buzz Kulik, its director (and co-producer with Bob Banner) had learned from long and much acclaimed television experience that strong material needs no frills, and here screenwriter Mann Rubin had woven good dramatic stuff from Whit Masterson's novel *711 – Officer Needs Help*, so Kulik gave it clear-cut treatment with not one of its 100 minutes wasted. David Janssen (right) played a cop who is suspended from the force after he, while on the trail of a psycho murderer, encounters an armed man in the dark, fires a shot and kills him – but the victim is a doctor, respectable and unarmed, or so it seems. It becomes a detective story as the cop quizzes witnesses and the dead man's associates; more killings occur before Janssen clears his name and the case. There was a whole gallery of colourful characterisations provided by a cast of extraordinary eminence for a movie of this type: Eleanor Parker, George Sanders, Walter Pidgeon, Lillian Gish (55 years after her film debut), Sam Wanamaker (left), Joan Collins, Keenan Wynn, Ed Begley, Stefanie Powers, Carroll O'Connor, George Grizzard, Steve Allen. In view of that salary list, good grosses were required, and they duly arrived.

◁ Michael Caine (right) and Oscar Homolka (left) impressively headed the cast of **Funeral In Berlin**, supported by Eva Renzi, Hugh Burden, Paul Hubschmid, Guy Doleman and Rachel Gurney. This over-plotted spy yarn, well directed by Guy Hamilton and produced by Charles Kasher from Evan Jones's dauntingly complex screenplay, centered on a plan to fake a defecting Russian general's funeral and smuggle him out of Berlin in a coffin. It was the second of three Len Deighton novels (the others: *The Ipcress File*, 1965, and *Billion Dollar Brain*, 1967) brought to the screen by Harry Saltzman – between his splashier James Bond productions – with different directors and scripters, but always Caine as the reluctant, low-key agent Harry Palmer.

▽ **Tarzan And The Great River** found our hero far from his old African stamping grounds, in a South America looking remarkably similar, stitched together from genuine stock shots and studio fakes. This is one of the latter, featuring a lion from Central Casting and Mike Henry, the fifteenth actor to don a Tarzan loincloth and take the swinging vine route through the jungle. Aside from the novelty of a hairy chest and quite a fluent line of chat, Mike was much the same as his predecessors. So, indeed, was the action, an exciting chase along the Amazon with Jan Murray, Manuel Padilla Jr, and Rafer Johnson. The screenplay was written by Bob Barbash, directed by Robert Day and produced by Sy Weintraub.

△ In **The President's Analyst** all hell bust loose for a psychiatrist after he was persuaded to take on the President of the United States as a patient. Spies of all nations start hounding him to make him reveal political secrets dropped from the couch until, driven almost psycho himself, the shrink flees to a hippie commune for peace. James Coburn (centre) was splendid in this role, supported by Godfrey Cambridge (right) and Severn Darden (left) – very funny as USA and Soviet agents, respectively – as well as Joan Delaney, Will Geer, Eduard Franz and Pat Harrington. As written and directed by Theodore Flicker and produced by Stanley Rubin, it scored with both espionage satire and slapstick fun.

△ According to Steve Fisher's **Red Tomahawk** script, the citizens of Deadwood live in fear of the Sioux after Custer's last stand at Little Big Horn. They need the guns Custer's men have left hidden, but only Dakota Lil knows where. Captain York, leader of the US Cavalry unit sent to defend Deadwood, has to do a lot of sweet talkin' to coax her to tell, and a lot of hard shootin' to rid the town of no-good gamblers before taking on the Sioux. This was a good old-fashioned Western with good old-fashioned stars in a cast typical of A.C. Lyles productions; one of his best line-up of familiar names was on view: Howard Keel (right) as York, Joan Caulfield as Lil, Broderick Crawford (left), Wendell Corey, Scott Brady, Richard Arlen, Tom Drake, Donald Barry and Ben Cooper. As usual, R.G. Springsteen directed briskly, and the outdoor action was all the better for Technicolor. Two decades earlier the durable Mr Keel had kept the rafters of London's Drury Lane ringing for years in *Oklahoma!*, and two decades later he would help to hold TV viewers agog for years in *Dallas*; proof that if you want to keep going, go West.

OTHER RELEASES OF 1967

Chuka
Rod Taylor, Ernest Borgnine, John Mills, Luciana Paluzzi. Dir: Gordon Douglas. Pro: Rod Taylor, Jack Jason. A gunfighter and a disgraced colonel are caught up in the battle to save a besieged western fort.

C'mon, Let's Live A Little
Bobby Vee, Jackie de Shannon, Eddie Hodges. Dir: David Butler. Pro: June Starr, John Hertelandy. Musical about an Arkansas country lad breaking into the swinging college crowd.

The Deadly Bees
Suzanna Leigh, Frank Finlay. Dir: Freddie Francis. Pro: Max Rosenberg, Milton Subotsky. Girl on a holiday island meets two beekeepers, discovers one is a madman who develops bees that kill. (British)

Easy Come, Easy Go
Elvis Presley, Dodie Marshall, Pat Prest, Frank McHugh. Dir: John Rich. Pro: Hal B. Wallis. Singing frogman discovers what looks like a sunken treasure, but it turns out to be worthless.

Fort Utah
John Ireland, Virginia Mayo, Scott Brady. Dir: Lesley Selander. Dir: A.C. Lyles. Western wanderer teams with a wagonmaster to break up an attack by Indians caused by a troublerouser whom they capture and kill.

The Gentle Giant
Dennis Weaver, Vera Miles, Ralph Meeker, Clint Howard. Dir: James Neilsen. Pro: Ivan Tors. A little boy's pet cub grows into a 650-pound bear and has to be sold to a circus; it escapes and finds its way back to the boy.

Gunn
Craig Stevens, Laura Devon, Edward Asner, Helen Traubel. Dir: Blake Edwards. Pro: Owen Crump. Private eye investigates murder of a gangster and his mistress; pins it on the transvestite madam of a brothel.

The Hired Killer
Robert Webber, Franco Nero, Jeanne Valerie. Dir: Frank Shannon. Pro: F.T. Gay. A professional hit-man wanting to retire is persuaded by $100,000 to accept his final assignment. (Italian/French)

The Long Duel
Yul Brynner, Trevor Howard, Charlotte Rampling, Harry Andrews. Dir. & Pro: Ken Annakin. A tribal leader, escaped from British internment in India, and the officer sent to catch him win mutual respect. (British)

The Sea Pirate
Gerard Barray, Terence Morgan, Antonella Lualdi. Dir. & Pro: Roy Rowland. Young Frenchman, who has to earn a fortune before he can marry his girl, becomes a pirate on the Indian Ocean. (French/Italian)

Smashing Time
Lynn Redgrave, Rita Tushingham, Michael York. Dir: Desmond Davis. Pro: Carlo Ponti, Roy Millichip. Comedy of two provincial girls' adventures with the trendy eccentrics of swinging London. (British)

Two Weeks In September
Brigitte Bardot, Laurent Terzieff, James Robertson Justice. Dir: Serge Bourguignon. Pro: Francis Cosne, Kenneth Harper. Paris model takes a young lover with her on a job in London and Scotland, then returns to her rich protector. (French)

The Upper Hand
Jean Gabin, George Raft, Gert Frobe, Nadja Tiller, Mireille Darc. Dir: Denys de la Patelliere. Pro: Maurice Jacquin. International underworld characters fall afoul of each other in a gold-smuggling conspiracy. (French)

The Vulture
Robert Hutton, Akim Tamiroff, Broderick Crawford, Diane Clare. Dir. & Pro: Lawrence Huntington. In Cornwall, people are attacked by a huge bird with a human head, product of a nuclear experiment in reincarnation. (British)

1968

▽ Graceful, colourful and charming, **Benjamin** often looked like a Fragonard painting in motion. Its appeal to the ear (at least in the dubbed version) and the intellect was a good deal less than to the eye, since its story of 18th century French beauties in an amorous flutter over a very young man had little substance. Pierre Clementi, Catherine Deneuve and Michele Morgan (left to right here); Michel Piccoli, Odile Versois, Francine Berge, Catherine Rouvel and Anna Gael were in the Mag Bodard production, elegantly directed by Michel Deville. The decorative presence of Mlle Deneuve, who had scored recent hits in *Repulsion* and *Belle De Jour*, and Mlle Morgan, an international star for 30 years, widened its appeal to English-speaking audiences.

△ A genuinely nerve-jarring thriller, **Targets** had one of the oddest inceptions in Hollywood's history. Roger Corman, that merchant of menace who wasted nothing, had a few days' work owed him by Boris Karloff under an old contract. This sparked off a screenplay by Corman's protégè, Peter Bogdanovich, about a horror movie star going into retirement and confronting a real killer during his final personal appearance. After killing his family and several random strangers, the gun-crazy youth (Tim O'Kelly, here, and very good) is cornered against a drive-in's huge screen – showing Karloff in Corman's 1963 *The Terror*. Bogdanovich made an impressive debut as director and producer of the new picture; Karloff, at the other end of his career, aged 81, gave one of his best performances; Nancy Hsueh, James Brown and Sandy Baron supported. Made for peanuts, which turned into gold nuggets.

▽ Dirk Bogarde, here zonked by an enemy agent's drug, to the amusement of fellow party guest Stuart Hoyle (left), led an adventurous life in **Sebastian**. This British movie, coming into a market flooded with spy stories, tried to be different in subject matter and treatment, and it worked. The tedious routine of code-breaking was depicted as a kind of bingo session, with joyous cries of 'Got it!' dispersing tense concentration. Bogarde, when not in charge of an office full of females cracking a Soviet cipher, had alternating episodes of romance and espionage action to share with a fine cast: Susannah York, John Gielgud, Lilli Palmer, Margaret Johnston, Nigel Davenport, Donald Sutherland, Janet Munro and Ronald Fraser. The Michael Powell-Herbert Brodkin production was written by Gerald Vaughan-Hughes from a story by Leo Marks, and directed with suitable panache by David Greene.

◁ A sixties version of the screwball genre so popular in the thirties, **The Bliss Of Mrs Blossom** was a disarmingly dotty comedy. It would have us believe that the wife (Shirley MacLaine, right) of a busy brassiere manufacturer (Richard Attenborough, left) kept a lover (James Booth, centre) in the attic without the husband's knowledge. The interloper had come to mend the lady's sewing machine, and so charmingly did he fix her bobbin that he was still there three years later; then hubby found out, sent the cad off to work and became the daytime romancer himself. Anything for a laugh, said writers Alec Coppel and Denis Norden, director Joseph McGrath and producer Josef Shaftel. An all-British cast, except for the delightful Shirley, included the versatile Freddie Jones, the gifted Patricia Routledge, and comics Bob Monkhouse and William Rushton.

▽ A foretaste of *The Godfather* came in **The Brotherhood**, a highly charged drama of feuds among the Mafia wolf-packs in America. While it gripped throughout, a lack of the ferocity evident in the later movie lessened its impact, and it was a box-office failure. Director Martin Ritt demonstrated his customary ability to bring out the best in his actors: Kirk Douglas (right), taut and thrusting as a 'family' leader faithful to the old style of organized crime; Alex Cord (left) as his younger brother, a follower of the modern big-business Syndicate methods; Luther Adler, Irene Papas, Susan Strasberg, Eduardo Ciannelli and Murray Hamilton. Ordered to follow the exiled Douglas to Sicily and kill him, Cord did so with a final kiss of death, in the tradition his brother had taught him – a memorable scene. The strong script was by Lewis John Carlino.

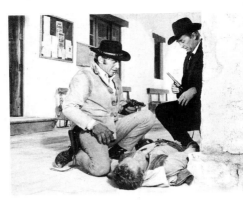

▷ Jane Fonda (right) zigzagged between Hollywood and Europe to make films in the sixties, in the midst of which she married director Roger Vadim. In his **Barbarella** he appeared to be turning her into another Brigitte Bardot (a previous Mme Vadim) by undressing her in a series of costumes designed to conceal practically nothing. While meeting the physical requirements (barely!) Fonda had too much mentally and histrionically to be wasted on any such attempt, and this movie – all visual flash and surface sensation – proved just a temporary aberration in her career. She played a 41st-century astronaut, whose escapades had made a naughty comic strip which was fashioned into a preposterous screenplay by eight writers, including author Jean-Claude Forest, Terry Southern and Vadim, who called it 'a sexual *Alice In Wonderland* of the future'. But critic Charles Champlin subtitled it '2002: A Space Idiocy'. Gulf & Western boss Charles Bluhdorn thought it unworthy of Paramount release, then let it go out, and it made a small fortune as a soft-porn extravaganza, a campy lark, a must-see-it cult item. The French-Italian production of Dino De Laurentiis had lush Technicolor photography by Claude Renoir, and John Phillip Law (left, as a sexy archangel Barbarella desires), Milo O'Shea, David Hemmings, Marcel Marceau, Anita Pallenberg, Claude Dauphin and Ugo Tognazzi in the cast.

△ Dean Martin (left) and Robert Mitchum (right) toted their six-shooters rather wearily through a saddle-sore Western, **Five Card Stud**, to which the box-office didn't react very briskly either. Marguerite Roberts adapted the Ray Gaulden novel about a crooked poker game, a murder and a lynching party whose members were made to bite the dust, one after another, by a religious maniac. A feminine touch was added by Inger Stevens as chief clipper in an all-girl barbershop, while other worthies were portrayed by Roddy McDowall, John Anderson, Whit Bissell, Yaphet Kotto, Katherine Justice and Ted de Corsia in the Hal B. Wallis production. Henry Hathaway directed during a drowsy spell.

▽ Don't let this couple's elegant appearance fool you. They're robbers, cooking up a scheme to heist $10 million worth of gems from the Brazilian Diamond Company. In **Grand Slam**, an Italian-Spanish-German production, Edward G. Robinson marked the 45th anniversary of his first screen performance by playing a schoolmaster who decides to take the crime route to prosperity. Janet Leigh, with him here, was a secretary with the key to an unbreakable safe, and Klaus Kinski, Adolfo Celi and Robert Hoffman had other major roles under Giuliano Montaldo's direction. The Mino Poli screenplay, produced by Harry Colombo and George Papi, kept the suspense taut for two hours. No mean feat.

△ It had been easy to see why **Half A Sixpence** was such a success for Tommy Steele in London and New York theatres. He and it displayed boundless energy and infectious enthusiasm that came across from stage to audience with immediate impact. On the screen, though, those qualities seemed forced, the songs got in the way of the story, and the dances, often shot in theatrical rather than cinematic style, had the look of outdated technique, as if the innovations of the MGM musical era – in which this British film's American director, George Sidney, had once participated – had never happened. Running two and a half hours, it could have dispensed with a few of its dozen numbers (composed by David Heneker, choreographed by Gillian Lynne) to the benefit of its story, about a poor boy inheriting and losing a fortune, winning and losing a society girl, and settling down with his first sweetheart. Created by H.G. Wells in his novel *Kipps* and filmed straight in 1941, the tale had a simple charm, here somewhat engulfed by Technicolor lavishness. The ebulliently talented star (left) was well supported by Julia Foster (right) as his true love, Cyril Ritchard, Elaine Taylor, James Villiers, Pamela Brown, Hilton Edwards, Grover Dale and Penelope Horner, and Beverley Cross's adaptation of his play allowed the Charles Schneer-Sidney co-production to refresh the eye with outdoor English scenery as well as elegant Edwardian interiors.

▽ The warm beauty of Genevieve Bujold (illustrated) shone through her performance in **Isabel** to such effect that she was next chosen to play another title role (*Anne Of The Thousand Days*) which made her an international star. The present film, a comparatively modest affair, was an off-beat thriller depending on brooding atmosphere rather than shock for its frissons. Set in the bleak countryside of Canada's Gaspe Peninsula, it told of a girl who returned to her farm home for her mother's funeral, stayed to look after an elderly uncle, and was haunted by visions of the past. Written, directed and produced by Paul Almond (Miss Bujold's husband and, like her, a Canadian), it featured Mark Strange, Elton Hayes and Gerard Parkes.

◁ Lloyd Bridges, Nico Minardos, Shepperd Strudwick and Joan Blackman (left to right) in **Daring Game**, an eventful if pretty confusing item about American inventors getting embroiled in a Caribbean political plot, from which they rescue a scientist. Much of the action took place under water or in the sky, giving cinematographer Edmund Gibson a chance to show how good colour filming could improve a B script. It was produced by Gene Levitt for the Ivan Tors unit, written by Andy White, and directed by Laslo Benedek, who understandably preferred to quote his credits on *Death Of A Salesman* and *The Wild One*.

▽ Not a whit discouraged by the disaster of *Oh Dad, Poor Dad. . . . .* two years before, Paramount took another crack at that difficult genre, zany black comedy, in **Skidoo**. The result was even more calamitous. The critics greeted it with such ferocious antagonism that even those moviegoers attracted by its big-name cast went into retreat. Otto Preminger, evidently while otherwise preoccupied, both directed and produced from a truly abysmal screenplay by Doran William Cannon – something about an ex-gangster avoiding an unwanted return to crime with the aid of California flower children. Scene after scene dropped with a dull thud, no matter how hard Carol Channing (left), Frankie Avalon (right), Groucho Marx, Mickey Rooney, Jackie Gleason, Peter Lawford, George Raft, Cesar Romero, John Phillip Law, Burgess Meredith and Fred Clark tried to inject genuine fun into it.

△ Little more than a dramatised version of a nervous breakdown, **Inadmissable Evidence** followed a 40-year-old lawyer's agonising journey to the breaking point in his private and professional lives, as he becomes more and more alienated from everyone connected with them. This extraordinary British film brought to a wider audience the performance by Nicol Williamson (left) which had electrified theatregoers in the West End and on Broadway. It was a richly detailed, disturbingly powerful depiction of emotions held under decreasing control, one that would have taxed any great screen veteran; Williamson, actually ten years younger than the character he played, was making his movie debut. Another newcomer, Anthony Page, directed him and Jill Bennett (right), Peter Sallis, Eileen Atkins, Isabel Dean, Eleanor Fazan and David Valla in John Osborne's adaptation of his own play. The Ronald Kinnoch production had photography by Kenneth Hodges, music by Dudley Moore. Still somewhat stage-bound, the drama would have been merely depressing with less penetrating dialogue and characterisation. In the event, only box-office accountants were depressed.

▽ What might occupy the leisure hours of a police constable in the swinging London of the sixties, according to **The Strange Affair**, is depicted here by Michael York with the assistance of Susan George. Relaxing into Stanley Mann's contemporary dialogue (undertaken between his movie bouts with the Bard in *The Taming Of The Shrew* and *Romeo And Juliet*), York gave an excellent performance as an ingenuous young cop who has to face blackmail when his honesty collides with the corruption of a superior officer (Jeremy Kemp). Produced by Mann and Howard Harrison, and directed by David Greene, this drama from Bernard Toms's novel was rather nasty but undeniably gripping. And our hero's nude frolics with a permissive nymphet, filmed by her kinky guardians, did it no harm whatever at the box-office.

▷ Witches seemed truly wicked when seen in the prosaic surroundings of a New York apartment house in **Rosemary's Baby**. This classic horror story was set in the legendary Dakota (scene of John Lennon's murder in 1980) where new tenants, an aspiring actor and his wife, gradually come under the fiendish influence of ostensibly friendly neighbours, who induce the man to become an instrument of the Devil by impregnating his wife with satanic seed. As the birth approaches, the girl's terror and the devil-worshippers' excitement mounts to a frenzy, infecting the movie's viewers, who were held spellbound throughout by the pervading malevolence. Director and scriptwriter Roman Polanski brilliantly established and sustained the atmosphere of evil without indulging in the nasty excesses of subsequent entries in Hollywood's horror cycle. A remarkable performance by Mia Farrow (right) as the wife had expert support from John Cassavetes (left) as the husband; Ralph Bellamy, Sidney Blackmer, Maurice Evans, Patsy Kelly, Elisha Cook Jr, Charles Grodin, Angela Dorian – and, especially, the ever remarkable Ruth Gordon, whose chilling study of a modern witch won her an Academy Award. Like the gripping Ira Levin novel on which it was based, William Castle's Technicolor production was a best-seller.

▽ Best known – and in the opinion of many moviegoers, simply the best – of all Neil Simon's comedies, **The Odd Couple** gave Walter Matthau (left) and Jack Lemmon (right) marvellous opportunities for funny characterisation, and they grabbed them with gusto. Simon had the bright idea of taking the familiar house-proud wife/sloppy husband conflict and switching the sex of the wife; with two men sharing that situation (no gayness implied) the jokes practically created themselves. John Fiedler, Herb Edelman, Monica Evans, Carole Shelley and Iris Adrian had supporting roles in the Howard W. Koch production which, like Simon's *Barefoot In The Park*, was directed by Gene Saks. A subsequent television series, with Tony Randall and Jack Klugman in the Lemmon and Matthau roles, was as big a success as the stage and cinema versions.

▽ Striving for a modernistic – or even futuristic – chic in costume and decor, **Danger: Diabolik** still came across as the old super-thief malarky that made *Arsene Lupin* popular a half-century earlier. John Phillip Law, here with Marisa Mell as his playmate-accomplice, enacted the slick anti-hero who rips off a $10 million haul, then goes after a fortune in gems, a caper which brings him up against a Syndicate boss. The Dino De Laurentiis production, shot in Italy by Mario Bava, had a wild script by Bava, Adriano Baracco and Dino Maiuri derived from a comic strip (what else?) with a big Continental circulation. Michel Piccoli and Terry-Thomas were featured.

△ **Tarzan And The Jungle Boy** marked the 50th anniversary of one of fiction's most popular figures of all time. The white baby left orphaned in the African wilderness to be raised by its denizens to manhood was first seen on screen in 1918 with Elmo Lincoln beating his chest as *Tarzan Of The Apes*. The half-century celebrations could have been given a more distinguished climax than this Sy Weintraub-Robert Day production, a fair-to-middling workout of the formula adventures, but the faithful crowds approved of it – and particularly its leading man. Ex-football star Mike Henry (right), the squarest jawed and most spectacularly muscled Tarzan of them all, was making his third appearance as the fabulous tree-swinger in Steven Lord's screenplay about his search, assisted through the jungle flora by some remarkably intelligent fauna, for a lost boy, played by Steve Bond (left); meanwhile two native brothers battle for tribal supremacy. Director Robert Gordon shot it mostly in Brazil, with Alizia Gur, Rafer Johnson and Ronald Gans also cast. As always, it was a profit-maker.

▽ Mexico's outlaw hero, at once a daring bandit, a violent revolutionary and a social reformer, was portrayed with zest (and hair) by Yul Brynner in **Villa Rides!** This Ted Richmond production concentrated on the rebel in Villa, and his battles were filmed in rousing style, but too many irrelevant scenes (like this one with Brynner and Diana Lorys) and too much footage given to a 1912 pioneer airman and gunrunner played by Robert Mitchum, made the movie seem over-full of action, yet at the same time dull – curiously, considering that the script came from the accomplished hands of Robert Towne and Sam Peckinpah. Buzz Kulik directed a big cast including Charles Bronson, Herbert Lom, Alexander Knox, Maria Grazia Buccella and Fernando Rey, and gained a spectacular plus in Jack Hildyard's photography.

◁ For **Uptight** Ruby Dee, Julian Mayfield and director Jules Dassin (left to right) rewrote Liam O'Flaherty's *The Informer*, making the main characters black and updating the background motivation from the Irish troubles to American blacks' reaction to the murder of Martin Luther King. They had to go some to match the 1935 triumph of screenwriter Dudley Nichols and director John Ford, and they didn't quite make it. However, this version did have dramatic intensity, as well as potent performances by Mayfield as the informer hounded by the militants he betrayed, Miss Dee as the prostitute who took pity on him, Raymond St Jacques, Roscoe Lee Browne and Frank Silvera. Dassin also produced, giving it a fine jazz score by Booker T. Jones.

▽ Joan Hackett, here disturbed by the menace of Bruce Dern, was the forthright and unsentimental heroine of a Western similarly free from movie conformity, **Will Penny**. Set in Montana, the grim story starred Charlton Heston, vivid and realistic as an over-the-hill cowboy facing up to persecution by the most bloodthirsty passel of no-goods ever to ride the plains. Rescued by the girl who then shares his ordeal, he realises that he has nothing but hardship to offer her, and they go their separate ways. The Fred Engel-Walter Seltzer production, also featuring Donald Pleasence, Lee Majors, Ben Johnson and Anthony Zerbe, was a credit to writer-director Tom Gries. Its sombre tone precluded box-office glory, but most audiences echoed the critics' applause.

▽ Leonard Whiting and Olivia Hussey (shown here) were possibly the best looking pair ever to have played **Romeo And Juliet**, and at 17 and 15, respectively, they were certainly the nearest in age to Shakespeare's intention. Unfortunately their youth was matched by their inexperience, and a good deal of the sense and poetry of the play got lost in those handsome young mouths. Altogether, director Franco Zeffirelli's treatment didn't bother too much about the verse; he was out for visual beauty, and he achieved it in abundance. The rich Technicolor cinematography of Pasqualino de Santis and the gorgeous costumes of Danilo Donati were both considered the year's best by the Academy voters, while Zeffirelli and the film itself were short-listed in their categories. Aside from the ravishing pictorial effects, the Italian-British production scored with its action scenes and vivid performances by Michael York (Tybalt), Pat Heywood (Nurse), John McEnery (Mercutio), Milo O'Shea, Robert Stephens, Paul Hardwick and Natasha Parry in the vast cast, with Laurence Olivier speaking the prologue. Franco Brusati, Masolino d'Amico and Zeffirelli screen-adapted and Anthony Havelock-Allan and John Brabourne produced this latest of many movie *Romeo and Juliet*s, which returned more money than any other Shakespeare film.

▷ Rod Steiger (illustrated) sank keen actor's teeth into a rich, juicy role in **No Way To Treat A Lady** – in fact, seven roles in one, as a psychopathic Broadway showman with a compulsion to kill women. He adopts bizarre disguises, using costumes and make-up from his theatre in order to get at his victims, meanwhile driving a detective bananas by taunting him with telephone calls. George Segal, also very good as the cop, figured in a romantic sub-plot with a witness (and the nut's intended next victim) played by the coolly delectable Lee Remick, while Eileen Heckart, Michael Dunn, Murray Hamilton, Barbara Baxley and Ruth White had effective scenes; all directed in smartly paced style by Jack Smight. The off-beat script, developed by John Gay from William Goldman's novel, indulged in unexpected mood changes, ranging through suspense, farce, horror and romance, to finish with a good old-fashioned chase, leaving an over-all impression of entertaining black comedy. Sol C. Siegel's production in Technicolor drew kind words from reviewers and satisfactory cash from exhibitors.

△ Just one of the many sensational incidents piled up in Roger Smith's adaptation of Nell Dunn's **Up The Junction** was this traffic smash-up with Dennis Waterman attending to the victim, watched by (left to right) Suzy Kendall, Adrienne Posta and Maureen Lipman. Based on a semi-documentary about London's free-wheeling life styles of the sixties, it traced the career of a girl (well played by Suzy) from the fashionable end of Chelsea, who goes down-market to Battersea to experience life, including work, love and pregnancy. Director Peter Collinson brought realism and dramatic punch to a depressing story, produced by Anthony Havelock-Allan and John Brabourne, with Liz Fraser, Hylda Baker and Alfie Bass also in the cast. It drew profitable business, especially in Britain.

△ Putting in a strong bid for election as least popular picture of the year was **The Long Day's Dying**, which delivered every ounce of depression promised by the title. Tom Bell, Tony Beckley and David Hemmings (left to right here) and Alan Dobie performed valiantly as a trio of British paratroopers, with their German prisoner, trying to find their way through a European battle zone to the rest of their unit, and dying one by one. The good anti-war intentions of director Peter Collinson, screenwriter Charles Wood and producer Harry Fine were praiseworthy, but they did nothing to transform Alan White's novel into valid movie material.

OTHER RELEASES OF 1968

Anyone Can Play
Ursula Andress, Virna Lisi, Claudine Auger. Dir: Luigi Zampa. Pro: Gianni Hecht Lucari. Sex comedy about Roman society beauties whose indiscretions result in assault, blackmail and scandal. (Italian)

Arizona Bushwhackers
Howard Keel, Yvonne De Carlo, Scott Brady, Brian Donlevy, Marilyn Maxwell. Dir: Lesley Selander. Pro: A.C. Lyles. Southerner, released from Northern war prison for Western law enforcement, is shunned in Arizona, but gets the job done.

Blue
Terence Stamp, Joanna Pettet, Karl Malden, Ricardo Montalban. Dir: Silvio Narizzano. Pro: Judd Bernard, Irwin Winkler. American, raised by Mexicans, is resented by his adoptive brothers, and violently conflicts with their bandit-chief father.

Buckskin
Barry Sullivan, Joan Caulfield, Wendell Corey, Lon Chaney Jr, Richard Arlen. Dir: Michael Moore. Pro: A.C. Lyles. Townspeople are cowed by a ruthless mine-owner, who dams the water supply until the marshal drives him out.

Fever Heat
Nick Adams, Jeannine Riley. Dir. & Pro: Russell Doughton Jr. Action drama in the dirt-track world of racing men, racy women and stock cars.

Maroc 7
Gene Barry, Cyd Charisse, Elsa Martinelli, Leslie Phillips. Dir: Gerry O'Hara. Pro: John Gale, Leslie Phillips. Undercover agent's hunt for jewel thieves leads him to a fashion photography jaunt in Morocco. (British)

Project X
Christopher George, Greta Baldwin. Dir. & Pro: William Castle. East versus West in the year 2118: an agent bearing a vital secret has his memory erased.

The Treasure Of San Gennaro
Nino Manfredi, Senta Berger, Harry Guardino, Claudine Auger. Dir: Dino Risi. Pro: Vetra-Lyre-Roxy. Three American crooks team up with a local hoodlum to steal a fabulous treasure in Naples. (Italian)

The Violent Four
Gian Maria Volonte, Thomas Milian, Margaret Lee. Dir: Carlo Lizzani. Pro: Dino De Laurentiis. Milan rids itself of a gang engaged in extortion, arson, prostitution, robbery and murder. (Italian)

1969

▽ Great stuff for the kiddies, **My Side Of The Mountain** was also enjoyed by adults with a yearning for back-to-nature escapism. It told the story of a 13-year-old boy who, inspired by reading Thoreau's celebration of the simple life, leaves home to live alone in the wild. Equipped only with some clothes, blankets, books and a microscope, he keeps himself fed, sheltered and happy. Ted Eccles (illustrated) did a fine job as the boy, seeming oblivious to the camera under the direction of James B. Clark, a specialist in family entertainment. Theodore Bikel had the only other important role, that of a retired folk singer, in the Ted Sherdeman-Jane Klove-Joanna Crawford screenplay from Jean George's book. Beautifully produced in Canada by Robert Radnitz.

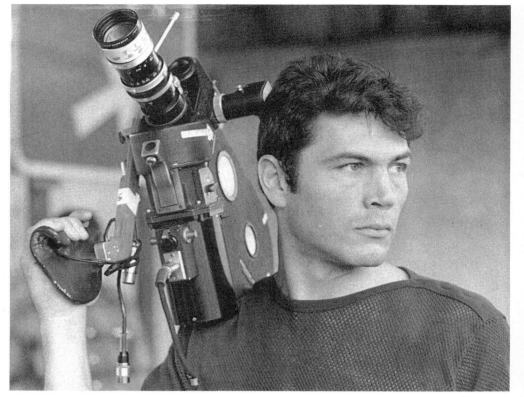

△ **Medium Cool** was the first movie directed by the award-winning cinematographer Haskell Wexler, who also wrote it and filmed it in Technicolor, scoring strongly in all three departments. His screenplay, developed from Jack Couffer's novel *The Concrete Wilderness*, probed the character of a news cameraman trying to keep his mind on his job while surrounded by the hate, hypocrisy and violence of a political convention; it also concerned his involvement with a schoolteacher searching for her lost little boy. More compelling than the plot was the background: the notorious 1968 Democratic convention in Chicago and its attendant riots. Wexler took his cameras and players into the thick of it, achieving an exciting semi-documentary realism seldom seen in a fiction film. The Tully Friedman-Wexler production had a cast – Robert Forster (illustrated), Verna Bloom, Peter Bonerz, Marianna Hill, Sid McCoy, Harold Blankenship – with more talent than name value, and the box-office results echoed the title (a play on Marshall McLuhan's description of television as 'the cool medium'). But the critics raved.

▷ After *Butch Cassidy And The Sundance Kid*, a colossal money-maker, Robert Redford (left) ranked in the very top echelon of 1969 names. Yet his next release, just one month later, might as well have starred Joe Klutz for all it got at the box-office. There seemed to be no good reason for **Downhill Racer** to trip up so badly, since besides the Redford charisma it had exhilarating action, beautifully photographed (by Brian Probyn) against spectacular Alpine scenery. Maybe it was because the locale wasn't the movie's only cold element: the central figure, an arrogant loner chosen for the US Olympics ski team, was pretty chilly too. James Salter's script, from the novel by Oakley Hall, took a penetrating look at athletic competition and the news media's hero-making. The Richard Gregson production featured Gene Hackman (right) as Redford's crusty coach and Camilla Sparv as his seductive off-ski interest. The feature debut of director Michael Ritchie marked him as a find.

▷ Just what Lindsay Anderson was trying to tell us in **If...** it was difficult to discern. That British boys' boarding schools are hell? That a community (or nation) governed by restrictions must break down in anarchy? That youth's eternal conflict with authority was entering an era of violence? Many analyses and arguments were batted around when this film arrived with a story (as obscure as its title, which might just as well have been 'But' or 'Or') about schoolboys' discontent culminating in a nightmarish attack on their assembled masters, whom they slaughter by gunfire. A disconcerting production detail was the switching back and forth between colour and black-and-white; some said this was caused by budget shortage. Others suggested that Anderson (who directed, co-produced with Michael Medwin, and wrote it with David Sherwin) was less concerned with making a serious allegory than with delivering a swift kick to formula-based movie traditions. Either way, it was a remarkable picture, easy to criticise, impossible to forget. Malcolm McDowell (illustrated), as the most rebellious of the students, was (like Richard Harris in documentary-maker Anderson's previous fiction film, *This Sporting Life*) propelled starwards; also cast were David Wood, Richard Warwick, Robert Swann, Peter Jeffrey, Christine Noonan, Arthur Lowe, Mona Washbourne and Anthony Nicholls.

△ Produced by Dino De Laurentiis with a lavish hand and directed by Alberto Lattuada with a good eye for period atmosphere but a wobbly dramatic sense, **Fraulein Doktor** was inspired by the real life story (it says here) of World War I German spy Anna Maria Lesser. Caught up in the lady's complicated exploits were Kenneth More (left), James Booth (right), Capucine, Alexander Knox, Nigel Green and Giancarlo Giannini, while Suzy Kendall valiantly impersonated Anna Maria herself. The screenplay concocted by Stanley Mann, H.C. Craig, Duilio Coletti, Vittoriano Petrilli and Lattuada, and filmed in Italy and Yugoslavia, had its exciting moments but occasionally lapsed into melodrama so ripe as to make you wish they'd made 'Carry On, Mata Hari' instead.

▷ No, director Sergio Leone didn't keep his **Once Upon A Time In The West** cast in line with that gun. He was just showing Claudia Cardinale how to handle it in a scene with Charles Bronson (left) who needed no instruction in gat-slinging. Into this super-spaghetti western's 165 minutes of shoot-'em-up action Leone crammed elements of virtually every similar winner ever filmed, not least the violence of his Clint Eastwood *Dollar* movies. The result fell short of his epic goal, but crowded audiences enjoyed a feast of blood-splattered excitement. Big surprise among the cliches: Henry Fonda cast as a vicious villain, coldly wiping out an entire family and leaving Jason Robards to be falsely accused of the slaughter. Keenan Wynn, Lionel Stander, Paolo Stoppa and Jack Elam acted in the Leone-Sergio Donati screenplay, produced by Fulvia Morsella.

▷ Everybody hit the floor when Terence Hill (who became a top Italian star when he dropped his real name, Mario Girotti), Eli Wallach, Brock Peters and Bud Spencer (left to right) made their entrance in **Ace High** (aka **Revenge In El Paso**) a lively spaghetti Western centring on Wallach as a bandit who relieves similarly shady characters of $300,000. He is tracked down by his victims, and they all have to join forces against a desperado (Kevin McCarthy). The rest was mostly chase. Giuseppe Colizzi, its writer, director and (with Bino Cicogna) producer, kept tongue in cheek amidst Spanish locations looking like Mississippi and points west. But its 120 minutes were about 30 too many.

△ Overweight, over-long and over budget, grumbled the critics (and Paramount's accountants) about **Paint Your Wagon**. But this outdoor musical, filmed in Oregon and with difficulty, had among its 166 minutes many which hit the heights – all of them during the great songs Frederick Loewe and Alan Jay Lerner wrote for the 1951 Broadway show, such as 'I Still See Elisa', 'There's a Coach Comin' In', 'I Talk To The Trees', 'They Call The Wind Maria' and 'Wand'ring Star'. That last, delivered in an astounding growl by Lee Marvin (right) turned out to be the surprise hit of the movie and a chart-topping disc. Lee and Clint Eastwood (left) played gold prospectors who shared one wife, Jean Seberg (centre right), in the rambling story written and produced by Lerner, with Harve Presnell, singing handsomely, Ray Walston and Alan Baxter in minor roles. Neither Paddy Chayefsky's adaptation nor Joshua Logan's direction improved on the stage original, but spectacular scenery did. Also spectacular was the $20 million cost, too much for even the sixth biggest receipts in Paramount's history (to 1969) to recoup.

▷ After forty years of loping through the Western ranges and other scenes of heroic action, John Wayne (illustrated) reached the Hollywood pinnacle with **True Grit**: it won him the Academy Award for best actor of the year. By now as much a symbol of American democracy (right wing) as Uncle Sam, 'Duke' Wayne had become more of an institution than a star, and some of his performances had taken on a monolithic stolidity. But he responded with renewed gusto to a rich role in this Marguerite Roberts screenplay (from a book by Charles Portis) about a grizzled, one-eyed lawman hired as a bounty-hunter by a young girl to catch the killer of her father. In company with a Texas Ranger searching for the same man on another charge, they hunt him down. Kim Darby was refreshing as the girl, pop singer Glen Campbell surprised with a good straight performance as the Texan, and Robert Duvall, Dennis Hopper, Jeff Corey, Donald Woods and Jeremy Slate did well for director Henry Hathaway, another veteran back in good form. Hal B. Wallis's production boasted Technicolor photography by Lucien Ballard and an Elmer Bernstein score, both fine. Wayne's career included many box-office winners but none so big as this one (North American rentals over $15 million), which cued his making a sequel, *Rooster Cogburn*, co-starring Katharine Hepburn, for Universal in 1975.

△ Liza Minnelli (left) got an Academy Award nomination for a performance in **The Sterile Cuckoo** (GB: **Pookie**) which trembled on the brink of ham, while extracting every ounce of pathos and comedy written into the role of an eccentric girl forcing a college love affair with a reluctant student. Her insecurity and vulnerability were sometimes touching, but eventually he (and the audience) found her non-stop talking and emotionalism just too much. Wendell Burton (right) impressed as the boy, with Tim McIntire, Austin Green and Sandra Faison also in producer-director Alan J. Pakula's cast. Alas, the Alvin Sargent screenplay from John Nicholson's story couldn't make use of Liza's dazzling song-and-dance talents, and the public waited for *Cabaret*.

◁ **The Italian Job**, a spectacular robbery of gold bullion in Turin, was masterminded by Noel Coward (right) from a British prison where he was lord of all he surveyed. Michael Caine (left) led his gang, disguised as visiting football fans, to grab the loot and make their getaway by creating traffic jams. Huge fun, especially when the improbable plot was jettisoned and stunt drivers took over for a long, breathtaking climax with a literally cliff-hanging finish. Raf Vallone, Tony Beckley, Rossano Brazzi, Margaret Blye, Benny Hill, Irene Handl, John Le Mesurier and Fred Emney joined in with spirit, Michael Deeley produced resourcefully, director Peter Collinson drew every ounce of suspense from Troy Kennedy Martin's script, and a good time was had by all – including its exhibitors.

▷ You can't fault Richard Attenborough for courage. After a quarter of a century as one of Britain's top screen actors, he took on as his first try as director the unclassifiable (some said unfilmable) Joan Littlewood-Charles Chilton stage hit **Oh! What A Lovely War**. This pageant-pantomime-satire-fantasy-history of World War I plunged deeply cutting barbs into the dark side of patriotism which makes international slaughter seem not only respectable but glorious. On the surface level it was a spectacular romp, constantly enlivened by songs of the time and by a truly stellar cast: Ralph Richardson (left), John Gielgud (right), Laurence Olivier, John Mills, Dirk Bogarde, Michael Redgrave, Vanessa Redgrave, Jack Hawkins, Maggie Smith, Kenneth More, Susannah York, John Clements, Phyllis Calvert, Jean Pierre Cassel, Paul Daneman, Joe Melia, Meriel Forbes. A few sequences didn't quite work, but on the whole Attenborough, his co-producer Brian Duffy, screenwriter Len Deighton, photographer Gerry Turpin and designer Don Ashton deserved all the praise they got.

△ The forbidding title of **Only When I Larf** cloaked a fast and often funny entertainment about a trio of confidence tricksters: David Hemmings (left), Alexandra Stewart (right), and Richard Attenborough (a hilarious performance) as their leader. Their exploits, climaxed by the fleecing of African diplomats in an arms deal, ranged from the ingenious to the addlepated, and were linked by a rivalry between Hemmings and Attenborough to dominate the partnership. John Salmon's screenplay from a novel by Len Deighton was produced by the latter and Brian Duffy in Britain. Director Basil Dearden's cast included Nicholas Pennell, Melissa Stribling, Terence Alexander and Calvin Lockhart.

△ Veteran shock producer William Castle (he titled his autobiography *I'm Gonna Scare The Pants Off America*) tested audiences' nerves with a first-rate melo, **Riot**. He sent a crew, headed by director Buzz Kulik, with actors Jim Brown (left), Gene Hackman (right), Mike Kellin, Ben Carruthers and Gerald O'Loughlin, into Arizona State Penitentiary to shoot James Poe's script, from a novel by Frank Elli. Nonprofessional cast members were already there, doing time. The movie's 97 minutes of incessant action included a take-over of part of the prison by bloodthirsty cons during the warden's absence; their kangaroo-court revenge on informers whose names they discovered during an office break-in; the torture of guards held as hostages; a depiction of sadistic transvestites' brutality, and assorted gunplay, knifing, clubbing and gas bombing. Special children's matinee Saturday.

▷ A curious mixture of hectic action, romantic melodrama, rowdy comedy and sordid realism in the stews of 18th century London, **Where's Jack?** didn't come off. Or rather, it did, after disappointing runs. Tommy Steele (right), bright and likeable as ever, threw plenty of gusto into the role of Jack Sheppard, a highwayman able to break into the most closely guarded house or out of the tightest prison. The British picture's producer, Stanley Baker (left) also scored as Jack's ruthless and corruptible nemesis. They, and Fiona Lewis, Alan Badel, Sue Lloyd, Noel Purcell and Dudley Foster were directed by James Clavell in a two-hour screenplay by Rafe and David Newhouse which had nothing wrong with it that a little cutting couldn't have helped.

△ Weird, wild and occasionally wonderful, **The Assassination Bureau** offered Diana Rigg (right) as a journalist, versus Oliver Reed (left) as the leader of a high-class murder mob, in a send-up of conspiracy thrillers. The inventive script by Michael Relph and Wolf Mankowitz zipped around 1906 Europe, taking in a bombing of a Zurich bank, an exploding sausage in Vienna, a spree in a chic Paris brothel and, finally, a zeppelin raid on an assemblage of monarchs. Relph also produced, and Basil Dearden directed the entertaining nonsense, with Telly Savalas, Curt Jurgens, Philippe Noiret, Warren Mitchell, Beryl Reid, Clive Revill and Kenneth Griffith in the cast.

▽ Newcomers Richard Benjamin (left) and Ali MacGraw (right) gave remarkably accomplished performances in **Goodbye Columbus**, the romance of a college drop-out, working as a librarian, with the headstrong daughter of a comparatively affluent family who don't think he's much of a catch. Low on narrative impetus but high on characterisation, it took a fresh, funny look at Jewish life styles of the 1950s in New York's suburbs. Director Larry Peerce, a native of the Bronx, worked from first-hand observation in handling the Oscar-nominated script Arnold Schulman wrote from Philip Roth's best-selling novella. Stanley Jaffe produced, giving good parts to Jack Klugman, Nan Martin, Michael Meyers and Lori Shelle. The fans don't usually flock to social satire, but they did to this one.

OTHER RELEASES OF 1969

Adalen 31
Peter Schildt, Anita Bjork, Kerstin Tidelius. Dir. & Pro: Bo Widerberg. True story of the 1931 general strike in Sweden, seen through the experiences of one worker's family. (Swedish)

The Brain
David Niven, Jean Paul Belmondo, Bourvil, Eli Wallach. Dir: Gerard Oury. Pro: Alain Poire. Comedy of a master crook posing as a NATO colonel, stealing $14,000,000 from a train and being chased by other thieves. (French)

Hello Down There
Tony Randall, Janet Leigh, Jim Backus, Roddy McDowall, Richard Dreyfuss. Dir: Jack Arnold. Pro: George Sherman. Undersea developer builds a home on the ocean floor and persuades his boss to try it out for 30 days.

Those Daring Young Men In Their Jaunty Jalopies (GB Monte Carlo Or Bust)
Tony Curtis, Peter Cook, Dudley Moore, Bourvil, Jack Hawkins, Susan Hampshire. Dir. & Pro: Ken Annakin An outrageous bunch of characters drive in the Monte Carlo Rally during the twenties. (Italian/French)

▽ With all their charm and skill, Mr and Mrs Paul Newman (Joanne Woodward) couldn't make much of **W.U.S.A.**, a misfired shot at combining personal drama and political tract. What power the original novel (*A Hall Of Mirrors* by Robert Stone) possessed became blurred on the screen, indicating that entrusting the script to the author may have been a mistake. The stars, seen here, played a pair of losers, like most of the characters – he as an announcer on New Orleans radio station WUSA who opposes its Fascist propaganda, she as a prostitute who, arrested during a political riot, hangs herself in jail. Others depressingly present were Anthony Perkins as a deranged welfare worker, Laurence Harvey as a bogus evangelist, Pat Hingle as a right-wing demagogue, Michael Anderson Jr, Bruce Cabot, Cloris Leachman and Moses Gunn. Director Stuart Rosenberg or producers John Forman and Newman should have done something about the dialogue, which was often so oblique as to be meaningless and sometimes unintentionally funny.

▷ Finishing off a week's fling in Rome, playboy Bekim Fehmiu here plans a new plunge into the fleshpots of *la dolce vita*, while Olivia de Havilland contemplates going back to prosaic domesticity in Texas. A rare moment of calm in **The Adventurers**, Harold Robbins's long, colourful, trashy novel turned into a ditto movie. Its tale of a Latin American ambassador's son, his jet-set philandering, and his eventual return to his native land to take revenge on the corrupt government official who raped and murdered his mother, encompassed nearly every lurid sensation known to humanity and best-sellerdom. Three hours of this proved too much for ticket-buying crowds, to the dismay of its sponsors. Lewis Gilbert directed and produced for Avco-Embassy, scripted (with Michael Hastings), and cast Candice Bergen, Ernest Borgnine, Charles Aznavour, Rossano Brazzi, Alan Badel, Leigh Taylor-Young, John Ireland, opera star Anna Moffo, and Fernando Rey in featured roles.

▽ Entering the box-office arena at the head of Paramount's parade of seventies releases, **Darling Lili** fell flat on its face and never got up again. The banana peel was a batch of terrible reviews, the critics being almost unanimous in blasting the musical comedy's painfully slow progress through a World War I romance between an American airman (Rock Hudson, left) and an English music-hall singer (Julie Andrews, right) who is really a German spy. Overlong, overelaborate and, worst of all, wildly over budget – producer-director Blake Edwards lavished more than $20 million on it; about one-quarter came back – what could have been a diverting skit on the Mata Hari legend buckled under a load of songs, aerobatics and sledgehammer whimsy. Not that it was all bad: pleasurable moments were scattered through its 136 minutes to save its talented stars and director from total embarrassment, and some people enjoyed it all, regardless. Jeremy Kemp, Lance Percival, Michael Witney, Jacques Marin, Andre Maranne and Gloria Paul had parts in the Edwards-William Peter Blatty screenplay, which was helped along by Technicolor photography of French scenery and Oscar-nominated music and costumes.

▽ A two-hour combination of hilarity and horror, **Catch 22** drew a mixed reception when it appeared nine years after author Joseph Heller hit the best-seller jackpot with it. The novel's black comedy somehow became blacker and less comic when the corpses of its World War II American airmen became visible on screen, and Buck Henry's screenplay was so episodic that it was more like a series of sketches (some of them highly amusing) than a coherent story. However, it did work up a fine froth of anti-war satire as its 'hero', a peace-loving pilot, thrashed about in the toils of military double-think, feigning insanity to avoid bombing missions; actually, he was the sanest man in his company of crackpots stationed in Italy. They were played in styles ranging from deadpan to hysterical by a cast so loaded with good names that they had to be billed alphabetically: Alan Arkin (deservedly first; he was fine in the lead), Martin Balsam (right), Richard Benjamin, Art Garfunkel, Jack Gilford, Buck Henry, Bob Newhart, Anthony Perkins, Paula Prentiss, Martin Sheen, Jon Voight (left) and Orson Welles. The expensive Martin Ransohoff-John Calley production in Technicolor, directed by Mike Nichols, had a hard time getting back its $18 million cost.

▽ Marseilles was the Chicago of France, and Alain Delon (left) and Jean-Paul Belmondo (right) were its Cagney and Bogart in **Borsalino**. This blood-spattered, bullet-riddled homage to Warner Bros.' palmy days drew huge crowds in Europe and did very nicely for producer Delon elsewhere too, his recent involvement in the scandal that rocked Paris when his bodyguard was murdered having done him no box-office damage at all. He played the more ruthless of a pair of hoodlums blasting their way to the top of the underworld until Belmondo decides his girl is more important than crime. Director Jacques Deray kept the excitement hot for over two hours and gave it the authentic look, sound and mood of 1930s low life. He, Jean Cau, Claude Sautet and Jean-Claude Carriere wrote the script, which gave roles to Arnoldo Foa, Catherine Rouvel, Michel Bouquet, Laura Adani and Corinne Marchand.

▽ A secret society called **The Molly Maguires** was a forerunner of today's labour unions in fighting for workers' rights, but it was violent and lawless, operating through brutal terrorism and even murder. In a Pennsylvania coal mining town, circa 1870, a detective is assigned to investigate the Maguires while posing as a prospective member. He is thoroughly tested by their tough leader before being accepted by the workers, who thus leave themselves open to betrayal, arrest and conviction. Richard Harris (right) and Sean Connery created powerful characters, the first as the undercover man struggling with his conscience, the second as the ruthless fanatic he deceives. Walter Bernstein's script, based on fact, shifted audience sympathy from one side to the other, and this ambivalent point of view reduced the drama's potency, but it was an impressive picture, praised by critics and shunned by ticket buyers: its income ($1½ million in North America) was dwarfed by the cost ($11 million) of a production so meticulous that a coal mine was constructed at the studio to augment footage of a real one used during long location shooting in a grim Pennsylvania town. Director Martin Ritt and his co-producer, Bernstein, gave the movie a hard realism furthered by James Wong Howe's Technicolor photography, and a cast also including Samantha Eggar (left), Frank Finlay, Anthony Zerbe, Art Lund, Bethel Leslie and Anthony Costello.

△ Neil Simon's first comedy written directly for the screen, **The Out-Of-Towners**, was originally intended to be a segment of his *Plaza Suite*, was discarded, then worked up into a full length screenplay. The stretching showed, with the basic joke – the bewilderment of provincials in New York – becoming tiresome before the finish. Jack Lemmon and Sandy Dennis, here vainly seeking help in a police station, nevertheless wrung many laughs from the calamities befalling a couple who are no match for the hectic pace of Fun City. They, and cameos by Anne Meara, Carlos Montalban, Billy Dee Williams, Sandy Baron and Anthony Holland, were directed in the Paul Nathan production by Arthur Hiller, who kept the action going at a fast clip and implausibility at bay.

◁ Barbra Streisand's self-assured manner, powerful voice and Nefertiti nose didn't really suit either of her personas in **On A Clear Day You Can See Forever**. Still, in the dual role of a confused college student and an 18th-century London damsel, a previous incarnation to which she regresses under hypnosis, she acted and sang with all the professional aplomb expected by her fans. They didn't, however, manage to boost Paramount's take above a low figure for a big 1970 musical; five years before, the stage version had also been a box-office disappointment. Howard W. Koch's handsome production had a major asset in its score by author/lyricist Alan Jay Lerner and composer Burton Lane. Oddly, their three best songs (the beautiful title ballad, the haunting 'Melinda' and the rousing 'Come Back To Me') went to co-star Yves Montand as Barbra's hypnotic psychiatrist. Here she dreams about him while boyfriend Larry Blyden coaxes her to join a roof party. Vincente Minnelli, ending a brilliant Hollywood career, directed them, together with Jack Nicholson, Bob Newhart and Simon Oakland.

△ **The Lawyer**, tough, ambitious and a bit of a slob, but likeable with it, gave Barry Newman (left) a starmaking role which he handled so well that he, and it, became internationally popular in the subsequent television series, *Petrocelli*. The movie, based on the 1954 Sam Sheppard case, concerned his efforts to defend a doctor accused of murdering his wife. A surplus of romantic scenes between the lawyer and his own wife slowed the tempo of the Sidney J. Furie-Harold Buchman script, but the courtroom sequences – always surefire when well directed, as by Furie here – had a powerful grip. Harold Gould, Diana Muldaur, Robert Colbert (right) and Kathleen Crowley were featured in Brad Dexter's production.

▷ In a year littered with expensive disasters, **Love Story** came to Paramount's rescue in a great big way. Modestly budgeted, with a small cast and no pretentions to being anything special, it was a simple story of boy meets girl, boy gets girl, boy loses girl to the grim reaper. But its impact on the public was instantaneous. Exhibitors had only to put the title up on their marquees and stand back to let the crowds pour in; Erich Segal's novel sold millions of copies; Francis Lai's theme tune swept the world; Ryan O'Neal and Ali MacGraw (both seen here), as students whose affair ripens into a marriage cut short by her illness and death, were catapulted into stardom; even its advertising slogan, 'Love means never having to say you're sorry', became a popular catchline. Studio chief Robert Evans had bought Segal's script for MacGraw (then Mrs Evans) but the male lead was rejected by Michael York, Jon Voight, Beau Bridges, Michael Sarrazin and Michael Douglas before a percentage-of-profits offer coaxed O'Neal, while directors Larry Peerce and Anthony Harvey bowed out before Arthur Hiller reluctantly accepted the job. Result: international income approaching $100 million, a new all-time record for the company. Ray Milland as O'Neal's rich father and John Marley as MacGraw's poor one were excellent; so was Dick Kratina's crisp colour photography of the attractive New England exteriors. Critics shrugged, but it got seven Oscar nominations.

◁ **Tell Me That You Love Me, Junie Moon** didn't have crowds battering down any theatre doors to get in – and no wonder, with a title like that. The movie itself was a good deal better. Setting out determined to achieve what is known in the trade as heart wallop, it occasionally slipped on a patch of sentimental molasses or tripped on a narrative snag. But director-producer Otto Preminger made it moving and helped his three leads, Liza Minnelli (right), Robert Moore and Ken Howard to bring conviction to wildly neurotic characters; a facially disfigured girl, a homosexual cripple and an epileptic drop-out. Marjorie Kellogg's story had them leaving hospital to set up housekeeping together in a cottage and to ameliorate each other's hang-ups. Minor roles went to James Coco, Kay Thompson, and Ben Piazza (left) as the psycho who scarred Liza.

OTHER RELEASES OF 1970

The Confession
Yves Montand, Simone Signoret, Gabriele Ferzetti. Dir: Constantin Costa-Gavras. Pro: Robert Dorfman, Bertrand Javal. True story of a Czech bureaucrat hounded and tortured into making a false confession. (French)

Little Fauss And Big Halsy
Robert Redford, Michael J. Pollard, Lauren Hutton. Dir: Sidney J. Furie. Pro: Albert S. Ruddy. Money and women float in and out of the lives of a motorcyclist and his mechanic as they tour the racing circuit.

Norwood
Glen Campbell, Kim Darby, Joe Namath, Carol Lynley, Pat Hingle. Dir: Jack Haley Jr. Pro: Hal B. Wallis. Ex-GI leaves his Texas home to seek a singing career and readjust to normal life.

Tropic Of Cancer
Rip Torn, Ellen Burstyn, James Callahan, Phil Brown, Laurence Ligneres. Dir. & Pro: Joseph Strick. Henry Miller's once-banned novel; a tour of Paris bistros and brothels in the 30s.

1971

∇ **Waterloo**, a huge steamroller of a historical drama, trundled its way through 123 minutes (originally longer) to make a strong impression on eyes and ears without ever touching the heart. The 1815 campaign that finished Napoleon's career, depicted with enormous panache, and as much noise and confusion as the real battle must have had, occupied almost half the running time; this was preceded by an account of the emperor's return from exile on Elba, and his defiance of Louis XVIII while rallying the army to fight the English-Prussian alliance. All this part of the movie was chiefly of interest to students of Rod Steiger's technique which, together with a padded *embonpoint*, was applied to the central figure to make, if not a convincing Napoleon, at least a memorable Rod Steiger (illustrated). Others present to considerable effect were Christopher Plummer as Wellington, Orson Welles as Louis, Dan O'Herlihy as Marshal Ney; Jack Hawkins, Virginia McKenna, Michael Wilding, Terence Alexander, Rupert Davies, Donal Donnelly and Ian Ogilvy. The Italian-Russian-British production, lavish and spectacular in Panavision and Technicolor, was sponsored by Dino De Laurentiis, written by H.A.L. Craig, Vittorio Bonicelli and Sergei Bondarchuk, and directed by the latter, whose previous epic, the Russian *War And Peace*, is said to be the longest, most expensive film ever made. This one cost another fortune and was a box-office calamity.

∇ Echoes of *The Blue Lagoon* wafted across an idyllic countryside as Sean Bury (left), an English boy neglected by his family, and Anicee Alvina (right), an orphaned French girl, made a world of their own in a secluded cottage. **Friends** reduced the usual age of the lovers in this type of story, edging towards the minimum possible for the arrival of a baby (he was 15, she 14), which gave the movie a certain notoriety that made a box-office counterweight to poor reviews. Lush Technicolor photography by Andreas Winding around Paris, Arles and Aix-en-Provence fitted the mood of the Jack Russell-Vernon Harris screenplay better than Elton John's and Bernie Taupin's rock-tinged music did. Ronald Lewis and Toby Robins had minor roles. Producer-director Lewis Gilbert made a sequel, *Paul and Michelle*, three years later.

△ English-speaking moviegoers couldn't get excited about (or even pronounce) Bekim Fehmiu, although Paramount had starred the handsome Yugoslav in *The Adventurers*. They tried again with **The Deserter**, a grim Southwestern which cast Fehmiu (left) as a US captain on the Mexican border in 1886, quelling savage raiders by the military book until he and his Indian guide (Ricardo Montalban, right) find his wife hanging, naked and mutilated. This sends him on a rampage, killing enough Apaches to satisfy the most bloodthirsty of the movie's none-too-numerous patrons. Richard Crenna, Chuck Connors, John Huston, Brandon De Wilde, Albert Salmi, Woody Strode and Slim Pickens acted under direction from Burt Kennedy in the Norman Baer-Ralph Serpe production, written by Clair Huffaker.

▷ One of the reasons why stage producers love Neil Simon's plays: they nearly always need just one set. So easy on the budget. **Plaza Suite** took this attribute to the limit by incorporating three separate plays with different characters but the same scenery, that of the title. Simon revised it only slightly for Howard W. Koch's film version, directed by Arthur Hiller with such expertise that you forgot it was virtually a photographed stage performance. Thanks were due also to the richly varied talents of Walter Matthau, playing successive occupants of Suite 719 in New York's Plaza Hotel, and his trio of leading ladies. First, Maureen Stapleton as a nice over-40 matron pathetically trying to infuse her businessman husband with enthusiasm for their honeymoon anniversary. Then Barbara Harris as the ex-flame of a movie producer, who found she didn't want a renewed affair, just the latest Hollywood gossip. Finally, and most uproariously funny, Lee Grant and Matthau (here) as the frantic parents of a bride who wouldn't come out of the bathroom to attend her wedding.

△ **Such Good Friends** sniped satirically at sexual foibles and medical methods, sometimes hit its targets with laugh-rousing accuracy and occasionally misfired completely. Dyan Cannon (background) starred as a wife who found her hospitalized husband's little black book which rated the prowess in bed of her best female friends. Her spree of revenge while he languished in intensive care took up the bulk of a comedy teetering between witty frankness and gross vulgarity, the latter exemplified by a long scene in which Dyan undressed her rotund doctor, played by James Coco. Jennifer O'Neill (centre), Ken Howard, Nina Foch, Laurence Luckinbill, Louise Lasser, Burgess Meredith, Sam Levene, Rita Gam and Nancy Guild also had parts in the Esther Dale (a pseudonym for Elaine May and others) script from Lois Gould's novel, produced and directed by Otto Preminger.

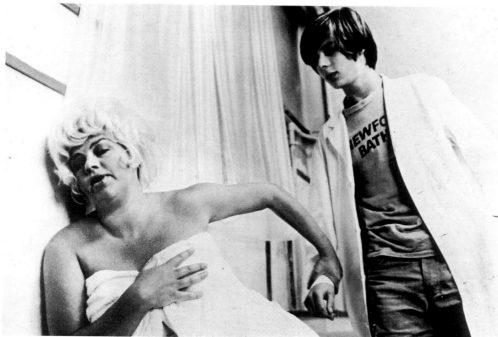

◁ A fascinating exploration of adolescent emotions, **Deep End** was so far off the beaten track that moviegoing crowds, rushing to the latest blockbuster, didn't notice it was there. It was made by the young Polish director, Jerzy Skolimowski, with even younger co-stars, John Moulder-Brown (right) and Jane Asher, the three giving their odd love story an authentic spirit of youthfulness in both its eroticism and its exuberant comedy. Moulder-Brown, an English boy in his first screen lead, was amazingly accomplished as a teenager just out of school who becomes an attendant at a seedy public bath-house and swimming pool in London. He promptly falls in love with his slightly older colleague (Asher, also excellent) whose already complicated affairs with a fiancé (Christopher Sandford) and a lover (Karl Michael Vogler) don't deter his pursuit of her until its gory climax in the baths. An atmosphere of corruption and the violent ending were balanced by sequences of broad fun, notably one in which the boy follows the girl and her fiancé into a pornographic cinema, and another featuring Diana Dors (left) as an eccentric bath-taker. Helmut Jedele produced the German-sponsored film with script by Skolimowski, J. Gruza and B. Sulik, colour photography by Charly Steinberger and music by Cat Stevens.

◁ A gloriously daft comedy arrived in Elaine May's first effort as director, **A New Leaf**. Its release got off to an unfortunate start when Miss May sued Paramount for removal of her name from it, on the grounds that the studio's version of it was not hers. Since she was the screenplay writer and co-star as well as director, the suit might have posed a problem, but it failed, and the picture didn't; her disapproval was shared by no one. Based on a short story by Jack Ritchie, the hilarious proceedings concerned the hunt for a rich wife by a newly impoverished luxury-lover (Walter Matthau, left) whose eccentricities are more than matched by those of the girl he gets (May, right), a short-sighted, accident-prone botanist and millionairess, a frump, but so appealing that the fortune hunter scraps his plan to become her widower, and they live happily ever after. Matthau and May made a marvellously dotty couple, and they were helped to get every kind of laugh from giggles to button-busters by their supporting cast: Jack Weston, George Rose (a delight as Matthau's butler), James Coco, William Redfield, Graham Jarvis, Doris Roberts and Renee Taylor. Produced by Joe Manduke in colour.

▽ The mounting fear which spread through the audience from an expert performance by David Hemmings (right) sustained **Unman, Wittering And Zigo** during some dull spots in the script Simon Raven wrote from Giles Cooper's broadcast play. The title, a paybox dampener if ever there was one, came from the last three names on the roll call of a boys' school, a sort of upper-class British *Blackboard Jungle*, in which the well-bred delinquents threatened a new master with murder and his wife with rape. Carolyn Seymour, Douglas Wilmer, Anthony Haygarth and Hamilton Dyce were in the Gareth Wigan production directed by John Mackenzie. Flawed drama, but hard to forget.

◁ If *A New Leaf* was dotty, **Harold and Maude** was downright certifiable. It offered the romance of a twenty-year-old youth with a woman sixty years older, both of them one step away from the laughing academy. More often funny-peculiar than funny-ha-ha, the Colin Higgins screenplay traced the couple's love story from their meeting as funeral fans who enjoy attending strangers' last ceremonies, to their finish as man and wife, their marriage having occurred on the eve of Maude's eightieth birthday. Despite their morbid hobby, she is a life-loving bundle of energy, a daredevil for speed on motorbike or truck; Harold, on the other hand, is given to suicide attempts by various spectacular means in vain efforts to impress his unflappable mother. To make the mismatching complete, Harold comes from the lap of luxury, while Maude lives in a converted railroad car. The vivacious performances of Ruth Gordon (left) and Bud Cort (right) in the title roles, and the deft direction of Hal Ashby, steered the comedy around the material's more embarrassing grotesqueries to a number of hilarious scenes, in which Vivian Pickles (as the mother), Cyril Cusack, Charles Tyner and Ellen Geer were among those present. Produced by Charles Mulverhill and author Higgins in Technicolor, it received a mixed reception but gradually developed into a cult classic.

OTHER RELEASES OF 1971

The Bear And The Doll
Brigitte Bardot, Jean-Pierre Cassel. Dir: Michel Deville. Pro: Mag Bodard. Collision of a cellist's Renault and a divorcee's Rolls-Royce sparks off a romance. (French)

Been Down So Long It Looks Like Up To Me
Barry Primus, Linda DeCoff, Susan Tyrell. Dir: Jeffrey Young. Pro: Robert Rosenthal. The trials, tribulations and girls in the life of a 1958 college man.

Black Beauty
Mark Lester, Walter Slezak, Patrick Mower, Peter Lee Lawrence. Dir: James Hill. Pro: Peter Andrews, Malcolm Hayworth. Anna Sewell's classic story of a beautiful horse's career as it passes from owner to owner. (British)

The Conformist
Jean-Louis Trintignant, Stefania Sandrelli, Dominique Sanda. Dir: Bernardo Bertolucci. Pro: Maurizio Lodi-Fe. Young Fascist becomes an assassin while striving for social and political acceptance. (Italian)

Desperate Characters
Shirley MacLaine, Kenneth Mars, Sada Thompson, Gerald S. O'Loughlin. Dir. & Pro: Frank D. Gilroy. Drama of a couple whose humdrum marriage is paralleled by the decaying New York area they live in.

A Gunfight
Kirk Douglas, Johnny Cash, Jane Alexander, Karen Black. Dir: Lamont Johnson. Pro: A. Ronald Rubin, Harold Jack Bloom. Two Westerners, once notorious trigger-men, become friends as they stage a gunfight for money.

Joe Hill
Thommy Berggren, Anja Schmidt, Kelvin Malave. Dir. & Pro: Bo Widerberg. A Swedish immigrant arrives in USA in 1910, becomes a leader of workers fighting for their rights, and the victim of a false murder charge. (Swedish)

Let's Scare Jessica To Death
Zohra Lampert, Barton Heyman, Kevin O'Connor. Dir: John Hancock. Pro: Charles B. Moss Jr. Resting in the country after a nervous breakdown, a wife is assailed by apparently supernatural menaces.

Murphy's War
Peter O'Toole, Sian Phillips, Phillipe Noiret, Horst Janson. Dir: Peter Yates. Pro: Michael Deeley. Merchant seaman in the tropics finds a wrecked plane, learns to fly it against the U-boat that sank his ship. (British)

The Red Tent
Peter Finch, Sean Connery, Claudia Cardinale, Hardy Kruger. Dir: Mikail K. Kalatozov. Pro: Franco Cristaldi. Haunted by shame, an old Italian relives a 1928 dirigible disasater in the Arctic, where he abandoned his men. (Italian/Russian)

The Star-Spangled Girl
Sandy Duncan, Tony Roberts, Elizabeth Allen, Todd Sussman. Dir: Jerry Paris. Pro: Howard Koch. Old-fashioned, patriotic girl's funny romance with the editors of an ultra-radical underground newspaper.

T.R. Baskin (GB Date With A Lonely Girl)
Candice Bergen, James Caan, Peter Boyle. Dir: Herbert Ross. Pro: Peter Hyams. Small-town girl finds that working as a secretary in Chicago and meeting a romantic partner can be tricky tasks.

Willy Wonka And The Chocolate Factory
Gene Wilder, Jack Albertson. Dir: Mel Stuart. Pro: David Wolper, Stan Margulies. Boy falls under the spell of a candy-making magician.

1972

∇ David Newman and Robert Benton, who first burst into movie fame as the writers of *Bonnie And Clyde*, delivered another winner in **Bad Company** with, however, a much milder response from the box-office, perhaps because it lacked the earlier film's sexual element. It did have something of the same gritty humour and lyrical recklessness in its footloose tale of two young men of opposite temperaments becoming fellow outlaws while dodging cut-throats, sheriffs and recruiting officers during the Civil War. Benton, who also directed (he was later to win an Oscar for *Kramer vs Kramer*), shared critics' praise with the leading actors, Barry Brown (right) and Jeff Bridges. Also in Stanley R. Jaffe's production were Jim Davis, David Huddleston and John Savage.

∇ The dare that led to disaster: Parker Stevenson (left) was challenged by John Heyl (right) to join him in a high dive from a tree in **A Separate Peace**. They were best friends, one an ebullient athlete, the other an introspective student, both confused by their feelings for each other. So was the audience, because scripter Fred Segal and director Larry Peerce kept it at arm's length from the drama with obscure motivations, understated emotions, muffled dialogue; all of which cancelled out a superb sense of time – war-haunted 1942 – and place, a New England prep school and the actual alma mater of John Knowles, whose novel was the basis of Robert Goldston's production. The two boys' performances shone through the narrative fog, and were adequately supported by Peter Brush, Victor Bevine and William Roerick.

△ **The Man** wasn't much of a picture, but it did have an intriguingly novel idea behind it: the rise of a black man to the presidency of the United States. This invention by novelist Irving Wallace had formed the basis of his best-seller, a tome running to 768 pages, which screenwriter Rod Serling boiled down to 93 minutes for a television movie picked up for theatrical release in America. With a splendid performance by James Earl Jones (illustrated) at its centre, the cast boasted five well-tested talents – Martin Balsam, Burgess Meredith, Lew Ayres, William Windom, Barbara Rush – plus the lesser known Janet MacLachlan as Jones's militant daughter, and Georg Stanford Brown as a guilty black he publicly defends, thereby damaging his presidency. His becoming president in the first place is not by election (equality hasn't got that far, even in fiction) but by a fortuitous combination of events, such as the former president's death when a palace ceiling falls in during a European conference. Joseph Sargent directed and Lee Rich produced. Now how about one about an American Margaret Thatcher?

∇ A very Grimm fairy tale indeed, **The Pied Piper** was directed in sombre mood by Jacques Demy, who had made light-as-air entertainments in his native France (*The Umbrellas Of Cherbourg*, *The Young Girls Of Rochefort*) to international acclaim. This one was received without enthusiasm, critics calling it an awkward mixture of legend too simple-minded for adults and drama too horribly detailed for children. Demy, who also wrote the script with Andrew Birkin and Mark Peploe, filled the 14th-century tale of the strolling minstrel of Hamelin with noisome images of plague victims, rotting vegetation and, of course, rats. The piper (pop singer Donovan, left) shared prominence in it with the wicked baron (Donald Pleasence), whose evil son burns his disobedient chemist at the stake, and marries an 11-year-old girl against her will. Some welcome comedy seemed likely from the latter's parents, in the ample persons of Roy Kinnear and Diana Dors, but in fact the only relief from the gloom came in Donovan's songs, which made a pleasing impression while his acting made none at all. Jack Wild, John Hurt, Michael Hordern and Cathryn Harrison were also in the handsome Technicolor production of David Puttnam and Sanford Lieberson, shot in England and on location in the Bavarian medieval city of Rothenburg.

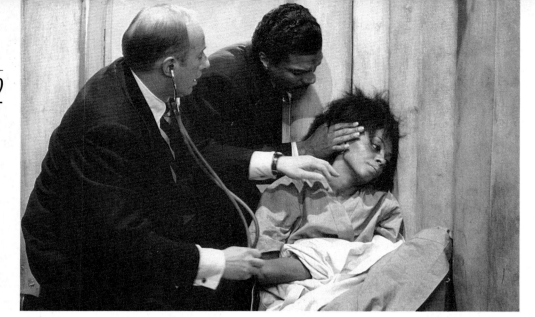

△ Diana Ross (right) glowed like a beacon through the murky drama of **Lady Sings The Blues**. The former lead singer of The Supremes deserved her Academy nomination for the best actress award and the predominantly excellent reviews greeting her performance as Billie Holiday, the legendary jazz singer. 'Lady Day' was inimitable, but Ross, although more beautiful and with a distinctive voice of her own, made you believe that this was how the tragic star looked and sounded. The Oscar nomination for the screenplay by Terence McCloy, Chris Clark and Suzanne de Passe was, however, hard to justify: while based on Holiday's autobiography, ghosted by William Duffy, it left out whole chunks of the life story and used fiction when facts didn't fit. Sidney J. Furie's direction and the Jay Weston-James S. White production, in luscious Eastmancolor and Panavision, combined to cast a glamorous, romantic aura over a story (encompassing child rape, brothel servitude, drug enslavement) requiring gritty realism. The result ranked among biofilms of addicted stars somewhere between the high of *I'll Cry Tomorrow* and the low of *The Helen Morgan Story*, but even the former was surpassed as a box-office success. Billy Dee Williams (centre) as Holiday's husband and Richard Pryor as her pianist, in a cast including Sid Melton, James Callahan, Paul Hampton, Virginia Capers, Yvonne Fair and Scatman Crothers, were very effective. So were the songs – all 18 of them.

△ Was the Catholic boarding school in **Child's Play** haunted by a demonic power? Was the Latin master (James Mason, centre) a victim of persecution or of paranoia? Did the English teacher (Robert Preston, right) lead the pupils in a conspiracy? Could the new gym instructor (Beau Bridges, left) be as innocent as he seemed? Did this release, so close to *If...*, *Unman, Wittering And Zigo* and *A Separate Peace*, mean that Paramount was inventing a new film cycle on boys' boarding schools? All these burning questions except the last were answered to exciting dramatic effect, but little box-office response, in Robert Marasco's play, as adapted to the screen by Leon Prochnik and produced by David Merrick, who did the same for it on Broadway. Skilful director Sidney Lumet handled the film's brooding atmosphere and violent climax with a good deal of panache.

▽ Director Gene Saks and writer Neil Simon got together at Paramount for the third time to film another of Simon's Broadway winners: **Last Of The Red Hot Lovers**. It didn't hit the comedy bulls-eye with the impact of *Barefoot In The Park* or *The Odd Couple* because the basic material wasn't so funny. Constructed as a three-act play, in which a seafood restaurateur makes three clumsy attempts to seduce three different girls in a flat borrowed from his mother, the movie stayed stubbornly stage-bound despite a little opening out, such as this scene with Alan Arkin (as the fish-handed Don Juan) and Paula Prentiss. Sally Kellerman and Renee Taylor were the other girls in the Howard W. Koch production. An overhead mike swinging into view from time to time added a disconcerting touch.

▷ Two contemporary vogues – a growing one for Woody Allen comedy and a posthumous one for Humphrey Bogart – collided in a shower of laughs called **Play It Again, Sam**. Woody's script, which he adapted from his Broadway play, dealt with a movie buff obsessed by memories of Bogie, whose hallucinated image (in brilliant mimicry by Jerry Lacy) manifested itself every once in a while to give helpful hints on woman winning. The Arthur Jacobs production, directed by Herbert Ross, finished with a wicked parody of the last scene in *Casablanca*. Woody, here feigning indifference to Diane Keaton (what an actor!) was supported also by Tony Roberts, Susan Anspach, Joy Bang and Viva.

▷ **The Godfather**, the picture that raised the gangster drama to epic proportions, had two outstanding performances: Marlon Brando (right) as the patriarch of a family which dominated organised crime in America, and Al Pacino (left) as his youngest son, a college boy who had to take a post-graduate course in killing. An instantaneous smash-hit, it returned about $150 million in world-wide rentals to Paramount, making it not only the company's, but the whole industry's biggest money-maker to date. Some critics deplored the romantic glow it cast over what was really a bunch of bloodthirsty criminals, but none could deny its dramatic strength, its ability to rivet attention for nearly three hours in the details of domestic and Mafia power-plays, and its occasional nerve-jolting shocks. Albert S. Ruddy's production gathered ten Academy Award nominations, three of them winners: the film itself as the year's best, Brando as best actor (despite the distractions of a stuffed-cheeks make-up and an almost inaudible hoarse whisper), and the screenplay by Mario Puzo (author of the original novel) and Francis Ford Coppola, also its masterly director. Brando caused an uproar by refusing to accept his Oscar, on the curious grounds that Hollywood was unfair to the American Indian. Three of the Academy's five nominees as best supporting actor were named for this one picture (a record): Pacino, Robert Duvall and James Caan. Scarcely less memorable were Diane Keaton, Talia Shire (Coppola's sister), Sterling Hayden, Richard Conte, John Cazale, Abe Vigoda, Gianni Russo, Morgana King, Al Lettieri, Richard Castellano, John Marley and Al Martino in a role rumoured to have been based on Frank Sinatra. *The Godfather*'s early history paralleled *Gone With The Wind*'s in that the book was bought from galley proofs for what turned out to be a bargain price when it became a runaway best-seller; and there was much publicity about casting the lead (Laurence Olivier and Edward G. Robinson were most strongly tipped) before Brando accepted a percentage deal that brought him $1 million.

OTHER RELEASES OF 1972

Four Flies On Grey Velvet
Michael Brandon, Mimsy Farmer, Jean-Pierre Marielle. Dir: Dario Argento. Pro: Salvatore Argento. Rock musician living it up in Rome gets involved in a bizarre series of murders. (Italian)

Hannie Caulder
Raquel Welch, Robert Culp, Ernest Borgnine. Dir: Burt Kennedy. Pro: Patrick Curtis. Raped and widowed by three outlaws, a woman learns how to shoot and searches the West to get revenge.

The Legend Of Nigger Charley
Fred Williamson, D'Urville Martin, Don Pedro Colley. Dir: Martin Goldman. Pro: Larry G. Spangler. A Virginia slave kills his cruel owner and travels to the West, pursued by a professional slave hunter.

The Possession Of Joel Delaney
Shirley MacLaine, Perry King, Lovelady Powell. Dir: Waris Hussein. Pro: Martin Poll. Wealthy divorcee thinks her young brother has become a drug addict; he is really haunted by the spirit of a dead killer.

ZPG: Zero Population Growth
Oliver Reed, Geraldine Chaplin, Diane Cilento, Don Gordon. Dir: Michael Campuss. Pro: Thomas F. Madigan. Young couple of the future defy a law making reproduction punishable by death. (British)

1973

▽ A must for surgery fans, **Ash Wednesday** was a musn't for lovers of good drama. A glance at its box-office returns confirmed that the second group had got the message, also that the combined multitudes of Elizabeth Taylor and Henry Fonda admirers had stayed well away, having read the reviews. These usually sure-fire stars were marooned in a witless story about a moribund marriage which the wife decides to resuscitate by reviving her beauty, no longer what it was after 50 years' wear and tear. So she checks into an Italian clinic and has her face lifted, along with practically everything else. Those in the audience who survived the sequences of flesh being sliced in Technicolor close-ups saw Liz (illustrated) emerge in all her familiar glory, with disappointing effect on husband Fonda; she has to be satisfied with young lovers. Helmut Berger, Keith Baxter, Maurice Teynac and Margaret Blye completed director Larry Peerce's cast in the Dominick Dunne production, written by Jean Claude Tramont. Before taking this role, Liz should have remembered that she had been at her all-time best, in *Who's Afraid Of Virginia Woolf?*, looking her worst throughout.

▷ An upsurge of interest in women's liberation brought about the coincidence of two screen treatments of **A Doll's House**, both from Britain, arriving at the same time. (There were three silent versions of Ibsen's play, one of which Paramount produced: see 1918.) Confusion was lessened in America by one of them, starring Jane Fonda under Joseph Losey's direction, being shunted straight into television, while the other was released by Paramount to cinemas. This was almost literally a filmed play, with the same star and director – Claire Bloom and Patrick Garland – who had brought its Christopher Hampton translation to London's West End, and Broadway in 1971, but the supporting cast was now made dazzling by Anthony Hopkins (left), Sir Ralph Richardson, Denholm Elliott, Anna Massey and Dame Edith Evans. As the toy wife who gradually realises that her comfortable marriage is stifling her and walks out of it, slamming the door on her smug husband, Bloom (right) met every demand of a complex role; she and Hopkins rose stirringly to the emotional heights of the final confrontation scene. Although the Hillard Elkins production ventured briefly into Norwegian exteriors, it was inevitably stage-bound and too static to attract mass audiences.

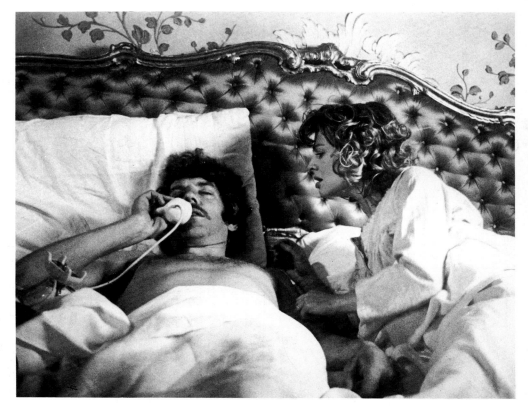

△ You needed to see **Don't Look Now** more than once to figure out what was going on much of the time, and even then you couldn't be sure. Director Nicolas Roeg took a fairly trivial plot, scripted by Alan Scott and Chris Bryant from a Daphne du Maurier short story, and turned it into a dream, or rather nightmare, of anxiety and the occult. The mystery of death covered the film like a shroud, from the first scene, the accidental drowning in England of a young couple's daughter, to the last, the father's funeral in Venice. In between, he (Donald Sutherland, left) is tormented by flashes of second sight and his wife (Julie Christie, right) is unnerved by a medium's contact with the dead girl, imagined glimpses of whom lead the father through the shadows of Venice's wintry alleys and canals in a mad pursuit ending with his murder. Roeg, formerly a great cameraman himself, had the aid of cinematographer Anthony Richmond to make the film a haunting visual experience, and of film editor Graeme Clifford to create its tricky flashback-and-forwards effects. The stars, both fine, had a beautifully composed nude love scene that caused much talk. Also cast in Peter Katz's British-Italian production in Technicolor: Hilary Mason, Clelia Matania, Massimo Serrato, Renato Scarpe. Alas, too many potential ticket-buyers obeyed the title.

△ Al Pacino (illustrated), who showed up so well among members of the lethal family of *The Godfather*, was rewarded with a movie of his own in **Serpico**, and his Oscar nomination for 'best supporting actor' in 1972 was upped to 'best actor' in 1973. His performance blazed with the integrity and conviction that motivated the real Serpico, a New York policeman whose refusal to join in the bribe-taking that riddled the force developed into a determination to expose it. This he does in the film with the help of one brave sergeant (Tony Roberts), following a series of confrontations, the final one almost fatal, with his fellow cops and their equally corrupt or indifferent superiors. In 1970 Serpico's testimony at a hearing ordered by the Mayor shook the New York Police Department from top to bottom, and in 1973 Peter Maas published a best-selling biography of him which Waldo Salt and Norman Wexler turned into a thrilling screenplay, making vivid not only the cop's anti-graft obsession, but his off-beat personality (a tough guy who wore beads, and liked ballet and classical music). Sidney Lumet's direction gave urgent intensity, except in a few superfluous romantic scenes, to the Dino De Laurentiis-Martin Bregman production in Technicolor, and to his cast, which also included John Randolph, Jack Kehoe, Biff McGuire, Barbara Eda-Young, Cornelia Sharpe, and John Medici. Payboxes boomed.

△ Offhand, one would say that a picture about a baseball team of lovable roughnecks, one of whom is slowly dying of Hodgkinson's disease, is something to be avoided at all cost. But **Bang The Drum Slowly** worked beautifully, both as a drama of man's mortality and as a comedy of professional sporting life. The script by Mark Harris, based on his highly regarded 1956 novel, had a strong pair of central roles; Robert De Niro (illustrated) was excellent as the fatally stricken catcher, a slow-witted guy wanting to stay on the team just one more season; and Michael Moriarty was even better as his bright roommate who helps him to do it. They were backed up by Vincent Gardenia as their manager, Phil Foster, Ann Wedgeworth, Patrick McVey, Barbara Babcock and Maurice Rosenfield (who produced the film with his wife, Lois) in a large cast made to look thoroughly at home on the diamond, in locker-rooms, bars and hotels, by director John Hancock. It attracted good reviews and business in its home country, but was practically ignored in overseas markets where baseball and incurable disease put a double hex on it. The title came from the 'Streets Of Laredo' song.

△ **Badge 373** arrived between the two *French Connection* movies made by Fox; all three were based on the exploits of Eddie Egan, who must be the most fully film-documented figure in the area of crime since Al Capone. He was, however, on the right side of the law, a real New York police detective, but he appeared here cast as Eddie's superior officer, while Eddie himself (right) was played by Robert Duvall (centre). (Confused? So was the picture.) This rambunctious cop, suspended from the force after accidentally killing a junkie, goes back to work unofficially when he hears his partner has been murdered by the mob. Through those dark streets he goes, doing what a man's gotta do, encountering a lot of exceptionally disgusting characters, and finishing with a breakneck bus chase across Manhattan. Until then, despite all the violence of its action and language, there wasn't much real excitement, and the box-office impact was minor. Howard W. Koch directed and produced the screenplay by Pete Hamill, who also appeared briefly in a cast featuring Verna Bloom as Eddie's girl and Henry Darrow as his most vicious adversary.

▷ It's movies like **Innocent Bystanders** that give spying a bad name. It opened in a nice comfortable way with the familiar situation of a burnt-out espionage agent being assigned one last mission; to bring in a great Russian scientist who has run away to Turkey. Then the complications start. The ageing agent (Stanley Baker, left) gets tangled up with Russians, the scientist (Vladek Sheybal), an American spy chief (Dana Andrews), a Turkish innkeeper (Warren Mitchell), a charming mystery woman (Geraldine Chaplin, right), his own boss (Donald Pleasence) and younger colleagues (Sue Lloyd, Derren Nesbitt), all of whom may or may not be double agents. The audience became engulfed in a who's-doing-what-to-whom? fog of complexities, pierced every now and then by a burst of exciting action. Director Peter Collinson's treatment of the James Mitchell screenplay, based on James Munro's novel, tended to value striking visual effects above narrative clarity, and George H. Brown's British-based production took in so many locations in the United States and Europe that where became as puzzling as what, who and whom.

▷ E.B. White's perennial children's classic, **Charlotte's Webb**, had a warm appeal for perennial children. They had bought more than five million copies of the book since its 1952 publication, and were happy to find that the movie version – a feature-length cartoon produced by Joseph Barbera and William Hanna, famous for their *Tom & Jerry* shorts – differed very little from the original. Charlotte is a benevolent spider who rescues her friend, Wilbur the pig, from becoming bacon and pork chops by weaving messages in praise of him into her web, to the amazement of one and all. Other creatures in the barn and farmyard are involved, most entertainingly a rat named Templeton who, to the tune of one of the movie's best numbers by Richard and Robert Sherman, 'A Veritable Smorgasbord', goes on an eating orgy at a county fair. The author described his work, dauntingly, as a tale of 'the miracle of birth, the miracle of friendship, the miracle of death' but most people, especially youngsters, enjoyed it anyway. Charles Nichols and Iwao Takamoto directed the Earl Hamner Jr adaptation, using the voices of Debbie Reynolds (Charlotte), Henry Gibson (Wilbur), Paul Lynde (Templeton), Agnes Moorehead, Rex Allen and Martha Scott.

◁ Jack Lemmon's study of a man in the toils of disillusion, self-pity and guilt brought **Save The Tiger** the Academy Award for the year's best actor. This accolade might have gone equally deservedly in several other years to Lemmon (illustrated), whose talent shone over a wide range, from farce to tragedy. His new film tended towards the latter, without quite reaching true pathos. A dispiriting affair, it examined a businessman who dumps his cherished moral values to fight off bankruptcy by fiddling the books, pimping for a prospective customer, and hiring an arsonist to burn down the insured factory. All this causes him to reflect ruefully on the emptiness of the American dream, as both his ethics and his happiness dwindle away. The audience didn't have much fun either, and in view of the Oscar publicity boost, business was disappointing. The picture was strongest in character insight, apparent in the direction of John G. Avildsen, the supporting performances of Jack Gilford (as Lemmon's partner, here telephoning), Patricia Smith (as his wife), Laurie Heineman, Norman Burton (foreground), Thayer David, and the screenplay of Steve Shagan, who also produced. Gilford's acting and Shagan's writing received Academy Award nominations too.

▷ Getting their act together and taking it on the road, Ryan and Tatum O'Neal (here detoured into a police station) made an extraordinary father-daughter team of co-stars and scored a resounding hit in **Paper Moon**. Dad played a smooth-talking trickster driving through depression-era Kansas with a carload of bibles and a list of newly widowed prospects to sell them to. Tatum was a cigarette-smoking nine-year-old toughie who attaches herself to Ryan, and manages to show that master con-man a new trick or two before lapsing into childish jealousy when a grown-up gal (Madeleine Kahn) comes along for the ride. Ryan let Tatum steal the picture; director-producer Peter Bogdanovich got an alarmingly assured performance from her, and the Academy made her its youngest winner ever of a competitive award, as Best Supporting Actress. Pop song recordings of the thirties helped to convey the sense of period needed by Alvin Sargent's script, from a novel by Joe David Brown. Mixed reviews, but large audiences loved it.

▽ A widely acclaimed novel by George V. Higgins, its background of Boston's underworld gaining authenticity from his experience as United States Assistant Attorney, **The Friends Of Eddie Coyle** was written mostly in unkeyed dialogue, making it hard for some readers to follow. The screen version was therefore an improvement: you could see who was saying what to whom. Robert Mitchum (left) had a splendid actor's control over every shrug and droop of the dejected Eddie, a born loser and an ex-con caught between the cops and the robbers, his quondam 'friends' on whom he informed in order to earn a living. Richard Jordan (right), Peter Boyle, Steven Keats, Alex Rocco and Mitchell Ryan created realistic types under Peter Yates's direction in producer Paul Monash's low-key screenplay, whose downbeat theme precluded wide popularity.

◁ Anyone going to **Brother Sun, Sister Moon** in search of an accurate history of St Francis of Assisi's life was out of luck. But an eye-filling feast awaited connoisseurs of ravishing scenery (Italy at its most photogenic) and handsome young people (Graham Faulkner, illustrated as Francis, Judi Bowker as his follower). As in his *Romeo And Juliet*, Franco Zeffirelli seemed oblivious to shortcomings in acting, dialogue and narrative while he concentrated on superb settings, costumes and camera effects, all of which made the film a masterpiece for the deaf. The script by Suso Cecchi d'Amico, Kenneth Ross, Lina Wertmuller and Zeffirelli, tracing Francis's departure from his affluent parents to commune with nature and spread the teachings of Christ, was the object of withering scorn from the critics, who had special barbs for an absurdly staged scene with Alec Guinness as Pope Innocent III receiving the earliest members of the Franciscan order; also the jarring effect of a soundtrack sicklied o'er by pop singer Donovan, whose score was arranged by Ken Thorne from authentic ancient melodies researched by Alfredo Bianchini. Players Valentina Cortese, Lee Montague, Leigh Lawson, Kenneth Cranham, Michael Feast, Nicholas Willatt and John Sharp got off lightly, while Ennio Guarnieri's photography of the costly Luciano Perugia production was showered with praise.

◁ **Jonathan Livingston Seagull** was a bird who soared in search of a rich, full life, saying 'You have the freedom to be yourself, your true self, here and now, and nothing can stand in your way!'. An amazing number of readers, attracted to Richard Bach's parable in the form of a novel, had made it a freak best-seller and Jonathan the best-loved feathered hero since Donald Duck. He was brought from book to film in a screenplay by Bach himself, with an all-seagull cast and disastrous box-office results. The scenes of birds in flight were gloriously beautiful, but while the eye was thus being enraptured, the ear became numbed by endlessly moralising dialogue (and monologue) and noisy Neil Diamond music. Producer-director Hall Bartlett gave it the expressive (and un-credited) off-screen voices of James Franciscus (as Jonathan), Juliet Mills, Hal Holbrook, Dorothy McGuire and Richard Crenna, a gifted artist in Oscar-nominated Jack Couffer behind the colour cameras; and, with 114 minutes, too much running time. Most critics said it was strictly for the birds, and the public flocked elsewhere.

OTHER RELEASES OF 1973

Alfredo, Alfredo
Dustin Hoffman, Stefania Sandrelli, Carla Gravina. Dir. & Pro: Pietro Germi. Meek bank clerk runs into some comic complications when he tries to divorce his temperamental, oversexed wife. (Italian)

Charley One-Eye
Richard Roundtree, Roy Thinnes, Nigel Davenport. Dir: Don Chaffey. Pro: James Swann. Two outcasts are drawn together by adversity: one a black army deserter, the other an Indian rejected by his own people.

Fear Is The Key
Barry Newman, Suzy Kendall, John Vernon. Dir: Michael Tuchner. Pro: Alan Ladd Jr., Jay Kanter. Deep-sea diver turns kidnapper to get to a crime czar whose gang has murdered his wife and child.

The First Circle
Gunther Malzacher, Elzbieta Czyzewska, Peter Steen. Dir: Alexander Ford. Pro: Mogens Skot-Hansen. Solzhenitsyn's story based on his experiences behind the barricades of a Stalinist labour camp. (Danish/German)

Hit!
Billy Dee Williams, Richard Pryor, Paul Hampton, Gwen Welles. Dir: Sidney J. Furie. Pro: Harry Korshak. Black government agent assembles a team of killers to wipe out major international drug traffickers.

Hitler: The Last Ten Days
Alec Guinness, Simon Ward, Diane Cilento, Adolfo Celi. Dir: Ennio de Concini. Pro: John Heyman. As Russian troops encircle Berlin, Hitler's insanity reaches new heights and depths in his bunker. (British/Italian)

The Mattei Affair
Gian Maria Volonte, Luigi Squarizina, Peter Baldwin. Dir: Francesco Rosi. Melodrama, based on fact, about the career of an Italian industrialist whose life ends with a mystery. (Italian)

The Optimists (GB **The Optimists Of Nine Elms**)
Peter Sellers, Donna Mullane, John Chaffey. Dir: Anthony Simmons. Pro: Adrian Gaye, Victor Lyndon. Comedy of a London street busker and two slum children who follow him. (British)

Save The Children
Isaac Hayes, Sammy Davis Jr., Nancy Wilson, Marvin Gaye. Dir: Stan Lathan. Pro: Matt Robinson. All-star documentary of a Chicago show put on by entertainers for charity.

Scalawag
Kirk Douglas, Mark Lester, Neville Brand, Lesley-Anne Down. Dir: Kirk Douglas. Pro: Anne Douglas. One-legged pirate and two children encounter mutinous cut-throats and hostile Indians while seeking a buried treasure.

The Soul Of Nigger Charley
Fred Williamson, D'Urville Martin, Denise Nicholas. Dir. & Pro: Larry G. Spangler. Black freedom fighter is joined by a Mexican bandit to crush a villain who captures slaves and takes them to Mexico.

Superfly T.N.T.
Ron O'Neil, Roscoe Lee Browne, Sheila Frazier, Jacques Sernas. Dir: Ron O'Neil. Pro: Sig Shore. Ex-drug pusher interrupts his lush life in Rome to help an African official to rid his little country of a ruthless dictator.

Tales That Witness Madness
Kim Novak, Joan Collins, Jack Hawkins, Donald Pleasence. Dir: Freddie Francis. Pro: Norman Priggen. Horror compendium in which a clinician relates four of his most fantastic cases. (British)

1974

▽ You had to have a taste for violent action to get full value from **The Longest Yard** (GB: **The Mean Machine**). Millions did have it, as director Robert Aldrich had proved several times before (*The Dirty Dozen*, etc), and in this movie he made it more palatable for gentler souls by adding liberal dashes of comedy and sex. These came mostly in the free-wheeling performance of Burt Reynolds (left) as an ex-pro footballer who, jailed after beating up his girl-friend and wrecking her car, is ordered by the foot-ball-crazy warden to train a team of prisoners to play his team of guards. After matching wits with the warden (splendidly played as a smiling cobra by Eddie Albert, right) and bodies with the warden's secretary (Bernadette Peters), Burt went into a very long (47 minutes, replete with slow motion and split-screen panels), very bloody battle, thinly disguised as a game, between the biggest convicts and the most sadistic guards. The cons won, and so did Paramount: the grosses were huge. Ed Lauter, Michael Conrad, Richard Kiel, Mike Henry, James Hampton, Harry Caesar and Anitra Ford figured in the Albert S. Ruddy production from his own story, with a screen-play by Tracy Keenan Wynn. Georgia State Prison was used for location filming.

▽ **Death Wish** was cowboys and Indians brought up to date, with a gun-toting, self-appointed sheriff roaming the badlands of New York City to hunt down the law-breakers. Charles Bronson (illustrated) played an average urban man transformed into a killer after his home has been invaded by young hoodlums who – in a scene so brutally realistic that many censors shortened it – rape his wife and daughter; the wife dies and the daughter becomes a mental cripple. Armed with a gun, he goes out every night and roams the streets, parks and subways of the city for muggers, rapists and vandals, whom he promptly shoots point-blank. There seemed to be an abundance of them that was improbable even for New York, but the film was made with such vivid intensity that audiences had no time for nit-picking: they were absolutely carried away by its theme of revenge on muggers. In several crime-infested cities people applauded and actually cheered every time Bronson slaughtered another sus-pect; as in the film, he became a kind of folk hero; all moral objections to vigilante action were forgotten. A box-office smash, the Wendell Mayes screenplay, based on a novel by Brian Garfield, was directed by Michael Winner and produced by Hal Landers and Bobby Roberts; with Hope Lange, Vincent Gardenia, William Redfield, Steven Keats and Stuart Margolin in the cast.

△ Paramount's third attempt to make a film of **The Great Gatsby** was given a bumpy ride by most critics, who seemed to be expecting the impossible. It is a superb novel, F. Scott Fitzgerald's masterpiece, but his fascinating style, revealing and concealing at the same time, so that the whole truth about his characters stays tantalisingly just out of reach, cannot survive the transplant to the screen. Jack Clayton, in his meticu-lous direction of Francis Ford Coppola's adaptation, came close to turning the trick; if he didn't quite make it, he certainly created a beautiful movie, constantly rewarding in its settings and costumes of the twenties' idle rich, its haunting tunes of the jazz age, its splendid acting by Robert Redford (right), miscast as the enig-matic Gatsby (but who wouldn't be, except perhaps Jack Nicholson?); Mia Farrow as the shallow, selfish beauty who obsesses him; Bruce Dern as her insensi-tive millionaire husband; Karen Black as his mistress, killed by his wife's reckless driving; Scott Wilson as her garage-mechanic husband who, thinking Gatsby responsible for the accident, murders him; and, best of all, Sam Waterston (left) as the observer and nar-rator of the drama. David Merrick's lavish production went way over schedule and budget, but just about broke even on the company's ledger.

▽ **Daisy Miller** was like a fine Renoir reproduction pasted on an empty chocolate box. With the interior scenes given a handsome mounting, and the Swiss and Italian exteriors a luminous beauty by cameraman Alberto Spagnoli, its visual style was worth the price of admission. But under this surface, narrative substance left much to be desired. Henry James's 1878 story used one of his favourite themes, the social clash of Americans and Europeans, in a fragile tale of a girl touring the Continent, falling in love, and dying of Roman fever. The central role needed a fascinating star personality, and producer-director Peter Bogdanovich's friend, Cybill Shepherd (right), was not quite that. Barry Brown, Cloris Leachman, Mildred Natwick, Eileen Brennan and Duilio Del Prete (left) also acted out Frederick Raphael's screenplay. Mixed reviews, dismal returns.

△ Even in a banner year for the company – Paramount had more than a normal share of box-office winners, and dominated the 1974 Academy Award lists with a record 38 nominations – **The Conversation** stood out as an extraordinary achievement. It was a fascinatingly original drama about an expert in bugging devices who investigates a murder plot and ends as a victim of his own obsession with overhearing others: he becomes convinced that surveillance is being turned on him, and paranoia takes over. The crux of Francis Ford Coppola's story was a tapped conversation the expert fatally misinterprets, and the movie was unique in making the eavesdropping microphone more important than the voyeuristic camera. It was a hit with the critics but less so with the public, perhaps because Gene Hackman's superbly acted central role (illustrated) ended in downbeat despair. The whole thing, indeed, was sombre and disturbing in its implications that anyone able to apply modern technology has anyone else's privacy at his mercy. Coppola's writing, direction and (with Fred Roos) production were constantly provocative and absorbing, with good performances by Allen Garfield, John Cazale, Robert Duvall, Frederic Forrest, Cindy Williams, Harrison Ford and Elizabeth MacRea. It was the Cannes Film Festival's grand prize winner.

◁ While Jack Clayton was recreating the twenties for *The Great Gatsby* on the East coast, Roman Polanski was turning the Los Angeles clock back to the thirties for **Chinatown**. A private-eye thriller in the manner of Dashiell Hammett or Raymond Chandler, this brilliant entertainment was one of the most highly praised and commercially successful releases of the year. It drew Academy Award nominations in eleven categories; the Oscar for best screenplay was won by Robert Towne for a multi-layered story in which crimes and corruption were unpeeled like onion skins, with a murder on the outside and land-grabbing fraud at the core. Jack Nicholson (centre) played a gumshoe suspecting, and then protecting, the victim's widow (Faye Dunaway), whose tycoon father is plotting control of LA's water supply. This villain (John Huston) also has a murky private life: he is the father of his daughter's child. Nicholson, who is disfigured most of the time by a slit nostril (administered by Polanski himself as one of the tycoon's goons), and Faye, who is killed in the violent finale, both scored strongly – he coolly humorous, she tautly distraught as the nasty tale unfolded. Perry Lopez, Diane Ladd, John Hillerman, Darrell Zwerling and Roy Jenson were also cast in the Robert Evans production, the misleading title of which – though redolent with atmosphere – had little to do with anything; the last scene just happened to occur in LA's Chinese district.

▽ That endangered species, the pure detective story, came back with a star-spangled bang in **Murder On The Orient Express**, which had no time for the tough violence of the modern private-eye school but plenty (over two hours of it) for the deduction and surprise denouement that have made Agatha Christie a perennial best-seller. That was its strength and its weakness: the plot and the characters held suspense and fascination, but there were so many interviews by a garrulous sleuth (Christie's immortal Hercule Poirot) with secret-hiding suspects in a confined setting (a snowbound train) that monotony increasingly threatened before the killers of an American millionaire were unmasked. Practically the whole cast of characters had been connected years before by a Lindbergh-type kidnap case – and *what* a cast! Albert Finney (left) dominated as Poirot, with Ingrid Bergman (winning her third Oscar), Richard Widmark, Sean Connery, Lauren Bacall, John Gielgud (centre left), Wendy Hiller, (right) Michael York, Anthony Perkins, Vanessa Redgrave, Jacqueline Bisset, Martin Balsam, Rachel Roberts (centre right), Jean-Pierre Cassel, Colin Blakely (centre), George Coulouris and Dennis Quilley. That lot ensured big box-office as well as accomplished performances. The Christie book's 1930s period was retained by Paul Dehn's screenplay, produced in England by John Brabourne and Richard Goodwin, and elegantly directed by Sidney Lumet.

◁ The popularity of *Friends* was enough to make a sequel seem viable, but **Paul And Michelle** sank without trace. Lewis Gilbert again produced and directed sensitively; Anicee Alvina (left) and Sean Bury (back to camera) and scriptwriter Vernon Harris (this time with Angela Huth as a collaborator) repeated their assignments capably. However, the adolescent lovers had now left their private Eden and, three years older in Paris, they looked like the romantic duos of too many other movies. Pleasant to watch, though, as was Keir Dullea (right) as the American whom Sean is nonplussed to find sharing Anicee's room. If that steady gaze seems familiar, you saw it unforgettably staring into infinity in *2001: A Space Odyssey*.

▽ A formula thriller about police versus a sex-mad murderer took on some novelty value through the injection of a clairvoyant character in **Man On A Swing**. Those sequences, played by Cliff Robertson (left) as the detective chief and Joel Grey (right) as the man with extra-sensory perception, tingled with suspense and made you wonder why Grey, even with an Academy Award to his credit (for *Cabaret*) was seen so seldom in pictures. The race to find the crazy killer before he struck again also carried dramatic urgency in David Z. Goodman's script, well directed by Frank Perry, but the denouement fell flat. Dorothy Tristan, George Voskovec and Elizabeth Wilson were others in Howard Jaffe's production.

△ Watching **The Godfather, Part II** was like enjoying a good read: it had the richness of a densely plotted, multi-character novel. At once a sequel and a preface to *The Godfather*, it should properly have been called parts I and III with the original film as part II. Aside from the confusion engendered by this format, and increased by producer-director Francis Ford Coppola's cross-cutting between past and present, it was a memorable cinematic experience, worthy of its many awards, including the 'best picture' Oscar. The script, by Coppola and Mario Puzo, traced the early life of the Godfather as a child orphaned by murder in Sicily and as a young immigrant (Robert De Niro, crouching left) learning the rackets in 1917 New York. It then jumped several decades to take up the story of the Godfather's heir (Al Pacino), his forays into Las Vegas and Cuba, his power struggles with other crime czars and conflicts with his family, all punctuated by brutal killings. Diane Keaton as Pacino's wife and Lee Strasberg, the method-actor guru, as a Jewish mob boss were prominent in the Gary Frederickson-Fred Roos co-production's cast of impressive actors, such as Robert Duvall, John Cazale, Talia Shire, Michael V. Gazzo, G.D. Spradlin, Richard Bright, and Morgana King. This follow-up was longer and more expensive than the first film, and returned only about a third as much money, but still its $30 million from American and Canadian rentals alone covered its cost twice. In 1977 a seven-hour combination of the two movies, plus out-takes, made a TV event.

▽ Karel Reisz makes them seldom, but he makes them well. **The Gambler**, one of only five pictures he directed between his first, *Saturday Night And Sunday Morning*, in 1960 and *The French Lieutenant's Woman* in 1981, dealt in attention-holding style with the tyranny of addiction. James Caan, here with Lauren Hutton, gave his best performance so far as a young Jewish intellectual, apparently cool and well adjusted, but in fact totally at the mercy of a compulsion to gamble. The story – updated, Americanized and re-arranged by James Toback from Dostoievsky – traced the New York and Las Vegas career of a man obsessed by the elation of winning and the perverse thrill of losing, no matter what it cost his family, his girl or himself. But to an audience, gambling lacks the tragic force of drink or drug addiction; the victim stirs more exasperation, less pity. So this Irwin Winkler-Robert Chartoff production proved only a minor success for Reisz, whose cast included Morris Carnovsky, Paul Sorvino, Jacqueline Brookes and Burt Young.

287

▽ Warren Beatty (illustrated) escaped sudden death in **The Parallax View** often enough to keep an old-time serial going. But this was a new-style thriller, all shocking realism and chic obfuscation. Beatty's reporter hero, having witnessed the Kennedy-like assassination of a senator and the murder of the assassin, discovers that all the witnesses are dying from unnatural causes too; will he be next? What is behind it all? His investigations indicate a vast, mysterious organisation that, for reasons never made clear, trains hit-men for political killings. By the end of the David Giler-Lorenzo Semple Jr screenplay (from a novel by Loren Singer) the wicked Parallax Corporation is triumphant and nearly everybody in the cast – which included Paula Prentiss, Hume Cronyn, William Daniels, Walter McGinn and Kelly Thorsden – is dead. The downbeat finish and the vagueness at the heart of the story may be why the movie was not a major attraction, for all its surface excitement, the skill of Alan J. Pakula's direction and production, and the popularity of its star.

◁ Alan Jay Lerner didn't have much luck with Paramount, and vice-versa. While his career elsewhere glittered with triumphs like *My Fair Lady* and *Gigi*, all three of this studio's musicals with screenplays and lyrics by Lerner were financial earaches: *Paint Your Wagon*, *On A Clear Day You Can See Forever*, and now **The Little Prince**. Composer Frederick Loewe, emerging from retirement, brought music to Antoine de Saint-Exupery's celebrated tale of a boy (Steven Warner, left) who appeared from an asteroid to revive an aviator (Richard Kiley, right) stranded in the Sahara, and to learn about earthly life from a fox (Gene Wilder), a snake (a marvellously sinuous Bob Fosse) and the pilot himself. As produced and directed by Stanley Donen, it had visual and aural charms but was a bit too diaphanous for cinema crowds. Also cast: dancer Donna McKechnie, and British actors Clive Revill, Joss Ackland, Graham Crowden and Victor Spinetti.

▷ There was a good deal of critical praise for **The White Dawn**, an unusual adventure story of three sailors separated from their ship during an Arctic hunt for whales, and their exploitation of the Eskimos – one of them seen here confronting a marauding polar bear – who saved them. Director Philip Kaufman caught magnificent location vistas in Canada's far north, and strong performances by Timothy Bottoms, Lou Gossett and Warren Oates, supported by natives of the region in which the story actually took place in 1896. James Houston turned it into a novel, then collaborated with Tom Rickman on the screenplay, impressively produced by Martin Ransohoff, who also did the adaptation. Alas, the icy atmosphere spread to the box-office.

OTHER RELEASES OF 1974

The Apprenticeship Of Duddy Kravitz
Richard Dreyfuss, Jack Warden, Joseph Wiseman. Dir: Ted Kotcheff. Pro: John Kemeny. Young Jewish hustler in 1948 Montreal cheats and schemes in order to buy a plot of land.

Captain Kronos, Vampire Hunter
Horst Janson, John Carson, Shane Briant. Dir: Brian Clemens. Pro: Albert Fennell, Brian Clemens. 19th century swashbuckler fights an outbreak of vampirism causing panic in a village. (British)

The Education Of Sonny Carson
Rony Clanton, Don Gordon, Joyce Walker. Dir: Michael Campus. Pro: Irwin Yablans. The exploits of a rebellious black youth in Brooklyn; adapted from his autobiography.

Frankenstein And The Monster From Hell
Peter Cushing, Shane Briant, Madeleine Smith. Dir: Terence Fisher. Pro: Roy Skeggs. Baron F. purloins various organs from an insane asylum's patients to create his legendary monster. (British)

The Klansman
Richard Burton, Lee Marvin, Cameron Mitchell, O.J. Simpson. Dir: Terence Young. Pro: William Alexander. A southern aristocrat fails to keep the peace when the blacks in a late 60s Alabama town are inflamed by the Klan's outrages.

Malizia (aka Malicious)
Laura Antonelli, Turi Ferro, Allessandro Momo, Tina Aumont. Dir: Salvatore Samperi. Pro: Silvio Clementelli. A widower and his three sons are thrown into turmoil by a seductive housekeeper. (Italian)

Phase IV
Nigel Davenport, Michael Murphy, Lynne Frederick. Dir: Saul Bass. Pro: Paul B. Radin. Scientists fight the onslaught of a huge army of intelligent ants which has become a menace to mankind.

Shanks
Marcel Marceau, Tsilla Chelton, Helena Kallioniotes. Dir: William Castle. Pro: Steven North. Fantasy about a deaf-mute puppeteer who takes over a scientist's invention: a magic box that brings the dead back to life.

Three Tough Guys
Lino Ventura, Isaac Hayes, Fred Williamson, Paula Kelly. Dir: Duccio Tessari. Pro: Dino De Laurentiis. Blacks and whites join forces to find a killer and the loot he has hidden after a bank robbery.

1975

▽ **Sheila Levine Is Dead And Living In New York** must have posed a problem in film editing. If you cut out all the unnecessary footage, you'd have nothing left. Jeannie Berlin (left, modelling the latest in don't-give-a-damn ensembles) delivered an exhausting performance as a suburban girl – grappling with a neurotic weight problem, among other fashionable hang-ups – who forsakes her nice comfortable family to search for a career and a husband in Manhattan, while the script frantically looked for laughs. Roy Scheider played the attractive doctor who preferred her roommate (Rebecca Dianne Smith, right), and Sidney J. Furie directed the Harry Korshak production, written by Kenny Solms and Gail Parent from the latter's novel, a simultaneously moving and hilarious best-seller. The movie was not.

▽ People who thought 'if you've seen one Western you've seen them all' got a nice surprise in **Posse**. With a minimum of violence, it extracted as much excitement from the hackneyed genre as any of the old shoot-'em-ups, and added a bonus of brain appeal. For this Kirk Douglas (seated) could take three bows, as producer, director and star, that last as a US marshal with a power complex in 1890 Texas. He pursues outlaws with his highly trained, uniformed posse as a means to political glory, until his prize captive (Bruce Dern, here with Douglas) turns the tables on him and holds him hostage. The William Roberts-Christopher Knopf script cleverly shifted audience sympathy from one man to the other, revealing the ostensible hero as a neurotic, and finally pathetic, fascist. Prominent in support were Bo Hopkins, James Stacey and Alfonso Arau.

▽ Something like *Uncle Tom's Cabin* rewritten for *Playboy* magazine came along in **Mandingo**. At Falconhurst, the plantation house in the old South imagined by author Kyle Onstott, the problems of being a slave lay in providing the white folks with not only free labour but sex and sadism too. Its owner (James Mason) buys and breeds his black serfs as if they were livestock, and is particularly pleased with his latest purchase, a magnificent young giant (Ken Norton, left), who arouses even more interest in the Massa's daughter-in-law (Susan George, right). Her husband, heir to Falconhurst (Perry King) shows his lack of racial prejudice, sort of, by regularly bedding a comely slave (Brenda Sykes) and so his neglected wife, who appears to be in a constant state of heat, goes to work on the muscular new stud. While this steamy stuff is going on, Massa Mason indulges in assorted lashings and tortures. Melodrama this purple could have made a riotous satire, but scripter Norman Wexler (working from Onstott's best-seller and Jack Kirkland's stage version) and director Richard Fleischer played it straight, with, lamentably, excellent box-office results. A publicity asset for the Dino De Laurentiis production was the screen debut of Norton, the boxer, a surprisingly able actor.

▷ **Once Is Not Enough** was a mink-lined rubbish bin into which the author threw everything that guaranteed bonanza sales: millionaire luxury, showbiz revelations, jet-set revelries, uninhibited promiscuity, a father fixation, a dash of lesbianism, and an innocent heroine surrounded by corruption. Deborah Raffin in this central role was supported by more famous players, led by Kirk Douglas (here with her) as her adored father, a Hollywood producer in financial trouble which he solves by marrying the richest woman in the world (Alexis Smith), who maintains a kinky affair with a movie star (Melina Mercouri) on the side. George Hamilton and David Janssen provided romantic complications for the girl, while Brenda Vaccaro walked off with the picture's acting honours as an amoral, sharp-tongued editor. Officially titled *Jacqueline Susann's Once Is Not Enough* in obeisance to the author, it was lushly produced by Howard W. Koch, directed by Guy Green and scripted by Julius J. Epstein, who rearranged the novel without deodorizing any of its basic qualities, including its sweet smell of success.

△ Flawed and overheated it may have been, but **The Day Of The Locust** was absolutely unforgettable, a one-off movie drama unlike any other. Director John Schlesinger and screenwriter Waldo Salt took Nathanael West's short novel, a minor classic about Hollywood's underlings, as the basis of nothing less than an apocalyptic vision of modern society in decline. It didn't always come off – there were awkward lapses in continuity, and some of West's astringency got lost – but it constantly fascinated as it ripped the surface tinsel off the film city to show the basic tinsel beneath, and the climax – in which a première crowd outside Grauman's Chinese Theatre becomes a mad, bloodthirsty mob – reached epic heights. William Atherton (left) played a young designer drawn to the booming Hollywood of the thirties, only to be disillusioned by his studio's cool reaction to a fatal set collapse, and by a pretty extra (Karen Black, right) too empty-headed to return his love. She also torments an older, retired introvert (Donald Sutherland) to the point of a brainstorm which triggers off the climactic riot. These three were surrounded by a sleazily colourful lot, vividly realised by a gifted supporting cast: Burgess Meredith, Geraldine Page, Richard Dysart, Bo Hopkins, Lelia Goldoni, Billy Barty, Madge Kennedy, Natalie Schafer, Paul Stewart and many more. The whole cast and the technical team on Jerome Hellman's production did great work, but financially it fell short of the previous Schlesinger-Salt-Hellman collaboration, *Midnight Cowboy*.

▷ All 24 principals in Robert Altman's **Nashville** had their moments, mostly comical or satirical in tone, although it was the more dramatic performances the Academy singled out for Oscar nominations: Ronee Blakley (left) as a singer experiencing a nervous breakdown, and Lily Tomlin as a mother involved in an extramarital fling. Altman, whose direction won the New York Critics Circle Award (so did the film), shook a kaleidoscope of disparate stories, personalities, songs and incidents into one of the most entertaining and exhilarating movies of the decade. Joan Tewkesbury's screenplay had a basis of sorts in a political campaign climaxed by an assassination, but the background of Nashville, with the offbeat types attracted to this Mecca of country and western music, was what made the picture so special. Many of its 27 numbers were written by cast members: Keith Carradine became the first performer to win an Oscar for his own composition ('I'm Easy'). The line-up of performers included Henry Gibson (right), Barbara Baxley (lower right), Barbara Harris, Keenan Wynn, Shelley Duvall, Allen Garfield and, wandering through it all as a bewildered journalist, Geraldine Chaplin, daughter of Charlie. Originally a United Artists project, the ABC-Altman production brought Paramount a rich return.

△ Director Robert Aldrich and star Burt Reynolds followed up their 1974 hit *The Longest Yard* with a more serious but equally violent picture in **Hustle**, another commercial winner. Both men excelled their previous work, Aldrich whipping the story along at a brisk pace without neglecting provocative details, and Reynolds injecting a trenchant cynicism into his role of a basically nice guy obliged to cope with nasty events in the hustle of Los Angeles police work. He is chiefly concerned with two prostitutes, one an elegant professional he is in love with, while hating her profession; the other a young amateur who has been drugged, debauched and drowned by persons unknown. While investigating the victim's past he become embroiled with her insanely vengeful father (Ben Johnson), her pathetic mother (Eileen Brennan) hiding ugly secrets, and a corrupt lawyer (Eddie Albert). Aided by his black partner (Paul Winfield) he clears up the sordid case, but dies in the shoot-out finale. France's international talent, Catherine Deneuve (here with Reynolds), making a rare Hollywood appearance, had an exquisite glow as the hero's call-girl mistress, while Ernest Borgnine, Jack Carter, Catherine Bach, David Spielberg and Sharon Kelly filled lesser roles in Steve Shagan's taut screenplay.

▽ With **Three Days Of The Condor** we were back in the hallucinatory world of conspiracy by a faceless organisation. Adapted from James Grady's novel *Six Days Of The Condor* (even Hollywood was economising, said wags), this was a first-rate thriller and easily the company's strongest money magnet of the year, extracting over $20 million from North American bookings. It opened with a sensational sequence in which a researcher (Robert Redford, left) at a New York office of the CIA comes back from lunch to find all his colleagues slaughtered. Director Sydney Pollack and scripters Lorenzo Semple Jr and David Rayfiel showed remarkable skill in avoiding a letdown after this shock start; tension never slackened as the survivor kept one jump ahead of the killers, his terror increased by the realisation that their employers and his – the CIA – are one and the same. After a series of breathtaking chases and escapes he can turn only to the *New York Times* for relief at the end (according to several recent films, the press is democracy's last bulwark). Faye Dunaway (right) as a stranger forced, and later willing, to be his confederate; Max Von Sydow as his sinister nemesis; and Cliff Robertson and John Houseman as his CIA superiors were, like Redford, excellent in Stanley Schneider's production for Dino De Laurentiis.

OTHER RELEASES OF 1975

Bug
Bradford Dillman, Joanna Miles, Richard Gilliland. Dir: Jeannot Szwarc. Pro: William Castle. A town is terrorised by enormous cockroaches, released from underground by an earthquake and setting on fire all they touch.

Dog-Pound Shuffle (aka Spot)
Ron Moody, David Soul. Dir. & Pro: Jeffrey Bloom. A pair of drifters, down on their luck, save the life of a little dog and are inspired to rescue their own lives.

The Dove
Joseph Bottoms, Deborah Raffin, John McLiam, Dabney Coleman. Dir: Charles Jarrott. Pro: Gregory Peck. The picturesque and sometimes dangerous adventures of a boy sailing around the world. He loses his cat but finds a wife.

Framed
Joe Don Baker, Conny Van Dyke, Gabriel Dell, Brock Peters. Dir: Phil Karlson. Pro: Mort and Joel Briskin. After four years' imprisonment because of legal corruption, an innocent man takes the law into his own hands.

Mahogany
Diana Ross, Billy Dee Williams, Anthony Perkins, Jean-Pierre Aumont. Dir: Berry Gordy. Pro: Rob Cohen, Jack Ballard. Chief men in the life of a top fashion designer are a black lover and a white photographer who mars her career.

1976

▽ The writing of Ron Koslow, direction by Daniel Petrie and production by Ron Silverman were all respectable jobs, yet **Lifeguard** remained persistently uninvolving. It presented the dilemma of a man lacking that essential attribute of the American hero: ambition. Well played by Sam Elliott (here being held back from attacking Mark Hall by Scott Lichtig, left, and Parker Stevenson, right), he enjoyed the easygoing life of a beach guard, but was nudged by his parents and girlfriend (Anne Archer) towards a more rewarding occupation – selling cars, for instance. A touching interlude with a young girl (Kathleen Quinlan) infatuated by his handsome muscularity petered out inconclusively, like the movie itself. Box-office cashiers had a restful week.

▷ John Wayne's last picture was one of his best. While not especially brilliant in story or production, **The Shootist** drew a poignancy unique in film history from the circumstance that while its fictional hero suffered from cancer, its real-life star was also a victim of the disease. And the audiences watching him knew it because, to encourage others similarly afflicted, Wayne publicised his recoveries from the illness during his many years of fighting it. In the screenplay by Miles Hood Swarthout and Scott Hale, from Glendon Swarthout's novel, Wayne (left) was an old-time outlaw returning to Carson City to consult a doctor friend (James Stewart, right) who tells him his illness is terminal. After finding peace with a sympathetic widow (Lauren Bacall – effectively cast against type) and her hero-worshipping son (Ron Howard) he decides to give his death some purpose by challenging the region's worst villains to a shoot-out. This was the blaze-of-glory climax of a Western that mostly eschewed violence and adroitly avoided any traps of mawkishness and gloom the subject-matter might have sprung. For this, credit must go to ace director Don Siegel, whose cast in the M.J. Frankovich-William Self production included Richard Boone, Hugh O'Brian, Harry Morgan, Sheree North and John Carradine. In 1979 Wayne died, aged 72, after nearly fifty years on the screen, during which he became one of the few real super-stars.

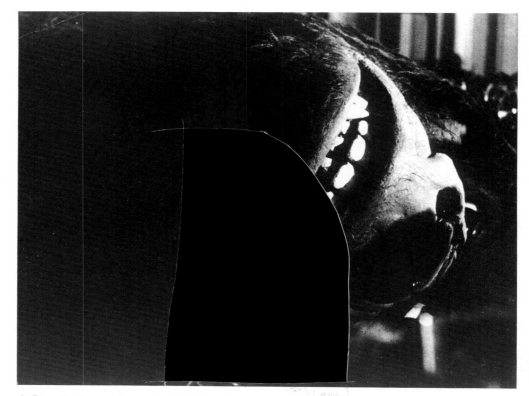

△ Dino De Laurentiis, the 'think big' producer, splurged $24 million on his super-gigantic remake of **King Kong** with the intention of equalling the phenomenal grosses of Universal's 1975 fright epic, *Jaws*. In that aim he was disappointed, but while the gorilla fell well short of the shark as a blockbuster, it did rise to fourth place among all Paramount winners so far, easily topping the company's other releases of 1976 in the process. The critics gave it a mixed reception, the original version (which cost RKO a mere $672,000 in 1933) having achieved the status of a classic: they weren't happy about the up-dated, campy elements Lorenzo Semple Jr injected into his rewrite of the Merian Cooper-Edgar Wallace story about an expedition into the South Pacific to find an uncharted island where the natives worship a giant gorilla. The latter captures a girl in the party and, after she has been rescued, he is transported to New York, escapes and, running amok through the skyscrapers in search of the girl, meets his inevitable fate. The fault-finders thought that the original's simple thrust had been blunted by over-elaborate spectacle, but thriller fans loved every bit of it. Jessica Lange (illustrated), Jeff Bridges, Charles Grodin, John Randolph and Rene Auberjonois led director John Guillermin's cast and the special effects won an Oscar.

◁ Totally fascinating, **The Tenant** was a display of the prodigious talents of Roman Polanski (right) as director, writer and actor. He gave himself a great part as an unassuming clerk who, having moved into a flat in a shabby Paris apartment house, discovers that its previous occupant had thrown herself out of the window and is dying in hospital. After visiting her and tentatively beginning a romance with her best friend (Isabelle Adjani, left), he becomes aware of strange the house and an increasing malevo- lord (Melvyn Douglas) and concierge s), while other tenants (Jo Van Fleet, ontribute to his descent into paranoia. tten with Gerard Brach and based on nd Torpor) and direction Polanski audience on tenterhooks, never quite e weird events shown by the probing Nykvist (Ingmar Bergman's usual re happening in reality or in the ten- ons. Produced in Paris by Andrew was a quieter thriller than Polan- nerve-wrackers (*Rosemary's Baby*, insinuating, and predictably having impact.

▽ **The Bad News Bears** whammed out a home-run at the box-office, a hit big enough to surprise even its director, Michael Ritchie, producer Stanley R. Jaffe and studio executives. The tale of a kids' baseball team at the bottom of California's mini-league ranks, and its rise when an ex-pro veteran of the game starts coaching it, had mass appeal for several reasons. It had plenty of laughs in a wise-cracking script by Bill Lancaster (Burt's son) and lively action in its treatment; plus Tatum O'Neal (right), a famous name since *Paper Moon*, as the team's leading light; plus, most importantly, the superb Walter Matthau (left) as the coach, a beer-guzzling loser reduced to cleaning swimming pools before training the kids makes him a winner. Vic Morrow, Joyce Van Patten, Ben Piazza, Jackie Earle Haley, Alfred Lutter and Brandon Cruz were in the cast. The more discriminating moviegoers found the precocity of the little ones and the foul language in their dialogue were hard to take; and, of course, the strong baseball element was a handicap in most foreign territories. Nevertheless, its domestic success prompted two sequels (*Bad News Bears In Breaking Training*, 1977, and *Bad News Bears Go To Japan*, 1978), but with diminishing results.

▽ Oddly enough, the children preten in **Bugsy Malone** were less offensive ing wise-guy children in *The Bad N though Bugsy and his companions w that sleazy underworld on which Wa the movie franchise in the thirties. T the dark streets, the nightclubs and were all there, but the mobsters, the m and the crooners were kids who had b resources of a film studio for their let's-play-grown-ups game. They played it in all seriousness, and in many cases with remarkable talent, but everything sordid and violent in the genre they parodied was cancelled out by such innocuous devices as guns firing marshmallows instead of bullets and cars propelled by pedals – also, of course, by the youthful zest of the performers themselves. They were led by Scott Baio as the eponymous hero, Florrie Dugger as his chorus-girl love, John Cassisi (right) as Mr Big of the rackets, and Jodie Foster (left), an astoundingly poised and mature actress, as Tallulah, the seductive cabaret singer; all of them involved in a gang war climaxed by a riotous custard-pie battle. Well deserved praise was won by Alan Parker's direction of his cleverly satirical script, Paul Williams's ten tuneful songs and Gillian Gregory's choreography for the Robert Stigwood presentation of this Alan Marshall production, set in 1929 New York, but filmed in England. A London stage version was produced in 1983.

▷ A glorious burlesque of practically all the multi-storied and/or disaster-type movies ever made, **The Big Bus** could be subtitled 'Earthquake At The Poseidon Airport Hotel'. Every cliché of such subjects was mercilessly knocked down, thoroughly gagged up and tickled to death. In the screenplay written and produced by Fred Freeman and Lawrence J. Cohen, the title role was filled by a nuclear-powered, 75-ton, 32-wheeled monster making its maiden trip from New York to Denver non-stop. Created by a mad scientist (Harold Gould) who is floored by an explosion, the bus is commanded by his daughter (Stockard Channing) who hires a de-licenced driver (Joseph Bologna, here with Miss Channing) and one afflicted by blackouts (John Beck) to pilot the giant, which runs into a series of uproarious catastrophies with a literally cliff-hanging climax. Among the passengers are an unfrocked priest (Rene Auberjonois), an old lady on a spree (Ruth Gordon), a disbarred veterinarian (Bob Dishy), an over-sexed actress (Lynn Redgrave) and a couple celebrating their divorce (Sally Kellerman, Richard Mulligan), while other hilarity-rousers included Jose Ferrer, Larry Hagman, and Ned Beatty. James Frawley's direction kept them, the loony incidents and the witty dialogue dashing along at a tempo that rarely slowed down. Unaccountably, the box-office didn't keep pace.

△ **Face To Face** told the harrowing story of a successful psychiatrist, the personification of cool, well organised professionalism, who suddenly disintegrates into madness. It was a major work of art, written, directed and produced by Ingmar Bergman, whose insight into the psychology of women had been demonstrated in several of his previous pictures, but never with such penetration as this. He was given great help by the performance of Liv Ullmann (illustrated), long his partner on screen and off; she seemed to be more living than acting the breathtaking drop into the depression that reaches its nadir as she takes a massive dose of sleeping pills. They propel her, and the film into a series of nightmares and hallucinations, chiefly concerning her orphaned childhood with her grandparents; repressed memories possess her, especially of ill treatment by her grandmother, for whom she feels new sympathy when she emerges from her collapse. Erland Josephson, as a doctor who would be her lover but for his homosexuality, and Gunnar Bjornstrand and Aino Taube-Henrikson, as the old couple, were outstanding in the Swedish production (originally made as a TV series) released by Paramount as a Dino De Laurentiis presentation. Ironically, Bergman himself suffered a nervous breakdown soon after completing the film, when he was arrested on a tax fraud charge, later dropped.

▽ Should your dentist say 'Open wide; this is going to hurt like hell!' you'd have some idea of the shock-horror-anxiety that **Marathon Man** flung at its audiences. Indeed, one of its most agonising scenes was of a dental torture performed by Laurence Olivier (left), of all people, on Dustin Hoffman (centre) to make him reveal a secret he didn't possess. Hoffman, as a New York student given to running for exercise, had to spend most of the film running for his life, pursued by mysterious CIA-type characters and an ex-Nazi from South America (Lord O.) while falling in love with an enigmatic Swiss Miss (Marthe Keller). The plot provided by William Goldman's script, from his own novel, was too complicated to describe, even by the movie itself, which left motives unexplained and loose ends dangling all over the place. John Schlesinger, directing, didn't bother about credibility; he followed the old Hollywood adage 'cut to the chase' and delivered a violent thriller, unremitting in its assault on the nerves. Roy Scheider, William Devane, Fritz Weaver, Marc Lawrence and Richard Bright were prominently cast in the Robert Evans-Sidney Beckerman production, which drew hefty business: over $16 million just from North American theatres.

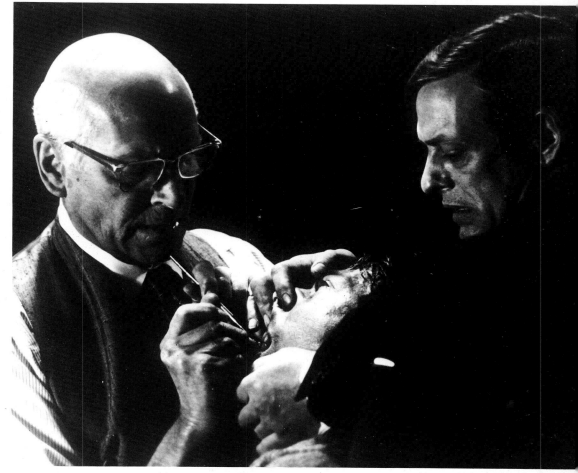

▽ Customers hoping for frissons of horror and sexuality were out of luck when **Lipstick**, well publicised as a frank story of rape, turned out to be an unconvincing, over-theatrical potboiler. Margaux Hemingway, a top flight photographic model, played just that in her screen debut, but neither she nor Mariel Hemingway, her younger sister, also playing just that, looked likely to achieve the renown of their forebear, Ernest. David Rayfiel's script told how Margaux was raped by mixed-up musician Chris Sarandon (here being restrained in a courtroom outburst) and legally frustrated when she had him charged. Her lawyer, Anne Bancroft, got nowhere with a women's rights plea, but little sister Mariel made virtue triumph by luring Chris into assaulting her too. Freddie Fields produced for Dino De Laurentiis; Lamont Johnson directed; Perry King (left) and Robin Gammell acted.

◁ **Won Ton Ton, The Dog Who Saved Hollywood** had its inspiration in Rin-Tin-Tin, the dog who saved Warner Bros. before the talkies did. That gem of an idea for satirical comedy was quickly lost in a rave-up of farcical situations in which the stray canine hero is adopted by a wacky would-be actress (Madeline Kahn, left) and an aspiring director (Bruce Dern, right) who strike it rich when a studio boss (Art Carney) spots the hound as star material. After many hits with Won Ton Ton performing some amazing feats, his public loses interest, he and his owners are fired and he is given to a travelling dog show; then the girl, whose acting would make Ruby Keeler look like Sarah Bernhardt, is hailed as a comic find and all's well. Michael Winner directed the chaotic Arnold Schulman-Cy Howard screenplay in anything-goes style, getting the best laugh results from Miss Kahn. Also in the David Picker-Schulman-Winner production were Phil Silvers, Teri Garr, Ron Leibman and Stepin Fetchit, with brief cameos of silent movie types (although most of them post-dated that era) by Richard Arlen, Janet Blair, Jackie Coogan, Andy Devine, Gloria de Haven, William Demarest, Rhonda Fleming, Dick Haymes, Dorothy Lamour, Victor Mature, The Ritz Brothers, Rudy Vallee, Johnny Weissmuller and others. It proved to be a dull dog at the box-office.

△ F. Scott Fitzgerald died before he could finish writing **The Last Tycoon**, yet even in its incomplete state it was considered to be one of his finest novels; also one of the best about Hollywood by anyone. He wrote it from personal observation of the studios, particularly MGM, on whose 'boy wonder' production chief, Irving Thalberg, he based his central character. Far from being the usual flamboyant movie czar imagined by the public, Thalberg was quiet, polite and businesslike, with a rare gift for hiring the the right people and guiding their talents in the right direction. Not an exciting person in visual terms – and neither was this picture. Like Robert De Niro (centre) in the leading role, it was serious, thoughtful and convincing. And dull. The Harold Pinter screenplay, directed by Elia Kazan, followed the studio chief through his dealings with temperamental stars, egotistical directors, a writer's conference, a rival executive (Robert Mitchum, left) and a union leader (Jack Nicholson). These scenes might have come from a Thalberg biography, but the romantic sequences with a vaguely characterised English girl (Ingrid Boulting) were pure fiction, and pure candyfloss. The Sam Spiegel production also featured Tony Curtis, Jeanne Moreau, Donald Pleasence, Ray Milland (right), Dana Andrews, Theresa Russell, John Carradine, Peter Strauss and Morgan Farley.

OTHER RELEASES OF 1976

Emmanuelle, The Joys Of A Woman
Sylvia Kristel, Umberto Orsini, Caroline Laurence. Dir: Francis Giacobetti. Pro: Yves Rousset-Rouard. Pleasure in the Orient is sought by a sex-obsessed adventuress. (French/Italian)

The First Nudie Musical
Stephen Nathan, Cindy Williams, Bruce Kimmel. Dir: Mark Haggard, Bruce Kimmel. Pro: Jack Reeves. To keep bankruptcy at bay, a Hollywood producer makes the first all-singing, all-dancing, all-naked movie.

Leadbelly
Roger E. Mosley, Paul Benjamin, Madge Sinclair. Dir: Gordon Parks. Pro: Marc Merson. Biopic tracing the ups and downs of the legendary black folk-singer's career from his later teens to his mid-forties.

The Memory Of Justice
Dir & Pro: Marcel Ophuls. 278-minute documentary examining war crimes; covers Germany, Vietnam, Hiroshima and Algeria.

Mikey And Nicky
Peter Falk, John Cassavetes, Ned Beatty, Joyce Van Patten. Dir: Elaine May. Pro: Michael Hausmann. Companionship and discord between two small-time criminals who were friends in childhood.

Survive!
Hugo Stiglitz, Norma Lazaran. Dir: Rene Cardona. Pro: Conacine, Cardona. The crash of a plane on an inaccessible South American mountain peak leaves 16 survivors, who have to resort to eating the dead. (Mexican)

1977

▽ So much advance publicity was given to Bernardo Bertolucci's **1900** during its production, and its pre-release exhibition at international film festivals (the young Italian director's name was news since his *Last Tango In Paris*) that its release should have been a major success. But there had been such an emphasis on its extreme length, necessitating its being shown in two separate parts in its European runs, that moviegoers were intimidated by a possible endurance test and avoided it. Mixed reviews didn't help: many critics complained that, even with its original five and a half hours reduced to four, the Franco Arcelli-Giuseppe and Bernardo Bertolucci screenplay looked over-inflated in attempting to cover the rise of Italy's Fascism and then Communism as well as a saga of two families, those of a landowner (Burt Lancaster) and a peasant (Sterling Hayden) and, later, their respective grandsons, a dilettante (Robert De Niro, left) and a union organiser (Gerard Depardieu). Also in the huge cast of the Alberto Grimaldi production were Donald Sutherland, Dominique Sanda (right), Laura Betti, Alida Valli, Roberto Maccanti and Stephania Sandrelli. Its epic qualities were appreciated by most of those taking the advice of critics like *Newsweek*'s Jack Kroll, who said, 'Everyone who cares about movies will have to see *1900* . . . It is a great film'.

▽ **Sorcerer** was William Friedkin's remake of a memorable French thriller, *The Wages Of Fear*, made by Henri-Georges Clouzot in 1955. The latter's main sequence was a *tour de force* of nail-biting suspense in which four men drove two truckloads of nitroglycerine across hundreds of miles of obstacle-strewn Latin American terrain to fight an oil-well fire. Occupying about one hour of the new movie, that sequence still held tremendous tension in Friedkin's reproduction. Unfortunately, he preceded it with another hour comprising detailed accounts – practically four short films in themselves – of how each driver came to be a fugitive from the law, stranded in tropical squalor and desperate enough to take on their death-defying job. As in the climactic section of the movie, the men in these prefaces were compellingly acted by Roy Scheider as an American gangster, Bruno Cremer as a French embezzler, Francisco Rabal as a Mexican killer and Amidou (illustrated) as an Arab terrorist. But the four-way build-up in Walon Green's screenplay (based, like the original, on a novel by Georges Arnaud) weakened the dramatic impact and, worse still from a commercial aspect, inflated the film's cost to about $22 million (not nearly recovered), hence its co-sponsorship by Paramount and Universal.

△ Pleasing visually in the beautiful scenery of a Bahamas isle photographed by Fred Koenekamp, and intellectually in the thoughtful performance of George C. Scott, **Islands In The Stream** was unsatisfying as a whole. Ernest Hemingway's book, on which Denne Bart Petticlerc based his screenplay was, like Fitzgerald's *The Last Tycoon*, an uncompleted, posthumously published work of a great novelist whose style couldn't be faithfully reproduced in screen terms. This was a very respectable attempt by the scriptwriter, director Franklin J. Schaffner, Scott (right) in the author's idealised self-portrait, and the supporting cast – Claire Bloom (left), David Hemmings, Gilbert Roland, Susan Tyrell, Richard Evans, Julius Harris, Hart Bochner, Michael-James Wixted, Brad Savage – but it achieved dramatic force only in fits and starts. The tale, much of of it invented by Petticlerc, dealt with a sculptor whose idyllic island life is disturbed in the summer of 1940 by the arrival of the three sons (Bochner, Wixted, Savage) of his two failed marriages. Long estranged from them, he makes their reunion a happy one, but has more trouble adjusting to the return of his first wife (Bloom), and he runs into violent danger while smuggling German Jewish refugees into Cuba, aided by his friend (Hemmings) who is killed. The Peter Bart-Max Palevski production was not a commercial success.

▷ The whole theatre fairly vibrated with excitement while the audience caught **Saturday Night Fever**. Starting with a rather shabby, slice-of-life look, it quickly developed into one of those rare pictures glowing with the aura of a smash-hit. Equally unmistakable was the super-star impact of a young actor virtually unknown in films, more often seen on US television: John Travolta (illustrated). Playing a paint store clerk in Brooklyn, a weekday nobody, he is transformed on Saturdays into a stunning stud; fascinated, we watch his ritual of dressing, pomading, perfuming, then his swaggering entrance into the dance hall where he is king, and where the movie's other sensation takes over: disco dancing. On a floor lit from below, to music by The Bee Gees (Barry, Robin and Maurice Gibb) at once stimulating and hypnotic, the dancing by ensembles, pairs, and particularly Travolta solo, was entertainment dynamite. Otherwise the action was fast in Norman Wexler's screenplay (from a story by Nik Cohn) about the hero's exploits with his gang, problems with his family, and romance with a girl (Karen Lynn Gorney) furthering his ambition to be a professional dancer. Barry Miller, Joseph Cali, Paul Pape and Bruce Ornstein were others directed by John Badham in the Robert Stigwood production, which ranked second only to *The Godfather* on Paramount's all-time list of money-makers. Another fortune was earned by the soundtrack album.

△ There were plenty of takers for what **Black Sunday** had to offer: 145 minutes of high-pressure plot and action about a terrorist group taking over a Goodyear blimp in order to explode it on Miami's Superbowl stadium during a big football match. With intrepid Robert Shaw (right) in hot helicopter pursuit, the conspirators hadn't a chance – but their 80,000 intended victims didn't know that. Neither did the cinema audience, so expert was director John Frankenheimer's command of pace and suspense. Bruce Dern, Marthe Keller, Fritz Weaver (left), Steven Keats, Bekim Fehmiu and Michael V. Gazzo had good parts in the Robert Evans production, written by Ernest Lehmann, Kenneth Ross and Ivan Moffat from Thomas Harris's best-seller. It was being made at the same time as Universal's similar football-stadium disaster epic, *Two Minute Warning*, which beat it to release but came second at the box-office.

△ **Citizens Band** (aka **Handle With Care**) cast a hilarious eye over the craze for personal broadcasting facilities that has grown, one shudders to learn, into a pastime for thirty million Americans. In the town under observation, almost everybody seems to have two identities, one real and the other invented for CB transmissions; the operators' radios are used for riding their hobbyhorses, exercising their imaginations, arousing their libidos and relieving their loneliness. Among the characters singled out by its author, Paul Brickman, and vividly presented by director Jonathan Demme in the Freddie Fields production, were a priest and a prostitute, both advertising their wares, a verbose drunk, and two sets of people in triangle situations: a pair of brothers (Paul Le Mat, Bruce McGill) competing for the same girl (Candy Clark, illustrated), and a bigamous truck-driver (Charles Napier) whose wives (Marcia Rodd, Anne Wedgeworth) discover each other in a riotously funny scene. Le Mat and Clark shared the happy ending; Roberts Blossom, Alix Elias, Richard Bright and Ed Begley Jr completed the cast. A change of title after the movie's release did little to stimulate business, but it has since become a cult favourite.

△ Judith Rossner's best selling novel, **Looking For Mr Goodbar**, came to the screen with some of its controversial frankness glossed over, but enough left to test the liberality of 1977 censors. (In Hays Office days it would have worn their scissors blunt.) The book's notoriety and the popularity of Diane Keaton (right), whose Oscar-winning *Annie Hall* (United Artists) was in current release, resulted in domestic rentals near $17 million, topped only by *Saturday Night Fever* during the year. Although not an obvious choice for the role, Miss Keaton made an excellent job of conveying the psychological hang-ups of the heroine, by day a teacher of deaf children, by night a habituée of bars, ready to be picked up and bedded down. Among those who oblige are a decent chap (William Atherton) who loves her; a sadistic stud (Richard Gere, left) on whose rough treatment she thrives; and ultimately a bisexual psychopath (Tom Berenger) who puts a stop to her instability – and her life. The distressing story was not relieved by the other characters influencing her: her worldly-wise sister (Tuesday Weld, very good), difficult parents (Richard Kiley, Priscilla Pointer) and original seducer (Alan Feinstein). In his screenplay and direction, Richard Brooks established big-city rootlessness and a mood of obsessive eroticism. Freddie Fields produced.

1978

▽ Telling the old, old story of one woman in love with two men, **Days Of Heaven** was lifted high above the commonplace by a series of scenes so beautiful that the viewer wanted the moving picture to stop occasionally and just be a picture. It was cinematographer Nestor Almendros (who won an Oscar for it) and his assistants who were the real stars of the movie, their cameras using natural light to make an enchanted vision of the Texas 'Panhandle' region, not usually listed among the world's beauty spots. There, in writer-director Terrence Malick's screenplay set in 1916, migrant workers from the big cities gather to harvest the wheat crop of a wealthy young farmer (Sam Shepard) who falls in love with one of them (Brooke Adams, left), a girl posing as the sister of her jealous boyfriend (Richard Gere, right). Her marriage to the supposedly terminally ill farmer, a prairie fire, a plague of locusts and a murder are among the events observed and commented on by the film's narrator, a sophisticated 12-year-old (Linda Manz). All four principals, plus Robert Wilke, Stuart Margolin, Tim Scott and Jackie Shultis, performed impressively for Malick, whose direction was voted the best of the year by the New York Film Critics Circle. But the Bert and Harold Schneider production reaped a scanty box-office harvest.

▽ To make an exquisitely lovely picture from a story set in a brothel, with a child prostitute as its central character, would seem to be something of a miracle. Louis Malle achieved it with **Pretty Baby**. The French director-producer's treatment of Polly Platt's screenplay (from their own original story) removed all trace of pornography from the sordid material: with the aid of one of the world's greatest cinematographers, Sven Nykvist, he cast a glow of romantic beauty over the notorious red-light district of New Orleans in 1917, and at the same time he gave the place and time an air of reality. The bordello, its inhabitants and customers were observed through the cool eyes of a 12-year-old girl (remarkably well played by Brooke Shields, left, at the same age) who saw nothing evil in it because it was simply her birthplace and home, where mother (Susan Sarandon) followed her profession. The girl becomes the favourite subject of a photographer (Keith Carradine, right, very moving in a role based on a real figure of the time) who haunts the place, uninvolved until he falls in love with her and takes her away after she has become its star attraction. Antonio Fargas as the brothel's pianist and Frances Faye as its madam stood out in a crowded cast. Theatres were also crowded: this was a financial as well as an artistic success.

▽ Renowned internationally as The Fonz, his character in Paramount's long-running television series *Happy Days*, Henry Winkler had a ready-made audience waiting for **The One And Only**. He also had an irritating role as a conceited, no-talent actor who finds fame at last as a professional wrestler (here being overpowered). Why the public should have cheered his ludicrous bouts, or why his wife (Kim Darby) was captivated by his antics in private life, remained unexplained by a script which kept straining for laughs with such other diversions as an oversexed midget (Herve Villechaize), a fight promoter (Gene Saks) obsessed by his gay son, and some remarkably coarse dialogue. Steve Gordon wrote it, and produced with David Picker, Carl Reiner directed it, and their combined efforts resulted in an incredible American return of $12 million.

◁ In a year loaded with massive Paramount money-makers, **Grease** was the biggest of them all. Released in the same month as *Heaven Can Wait* (which itself outgrossed all the company's other winners except *The Godfather, Saturday Night Fever* and *Love Story*) it actually doubled that film's figures and became the all-time champion to date. Why? Because, said some, it had the new star sensation, John Travolta, and the skyrocketing disc favourite, Olivia Newton-John (both illustrated); but the original stage show didn't have them, and that was still enjoying the longest run (1972-80) in Broadway's history. Others said it was just because of its being a lively, tuneful musical; but there had been many better ones on stage and screen. Whatever it was, *Grease* had it in a great big way, and the crowds contained lots of repeat customers – especially young ones, who identified with the exuberant kids in a 1950's high school led by the co-stars as off-and-on sweethearts (the Bronte Woodard script adapted by Allan Carr from the Jim Jacobs-Warren Casey play amounted to little more plot than that) and including Stockard Channing, Jeff Conaway, Didi Conn and Lorenzo Lamas, all a bit long in the tooth for their roles, but singing and dancing with teenage gusto through 22 numbers ranging from solid rock to disco ballad. (The record album was also a multi-million seller.) Their elders in the Robert Stigwood-Allan Carr production, directed by Randal Kleiser, were played by such good troupers as Eve Arden, Frankie Avalon, Joan Blondell, Sid Caesar, Edd Byrnes, Alice Ghostley and Dodie Goodman.

△ 'Breathtaking' was the word many critics used to describe **The Duellists**. Even more than in the case of *Days Of Heaven*, this reaction was caused by the picture's extraordinary visual beauty: cinematography as an art form has never been more ravishingly demonstrated as in the compositions of light, shade and colour created by Frank Tidy's cameras, with the collaboration of director Ridley Scott and the crew of David Puttnam's production. Again like the other visual masterpiece, its triumph didn't extend to the box-office. This was because the screenplay, written by Gerald Vaughan-Hughes from a Joseph Conrad novella, could not find enough dramatic substance in the original story to sustain 101 minutes of film. Monotonous and thinly motivated, it consisted almost entirely of a series of duels by swords and pistols between two officers in Napoleon's army, whose obsessive feud over a period of thirty years became increasingly incredible. Their confrontations were stirringly enacted by Harvey Keitel (left) as a demented grudge-bearer and Keith Carradine (right) as his saner antagonist whose ethical strength is gradually worn down to the other's level. Aside from three Americans, the leading men and Christina Raines (briefly seen as Carradine's bride), the excellent cast was British: Albert Finney, Edward Fox, Robert Stephens, Tom Conti, John McEnery, Diana Quick, Alun Armstrong, Maurice Colbourne, Meg Wynn Owen, Jenny Runacre and Alan Webb.

▽ Everything about **Death On The Nile** was almost, but not quite as good as it should have been to equal the success of *Murder On The Orient Express*, the previous filming of an Agatha Christie whodunit by the same British producers, John Brabourne and Richard Goodwin. It had approximately as dazzling a starburst of famous names in its cast including Mia Farrow, Harry Andrews, Olivia Hussey and Jane Birkin, along with – illustrated here from left to right: David Niven, George Kennedy, Peter Ustinov, Lois Chiles, Simon MacCorkindale, Bette Davis, Jack Warden, Maggie Smith, Jon Finch, Angela Lansbury and I.S. Johar. But many of them were given little chance for character development by Anthony Shaffer's script, and fell back on displays of familiar mannerisms. Miss Lansbury, camping up her role hilariously, came off best, and Ustinov worst, since as Hercule Poirot he was interminably on-screen, probing the murder of one of the Nile cruise's passengers (Miss Chiles), an unpleasant heiress nearly everyone had good reason to kill. Sumptuously filmed in England and on location in Egypt, the riverboat trip lasted a long time (140 minutes) and could have been piloted with more full-steam-ahead by director John Guillermin. The critics gave it a faint send-off – only Anthony Powell's Oscar-winning costumes got unanimous cheers – and, while not a flop, it drew only about half as many customers as its predecessor.

▷ Warren Beatty's enormous successes as producer and star of *Bonnie And Clyde* (Warner Bros. 1967) and *Shampoo* (Columbia 1974) were dwarfed by **Heaven Can Wait**, for which he added co-scripting, with Elaine May, and co-directing, with Buck Henry (right), to his acting and producing chores. Lacking the sensational come-ons of the first hit's violence and the second's sex, this charmer was a blithe sprite of a movie whose pace was its fortune. And what a fortune: its worldwide dollar total soared into the nine-figure region achieved by very few attractions. The story was both ingenuous and ingenious, a fable of disarming innocence spiced with adult complications as its foot-ball-star hero (Beatty, centre) is whisked from life into death years ahead of schedule by a heavenly mess-enger (James Mason, left) who's got his despatch list mixed. So that he can live out his allotted time he is reincarnated as a financier, whose wife (Dyan Cannon) and her lover (Charles Grodin) plot his murder, while he falls in love with an English girl (Julie Christie) who recognises his former self. Many funny involvements preceded the happy ending of this winner of eight Academy nominations and two actual Oscars. It was based on Harry Segall's play *Heaven Can Wait*, which was filmed with Robert Montgomery as *Here Comes Mr Jordan* (Columbia 1941), but had no connection with *Heaven Can Wait* (Fox 1943).

△ The good news about **Up In Smoke** was its phenomenal box-office power: produced for peanuts, as modern costs go, it returned an awe-inspiring $28 million from US and Canada bookings alone, to become the surprise hit of the year. The bad news was that it didn't deserve all that good news. 'It will make you feel very funny' was the advertising slogan, refer-ring to both the movie and its subject, marijuana, and it brought a delighted response from millions who caught the double inference, while a minority found that funny meant queasy. The picture starred Cheech Marin (right) and Tommy Chong (left), a Mexican-Chinese-American duo previously known for their comedy recordings; over ten million Cheech and Chong discs had been sold in a decade. They played a couple of lame-brained slobs totally devoted to dope; in a tarted-up rattletrap they drive around some less attractive areas of California, smoking the weed and/or avidly searching for more, and wind up, stoned out of their minds, performing in fancy dress at an LA rock-and-roll bash. Characters encountered on the way were played by Stacy Keach, Edie Adams, Tom Skerritt and Strother Martin. Only those flinching from dope addiction as a comic subject, and those allergic to witless vulgarity, disliked the Lou Adler-Lou Lombardo production, directed by Adler and written by Cheech and Chong.

◁ **Foul Play** provided a rewarding vehicle for the talents of Goldie Hawn, the most delightful portrayer since Judy Holliday of blonde charmers who are not exactly dumb, but playing without a full deck. The game she was forced to play in this Colin Higgins picture (he wrote and directed it) was a risky one, starting with her picking up a hitchhiker with whom she goes to a movie, halfway through which he mur-murs 'Beware of the dwarf' and dies. From that moment, on, Goldie's life becomes a phantasmagoria of frights, puzzles, pursuits and narrow escapes in a plot of indescribable complexity, somehow concern-ing an assassination of the Pope. She is accompanied by a handsome San Francisco detective (Chevy Chase, the television star in his first film lead, seen with her here) who remains less flappable than she does in involvements with Burgess Meredith, Rachel Roberts, Eugene Roche, Marc Lawrence, Billy Barty and, as a sex-mad would-be swinger who takes her to his pad for a wildly funny seduction attempt, Dudley Moore. Whipped along by Higgins at a hectic pace, the whole thing was hugely entertaining. Producers Thomas L. Miller and Edward Milkis were able to chalk up a major success which brought in over $27 million from domestic rentals plus approximately the same from the international market.

▷ You needed a strong pair of eardrums and a hearty appetite for rock-and-roll to enjoy **American Hot Wax**. A vogue for that pop music furore of the 50s was sparked off in the 70s by the phenomenal success of *Grease*, so it seemed a good time for dusting off the central character of Paramount's 1957 release, *Mr Rock And Roll*: Alan Freed, 'the father of R&R'. Then he had played himself; now Tim McIntire played the New York disc jockey who ruled the air waves until he was toppled by a payola investigation. The fragmen-tary story by John Kaye had Freed staging the First Anniversary Rock 'n' Roll Show at the Brooklyn Para-mount Theatre, despite a plot by the District Attorney to close it down. Among those performing at full blast were Chuck Berry (illustrated), – repeating from the 1957 movie – Jerry Lee Lewis, Screaming Jay Haw-kins, and The Chesterfields, a group created solely for the film. It was produced by Art Linson, and di-rected by Floyd Mutrux.

OTHER RELEASES OF 1978

The Bad News Bears Go To Japan
Tony Curtis, Jackie Earle Haley. Dir: John Berry. Pro: Michael Ritchie. The junior baseballers are conned by a hustler into playing a much stronger Japanese team in Tokyo.

Goin' South
Jack Nicholson, Mary Steenburgen, Christopher Lloyd. Dir: Jack Nicholson. Pro: Harry Gittes, Harold Schneider. Spin-ster saves a ne'er-do-well from a lynching and he helps her to keep her mining property from the railroad.

Joseph Andrews
Peter Firth, Ann-Margret, Jim Dale, Michael Hordern. Dir: Tony Richardson. Pro: Neil Hartley. Henry Fielding's 18th century comedy about an innocent lad fending off seduc-tions, robberies and rogues as the personal servant of a lady.

King Of The Gypsies
Sterling Hayden, Shelley Winters, Eric Roberts, Susan Sarandon, Brooke Shields. Dir: Frank Pierson. Pro: Fre-derico De Laurentiis. The saga of three generations of a violent gypsy family.

Oliver's Story
Ryan O'Neal, Candice Bergen, Nicola Pagett, Ray Milland. Dir: John Korty. Pro: David V. Picker. Sequel to *Love Story* (1970); the young widower finds consolation in a lovely, rich divorcee.

The Serpent's Egg
Liv Ullman, David Carradine, Gert Frobe. Dir: Ingmar Bergman. Pro: Dino De Laurentiis. Berlin depravity and the rise of the Nazis background the romance of a circus acrobat and a cabaret girl.

1979

∇ In one respect **Players** was the most successful movie ever made: it was by far the best depiction of the tennis world. Although used incidentally many times on the screen, notably in Hitchcock's *Strangers On A Train* (Warner Bros., 1951) and the Hepburn-Tracy *Pat And Mike* (MGM, 1952) tennis has been the chief subject in only one film that memory can summon, Ida Lupino's *Hard, Fast And Beautiful* (RKO, 1951); which is strange, considering the sport's booming popularity. It was given a keen-eyed once-over in the new Robert Evans production, the realism extending to the use of Wimbledon's centre court for the climax in which thousands cheered the tournament's final between the hero (Dean-Paul Martin, left) and champion Guillermo Vilas. Other top players appearing were John McEnroe, Ilie Nastase, John Alexander, Tom Gullikson, John Lloyd and Pancho Gonzales (right), the latter giving an amazingly good performance as the coach who puts Martin through the long, tough training needed to lift him from tennis tramp to champ. Martin (Dean's son) was also effective both on and off the court, under Anthony Harvey's direction. Unfortunately the screenplay, which was contrived by Arnold Schulman tacked on a ludicrously inept romance between the boy and an older woman (Ali MacGraw, centre) kept by a millionaire (Maximilian Schell), which made the movie serve a double fault: rotten reviews and feeble business.

∇ Corrosive reviews and unenthusiastic word-of-mouth neutralised the elaborate production and big-name values of **Bloodline**. The Sidney Sheldon novel, a 1978 best-seller, was so wide-ranging in locales and characters, and so relentlessly soap-operatic, that it seemed ideal material for a television serial. Condensed into feature film length by Laird Koenig's script, its complex plot jumped all over the place, leaving a trail of loose ends and losing its grip on the audience. Audrey Hepburn (right) came out of retirement to play the inheritor of a vast chemical company; her shareholding relatives want to sell out, she doesn't and so must be eliminated, permanently. Her potentially lethal cousins – James Mason in London, Romy Schneider in Paris, Irene Papas in Rome – who are having marriage and money hang-ups (involving Omar Sharif, Claudia Mori, Maurice Ronet, Michelle Phillips), gather in Zurich, where a police chief (Gert Frobe) announces that the girl's father was murdered; then the latter's secretary (Beatrice Straight) is too, and it looks like curtains for Audrey next, with even her husband (Ben Gazzara, left) seeming a menace ... Terence Young, who had directed Miss Hepburn's last Hollywood picture, *Wait Until Dark* (Warner Bros., 1967) to better effect, handled this David Picker-Sidney Beckerman production, which was officially titled *Sidney Sheldon's Bloodline* as if to make clear who was to blame.

△ Ranked by critics and fans as the best novel about American professional football, Peter Gent's **North Dallas Forty** kept that same status as a film. A long way closer to the realities of the game than the college heroics and last-minute touchdowns of previous football movies, this trenchant screenplay written by its director, Ted Kotcheff, and producer, former Paramount studio chief Frank Yablans, in collaboration with Gent, starred Nick Nolte as a veteran player. Still a powerful asset to his team, he feels he is starting to go over the hill and, encouraged by a perceptive woman (Dayle Haddon, illustrated with Nolte) he plans to develop wider interests than the football world can offer. His fight against the stultifying conformity demanded by the team's owner (Steve Forrest) and coaches (Charles Durning, G.D. Spradlin) made a drama more gripping than the action on the gridiron, rousing as that was, and a good deal of locker-room humour came through in the performances, of Mac Davis, the TV and nightclub entertainer in his acting debut, Bo Svenson and several football pros. While foreign income, which normally averages one-half of the total, was restricted by the picture's subject, domestic rentals alone reached a handsome $16 million.

△ For years a pet project of producer Dino De Laurentiis, **Hurricane** was planned as a bigger and better version of the Samuel Goldwyn picture that blew up a storm of popularity as a 1937 United Artists release. The new one was bigger, yes. Better, no. The revised script Lorenzo Semple Jr based on the novel by Charles Nordhoff and James Norman Hall had a tedious solemnity not enlivened by Jan Troell's sluggish direction. One waited, stifling yawns, for the promised wind to freshen up while the heroine (Mia Farrow), daughter of the American governor of Pago Pago (Jason Robards), arrives on the Samoan isle to join her fiancé (Timothy Bottoms) and is passionately aroused by the sight of a young native (Dayton Ka'Ne, with her here) who becomes her lover and the new chief of a nearby island. Despite discouragement from father, fiancé, the local doctor (Max von Sydow) and priest (Trevor Howard), their flame burns on until it's temporarily doused by the long-awaited hurricane, a magnificently spectacular calamity that wipes out the entire cast except Mia and Ka'Ne. Special effects for this sequence by Glen Robinson (who worked on the 1937 film too), Joe Day and Aldo Puccini, and Sven Nykvist's photography throughout, were superb. But the real disaster was financial: shooting the whole massive production on the remote island of Bora Bora resulted in a cost of $22 million, and Paramount's USA-Canada release returned only $4.5 million.

▷ **Escape From Alcatraz** was one of the best prison movies ever made, and a major hit for the company in 1979, when its outdrew all except *Star Trek*. Much of this success stemmed from the popularity of Clint Eastwood (illustrated), the only star voted by exhibitors every year for the previous eleven years into their top ten list of box-office magnets. He played a real-life role: Richard Tuggle's screenplay was based on a factual book by J. Campbell Bruce about the break-out of three convicts from Alcatraz on June 11, 1962, the only successful escape from America's Devil's Island in its history. They were Frank Morris (Eastwood) and brothers John and Clarence Anglin (Fred Ward and Jack Thibeau) who, having laboriously made dummies for their bunks, and water-wings from raincoats, bored through their cells' ventilation grilles to the main shaft and the roof, then plunged into San Francisco Bay. They were never found, alive or dead, and a year later Alcatraz was closed, its maximum-security status discredited. Producer-director Don Siegel brought all his well-known talent for conveying realism and suspense, not only to the minutely detailed escape sequence but also to Morris's earlier encounters with the warden (Patrick McGoohan), a knife-wielding killer (Bruce Fischer) and other cons (Larry Hankin, Roberts Blossom, Paul Benjamin and Frank Ronzio).

△ The big surprise in **Starting Over** was Burt Reynolds. He had reached the top of the box-office heap by developing the image of a muscular hunk who caused palpitations among female fans and supplied tough action for the males. Now the element of self-deprecating humour he had allowed to surface occasionally was given full rein as he ventured into Cary Grant territory with a straight romantic comedy performance, and he did it with sincerity, finesse and no show-off tricks. Well written by James L. Brooks from a novel by Dan Wakefield, his role was that of an ordinary middle-class husband stumbling through the crisis of divorce. His wife wants freedom to express herself as a songwriter; also, he discovers, to continue her affair with her boss. He walks out on her and his job, falls in love with a charming lady who can't say yes because of a past unhappy experience with a divorced man, and finds himself drawn back to his wife. Before he and the new love finally got together, many funny scenes were deftly handled by director Alan J. Pakula, notably those in which the wife renders her own songs screechingly off-key, and in a discussion group for divorced men. Jill Clayburgh (the new love, illustrated with Reynolds), Candice Bergen (the wife), Charles Durning, Frances Sternhagen, Austin Pendleton and Mary Kay Place contributed strongly to the Pakula-Brooks production.

▽ With a decade of phenomenal television success behind it in the form of a series watched by millions every week, **Star Trek: The Motion Picture** seemed to be a sold-in-advance winner, and so it proved. Another factor motivating the studio's lavish investment was the almost unbelievable record established by the similar *Star Wars* (20th Century-Fox, 1977); the new movie brought in little more than one-third as much but, even so, it was the industry's second biggest money-maker of 1979, and the fourth biggest in Paramount's history. Commerical considerations aside, it was good science-fiction entertainment for all but the discriminating minority who deplored a lack of novelty in the Harold Livingston script (based on a story by Alan Dean Foster), which had some nasty 23rd-century hardware from outer space menacing Earth, causing the *USS Enterprise* to be reactivated, to leave its orbital drydock over San Francisco, race towards the invaders lickety-split, and engage them in battles which save mankind. This high-flying tosh was a bit of a comedown for Robert Wise, who directed the Gene Roddenberry production with a cast mostly from the TV series (led by William Shatner as Captain Kirk, centre; Leonard Nimoy as Mr Spock, left; DeForest Kelley as Dr McCoy, right) who seemed somewhat numbed by over-familiarity with their roles.

▽ '**Sunburn** is not meant to be taken seriously,' announced co-producer John Daly unnecessarily. 'The aim was to take the audience on a two-hour roller-coaster ride with intriguing people, an entertaining yarn and a Panavision profile of Acapulco.' The intriguing and entertaining were open to debate, but Acapulco, that Mexican mecca of the jet set, looked luscious as Charles Grodin and Farrah Fawcett (who dropped Majors from her married surname between production and release) arrived to investigate a $5 million insurance claim on the death of a tycoon. Was it murder? Involved in the answer were Eleanor Parker as his widow, Robin Clarke and Joan Goodfellow as his children, Alejandro Rey as his lawyer, Joan Collins as the latter's wife and Jack Kruschen as a mob chief. Grodin (right) and private eye Art Carney sorted them out, and gave the movie's best performances; Farrah (left) wore knockout clothes and got, in turn, kissed, chased, kidnapped and rescued. With William Daniels, John Hillerman and Keenan Wynn also featured, the Daly-Stephen Oliver-James Booth screenplay (from a Stanley Ellin novel), co-produced by Gerald Green and directed by Richard C. Sarafian, was determinedly chic and decidely weak.

△ Street gangs don't come any tougher than **The Warriors**, a bunch of hoodlums who made the roughnecks of *West Side Story* look like a ballet class. They had no time for dancing; they were too busy battling other gangs and the police in order to keep hold of their slice of the slums of New York. In Lawrence Gordon's production, given awesome realism by director Walter Hill, the Warriors are summoned from their home 'turf' in Coney Island to the Bronx for a meeting with all the other teenage (or just over) mobs in town; one leader (Roger Hill) tells the huge assembly that they must unite and take over the control of the city. Before he can finish speaking he is shot dead by a rival chief (David Patrick Kelly); the latter shouts that he saw the fatal shot fired by one of the Warriors (Dorsey Wright) who is beaten to death by the throng. In the *mêlée* the other Warriors (Michael Beck, centre right; James Remar; Thomas Waites; Brian Tyler, right; David Harris; Tom McKitterick, left; Marcelino Sanchez, 2nd left; Terry Michos, centre left – with Deborah Van Valkenburg, 2nd right) escape and make the long journey home through Manhattan's streets and subway trains, constantly menaced by enemy mobs. High-voltage excitement, never relaxed in the screenplay David Shaber and Hill based on Sol Yurick's 1965 novel, was intensified by Andrew Laszlo's vivid photography, shot during 60 New York nights. The audience impact was so strong that actual riots occurred in some of the crowds watching it. In its raw, brutal way, this movie was a work of art.

OTHER RELEASES OF 1979

An Almost Perfect Affair
Keith Carradine, Monica Vitti, Raf Vallone. Dir: Michael Ritchie. Pro: Terry Carr. During the Cannes Film Festival the romance between an American and an Italian producer's wife proves bitter-sweet.

The Dance Of Death
Laurence Olivier, Geraldine McEwan, Robert Lang, Malcolm Reynolds, Janina Faye. Dir: David Giles. Pro: John Brabourne. The National Theatre of Great Britain production of Strindberg's matrimonial drama.

French Postcards
Miles Chapin, Blanche Baker, Debra Winger, Mandy Patinkin. Dir: Willard Huyck. Pro: Gloria Katz. Comedy of three American students at the Institute of French Studies looking for lessons in love.

Meatballs
Bill Murray, Harvey Atkin, Kate Lynch, Russ Banham. Dir: Ivan Reitman. Pro: Dan Goldberg. Frantic send-up of summer camps in which slapstick escapades and scrambled flirtations get sorted out.

Nest Of Vipers
Ornella Muti, Senta Berger, Christian Borromeo, Capucine. Dir: Tonino Cervi. Pro: Piero La Mantia. In Venice a beautiful teacher seduces her son's teen-age friend, who plans to marry one of her students. (Italian)

Prophecy
Talia Shire, Robert Foxworth, Armand Assante, Victoria Racimo. Dir: John Frankenheimer. Pro: Robert L. Rosen. Doctor and wife investigate ecology problems in the Maine woods, and find terrifying freaks of nature.

Real Life
Albert Brooks, Charles Grodin, Frances Lee McCain. Dir: Albert Brooks. Pro: Penelope Spheeris. What happens to a typical American family when a film-making crew moves into their home for 'real life' scenes.

1980

▽ Most of **Urban Cowboy** took place in the biggest honky-tonk in America, a Houston roadhouse where everybody whoops it up the way Westerners did in the good old days. Instead of gun-slinging and horsemanship, its modern test of virile daring is a mechanical bull on which the 1980 buckaroos compete to see who can last longest before being thrown off. John Travolta (right), as a Texan farm boy in town for an oil refinery job, joins in the carousing and bull-riding, falls for an attractive slut (Debra Winger) and marries her. They soon break up, John pairing off with an heiress slumming at the tavern (Madolyn Smith, left), while Debra moves in with an ex-con (Scott Glenn) captivated by her prowess on the bull. John wins top prize on this contraption at a rodeo night, then catches Glenn stealing the takings. John and Debra re-merge, and the audience emerged wishing the director (James Bridges) and producers (Robert Evans, Irving Azoff) had blown a fuse in that bucking bull. There was just too much of it, and the screenplay by Bridges and Aaron Latham, from the latter's story, could well have stood cutting from its misguidedly generous 135 minutes. Travolta's magnetic presence, nearly equalled by badman Glenn's, was doubtless responsible for the picture's highly profitable income.

▽ Fans of Popeye the Sailor – there have been millions of them, ever since E.C. Segar created him for a newspaper comic strip in 1929 – rejoiced when producer Robert Evans announced a live-action feature about their hero. It took Evans and screenwriter Jules Feiffer nearly three years to get **Popeye** before the cameras, with Robert Altman directing it as a $20 million co-production by Paramount (which had once had a long series of *Popeye* cartoon shorts) and the Walt Disney company. Clever casting helped to bring the inhabitants of Sweethaven, built and filmed in Malta, to colourful life; they were led by the muttering old tar himself (Robin Williams, right), Olive Oyl (Shelley Duvall, left), villainous Bluto (Paul L. Smith), hamburger-gulping Wimpy (Paul Dooley), Olive's family (MacIntyre Dixon, Roberta Maxwell, Donovan Scott) and Poopdeck Pappy (Ray Walston). The early reels dragged as Popeye was established as a wayfarer abandoned by his father; he searches for him, meets Olive Oyl, takes on a baby foundling, and inspires the wrath of Olive's jealous suitor, Bluto, who kidnaps her. Then the movie really took off, in a riot of chases and fights – won by the spinach-propelled hero, of course. A dozen songs by Harry Nilsson enlivened the soundtrack. Whether so much time, talent and money should have been expended on such crude comic-strip characters is debatable; anyhow, it entertained many customers and paid its way.

△ **Little Darlings** was the sarcastic title of a comedy about a formidable bunch of girls living it up in a summer camp. Although they were young enough to know better, these holiday-makers, ranging from 11 to 15 years old, seemed to be almost exclusively interested in sex, and were hardly settled in their lakeside cabins before organising a contest to be won by the first girl to have her first man. Prominent competitors were played by Tatum O'Neal (left) as a rich kid who zeroes in on the camp's handsome athletic instructor (Armand Assante), and Kristy McNichol (right) as a street-wise tomboy who starts a panting affair with a lad from a nearby boys' camp (Matt Dillon), while other girls indulge in such larks as raiding a men's room to break open a condom-vending machine. Viewers who found all this a bit much were more impressed by the character development of Tatum and Kristy, from the instant enmity of sheltered wealth versus tough poverty to a friendship presaging adult understanding. This and the rowdier aspects of Kimi Peck's story, scripted by her and Dalene Young, were adeptly handled by director Ronald Maxwell in Stephen Friedman's production, a box-office winner. Maggie Blye as Kristy's floozie mother, Nicholas Coster as Tatum's father and Krista Errickson as a teenage siren stood out in the supporting cast.

△ Steve McQueen died in 1980 soon after the release of **The Hunter**, which he had originally intended to direct as well as star in; the ill health that had reduced his appearances in recent years obliged him to hand over direction of the Mort Engelberg production to Buzz Kulik. The result didn't measure up to the McQueen successes that had made him one of the most popular and highly paid stars in pictures, but it had its moments. Scripters Ted Leighton and Peter Hyams, working from a book by Christopher Keane and the life story of Ralph Thorson (who played a bartender bit in the film) strung together a loose series of episodes about a bounty hunter tracking down fugitives who have jumped bail, and returning them to the police. He is paid by a bail bondsman (Eli Wallach) whose most dangerous assignment is to catch a felon (Tom Rosales) in Chicago, where a breakneck chase through the streets and elevated railroad is successful. McQueen (illustrated) returns home to LA to find his schoolteacher girlfriend (Kathryn Harrold) has been kidnapped by a revenge-seeking thug he once captured (Tracey Walter). LeVar Burton and Ben Johnson were also featured. The climax – in which hero finally despatches bad guy by cornering him in a school's science lab, filling it with gas and blowing it up – was a real thriller, which is more than can be said for the whole movie.

▷ With directors Jim Abrahams and David and Jerry Zucker at the controls and Jon Davison on the production joystick, **Airplane!** flew very high indeed. Inspired by the quite serious Paramount drama *Zero Hour*, which in 1957 started a vogue for television and movie air disasters, this was a send-up which let down very seldom in its jet-powered satirical sweep. Prominent in the cliché-crushing were Lloyd Bridges (left) as a harassed ground officer, Stephen Stucker as his wisecracking sidekick, Peter Graves as the rugged if gay pilot, basketball star Kareem Abdul-Jabbar as the 7-foot co-pilot, Lorna Patterson as a singing stewardess, Leslie Nielsen as a most peculiar doctor, and Robert Stack (centre, with Lee Terri, right) as the captain called in to 'talk down' hero Robert Hays when, aided by girlfriend Julie Hagerty, Hays has to change from passenger to pilot. Everybody else in the plane has collapsed with food poisoning. By the time it landed safely, most of the audience had collapsed with laughter. The Howard W. Koch production, written by the trio of directors (this, incidentally, was the first time three had shared overall directorial credit), had fantastic success around the world; the company received almost $80 million as its share from exhibitors.

△ They don't make high-styled comedies about sophisticated crooks any more, at least not like those of the thirties – but they try, every now and then. **Rough Cut** was one of the better shots, but it didn't really come off. Burt Reynolds and Lesley-Anne Down (illustrated together) were not Cary Grant and Myrna Loy when it came to making pseudo-sophisticated dialogue sound unpseudo, and David Niven was looking distressingly frail (his fatal illness already evident) as a Scotland Yard chief forcing socialite kleptomaniac Lesley-Anne to trap gentleman thief Reynolds. The action shifted from London's Mayfair to Amsterdam for their $30 million diamond hijack, the movie's most engrossing sequence; then to Hawaii for a totally unconvincing surprise ending, tacked on six months after principal shooting was completed in England. Director Don Siegel's cast included Timothy West, Patrick Magee, Al Matthews, Susan Littler, Joss Ackland, Isabel Dean and Andrew Ray. Rumour had it that Francis Burns, billed as writer of the screenplay (from Derek Lambert's novel, *Touch The Lion's Paw*) was a *nom de plume* for Larry Gelbart, and that the production was a stormy one, with director and writer at odds with producer David Merrick, the Broadway impresario. He certainly gave it elegance, evident in Freddie Young's photography and a music score by Duke Ellington.

▽ In the wrong hands, **The Elephant Man** might have been filmed as either a shock-horror epic or a pale imitation of *The Hunchback Of Notre Dame*. Miraculously, everything about David Lynch's sensitive direction, Jonathan Sanger's meticulous production and the work of a remarkable British (with one exception) cast was perfectly attuned to creating a little masterpiece. All its contributors were evidently inspired by the quality of the writing by Christopher DeVore, Eric Bergren and Lynch, whose sources were *The Elephant Man And Other Reminiscences* by Sir Frederick Treves, *The Elephant Man: A Study In Human Dignity* by Ashley Montagu, and the true life story of John Merrick, a man so hideously deformed since childhood that he was condemned to exist as a circus sideshow freak until he was rescued by a brilliant London surgeon (Treves) and given a chance to live his remaining years with dignity and grace. John Hurt (left) invested the title role with extraordinary poignancy, somehow making the man's thoughts and emotions shine through his monstrous make-up. Very fine too were Anthony Hopkins (right) as Treves; Anne Bancroft, the one American principal, as the stage star who befriended Merrick; Freddie Jones as his cruel exploiter; John Gielgud as the hospital chief, Wendy Hiller as the matron, Hannah Gordon as Mrs Treves and Michael Elphick as a heartless night porter who, in a particularly painful scene, torments the Elephant Man. Commercially as well as artistically, the film was an international success.

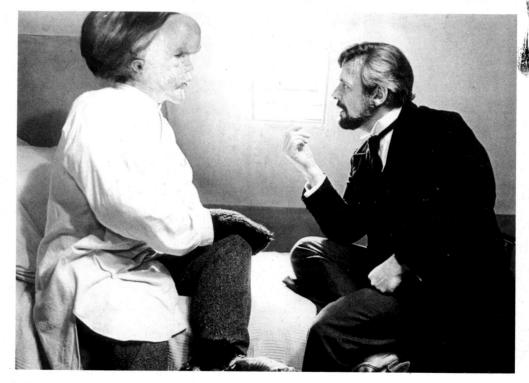

◁ Independent producer-director Sean S. Cunningham shot **Friday The 13th** entirely in New Jersey and on what passes for a shoestring in the eighties: just over $500,000. He sold distribution rights to Paramount, which pulled in *sixty times* that cost from world-wide rentals, according to the trade's bible, *Variety* – a journal not prone to exaggeration. The other astounding fact about this legendary movie is that it was dismissed by every reviewer as a disastrous flop, devoid of merit in all departments. They were right – but, as Adolph Zukor was wont to remark, 'the public is never wrong'. The public got what it evidently wanted in Victor Miller's blood-drenched screenplay set in a New Jersey summer camp, reopening after 20 years' closure due to a series of mysterious deaths. Seven dumb but happy young employees, ignoring the local folks' dire warnings, arrive to refurbish it and, while a violent storm rages and the lights fail, six of them – Laurie Bartram, Mark Nelson, Jeannine Taylor, Kevin Bacon (in background), Robbi Morgan and Harry Crosby, Bing's son, right) are stabbed, speared or axed, leaving one (Adrienne King, left) to survive the insane killer (Betsy Palmer) and get ready for a sequel. Or two.

▷ The unexpected triumph of Robert Redford's career to date was not as an actor – although he'd been one of the few genuine super-stars for a decade – but as the director of **Ordinary People**. This first venture brought him the supreme directorial prize, the Academy Award, while other year's-best Oscars went to screenwriter Alvin Sargent, supporting actor Timothy Hutton (right) and, most important of all, the film itself. That it also collected critics' laurels everywhere was less surprising than its world-wide return of $60 million-plus – a science-fiction result for a quiet, unspectacular family drama. Redford and Sargent retained the warmth and insight of Judith Guest's 1976 best-seller and gave it additional intensity via condensation, illuminating dialogue and performances: Donald Sutherland and Mary Tyler Moore (left) as an upper-middle-class couple living in surface harmony, under which an emotional gap is revealed by the breakdown of their younger son (Hutton). He is haunted by guilt over the accidental death of his older brother, drops out of school activities, can't communicate with his parents and needs the aid of a psychiatrist (Judd Hirsch); by the time he is straightened out the schism between mother and father has become irreparable. Meg Mundy, M. Emmet Walsh and Elizabeth McGovern also scored in the Wildwood (Redford's company) production, made in Chicago and the Paramount studio; Ronald Schwary produced.

△ Set in the time and place of an explosion of artistic creativity, and peopled by a whole gaggle of geniuses, **Nijinsky** somehow managed to be quite dull. Not in its stage sequences, which were brilliant, but in the long narrative stretches dealing with the great dancer's off-stage life. George de la Pena, a young member of the American Ballet Theatre, looked the part and certainly danced it; his energy and grace thrilled with gravity-defying leaps in *Le Spectre de la Rose* (illustrated) and erotic writhing in *L'Apres Midi d'un Faune*. But, like the film, his performance lacked fire in Hugh Wheeler's screenplay centred on the homosexual/heterosexual triangle of Nijinsky, his mentor Diaghilev (Alan Bates, not ideally cast) and his wife Romola (Leslie Browne). The trouble seemed to be that Nijinsky himself was an enigma, never solved by the stronger characters pushing him this way and that until he retreated into insanity, nor by the present film-makers: director Herbert Ross, producers Nora Kaye (the ballerina, now Mrs Ross) and Stanley O'Toole, and the many gifted people working with them to make a feast for balletomanes. *Jeux, Sacre du Printemps* and *Scheherazade* were other ballets sumptuously staged, and other celebrities reincarnated included Karsavina (Carla Fracci), Stravinsky (Ronald Pickup), Bakst (Ronald Lacey) and Fokine (Jeremy Irons), with Alan Badel, Colin Blakely and Anton Dolin appearing in major roles. But as a mass attraction it limped along badly.

▽ With the release of **American Gigolo** Richard Gere (right) made a bid for the sex-symbol throne occupied by John Travolta. An experienced actor on stage (coincidentally, he played Travolta's *Grease* role in London) and screen, he had scored in *Looking For Mr Goodbar* and *Days Of Heaven* when producer Freddie Fields picked him for the tricky task of winning audience acceptance of a male prostitute as hero. Strictly high-class, mind you, and catering only for women, but this professional stud needed all of writer-director Paul Schrader's finesse as well as the star's to hold sympathy while he dashed around the fashionable areas of Los Angeles in his Mercedes convertible, filling dates fixed by his 'contact' (Nina van Pallandt), enjoying non-professional ones with a senator's wife (Lauren Hutton) and, when a client is found dead after his service visit, evading investigation by a detective (Hector Elizondo, left). A scene devoted to his narcissistic preening and dressing, like Travolta's in *Saturday Night Fever*, was very similar to Rudolph Valentino's in several Paramount silents – although neither of those gents gave the camera his unadorned all, as Gere did. Was the studio, second to none (well, maybe MGM) in glorifying female glamour through the years, now reviving Rudy's ploy? The mind boggled.

OTHER RELEASES OF 1980

Bon Voyage, Charlie Brown
Cartoon feature. Dir: Bill Melendez. Pro: Melendez, Lee Mendelson. With some of his 'Peanuts' gang, Charlie travels to a mysterious French chateau, stopping off to play at Wimbledon en route.

Breaking Glass
Hazel O'Connor, Phil Daniels, Jon Finch, Jonathan Pryce. Dir: Brian Gibson. Pro: Davina Belling, Clive Parsons. Drama of a band and a girl singer rising in the rock music world. (British)

Coast To Coast
Dyan Cannon, Robert Blake, Quinn Redeker, Michael Lerner. Dir: Joseph Sargent. Pro: Steve Tisch, Jon Avnet. Rich woman, on the run from her husband, takes up with a tough truck driver, finds fun and romance.

The Outsider
Craig Wasson, Sterling Hayden, Patricia Quinn, Niall O'Brien, T.P. McKenna. Dir: Tony Luraschi. Belfast life in the raw, as a young Irish-American joins the IRA, which plans to kill him with a British bullet, use him as a martyr.

Serial
Martin Mull, Tuesday Weld, Sally Kellerman, Christopher Lee. Dir: Bill Persky. Pro: Sidney Beckerman. Comedy examining the trendy husbands and wives in an affleunt suburb of San Francisco.

1981

▽ Coming along pretty late in the mass-murder cycle, **My Bloody Valentine** delivered nothing like the stratospheric grosses of *Friday The 13th*, which it nevertheless resembled in body count and idiotic narrative. Twelve corpses, including that of Helene Udy (left), littered the scenery before the lethal pickaxe of an insane coal miner was laid down. The man inside the miner's gear (Peter Cowper, right) remained an impersonal menace throughout, and his victims were equally blank: mostly handsome young people able to look terrified on cue from director George Mihalka. He did succeed in getting some good shock effects for the gore fans, and the production values provided by Canadians John Dunning and Andre Link (whose previous Paramount pickup, *Meatballs*, was a gold-mine) and Stephen Miller (whose story concept sparked John Beaird's script) had technical polish. Paul Kelman, Lori Hallier and Neil Affleck headed the less-than-charismatic cast.

△ A sport movie less orientated than usual towards the North American market, arrived in **Victory** (GB: **Escape To Victory**). Wherever soccer is king – in Europe, South America, *etc* – it drew in the fans, and entertained them with a novel, well-crafted drama that mixed the game into a World War II theme, displaying such great soccer exponents as Pelé of Brazil, Bobby Moore of England, Paul Van Himst of Belgium and Osvaldo Ardiles of Argentina, among many others, acting alongside Sylvester Stallone (right), Michael Caine (left), Max von Sydow, Daniel Massey, Anton Diffring and Carole Laure in an international cast of players in either sense of the word. They had a celebrated director in John Huston, who made the Evan Jones-Yabo Yablonsky script (from a story by Yablonsky, Djordje Milicevic and Jeff Maguire) as a kind of morality play in which a football replaced the guns and bombs of warfare. A German officer sets up a match between a polyglot bunch of Allied prisoners and the German national team as a morale builder; his superiors boost it into a huge scheme for Nazi propaganda, staging it in a stadium in occupied Paris and broadcasting commentaries to the world. Thus winning the match becomes even more important to the prisoners than the chance it offers to escape... The Lorimar film was produced by Freddie Fields entirely in Hungary.

▽ People can't help, either at a zoo or in a cinema, getting a few giggles from the antics of orang-utans – and that's about all they got from **Going Ape!** The Hemdale production, written and directed by Jeremy Joe Kronsberg, was a minor addition to Paramount's release list, a clumsy comedy about a millionaire's son who could inherit only if he kept his late father's monkeys happy for five years. Tony Danza (left), Stacey Nelkin (centre left) as his girlfriend, Jessica Walter (centre right) as her scheming mother, and Danny De Vito (right, like Danza, best known in television's *Taxi* series) contended gamely with scene-stealing apes like the almost human invalid, Rusty (illustrated). Producer Robert Rosen proved that monkey business doesn't always pay off.

▽ Fond memories of *Adam's Rib* and other Spencer Tracy-Katharine Hepburn gems were aroused by Walter Matthau (left) and Jill Clayburgh (right) in **First Monday In October**. Of course, the old star magic couldn't be duplicated, but there was much of the same piquant interplay of personalities, the same expert timing of dialogue, in a comedy about well-matched professionals. Adapted by Jerome Lawrence and Robert E. Lee from their play (a hit on Broadway with Henry Fonda in Matthau's role), it dealt with the consternation in the US Supreme Court when the first female Justice is appointed. She, a conservative, and Matthau, a liberal, become good friends while engaged in conflicts over malpractice by a multinational firm and pornography by a film-maker. Produced by Paul Heller and actress Martha Scott, it featured Barnard Hughes, Jan Sterling and James Stephens in a cast well directed by British veteran Ronald Neame. Soon after the finish of production, President Reagan appointed the first woman to the real Supreme Court, making the movie remarkably topical – but still not very hot box-office.

△ The romantic glow that director Louis Malle cast over a squalid milieu in *Pretty Baby*, his first American picture, was spread again on his next, **Atlantic City**, to equally fascinating effect. This one also had a seamy background, the demi-monde of the town that was one of the most famous USA resorts in the early 1900s, became an underworld mecca in the twenties and, except for a spell of World War II prosperity, sank into neglect until gambling was legalised there in 1978 and it boomed into the Las Vegas of the east coast. John Guare's script centred on a survivor (Burt Lancaster, left) of the last forty years of that history; living off an ageing ex-beauty queen (Kate Reid) and some petty lawbreaking, he strikes it rich when a drug-pusher (Robert Joy) stashes a load of dope with him and is killed by mobsters. He befriends the victim's young widow (Susan Sarandon, right), a casino employee, and despite their age disparity they have a tender affair before she leaves to follow her dream of being a Monte Carlo croupier and he returns to the older woman. Malle brought out fine performances from his cast (Lancaster had never been better in his 45-year career) which also featured Michel Piccoli and Hollis McLaren, while Michel Legrand's music was a large plus. Shot in Atlantic City with Denis Heroux as producer and 'With the participation of Famous Players' (a Canadian company), a credit echoing Paramount's past.

▷ **Raiders Of The Lost Ark** was a solid gold, super-colossal, one hundred percent blockbuster. From the opening sequence – a perilous escape from a cave booby-trapped in fiendish ways – it kept up a breathtaking pace for 115 minutes. George Lucas, who conceived it, wrote the story with Philip Kaufman and shared executive producer duties with Howard Kazanjian, admitted that the old movie serials were his inspiration. The story, of an adventurous American archaeologist beating the Nazis to it in a search for the magical power-giving chest said to contain the Ten Commandments tablets, was virtually a non-stop succession of thrills, uninhibited by logic, and rarely pausing for explanations. When the heroine, last seen in a van blown to smithereens, turned up unscathed a reel or so later, the hero remarked, 'I thought you were dead', and changed the subject. Soon they were in a pit with 6000 snakes, then in an exploding plane, then trapped in a submarine base, and so on, to an eye-popping special effects climax. Shot mostly at the EMI Elstree Studios near London, with location trips to France, Tunisia and Hawaii, it cost $20 million, looked it, and returned about ten times as much. Frank Marshall produced the Lawrence Kasdan screenplay and Steven Spielberg directed with zest. It was the first collaboration of Spielberg (*Jaws*, *Close Encounters Of The Third Kind*) and Lucas (*Star Wars*, *The Empire Strikes Back*), making their score five of the top box-office hits of all time. Harrison Ford (illustrated) headed a cast that also included Karen Allen, Paul Freeman, Ronald Lacey, John Rhys-Davies and Denholm Elliott.

△ Considered by censorship bodies in the thirties to be too hot for Hollywood to handle, James M. Cain's novella **The Postman Always Rings Twice** was laundered by MGM for a 1946 Lana Turner-John Garfield starrer, following the success of Paramount's 1944 *Double Indemnity*, also by Cain (and basically the same story). Meanwhile the postman had rung twice at European studios, in 1939 for the French *Le Dernier Tourant* and in 1942 for the Italian *Ossessione*. The fourth delivery was a long time coming, but in 1981 it rang the box-office bell with a powerful adaptation by David Mamet of the sordid tale of a drifter who gets a job in a California roadside cafe, where he and the owner's wife spark off a blaze of sensual lust which, together with greed for the husband's property and insurance, leads them to murder him via a faked car crash. Arrested, then freed through a legal loophole, the guilty lovers are caught in a genuine road accident that kills the girl. Director Bob Rafelson gave Jack Nicholson and Jessica Lange (both illustrated) a chance, brilliantly seized, for impassioned histrionics (although the sex scenes which had Hollywood abuzz during production were toned down before release), while other sharp performances in Andrew Braunsberg's Lorimar production came from John Colicos, Michael Lerner, John P. Ryan and Angelica Huston. Produced by Charles Mulvehill and Rafelson.

▽ The Australian film industry, already riding high on the shoulders of *Picnic At Hanging Rock*, *The Last Wave* and several other outstanding creations of the seventies, received a tremendous boost in 1981 from **Gallipoli**. Overseas acclaim, especially in the US and Britain where it was distributed by Paramount, made its leading men, Mel Gibson (right) and Mark Lee (left), international names, and buttressed the prestige of director Peter Weir, producer Patricia Lovell and cinematographer Russell Boyd, who had worked together before on *Hanging Rock*. Weir's story (screenplay by David Williamson) followed two young men from different spheres of Australian life, through their initial rivalry and personality clash, to comradeship in the Anzac forces fighting World War I. It had a basic similarity to *Chariots Of Fire* (made in Britain at about the same time), even to a foot-race sequence, but, instead of the Olympics, these lads' testing ground was the appalling, ill-planned battle against the Turks in 1915, a defeat which, like Dunkirk in World War II, became a legendary triumph of spirit. Bill Kerr, Robert Grubb, David Argue, Bill Hunter and Tim McKenzie stood out in support of the two excellent leads. Presented by Robert Stigwood (co-producer) and Rupert Murdoch – a Midas-touch pair indeed – it was costly to make, involving an Egyptian location trip and hordes of extras, but profitable.

▷ In 1970, hit-maker Blake Edwards slipped up for the first time with *Darling Lili*, a monumental Paramount flop starring his wife, Julie Andrews. Lap-dissolve to 1980: Edwards was now writing, producing and directing **S.O.B.**, another Paramount release, again starring Julie (left), and it was all about a successful producer whose latest vehicle for his wife, the screen's most wholesome singing star, is a disastrous dud. From that point on, Edwards's chunk of autobiography launched into fiction – and wild hilarity. After a few daft suicide attempts while his wife leaves him, his studio executives (Larry Hagman, Robert Vaughn) hack at his film, and an agent (Shelley Winters) and a gossip columnist (Loretta Swit) bedevil him, the producer (Richard Mulligan, centre right) gets his director (William Holden, right) to turn the flop into a hit by reshooting scenes with his wife, who co-operates for financial reasons, appearing scandalously topless. Edwards, too, had a winner this time, whipping up a fine froth of comedy that included witty dialogue, slapstick action, stinging jabs at Hollywood chicanery, an original score by Henry Mancini, and two songs for Julie. Other good performers in the Lorimar film, co-produced by Tony Adams, were Robert Preston, Marisa Berenson, Robert Webber (centre left), Craig Stevens, Robert Loggia, Paul Stewart and Gene Nelson.

◁ No daughter who felt ill-used by her mother ever got her own back with such venomous thoroughness as Christina Crawford did when she published **Mommie Dearest**, a memoir of her life as the adopted child of Joan Crawford. Brought to the screen by producer Frank Yablans and director Frank Perry in outrageously melodramatic style, it gave the impression that Joan, one of the most successful stars made by MGM, was not so much a neurotic case for the couch as a psychotic candidate for the cuckoo farm, whose maternal devotion in public masked a despotic cruelty in private. Given the hysterical tone of the movie, Faye Dunaway (right) gave an immense performance, throwing herself with gusto into scenes of berserk rage when finding a wire hanger in the girl's wardrobe, or trying to kill her by strangulation, or hacking down the rose bushes in the garden. These were so far over the top that audiences laughed and developed a cult for jeering at the picture; more the fault of the director and the Yablans-Perry-Tracy Hotchanuer-Robert Getchell script than of Miss Dunaway, who even managed to look like Crawford as the studio queen battling Louis B. Mayer (Howard Da Silva), her lawyer (Steve Forrest, left) and her daughter (at different ages, Mara Hobel and Diana Scarwid), and on the alcoholic skids as the widow of the Pepsi-Cola boss (Harry Goz). Despite – or maybe because of – its purple patches, it was enjoyable stuff for all except the Crawford fan club.

▽ Novelty wasn't the strong point of **The Fan** but it had plenty of power to arouse and maintain suspense in its watchers. The well-worn theme of a woman menaced by a deranged killer was given a new look by the Priscilla Chapman-John Hartwell adaptation of a novel by Bob Randall, with the bright lights of New York's theatre district contrasting with the shadows where a young man's adoration of a stage star turns to murderous hatred when she ignores his fan letters. As she rehearses for a new show, he knifes her secretary and permanently disposes of another protective associate; she is alone when he confronts her at last. . . . Edward Bianchi directed his first feature with a sure grip on tension, and Robert Stigwood's production, shot entirely in New York, was redolent of the city. Lauren Bacall had no trouble giving star quality to the actress, and was well supported by James Garner as her ex-husband, Maureen Stapleton as her secretary, Hector Elizondo as a detective, Kurt Johnson as the victim of a gory swimming-pool murder, and especially, Michael Biehn (illustrated), whose college-boy good looks made him an unusual villain. Between completion and release, the story found a grim parallel in the killing of John Lennon by a fan in New York.

△ Devised as a showcase for the comedy flair and sex appeal of Burt Reynolds, **Paternity** achieved its purpose, but left something to be desired both as entertainment and as a box-office attraction. The basic idea of Charlie Peters's script – a bachelor-about-town wanting to be a father but not a husband – promised more in the opening reels than it delivered subsequently, as the protagonist got involved with one girl after another and comedy descended into farce. Burt settled on a cornet-playing waitress (Beverly D'Angelo, with him here) to be the unwed mother of his child and, needing the fee offered, she agreed. More to their surprise than the audience's, love bloomed, and while she was being wheeled to the delivery room they were married. Burt, Beverly, Norman Fell, Paul Dooley, distinguished Broadway actress Elizabeth Ashley, Lauren Hutton and Juanita Moore responded brightly to director David Steinberg. Producers Lawrence Gordon and Hank Moonjean provided 'diamonds by Tiffany' (credits don't come classier) and a plug for Paramount's fellow Gulf & Western company, Madison Square Garden, of which Reynolds played the manager.

△ E.L. Doctorow's **Ragtime** was immensely successful as a book – an example of 'faction', mixing actual people and events with fictional ones in a tantalising way – but not everybody's cup of tease as a film. Although highly praised in many quarters for its impressive production by Dino De Laurentiis and dexterous direction by Milos Forman, it failed to attract nearly enough moviegoers to pay for its huge $32 million cost. A kaleidoscope of American life (mostly filmed at London's Shepperton studios) in 1906, it linked a real story – the notorious case of Evelyn Nesbit (Elizabeth McGovern, left), whose millionaire husband (Robert Joy) murdered her ex-lover (Norman Mailer) – with an invented one about a family disrupted when they shelter a black foundling whose father (Howard E. Rollins) develops a lethal feud with a white firemen's chief (Kenneth McMillan) which escalates into a major blacks-vs-white confrontation. New York Police and Fire Commissioner Waldo (James Cagney, 81, emerged from 20 years' retirement to play this actual character) defeats the militants when, entrenched in the famous J.P. Morgan Library, they threaten to blow it up. Other real characters in Michael Weller's sometimes confusing, often compelling screenplay were Morgan, President Theodore Roosevelt, black leader Booker T. Washington, Houdini and a Nesbit case lawyer (Cagney's old co-star, Pat O'Brien, also 81), while in fictional roles were Brad Dourif, Mandy Patinkin, James Olson, Mary Steenburgen, Debbie Allen and Donald O'Connor (right).

▽ Long (over three hours), hugely expensive and vast in scope, **Reds** was produced, directed and (with Trevor Griffiths) co-written by Warren Beatty, who also starred. A remarkable one-man achievement, acknowledged by the Academy Award for best direction and the New York Critics Award for best picture. Significantly, though, it didn't sweep the board as a complete triumph: only supporting actress Maureen Stapleton and cinematographer Vittorio Storaro won other Oscars. Big and brilliant as it was, this gem had a serious flaw: trying to be at once a history of Marxism, an account of the Russian revolt and the love story of American writers John Reed and Louise Bryant (all the leading characters were real), it failed to focus on any theme long enough to involve the audience totally. Diane Keaton and Beatty (together, centre) won high praise at the head of a fine cast including Jack Nicholson (as Eugene O'Neill), Edward Hermann, Gene Hackman, Jerzy Kosinski, Paul Sorvino, Ian Wolfe and Bessie Love. Contemporary 'witnesses' ranging from Henry Miller to Rebecca West commented on the events – a unique touch.

OTHER RELEASES OF 1981

Dragonslayer
Peter MacNicol, Caitlin Clarke, Ralph Richardson. Dir: Matthew Robbins. Pro: Hal Barwood. Adventures of an apprentice sorcerer who frees 6th century Britain from the thrall of a mighty dragon. (Walt Disney Studios co-production)

Friday The 13th, Part 2
Adrienne King, Amy Steel, John Furey. Dir. & Pro: Steve Miner. Undaunted by the killings related in *Friday The 13th* (1980), another group of young camp counselors comes to the lake and is hideously slain.

Gas
Donald Sutherland, Susan Anspach, Sterling Hayden, Peter Aykroyd. Dir: Les Rose. Pro: Claude Heroux. Comedies, dramas and crashes among American car drivers, infuriated by a fuel shortage. (Canadian)

Glen Or Glenda
Edward D. Wood Jr. Dir. & Pro: Wood. Wild melodrama about a transvestite husband, made on a shoestring so ineptly that it has grown into a comedy classic and Wood has become a cult favourite.

Night School
Leonard Mann, Rachel Ward, Drew Snyder. Dir: Kenneth Hughes. Pro: Larry Babb. A professor is chief suspect as decapitating killer, while heads roll at a women's college.

The Sea Wolves
Gregory Peck, Roger Moore, David Niven. Dir: Andrew V. McLaglen. Pro: Evan Lloyd. British officers recruit amateur commandos to raid a German spy ship in the Indian Ocean.

Second Hand Hearts
Robert Blake, Barbara Harris. Dir: Hal Ashby. Pro: James William Guericio. Off-beat newlyweds, a car-wash boy and a singing waitress, collect her three children and drive from Texas to California.

Student Bodies
Kristen Riter, Matt Goldsby, Richard Brando. Dir: Mickey Rose. Pro: Allen Smithee. Send-up of horror movies in which a mad killer stalks high school teenagers.

1982

▽ There's a good story lurking in the idea of two cops, one of them homosexual, working as a team, but **Partners** wasn't it. Instead of dealing with the dramatic and humorous possibilities inherent in their personality clash, screenwriter-executive producer Francis Veber settled for easy laughs and caricatured characters. Straight man Ryan O'Neal (right) and gay John Hurt (left) are assigned by their captain to pose as a loving couple and probe the Los Angeles gay community for clues in a murder case. Both actors were stymied by the script and James Burrows's direction which made O'Neal's apparently sophisticated detective show shocked alarm at the swooning reaction of every gay to his mere presence, and Hurt's presumably intelligent deviate behave like a limp-wristed dimwit. The mystery they investigated lacked grip, leaving the customers short-changed for their money and the critics entirely unsatisfied. Aaron Russo produced; Kenneth McMillan, Robyn Douglass, Jay Robinson and Rick Jason acted.

△ Biggest disappointment of 1982: the flop of **Grease 2**. Of course, its failure was only in comparison with the phenomenal success of the 1978 *Grease*, the strongest money-maker of all musicals; in absolute terms the new movie's grosses could be called pretty good. As entertainment, too, it could claim a fair share of the original's assets: loads of songs and colour, hordes of attractive young people throwing themselves into lavishly staged numbers, a general air of high spirits and jolly sex. But producers Robert Stigwood and Allan Carr obviously pinned too much faith in the drawing power of the title. It wasn't enough to make up for the absence of John Travolta and Olivia Newton-John, who were replaced by Maxwell Caulfield (right) and Michelle Pfeiffer (left), both good to look at and talented, but bland and dull. Another drawback was Ken Finkleman's story, so slight as to verge upon nonexistence. Patricia Birch directed what there was of it proficiently, and did even better with her choreography – although the finale recalled that famous Chinese act, On Too Long. Cast included Lorna Luft (Judy Garland's daughter, centre) and Adrian Zmed as students, Tab Hunter, Eve Arden, and Sid Caesar as faculty members at dear old Rydell High.

△ Customers expecting a peppy musical when they went into **I'm Dancing As Fast As I Can** were out of luck. They got nothin' but the blues, as this depressing saga of a Valium addict traced a woman's downward path from prestige as a TV documentary maker to madness in an asylum. Jill Clayburgh (centre), a fine actress, wasn't given much help by screenwriter David Rabe (her husband in real life) or director Jack Hofsiss (his debut) to make the pill-popper a credible, sympathetic character. And when the audience could have done with some light relief from her spaced-out or frenzied traumas, it had to watch Nicol Williamson as her lover (left) succumbing to alcoholism, and Geraldine Page as her documentary subject dying of cancer. Entertainment it wasn't. They were cast with Dianne Wiest, Joe Pesci, Richard Masur (right), Daniel Stern and Joseph Maher in the Edgar Scherick-Scott Rudin production, based on a autobiography by Barbara Gordon.

▷ Somebody should strike a medal for Ken Finkleman. This brave man made his feature film debut by taking over both the writing and directing of **Airplane II: The Sequel** when the creators of the riotously funny 1980 hit *Airplane!* decided against tackling its successor. They were right. Virtually every joke that could be invented for a satire on the air-disaster movie had been mopped up by the original (and some of those were leftovers from *The Big Bus*). Finkleman did manage to find a few new ones for Howard W. Koch's production, and he replaced the air liner with a space shuttle, but it was otherwise a case of familiarity breeding discontent. The only customers fully satisfied were those who had missed the first picture, but not many had. A number of good players from the original popped up again: Robert Hays as the reluctant pilot of Mayflower One on its maiden voyage to the moon; Julie Hagerty (left) as his bubble-brained girl, in charge of the shuttle's computers; Peter Graves (right) as the clean-cut captain with a weakness for boys; Lloyd Bridges heading the Mission Control where pandemonium reigns as wildly on the ground as among the passengers aloft; Stephen Stucker as his hilarious assistant. Cast newcomers included Chad Everett, William Shatner, Chuck Connors, Raymond Burr (TV's *Perry Mason*), Rip Torn and John Dehner.

△ Star Trek: The Wrath Of Khan was a better show than *Star Trek: The Motion Picture*, boasting a more coherent story; and its failure to reach quite the same enormous grosses as its predecessor still left plenty of scope for a hefty profit. It retained the zest of Paramount Television's seemingly everlasting series as well as many of the regular personnel of the Starship *Enterprise*. Its sister ship *Reliant*, in Jack Soward's script (from his and executive producer Harve Bennett's original), landed on a planet ruled by Khan – a richly evil performance by Ricardo Montalban – who had been marooned there years before by Kirk's *Enterprise*. He captured *Reliant* and went into revenge action against Kirk, partly by deploying a particularly horrible Thing which invaded its victim's brain via the ear. Ensuing space battles culminated in *Enterprise*'s Spock (Leonard Nimoy, as ever) giving his life to save the rest of the crew, in a display of special effects at once dazzling and opening the way for another sequel. Producer Robert Sallin and director Nicholas Meyer supplied lots of eye-popping visuals, a fast pace, and even good acting opportunities for (here, left to right, watching a cosmic event on their viewscreen) DeForest Kelley, Merritt Buttrick, Bibi Besch, Kirstie Alley and William Shatner.

△ Fast and furious cops-and-robbers stuff, salted with ingratiating humour, put **48 Hrs.** over as an immensely popular release. (Never spell out the title as *48 Hours*, warned a press release without explanation.) Its pace on the screen reflected the alacrity of its production: pages of the Walter Hill-Roger Spottiswoode-Larry Gross-Steven de Souza script were being delivered to director Hill as he shot location sequences in San Francisco, where the city's streets and subway system provided the backgrounds for most of the hectic action. This involved Nick Nolte (right) as a hard-bitten police detective and Eddie Murphy (left) as a convict he has sprung from jail long enough (48 hrs) to help the hunt for a pair of vicious cop-killers, played by James Remar and Sonny Landham, who lead them on a gory chase through the underworld. While gunshots and four-letter oaths vied for dominance of the soundtrack (the latter won by a short head), the relationship of cop and convict gradually developed from conflict to friendship, both cleverly conveyed by Nolte and Murphy, the black TV comedian in his movie debut. Annette O'Toole (as Nolte's bartender girlfriend), Frank McRae, David Patrick Kelly, Brion James and Kerry Sherman supported in the Lawrence Gordon production, a powerful box-office performer.

▷ After a slight slump with *Friday The 13th, Part 2* (still hugely profitable) from the dizzy box-office heights of *Friday The 13th* (see 1980), **Friday The 13th, Part 3** zoomed back to match the original movie's figures. 3-D was the shot in the arm for this one, with the dimensional illusion which had become a craze in the early fifties returning in an improved form to keep the fans goggle-eyed. Commenting on the perfected projectors being used to show it and plans for a single-camera filming system, the new picture's 3-D supervisor, Martin Jay Sadoff, said 'We hope to obliterate the screen and have entire scenes playing over the heads of the audience'. There was no danger whatever of this movie going over the heads of even the lowest-brow audience. Not so much a sequel as a regurgitation, it was the same old junk about teenagers vacationing at Lake Crystal, the resort equipped with a mad killer behind every tree and hot and cold running blood in every cabin. Crazy Jason (this time played by Richard Brooker) the only character to survive all three horror epics, despite having been drowned in 1 and hacked to pieces in 2, terrorized Dana Kimmell (left), Catherine Parks, Paul Kratka (right), Jeff Rogers and everybody else in the Martin Kitrosser-Carol Watson rewrite, produced by Frank Marcuso Jr.

▽ Although a commercial failure, **Love And Money** had a distinctive style that made it stick in the memory longer than the average romantic melodrama. Written, directed and produced by one of the new generation of film-makers, James Toback, it was a story of the obsession aroused in a Los Angeles bank manager when he is exposed to the allure of a woman, the seductive young wife of a financier. She makes him abandon his job, home, dependent grandfather and live-in girlfriend in order to fly to Central America, where her financier husband wants his help in wresting control of silver mines from a dictator who was once the college room-mate of the hero. The latter disentangles himself from their conflict and an

assassination plot, but not from his infatuation with the wife, whom he takes back to the Sates for a dubiously happy ending. Not the least interesting aspect of the Lorimar production was its cast, with newcomer Ray Sharkey (left) as the sex-struck banker; the stunningly beautiful Ornella Muti (right), Italy's top box-office star in her Hollywood debut, as the wife; Klaus Kinski, as charismatic as ever, playing the ruthless financier; Armand Assante as the Castro-like dictator, Susan Heldfond as the girl back home; and the big surprise as Grandpa, 87-year-old King Vidor, one of the most renowned directors in screen history. Music by Bach and Aaron Copland, conducted by Copland himself, was an additional enhancement.

▽ How many times have you seen this? ... Brash young recruit arrives at training camp; proves himself physically and mentally superior to, but doesn't mix much with, his mates; is singled out by the toughest sergeant for severe treatment, until he learns *esprit de corps* ... **An Officer And A Gentleman** fleshed out that venerable story line with believable incidents, robust dialogue, and characters who looked and sounded like real people. Credits due all round to director Taylor Hackford, writer Douglas Day Stewart, producer Martin Elfand, and cast, here left to right: Richard Gere, Gerald Eyestone, Shannon Lynn, Keith Haar, David Keith, William Franklin, Lou Gossett Jr. Also: Debra Winger, Robert Loggia, Lisa Blount, Lisa Eilbacher. Gere starred impressively as the loner who found himself during 13 weeks of relentless training at the Naval Aviation Academy; Winger scored as his girl, not the customary admiral's daughter but a sluttish factory-hand, and Gossett won the best supporting actor Oscar as the drill sergeant. It was Paramount's biggest 1982 money-maker.

▽ Having stirred up a furore, not to mention a hefty profit, with his 1974 production, *Death Wish*, Dino De Laurentiis sponsored another modern vigilante thriller in **Fighting Back** with much milder results. There was nothing wrong with it that a few surprises wouldn't have cured, but the theme had been played too often by 1982 and *déjà vu* kept raising its tired head. Even so, action fans got their money's worth (the credits listed no fewer than 38 stunt men and women) in the Tom Hedley-David Z. Goodman story about a Philadelphia food-shop owner (Tom Skerritt, right) whose temper hits the fan when, after a series of local muggings, rapes and burglaries, hoodlums cut a finger off his mother (Gina De Angelis), and cause his wife (Patti LuPone, left) to miscarry. He forms the People's Neighbourhood Patrol, an armed band of citizens who find they have to fight the law, including his policeman pal (Michael Sarrazin), as well as the lawbreakers. Director Lewis Teague kept the conflicts moving, and D. Constantine Conte produced, with Yaphet Kotto, David Rasche, Donna DeVarona and Pat Cooper supporting stars Skerritt, of TV fame, Miss LuPone, acclaimed in the title role of Broadway's *Evita*, and the always excellent Sarrazin.

1984

△ A teenage comedy-drama festooned with tunes and terpsichore, **Footloose** launched the 1984 release schedule in fine style. The young video-oriented crowds it was made for were right on its beat, and there was plenty in director Herbert Ross's treatment of a cleverly wrought screenplay by Dean Pitchford to keep the adults entertained too. Proving that the generation-gap formula hadn't yet been done to death, it related the problems of a Chicago boy (Kevin Bacon, left) shunted into a small town where the adolescent inhabitants simmer under the lid clamped on them by an autocratic clergyman (John Lithgow) who bans rock music and dancing. The newcomer fosters rebellion in the reverend's daughter (Lori Singer) and their schoolmates, and leads everybody, including the oldsters, to a happy ending. Nine songs, written by Pitchford with various collaborators were, although essential to the action, sung off screen and heard usually via on-screen stereos, etc; they were actually composed after filming was completed. The top-speed dancing highlights were very much on-screen and bang on target, as were the performances of Christopher Penn (right), Dianne Wiest, Jim Youngs, Frances Lee McCain and the three leads. Lewis J. Rachmil and Craig Zadan produced for executive Daniel Melnick.

▽ The success of **Falling In Love** lay in the safe hands of Meryl Streep and Robert De Niro (both illustrated), whose talents and popularity had never stopped growing since their 1978 appearance together in *The Deer Hunter* (EMI-Universal). Sensitively guided by Ulu Grosbard, long a top Broadway and Hollywood director, they played commuters who daily take the train to Manhattan from their neighbouring suburbs. Although both are married, they feel a mutual attraction that becomes impossible to ignore; a tender love affair develops but, loath to risk wrecking their home lives, the woman refuses to consummate it. Her father's death triggers a nervous collapse and she discontinues her clandestine meetings with the man, who leaves to work in Texas after his wife has extracted a confession. But a year later the platonic lovers meet again. ... This bittersweet drama, something like a modern American *Brief Encounter*, was lightened by touches of comedy in the script by playwright Michael Cristofer, making his screen-writing debut. Grosbard took his crew, stars and some of the supporting cast (which included Harvey Keitel, Dianne Wiest, George Martin, David Clennon and Jane Kaczmarek) on a tour of New York City locations – an additional pleasure for the Marvin Worth production's big audiences.

▷ There was hardly an unbitten fingernail in the house by the time **Indiana Jones And The Temple Of Doom** had finished bombarding its audience with 118 minutes of unnerving climaxes. They came at you even thicker and faster than in Indiana's first adventure, the 1981 record-smasher *Raiders Of The Lost Ark*. Whereas that movie sometimes resembled half a dozen old-time serial episodes strung together, this one was like a full dozen with all the non-action moments omitted. It was really too much of a good thing, but nobody minded (except a few critics) as it wowed huge crowds and soared into the stratosphere of nine-figure dollar earners. Unexpectedly starting in super-musical style, with a full-scale production number to the tune of Cole Porter's 'Anything Goes', it then proceeded to illustrate that title in a pell-mell succession of fights, pursuits, hairsbreadth escapes, tortures (some of these a bit raw for the kiddies it attracted) and cliff-hangers, topped by an underground rail-car chase as a terrific finale. Harrison Ford (right) was again the heroic Indiana, Kate Capshaw (centre) his singing (and screaming) heroine, and Ke Huy Quan (left) an Oriental boy who joined their wild jaunt across China and India – actually Sri Lanka, Macao, California and London's Elstree studios, where Steven Spielberg directed with his customary panache. In their script, based on a true story by George Lucas (also co-executive producer with Frank Marshall), Willard Huyck and Gloria Katz restrained themselves only in not tying Indiana or his girl to a railroad track or a buzz-sawn log. Something had to be left for the next instalment. This obviously complicated and expensive film was produced by Robert Watts.

△ **Racing With The Moon** had links with two other pictures about small-town American youth: *Summer Of '42* (Warner Bros., 1971), filmed in the same place, the northern California coast, and set in the same year; and *The Last Picture Show* (Columbia, 1971), dealing, among other things, with boyhood on the verge of war-service manhood. But it had a warm, very likeable quality of its own. Director Richard Benjamin, well known as an actor himself, showed a talent for making his players behave like real teenagers, and his leads – Sean Penn (left) as a sort of older Tom Sawyer, Nicolas Cage (right) as his Huck Finn pal, and Elizabeth McGovern, lovely as his girl – brought convincing emotionalism to their dramatic scenes as well as sparkle to the funny ones. Parallel love affairs involved the tender conquest by Penn of a poor girl who he thinks is rich (the only artificial contrivance in Steven Kloves's script), and the seduction by Cage of another, whose abortion causes the boys' friendship to break up before they leave, reunited, for World War II duty. The uninformative title referred to their daredevil stunt, shown in the film's first and last scenes, of leaping onto moving trains. Supporting performances by John Karlen, Rutanya Alda and Suzanne Adkinson enhanced the Alain Bernheim-John Kohn production.

▽ 'This isn't reality; this is fantasy', remarks one of the 23rd-century characters in **Star Trek III: The Search For Spock**. Very real, however, was the fantastic success of this chapter in a seemingly endless saga. Costing $16 million to make, it grossed slightly more than that in just its first three days of American release – a new record for the industry, and a triumph for Leonard Nimoy (on screen, left) promoted from series co-star to director. He handled his new job well, and added a brief appearance as Mr Spock, who had apparently been killed in *Star Trek II: The Wrath Of Khan* (1982) and whose restoration in body and spirit formed the motivation for the new adventures herein. They included a trip from Earth to Spock's native planet Vulcan by the *USS Enterprise*, skippered as ever by Commander Kirk (William Shatner, right), while his scientists (Merritt Buttrick, Robin Curtis) explore the new planet Genesis, which holds the secret of life renewal. All are menaced by malevolent warlord Kruge (Christopher Lloyd) who stops at nothing to steal the secret, but Spock's regeneration is finally achieved at a Vulcan ceremony conducted by a priestess, played by none other than 85-year-old Dame Judith Anderson. (One quelled the question 'What's a nice classical actress like you doing on a planet like this?'.) DeForest Kelley (on screen, right), James Doohan, Walter Koenig, George Takei and Nichelle Nichols, veterans of the TV series that began way back in 1966, helped to rivet audience attention on producer-writer Harve Bennett's winner.

▽ The studio closed out the year by breaking the box-office bank with **Beverly Hills Cop** which averaged an incredible daily gross of $3 million throughout its first few weeks. The movie's simplistic, B-picture title belied its chic, glossy locations and action-packed plot which capitalised on a number of sure-fire ingredients – of which the surest was its star, Eddie Murphy (illustrated). Murphy, the biggest black attraction since Sidney Poitier, harnessed his brash, energetic and wildly appealing personality to the role of Axel Foley, an impulsive and unorthodox Detroit cop, whose well-meant disregard for the rules gets him into regular trouble. When a close pal is brutally murdered, Foley takes matters into his own hands and follows a trail that leads him to Beverly Hills and the glitzy clubs, galleries and mansions of the corrupt rich. The beleaguered hero is helped by a childhood friend (Lisa Eilbacher) who works for a wealthy gallery owner (Steven Berkoff), a man of dubious character. A pacy screenplay by Daniel Petrie Jr (from a story by himself and Danilo Bach) was matched by Martin Brest's direction for an absorbing piece of entertainment. Hats off to producers Don Simpson and Jerry Bruckheimer, and an excellent supporting cast that included Judge Reinhold, John Ashton, Gilbert R. Hill (as Murphy's put-upon superior), Ronny Cox and Paul Reiser.

△ A three-headed Oscar should have been struck in 1980 for Jim Abrahams, David Zucker and Jerry Zucker as the writer-directors of *Airplane!* They had to be satisfied with box-office records – but not even those were forthcoming for **Top Secret!**, their 1984 follow-up. While not exactly a flop, either as a ticket seller or as a laugh raiser, the new movie certainly failed to match their previous triple triumph – perhaps because their satirical darts were aimed at two targets (espionage dramas and pop-star musicals) instead of one (air disaster thrillers), thus confusing some viewers. Nevertheless, the cliché-kidding gags flowed

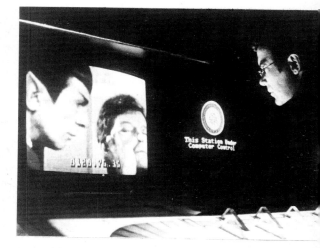

freely as a Presley-like American singing idol became embroiled in an East German plot to take over West Germany. He falls in love with a girl who, of course has a scientist father requiring rescue from the baddies. Martyn Burke collaborated on the screenplay, produced in England by Jon Davison and Hunt Lowry (who were also involved in *Airplane!*), with a lively cast headed by newcomer Val Kilmer (left) – excellent in his song numbers and comedy acting – Lucy Gutteridge (the girl, right), Michael Gough (the father), Jeremy Kemp and Christopher Villiers, plus a hilarious cameo by Omar Sharif.

OTHER RELEASES OF 1984

Best Defense
Dudley Moore, Eddie Murphy, Kate Capshaw. Dir: Willard Huyck. Pro: Gloria Katz. Parallel stories of engineer who gets his hands on plan for a new supertank, and army officer in Kuwait sent to test it in critical circumstances.

Firstborn
Teri Garr, Peter Weller, Christopher Collet. Dir: Michael Apted. Pro: Paul Junger Witt, Tony Thomas. Teenager copes with the problem of his divorced mother's dangerous love affair.

Friday The 13th – The Final Chapter
Kimberly Beck, Corey Feldman, E. Erich Anderson. Dir: Joseph Zito. Pro: Frank Mancuso Jr. Indestructible mass-murderer Jason lives again to run another bloodbath into Lake Crystal.

Joy Of Sex
Ernie Hudson, Colleen Camp, Christopher Lloyd. Dir: Martha Coolidge. Pro: Frank Konigsberg. Boys meet girls at a high school where studies rarely interfere with the urge to merge.

The River Rat
Tommy Lee Jones, Brian Dennehy, Martha Plimpton. Dir: Tom Rickman. Pro: Bob Larson. On the Mississippi, the reunion of a girl and her paroled convict father is disrupted by a prison officer seeking hidden loot.

Thief Of Hearts
Steven Baur, Barbara Williams, John Getz. Dir: Douglas Day Stewart. Pro: Don Simpson, Jerry Bruckheimer. A love affair between a wife and a burglar develops from his theft of her diaries; her husband intervenes.

RUGGLES OF RED GAP

The Rest of 'The Best Shows in Town'

The number of films distributed by Paramount from 1916 to 1925, the period covered by this book's first chapter, was so enormous that it is necessary to list the bulk of them in abbreviated form. Every week in the six years up to and including 1921 saw the arrival of at least two – frequently three – new full-length features at American theatres. During the next four years this prolific pace slackened somewhat, but there were still usually one or two releases every week.

Together with the films on pages 14 to 35, the following forms a complete list of the company's output from September 1916 (when Paramount distribution and Famous Players-Lasky amalgamated) through December 1925. It gives titles, with alternatives where applicable ('aka' means 'also known as'), leading players, directors, story types, and authors when notable; overseas production sources are also indicated. Space limitation is not the only reason for the entries' brevity: despite exhaustive research, full data on the earlier years' product often remains lost in the mists of time, and a great many of the films themselves no longer exist.

In such an abundance of movies, it is hardly surprising that some of them failed to live up to that era's most famous entertainment slogan: 'If It's a Paramount Picture It's the Best Show in Town'. The wonder is that so many of them did.

THE KING ON MAIN STREET

BEGGAR ON HO[...]

THE COAST OF FOLLY

THE SWAN

1916

Anton The Terrible
Theodore Roberts, Anita King, Edythe Chapman. Dir: William C. de Mille. Russian melodrama.

Ashes Of Embers
Pauline Frederick, Earle Foxe. Dir: Joseph Kaufman. Romantic drama of twin sisters.

Coney Island Princess
Irene Fenwick, Owen Moore. Dir: Del Henderson. New York comedy-drama, from play by Edward Sheldon.

The Daughter Of MacGregor
Valentine Grant, Sidney Mason. Dir: Sidney Olcott. Romantic drama filmed in Scotland.

The Evil Eye
Blanche Sweet, Tom Forman. Dir: George Melford. Drama of woman doctor.

The Happiness Of Three Women
House Peters, Myrtle Stedman. Dir: William Desmond Taylor. Drama by Albert Payson Terhune.

The Heir To The Hoorah
Thomas Meighan. Dir: William C. de Mille. Action drama.

Her Father's Son
Vivian Martin. Dir: William Desmond Taylor. Family drama.

Intrigue
Dustin Farnum, Lenore Ulric. Dir: Frank Lloyd. Mystery drama.

The Kiss
Owen Moore. Dir: Del Henderson. Romance.

The Lash
Marie Doro, Elliott Dexter. Dir: James Young. Romantic melodrama.

Less Than The Dust
Mary Pickford, David Powell. Dir: John Emerson. Drama of India.

The Martyrdom Of Philip Strong
Mabel Trunnelle. Dir: none listed. Religious drama from C.M. Sheldon's novel 'In His Steps'.

Miss George Washington
Marguerite Clark, Niles Welch. Dir: J. Searle Dawley. Romantic comedy of truth and lies.

Nanette Of The Wilds
Pauline Frederick. Dir: Joseph Kaufman. Outdoor drama, by Willard Mack.

The Plow Girl
Mae Murray, Elliott Dexter. Dir: Robert Z. Leonard. Rural romance.

The Quest Of Life
Julian L'Estrange, Florence Walton. Dir: Ashley Miller. Drama by Edmund Goulding.

The Rainbow Princess
Ann Pennington. Dir: J. Searle Dawley. Romance.

Redeeming Love
Kathlyn Williams, Thomas Holding. Dir: William Desmond Taylor. Romantic drama.

The Right Direction
Vivian Martin. Dir: E. Mason Hopper. Romantic drama.

The Road To Love
Lenore Ulric. Dir: Scott Sidney. Romantic melodrama.

Seventeen
Jack Pickford, Louise Huff. Dir: Robert Vignola. Comedy-drama of adolescence, from play by Booth Tarkington.

The Slave Market
Pauline Frederick, Thomas Meighan. Dir: Hugh Ford. West Indies drama, from play by Frederick Arnold Kummer.

A Son Of Erin
Dustin Farnum, Winifred Kingston. Dir: Julia Ivers. Drama.

The Soul Of Kura San
Sessue Hayakawa. Dir: E.J. Le Saint. Japanese drama.

The Storm
Blanche Sweet, Thomas Meighan, Theodore Roberts. Dir: Frank Reicher. Drama of a girl and a clergyman.

The Traveling Salesman
Frank McIntyre, Doris Kenyon. Dir: Joseph Kaufman. Comedy.

Unprotected
Blanche Sweet, Tom Forman. Dir: James Young. Drama of women in prison.

The Victoria Cross
Lou Tellegen, Mabel van Buren. Dir: Edward Le Saint. Drama of war in the East.

Witchcraft
Fannie Ward. Dir: Frank Reicher. Thriller.

The Years Of The Locust
Fannie Ward, Jack Dean. Dir: George Melford. Drama from novel by Albert Payson Terhune.

The Yellow Pawn
Wallace Reid, Cleo Ridgely. Dir: George Melford. Drama of artist's romance, from novel by Frederick Arnold Kummer.

1917

The Amazons
Marguerite Clark, Jack Standing. Dir: Joseph Kaufman.. Comedy of emancipated sisters, from play by Arthur Wing Pinero.

The American Consul
Theodore Roberts. Dir: Rollin Sturgeon. Drama of diplomacy.

The Antics Of Ann
Ann Pennington. Dir: Edward Dillon. Romantic comedy.

Arms And The Girl
Billie Burke. Dir: Joseph Kaufman. Romantic comedy.

As Men Love
House Peters, Myrtle Stedman. Dir: E. Mason Hopper. Dramatic romance.

At First Sight
Mae Murray. Dir: Robert Z. Leonard. Romantic comedy.

Bab's Burglar
Marguerite Clark, Richard Barthelmess. Dir: J. Searle Dawley. Romantic comedy of a teenager asserting independence.

Bab's Diary
Marguerite Clark, Richard Barthelmess. Dir: J. Searle Dawley. Romantic comedy of the teenager's invented drama. 'Bab' series by Mary Roberts Rinehart.

Bab's Matinee Idol (aka **Her Shattered Idol**)
Marguerite Clark, Nigel Barrie. Dir: J. Searle Dawley. Romantic comedy of the teenager adoring an actor.

Barbary Sheep
Elsie Ferguson, Pedro de Cordoba. Dir: Maurice Tourneur. Drama of an Englishwoman in Algiers, by Robert Hichens.

Betty To The Rescue
Fannie Ward, Jack Dean. Dir: Frank Reicher. Action comedy by Beatrice de Mille.

Big Timber
Wallace Reid, Kathlyn Williams. Dir: William Desmond Taylor. Logging camp drama.

The Black Wolf
Lou Tellegen, Nell Shipman. Dir: Frank Reicher. Melodrama.

The Bond Between
George Beban, Vona Vale. Dir: Donald Crisp. Melodrama.

The Bottle Imp
Sessue Hayakawa. Dir: Marshall Neilan. Adventure tale by Robert Louis Stevenson.

Broadway Jones
George M. Cohan, Marguerite Snow. Dir: Joseph Kaufman. Comedy-drama from play by Cohan.

The Call Of The East
Sessue Hayakawa, Jack Holt. Dir: George Melford. Melodrama.

Castles For Two
Marie Doro, Elliott Dexter. Dir: Frank Reicher. Romantic drama by Beatrice de Mille.

The Clever Mrs Carfax
Julian Eltinge. Dir: Donald Crisp. Female impersonation comedy.

The Cook Of Canyon Camp
George Beban, Florence Vidor. Dir: Donald Crisp. Western comedy-drama by Crisp.

The Cost Of Hatred
Theodore Roberts, Kathlyn Williams. Dir: George Melford. Melodrama.

Countess Charming
Julian Eltinge. Dir: Donald Crisp. Female impersonation comedy.

The Crystal Gazer
Fannie Ward, Jack Dean. Dir: George Melford. Fortune telling drama.

The Devil-Stone
Geraldine Farrar, Wallace Reid, Hobart Bosworth. Dir: Cecil B. DeMille. Romantic drama set in Brittany.

Double-Crossed
Pauline Frederick. Dir: Robert Vignola and Emile Chautard. Melodrama of wife forced to steal.

Down To Earth
Douglas Fairbanks, Eileen Percy. Dir: John Emerson. Comedy about a hypochondriac, by Emerson and Anita Loos.

The Dummy
Jack Pickford. Dir: Francis Grandon. Kidnapping drama.

Each To His Kind
Sessue Hayakawa. Dir: Edward Le Saint. Japanese drama.

The Eternal Temptress
Lina Cavalieri. Dir: Emile Chautard. Romantic melodrama.

Exile
Olga Petrova. Dir: Maurice Tourneur. Romantic drama.

The Fair Barbarian
Vivian Martin, Douglas MacLean. Dir: Robert Thornby. Romance from novel by Frances Hodgson Burnett.

Forbidden Paths
Sessue Hayakawa, Vivian Martin. Dir: R.L. Thornby. Interracial drama.

The Fortunes Of Fifi
Marguerite Clark, William Sorelle. Dir: Robert Vignola. Backstage romance in Napoleonic Paris.

Freckles
Jack Pickford, Louise Huff. Dir: Marshall Neilan. Comedy of youth from novel by Gene Stratton Porter.

The Ghost House
Jack Pickford, Louise Huff. Dir: William C. de Mille. Comedy thriller.

The Girl At Home
Jack Pickford, Vivian Martin. Dir: Marshall Neilan. Romantic comedy.

A Girl Like That (aka **The Turning Point**)
Irene Fenwick, Olive Thomas, Owen Moore. Dir: Hugh Ford. Romantic drama.

Giving Becky A Chance
Vivian Martin, Jack Holt. Dir: Howard Estabrook. Romantic comedy.

The Golden Fetter
Wallace Reid, Anita King. Dir: Edward Le Saint. Western mining drama.

Great Expectations
Jack Pickford, Louise Huff. Dir: Robert Vignola. Drama from novel by Charles Dickens.

Hashimura Togo
Sessue Hayakawa, Florence Vidor. Dir: William C. de Mille. Japanese drama.

Heart's Desire
Marie Doro. Dir: Francis Grandon. Romantic drama.

The Heir Of The Ages
House Peters. Dir: Edward Le Saint. Drama.

Her Better Self
Pauline Frederick, Thomas Meighan. Dir: Robert Vignola. Romance of heiress and doctor.

Her Own People
Lenore Ulric. Dir: Scott Sidney. Romantic melodrama.

Her Strange Wedding
Fannie Ward, Jack Dean. Dir: George Melford. Romantic drama.

The Highway Of Hope
Kathlyn Williams, House Peters. Dir: Howard Estabrook. Romantic drama.

His Mother's Boy
Charles Ray, Doris Lee. Dir: Victor Schertzinger. Comedy of tenderfoot out West.

His Sweetheart
George Beban. Dir: Donald Crisp. Romantic comedy-drama.

The Hostage
Wallace Reid. Dir: Robert Thornby. Satirical story of backwoods feud.

The Hungry Heart
Pauline Frederick, Robert Cain. Dir: Robert Vignola. Drama of neglected wife.

In Again, Out Again
Douglas Fairbanks. Dir: John Emerson. Comedy about a pacifist, by Emerson and Anita Loos.

The Inner Shrine
Margaret Illington, Elliott Dexter. Dir: Frank Reicher. Romantic drama.

Jack And Jill
Jack Pickford, Louise Huff. Dir: William Desmond Taylor. Romance.

The Jaguar's Claws
Sessue Hayakawa. Dir: Marshall Neilan. Action melodrama.

The Judgment House
Violet Heming. Dir: J. Stuart Blackton. Drama from novel by Sir Gilbert Parker.

A Kiss For Susie
Vivian Martin, Tom Forman. Dir: Robert Thornby. Comedy romance.

The Land Of Promise
Billie Burke, Thomas Meighan. Dir: Joseph Kaufman. Drama of Englishwoman on Canadian farm, from play by W. Somerset Maugham.

The Law Of The Land
Olga Petrova. Dir: Maurice Tourneur. Romantic melodrama.

The Little Boy Scout
Ann Pennington, Owen Moore. Dir: Francis Grandon. Comedy.

Little Miss Optimist
Vivian Martin, Tom Moore. Dir: Robert Thornby. Romantic comedy.

The Little Princess
Mary Pickford, Norman Kerry, ZaSu Pitts. Dir: Marshall Neilan. Romantic fantasy by Francis Hodgson Burnett.

The Lonesome Chap
House Peters, Louise Huff. Dir: Edward Le Saint. Romantic drama.

The Long Trail
Lou Tellegen, Mary Fuller. Dir: Howell Hansell. Adventure drama.

Lost And Won
Marie Doro, Elliott Dexter. Dir: Frank Reicher. Cinderella story from play by Channing Pollock.

Lost In Transit
George Beban, Helen Jerome Eddy. Dir: Donald Crisp. Comedy.

Love Letters
Dorothy Dalton. Dir: Roy William Neill. Romantic drama.

The Love That Lives
Pauline Frederick, Pat O'Malley. Dir: Robert Vignola. Drama of maternal love.

The Man From Painted Post
Douglas Fairbanks, Eileen Percy. Dir: Joseph Henabery. Western action comedy.

The Marcellini Millions
George Beban. Dir: Donald Crisp. Inheritance drama.

A Modern Musketeer
Douglas Fairbanks, Marjorie Daw. Dir: Allan Dwan. Adventure comedy of would-be d'Artagnan, by Dwan.

Molly Entangled
Vivian Martin, Harrison Ford. Dir: Robert Thornby. Romantic comedy.

A Mormon Maid
Mae Murray, Frank Borzage. Dir: Robert Z. Leonard. Romance of early America. (Released by Freedman Enterprises)

The Mysterious Miss Terry
Billie Burke. Dir: J. Searle Dawley. Romantic comedy.

Nan Of Music Mountain
Wallace Reid, Ann Little, Theodore Roberts. Dir: George Melford. Railroad action drama.

The Narrow Trail
William S. Hart. Dir: Lambert Hillyer. Western drama by Hart.

On Record
Mae Murray, Tom Forman. Dir: Robert Z. Leonard. Drama.

On The Level
Fannie Ward, Jack Dean. Dir: George Melford. Action drama.

Out Of The Wreck
Kathlyn Williams. Dir: William Desmond Taylor. Romantic melodrama.

The Poor Little Rich Girl
Mary Pickford. Dir: Maurice Tourneur. Romance from novel and play by Eleanor Gates.

The Price Mark
Dorothy Dalton. Dir: Roy William Neill. Romantic melodrama.

The Pride Of The Clan
Mary Pickford, Matt Moore. Dir: Maurice Tourneur. Scottish romantic drama.

The Primrose Ring
Mae Murray, Tom Moore. Dir: Robert Z. Leonard. Romantic drama.

A Prison Without Walls
Wallace Reid, Myrtle Stedman. Dir: E. Mason Hopper. Prison reform drama.

Reaching For The Moon
Douglas Fairbanks, Eileen Percy. Dir: John Emerson. Action comedy by Emerson and Anita Loos.

The Rise Of Jennie Cushing
Elsie Ferguson, Elliott Dexter. Dir: Maurice Tourneur. Drama of girl with a past.

A Roadside Impresario
George Beban. Dir: Donald Crisp. Comedy by Beban.

A Romance Of The Redwoods
Mary Pickford, Elliott Dexter. Dir: Cecil B. DeMille. Outdoor drama by DeMille and Jeanie Macpherson.

Sacrifice
Margaret Illington, Jack Holt. Dir: Frank Reicher. Domestic drama.

Sapho
Pauline Frederick, Thomas Meighan. Dir: Emile Chautard. Parisian romantic drama, from novel by Alphonse Daudet.

The School For Husbands
Fannie Ward. Dir: George Melford. Matrimonial comedy.

The Secret Game
Sessue Hayakawa, Florence Vidor. Dir: William C. de Mille. Romantic drama.

The Seven Swans
Marguerite Clark, Richard Barthelmess. Dir: J. Searle Dawley. Fairy tale by Hans Christian Andersen.

The Silent Man
William S. Hart. Dir: Hart. Outdoor drama.

The Silent Partner
Blanche Sweet, Thomas Meighan. Dir: Marshall Neilan. Drama of secretary and boss, by Edmund Goulding.

Sleeping Fires
Pauline Frederick, Thomas Meighan. Dir: Hugh Ford. Murder trial drama.

The Son Of His Father
Charles Ray. Dir: Victor Schertzinger. Business comedy-drama.

The Spirit Of Romance
Vivian Martin. Dir: E. Mason Hopper. Love story.

The Squaw Man's Son
Wallace Reid, Dorothy Davenport. Dir: Edward Le Saint. Anglo-Western drama.

The Sunset Trail
Vivian Martin, Harrison Ford. Dir: George Melford. Outdoor romance.

Those Without Sin
Blanche Sweet, Tom Forman. Dir: Marshall Neilan. Civil War drama.

The Tides Of Barnegat
Blanche Sweet, Elliott Dexter. Dir: Marshall Neilan. Drama of sacrifice.

The Trouble Buster
Vivian Martin, Paul Willis. Dir: Frank Reicher. Outdoor drama.

Unconquered
Fannie Ward, Jack Dean. Dir: Frank Reicher. Outdoor drama by Beatrice de Mille.

The Undying Flame
Olga Petrova. Dir: Maurice Tourneur. Romantic drama.

The Valentine Girl
Marguerite Clark, Richard Barthelmess. Dir: J. Searle Dawley. Romantic drama by Dawley.

The Varmint
Jack Pickford, Louise Huff. Dir: William Desmond Taylor. Outdoor comedy-drama.

The Wax Model
Vivian Martin. Dir: E. Mason Hopper. Romantic drama.

What Money Can't Buy
Jack Pickford, Louise Huff. Dir: Lou Tellegen. Comedy-drama from play by George Broadhurst.

Wild And Woolly
Douglas Fairbanks. Dir: John Emerson. Action comedy by Emerson and Anita Loos.

The Winning Of Sally Temple
Fannie Ward, Jack Dean. Dir: George Melford. Romantic melodrama.

The World Apart
Wallace Reid, Myrtle Stedman. Dir: William Desmond Taylor. Western mining drama.

1918

Amarilly Of Clothesline Alley
Mary Pickford. Dir: Marshall Neilan. Comedy romance.

Arizona
Douglas Fairbanks. Dir: Fairbanks, Albert Parker. Western action comedy from play by Augustus Thomas.

Battling Jane
Dorothy Gish, George Nichols. Dir: Elmer Clifton. Small town comedy drama.

Believe Me, Xantippe
Wallace Reid, Ann Little. Dir: Donald Crisp. Romantic comedy of a perilous wager.

The Biggest Show On Earth
Enid Bennett. Dir: Jerome Storm. Circus drama.

The Blue Bird
Tula Belle, Robin MacDougall. Dir: Maurice Tourneur. Metaphysical fantasy-drama by Maurice Maeterlinck.

Blue Blazes Rawden
William S. Hart. Dir: Hart. Western drama.

The Border Wireless
William S. Hart. Dir: Hart. Outdoor drama.

Bound In Morocco
Douglas Fairbanks, Pauline Curley. Dir: Allan Dwan. Adventure comedy of American tourists.

Branding Broadway
William S. Hart. Dir: Hart. Action drama.

The Bravest Way
Sessue Hayakawa, Florence Vidor. Dir: George Melford. Romantic drama.

The City Of Dim Faces
Sessue Hayakawa. Dir: George Melford. San Francisco melodrama by Frances Marion.

The Claws Of The Hun
Charles Ray, Jane Novak. Dir: Victor Schertzinger. World War melodrama.

Come On In
Shirley Mason, Ernest Truex. Dir: John Emerson. Comedy by Emerson and Anita Loos.

The Cruise Of The Make-Believe
Lila Lee, Harrison Ford. Dir: George Melford. Adventure romance.

The Danger Mark
Elsie Ferguson, Mahlon Hamilton. Dir: Hugh Ford. Drama of alcoholism from novel by Robert W. Chambers.

A Daughter Of The Old South
Pauline Frederick, Pedro de Cordoba. Dir: Emile Chautard. Romantic drama.

A Desert Wooing
Enid Bennett, Jack Holt. Dir: Jerome Storm. Romantic drama.

Eve's Daughter
Billie Burke. Dir: James Kirkwood. Romantic comedy.

The Family Skeleton
Charles Ray, Sylvia Breamer. Dir: Victor Schertzinger. Domestic comedy-drama.

Fedora
Pauline Frederick, Alfred Hickman. Dir: Edward Jose. Romantic drama of Czarist Russia, from play by Victorien Sardou.

The Firefly Of France
Wallace Reid, Ann Little. Dir: Donald Crisp. Wartime spy drama.

Flare-Up Sal
Dorothy Dalton. Dir: Roy William Neill. Romantic comedy.

Fuss And Feathers
Enid Bennett, Douglas MacLean. Dir: Fred Niblo. Romantic comedy.

The Girl Who Came Back
Ethel Clayton, Elliott Dexter. Dir: Robert Vignola. Jewel theft drama.

The Goat
Fred Stone. Dir: Donald Crisp. Comedy set in Hollywood studio, by Frances Marion.

Goodbye, Bill
Shirley Mason, Ernest Truex. Dir: John Emerson. Romantic comedy by Emerson and Anita Loos.

The Great Love
Lillian Gish, Robert Harron. Dir: D.W. Griffith. Romantic drama during World War.

Green Eyes
Dorothy Dalton, Jack Holt. Dir: Roy William Neill. Drama of jealousy.

The Guilty Man
William Gardwood, Vivian Reed. Dir: Irvin Willat. Mystery drama.

The Gypsy Trail
Bryant Washburn, Wanda Hawley. Dir: Walter Edwards. Outdoor romance.

He Comes Up Smiling
Douglas Fairbanks, Marjorie Daw. Dir: Allan Dwan. Adventure comedy.

Headin' South
Douglas Fairbanks, Katherine MacDonald. Dir: Arthur Rosson. Western adventure comedy by Allan Dwan.

Heart Of The Wilds
Elsie Ferguson, Thomas Meighan. Dir: Marshall Neilan. Canadian drama from play by Edgar Selwyn.

Her Country First
Vivian Martin. Dir: Rollin Sturgeon. Wartime drama from novel by Mary Roberts Rinehart.

Her Final Reckoning
Pauline Frederick, Robert Cain. Dir: Emile Chautard. Romance of prince and gypsy.

Here Comes The Bride
John Barrymore. Dir: John S. Robertson. Matrimonial comedy.

The Hidden Pearls
Sessue Hayakawa. Dir: George Melford. Mystery drama.

The Hired Man
Charles Ray, Doris Lee. Dir: Victor Schertzinger. Romantic comedy of farm boy.

His Majesty Bunker Bean
Jack Pickford, Louise Huff. Dir: William Desmond Taylor. Comedy romance from novel by Harry Leon Wilson.

His Own Home Town
Charles Ray, Katherine MacDonald. Dir: Victor Schertzinger. Comedy-drama of clergyman's son.

Hit-The-Trail Holliday
George M. Cohan. Dir: Marshall Neilan. Adventure comedy-drama from play by Cohan.

The Honor Of His House
Sessue Hayakawa, Florence Vidor. Dir: William C. de Mille. Japanese drama.

The Hope Chest
Dorothy Gish, Richard Barthelmess. Dir: Elmer Clifton. Romantic comedy.

The House Of Silence
Wallace Reid, Ann Little. Dir: Donald Crisp. Detective melodrama.

How Could You, Jean?
Mary Pickford. Dir: William Desmond Taylor. Romantic comedy.

Huck And Tom
Jack Pickford, Robert Gordon. Dir: William Desmond Taylor. Adventure comedy-drama, from Mark Twain novels.

The Hun Within (aka **The Peril Within**)
Dorothy Gish, Douglas MacLean. Dir: Chet Withey. Wartime melodrama.

In Pursuit Of Polly
Billie Burke. Dir: Chet Withey. Romantic comedy.

Jane Goes A-Wooing
Vivian Martin, Niles Welch. Dir: George Melford. Comedy romance.

Johanna Enlists
Mary Pickford, Douglas MacLean. Dir: William Desmond Taylor. Wartime comedy-drama by Rupert Hughes.

Jules Of The Strong Heart
George Beban. Dir: Donald Crisp. Outdoor drama.

The Kaiser's Shadow
Dorothy Dalton. Dir: Roy William Neill. Wartime melodrama by Octavus Roy Cohen.

The Keys Of The Righteous
Enid Bennett. Dir: Jerome Storm. Drama.

The Law Of The North
Charles Ray, Doris Lee. Dir: Irvin Willat. Canadian adventure drama.

Less Than Kin
Wallace Reid, Ann Little. Dir: Donald Crisp. Impersonation drama from novel by Alice Duer Miller.

Let's Get A Divorce
Billie Burke. Dir: Charles Giblyn. Matrimonial comedy from play by Victorien Sardou.

The Lie
Elsie Ferguson, David Powell, Percy Marmont. Dir: J. Searle Dawley. Drama of slandered lady.

Little Miss Hoover
Marguerite Clark, Eugene O'Brien. Dir: John S. Robertson. Washington comedy of win-the-war efforts.

Love Me
Dorothy Dalton, Jack Holt. Dir: Roy William Neill. Romantic drama.

Love's Conquest
Lina Cavalieri. Dir: Edward Jose. Romantic melodrama from play by Victorien Sardou.

Madame Jealousy
Pauline Frederick, Thomas Meighan. Dir: Robert Vignola. Modern morality drama.

The Make-Believe Wife
Billie Burke. Dir: John S. Robertson. Romantic comedy.

The Man From Funeral Range
Wallace Reid, Ann Little. Dir: Walter Edwards. Revenge drama.

The Marriage Ring (aka **Coals Of Fire**)
Enid Bennett, Jack Holt. Dir: Fred Niblo. Matrimonial drama.

The Mating Of Marcella
Dorothy Dalton. Dir: Roy William Neill. Romantic drama.

Mile-A-Minute Kendall
Jack Pickford, Louise Huff. Dir: William Desmond Taylor. Action comedy-drama from play by Owen Davis.

Mirandy Smiles
Vivian Martin, Douglas MacLean. Dir: William C. de Mille. Romantic comedy.

Missing
Thomas Meighan, Sylvia Breamer, Robert Gordon. Dir: James Young, J. Stuart Blackton. Wartime drama.

M'Liss
Mary Pickford, Thomas Meighan, Theodore Roberts. Dir: Marshall Neilan. Western drama.

Mr Fix-It
Douglas Fairbanks, Wanda Hawley, Katherine MacDonald, Jack Pickford. Dir: Allan Dwan. New York comedy.

Mrs Dane's Defense
Pauline Frederick, Frank Losee. Dir: Hugh Ford. Drama of lady with a past, from play by Henry Arthur Jones.

My Cousin
Enrico Caruso. Dir: Edward Jose. Comedy-drama.

The Mystery Girl
Ethel Clayton. Dir: William C. de Mille. Jewel theft drama.

Naughty, Naughty!
Enid Bennett. Dir: Jerome Storm. Romantic farce.

A Nine O'Clock Town
Charles Ray, Jane Novak. Dir: Victor Schertzinger. Small-town romantic comedy.

Old Wives For New
Florence Vidor, Elliott Dexter. Dir: Cecil B. DeMille. Matrimonial drama.

On The Quiet
John Barrymore, Lois Meredith. Dir: Chet Withey. Romantic comedy of playboy, from play by Augustus Thomas.

One More American
Charles Beban. Dir: William C. de Mille. Patriotic drama by de Mille.

Out Of A Clear Sky
Marguerite Clark, Thomas Meighan. Dir: Marshall Neilan. Drama of Belgian war refugee in Tennessee.

A Petticoat Pilot
Vivian Martin, Harrison Ford. Dir: Rollin Sturgeon. Aviation comedy.

Playing The Game
Charles Ray, Doris Lee. Dir: Victor Schertzinger. Drama of playboy's reformation.

Private Peat
Harold Peat. Dir: Edward Jose. Wartime comedy-drama from Peat's autobiography.

Prunella
Marguerite Clark, Jules Raucourt. Dir: Maurice Tourneur. Romance of a Paris actress, from play by Laurence Houseman and Granville Barker.

The Pursuit
Wallace Reid, Ann Little. Dir: Donald Crisp. Romantic drama.

Quicksands
Dorothy Dalton. Dir: Victor Schertzinger. Romantic melodrama.

Resurrection
Pauline Frederick, Robert Elliott. Dir: Edward Jose. Drama of Czarist Russia, from novel by Leo Tolstoy.

Rich Man, Poor Man
Marguerite Clark, Richard Barthelmess. Dir: J. Searle Dawley. Romance of a slavey.

Rimrock Jones
Wallace Reid, Ann Little. Dir: Donald Crisp. Mining drama.

Rose Of The World
Elsie Ferguson, Wyndham Standing. Dir: Maurice Tourneur. Drama of British in India.

Sandy
Jack Pickford, Louise Huff. Dir: George Melford. Comedy-drama of youth.

Say, Young Fellow
Douglas Fairbanks, Marjorie Daw. Dir: Joseph Henabery. Adventure comedy of big-city reporter in small town.

Selfish Yates
William S. Hart, Jane Novak. Dir: Hart. Outdoor action drama.

Shark Monroe
William S. Hart. Dir: Hart. Outdoor action drama.

The Song Of Songs
Elsie Ferguson, Crauford Kent. Dir: Joseph Kaufman. Drama of a woman's downfall, from novel by Hermann Sudermann, play by Edward Sheldon.

The Source
Wallace Reid, Ann Little. Dir: Donald Crisp. Lumber camp drama.

The Spirit of '17
Jack Pickford, Katherine MacDonald. Dir: William Desmond Taylor. Wartime drama.

Sporting Life
Constance Binney, Ralph Graves. Dir: Maurice Tourneur. Romantic comedy.

String Beans
Charles Ray, Jane Novak. Dir: Victor Schertzinger. Comedy of runaway farm boy.

Such A Little Pirate
Lila Lee, Harrison Ford. Dir: George Melford. Romantic comedy by James Oliver Curwood.

Sunshine Nan
Ann Pennington. Dir: Charles Giblyn. Romantic comedy.

The Thing We Love
Wallace Reid, Kathlyn Williams. Dir: Lou Tellegen. Patriotic drama.

The Tiger Man
William S. Hart. Dir: Hart. Action drama.

Till I Come Back To You
Bryant Washburn, Florence Vidor. Dir: Cecil B. DeMille. Wartime drama by Jeanie Macpherson.

Too Many Millions
Wallace Reid, Tully Marshall. Dir: James Cruze. Inheritance comedy.

The Tyrant – Fear
Dorothy Dalton. Dir: Roy William Neill. Melodrama.

Unclaimed Goods
Vivian Martin. Dir: Rollin Sturgeon. Romantic drama.

Under The Greenwood Tree
Elsie Ferguson, Eugene O'Brien. Dir: Emile Chautard. Drama of lady posing as gypsy, from play by Henry Osmond.

The Vamp
Enid Bennett, Douglas MacLean. Dir: Jerome Storm. Romantic comedy.

Vive La France!
Dorothy Dalton, Edmund Lowe. Dir: Roy William Neill. Wartime drama.

Viviette
Vivian Martin, Harrison Ford. Dir: Walter Edwards. Romantic drama from novel by William J. Locke.

The Way Of A Man With A Maid
Bryant Washburn, Wanda Hawley. Dir: Donald Crisp. Romantic drama.

We Can't Have Everything
Elliott Dexter, Kathlyn Williams. Dir: Cecil B. DeMille. Drama from novel by Rupert Hughes.

When Do We Eat?
Enid Bennett. Dir: Fred Niblo. Farce.

White Man's Law
Sessue Hayakawa, Florence Vidor. Dir: James Young. Racial drama.

The Widow's Might
Julian Eltinge, Florence Vidor. Dir: William C. de Mille. Female impersonation comedy.

Wild Youth
Louise Huff, Jack Mulhall. Dir: George Melford. Romantic drama from novel by Sir Gilbert Parker.

Wolves Of The Rail
William S. Hart. Dir: Hart. Outdoor adventure drama.

A Woman Of Impulse
Lina Cavalieri. Dir: Edward Jose. Romantic drama.

Women's Weapons
Ethel Clayton, Elliott Dexter. Dir: Robert Vignola. Romantic drama.

The World For Sale
Conway Tearle, Ann Little. Dir: J. Stuart Blackton. Drama from novel by Sir Gilbert Parker.

1919

Adventure in Hearts (aka **Captain Dieppe**)
Robert Warwick. Dir: James Cruze. Romantic adventure story by Anthony Hope.

Alias Mike Moran
Wallace Reid, Ann Little. Dir: James Cruze. Patriotic melodrama.

The Avalanche
Elsie Ferguson, Warner Oland. Dir: George Fitzmaurice. Drama of gambling fever, from novel by Gertrude Atherton.

Behind The Door
Hobart Bosworth, Jane Novak. Dir: Irvin Willat. Mystery drama.

Bill Henry
Charles Ray, Edith Roberts. Dir: Jerome Storm. Small-town romantic comedy.

Boots
Dorothy Gish, Richard Barthelmess. Dir: Elmer Clifton. Romantic comedy of wartime London.

The Breed Of Men
William S. Hart. Dir: Hart. Adventure drama.

The Busher
Charles Ray, Colleen Moore, John Gilbert. Dir: Jerome Storm. Baseball comedy-drama.

Captain Kidd, Jr
Mary Pickford, Douglas MacLean. Dir: William Desmond Taylor. Comedy-drama.

The Career Of Catherine Bush
Catherine Calvert. Dir: Roy William Neill. Romantic melodrama from novel by Elinor Glyn.

The Cinema Murder
Marion Davies, Nigel Barrie. Dir: George D. Baker. Mystery drama from novel by E. Phillips Oppenheim.

Come Out Of The Kitchen
Marguerite Clark, Eugene O'Brien. Dir: John S. Robertson. Romantic comedy from novel by Alice Duer Miller, play by A.E. Thomas.

The Counterfeit
Elsie Ferguson, David Powell. Dir: George Fitzmaurice. Drama of high society crooks.

Crooked Straight
Charles Ray, Margery Wilson. Dir: Jerome Storm. Big-city crime drama.

The Dark Star
Marion Davies, Norman Kerry. Dir: Allan Dwan. Romantic drama from novel by Robert W. Chambers.

Daughter Of The Wolf
Lila Lee, Elliott Dexter. Dir: Irvin Willat. Melodrama.

Don't Change Your Husband
Gloria Swanson, Elliott Dexter, Lew Cody. Dir: Cecil B. DeMille. Marital comedy-drama.

The Dub
Wallace Reid, Nina Byron. Dir: James Cruze. Crime melodrama.

The Egg-Crate Wallop (aka **The Knock-Out Blow**)
Charles Ray, Colleen Moore. Dir: Jerome Storm. Prizefighting comedy.

Erstwhile Susan
Constance Binney. Dir: John S. Robertson. Romance.

Everywoman
Monte Blue, Wanda Hawley, Bebe Daniels, Theodore Roberts. Dir: George Melford. Modern morality drama.

Extravagance
Dorothy Dalton. Dir: Victor Schertzinger. Romantic drama.

The Eyes Of The Soul
Elsie Ferguson, Wyndham Standing. Dir: Emile Chautard. Drama of chorus girl and blind soldier.

False Faces
Henry B. Walthall, Lon Chaney. Dir: Irvin Willat. Naval spy drama from novel by Louis Joseph Vance.

The Final Close-Up
Shirley Mason. Dir: Walter Edwards. Film studio drama.

The Fires Of Faith
Eugene O'Brien. Dir: Edward Jose. Melodrama.

The Firing Line
Irene Castle. Dir: Charles Maigne. Wartime drama from novel by Robert W. Chambers.

For Better, For Worse
Gloria Swanson, Elliott Dexter. Dir: Cecil B. DeMille. Matrimonial drama.

The Girl Dodger
Charles Ray, Doris Lee. Dir: Jerome Storm. Comedy of would-be author.

A Girl Named Mary
Marguerite Clark, Wallace MacDonald. Dir: Walter Edwards. Romantic drama of poor girl coming into fortune.

Girls
Marguerite Clark, Harrison Ford. Dir: Walter Edwards. New York comedy about man-haters, from play by Clyde Fitch.

Good Gracious, Annabelle!
Billie Burke. Dir: George Melford. Romantic comedy from play by Clare Kummer.

Greased Lightning
Charles Ray, Wanda Hawley. Dir: Jerome Storm. Racing car comedy.

The Grim Game
Houdini, Ann Forest. Dir: Irvin Willat. Drama of miraculous escapes.

Happy Though Married
Enid Bennett, Douglas MacLean. Dir: Fred Niblo. Domestic comedy.

Hard-Boiled
Dorothy Dalton. Dir: Victor Schertzinger. Crook comedy-drama.

The Haunted Bedroom
Enid Bennett, Lloyd Hughes. Dir: Fred Niblo. Comedy thriller.

Hawthorne Of The U.S.A. (aka **Hawthorne The Adventurer**)
Wallace Reid, Lila Lee. Dir: James Cruze. Mythical kingdom comedy from play by James Fagan.

Hay Foot, Straw Foot
Charles Ray, Doris Lee. Dir: Jerome Storm. Comedy of rural army recruit.

The Heart Of Youth
Lila Lee, Tom Forman. Dir: Robert Vignola. Adventure drama.

His Official Fiancee
Vivian Martin, Forrest Stanley. Dir: Robert Vignola. Romantic drama.

His Parisian Wife
Elsie Ferguson, David Powell. Dir: Emile Chautard. Domestic drama.

His Wife's Friend
Dorothy Dalton. Dir: Joseph de Grasse. Romantic drama.

The Home Breaker
Dorothy Dalton, Douglas MacLean. Dir: Victor Schertzinger. Domestic comedy drama.

Home Town Girl
Vivian Martin, Ralph Graves. Dir: Robert Vignola. Comedy romance.

I'll Get Him Yet
Dorothy Gish, Richard Barthelmess. Dir: Elmer Clifton. Romance of heiress and reporter.

In Mizzoura
Robert Warwick, Eileen Percy. Dir: Hugh Ford. Country comedy-drama from play by Augustus Thomas.

An Innocent Adventuress
Vivian Martin. Dir: Robert Vignola. Romantic drama.

The Invisible Bond
Irene Castle. Dir: Charles Maigne. Romantic drama.

It Pays To Advertise
Bryant Washburn, Lois Wilson. Dir: Donald Crisp. Business comedy from play by Walter Hackett, Roi Megrue.

John Petticoats
William S. Hart. Dir: Lambert Hillyer. Outdoor action drama.

Johnny Get Your Gun
Fred Stone, Casson Ferguson. Dir: Donald Crisp. Comedy.

The Knickerbocker Buckaroo
Douglas Fairbanks, Marjorie Daw. Dir: Albert Parker. Comedy of Easterner out West, by Fairbanks.

L'Apache
Dorothy Dalton. Dir: Joseph de Grasse. Melodrama of Paris underworld.

The Lady Of Red Butte
Dorothy Dalton. Dir: Victor Schertzinger. Adventure drama.

The Law Of Men
Enid Bennett, Niles Welch. Dir: Fred Niblo. Crime drama.

Let's Elope (aka **The Naughty Wife**)
Marguerite Clark, Gaston Glass. Dir: John S. Robertson. Comedy from play by Fred Jackson, Edgar Selwyn.

The Life Line (aka **Romany Rye**)
Pauline Starke, Jack Holt. Dir: Maurice Tourneur. Gypsy drama.

Little Comrade
Vivian Martin, Niles Welch. Dir: Chet Withey. Romance.

The Lottery Man
Wallace Reid, Wanda Hawley. Dir: James Cruze. Romantic comedy from play by Rida Johnson Young.

Louisiana
Vivian Martin, Robert Ellis. Dir: Robert Vignola. Romance of the South, from novel by Frances Hodgson Burnett.

The Love Burglar
Wallace Reid, Anna Q. Nilsson. Dir: James Cruze. Underworld drama.

Love Insurance
Bryant Washburn, Lois Wilson. Dir: Donald Crisp. Romantic comedy from novel by Earl Derr Biggers.

Luck In Pawn
Marguerite Clark, Charles Meredith. Dir: Walter Edwards. Romantic comedy.

Maggie Pepper
Ethel Clayton, Elliott Dexter. Dir: Chet Withey. Comedy-drama.

The Market Of Souls
Dorothy Dalton. Dir: Joseph de Grasse. Melodrama.

The Marriage Price
Elsie Ferguson, Wyndham Standing. Dir: Emile Chautard. Drama of marriage for money.

Men, Women And Money
Ethel Clayton. Dir: George Melford. Drama of conspiracy by Cosmo Hamilton.

The Miracle Of Love
Mae Murray. Dir: Robert Z. Leonard. Romantic drama by Cosmo Hamilton.

The Misleading Widow (aka **Billeted**)
Billie Burke, James Crane. Dir: John S. Robertson. Wartime comedy from play by F. Tennyson Jesse, H.M. Harwood.

The Money Corral
William S. Hart, Jane Novak. Dir: Hart. Western action drama by Hart and Lambert Hillyer.

More Deadly Than The Male
Ethel Clayton. Dir: Robert Vignola. Melodrama.

Mrs Wiggs Of The Cabbage Patch
Marguerite Clark, Mary Carr. Dir: Hugh Ford. Comedy-drama of poor family, from novel by Alice Hegan Rice.

The Mystery Of The Yellow Room
Ethel Grey Terry. Dir: Emile Chautard. Detective thriller.

Nugget Nell
Dorothy Gish, David Butler. Dir: Elmer Clifton. Burlesqued Western drama.

Oh, You Women!
Ernest Truex, Louise Huff. Dir: John Emerson. Postwar comedy by Anita Loos and Emerson.

Other Men's Wives
Dorothy Dalton, Forrest Stanley. Dir: Victor Schertzinger. Infidelity drama.

Out of Luck (aka Nobody Home)
Dorothy Gish, Ralph Graves. Dir: Elmer Clifton. Comedy of superstition.

Out Of The Shadow
Pauline Frederick, Wyndham Standing. Dir: Emile Chautard. Melodrama.

Paid In Full
Pauline Frederick, Wyndham Standing. Dir: Emile Chautard. Romantic drama from play by Eugene Walter.

Partners Three
Enid Bennett. Dir: Fred Niblo. Triangle comedy-drama.

Peppy Polly
Dorothy Gish, Richard Barthelmess. Dir: Elmer Clifton. Comedy of reckless girl.

Pettigrew's Girl
Ethel Clayton, Monte Blue. Dir: George Melford. Romance of actress and soldier, by Dana Burnett.

The Poor Boob
Bryant Washburn. Dir: Donald Crisp. Comedy from play by Margaret Mayo.

The Poppy Girl's Husband
William S. Hart, Juanita Hansen. Dir: Hart. Action drama.

Puppy Love
Lila Lee, Harold Goodwin. Dir: Roy William Neill. Romantic comedy.

Putting It Over
Bryant Washburn, Shirley Mason. Dir: Donald Crisp. Village comedy.

Red Hot Dollars
Charles Ray, Gladys George. Dir: Jerome Storm. Big business comedy.

The Rescuing Angel
Shirley Mason, Forrest Stanley. Dir: Walter Edwards. Comedy-drama from play by Clare Kummer.

The Roaring Road
Wallace Reid, Ann Little, Theodore Roberts. Dir: James Cruze. Car racing comedy-drama.

A Romance Of Happy Valley
Lillian Gish, Robert Harron. Dir: D.W. Griffith. Rural comedy-drama.

Rose O' The River
Lila Lee. Dir: Robert Thornby. Outdoor romance from novel by Kate Douglas Wiggin.

Rustling A Bride
Lila Lee, Monte Blue. Dir: Irvin Willat. Western romance.

Sadie Love
Billie Burke. Dir: John S. Robertson. Romantic comedy from play by Avery Hopwood.

Scarlet Days
Richard Barthelmess, Carol Dempster. Dir: D.W. Griffith. Western romantic drama.

The Secret Garden
Lila Lee. Dir: G. Butler Clonebaugh. Romance of childhood, from novel by Frances Hodgson Burnett.

Secret Service
Robert Warwick, Wanda Hawley. Dir: Hugh Ford. Espionage drama from play by William Gillette.

The Sheriff's Son
Charles Ray, Seena Owen. Dir: Victor Schertzinger. Western drama.

The Silver King
William Faversham. Dir: George Irving. Melodrama from play by Henry Arthur Jones.

A Society Exile
Elsie Ferguson, Henry Stephenson. Dir: George Fitzmaurice. Drama of Englishwoman in Venice, from play by Henry Arthur Jones.

Soldiers Of Fortune
Norman Kerry, Anna Q. Nilsson, Wallace Beery. Dir: Allan Dwan. Adventure drama by Richard Harding Davis.

Something To Do
Bryant Washburn, Ann Little. Dir: Donald Crisp. Comedy-drama.

A Sporting Chance
Ethel Clayton, Jack Holt. Dir: George Melford. Comedy-drama.

Square Deal Sanderson
William S. Hart, Ann Little. Dir: Hart. Western drama.

Stepping Out
Enid Bennett, Niles Welch. Dir: Fred Niblo. Domestic comedy.

The Teeth Of The Tiger
David Powell. Dir: Chet Withey. Arsene Lupin detective drama by Maurice LeBlanc.

The Test Of Honor
John Barrymore, Constance Binney. Dir: John S. Robertson. Drama of conscience, by E. Phillips Oppenheim.

The Third Kiss
Vivian Martin, Harrison Ford. Dir: Robert Vignola. Romantic comedy.

Three Men And A Girl
Marguerite Clark, Richard Barthelmess, Percy Marmont. Dir: Marshall Neilan. Romantic comedy.

Told In The Hills
Robert Warwick, Ann Little. Dir: George Melford. Backwoods drama.

Turning The Tables
Dorothy Gish, George Fawcett. Dir: Elmer Clifton. Comedy of girl in sanitarium.

23½ Hours' Leave
Douglas MacLean, Doris May. Dir: Henry King. Wartime comedy by Mary Roberts Rinehart.

The Two Brides
Lina Cavalieri. Dir: Edward Jose. Romantic drama.

Under The Top
Fred Stone, Ella Hall. Dir: Donald Crisp. Circus comedy-drama by Anita Loos and John Emerson.

The Valley Of The Giants
Wallace Reid, Grace Darmond. Dir: James Cruze. Outdoor adventure drama, from novel by Peter B. Kyne.

Venus In The East
Bryant Washburn, Anna Q. Nilsson. Dir: Donald Crisp. Comedy-drama.

A Very Good Young Man
Bryant Washburn. Dir: Donald Crisp. Romantic comedy.

Vicky Van (aka The Woman Next Door)
Ethel Clayton. Dir: Robert Vignola. Romantic drama.

Victory
Jack Holt, Seena Owen, Lon Chaney. Dir: Maurice Tourneur. Drama on South Seas island, from novel by Joseph Conrad.

The Virtuous Thief
Enid Bennett. Dir: Fred Niblo. Romantic drama.

Wagon Tracks
William S. Hart, Jane Novak. Dir: Lambert Hillyer. Western drama.

Wanted: A Husband
Billie Burke. Dir: Lawrence Windom. Romantic comedy from novel by Samuel Hopkins Adams.

What Every Woman Learns
Enid Bennett. Dir: Fred Niblo. Romantic comedy.

The White Heather
Mabel Ballin, Ralph Graves. Dir: Maurice Tourneur. Action melodrama.

Why Smith Left Home
Bryant Washburn, Lois Wilson. Dir: Donald Crisp. Domestic comedy from play by George Broadhurst.

Widow By Proxy
Marguerite Clark, Nigel Barrie, John Gilbert. Dir: Walter Edwards. Romantic comedy.

The Winning Girl
Shirley Mason, Niles Welch. Dir: Robert Vignola. Outdoor comedy-drama.

Witness For The Defense
Elsie Ferguson, Warner Oland. Dir: George Fitzmaurice. Courtroom drama from play by A.E.W. Mason.

The Woman Thou Gavest Me
Jack Holt, Katherine MacDonald. Dir: Hugh Ford. Romantic melodrama from novel by Hall Caine.

You Never Saw Such A Girl
Vivian Martin, Harrison Ford. Dir: Robert Vignola. Comedy romance.

You're Fired
Wallace Reid, Wanda Hawley. Dir: James Cruze. Romantic comedy from a story by O. Henry.

1920

Alarm Clock Andy
Charles Ray, Millicent Fisher. Dir: Jerome Storm. Comedy of bashful salesman.

All Of A Sudden Peggy
Marguerite Clark, Jack Mulhall. Dir: Walter Edwards. English romantic comedy.

Always Audacious
Wallace Reid, Margaret Loomis. Dir: James Cruze. Impersonation drama by Ben Ames Williams.

An Amateur Devil
Bryant Washburn. Dir: Maurice Campbell. Romantic comedy.

The Amateur Wife
Irene Castle. Dir: Edward Dillon. Matrimonial comedy.

April Folly
Marion Davies. Dir: Robert Z. Leonard. Romantic comedy.

Away Goes Prudence
Billie Burke. Dir: John S. Robertson. Romantic comedy.

Behold My Wife
Elliott Dexter, Milton Sills. Dir: George Melford. Drama from novel by Sir Gilbert Parker.

Below The Surface
Hobart Bosworth. Dir: Irvin Willat. Action drama.

Black Is White
Dorothy Dalton, Holmes Herbert. Dir: Charles Giblyn. Drama.

Black Birds
Justine Johnstone. Dir: John Francis Dillon. Crook drama.

Burglar-Proof
Bryant Washburn, Lois Wilson. Dir: Maurice Campbell. Comedy thriller.

The City Of Masks
Robert Warwick, Lois Wilson. Dir: Thomas Heffron. Melodrama.

A City Sparrow
Ethel Clayton, Clyde Fillmore. Dir: Sam Wood. Romantic drama.

Civilian Clothes
Thomas Meighan, Martha Mansfield. Dir: Hugh Ford. Post-war drama.

Conrad In Quest Of His Youth
Thomas Meighan, Kathlyn Williams. Dir: William C. de Mille. Drama from novel by Leonard Merrick.

The Cost
Violet Heming, Ralph Kellard. Dir: Harley Knoles. Romantic drama.

The Cradle Of Courage
William S. Hart, Ann Little. Dir: Lambert Hillyer. Action drama.

Crooked Streets
Ethel Clayton, Jack Holt. Dir: Paul Powell. Suspense drama.

The Cumberland Romance
Mary Miles Minter, Monte Blue. Dir: Charles Maigne. Rural drama from novel by John Fox Jr.

The Dancin' Fool
Wallace Reid, Bebe Daniels. Dir: Sam Wood. Ballroom dancing comedy.

Dangerous Hours
Barbara Castleton, Lloyd Hughes. Dir: Fred Niblo. Action drama by Donn Byrne.

The Dark Lantern
Alice Brady, James Crane, Reginald Denny. Dir: John S. Robertson. Triangle drama.

The Dark Mirror
Dorothy Dalton, Huntley Gordon. Dir: Charles Giblyn. Romantic drama from novel by Louis J. Vance.

The Deep Purple
Miriam Cooper, Helen Ware. Dir: Raoul Walsh. Melodrama from play by Paul Armstrong, Wilson Mizner.

Deep Waters
John Gilbert, Barbara Bedford. Dir: Maurice Tourneur. Deep-sea diving drama.

Double Speed
Wallace Reid, Wanda Hawley, Theodore Roberts. Dir: Sam Wood. Racing car comedy-drama.

Easy To Get
Marguerite Clark, Harrison Ford, Rod La Rocque. Dir: Walter Edwards. Marital comedy.

Excuse My Dust
Wallace Reid, Ann Little, Theodore Roberts. Dir: Sam Wood. Racing car comedy-drama.

The Eyes Of The Heart
Mary Miles Minter, Edmund Burns. Dir: Paul Powell. Drama of blindness by Dana Burnett.

The False Road
Enid Bennett, Lloyd Hughes. Dir: Fred Niblo. Action drama.

The Fear Market
Alice Brady, Frank Losee. Dir: Kenneth Webb. Drama of father and daughter.

The Fighting Chance
Conrad Nagel, Anna Q. Nilsson. Dir: Charles Maigne. Adventure drama from novel by Robert W. Chambers.

Flying Pat
Dorothy Gish, James Rennie. Dir: N. Richard Jones. Aviation romance.

Food For Scandal
Harrison Ford, Wanda Hawley. Dir: James Cruze. Romantic comedy.

The Fourteenth Man (aka **The Man From Blankleys**)
Robert Warwick, Bebe Daniels. Dir: Joseph Henabery. Comedy of hired guest, from play by F. Anstey.

The Frisky Mrs Johnson
Billie Burke. Dir: Edward Dillon. Comedy from play by Clyde Fitch.

A Full House
Bryant Washburn. Dir: James Cruze. Comedy.

The Furnace
Agnes Ayres, Milton Sills. Dir: William Desmond Taylor. Romantic melodrama.

Guilty Of Love
Dorothy Dalton. Dir: Harley Knoles. Romantic drama from play by Avery Hopwood.

Hairpins
Enid Bennett. Dir: Fred Niblo. Romantic comedy.

Half An Hour
Dorothy Dalton, Charles Richman. Dir: Harley Knoles. Matrimonial drama from play by Sir James Barrie.

Held By The Enemy
Agnes Ayres, Lewis Stone. Dir: Donald Crisp. Civil War drama from play by William Gillette.

Heliotrope
Frederick Burton. Dir: George D. Baker. Drama of father's self-sacrifice, by Richard Washburn Child.

Her Beloved Villain
Wanda Hawley. Dir: Sam Wood. Romantic comedy-drama from play by Clyde Fitch.

Her First Elopement
Wanda Hawley. Dir: Sam Wood. Romantic comedy.

Her Husband's Friend
Enid Bennett. Dir: Fred Niblo. Triangle romance.

His House In Order
Elsie Ferguson, Holmes Herbert. Dir: Hugh Ford. Romantic drama from a play by Arthur Wing Pinero.

Homer Comes Home
Charles Ray, Priscilla Bonner. Dir: Jerome Storm. Small-town romantic drama.

Huckleberry Finn
Lewis Sargent, Gordon Griffith. Dir: William Desmond Taylor. Adventure comedy-drama from novel by Mark Twain.

Idols Of Clay
Mae Murray, David Powell. Dir: George Fitzmaurice. Romantic drama.

Jack Straw
Robert Warwick. Dir: William C. de Mille. Comedy-drama from play by W. Somerset Maugham.

The Jailbird
Douglas MacLean. Dir: Lloyd Ingraham. Comedy.

Jenny, Be Good
Mary Miles Minter. Dir: William Desmond Taylor. Romantic comedy.

The Jucklins
Monte Blue. Dir: George Melford. Comedy-drama.

Judy Of Rogue's Harbor
Mary Miles Minter. Dir: William Desmond Taylor. Romance.

The Ladder of Lies
Ethel Clayton, Clyde Fillmore. Dir: Tom Forman. Romantic drama.

A Lady In Love
Ethel Clayton, Harrison Ford. Dir: Walter Edwards. Romantic drama.

Lady Rose's Daughter
Elsie Ferguson, David Powell. Dir: Hugh Ford. Drama of illegitimacy, from novel by Mrs Humphrey Ward.

The Law Of The Yukon
June Elvidge. Dir: Charles Miller. Outdoor drama.

Let's Be Fashionable
Douglas MacLean, Doris May. Dir: Lloyd Ingraham. Romantic comedy.

The Life Of The Party
Roscoe 'Fatty' Arbuckle. Dir: Joseph Henabery. Slapstick comedy from story by Irvin S. Cobb.

Little Miss Rebellion
Dorothy Gish, Ralph Graves. Dir: George Fawcett. Comedy of royal exile in New York.

The Luck Of The Irish
James Kirkwood, Anna Q. Nilsson. Dir: Allan Dwan. Adventure comedy-drama.

Mary Ellen Comes To Town
Dorothy Gish, Ralph Graves. Dir: Elmer Clifton. Comedy of country girl's romance.

Mary's Ankle
Douglas MacLean, Doris May. Dir: Lloyd Ingraham. Romantic comedy.

Midsummer Madness
Lois Wilson, Jack Holt, Lila Lee. Dir: William C. de Mille. Triangle drama by Cosmo Hamilton.

Miss Hobbs
Wanda Hawley, Jack Mulhall. Dir: Donald Crisp. Romantic comedy by Jerome K. Jerome.

Mrs Temple's Telegram
Bryant Washburn, Wanda Hawley. Dir: James Cruze. Comedy-drama.

My Lady's Garter
Sylvia Breamer, Wyndham Standing. Dir: Maurice Tourneur. Romance.

The New York Idea
Alice Brady, Lowell Sherman. Dir: Herbert Blaché. Divorce comedy.

Nineteen And Phyllis
Charles Ray, Clara Horton. Dir: Joseph de Grasse. Comedy of beau without money.

Nurse Marjorie
Mary Miles Minter. Dir: William Desmond Taylor. Romantic drama from novel by Israel Zangwill.

Oh Lady, Lady!
Bebe Daniels, Harrison Ford. Dir: Maurice Campbell. Impersonation comedy from play by P.G. Wodehouse and Guy Bolton.

An Old-Fashioned Boy
Charles Ray, Ethel Shannon. Dir: Jerome Storm. Romantic comedy.

On With The Dance
Mae Murray. Dir: George Fitzmaurice. Romantic drama.

Paris Green
Charles Ray, Ann May. Dir: Jerome Storm. Comedy of small-town boy and French girl.

The Prince Chap
Thomas Meighan, Lila Lee, Ann Forrest. Dir: William C. de Mille. Drama of adopted daughter.

The Restless Sex
Marion Davies, Carlyle Blackwell. Dir: Robert Z. Leonard, Leo d'Usseau. Romantic comedy-drama.

The Right To Love
Mae Murray, David Powell. Dir: George Fitzmaurice. French romantic drama.

A Romantic Adventuress
Dorothy Dalton. Dir: Harley Knoles. Romantic comedy-drama.

The Round-Up
Roscoe 'Fatty' Arbuckle. Dir: George Melford. Western comedy.

Sand
William S. Hart. Dir: Lambert Hillyer. Outdoor action drama.

The Sea Wolf
Tom Forman, Noah Beery. Dir: George Melford. Adventure drama from novel by Jack London.

Sick A-Bed
Wallace Reid, Bebe Daniels. Dir: Sam Wood. Comedy of hypochondriac and nurse.

Silk Hosiery
Enid Bennett. Dir: Fred Niblo. Romantic comedy-drama.

Sinners
Alice Brady, James Crane. Dir: Kenneth Webb. Romantic drama of country girl in New York.

The Sins Of Rosanne
Ethel Clayton, Jack Holt. Dir: Tom Forman. Romantic drama.

The Sins Of St Anthony
Bryant Washburn. Dir: James Cruze. Drama by Charles Collins.

The Six Best Cellars
Bryant Washburn, Wanda Hawley. Dir: Donald Crisp. Comedy.

Something Different
Constance Binney. Dir: Roy William Neill. Romantic adventure from novel by Alice Duer Miller.

Something To Think About
Gloria Swanson, Elliott Dexter, Theodore Roberts. Dir: Cecil B. DeMille. Comedy-drama.

The Soul Of Youth
Lila Lee, Lewis Sargent. Dir: William Desmond Taylor. Drama of young love.

The Stolen Kiss
Constance Binney. Dir: Kenneth Webb. Love story.

Sweet Lavender
Mary Miles Minter, Milton Sills, Theodore Roberts. Dir: Paul Powell. Romantic drama from play by Arthur Wing Pinero.

Terror Island
Houdini. Dir: James Cruze. Adventure thriller.

The Testing Block
William S. Hart. Dir: Lambert Hillyer. Western drama.

The Thirteenth Commandment
Ethel Clayton. Dir: Robert Vignola. Drama from novel by Rupert Hughes.

39 East
Constance Binney, Reginald Denny. Dir: John S. Robertson. Romantic drama.

Thou Art The Man
Robert Warwick, Lois Wilson. Dir: Thomas Heffron. Drama from novel by F.E. Mills-Young.

To Please One Woman
Claire Windsor. Dir: Lois Weber. Romantic drama.

The Toll Gate
William S. Hart, Anna Q. Nilsson. Dir: Lambert Hillyer. Western drama.

Too Much Johnson
Bryant Washburn, Monte Blue. Dir: Donald Crisp. Comedy-drama from play by William Gillette.

The Tree Of Knowledge
Robert Warwick, Kathlyn Williams. Dir: William C. de Mille. Romantic drama.

The Village Sleuth
Charles Ray, Winifred Westover. Dir: Jerome Storm. Rural detective comedy.

What Happened To Jones
Bryant Washburn. Dir: James Cruze. Comedy from play by George Broadhurst.

What's Your Hurry?
Wallace Reid, Lois Wilson. Dir: Sam Wood. Car racing comedy-drama.

What's Your Husband Doing?
Douglas MacLean, Doris May. Dir: Lloyd Ingraham. Romantic comedy.

The White Circle
John Gilbert. Dir: Maurice Tourneur. Drama from novel by Robert Louis Stevenson.

The Woman In The Suitcase
Enid Bennett. Dir: Fred Niblo. Comedy drama.

The World And His Wife
Alma Rubens, Gaston Glass. Dir: Robert Vignola. Triangle drama.

You Never Can Tell (aka Class)
Bebe Daniels, Jack Mulhall. Dir: Chester Franklin. Comedy of hat-check girl seeking millionaire.

Young Mrs Winthrop
Ethel Clayton, Harrison Ford. Dir: Walter Edwards. Romantic comedy.

1921

After The Show
Jack Holt, Lila Lee. Dir: William C. de Mille. Backstage drama.

All Souls' Eve
Mary Miles Minter, Jack Holt. Dir: Chester Franklin. Matrimonial drama.

Appearances
David Powell, Mary Glynne. Dir: Donald Crisp. Society drama. (Paramount-British)

At The End Of The World
Milton Sills, Betty Compson. Dir: Penrhyn Stanlaws. Shanghai adventure drama.

The Bait
Hope Hampton. Dir: Maurice Tourneur. Crime drama.

Beau Revel
Lewis Stone, Florence Vidor. Dir: John Griffith Wray. Society drama by Louis J. Vance.

Behind Masks (aka Jeanne Of The Marshes)
Dorothy Dalton. Dir: Frank Reicher. Adventure melodrama by E. Phillips Oppenheim.

Beyond
Ethel Clayton. Dir: William Desmond Taylor. Spiritualism drama from play by Henry Arthur Jones.

The Bonnie Briar Bush (GB Beside The Bonnie Briar Bush)
Donald Crisp, Mary Glynne. Dir: Crisp. Scottish drama by Ian MacLaren. (Paramount-British)

Brewster's Millions
Roscoe 'Fatty' Arbuckle. Dir: Joseph Henabery. Inheritance comedy from play by George Barr McCutcheon.

The Bronze Bell
Courtenay Foote, Doris May. Dir: James Horne. East Indian drama from novel by Louis J. Vance.

Buried Treasure
Marion Davies, Norman Kerry. Dir: George D. Baker. Reincarnation drama by F. Britten Austin.

The Call Of The North (aka The Conjurer's House)
Jack Holt, Madge Bellamy. Dir: Joseph Henabery. Canadian melodrama from play by George Broadhurst.

The Call Of Youth
Mary Glynne, Jack Hobbs. Dir: Hugh Ford. Drama by Henry Arthur Jones. (Paramount-British)

Cappy Ricks
Thomas Meighan, Agnes Ayres. Dir: Tom Forman. Sea adventure drama from novel by Peter B. Kyne.

The Case Of Becky
Constance Binney, Glenn Hunter. Dir: Chester Franklin. Hypnotism drama.

Chickens
Douglas MacLean, Gladys George. Dir: Jack Nelson. Rural comedy-drama.

The City Of Silent Men
Thomas Meighan, Lois Wilson. Dir: Tom Forman. Crime drama.

The Conquest Of Canaan
Thomas Meighan, Doris Kenyon. Dir: Roy William Neill. Drama of small town politics by Booth Tarkington.

Crazy To Marry
Roscoe 'Fatty' Arbuckle, Lila Lee. Dir: James Cruze. Romantic farce.

Dangerous Lies
David Powell, Mary Glynne. Dir: Paul Powell. Swindling drama. (Paramount-British)

Dawn Of The East
Alice Brady, Kenneth Harlan. Dir: Edward H. Griffith. Bigamy and blackmail drama.

The Dollar-A-Year Man
Roscoe 'Fatty' Arbuckle, Lila Lee. Dir: James Cruze. Yacht club comedy.

Don't Call Me Little Girl
Mary Miles Minter. Dir: Joseph Henabery. Romantic comedy.

Don't Tell Everything
Gloria Swanson, Wallace Reid, Elliott Dexter. Dir: Sam Wood. Comedy-drama of jealousy.

Ducks And Drakes
Bebe Daniels, Jack Holt. Dir: Maurice Campbell. Comedy of a flirt.

The Easy Road
Thomas Meighan, Lila Lee, Gladys George. Dir: Tom Forman. Regeneration drama.

The Education Of Elizabeth
Billie Burke. Dir: Edward Dillon. Comedy of showgirl in society.

Enchantment
Marion Davies, Forrest Stanley. Dir: Robert Vignola. Comedy of rich flapper.

Everything For Sale
May McAvoy, Eddie Sutherland. Dir: Frank O'Connor. Mother-love drama.

Exit The Vamp
Ethel Clayton, T. Roy Barnes. Dir: Frank Urson. Triangle comedy-drama.

Experience
Richard Barthelmess, Nita Naldi. Dir: George Fitzmaurice. Allegorical drama.

The Faith Healer
Milton Sills, Ann Forrest, Adolphe Menjou. Dir: George Melford. Religious drama.

First Love
Constance Binney, Warner Baxter. Dir: Maurice Campbell. Romantic comedy.

Footlights
Elsie Ferguson, Reginald Denny. Dir: John S. Robertson. Backstage romantic comedy.

Frontier Of The Stars
Thomas Meighan. Dir: Charles Maigne. Crook regeneration drama.

Gasoline Gus
Roscoe 'Fatty' Arbuckle, Lila Lee. Dir: James Cruze. Oil-well comedy. (Withdrawn from distribution prior to general release).

Get-Rich-Quick Wallingford
Sam Hardy, Doris Kenyon, Norman Kerry. Dir: Frank Borzage. Crook comedy-drama.

The Ghost In The Garret
Dorothy Gish. Dir: N. Richard Jones. Comedy of haunted house.

The Gilded Lily
Mae Murray, Lowell Sherman. Dir: Robert Z. Leonard. New York romantic drama.

The Golem
Paul Wegener. Dir: Wegener, Carl Boese. Drama based on the Prague ghetto legend. (German).

The Great Day
Meggie Albanesi, Bertram Burleigh. Dir: Hugh Ford. Blackmail drama. (Paramount-British).

The Great Impersonation
James Kirkwood, Ann Forrest. Dir: George Melford. Spy melodrama by E. Phillips Oppenheim.

The Great Moment
Gloria Swanson, Milton Sills. Dir: Sam Wood. Romantic drama by Elinor Glyn.

A Heart To Let
Harrison Ford, Justine Johnstone. Dir: Edward Dillon. Romance of heiress and blind man.

The Hell Diggers (aka The Gold Dredgers)
Wallace Reid, Lois Wilson. Dir: Frank Urson. Drama of miners vs. farmers.

Her Face Value
Wanda Hawley, T. Roy Barnes. Dir: Thomas Heffron. Romantic drama of movie star.

Her Sturdy Oak
Wanda Hawley, Walter Hiers. Dir: Thomas Heffron. Romantic comedy by Elmer Harris.

Her Winning Way
Mary Miles Minter. Dir: Joseph Henabery. Comedy romance from novel by Edgar Jepson.

The Home Stretch
Douglas MacLean. Dir: Jack Nelson. Racetrack comedy-drama.

The House That Jazz Built
Wanda Hawley, Forrest Stanley, Gladys George. Dir: Penrhyn Stanlaws. Domestic comedy by Sophie Kerr.

Hush Money
Alice Brady, George Fawcett. Dir: Charles Maigne. Drama of blackmailed society girl.

The Idol Of The North
Dorothy Dalton. Dir: Roy William Neill. Canadian action drama.

The Inside Of The Cup
William Carleton, David Torrence. Dir: Albert Capellani. Religious drama.

Just Around The Corner
Fred Thomson, Sigrid Holmquist. Dir: Frances Marion. New York family drama by Fannie Hurst.

The Kentuckians (aka The Fighting Schoolmaster)
Monte Blue. Dir: Charles Maigne. Drama of rural rivalry.

King, Queen, Joker
Sydney Chaplin, Lottie MacPherson. Dir: Chaplin. Ruritanian farce by Chaplin.

A Kiss In Time
Wanda Hawley, T. Roy Barnes. Dir: Thomas Heffron. Romantic comedy.

Ladies Must Live
Betty Compson, John Gilbert, Leatrice Joy. Dir: George Loane Tucker. Romantic drama by Alice Duer Miller.

The Land Of Hope
Alice Brady, Jason Robards. Dir: Edward H. Griffith. Drama of immigrants.

The Last Payment
Pola Negri. Dir: George Jacoby. German drama from *The Merry-Go-Round Of Life*. (UFA, German)

Life
Nita Naldi, Herbert Druce. Dir: Travers Vale. New York drama from play by William A. Brady, T. Buchanan.

The Little Clown
Mary Miles Minter, Jack Mulhall. Dir: Thomas Heffron. Circus comedy-drama from play by Avery Hopwood.

Little Italy
Alice Brady, Norman Kerry. Dir: George Terwilliger. Comedy-drama of Italian girl in New York.

The Lost Romance
Jack Holt, Lois Wilson. Dir: William C. de Mille. Domestic triangle drama from play by Edward Knoblock.

The Love Charm
Wanda Hawley, Warner Baxter. Dir: Thomas Heffron. Romantic comedy.

The Love Special
Wallace Reid, Agnes Ayres. Dir: Frank Urson. Railroad drama.

The Magic Cup
Constance Binney. Dir: John S. Robertson. Crook drama.

Moonlight And Honeysuckle
Mary Miles Minter, Monte Blue. Dir: Joseph Henabery. Romantic comedy.

The Mystery Road
David Powell, Mary Glynne. Dir: Paul Powell. Adventure drama. (Paramount-British)

O'Malley Of The Mounted
William S. Hart, Eva Novak. Dir: Lambert Hillyer. Outdoor action drama.

One A Minute
Douglas MacLean. Dir: Jack Nelson. Business comedy.

One Wild Week
Bebe Daniels, Frank Kingsley. Dir: Maurice Campbell. Inheritance comedy-drama.

Out Of The Chorus
Alice Brady, Vernon Steele. Dir: Herbert Blaché. Drama of showgirl's wealthy marriage.

The Outside Woman
Wanda Hawley. Dir: none credited. Comedy of foolish bride.

Passin' Thru
Douglas MacLean, Madge Bellamy. Dir: William A. Seiter. Rural comedy.

The Passionate Pilgrim
Matt Moore, Mary Newcombe. Dir: Robert Vignola. Newspaper drama.

Paying The Piper
Dorothy Dickson, Rod La Rocque, Alma Tell. Dir: George Fitzmaurice. Drama of a spendthrift.

The Plaything Of Broadway
Justine Johnstone, Crauford Kent. Dir: John Francis Dillon. Romance of dancer and doctor.

The Price Of Possession
Ethel Clayton, Rockliffe Fellowes. Dir: Hugh Ford. Inheritance drama. (Paramount-British)

A Prince There Was
Thomas Meighan, Mildred Harris. Dir: Tom Forman. Society comedy-drama from play by George M. Cohan.

The Princess Of New York
Mary Glynne, David Powell. Dir: Donald Crisp. Drama of American heiress in London. (Paramount-British)

A Private Scandal
May McAvoy, Ralph Lewis. Dir: Chester Franklin. Drama of Belgian orphan in California.

Proxies
Norman Kerry, Zena Keefe. Dir: George D. Baker. Drama of reformed crooks.

The Rookie's Return
Douglas MacLean, Doris May. Dir: Jack Nelson. Comedy. (Sequel to 23½ Hours' Leave, 1919)

Room And Board
Constance Binney. Dir: Alan Crosland. Drama of Irish estate.

Sacred And Profane Love
Elsie Ferguson, Conrad Nagel. Dir: William Desmond Taylor. Romantic drama by Arnold Bennett.

Sentimental Tommy
Gareth Hughes, May McAvoy. Dir: John S. Robertson. Romantic drama of Scottish village, by Sir James Barrie.

Sham
Ethel Clayton, Theodore Roberts. Dir: Thomas Heffron. Drama of impoverished heiress.

She Couldn't Help It
Bebe Daniels. Dir: Maurice Campbell. Crook reformation comedy. (Remake of In The Bishop's Carriage, 1913)

Sheltered Daughters
Justine Johnstone, Warner Baxter. Dir: Edward Dillon. New York melodrama.

The Snob
Wanda Hawley, Walter Hiers. Dir: Sam Wood. Social comedy.

The Speed Girl
Bebe Daniels, Theodore von Eltz. Dir: Maurice Campbell. Comedy of movie stunt girl.

Straight Is The Way
Matt Moore. Dir: Robert Vignola. Crook comedy-drama.

Such A Little Queen
Constance Binney. Dir: George Fawcett. Romantic comedy.

The Three-Word Brand
William S. Hart, Jane Novak. Dir: Lambert Hillyer. Western drama.

Too Much Speed
Wallace Reid, Agnes Ayres, Theodore Roberts. Dir: Frank Urson. Car racing drama.

Too Wise Wives
Claire Windsor, Louis Calhern. Dir: Lois Weber. Domestic drama.

The Traveling Salesman
Roscoe 'Fatty' Arbuckle. Dir: Joseph Henabery. Comedy. (Re-make of 1916 film)

Two Weeks With Pay
Bebe Daniels, Jack Mulhall. Dir: Maurice Campbell. Impersonation comedy.

Under The Lash
Gloria Swanson, Mahlon Hamilton. Dir: Sam Wood. South African triangle drama.

Wealth
Ethel Clayton, Herbert Rawlinson. Dir: William Desmond Taylor. Drama of wife vs. mother-in-law.

What's Worth While
Claire Windsor, Louis Calhern. Dir: Lois Weber. Western romance.

The Whistle
William S. Hart. Dir: Lambert Hillyer. Drama of mill accident.

White And Unmarried
Thomas Meighan, Jacqueline Logan. Dir: Tom Forman. Crook comedy-drama.

White Oak
William S. Hart. Dir: Lambert Hillyer. Action drama.

The Wild Goose
Norman Kerry, Mary MacLaren. Dir: Albert Capellani. Infidelity drama by Gouverneur Morris.

A Wise Fool (aka The Money Master)
James Kirkwood, Ann Forrest. Dir: George Melford. Canadian romantic drama by Sir Gilbert Parker.

The Woman God Changed
Seena Owen. Dir: Robert Vignola. Regeneration drama.

1922

Across The Continent
Wallace Reid, Mary MacLaren, Theodore Roberts. Dir: Philip Rosen. Car race drama.

Anna Ascends
Alice Brady, David Powell, Nita Naldi. Dir: Victor Fleming. Romantic comedy-drama of Syrian immigrant.

The Bachelor Daddy
Thomas Meighan, Leatrice Joy. Dir: Alfred E. Green. Adoption comedy.

Back Pay
Seena Owen, Matt Moore. Dir: Frank Borzage. Romantic drama by Fannie Hurst.

The Beauty Shop
Raymond Hitchcock. Dir: Edward Dillon. Comedy of cosmetics business from play by Channing Pollock.

Beauty's Worth
Marion Davies. Dir: Robert Vignola. Romance of society girl by Sophie Kerr.

Bobbed Hair
Wanda Hawley, William Boyd. Dir: Thomas Heffron. Romantic comedy.

The Bonded Woman
Betty Compson, Richard Dix. Dir: Philip Rosen. Romantic sea drama.

Boomerang Bill
Lionel Barrymore. Dir: Tom Terriss. Underworld drama.

Borderland
Milton Sills, Agnes Ayres. Dir: Paul Powell. Drama of the supernatural.

Bought And Paid For
Agnes Ayres, Jack Holt. William C. de Mille. Matrimonial drama from play by George Broadhurst.

The Bride's Play
Marion Davies, Wyndham Standing. Dir: George Terwilliger. Historical romance by Donn Byrne.

Burning Sands
Milton Sills, Wanda Hawley, Jacqueline Logan. Dir: George Melford. Desert melodrama.

The Cowboy And The Lady
Mary Miles Minter, Tom Moore. Dir: Charles Maigne. Western romance from play by Clyde Fitch.

The Cradle
Ethel Clayton, Charles Meredith. Dir: Paul Powell. Domestic drama from play by Eugene Brieux.

The Crimson Challenge
Dorothy Dalton. Dir: Paul Powell. Western drama.

A Daughter Of Luxury
Agnes Ayres, Tom Gallery. Dir: Paul Powell. Impersonation drama.

The Devil's Pawn
Pola Negri. Dir: Paul Stein. Girl's search for her father in Petrograd. (UFA, German)

The Dictator
Wallace Reid, Lila Lee. Dir: James Cruze. Adventure in South America, from play by Richard Harding Davis. (Remake of 1915 film)

Ebb Tide
James Kirkwood, Lila Lee, Noah Beery. Dir: George Melford. Adventure drama from novel by Robert Louis Stevenson and Lloyd Osbourne.

The Eyes Of The Mummy
Emil Jannings, Pola Negri. Dir: Ernst Lubitsch. Egyptian drama; Das Augen der Mumie Ma (UFA, German)

A Face In The Fog
Lionel Barrymore, Seena Owen. Dir: Alan Crosland. 'Boston Blackie' mystery drama.

Find The Woman
Alma Rubens, Norman Kerry, Harrison Ford. Dir: Tom Terriss. Murder mystery by Arthur Somers Roche.

For The Defense
Ethel Clayton, Vernon Steele. Dir: Paul Powell. Murder mystery by Elmer Rice.

The Game Chicken
Bebe Daniels, Pat O'Malley. Dir: Chester Franklin. Smuggling comedy-drama.

The Good Provider
Vera Gordon. Dir: Frank Borzage. Drama of small-town Jews in New York, by Fannie Hurst.

The Greatest Truth
Mia May. Dir: Joe May. (UFA, German)

The Green Temptation
Betty Compson. Dir: William Desmond Taylor. Drama of jewel thieves.

The Heart Specialist
Mary Miles Minter. Dir: Frank Urson. Drama of mistaken identity.

Her Gilded Cage
Gloria Swanson, David Powell. Dir: Sam Wood. Comedy-drama of French actress, from a play by Anne Nichols.

Her Husband's Trademark
Gloria Swanson. Dir: Sam Wood. Romantic triangle drama.

Her Own Money
Ethel Clayton, Warner Baxter. Dir: Joseph Henabery. Domestic comedy-drama.

A Homespun Vamp
May McAvoy. Dir: Frank O'Connor. Comedy-drama of country drudge.

If You Believe It, It's So
Thomas Meighan, Pauline Starke. Dir: Tom Forman. Crook rehabilitation drama.

The Impossible Mrs Bellew
Gloria Swanson, Conrad Nagel. Dir: Sam Wood. Matrimonial drama.

Is Matrimony A Failure?
Lois Wilson, T. Roy Barnes, Lila Lee, Adolphe Menjou. Dir: James Cruze. Comedy of bungled weddings.

The Lane That Had No Turning
Agnes Ayres, Theodore Kosloff. Dir: Victor Fleming. Romantic drama by Sir Gilbert Parker.

The Law And The Woman
Betty Compson, William P. Carleton. Dir: Penrhyn Stanlaws. Murder melodrama from play by Clyde Fitch. (Remake of The Woman In The Case, 1916)

Love's Boomerang (aka Perpetua)
David Powell, Ann Forrest. Dir: John S. Robertson. Romantic drama. (Paramount-British)

Making A Man
Jack Holt, Eva Novak. Dir: Joseph Henabery. Drama of a snob transformed, by Peter B. Kyne.

The Man From Home
James Kirkwood, Anna Q. Nilsson. Dir: George Fitzmaurice. Blackmail and murder drama. (Paramount-British)

The Man Unconquerable
Jack Holt, Sylvia Breamer. Dir: Joseph Henabery. South Seas melodrama.

The Man Who Saw Tomorrow
Thomas Meighan, Leatrice Joy. Dir: Alfred E. Green. Hypnotism drama.

Midnight
Constance Binney, William Courtleigh. Dir: Maurice Campbell. Mystery drama.

Missing Millions
Alice Brady, David Powell. Dir: Joseph Henabery. 'Boston Blackie' crook drama.

Morals
May McAvoy. Dir: William Desmond Taylor. Romantic drama from novel by William J. Locke.

Moran Of The Lady Letty
Rudolph Valentino, Dorothy Dalton. Dir: George Melford. Adventure drama from novel by Frank Norris.

Mysteries Of India
Conrad Veidt, Lya De Putti, Mia May. Dir: Joe May. Indian melodrama. (UFA, German)

Nancy From Nowhere
Bebe Daniels, Eddie Sutherland. Dir: Chester Franklin. Comedy of modern Cinderella.

Nice People
Wallace Reid, Bebe Daniels, Conrad Nagel. Dir: William C. de Mille. Jazz-age comedy-drama, from play by Rachel Crothers.

North Of The Rio Grande
Jack Holt, Bebe Daniels. Dir: Rollin Sturgeon. Western drama.

The Old Homestead
Harrison Ford, Theodore Roberts. Dir: James Cruze. Rural drama.

On The High Seas
Jack Holt, Dorothy Dalton. Dir: Irvin Willat. Adventure drama by Edward Sheldon.

One Glorious Day
Will Rogers, Lila Lee. Dir: James Cruze. Transformation comedy.

The Ordeal
Agnes Ayres, Conrad Nagel. Dir: Paul Powell. Domestic drama by W. Somerset Maugham.

Our Leading Citizen
Thomas Meighan, Lois Wilson. Dir: Alfred E. Green. Small town comedy-drama by George Ade.

Outcast
Elsie Ferguson, David Powell. Dir: Chet Withey. Romantic drama.

Over The Border
Tom Moore, Betty Compson. Dir: Penrhyn Stanlaws. Canadian Mounties drama. (re-make of *Heart Of The Wilds*, 1918)

Pink Gods
Bebe Daniels, James Kirkwood, Anna Q. Nilsson, Adolphe Menjou. Dir: Penrhyn Stanlaws. South African mine drama.

The Pride Of Palomar
Forrest Stanley, Marjorie Daw. Dir: Frank Borzage. Outdoor drama from novel by Peter B. Kyne.

The Red Peacock
Pola Negri. Dir: Paul L. Stein. Romantic drama based on 'Camille' by Alexandre Dumas fils. (UFA, German)

Rent Free
Wallace Reid, Lila Lee. Dir: Howard Higgin. Romantic comedy.

Saturday Night
Leatrice Joy, Conrad Nagel. Dir: Cecil B. DeMille. Drama of social conflicts, by Jeanie Macpherson.

Singed Wings
Bebe Daniels, Conrad Nagel, Adolphe Menjou. Dir: Penrhyn Stanlaws. Drama of jealousy.

The Siren Call
Dorothy Dalton, David Powell. Dir: Irvin Willat. Northwest action drama by Edward Sheldon.

The Sleep Walker
Constance Binney, Jack Mulhall. Dir: Edward Le Saint. Comedy-drama of somnambulist.

South Of Suva
Mary Miles Minter, John Bowers. Dir: Frank Urson. Adventure drama.

The Spanish Jade
David Powell, Evelyn Brent. Dir: John S. Robertson. Romantic melodrama. (Paramount-British)

Thirty Days
Wallace Reid, Wanda Hawley. Dir: James Cruze. Comedy of jealousy.

Three Live Ghosts
Norman Kerry, Anna Q. Nilsson. Dir: George Fitzmaurice. Post-war comedy. (Paramount-British)

Through A Glass Window
May McAvoy, Raymond McKee. Dir: Maurice Campbell. Drama of poor New York family.

Tillie
Mary Miles Minter, Noah Beery. Dir: Frank Urson. Drama of Pennsylvania Dutch family.

To Have And To Hold
Betty Compson, Bert Lytell. Dir: George Fitzmaurice. Romance of American colonial days. (Re-make of 1916 film)

Too Much Wife
Wanda Hawley, T. Roy Barnes. Dir: Thomas Heffron. Matrimonial comedy.

The Top Of New York
May McAvoy, Walter McGrail. Dir: William Desmond Taylor. Tenements drama.

Travelin' On
William S. Hart. Dir: Lambert Hillyer. Western drama.

The Truthful Liar
Wanda Hawley. Dir: Thomas Heffron. Drama of blackmail and murder.

The Valley Of Silent Men
Lew Cody, Alma Rubens. Dir: Frank Borzage. Northwest drama by James Oliver Curwood.

A Virginia Courtship
May McAvoy. Dir: Frank O'Connor. Romantic comedy-drama.

While Satan Sleeps
Jack Holt. Dir: Joseph Henabery. Western drama by Peter B. Kyne. (Remake of *The Parson Of Panamint*, 1916)

The Wife Trap
Mia May. Dir: Robert Wullner. (UFA, German)

The Woman Who Walked Alone
Dorothy Dalton, Milton Sills. Dir: George Melford. Romantic melodrama.

The World's Champion
Wallace Reid, Lois Wilson. Dir: Philip Rosen. Comedy of aristocratic boxer.

The Young Diana
Marion Davies. Dir: Robert Vignola and Albert Capellani. Romantic drama.

The Young Rajah
Rudolph Valentino, Wanda Hawley. Dir: Philip Rosen. Romantic drama.

1923

Adam And Eva
Marion Davies, T. Roy Barnes, Edward Douglas. Dir: Robert Vignola. Society comedy.

Adam's Rib
Milton Sills, Anna Q. Nilsson. Dir: Cecil B. DeMille. Romantic drama by Jeanie Macpherson.

Around The World In Speejacks
Documentary travelogue of Commodore and Mrs A.Y. Gowen's honeymoon cruise around the South Sea islands.

Big Brother
Tom Moore, Edith Roberts. Dir: Allan Dwan. Drama of reformed criminal, by Rex Beach.

The Call Of The Canyon
Richard Dix, Lois Wilson, Ricardo Cortez. Dir: Victor Fleming. Western drama by Zane Grey.

The Cheat
Pola Negri, Jack Holt. Dir: George Fitzmaurice. Melodrama of wayward wife. (Remake of 1915 Fannie Ward film)

Children Of Jazz
Ricardo Cortez, Eileen Percy. Dir: Jerome Storm. Comedy-drama of modern youth.

Dark Secrets
Dorothy Dalton. Dir: Victor Fleming. Romantic melodrama.

Don't Call It Love
Agnes Ayres, Jack Holt, Nita Naldi. Dir: William C. de Mille. Comedy of prima donna.

Drums Of Fate
Mary Miles Minter, Maurice Flynn. Dir: Charles Maigne. Matrimonial drama.

The Exciters
Bebe Daniels, Antonio Moreno. Dir: Maurice Campbell. Rum-running drama.

Fog Bound
Dorothy Dalton, David Powell. Dir: Irvin Willat. Melodrama of Prohibition era.

A Gentleman Of Leisure
Jack Holt. Dir: Joseph Henabery. Romantic comedy from play by P.G. Wodehouse.

The Glimpses Of The Moon
Bebe Daniels, Nita Naldi, David Powell. Dir: Allan Dwan. Matrimonial drama from novel by Edith Wharton.

The Go-Getter
T. Roy Barnes, Seena Owen. Dir: Edward H. Griffith. Comedy of salesman, by Peter B. Kyne.

Grumpy
Theodore Roberts, May McAvoy, Conrad Nagel. Dir: William C. de Mille. Comedy-drama of retired lawyer.

The Heart Raider
Agnes Ayres, Charles Ruggles. Dir: Wesley Ruggles. Comedy of speed-mad girl.

His Children's Children
Bebe Daniels, Dorothy Mackaill. Dir: Sam Wood. Drama of wealthy family's problems, from novel by Arthur Train.

Homeward Bound
Thomas Meighan, Lila Lee. Dir: Ralph Ince. Sea adventure drama by Peter B. Kyne.

Java Head
Leatrice Joy, Jacqueline Logan, Albert Roscoe. Dir: George Melford. Adventure drama by Joseph Hergesheimer.

Kick In
Betty Compson, Bert Lytell, May McAvoy. Dir: George Fitzmaurice. Crime drama from play by Willard Mack.

The Law Of The Lawless
Dorothy Dalton, Theodore Kosloff. Dir: Victor Fleming. Gypsy melodrama.

Lawful Larceny
Hope Hampton, Conrad Nagel. Dir: Allan Dwan. Gambling drama from play by Samuel Shipman.

The Leopardess
Alice Brady, Montagu Love. Dir: Henry Kolker. Drama of half-caste woman.

The Marriage Maker
Agnes Ayres, Jack Holt. Dir: William C. de Mille. Romantic fantasy from play by Edward Knoblock.

Mr Billings Spends His Dime
Walter Hiers, Jacqueline Logan. Dir: Wesley Ruggles. Adventure comedy by Dana Burnett.

My American Wife
Gloria Swanson, Antonio Moreno. Dir: Sam Wood. Romantic drama set in South America.

The Ne'er-Do-Well
Thomas Meighan, Lila Lee. Dir: Alfred E. Green. Drama of soldier of fortune, from novel by Rex Beach.

Nobody's Money
Jack Holt, Wanda Hawley. Dir: Wallace Worsley. Impersonation comedy-drama by William LeBaron.

The Nth Commandment
Colleen Moore. Dir: Frank Borzage. Domestic drama by Fannie Hurst.

Only 38
Lois Wilson, Elliott Dexter, May McAvoy. Dir: William C. de Mille. Comedy-drama of widow, by A.E. Thomas.

Peter The Great
Emil Jannings. Dir: Dimitri Buchowetzki. Historical drama of the Russian tsar. (UFA, German)

Prodigal Daughters
Gloria Swanson, Vera Reynolds, Ralph Graves. Dir: Sam Wood. Drama of jazz-age sisters.

The Purple Highway
Madge Kennedy, Monte Blue. Dir: Henry Kolker. Comedy of Broadway stage.

Racing Hearts
Richard Dix, Agnes Ayres. Dir: Paul Powell. Racing car comedy-drama.

Ruggles Of Red Gap
Edward Everett Horton, Lois Wilson, Louise Dresser. Dir: James Cruze. Comedy of English butler in America.

The Rustle Of Silk
Betty Compson, Conway Tearle, Anna Q. Nilsson. Dir: Herbert Brenon. Romantic drama.

Salomy Jane
Jacqueline Logan, Maurice Flynn. Dir: George Melford. Western drama from novel by Bret Harte.

The Silent Partner
Leatrice Joy, Owen Moore. Dir: Charles Maigne. Stock market drama.

Sixty Cents An Hour
Walter Hiers, Jacqueline Logan, Ricardo Cortez. Dir: Joseph Henabery. Comedy.

The Snow Bride
Alice Brady, Maurice Flynn. Dir: Henry Kolker. Canadian Northwest drama.

The Spanish Dancer
Pola Negri, Antonio Moreno, Adolphe Menjou. Dir: Herbert Brenon. Romance of old Spain.

Stephen Steps Out
Douglas Fairbanks Jr, Theodore Roberts. Dir: Joseph Henabery. Student's adventure in Turkey, by Richard Harding Davis.

The Tiger's Claw
Jack Holt, Eva Novak. Dir: Joseph Henabery. Melodrama in India.

To The Ladies
Edward Everett Horton, Louise Dresser, Theodore Roberts. Dir: James Cruze. Comedy of business rivalry, from play by George Kaufman, Marc Connelly.

To The Last Man
Richard Dix, Lois Wilson, Noah Beery. Dir: Victor Fleming. Western feud drama by Zane Grey.

The Trail Of The Lonesome Pine
Antonio Moreno, Mary Miles Minter. Dir: Charles Maigne. Backwoods feud drama. (Remake of 1916 film)

West Of The Water Tower
Glenn Hunter, May McAvoy. Dir: Rollin Sturgeon. Illegitimacy drama.

The White Flower
Betty Compson, Edmund Lowe. Dir: Julia Crawford Ivers. Hawaiian romance.

Wild Bill Hickok
William S. Hart. Dir: Clifford Smith. Western drama.

Woman-Proof
Thomas Meighan, Lila Lee. Dir: Alfred E. Green. Inheritance comedy by George Ade.

The Woman With Four Faces
Betty Compson, Richard Dix. Dir: Herbert Brenon. Underworld drama from play by Bayard Veiller.

The World's Applause
Bebe Daniels, Lewis Stone, Adolphe Menjou. Dir: William C. de Mille. Backstage murder drama.

You Can't Fool Your Wife
Leatrice Joy, Lewis Stone, Nita Naldi. Dir: George Melford. Romantic drama.

1924

The Alaskan
Thomas Meighan, Estelle Taylor. Dir: Herbert Brenon. Adventure drama by James Oliver Curwood.

Argentine Love
Bebe Daniels, Ricardo Cortez. Dir: Allan Dwan. Romantic drama by Vicente Blasco Ibanez.

The Bedroom Window
May McAvoy, Ricardo Cortez, Malcolm MacGregor. Dir: William C. de Mille. Murder mystery.

Bluff
Agnes Ayres, Antonio Moreno. Dir: Sam Wood. Impersonation drama.

The Border Legion
Antonio Moreno, Helene Chadwick. Dir: William K. Howard. Western drama by Zane Grey.

The Breaking Point
Nita Naldi, Matt Moore. Dir: Herbert Brenon. Mystery drama from play by Mary Roberts Rinehart.

Changing Husbands
Leatrice Joy, Victor Varconi. Dir: Frank Urson and Paul Iribe. Matrimonial comedy.

The City That Never Sleeps
Louise Dresser, Virginia Lee Corbin, Ricardo Cortez. Dir: James Cruze. Drama of mother-love.

The Code Of The Sea
Rod La Rocque, Jacqueline Logan. Dir: Victor Fleming. Adventure drama.

The Confidence Man
Thomas Meighan, Virginia Valli. Dir: Victor Heerman. Crook drama.

Dangerous Money
Bebe Daniels, Tom Moore, William Powell. Dir: Frank Tuttle. Inheritance drama.

The Dawn Of A Tomorrow
Jacqueline Logan, Raymond Griffith. Dir: George Melford. Crook drama from play by Frances Hodgson Burnett. (Remake of 1915 Mary Pickford film)

Empty Hands
Jack Holt, Norma Shearer. Dir: Victor Fleming. Canadian adventure drama by Arthur Stringer.

The Enemy Sex
Betty Compson, Percy Marmont, Huntley Gordon. Dir: James Cruze. Romantic drama of chorus girl.

Fair Week
Walter Hiers, Carmen Phillips. Dir: Rob Wagner. Small-town comedy.

The Female
Betty Compson, Warner Baxter. Dir: Sam Wood. South African romantic drama.

The Fighting Coward
Cullen Landis, Mary Astor, Ernest Torrence. Dir: James Cruze. Southern comedy-drama by Booth Tarkington.

Flaming Barriers
Antonio Moreno, Jacqueline Logan. Dir: George Melford. Fire-fighting drama.

The Garden Of Weeds
Betty Compson, Warner Baxter. Dir: James Cruze. Matrimonial drama from play by Leon Gordon.

The Guilty One
Agnes Ayres, Edward Burns. Dir: Joseph Henabery. Mystery drama.

Her Love Story
Gloria Swanson, Ian Keith. Dir: Allan Dwan. Ruritanian romantic drama by Mary Roberts Rinehart

The Heritage Of The Desert
Bebe Daniels, Lloyd Hughes, Ernest Torrence. Dir: Irvin Willat. Western drama by Zane Grey.

Icebound
Richard Dix, Lois Wilson, Vera Reynolds. Dir: William C. de Mille. Rural drama from play by Owen Davis.

Lily Of The Dust
Pola Negri, Ben Lyon. Dir: Dimitri Buchowetzki. Romantic drama. (Remake of *The Song of Songs*, 1918).

The Man Who Fights Alone
William Farnum, Lois Wilson. Dir: Wallace Worsley. Drama of jealousy.

Manhattan
Richard Dix, Jacqueline Logan. Dir: R.H. Burnside. Crime comedy-drama by Jeffrey Farnol.

Men
Pola Negri, Robert Frazer. Dir: Dimitri Buchowetzki. Drama of man-hating actress.

Montmartre
Pola Negri. Dir: Ernst Lubitsch. Romantic drama; *Die Flamme*, (UFA, German)

The Moral Sinner
Dorothy Dalton. Dir: Ralph Ince. Drama of jewel thief. (Remake of *The Girl Who Came Back*, 1918).

The Next Corner
Lon Chaney, Dorothy Mackaill, Ricardo Cortez. Dir: Sam Wood. Drama of infidelity.

North Of 36
Jack Holt, Lois Wilson, Ernest Torrence. Dir: Irvin Willat. Western adventure drama.

Open All Night
Viola Dana, Jetta Goudal, Raymond Griffith. Dir: Paul Bern. Comedy-drama by Paul Morand.

Pied Piper Malone
Thomas Meighan, Lois Wilson. Dir: Alfred E. Green. Sea-going comedy-drama by Booth Tarkington.

A Sainted Devil
Rudolph Valentino, Nita Naldi. Dir: Joseph Henabery. Adventure romance by Rex Beach.

Shadows Of Paris
Pola Negri, Adolphe Menjou. Dir: Herbert Brenon. Drama of Apache girl in Paris society.

The Side-Show Of Life
Ernest Torrence, Anna Q. Nilsson. Dir: Herbert Brenon. Drama of circus juggler, by William J. Locke.

Sinners In Heaven
Richard Dix, Bebe Daniels. Dir: Alan Crosland. South Seas island romance.

A Society Scandal
Gloria Swanson, Rod La Rocque. Dir: Allan Dwan. Divorce drama from Alfred Sutro's 'The Laughing Lady'.

The Story Without A Name (aka **Without Warning**)
Agnes Ayres, Antonio Moreno. Dir: Irvin Willat. Adventure drama by Arthur Stringer.

The Stranger
Richard Dix, Betty Compson. Dir: Joseph Henabery. Murder drama from John Galsworthy's 'The First and The Last'.

Tiger Love
Antonio Moreno, Estelle Taylor. Dir: George Melford. Spanish bandit romance.

Tongues Of Flame
Thomas Meighan, Bessie Love. Dir: Joseph Henabery. Drama of property.

Unguarded Women
Bebe Daniels, Richard Dix, Mary Astor. Dir: Alan Crosland. Drama of war widows.

The Wages Of Virtue
Gloria Swanson, Ben Lyon. Dir: Allan Dwan. Drama of the Foreign Legion, by P.C. Wren.

Wanderer Of The Wasteland
Jack Holt, Billie Dove. Dir: Irvin Willat. Western drama by Zane Grey. (Technicolor).

Worldly Goods
Agnes Ayres, Victor Varconi. Dir: Paul Bern. Domestic comedy-drama.

1925

Adventure
Tom Moore, Pauline Starke, Wallace Beery. Dir: Victor Fleming. Melodrama set in Solomon Islands, from novel by Jack London.

The Air Mail
Warner Baxter, Billie Dove. Dir: Irvin Willat. Aviation drama of pilot vs. smugglers.

The Ancient Highway
Jack Holt, Billie Dove. Dir: Irvin Willat. Canadian adventure drama by James Oliver Curwood.

Any Woman
Alice Terry. Dir: Henry King. Drama of heiress becoming secretary, by Arthur Somers Roche.

Beggar On Horseback
Edward Everett Horton, Esther Ralston. Dir: James Cruze. Comedy-drama of dream and reality, from play by George S. Kaufman, Marc Connelly.

The Best People
Warner Baxter, Esther Ralston. Dir: Sidney Olcott. Drama of family conflicts, from play by Avery Hopwood.

The Charmer
Pola Negri, Robert Frazer. Dir: Sidney Olcott. Drama of dancer, chauffeur and millionaire.

The Coast Of Folly
Gloria Swanson, Anthony Jowitt. Dir: Allan Dwan. Drama of mother and daughter.

Code Of The West
Owen Moore, Constance Bennett. Dir: William K. Howard. Drama of flapper on Western ranch, from novel by Zane Grey.

Coming Through
Thomas Meighan, Lila Lee, Wallace Beery. Dir: Edward Sutherland. Mining camp melodrama.

Contraband
Lois Wilson, Noah Beery, Raymond McKee. Dir: Alan Crosland. Melodrama of girl versus gang.

The Crowded Hour
Bebe Daniels, Kenneth Harlan. Dir: E. Mason Hopper. Wartime backstage drama.

The Devil's Cargo
William Collier Jr, Pauline Starke, Wallace Beery. Dir: Victor Fleming. Action drama of 1849 California.

The Dressmaker From Paris
Leatrice Joy, Ernest Torrence. Dir: Paul Bern. Romantic comedy-drama.

East Of Suez
Pola Negri, Edmund Lowe. Dir: Raoul Walsh. Romance of half-caste and Englishman in China, from play by W. Somerset Maugham.

Eve's Secret
Betty Compson, Jack Holt. Dir: Clarence Badger. Comedy of peasant girl made into lady.

Flower Of Night
Pola Negri, Warner Oland. Dir: Paul Bern. Melodrama of California gold mine, from novel by Joseph Hergesheimer.

Forty Winks
Raymond Griffith, Viola Dana, Theodore Roberts. Dir: Frank Urson and Paul Iribe. Comedy drama of secret service agent, from play by David Belasco, Henry de Mille.

The Golden Princess
Betty Bronson, Neil Hamilton, Phyllis Haver, Rockliffe Fellowes. Dir: Clarence Badger. Melodrama of California gold mine. (Remake of *Tennessee's Pardner*, 1916)

The Goose Hangs High
Constance Bennett, Esther Ralston. Dir: James Cruze. Comedy-drama of selfish children.

Grass
Documentary of Persian tribe's migration through mountainous country to grazing lands. Filmed in Arabia by Ernest B. Schoedsack and Merian C. Cooper.

Grounds For Divorce
Florence Vidor, Matt Moore. Dir: Paul Bern. Comedy of Paris lawyer and his wife, from play by Ernest Vajda.

In The Name Of Love
Ricardo Cortez, Greta Nissen, Richard Arlen. Dir: Howard Higgin. Romantic comedy of business man and social climber, from play by Edward Bulwer-Lytton.

Irish Luck
Thomas Meighan, Lois Wilson. Dir: Victor Heerman. Inheritance comedy-drama.

The King On Main Street
Adolphe Menjou, Bessie Love, Greta Nissen. Dir: Monta Bell. Comedy of European king in America.

A Kiss In The Dark
Adolphe Menjou, Aileen Pringle, Lillian Rich, Kenneth MacKenna. Dir: Frank Tuttle. Comedy of mixed couples, from Frederick Lonsdale's 'Aren't We All'.

The Little French Girl
Mary Brian, Alice Joyce, Neil Hamilton. Dir: Herbert Brenon. Romantic drama.

Locked Doors
Betty Compson, Theodore von Eltz, Theodore Roberts. Dir: William C. de Mille. Romantic triangle drama.

Lord Jim
Percy Marmont, Shirley Mason, Noah Beery. Dir: Victor Fleming. Drama of vagabond sailor, by Joseph Conrad.

Lost – A Wife
Adolphe Menjou, Greta Nissen. Dir: William C. de Mille. Comedy of compulsive gambler.

Lovers In Quarantine
Bebe Daniels, Harrison Ford, Alfred Lunt. Dir: Frank Tuttle. Romantic comedy by F. Tennyson Jesse.

The Lucky Devil
Richard Dix, Esther Ralston. Dir: Frank Tuttle. Car racing comedy-drama.

A Man Must Live
Richard Dix, Jacqueline Logan. Dir: Paul Sloane. Drama of reporter and divorcee, from novel by I.A.R. Wylie.

The Man Who Found Himself
Thomas Meighan, Virginia Valli, Frank Morgan, Lynn Fontanne. Dir: Alfred E. Green. Drama of embezzlement, by Booth Tarkington.

The Manicure Girl
Bebe Daniels, Edmund Burns. Dir: Frank Tuttle. Comedy-drama of gold-digger.

Marry Me
Florence Vidor, Edward Everett Horton. Dir: James Cruze. Comedy of school teacher and hypochondriac.

Men And Women
Richard Dix, Neil Hamilton. Dir: William C. de Mille. Drama of embezzling bank clerks. (Remake of 1914 film).

Miss Bluebeard
Bebe Daniels, Raymond Griffith. Dir: Frank Tuttle. Farce about bigamous actress.

New Brooms
Neil Hamilton, Bessie Love, Phyllis Haver. Dir: William C. de Mille. Comedy of family conflict, by Frank Craven.

New Lives For Old
Betty Compson, Theodore Kosloff. Dir: Clarence Badger. Wartime drama of French spy and American officer.

The Night Club
Raymond Griffith, Vera Reynolds, Wallace Beery. Dir: Frank Urson and Paul Iribe. Comedy of misogynist in love, from play by Cecil B. DeMille, William C. de Mille.

Night Life Of New York
Dorothy Gish, Rod La Rocque. Dir: Allan Dwan. Comedy-romance of telephonist and Westerner.

Not So Long Ago
Betty Bronson, Ricardo Cortez. Dir: Sidney Olcott. Romance of seamstress and rich youth.

Old Home Week
Thomas Meighan, Lila Lee. Dir: Victor Heerman. Small-town comedy-drama by George Ade.

The Pony Express
Ricardo Cortez, Betty Compson, George Bancroft. Dir: James Cruze. Western drama.

A Regular Fellow (aka He's A Prince)
Raymond Griffith, Mary Brian. Dir: Edward Sutherland. Comedy of Ruritanian prince.

Rugged Water
Warner Baxter, Lois Wilson, Wallace Beery, Phyllis Haver. Dir: Irvin Willat. Drama of lifeboat captains.

Sackcloth And Scarlet
Alice Terry, Dorothy Sebastian. Dir: Henry King. Drama of sisters, good and bad.

Sally Of The Sawdust
Carol Dempster, W.C. Fields, Alfred Lunt. Dir: D.W. Griffith. Circus comedy-drama from the play 'Poppy' by Dorothy Donnelly. (Released by United Artists).

Salome Of The Tenements
Jetta Goudal, Godfrey Tearle. Dir: Sidney Olcott. Drama of slum girl's rise.

Seven Keys To Baldpate
Douglas MacLean, Edith Roberts. Dir: Fred Newmeyer. Comedy thriller. (Remake of 1917 film)

The Shock Punch
Richard Dix, Frances Howard. Dir: Paul Sloane. Action drama of boxing champion, by John Monk Saunders.

A Son Of His Father
Warner Baxter, Bessie Love. Dir: Victor Fleming. Western melodrama by Harold Bell Wright.

The Spaniard (aka Spanish Love)
Ricardo Cortez, Jetta Goudal. Dir: Raoul Walsh. Romance of bullfighter and English lady.

The Splendid Crime
Bebe Daniels, Neil Hamilton. Dir: William C. de Mille. Drama of reformed thief. (Remake of *Ragamuffin*, 1916).

The Street Of Forgotten Men
Percy Marmont, Mary Brian, Neil Hamilton. Dir: Herbert Brenon. Drama of beggar's sacrifice for daughter.

The Swan
Frances Howard, Adolphe Menjou, Ricardo Cortez. Dir: Dimitri Buchowetzki. Romantic comedy-drama from play by Ferenc Molnar.

The Thundering Herd
Jack Holt, Lois Wilson, Noah Beery. Dir: William K. Howard. Action drama of hunters vs. Indians, by Zane Grey.

Tomorrow's Love
Agnes Ayres, Pat O'Malley. Dir: Paul Bern. Drama of cancelled divorce, by Charles Brackett.

Too Many Kisses
Richard Dix, Frances Howard, William Powell, Harpo Marx. Dir: Paul Sloane. Comedy of American playboy in Spain, by John Monk Saunders.

The Top Of The World
James Kirkwood, Anna Q. Nilsson. Dir: George Melford. South African melodrama.

The Trouble With Wives
Florence Vidor, Tom Moore, Esther Ralston. Dir: Malcolm St Clair. Comedy of jealousy.

The Wanderer
William Collier Jr, Greta Nissen, Ernest Torrence, Wallace Beery. Dir: Raoul Walsh. Biblical drama of the prodigal son.

Welcome Home
Warner Baxter, Lois Wilson, Luke Cosgrave. Dir: James Cruze. Comedy of problem father, from play by Edna Ferber, George S. Kaufman.

Wild Horse Mesa
Jack Holt, Billie Dove, Douglas Fairbanks Jr. Dir: George B. Seitz. Western drama of horse tamer, by Zane Grey.

Wild, Wild Susan
Bebe Daniels, Rod La Rocque. Dir: Edward Sutherland. Action comedy of heiress and author.

Woman-Handled
Richard Dix, Esther Ralston. Dir: Gregory La Cava. Comedy of a society playboy out West.

RAY MILLAND (1945)

OLIVIA de HAVILLAND (1946 & 1949)

Academy Nominations and Awards

The Academy of Motion Picture Arts and Sciences was founded in the early part of 1927 and, although an Awards of Merit committee was appointed soon after inauguration, it was not until July the following year that it suggested a procedure for recognising meritorious achievement in the industry. Studios were invited to submit lists of films released in the Los Angeles area between 1st August 1927 and 31st July 1928. From these lists the Academy's membership made its nominations in each of twelve categories of achievement, and the winners were decided by an appointed board of judges. The results were announced publicly on 18th February 1929 and the awards themselves were presented three months later. The Academy has honoured members of the movie-making profession in this way every year since, and the annual ceremonial of presenting the Oscars (as the statuette trophies have been nicknamed) is perhaps the best known of all the Academy's activities.

The eligibility period of August to July remained in force until 1933, when the decision was taken to change to the calendar year. The last split-year period was therefore an extended one, from 1st August 1932 to 31st December 1933. The other eligibility qualification – release in the Los Angeles area – has been unchanged throughout.

The following section gives details of all the nominations and awards that Paramount has received over the years. For the sake of completeness, those not related to feature films are also given; these include short subjects, scientific or technical achievements and honorary, special or memorial awards given to individuals who, at least at some time in their career, made a particularly important contribution to Paramount's fortunes.

Award-winners in competitive categories where there were other nominations are identified by means of a star. Black spots denote recipients of awards that

were presented at the Academy's discretion and were not competitive in the sense that other contenders, if indeed there were any, were not publicly nominated.

Occasionally the reader may discover a discrepancy between the year in which a film is nominated and the release year to which it is assigned in this book. Establishing the release year with precision is sometimes a difficult task and there are several ways in which a confusion can arise. A film may be withdrawn for revision after an initial showing of short duration, and does not enjoy 'full' release until the following year or it may open outside Los Angeles late one year and not move into the qualifying area until the next. . It also sometimes happens that a film is given a very limited release in the Los Angeles area simply to qualify for that year's awards, even though the main release is not planned until the following year, when the presentation ceremony gives it valuable publicity at the most effective time.

ANNA MAGNANI (1955)

JAMES L. BROOKS, SHIRLEY MacLAINE, JACK NICHOLSON (1983)

WARREN BEATTY (1981)

1927/1928

Picture
The Last Command
The Racket
The Way Of All Flesh
★ *Wings*

Actor
★ Emil Jannings *The Last Command*
and *The Way Of All Flesh*

Direction (comedy)
Ted Wilde *Speedy*

Writing (original story)
★ Ben Hecht *Underworld*
Lajos Biro *The Last Command*

Artistic Quality Of Production
Chang

Engineering Effects
★ Roy Pomeroy *Wings*

1928/1929

Picture
The Patriot

Actor
George Bancroft *Thunderbolt*
Lewis Stone *The Patriot*

Actress
Jeanne Eagels *The Letter*

Direction
Ernst Lubitsch *The Patriot*

Writing
★ Hans Kraly *The Patriot*

Art Direction
Hans Dreier *The Patriot*

1929/1930

Picture
The Love Parade

Actor
Maurice Chevalier *The Love Parade* and
The Big Pond

Actress
Nancy Carroll *The Devil's Holiday*
Ruth Chatterton *Sarah And Son*

Direction
Ernst Lubitsch *The Love Parade*

Writing
Howard Estabrook *Street Of Chance*

Cinematography
★ Joseph Rucker, Willard Van der Veer *With Byrd
At The South Pole*
Victor Milner *The Love Parade*

Art Direction
Hans Dreier *The Love Parade*
Hans Dreier *The Vagabond King*

Sound Recording
Franklin Hansen *The Love Parade*

1930/1931

Picture
Skippy

Actor
Jackie Cooper *Skippy*
Fredric March *The Royal Family Of Broadway*

Actress
Marlene Dietrich *Morocco*

Direction
★ Norman Taurog *Skippy*
Josef von Sternberg *Morocco*

**Writing
(adaptation)**
Joseph Mankiewicz, Sam Mintz *Skippy*
(original story)
Harry d'Abbadie d'Arrast, Douglas Doty,
Donald Ogden Stewart *Laughter*

Cinematography
★ Floyd Crosby *Tabu*
Lee Garmes *Morocco*
Charles Lang *The Right To Love*

Art Direction
Hans Dreier *Morocco*

Sound Recording
★ Paramount Studio Sound Department

1931/1932

Picture
One Hour With You
Shanghai Express
The Smiling Lieutenant

Actor
★ Fredric March *Dr Jekyll And Mr Hyde*
(tied with Wallace Beery *The Champ*, MGM)

Direction
Josef von Sternberg *Shanghai Express*

**Writing
(adaptation)**
Percy Heath, Samuel Hoffenstein *Dr Jekyll And
Mr Hyde*
(original story)
Grover Jones, William Slavens McNutt *Lady
And Gent*

Cinematography
★ Lee Garmes *Shanghai Express*
Karl Struss *Dr Jekyll And Mr Hyde*

Sound Recording
★ Paramount Studio Sound Department

Short Subjects (novelty)
Screen Souvenirs

1932/1933

Picture
A Farewell To Arms
She Done Him Wrong

Cinematography
★ Charles Bryant Lang Jr. *A Farewell To Arms*
Karl Struss *The Sign Of The Cross*

Art Direction
Hans Dreier, Roland Anderson *A Farewell To Arms*

Sound Recording
★ Harold C. Lewis *A Farewell To Arms*

Assistant Director
★ Charles Barton

1934

Picture
Cleopatra

Cinematography
★ Victor Milner *Cleopatra*

Sound Recording
Franklin Hansen *Cleopatra*

Film Editing
Anne Bauchens *Cleopatra*

Music (song)
Ralph Rainger (music), Leo Robin (lyrics) 'Love
In Bloom' in *She Loves Me Not*

Assistant Director
Cullen Tate *Cleopatra*

1935

Picture
The Lives Of A Bengal Lancer
Ruggles Of Red Gap

Actress
Claudette Colbert *Private Worlds*

Direction
Henry Hathaway *The Lives Of A Bengal Lancer*

**Writing
(original story)**
★ Ben Hecht, Charles MacArthur *The Scoundrel*
(screenplay)
Achmed Abdullah, John Balderston, Grover
Jones, William Slavens McNutt, Waldemar
Young *The Lives Of A Bengal Lancer*

Cinematography
Victor Milner *The Crusades*

Art Direction
Hans Dreier, Roland Anderson *The Lives Of A
Bengal Lancer*

Sound Recording
Franklin Hansen *The Lives Of A Bengal Lancer*

Film Editing
Ellsworth Hoagland *The Lives Of A Bengal Lancer*

Music (score)
Ernst Toch *Peter Ibbetson*

Assistant Director
★ Clem Beauchamp, Paul Wing *The Lives Of A
Bengal Lancer*

Dance Direction
Leroy Prinz *The Big Broadcast Of 1936* and
All The King's Horses

Scientific or Technical
● Paramount Productions, Inc., for the design and
construction of the Paramount transparency air
turbine developing machine

1936

Actress
Gladys George *Valiant Is The Word For Carrie*

Supporting Actor
Akim Tamiroff *The General Died At Dawn*

Cinematography
Victor Milner *The General Died At Dawn*

Sound Recording
Franklin Hansen *The Texas Rangers*

Music
(song)
Louis Alter (music), Sidney Mitchell (lyrics) 'A Melody From The Sky' in *The Trail Of The Lonesome Pine*
(score)
Werner Janssen *The General Died At Dawn*

Short Subjects
(cartoon)
Sinbad The Sailor
(one-reel)
Moscow Moods
(colour)
Popular Science J-6-2

1937

Art Direction
Hans Dreier, Roland Anderson *Souls At Sea*
Wiard Ihnen *Every Day's A Holiday*

Music
(song)
★ Harry Owens (music and lyrics) 'Sweet Leilani' in *Waikiki Wedding*
Frederick Hollander (music), Leo Robin (lyrics) 'Whispers In The Dark' in *Artists And Models*
(score)
W. Franke Harling, Milan Roder *Souls At Sea*

Sound Recording
L. L. Ryder *Wells Fargo*

Assistant Director
Hal Walker *Souls At Sea*

Dance Direction
Leroy Prinz *Waikiki Wedding*

Short Subjects
(cartoon)
Educated Fish
(colour)
Popular Science J-7-1

Scientific or Technical
● Farciot Edouart and Paramount Pictures, Inc., for the development of the Paramount dual screen transparency camera set-up
● Joseph E. Robbins and Paramount Pictures, Inc., for an exceptional application of acoustic principles to the soundproofing of gasoline generators and water pumps

1938

Supporting Actor
Basil Rathbone *If I Were King*

Cinematography
Victor Milner *The Buccaneer*

Art Direction
Hans Dreier, John Goodman *If I Were King*

Sound Recording
Loren Ryder *If I Were King*

Music
(song)
★ Ralph Rainger (music), Leo Robin (lyrics) 'Thanks For The Memory' in *The Big Broadcast Of 1938*
(scoring)
Boris Morros *Tropic Holiday*
(original score)
Richard Hageman *If I Were King*

Short Subjects (cartoon)
Hunky and Spunky

Special Awards
● For outstanding achievement in creating special photographic and sound effects in the Paramount production *Spawn Of The North*: special effects by Gordon Jennings assisted by Jan Domela, Dev Jennings, Irmin Roberts and Art Smith; transparencies by Farciot Edouart assisted by Loyal Griggs; sound effects by Loren Ryder assisted by Harry Mills, Louis H. Mesenkop and Walter Oberst

1939

Supporting Actor
Brian Donlevy *Beau Geste*

Art Direction
Hans Dreier, Robert Odell *Beau Geste*

Music
(song)
Ralph Rainger (music), Leo Robin (lyrics) 'Faithful Forever' in *Gulliver's Travels*
(scoring)
Phil Boutelje, Arthur Lange *The Great Victor Herbert*
(original score)
Victor Young *Gulliver's Travels*

Sound Recording
Loren Ryder *The Great Victor Herbert*

Special Effects
Farciot Edouart, Gordon Jennings, Loren Ryder *Union Pacific*

Short Subjects (one-reel)
★ *Busy Little Bears*

Scientific or Technical
● Farciot Edouart, Joseph E. Robbins, William Rudolph and Paramount Pictures, Inc., for the design and construction of a quiet, portable treadmill

1940

Writing
(original story)
★ Benjamin Glazer, John Toldy *Arise, My Love*
(original screenplay)
★ Preston Sturges *The Great McGinty*

Cinematography
(black and white)
Charles Lang Jr. *Arise, My Love*
(colour)
Victor Milner, W. Howard Greene *Northwest Mounted Police*

Special Effects
Farciot Edouart, Gordon Jennings *Dr Cyclops*

Film Editing
★ Anne Bauchens *Northwest Mounted Police*

Art Direction
(black-and-white)
Hans Dreier, Robert Usher *Arise, My Love*
(colour)
Hans Dreier, Roland Anderson *Northwest Mounted Police*

Sound Recording
Loren Ryder *Northwest Mounted Police*

Music
(song)
Artie Shaw (music), Johnny Mercer (lyrics) 'Love Of My Life' in *Second Chorus*
James V. Monaco (music), Johnny Burke (lyrics) 'Only Forever' in *Rhythm On The River*
(score)
Victor Young *Arise, My Love*
Artie Shaw *Second Chorus*
(original score)
Victor Young *Northwest Mounted Police*

Special Award
● To Bob Hope, in recognition of his unselfish services to the motion picture industry.

1941

Picture
Hold Back The Dawn

Actress
Olivia de Havilland *Hold Back The Dawn*

Writing
(original story)
Monckton Hoffe *The Lady Eve*
(screenplay)
Charles Brackett, Billy Wilder *Hold Back The Dawn*

Cinematography
(black and white)
Leo Tover *Hold Back The Dawn*
(colour)
Wilfred Cline, Karl Struss, William Snyder *Aloma Of The South Seas*
Harry Hallenberger, Ray Rennahan *Louisiana Purchase*

Special Effects
★ Farciot Edouart, Gordon Jennings, Louis Mesenkop *I Wanted Wings*
Farciot Edouart, Gordon Jennings, Louis Mesenkop *Aloma Of The South Seas*

Sound Recording
Loren Ryder *Skylark*

Music
(song)
Lou Alter (music), Frank Loesser (lyrics) 'Dolores' in *Las Vegas Nights*
(scoring of a dramatic picture)
Victor Young *Hold Back The Dawn*
(scoring of a musical picture)
Robert Emmett Dolan *Birth Of The Blues*

Art Direction/Interior Decoration
(black and white)
Hans Dreier, Robert Usher/Sam Comer *Hold Back The Dawn*
(colour)
Raoul Pene du Bois/Stephen A. Seymour *Louisiana Purchase*

Short Subjects
(cartoon)
Rhythm In The Ranks (George Pal Puppetoon)
Superman No. 1
(one-reel)
Beauty And The Beach (Headliner Series)
Down On The Farm (Speaking of Animals)

Scientific and Technical (class 3)
- Wilbur Silvertooth and the Paramount Studio Engineering Department for the design and computation of a relay condenser system applicable to transparency process projection, delivering considerably more usable light
- Paramount Pictures, Inc., and 20th Century-Fox Film Corporation for the development and first practical application to motion picture production of an automatic scene slating device
- Douglas Shearer and the Metro-Goldwyn-Mayer Studio Sound Department and to Loren Ryder and the Paramount Studio Sound Department for pioneering the development of fine grain emulsions for variable density original sound recording in studio production

1942

Picture
Wake Island

Supporting Actor
William Bendix *Wake Island*

Direction
John Farrow *Wake Island*

Writing
(original story)
Irving Berlin *Holiday Inn*
(original screenplay)
Frank Butler, Don Hartman *The Road To Morocco*
W. R. Burnett, Frank Butler *Wake Island*

Special Effects
★ Farciot Edouart, Gordon Jennings, William Pareira, Louis Mesenkop *Reap The Wild Wind*

Cinematography
(black-and-white)
John Mescall *Take A Letter, Darling*
(colour)
Victor Milner, William V. Skall *Reap The Wild Wind*

Art Direction/Interior Decoration
(black-and-white)
Hans Dreier, Roland Anderson/Sam Comer *Take A Letter, Darling*
(colour)
Hans Dreier, Roland Anderson/George Sawley *Reap The Wild Wind*

Sound Recording
Loren Ryder *The Road To Morocco*

Music
(song)
★ Irving Berlin (music and lyrics) 'White Christmas' from *Holiday Inn*
(scoring of a dramatic or comedy picture)
Victor Young *Take A Letter, Darling*
(scoring of a musical picture)
Robert Emmett Dolan *Holiday Inn*

Short Subjects
(cartoon)
Tulips Shall Grow (George Pal Puppetoon)
(one-reel)
★ *Speaking Of Animals And Their Families*

Scientific or Technical
- Robert Henderson and the Paramount Studio Engineering and Transparency Departments for the design and construction of adjustable light bridges and screen frames for transparency process photography

1943

Picture
For Whom The Bell Tolls

Actor
Gary Cooper *For Whom The Bell Tolls*

Actress
Ingrid Bergman *For Whom The Bell Tolls*

Supporting Actor
Akim Tamiroff *For Whom The Bell Tolls*

Supporting Actress
Paulette Goddard *So Proudly We Hail*
★ Katina Paxinou *For Whom The Bell Tolls*

Writing (original screenplay)
Allan Scott *So Proudly We Hail*

Cinematography
(black-and-white)
John Seitz *Five Graves To Cairo*
Charles Lang *So Proudly We Hail*
(colour)
Ray Rennahan *For Whom The Bell Tolls*

Art Direction/Interior Decoration
(black-and-white)
Hans Dreier, Ernst Fegte/Bertram Granger *Five Graves To Cairo*
(colour)
Hans Dreier, Haldane Douglas/Bertram Granger *For Whom The Bell Tolls*

Film Editing
Doane Harrison *Five Graves To Cairo*
Sherman Todd, John Link *For Whom The Bell Tolls*

Sound Recording
Loren Ryder *Riding High*

Special Effects
Farciot Edouart, Gordon Jennings, George Dutton *So Proudly We Hail*

Music
(song)
Harold Arlen (music), Johnny Mercer (lyrics) 'That Old Black Magic' in *Star Spangled Rhythm*
(scoring of a dramatic or comedy picture)
Victor Young *For Whom The Bell Tolls*
(scoring of a musical picture)
Robert Emmett Dolan *Star Spangled Rhythm*

Short Subjects
(cartoon)
500 Hats Of Bartholomew Cubbins (Puppetoon)
(one-reel)
★ *Amphibious Fighters*
(two-reel)
Mardi Gras (Musical Parade)

Special Awards
- To George Pal for the development of novel methods and techniques in the production of short subjects known as Puppetoons

Scientific or Technical
- Farciot Edouart, Earle Morgan, Barton Thompson and the Paramount Studio Engineering and Transparency Departments for the development and practical application to motion picture production of a method of duplicating and enlarging natural color photographs, transferring the image emulsions to glass plates and projecting these slides by especially designed stereopticon equipment
- Farciot Edouart and the Paramount Studio Transparency Department for an automatic electric transparency cueing timer

1944

Picture
Double Indemnity
★ *Going My Way*

Actor
★ Bing Crosby *Going My Way*
Barry Fitzgerald *Going My Way*

Actress
Barbara Stanwyck *Double Indemnity*

Supporting Actor
★ Barry Fitzgerald *Going My Way*

Direction
★ Leo McCarey *Going My Way*
Billy Wilder *Double Indemnity*

Writing
(original story)
★ Leo McCarey *Going My Way*
(original screenplay)
Preston Sturges *Hail The Conquering Hero*
Preston Sturges *The Miracle Of Morgan's Creek*
(screenplay)
★ Frank Butler, Frank Cavett *Going My Way*
Raymond Chandler, Billy Wilder *Double Indemnity*

Cinematography
(black-and-white)
John Seitz *Double Indemnity*
Charles Lang *The Uninvited*
Lionel Lindon *Going My Way*
(colour)
Ray Rennahan *Lady In The Dark*

Art Direction/Interior Decoration
(black-and-white)
Hans Dreier, Robert Usher/Sam Comer *No Time For Love*
(colour)
Hans Dreier, Raoul Pene du Bois/Ray Moyer *Lady In The Dark*

Film Editing
Leroy Stone *Going My Way*

Special Effects
Farciot Edouart, Gordon Jennings, George Dutton *The Story Of Dr. Wassell*

Sound Recording
Loren Ryder *Double Indemnity*

Music
(song)
★ James Van Heusen (music), Johnny Burke (lyrics) 'Swinging On A Star' in *Going My Way*
(scoring of a dramatic or comedy picture)
Miklos Rozsa *Double Indemnity*
(scoring of a musical picture)
Robert Emmett Dolan *Lady In The Dark*

Short Subjects
(cartoon)
And To Think I Saw It On Mulberry Street (Puppetoon)
(one-reel)
★ *Who's Who In Animal Land* (Speaking of Animals)
(two-reel)
Bombalera (Musical Parade)

Special Awards
- To Bob Hope, for his many services to the Academy, a Life Membership in the Academy of Motion Picture Arts and Sciences

Scientific or Technical
- Russell Brown, Ray Hinsdale and Joseph E. Robbins for the development and production use of the Paramount floating hydraulic boat rocker
- Gordon Jennings for the design and construction of the Paramount nodal point tripod
- Paul Lerpae for the design and construction of the Paramount travelling matte projection and photographing device

1945

Picture
★ *The Lost Weekend*

Actor
★ Ray Milland *The Lost Weekend*

Actress
Jennifer Jones *Love Letters*

Supporting Actor
J. Carrol Naish *A Medal For Benny*

Direction
★ Billy Wilder *The Lost Weekend*

Writing
(original story)
Laszlo Gorog, Thomas Monroe *The Affairs Of Susan*
John Steinbeck, Jack Wagner *A Medal For Benny*
(original screenplay)
Milton Holmes *Salty O'Rourke*
(screenplay)
★ Charles Brackett, Billy Wilder *The Lost Weekend*

Cinematography
(black-and-white)
John Seitz *The Lost Weekend*

Art Direction/Interior Decoration
(black-and-white)
Hans Dreier, Roland Anderson/Sam Comer, Ray Moyer *Love Letters*
(colour)
★ Hans Dreier, Ernst Fegté/Sam Comer *Frenchman's Creek*

Sound Recording
Loren Ryder *The Unseen*

Film Editing
Doane Harrison *The Lost Weekend*

Music
(song)
Harold Arlen (music), Johnny Mercer (lyrics) 'Accentuate The Positive' in *Here Come The Waves*
Victor Young (music), Edward Heyman (lyrics) 'Love Letters' in *Love Letters*
(scoring of a dramatic or comedy picture)
Miklos Rozsa *The Lost Weekend*
Victor Young *Love Letters*
(scoring of a musical picture)
Robert Emmett Dolan *Incendiary Blonde*

Short Subjects
(cartoon)
Jasper And The Beanstalk (Puppetoon)
(one-reel)
White Rhapsody (Sportlight)
(two-reel)
The Little Witch (Musical Parade)

Scientific or Technical
- Loren L. Ryder, Charles R. Daily and the Paramount Studio Sound Department for the design, construction and use of the first dial-controlled step-by-step sound channel line-up and test circuit

1946

Actress
★ Olivia de Havilland *To Each His Own*

Writing
(original story)
Jack Patrick *The Strange Love Of Martha Ivers*
Charles Brackett *To Each His Own*
(original screenplay)
Raymond Chandler *The Blue Dahlia*
Norman Panama, Melvin Frank *The Road To Utopia*

Art Direction/Interior Decoration
(black-and-white)
Hans Dreier, Walter Tyler/Sam Comer, Ray Moyer *Kitty*

Music
(song)
Irving Berlin (music and lyrics) 'You Keep Coming Back Like A Song' in *Blue Skies*
(scoring of musical picture)
Robert Emmett Dolan *Blue Skies*

Short Subjects
(cartoon)
John Henry And The Inky Poo (Puppetoon)
(one-reel)
Dive-Hi Champs (Sportlight)
(two-reel)
College Queen (Musical Parade)

Special Award
- To Ernst Lubitsch for his distinguished contributions to the art of the motion picture

Scientific or Technical
- Harlan L. Baumbach and the Paramount West Coast Laboratory for an improved method for the quantitative determination of hydroquinone and metol in photographic developing baths

1947

Special Effects
Farciot Edouart, Devereux Jennings, Gordon Jennings, Wallace Kelley, Paul Lerpae, George Dutton *Unconquered*

Music
(song)
Frank Loesser (music and lyrics) 'I Wish I Didn't Love You So' in *The Perils Of Pauline*
(scoring of musical picture)
Robert Emmett Dolan *The Road To Rio*

Short Subjects
(cartoon)
Tubby The Tuba (Puppetoon)
(one-reel)
Moon Rockets (Popular Science)
(two-reel)
Champagne For Two (Musical Parade)

Scientific or Technical
- C. R. Daily and the Paramount Studio Film Laboratory, Still and Engineering Departments for the development and first practical application to motion picture and still photography of a method of increasing film speed as first suggested to the industry by E. I. duPont de Nemours & Co.
- Farciot Edouart, C. R. Daily, Hal Corl, H. G. Cartwright and the Paramount Studio Transparency and Engineering Departments for the first application of a special anti-solarizing glass to a high intensity background and spot arc projectors

1948

Actress
Barbara Stanwyck *Sorry, Wrong Number*

Writing (screenplay)
Charles Brackett, Billy Wilder, Richard Breen *A Foreign Affair*

Cinematography (black-and-white)
Charles Lang *A Foreign Affair*

Costume Design (colour)
Edith Head, Gile Steele *The Emperor Waltz*

Short Subjects (two-reel)
Samba Mania (Musical Parade)

Music
(song)
★ Jay Livingston and Ray Evans (music and lyrics) 'Buttons And Bows' in *The Paleface*
(scoring of musical picture)
Victor Young *The Emperor Waltz*

Special Award
- To Adolph Zukor, a man who has been called the father of the feature film in America, for his services to the industry over a period of forty years

Scientific or Technical
- Victor Caccialanza, Maurice Ayers and the Paramount Studio Set Construction Department for the development and application of 'Paralite', a new lightweight plaster process for set construction

1949

Picture
The Heiress

Actress
★ Olivia de Havilland *The Heiress*

Supporting Actor
Ralph Richardson *The Heiress*

Direction
William Wyler *The Heiress*

Cinematography (black-and-white)
Leo Tover *The Heiress*

Art Direction/Set Decoration
(black-and-white)
★ John Meehan, Harry Horner/Emile Kuri *The Heiress*

Music
(scoring of a dramatic or comedy picture)
★ Aaron Copland *The Heiress*

Costume Design (black-and-white)
★ Edith Head, Gile Steele *The Heiress*

Short Subjects (one-reel)
★ *Aquatic House Party* (Sportlights)
Roller Derby Girl (Pacemaker)

Special Award
- To Cecil B. DeMille, distinguished motion picture pioneer, for 37 years of brilliant showmanship

Scientific or Technical
- Loren L. Ryder, Bruce H. Denney, Robert Carr and the Paramount Studio Sound Department for the development and application of the supersonic playback and public address system
- Charles R. Daily, Steve Csillag and the Paramount Studio Engineering, Editorial and Music Departments for a new precision method of computing variable tempo-clock tracks

1950

Picture
Sunset Boulevard

Actor
William Holden *Sunset Boulevard*

Actress
Gloria Swanson *Sunset Boulevard*

Supporting Actor
Erich von Stroheim *Sunset Boulevard*

Supporting Actress
Nancy Olson *Sunset Boulevard*

Direction
Billy Wilder *Sunset Boulevard*

Writing (story and screenplay)
★ Charles Brackett, Billy Wilder, D. M. Marshman Jr *Sunset Boulevard*

**Cinematography
(black-and-white)**
Victor Milner *The Furies*
John F. Seitz *Sunset Boulevard*
(colour)
George Barnes *Samson And Delilah*

**Art Direction/Set Decoration
(black-and-white)**
★ Hans Dreier, John Meehan/Sam Comer, Ray Moyer *Sunset Boulevard*
(colour)
★ Hans Dreier, Walter Tyler/Sam Comer, Ray Moyer *Samson And Delilah*

Costume Design (colour)
★ Edith Head, Dorothy Jeakins, Elois Jenssen, Gile Steele, Gwen Wakeling *Samson And Delilah*

Sound Recording
Rank-Sydney Box *Trio*

Film Editing
Arthur Schmidt, Doane Harrison *Sunset Boulevard*

**Music
(song)**
★ Ray Evans (music), Jay Livingston (lyrics) 'Mona Lisa' in *Captain Carey, U.S.A.*
(scoring of a dramatic or comedy picture)
★ Franz Waxman *Sunset Boulevard*
Victor Young *Samson And Delilah*

Scientific or Technical
● Loren L. Ryder and the Paramount Studio Sound Department for the first studio-wide application of magnetic sound recording to motion picture production

1951

Picture
A Place In The Sun

Actor
Montgomery Clift *A Place In The Sun*

Actress
Eleanor Parker *Detective Story*
Shelley Winters *A Place In The Sun*

Supporting Actress
Lee Grant *Detective Story*
Thelma Ritter *The Mating Season*

Direction
★ George Stevens *A Place In The Sun*
William Wyler *Detective Story*

**Writing
(original story)**
Robert Riskin, Liam O'Brien *Here Comes The Groom*
(screenplay)
★ Michael Wilson, Harry Brown *A Place In The Sun*
Philip Yordan, Robert Wyler *Detective Story*
(story and screenplay)
Billy Wilder, Lesser Samuels, Walter Newman *Ace In The Hole*

Film Editing
★ William Hornbeck *A Place In The Sun*

**Cinematography
(black-and-white)**
★ William Mellor *A Place In The Sun*
(colour)
John Seitz, W. Howard Greene *When Worlds Collide*

Costume Design (black-and-white)
★ Edith Head *A Place In The Sun*

**Music
(song)**
★ Hoagy Carmichael (music), Johnny Mercer (lyrics) 'In The Cool, Cool, Cool Of The Evening' in *Here Comes The Groom*
(scoring of a dramatic or comedy picture)
★ Franz Waxman *A Place In The Sun*

Special Effects
● *When Worlds Collide*

Short Subjects (one-reel)
Ridin' The Rails (Sportlights)

Scientific or Technical
● Gordon Jennings, S. L. Stancliffe and the Paramount Studio Special Photographic and Engineering Departments for the design, construction and application of a servo-operated recording and repeating device

1952

Picture
★ *The Greatest Show On Earth*

Actress
★ Shirley Booth *Come Back, Little Sheba*

Supporting Actress
Terry Moore *Come Back, Little Sheba*

Direction
Cecil B. DeMille *The Greatest Show On Earth*

**Writing
(motion picture story)**
★ Frederick Frank, Theodore St. John, Frank Cavett *The Greatest Show On Earth*
Leo McCarey *My Son John*
(story and screenplay)
Sydney Boehm *The Atomic City*

**Art Direction/Set Decoration
(black-and-white)**
Hal Pereira, Roland Anderson/Emile Kuri *Carrie*

**Costume Design
(black-and-white)**
Edith Head *Carrie*
(colour)
Edith Head, Dorothy Jeakins, Miles White *The Greatest Show On Earth*

Film Editing
Warren Low *Come Back, Little Sheba*
Anne Bauchens *The Greatest Show On Earth*

Music (song)
Jack Brooks (music and lyrics) 'Am I In Love' in *Son Of Paleface*
Harry Warren (music), Leo Robin (lyrics) 'Zing A Little Zong' in *Just For You*

Short Subjects (one-reel)
Athletes Of The Saddle (Sportlights)

Honorary and Other Awards
● To Bob Hope for his contribution to the laughter of the world, his service to the motion picture industry, and his devotion to the American premise

Irving G. Thalberg Memorial Award
● Cecil B. DeMille

1953

Picture
Roman Holiday
Shane

Actor
★ William Holden *Stalag 17*

Actress
★ Audrey Hepburn *Roman Holiday*

Supporting Actor
Eddie Albert *Roman Holiday*
Brandon de Wilde *Shane*
Jack Palance *Shane*
Robert Strauss *Stalag 17*

Direction
George Stevens *Shane*
Billy Wilder *Stalag 17*
William Wyler *Roman Holiday*

**Writing
(motion picture story)**
★ Ian McLellan Hunter *Roman Holiday*
(screenplay)
Ian McLellan Hunter, John Dighton *Roman Holiday*
A.B. Guthrie Jr *Shane*

**Cinematography
(black-and-white)**
Frank Planer, Henri Alekan *Roman Holiday*
(colour)
★ Loyal Griggs *Shane*

**Art Direction/Set Decoration
(black-and-white)**
Hal Pereira, Walter Tyler *Roman Holiday*

Costume Design (black-and-white)
★ Edith Head *Roman Holiday*

Film Editing
Everett Douglas *The War Of The Worlds*
Robert Swink *Roman Holiday*

Sound Recording
Loren Ryder *The War Of The Worlds*

Special Effects
★ *The War Of The Worlds*

Music (song)
Harry Warren (music), Jack Brooks (lyrics) 'That's Amore' in *The Caddy*

Short Subjects (one-reel)
Wee Water Wonders (Sportlight)

1954

Picture
The Country Girl

Actor
Bing Crosby *The Country Girl*

Actress
Audrey Hepburn *Sabrina*
★ Grace Kelly *The Country Girl*

Direction
Alfred Hitchcock *Rear Window*
George Seaton *The Country Girl*
Billy Wilder *Sabrina*

Writing
(screenplay)
★ George Seaton *The Country Girl*
John Michael Hayes *Rear Window*
Billy Wilder, Samuel Taylor, Ernest Lehman
Sabrina
(story and screenplay)
Norman Panama, Melvin Frank *Knock On Wood*

Cinematography
(black-and-white)
John F. Warren *The Country Girl*
Charles Lang Jr. *Sabrina*
(colour)
Robert Burks *Rear Window*

Art Direction/Set Decoration
(black-and-white)
Hal Pereira, Roland Anderson/Sam Comer,
Grace Gregory *The Country Girl*
Hal Pereira, Walter Tyler/Sam Comer, Ray
Moyer *Sabrina*
(colour)
Hal Pereira, Roland Anderson/Sam Comer,
Ray Moyer *Red Garters*

Costume Design (black-and-white)
★ Edith Head *Sabrina*

Sound Recording
Loren Ryder *Rear Window*

Music (song)
Irving Berlin (music and lyrics) 'Count Your
Blessings' in *White Christmas*

Scientific or Technical
● Paramount Pictures, Inc., Loren L. Ryder, John
R. Bishop and all the members of the technical
and engineering staff for developing a method of
producing and exhibiting motion pictures known
as VistaVision

1955

Picture
The Rose Tattoo

Actress
★ Anna Magnani *The Rose Tattoo*

Supporting Actress
Marisa Pavan *The Rose Tattoo*

Writing
(motion picture story)
Beirne Lay Jr *Strategic Air Command*
(story and screenplay)
Melville Shavelson, Jack Rose *The Seven
Little Foys*

Cinematography
(black-and-white)
★ James Wong Howe *The Rose Tattoo*
(colour)
★ Robert Burks *To Catch A Thief*

Art Direction/Set Decoration
(black-and-white)
★ Hal Pereira, Tambi Larsen/Sam Comer,
Arthur Krams *The Rose Tattoo*
(colour)
Hal Pereira, Joseph M. Johnson/Sam Comer,
Arthur Krams *To Catch A Thief*

Costume Design
(black-and-white)
Edith Head *The Rose Tattoo*
(colour)
Edith Head *To Catch A Thief*

Film Editing
Alma Macrorie *The Bridges At Toko-Ri*
Warren Low *The Rose Tattoo*

Special Effects
★ *The Bridges At Toko-Ri*

Music
(scoring of a dramatic or comedy picture)
Alex North *The Rose Tattoo*

Short Subjects (one-reel)
Three Kisses

Scientific or Technical
● Farciot Edouart, Hal Corl and the Paramount
Studio Transparency Department for the
engineering and development of a double-
frame, triple-head background projector
● Loren L. Ryder, Charles West, Henry Fracker
and Paramount Studio for a projection film
index to establish proper framing for various
aspect ratios
● Farciot Edouart, Hal Corl and the Paramount
Studio Transparency Department for an
improved dual stereopticon background
projector

1956

Picture
The Ten Commandments

Actress
Katharine Hepburn *The Rainmaker*

Direction
King Vidor *War And Peace*

Cinematography (colour)
Loyal Griggs *The Ten Commandments*
Jack Cardiff *War And Peace*

Art Direction/Set Decoration
(black-and-white)
Hal Pereira, A. Earl Hedrick/Samuel M.
Comer, Frank R. McKelvy *The Proud And
The Profane*
(colour)
Hal Pereira, Walter Tyler, Albert Nozaki/Sam
M. Comer, Ray Moyer *The Ten Commandments*

Special Effects
★ John Fulton *The Ten Commandments*

Costume Design
(black-and-white)
Edith Head *The Proud And The Profane*
(colour)
Edith Head, Ralph Jester, John Jensen, Dorothy
Jeakins, Arnold Friberg *The Ten Commandments*
Marie De Matteis *War And Peace*

Film Editing
Anne Bauchens *The Ten Commandments*

Sound Recording
Loren Ryder *The Ten Commandments*

Music
(song)
★ Jay Livingston (music), Ray Evans (lyrics)
'Whatever Will Be, Will Be' ('Que Sera, Sera')
in *The Man Who Knew Too Much*
(scoring of a dramatic or comedy picture)
Alex North *The Rainmaker*

Jean Hersholt Humanitarian Award
● Y. Frank Freeman

Scientific or Technical
● The technical departments of Paramount
Pictures Corporation for the engineering and
development of the Paramount lightweight
horizontal-movement VistaVision camera
● Roy C. Stewart and Sons of Stewart-Trans Lux
Corporation, Dr C. R. Daily and the
Transparency Department of Paramount
Pictures Corporation for the engineering and
development of the HiTrans and Para-HiTrans
rear projection screens

1957

Actor
Anthony Quinn *Wild Is The Wind*

Actresss
Anna Magnani *Wild Is The Wind*

**Writing (story and screenplay – written
directly for the screen)**
Leonard Gershe *Funny Face*
Barney Slater, Joel Kane, Dudley Nichols
The Tin Star

Cinematography
Ray June *Funny Face*

Art Direction/Set Decoration
Hal Pereira, George W. Davis/Sam Comer,
Ray Moyer *Funny Face*

Costume Design
Edith Head, Hubert de Givenchy *Funny Face*

Sound Recording
George Dutton and staff *Gunfight At The
O.K. Corral*

Film Editing
Warren Low *Gunfight At The O.K. Corral*

Music (song)
★ James Van Heusen (music), Sammy Cahn
(lyrics) 'All The Way' in *The Joker Is Wild*
Dimitri Tiomkin (music), Ned Washington
(lyrics) 'Wild Is The Wind' in *Wild Is The Wind*

Scientific or Technical
● Charles E. Sutter, William B. Smith, Paramount
Pictures Corporation and General Cable
Corporation for the engineering and application
to studio use of aluminium lightweight electrical
cable and connectors

1958

Supporting Actor
Gig Young *Teacher's Pet*

**Writing (story and screenplay – written
directly for the screen)**
Melville Shavelson, Jack Rose *Houseboat*
Fay and Michael Kanin *Teacher's Pet*

Cinematography (black-and-white)
Daniel Fapp *Desire Under The Elms*

Art Direction/Set Decoration
Hal Pereira, Henry Bumstead/Sam Comer,
Frank McKelvy *Vertigo*

Costume Design
Ralph Jester, Edith Head, John Jensen
The Buccaneer

Sound
George Dutton and staff *Vertigo*

Music (song)
Jay Livingston (music), Ray Evans (lyrics)
'Almost In Your Arms' in *Houseboat*

Honorary and Other Awards
● To Maurice Chevalier for his contributions to
the world of entertainment for more than half a
century

1959

Cinematography
(black-and-white)
Joseph LaShelle *Career*
(colour)
Daniel L. Fapp *The Five Pennies*

Art Direction/Set Decoration
(black-and-white)
Hal Pereira, Walter Tyler/Sam Comer, Arthur
Krams *Career*

Costume Design
(black-and-white)
Edith Head *Career*
(colour)
Edith Head *The Five Pennies*

Music
(song)
Sylvia Fine (music and lyrics) 'The Five
Pennies' in *The Five Pennies*
(scoring of musical picture)
Leith Stevens *The Five Pennies*
Nelson Riddle, Joseph Lilley *Li'l Abner*

Jean Hersholt Humanitarian Award
● Bob Hope

1960

Supporting Actress
Janet Leigh *Psycho*

Direction
Alfred Hitchcock *Psycho*

Cinematography (black-and-white)
John L. Russell *Psycho*

Art Direction/Set Decoration
(black-and-white)
Joseph Hurley, Robert Clatworthy/George
Milo *Psycho*
Hal Pereira, Walter Tyler/Sam Comer, Arthur
Krams *Visit To A Small Planet*
(colour)
Hal Pereira, Roland Anderson/Sam Comer,
Arrigo Breschi *It Started In Naples*

Short Subjects (live action)
A Sport Is Born

Honorary and Other Awards
● To Gary Cooper for his many memorable
screen performances and the international
recognition he, as an individual, has gained for
the motion picture industry

1961

Actress
Audrey Hepburn *Breakfast At Tiffany's*
Geraldine Page *Summer And Smoke*

Supporting Actress
Una Merkel *Summer And Smoke*

**Writing (screenplay – based on material
from another medium)**
George Axelrod *Breakfast At Tiffany's*

Cinematography (colour)
Charles Lang Jr *One-Eyed Jacks*

Art Direction/Set Decoration (colour)
Hal Pereira, Roland Anderson/Sam Comer,
Ray Moyer *Breakfast At Tiffany's*
Hal Pereira, Walter Tyler/Sam Comer, Arthur
Krams *Summer And Smoke*

Music
(song)
★ Henry Mancini (music), Johnny Mercer (lyrics)
'Moon River' in *Breakfast At Tiffany's*
(scoring of a dramatic or comedy picture)
★ Henry Mancini *Breakfast At Tiffany's*
Elmer Bernstein *Summer And Smoke*

1962

Cinematography (colour)
Russell Harlan *Hatari!*

Art Direction/Set Decoration
(black-and-white)
Hal Pereira, Roland Anderson/Sam Comer,
Frank R. McKelvy *The Pigeon That Took Rome*

Costume Design
(black-and-white)
Edith Head *The Man Who Shot Liberty Valance*
(colour)
Edith Head *My Geisha*

Scientific or Technical
● Charles E. Sutter, William Bryson Smith and
Louis C. Kennell of Paramount Pictures Corp.
for the engineering and application to motion
picture production of a new system of electric
power distribution

1963

Actor
Paul Newman *Hud*

Actress
★ Patricia Neal *Hud*
Natalie Wood *Love With The Proper Stranger*

Supporting Actor
★ Melvyn Douglas *Hud*

Direction
Martin Ritt *Hud*

Writing
**(screenplay – based on material from
another medium)**
Irving Ravetch, Harriet Frank Jr *Hud*
**(story and screenplay – written directly for
the screen)**
Arnold Schulman *Love With The Proper Stranger*

Cinematography (black-and-white)
★ James Wong Howe *Hud*
Milton Krasner *Love With The Proper Stranger*

**Art Direction/Set Decoration
(black-and-white)**
Hal Pereira, Tambi Larsen/Sam Comer,
Robert Benton *Hud*
Hal Pereira, Roland Anderson/Sam Comer,
Grace Gregory *Love With The Proper Stranger*
(colour)
Hal Pereira, Roland Anderson/Sam Comer,
James Payne *Come Blow Your Horn*

**Costume Design
(black-and-white)**
Edith Head *Love With The Proper Stranger*
Edith Head *Wives And Lovers*
(colour)
Edith Head *A New Kind of Love*

**Music
(song)**
★ James Van Heusen (music), Sammy Cahn
(lyrics) 'Call Me Irresponsible' in *Papa's Delicate
Condition*
(scoring of music – adaptation or treatment)
Leith Stevens *A New Kind Of Love*

1964

Picture
Becket

Actor
Richard Burton *Becket*
Peter O'Toole *Becket*

Supporting Actor
John Gielgud *Becket*
Edmond O'Brien *Seven Days In May*

Direction
Peter Glenville *Becket*

**Writing (screenplay – based on material for
another medium)**
★ Edward Anhalt *Becket*

Cinematography (colour)
Geoffrey Unsworth *Becket*

**Art Direction/Set Decoration
(black-and-white)**
Cary Odell/Edward G. Boyle *Seven Days In May*
(colour)
John Bryan, Maurice Carter/Patrick
McLoughlin, Robert Cartwright *Becket*

Costume Design (colour)
Margaret Furse *Becket*

Sound
John Cox and Shepperton Sound Dept *Becket*

Film Editing
Anne Coates *Becket*

**Music
(song)**
James Van Heusen (music), Sammy Cahn
(lyrics) 'Where Love Has Gone' in *Where Love
Has Gone*
(music score – substantially original)
Laurence Rosenthal *Becket*
Dimitri Tiomkin *The Fall Of The Roman Empire*

1965

Actor
Richard Burton *The Spy Who Came In From The Cold*

Cinematography (black-and-white)
Loyal Griggs *In Harm's Way*

Art Direction/Set Decoration (black-and-white
Hal Pereira, Jack Poplin/Robert Benton, Joseph Kish *The Slender Thread*
Hal Pereira, Tambi Larsen, Edward Marshall/Josie MacAvin *The Spy Who Came In From The Cold*

Costume Design (black-and-white)
Edith Head *The Slender Thread*

Honorary and Other Awards
● To Bob Hope for unique and distinguished service to our industry and the Academy

1966

Picture
Alfie

Actor
Michael Caine *Alfie*

Supporting Actress
Vivien Merchant *Alfie*

**Writing
(screenplay – based on material from another medium)**
Bill Naughton *Alfie*
(story and screenplay – written directly for the screen)
Clint Johnston, Don Peters *The Naked Prey*

Cinematography (black-and-white)
Marcel Grignon *Is Paris Burning?*
James Wong Howe *Seconds*

Art Direction/Set Decoration (black-and-white)
Willy Holt/Marc Frederix, Pierre Guffroy *Is Paris Burning?*

Music (song)
Burt Bacharach (music), Hal David (lyrics) 'Alfie' in *Alfie*

Short Subjects (cartoon)
★ *Herb Alpert And The Tia Juana Brass Double Feature*
(live action)
The Winning Strain

Honorary and Other Awards
● To Y. Frank Freeman for unusual and outstanding service to the Academy during his thirty years in Hollywood

1967

Supporting Acresss
Mildred Natwick *Barefoot In The Park*

1968

Picture
Romeo And Juliet

Supporting Actress
★ Ruth Gordon *Rosemary's Baby*

Direction
Franco Zeffirelli *Romeo And Juliet*

Writing (screenplay – based on material from another medium)
Neil Simon *The Odd Couple*
Roman Polanski *Rosemary's Baby*

Cinematography
★ Pasqualino de Santis *Romeo And Juliet*

Costume Design
★ Danilo Donati *Romeo And Juliet*

Film Editing
Frank Bracht *The Odd Couple*

Short Subjects (cartoon)
Windy Day (Hubley Studios)

1969

Actor
★ John Wayne *True Grit*

Actress
Liza Minnelli *The Sterile Cuckoo*

Writing (screenplay – based on material from another medium)
Arnold Schulman *Goodbye Columbus*

**Music
(song)**
Fred Karlin (music), Rory Previn (lyrics) 'Come Saturday Morning' in *The Sterile Cuckoo*
Elmer Bernstein (music), Don Black (lyrics) 'True Grit' in *True Grit*
(score of musical picture)
Nelson Riddle *Paint Your Wagon*

Short Subjects (cartoon)
Of Men And Demons (Hubley Studios)

1970

Picture
Love Story

Actor
Ryan O'Neal *Love Story*

Actress
Ali MacGraw *Love Story*

Supporting Actor
John Marley *Love Story*

Direction
Arthur Hiller *Love Story*

Writing (story and screenplay – based on factual material or material not previously published or produced)
Erich Segal *Love Story*

Art Direction/Set Decoration
Tambi Larsen/Darrell Silvera *The Molly Maguires*

Costume Design
Donald Brooks, John Bear *Darling Lili*

**Music
(song)**
Henry Mancini (music), Johnny Mercer (lyrics) 'Whistling Away The Dark' in *Darling Lili*
(original score)
★ Francis Lai *Love Story*
(original song score)
Henry Mancini, Johnny Mercer *Darling Lili*

1971

Writing (screenplay – based on material from another medium)
Bernardo Bertolucci *The Conformist*

Short Subject (live action)
★ *Sentinels Of Silence* (Producciones Concord)

**Music
(scoring: adaptation and original song score)**
Leslie Bricusse, Anthony Newley, Walter Scharf *Willy Wonka And The Chocolate Factory*

Documentary (short subjects)
★ *Sentinels Of Silence* (Producciones Concord)

1972

Picture
★ *The Godfather*

Actor
★ Marlon Brando *The Godfather*

Actress
Diana Ross *Lady Sings The Blues*

Supporting Actor
Al Pacino *The Godfather*
James Caan *The Godfather*
Robert Duvall *The Godfather*

Direction
Francis Ford Coppola *The Godfather*

**Writing
(screenplay – based on material from another medium)**
★ Mario Puzo, Francis Ford Coppola *The Godfather*
(story and screenplay – based on factual material not previously published or produced)
Terence McCloy, Chris Clark, Suzanne de Passe *Lady Sings The Blues*

Art Direction/Set Decoration
Carl Anderson/Reg Allen *Lady Sings The Blues*

Costume Design
Anna Hill Johnstone *The Godfather*
Bob Mackie, Ray Aghayan, Norma Koch *Lady Sings The Blues*

Sound
Bud Grenzbach, Richard Portman, Christopher Newman *The Godfather*

Film Editing
William Reynolds, Peter Zinner *The Godfather*

**Music
(scoring: adaptation and original song score)**
Gil Askey *Lady Sings The Blues*

1973

Actor
★ Jack Lemmon *Save The Tiger*
Al Pacino *Serpico*

Supporting Actor
Vincent Gardenia *Bang The Drum Slowly*
Jack Gilford *Save The Tiger*

Supporting Actress
Madeline Kahn *Paper Moon*
★ Tatum O'Neal *Paper Moon*

**Writing
(screenplay – based on material from another medium)**
Alvin Sargent *Paper Moon*
Waldo Salt, Norman Wexler *Serpico*
(story and screenplay – based on factual material or material not previously published or produced)
Steve Shagan *Save The Tiger*

Cinematography
Jack Couffer *Jonathan Livingston Seagull*

Art Direction/Set Decoration
Lorenzo Monzlardino, Gianni Quaranta/ Carmelo Patrono *Brother Sun, Sister Moon*
Sound
Richard Portman, Les Fresholtz *Paper Moon*

Film Editing
Frank P. Keller, James Galloway *Jonathan Livingston Seagull*

1974

Picture
Chinatown
The Conversation
★ *The Godfather, Part II*

Actor
Albert Finney *Murder On The Orient Express*
Jack Nicholson *Chinatown*
Al Pacino *The Godfather, Part II*

Actress
Faye Dunaway *Chinatown*

Supporting Actor
★ Robert De Niro *The Godfather, Part II*
Michael V. Gazzo *The Godfather, Part II*
Lee Strasberg *The Godfather, Part II*

Supporting Actress
★ Ingrid Bergman *Murder On The Orient Express*
Talia Shire *The Godfather, Part II*

Direction
★ Francis Ford Coppola *The Godfather, Part II*
Roman Polanski *Chinatown*

**Writing
(original screenplay)**
★ Robert Towne *Chinatown*
Francis Ford Coppola *The Conversation*
(screenplay adapted from other material)
★ Francis Ford Coppola, Mario Puzo *The Godfather, Part II*
Paul Dehn *Murder On The Orient Express*
Mordecai Richler, Lionel Chetwynd *The Apprenticeship Of Duddy Kravitz*

Cinematography
John Alonzo *Chinatown*
Geoffrey Unsworth *Murder On The Orient Express*

Art Direction/Set Decoration
★ Dean Tavoularis, Angelo Graham/ George R. Nelson *The Godfather, Part II*
Richard Sylbert, W. Stewart Campbell/Ruby Levitt *Chinatown*

Costume Design
★ Theoni Aldredge *The Great Gatsby*
Anthea Sylbert *Chinatown*
John Furness *Daisy Miller*
Theadora Van Runcle *The Godfather, Part II*
Tony Walton *Murder On The Orient Express*

Sound
Bud Grenzbach, Larry Jost *Chinatown*
Walter Murch, Arthur Rochester *The Conversation*

Film Editing
Sam O'Steen *Chinatown*
Michael Luciano *The Longest Yard*

**Music
(song)**
Frederick Loewe (music), Alan Jay Lerner (lyrics) 'Little Prince' in *The Little Prince*
(original dramatic score)
★ Nino Rota, Carmine Coppola *The Godfather, Part II*
Jerry Goldsmith *Chinatown*
Alex North *Shanks*
Richard Rodney Bennett *Murder On The Orient Express*
(scoring: original song score and/or adaptation)
★ Nelson Riddle *The Great Gatsby*
Alan Jay Lerner, Frederick Loewe, Angela Morley, Douglas Gamley *The Little Prince*

1975

Picture
Nashville

Supporting Actor
Burgess Meredith *The Day Of The Locust*

Supporting Actress
Ronee Blakley *Nashville*
Lily Tomlin *Nashville*
Brenda Vaccaro *Once Is Not Enough*

Direction
Robert Altman *Nashville*

Cinematography
Conrad Hall *The Day Of The Locust*

Film Editing
Frederic Steinkamp, Don Guidice *Three Days Of The Condor*

Music (original song)
★ Keith Carradine (music and lyrics) 'I'm Easy' in *Nashville*
Michael Masser (music), Gerry Goffin (lyrics) 'Do You Know Where You're Going To?' in *Mahogany*

1976

Actress
Liv Ullman *Face To Face*

Supporting Actor
Laurence Olivier *Marathon Man*

Direction
Ingmar Bergman *Face To Face*

Cinematography
Richard H. Kline *King Kong*

Art Direction/Set Decoration
Gene Callahan, Jack Collis/Jerry Wunderlich *The Last Tycoon*
Robert F. Boyle, Arthur Jeph Parker *The Shootist*
Sound
Harry W. Tetrick, William McCaughey, Aaron Rochin, Jack Solomon *King Kong*

Music (original song score and its adaptation, or adaptation score)
Paul Williams *Bugsy Malone*

Special Achievement Award
● For visual effects: Carlo Rambaldi, Glen Robinson, Frank van der Veer *King Kong*

1977

Actor
John Travolta *Saturday Night Fever*

Supporting Actress
Tuesday Weld *Looking For Mr. Goodbar*

Cinematography
Fred J. Koenekamp *Islands In The Stream*
William A. Fraker *Looking For Mr. Goodbar*

Sound
Robert Knudson, Robert J. Glass, Richard Tyler, Jean-Louis Ducarme *Sorcerer*, Paramount-Universal

1978

Picture
Heaven Can Wait

Actor
Warren Beatty *Heaven Can Wait*

Supporting Actor
Jack Warden *Heaven Can Wait*

Supporting Actress
Dyan Cannon *Heaven Can Wait*

Direction
Warren Beatty, Buck Henry *Heaven Can Wait*

Writing (screenplay based on material from another medium)
Warren Beatty, Elaine May *Heaven Can Wait*

Cinematography
★ Nestor Almendros *Days of Heaven*
William A. Fraker *Heaven Can Wait*

Art Direction/Set Decoration
★ Paul Sylbert, Edwin O'Donovan/George Gaines *Heaven Can Wait*

Costume Design
★ Anthony Powell *Death On The Nile*
Patricia Norris *Days Of Heaven*

Sound
John K. Wilkinson, Robert Glass Jr, John T. Reitz, Barry Thomas *Days Of Heaven*

**Music
(original score)**
Ennio Morricone *Days Of Heaven*
David Grusin *Heaven Can Wait*
(original song score and its adaptation, or adaptation score)
Jerry Wexler *Pretty Baby*
(original song)
John Farrar (music and lyrics) 'Hopelessly Devoted To You' in *Grease*
Charles Fox (music), Norman Gimbel (lyrics) 'Ready To Take A Chance Again' in *Foul Play*

1979

Actress
Jill Clayburgh *Starting Over*

Supporting Actress
Candice Bergen *Starting Over*

Art Direction/Set Decoration
Harold Michelson, Joe Jennings, Leon Harris, John Vallone/Linda Descenna *Star Trek—The Motion Picture*

Music (original score)
Jerry Goldsmith *Star Trek—The Motion Picture*

Visual Effects
Douglas Trumbull, John Dykstra, Richard Yuricich, Robert Swarthe, Dave Stewart, Grant McCune *Star Trek—The Motion Picture*

1980

Picture
★ *Ordinary People*
The Elephant Man

Actor
John Hurt *The Elephant Man*

Actress
Mary Tyler Moore *Ordinary People*

Supporting Actor
★ Timothy Hutton *Ordinary People*
Judd Hirsch *Ordinary People*

Direction
David Lynch *The Elephant Man*
★ Robert Redford *Ordinary People*

Writing (screenplay – based on material from another medium)
★ Alvin Sargent *Ordinary People*
Christopher DeVore, Eric Bergren, David Lynch *The Elephant Man*

Film Editing
David Blewitt *The Elephant Man*

Art Direction/Set Decoration
Stuart Craig, Bob Cartwright/Hugh Scaife *The Elephant Man*

Costume Design
Patricia Norris *The Elephant Man*

Music (original score)
John Morris *The Elephant Man*

Short Films (dramatic live action)
★ *The Dollar Bottom* (Rocking Horse Films Ltd)

1981

Picture
Atlantic City
Raiders Of The Lost Ark
Reds

Actor
Warren Beatty *Reds*
Burt Lancaster *Atlantic City*

Actress
Diane Keaton *Reds*
Susan Sarandon *Atlantic City*

Supporting Actor
Jack Nicholson *Reds*
Howard E. Rollins Jr *Ragtime*

Supporting Actress
Elizabeth McGovern *Ragtime*
★ Maureen Stapleton *Reds*

Direction
★ Warren Beatty *Reds*
Louis Malle *Atlantic City*
Steven Spielberg *Raiders Of The Lost Ark*

Writing (screenplay written directly for the screen)
John Guare *Atlantic City*
Warren Beatty, Trevor Griffiths *Reds*
(screenplay – based on material from another medium)
Michael Weller *Ragtime*

Cinematography
★ Vittorio Storaro *Reds*
Douglas Slocombe *Raiders Of The Lost Ark*
Miroslav Ondricek *Ragtime*

Film Editing
★ Michael Kahn *Raiders Of The Lost Ark*
Dede Allen, Craig McKay *Reds*

Music (original score)
Alex North *Dragonslayer*
Randy Newman *Ragtime*
John Williams *Raiders Of The Lost Ark*
(original song)
Randy Newman (music and lyrics) 'One More Hour' in *Ragtime*

Art Direction/Set Direction
★ Norman Reynolds, Leslie Dilley/Michael Ford *Raiders Of The Lost Ark*
John Graysmark, Patrizia von Brandenstein, Anthony Reading/George de Titta Sr, George de Titta Jr, Peter Howitt *Ragtime*
Richard Sylbert/Michael Seirton *Reds*

Costume Design
Shirley Russell *Reds*
Anna Hill Johnstone *Ragtime*

Sound
★ Billy Varney, Steve Maslow, Gregg Landaker, Roy Charman *Raiders Of The Lost Ark*
Dick Vorisek, Tom Fleischman, Simon Kaye *Reds*

Visual Effects
★ Richard Edlund, Kit West, Bruce Nicholson, Joe Johnston *Raiders Of The Lost Ark*
Dennis Muren, Phil Tippett, Ken Ralston, Brian Johnson *Dragonslayer*

1982

Actress
Debra Winger *An Officer And A Gentleman*

Supporting Actor
★ Louis Gossett Jr *An Officer And A Gentleman*

Writing (screenplay written directly for the screen)
Douglas Day Stewart *An Officer And A Gentleman*

Film Editing
Peter Zinner *An Officer And A Gentleman*

Music (original score)
Jack Nitzsche *An Officer And A Gentleman*
(original song)
★ Jack Nitzsche, Buffy Sainte-Marie, Will Jennings 'Up Where We Belong' in *An Officer And A Gentleman*

1983

Picture
★ *Terms Of Endearment*

Direction
★ James L. Brooks *Terms Of Endearment*

Actress
Jane Alexander *Testament*
★ Shirley MacLaine *Terms Of Endearment*
Debra Winger *Terms Of Endearment*

Supporting Actor
John Lithgow *Terms Of Endearment*
★ Jack Nicholson *Terms Of Endearment*

Writing (screenplay – based on material from another medium)
★ James L. Brooks *Terms Of Endearment*

Cinematography
Don Peterman *Flashdance*

Film Editing
Bud Smith, Walt Mulconery *Flashdance*
Richard Marks *Terms Of Endearment*

Music (original score)
Michael Gore *Terms of Endearment*
(original song score and its adaptation, or adaptation score)
Elmer Bernstein *Trading Places*
(original song)
★ Giorgio Moroder (music), Keith Forsey, Irena Cara (lyrics) 'Flashdance .. What A Feeling' in *Flashdance*
Michael Sembello, Dennis Matkosky (music and lyrics) 'Maniac' in *Flashdance*

Art Direction/Set Decoration
Polly Platt/Tom Pedigo *Terms Of Endearment*

Sound
Donald Mitchell, Rick Kline, Kevin O'Connell, James Alexander *Terms Of Endearment*

1984

Writing (screenplay written directly for the screen)
Daniel Petrie Jr, Danilo Bach *Beverly Hills Cop*

Music (original score)
John Williams *Indiana Jones And The Temple Of Doom*
(original song)
Kenny Loggins, Dean Pitchford (music and lyrics) 'Footloose' in *Footloose*
Tom Snow, Dean Pitchford (music and lyrics) 'Let's Hear It For The Boy' in *Footloose*

Visual Effects
★ Dennis Muren, Michael McAlister, Lorne Peterson, George Gibbs *Indiana Jones And The Temple Of Doom*

Index of Films

This index lists every feature film mentioned on pages 7–333 inclusive. Films mentioned in the Academy Nominations and Awards appendix on pages 334 to 344 are not indexed.

The main entry in the book for each Paramount film (whether it is an illustrated full-text entry or an abbreviated entry) is denoted by the page number in bold type. Page numbers in the lighter type relate to passing mentions of the film, either in an introduction or in another film's entry. If no bold page number is given, the film is not one released by Paramount between September 1916 and December 1984.

Where a film title begins with an arabic numeral, for example *40 Pounds Of Trouble*, it will be found under F, as if it were *Forty Pounds Of Trouble*.

Different films with the same or closely similar title are given separate index entries and are distinguished by the year of release, placed in brackets after the title.

Index of Personnel

This index lists the names of every real person mentioned on pages 7 to 333 inclusive. Individuals mentioned in the Academy Nominations and Awards appendix on pages 334 to 344 are not indexed, nor are any fictional characters.

Where a person is depicted in an illustration, the page number is given in italics, and that number refers to the page on which the related text or caption appears. Different mentions of the same person on the same page, but in different contexts or in relation to different films, are denoted by the insertion of a number in brackets after the page number.

The alphabetic position of people whose surnames are preceded by Von or De is under V or D, and not under the initial letter of their surname proper. Unhyphenated double surnames are indexed under the initial of the last of the two names; hyphenated double surnames are indexed under the initial of the first name of the pair. Surnames of Scottish origin beginning Mc- are separated from those beginning Mac- by all names beginning Mad- to Maz-.

Anyone familiar with movie literature will have discovered that different sources may give different spellings or versions of a person's name. In many cases they are correct to do so, because the people concerned (particularly if they were performers) did use more than one form of their name, either arbitrarily or for different periods of their career. Where we know this to be the case we have indicated the alternatives in brackets, the index entry proper being the form of the name which seems to have been used most widely; the mention in the text may use any one of the various forms. In those cases where there seems to be widespread confusion throughout the literature as to how a name should be spelt we have tried to standardise as far as possible on the basis of majority usage and/or by following the form used in 'The New York Times Directory Of The Film'.

X

Y

Z